GW00492795

Craigavon...
the future is here

THE place to live, work, visit & invest

For further details contact: **028 3831 2400**

NORTHERN IRELAND YEARBOOK 2003

A Comprehensive Reference Guide to the Political, Economic and Social Life of Northern Ireland

Written and Produced by Lagan Consulting 028 9261 3216
Editor: Michael McKernan
Public Affairs Editor: Owen McQuade
Research Managers: Joanne Fagan, Sandra Dane
Design: Gareth Duffy

© Lagan Consulting 2002

Published by bmf Publishing
76 Main Street
Moira
Co. Down, BT67 0LQ
028 9261 9933

Distribution and Marketing by tSO Ireland
16 Arthur Street
Belfast, BT1 4GD
028 9023 5401

Print Management by The Northern Whig, Belfast

ISBN: 0-9537672-5-6

The Publishers regret that while every effort has been made during the compilation of this
yearbook to ensure the accuracy of information obtained and published, they cannot be held
responsible in any way for inaccuracies in the information supplied to them for publication, nor for
any errors or omissions. Users of the yearbook should satisfy themselves that all the services
offered by those listed are acceptable, before commissioning.

Inclusion of a company or individual in this yearbook should not be interpreted as a
recommendation of that company or individual listed to undertake particular instructions. Similarly,
no criticism is implied of any company or individual who may for any reason have been omitted
from the yearbook.

A Comprehensive Guide to Northern Ireland
Foreword

Welcome to the second Edition of the Northern Ireland Yearbook - a comprehensive guide to Northern Ireland. It remains the only substantial book published that draws together all strands of public life in Northern Ireland and presents detailed information in a useful and insightful format.

Last year's edition of the book was completely sold out, so we have doubled the print run for this year and we feel we are getting closer to our goal of ensuring that the book features in the offices of most organisations in Northern Ireland, public, private and voluntary sectors and specifically on the desks of all of Northern Ireland's top decision makers. We also expect it will be available in all libraries, schools and institutions as well as in high street bookshops. Certainly the advertising community has appreciated the targeted penetration of the book where around 100 organisations have sought profile in the publication.

Most sections of the book have been expanded in scope and detail including the much-prized guide to the Civil Service and Public Bodies. We have also added a new guide to 'Doing Business in Northern Ireland' and an extra chapter on the European dimension.

It is entirely right that Northern Ireland should have its own substantial Yearbook covering the entire political, economic and social spectrum, and we are determined to make this publication a model of its kind. We are already considering ideas for enhancements to next year's edition. In this respect we would welcome any suggestions and comments from readers.

I hope you find this a useful and satisfying addition to your library and office.

Michael McKernan
Editor

Acknowledgements

The authors and publishers owe a debt of gratitude to many people who have contributed their advice and efforts to this substantial publication. Firstly we are indebted to the suppliers of copyright material incorporated into parts of the Yearbook, in particular the Ordnance Survey (OSNI), the Northern Ireland Statistical Research Agency (NISRA), the Northern Ireland Economic Research Council (NIERC), the Northern Ireland Tourist Board (NITB) and Translink. We have made every effort to ensure that permission has been obtained for all copyrighted material used, and to attribute the source. If there is any lapse in this respect it is entirely accidental.

We are also very appreciative of those whose photographs adorn the Yearbook, particularly the Northern Ireland Tourist Board, and those organisations and individuals who supplied their own material. (All photographic sources are acknowledged specifically below).

Thanks are due also to the many individuals who helped with the compilation of Chapter 4 including the listings of Civil Servants and other officials and appointees. The result, while by no means complete, remains the most comprehensive presentation of Northern Ireland's senior Civil Service ever produced.

We would like to acknowledge also the many expert individuals who contributed their advice and wisdom to the publication including politicians, leading economists, educationalists and health professionals. Hopefully the book does them justice.

Finally thanks are due to all the 'hands-on' people who worked so hard to actually produce the 2003 Yearbook. The team at Lagan Consulting, Owen, for all the government insight, Joanne and Sandra for research and production, Gareth for all the long hours of design work, also Des and Davy, Eilish for managing the advertising and the group of checkers and proof readers. Thanks also to Dan and Nicola at TSO; Peter and Trevor at Northern Whig, Russell at Ulster Business and all other contributors and advertisers.

Photographic sources (page nos)

Northern Ireland Tourist Board (10, 14, 24, 26, 27, 508, 517, 537, 539, 544)
Ordnance Survey (20, 97)
The Northern Ireland Assembly Press Office (44)
Northern Ireland Executive Press Service (60, 65)
House of Commons Information Office (91)
Alton Constituency Office (140)
Northern Ireland Office (155)
Pacemaker (155)
Lisburn City Council (210)
Banbridge District Council (217)
Belfast City Hospital (242, 247, 257, 274)
The Royal Hospitals (245, 258, 279)
Altnagelvin Hospital (Cover, 251, 263)
Northern Ireland Housing Executive (280)
Queen's University, Belfast (Cover, 290 292, 299)
CCEA (296, 297)
Central Library Belfast (305)
Linenhall Library (306)

Brownlow College (309)
Galen (326, 358)
Bombardier Aerospace (Cover, 328)
Invest Northern Ireland (402)
EU Representation in Belfast (414, 416)
The European Parliament UK Office (418)
The Irish Linen Guild (357)
BBC (446, 458)
Belfast Telegraph (443, 447, 457)
City Beat (458)
UTV (458)
Translink (512, 513)
Park Avenue Hotel (533)
Daniel McGeown Estate Agents (21)
Irish News (Cover, 542)
Police Service of Northern Ireland (Cover)
Halifax (Cover)
Belfast Giants (Cover)

Contents

CHAPTER 1

The Place and Its People

The Place and its People

Northern Ireland: A Brief History

Northern Ireland is a relatively young political entity, having been created in 1920 by the Government of Ireland Act, which partitioned Ireland into two separate jurisdictions. Each were awarded their own executive and Home Rule parliament; a 26 county Southern Ireland was given relative independence but the remaining six counties of Armagh, Antrim, Down, Fermanagh, Londonderry and Tyrone were retained within the United Kingdom, establishing their own devolved administration. Despite its brevity, Northern Ireland's history has been coloured with conflict and controversy, characterised by deep and festering divisions between its people, based largely on issues of religion and nationality. In very general terms the division is thus: the Protestant or unionist community look to Britain for political parentage, whilst the Catholic or nationalist community believe this role should be fulfilled by the Irish Republic.

The debate over the terminology used to refer to Northern Ireland is indicative of the difficulties inherent in providing an objective commentary on its past. Because Northern Ireland is composed of only six of the nine counties of the ancient Irish province of Ulster, use of the terms "Ulster", or the "Province" is perceived as inaccurate by nationalists. They tend to prefer "Six Counties" or "the north of Ireland" which in turn often irritate unionists. This example highlights how events, which to an outside observer seem clear-cut and straightforward can be interpreted by different people in different ways. It is generally accepted that no presentation of facts can be considered universally objective. The representation of Northern Ireland's history which follows may therefore be perceived as too 'orange' or too 'green', depending on the sensitivities of the reader; it has however been intended as neither.

Pre-Christian Era

The early history of Ireland as a whole is shrouded in semi-myth and legend; indeed anything before around 500AD is extremely difficult to prove. Historians estimate that the Celts came to Ireland from the Rhine and Danube areas in Europe, around 400 BC. They introduced the Gaelic language, along with their own culture and beliefs. Only culture and language unified Celtic Ireland at this

stage: the country was divided into about 150 small communities (tuatha). A king ruled each tuath, and an overking ruled a group of tuatha. Similarly, a group of overkings would hold allegiance to a provincial king. Ireland was roughly divided into five provinces: Ulster, Munster, Leinster, Connacht and Mide, although the number and precise boundaries of provinces were in a constant state of flux. The rulers of Ireland fought each other frequently, and individual leaders variously assumed the title of "High King" of Ireland, but no one person ruled all of Ireland at this time. According to legend, in 300 BC High King Fiachadh founded the Fianna. This was the military elite of Ireland, charged with guarding the High King, although at first it is said to have been a somewhat undisciplined and incoherent group. This changed with the arrival of Fionn mac Cumhail, more commonly known as Finn MacCool who is celebrated as the Fianna's greatest ever leader. Finn challenged the Fianna to become champions of the people, and implemented a code of honour, chivalry and justice.

There are many legends surrounding Finn MacCool and the Fianna; one of the most famous gives an account of the creation of the "Giant's Causeway", a hexagonal-shaped volcanic rock formation on the north coast of Ireland, which has become Northern Ireland's most popular visitor attraction. A Scottish giant angered Finn by questioning his fighting ability, but was unable to accept the resulting challenge because he could not swim to Ireland. The story says that Finn tore great strips of rock from the coast, and made them into pillars to stretch from Ireland to Scotland. The giant was forced to cross over to Ireland, and Finn chased him back to Scotland, flinging huge chunks of earth at him. The biggest crater caused by this flooded with water and became Lough Neagh, the largest lake in Ireland or Britain, whilst a huge lump of earth fell into the Irish Sea and became the Isle of Man. A similar myth tells how Ulster got its symbol, the Red Hand. Two chiefs, one of whom was of the ancient House of O'Neill, disputed ownership of a piece of land (often claimed to be Ulster). The dispute was to be settled by a race: the chiefs would sail to the shore, and whoever touched it first with his right hand would win the land. O'Neill saw his opponent leading and about to step out of his boat, and so he cut off his right hand with his sword and threw it onto the shore, thus winning the contest.

The Giant's Causeway, County Antrim

Perhaps the most famous Ulster hero from the early period is Cu Chulainn, said to have been born around 500 BC. His name was originally Setanta, but as a young man he accidentally killed the guard dog of Culainn, a local warrior, who was distraught at its loss. Setanta took the dog's place to guard Culainn, and was thereafter known as Cu Chulainn, the Hound of Culainn. Cu Chulainn led the so-called "Red Branch" of Ulster warriors, mainly against forces led by Queen Maeve of Connacht.

Early Christian Era

The Celts followed a religion based on natural phenomena and spiritual beliefs until the introduction of Christianity to Ireland, during the 5th century AD. The establishment of Christianity in Ireland is accredited to St. Patrick, although he was by no means the first Christian in Ireland. St Patrick is believed to have been born in western Britain, possibly Wales; a Romanised Celt who was kidnapped and sold into slavery in Ireland. Patrick eventually escaped to the Continent, where he studied for the priesthood until he decided to return to Ireland, traditionally dated 432 AD.

Armagh, once a site associated with pagan rituals, became the centre of Christianity in Ireland after St Patrick supposedly received a cauldron from a powerful Druid (Celtic priest), but angered the druid by saying just a small word of thanks. When the druid demanded the cauldron back, Patrick said the same word of thanks, which induced the druid to repent, giving Patrick not only the cauldron back, but also a piece of land on which to build a church. Armagh still remains the ecclesiastical capital of Ireland, with both Catholic and Church of Ireland cathedrals built on two hilltops overlooking the city. Ireland, north and south, has a plethora of churches named after the island's patron saint. Probably one of the best-known legends about St Patrick is his supposed banishment of all snakes from Ireland. This is probably a metaphor for Patrick's having banished the "demons of paganism", as it had been documented two centuries earlier that Ireland had no indigenous snakes. 1500 years later, St Patrick has become a symbol of both inspiration and division within Northern Ireland today. He is Ireland's patron saint, celebrated on his feast day, 17th March, by Irish people across the globe. However, in Northern Ireland St Patrick is viewed in different ways. To the majority of Catholics and nationalists, he is a Catholic saint on account of his

having been in Ireland long before the Protestant Reformation. The Protestant and unionist majority in Northern Ireland, however, tend to waver between rejecting the saint, and embracing him as a British preacher who civilised the native Irish. Both communities lay claim to St Patrick's final resting place: either at Saul, near Downpatrick (the Catholic view), or in the grounds of Downpatrick Church of Ireland Cathedral (the Protestant belief).

A distinctive feature of the development of early Christianity was the role of monasticism. During the Dark Ages (500-800 AD) religion and scholarship almost disappeared in other European countries, largely as a result of barbarian invasions that did not reach Ireland. Irish monks established communities all over Europe, such as those at St Fursey at Peronne in France and St Columbanus at Bobbio in Italy. In the early centuries AD, missionary success was complemented by Ireland's cultural achievements. Ornate chalices and jewellery were created, while scribes produced magnificently illuminated manuscripts. The Book of Kells is the most famous example, begun around 800 AD. Its name derives from the Abbey of Kells, Co Meath, its home until 1541, although it was probably begun on the island of Iona, between Ireland and Scotland. The Book of Kells marks what many have called the Golden Age of Irish history, the period when Ireland was the "land of saints and scholars". The Book of Kells is now permanently on display at Trinity College, Dublin, where a page is turned every day.

From around 800 AD Ireland was initially attacked and then settled by Vikings, raiders and traders from Northern Europe, who founded Dublin, Limerick, Cork and Waterford. Ireland's disunity made the country vulnerable to attacks, and the southern half was conquered easily, while the relative strength of the O'Neill dynasty of kings enabled the northern half to withstand assault. Towards the end of the 10th century Brian Boru became king of Munster, and engaged the Vikings in a battle, which they were ultimately to lose. At the turn of the century Boru gained control of the whole country and was crowned High King of all Ireland. For the first time the country was united under his solid leadership. After Brian Boru's death in 1014 other Irish kings sought to follow his example; the trend was towards the development of a strong, centralised monarchy, as seen elsewhere in Europe, until the arrival of Norman forces in 1167-9. Brian Boru's grave may still be visited in Armagh.

The first Normans in Ireland were effectively mercenaries, invited to assist the King of Leinster in his claim to the High Kingship in 1169. Their leader, Richard de Clare, nicknamed Strongbow, succeeded the Leinster throne, and in 1171 the Normans' overlord, Henry II of England, declared himself overlord of the whole of Ireland. Led by John de Courcy, Normans settled in many parts of Ireland, establishing similar systems of law, parliament and administration as they had in England. Norman influence in Ireland was never as strong as it had been in England following the battle of Hastings in 1066; the Normans tended to assimilate themselves into Irish culture, rather than the other way round. French names gradually evolved into Irish forms, for example de Burgh became Burke, and the prefix Fils became Fitz, as in FitzGerald and FitzWilliam. Meanwhile, the native Gaelic population remained numerous and intermarried with the Normans. By 1500 English control (previously Norman) had receded to a small area around Dublin called "the Pale", as Normans in Ireland became increasingly integrated. The modern expression "beyond the pale" refers to this time, when everything outside the Pale area was considered dangerous and uncivilised. It is interesting that, despite colonising Ireland, the Normans eventually came to be described as "more Irish than the Irish".

The Plantation of Ulster

From the 16th century English Tudor monarchs began a conquest of Ireland. Henry VIII became the first English ruler to declare himself king of Ireland in 1541 but the most significant event in the development of the modern Northern Ireland could be said to be the Plantation of Ulster. This involved the systematic introduction of English and Scottish settlers, designed to establish English rule and suppress the native Irish. Mary I was the first English monarch to attempt plantation, mainly in Ulster, from 1556, but it was left to her successor, Elizabeth I, to secure Ireland. Land was taken from the native population and redistributed to settlers, often as a reward for services rendered in Britain. This was not without resistance: by 1594 Hugh O'Neill, Earl of Ulster, had united the ruling families of the north of Ireland, and begun a rebellion against the English crown that was to last nine years. O'Neill was strengthened by some assistance from Spain, traditional enemies of England, but the battle of Kinsale in 1601 was decisive in quashing the uprising. This was the first time that England had ever established control over the whole of Ireland, and in 1603 O'Neill and other rebellious Gaelic nobles fled to France (the "Flight of the Earls").

Having united the English and Scottish thrones, King James I continued with the plantation of Armagh, Derry, Cavan, Donegal, Tyrone and Fermanagh, later adding Down and Antrim. In 1613 James formed the new county of "Londonderry", renaming the ancient city by royal charter. The Honourable The Irish Society in London paid for defensive walls to be erected around the perimeter of the city, which was to serve as headquarters for many of its commercial projects.

The British government invited their people to settle throughout Ulster, and the skill and motivation of many English and French Huguenots formed the basis of a linen industry that was eventually to become the biggest in the world. From being the poorest province of Ireland, Ulster gradually became the most prosperous. Its place as the most industrialised region of Ireland continued until relatively recent times and it was accepted by many as being attributable to the British influence on this part of the country.

The influx into the province of Protestant colonists, primarily Presbyterians from Scotland, meant that Ulster became the only part of Ireland where the Protestant religion was established with any real success. As with the Normans some centuries earlier, the Ulster-Scots settlers brought their own culture, the difference being that, unlike the Normans, Ulster-Scots tended to retain their distinct identity rather than integrate themselves into the native culture. Two separate cultural, political and religious identities began to emerge in the north of Ireland: the vast majority of native Irish people were Catholic, and held their allegiance to their native Ireland, whilst Protestant settlers, including Anglican, Methodist and other denominations, considered themselves loyal to Britain. It is argued by many that the Plantation was the event in which much of today's conflict has its roots.

Seventeenth Century Conflict

The 17th century English civil war between Charles I and Parliament also had far-reaching consequences in Ireland. Oliver Cromwell, leader of the victorious parliamentary forces, maintained the English presence in Ireland and consolidated his success in Britain by quashing ensuing Irish rebellions. Following Cromwell's military success, the 1653 Act of Settlement involved large-scale confiscation of land. Further colonisation ensured that property and political power passed to loyal Protestants: before 1641, Catholics owned about three-fifths of the land; by the 1680s, they owned one-fifth of it. However, many Catholics did not own land, and were tenants or serfs already. For them, the change was in landlord and in attitude towards them, but they perceived themselves and their people as dispossessed.

The accession of the Catholic James II to the British throne in 1685 sparked a new wave of discord in Ireland. The Protestant aristocracy in Britain vehemently opposed the Catholic king who sought to expand his power at their expense. On being deposed, James fled to Ireland, where he found support everywhere apart from the Protestant community in the north. In what have become famous historical events, the predominantly Protestant towns of Derry and Enniskillen closed their gates against James and defied his authority. In the face of a strong military

City of Derry Walls

force the governor of Derry, Robert Lundy, was initially prepared to negotiate with James, but Lundy was overthrown and the gates remained closed. In modern-day loyalist circles the name Lundy has become synonymous with 'traitor', and his effigy is ritually burned on loyalist bonfires across Northern Ireland in a celebration of the famous siege. James besieged Derry for three months but failed to breach the city's fortified walls. On account of this, Derry became known as "the Maiden City".

The British throne, meanwhile, had been offered to a Protestant Dutch prince, William of Orange, as part of a pan-European coalition (supported by the Pope) against the dominant, Catholic French king Louis XIV. William

followed James to Ireland as part of a Europe-wide conflict, and fought a number of battles, most notably the militarily decisive Battle of Aughrim and the less significant but more famous Battle of the Boyne in 1690. The Catholic population supported James, who had been sympathetic to their situation, while Protestant settlers (some of whose families had lived in Ireland for several generations) sided with William. The war ended in victory for William and subsequently brought the longest peace that Ulster had ever known. Today "Protestant King Billy" is a loyalist hero, and is depicted on many Orange banners and also in street murals across the province. Like the Siege of Derry, the Battle of the Boyne has been celebrated enthusiastically by many within the Ulster Protestant community as part of Orange Order demonstrations. The anthem of Ulster loyalism, "The Sash", refers to an Orange sash (still a symbol of the Orange Order) being worn in "Derry, Aughrim, Enniskillen and the Boyne", although the Orange Order itself was not founded until a century later.

Throughout the 18th century Catholics throughout the British Isles were perceived as a potential threat to the Protestant monarchy, and Ireland in particular was considered a platform for the creation of instability in Britain. Despite the Plantation the Protestant establishment remained a minority in Ireland, although Scots Presbyterian in Ulster had risen in strength alongside the established Church of Ireland (Anglican) ascendancy. A series of Penal Laws were passed which kept the bulk of the Catholic population in a state of relative poverty and without many of the most basic civil rights. As the Penal Laws applied to all non-Anglicans, Presbyterians in Ulster were also denied full civil rights, though to a somewhat lesser extent. This meant that members of the Established Church were the chief beneficiaries of Ulster's newfound prosperity.

By 1782, British rule in Ireland was stable enough to allow the Westminster government to grant full legislative independence to the Irish Parliament (Grattan's Parliament), effectively making Ireland a separate kingdom sharing the British monarch as head of state (although the Dublin administration would be directly appointed by the British king). Towards the end of the eighteenth century the British government also began to relax the Penal Laws and proposed Catholic Emancipation (repeal of some of the anti-Catholic legislation) in 1795.

Late 18th century Co Armagh land skirmishes between Protestant Peep o' Day Boys and Catholic

Defenders, which culminated in the Battle of the Diamond in September 1795, led to the formation of the Orange Order. The Order was created primarily as a Protestant defence association in support of the British King and the wider Protestant Ascendancy. It had the aim of galvanising the minority Protestant population against rising Catholic power and confidence. The Order, taking its name from William of Orange two or three generations earlier, was oathbound, making use of passwords and signs and was comprised mainly of Protestant weaver-farmers, with initially very few members from the landed gentry. Apart from economic and other considerations the members of the Orange Order feared the historical authoritarianism of Catholicism, and saw the Order as a vehicle for preserving Protestant liberties. Orangemen formed associations know as lodges throughout Ireland (although it was predominant in the North) and organised marches to commemorate the Battle of the Boyne and other events; these marches often led to rioting between Catholics and Protestants. By 1836 the British government had banned Orange marches on account of the rioting that followed, but this ban was defied from 1849 onwards. Over the years the Orange Order founded lodges all over the world with the "Twelfth of July", the historical date of the Battle of the Boyne, becoming the focal point for Orange parades.

Act of Union to the Land War

The United Irishmen, formed in 1791, was a revolutionary group of idealists, inspired by the thinking behind the French Revolution, who aimed to unite Catholic, Protestant and Dissenter against British rule. Inspired as much by radical Protestant liberals as by Catholics, and led by Theobald Wolfe Tone and Lord Edward Fitzgerald the United Irishmen attempted a rebellion against Britain in 1798. Despite French assistance the rebellion, which was accompanied by a smaller uprising in Ulster, was easily suppressed. One result of which was to strengthen the case (which had been growing in the minds of British politicians since the early 1770s) for a legislative union between Britain and Ireland, on the grounds that Ireland represented a security threat to Britain. Although the idea was opposed by many and varied groups throughout the country (including representatives from Dublin commerce, the law, country gentlemen and the Orange Order) due to the unrepresentative nature of the Irish parliament and the

strength of the Unionist position at Westminster, their arguments had little impact. It took just over a year (and the distribution of much political patronage) to persuade the Irish parliament to vote itself out of existence and the Act of Union took effect from 1 January 1801.

Under the terms of the Act of Union, all Irish parliamentary business was conducted at Westminster with Ireland represented in the new united parliament by 100 MPs who were actually more representative of the Irish population than their predecessors in the Irish parliament had been. The Catholic community, however, remained largely excluded from politics, both in terms of the right to vote and the right to stand for parliament. Various Catholic relief bills were rejected by both the House of Commons and the House of Lords in the early 19th century and proponents of the issue remained largely divided until the 1820s and the formation of the Catholic Association under lawyer Daniel O'Connell. O'Connell made membership of the Association accessible to everyone with associate membership costing just a penny a month. By mobilising those few Catholics who did have the right to vote, along with liberal Protestant sympathisers, O'Connell was successful in getting first his supporters, and then himself, elected to parliament. The government was faced with the fact that O'Connell had been elected, but due to the nature of the constitution was unable to take his seat, a situation they realised could quickly lead to an uprising in Ireland. In response, parliament passed an emancipation bill in 1829, opening the way to Catholic participation in parliament and to public office.

In the late 1840s Ireland suffered enormous hardship due to the "Great Famine", precipitated by successive failures of the potato crop, upon which Ireland's labouring poor were dependent as their staple foodstuff. The Famine devastated many parts of Ireland, causing many of its survivors to emigrate, and the population of the island fell from almost 8 million to around 4 million, a combination of death by starvation and disease, and emigration. The industrialised northeast was less affected by this struggle than the rest of Ireland because tenant farming was not the sole local economy, although the Famine was an issue of grievance throughout the island.

The Famine had a profound impact on not just the Irish population but the entire way of life. Death, migration and eviction of the very poorest cottiers and labourers, combined with the financial difficulties experienced by the gentry led to the dominance of the farmer class in Irish agricultural society. This was accompanied by a change in farming methods with a move away from tillage towards animal husbandry and pastoral farming. Living standards for those who remained also rose with real wages increasing and housing stock and literacy levels improving. In political terms, the most enduring legacy of the Famine was the way in which it highlighted the problems with the Irish land system and popularised the struggle which became associated with these. It was via the land issue that the issue of Irish nationalism came again to the fore towards the end of the 19th century.

Home Rule

It was out of the struggle for land reform in the 1870s and 1880s that the movement for 'home government', in the form of restoration of an Irish parliament, gained support, firstly under the leadership of Isaac Butt and then Charles Stuart Parnell. Parnell was successful in creating a modern, highly disciplined political party, the Irish Parliamentary Party, which had Home Rule as its first objective. By 1886, the IPP had won enough seats at Westminster to hold the 'balance of power' thereby forcing Gladstone to introduce a Home Rule Bill in order to restore the Liberal party to power.

Although Parnell had won 85 Westminster seats in Ireland, including a majority of those in Ulster, Home Rule enjoyed far from universal support, both within parliamentary circles and outside. A huge number of Gladstone's own party voted with the opposition to defeat the Bill, a move which was applauded loudly in Ulster and which actually led the worst riots of the 19th century in Belfast, as Protestants asserted their victory over their Catholic neighbours and colleagues.

By the late nineteenth century Belfast had become a prosperous and growing city, and in 1891 bypassed Dublin to become the largest city in Ireland. In terms of industry Belfast had become renowned worldwide for its linen, engineering, aerated waterworks, tobacco works, distilleries and shipyards. In fact Belfast's shipbuilding and engineering prowess captured the imagination of the world in the form of the most famous ship in history, Titanic, which was built at the Belfast shipyard, Harland and Wolff. Although her maiden voyage ended in disaster, Titanic still brings recognition to Belfast, and to a yard

that at its peak employed over 30,000 men on site.

Belfast's industrial and commercial success and the prosperity of the north east of Ulster in general, was largely attributable to its strong links with Britain. Coal and raw materials for Belfast's industries came from mainland Britain, and it was Britain and the Empire which were the destination for many of the province's manufactured goods. Increasingly, this prosperous region was unwilling to be subsumed into a larger but poorer, nationalist Ireland. It was widely felt that a Dublin parliament, dominated by the landed interest, would impose heavy taxes on northern industry and introduce protective tariffs to promote southern self-sufficiency. Economic fears combined with religious and cultural differences to ensure that the suggestion of Home Rule for Ireland, or indeed any degree of self-rule by the Irish, was, in the main, met with what ranged from vociferous opposition to, at times, civil unrest in Ulster.

It was in opposition to Home Rule that Conservatives in Ireland organised themselves into a coherent Unionist grouping, under the leadership of Ulster landowner Sir Edward Saunderson. This group enjoyed the support of prominent British Conservatives and were successful in seeing Gladstone's Second Home Rule Bill defeated in the House of Lords in 1893.

The Home Rule issue, although in hibernation for almost twenty years re-emerged on the political agenda in 1910, when the Irish Parliamentary Party, under the leadership of John Redmond, was again able to force the Liberals to support Home Rule. The 1911 Parliament Bill reduced the power of the House of Lords to delaying legislation for two years so that when Asquith introduced the Third Home Rule Bill in April 1912 it seemed certain to become law by 1914. Sure in the knowledge that the permanent Conservative majority in the Lords would never accept Home Rule, Unionists had, in 1886 and 1893 been content to confine their objections to Irish self-government to parliamentary means. By 1912, it had become clear that they could only depend on themselves to defend against any Home Rule measure and began to make provisions for less constitutional means of opposition.

Under the leadership of Dublin lawyer Sir Edward Carson and Ulster whiskey millionaire James Craig, Unionist resistance to Home Rule was organised. Preparations were made for a Unionist Provisional Government to come into effect with the passage of any measure of Home Rule; mass demonstrations were organised in Ulster and in Britain; the Solemn League and Covenant was signed, by some in their own blood; the UVF formed and drilling and marching began; guns were brought into Ulster by night. Unionists were showing themselves to be serious in their opposition to Home Rule.

Nationalists were, at the same time, showing themselves to be just as serious in their pursuit of their long-time political objective. An Irish Volunteer Force was formed in opposition to 'Carson's Army' and guns were brought by night into Howth, just as they had been into Larne several months earlier.

Despite all this bravado, negotiations were ongoing in the period 1912-14 to try and find a peaceful resolution to the Home Rule crisis. Despite Carson's reluctance as a Southern Unionist, as time went on it became increasingly obvious that Unionists could only, realistically, 'save' only Ulster from the fate of Home Rule. Their minority was too small to have any hope of preventing the measure taking effect for the rest of Ireland and they preferred to retain an area that they could easily control. By the spring of 1914 the idea of partition seemed to have been accepted in principle by all parties concerned. Divisions did however still exist on the precise nature of any agreement which excluded some Ulster counties from Home Rule and focused on whether exclusion should be temporary or permanent and to how many counties it should apply.

Partition

Thus was the situation with the outbreak of World War I in August 1914. Redmond gave his support to the war effort in return for a promise of Home Rule at the end of the war. Although passed on 18 September 1914, Home Rule was suspended for the duration of the war when amending legislation would make special provision for Ulster. Attempts by Lloyd-George to reach a solution during the war came to nothing and when the issue was re-visited at the end of the conflict the result was the 1920 Government of Ireland Act, which effectively combined the principles of Home Rule with those of Unionism, creating a six-county Northern Ireland and a 26-county Southern Ireland, each with their own executive and parliament. It has been commented as being somewhat ironic that the one part of Ireland which so vehemently opposed Home Rule, is the one part where the principle can be considered to have actually worked, in the form of Northern Ireland. The powers of the two

new jurisdictions were initially limited and provision was made, in the shape of the Council of Ireland, for their amalgamation. This body was never to meet, however and Northern Ireland was there to stay. The Irish 'War of Independence' was fought in the south in the period 1919-21 and led to the signing of the Anglo-Irish Treaty in December 1921, whereby the remaining 26 counties were given the name Irish Free State and dominion status within the British Empire.

Northern Ireland

The new Northern Ireland government (which became known as the Stormont government, after the building in which it sat after 1932) established by the Government of Ireland Act was from the outset dominated by the Ulster Unionist Party, led by James Craig. The executive consisted of Prime Minister Craig and a Cabinet of 6 Unionist Ministers representing Finance, Home Affairs, Labour, Education, Agriculture and Commerce.

The new government had a less than auspicious start, facing threats and difficulties from every direction. Internally, it had to cope with sectarian rioting which in the period 1920-22 killed 455 and wounded 1766 people in Belfast alone. By the end of 1920 7,400 people had been driven from their jobs and nearly 23,000 from their homes. This was a situation the new administration found difficult to contain since although having responsibility, it was largely devoid of power to act.

Craig also felt his new state faced an external threat from the Free State Army, a fear which was in part confirmed in May 1922 when Irish troops occupied a triangle of land at Belleek on the Co Fermanagh border and defeated the local Ulster Special Constabulary garrison.

From the outset, the Stormont government was beset with financial difficulties. Its allocation of funds from Westminster were based on the boom years of 1920-21 which showed that the Northern Ireland government would have a surplus of £2.5 million but in reality the situation was the opposite and the Finance Minister experienced a permanent shortfall. Most of the money allocated to Northern Ireland was actually collected by the London Treasury, and only 'handed over' after the imperial contribution and other levies for legal and customs services were deducted. The result in Northern Ireland was uncertainty as to how much money the government would get each year which made budgeting somewhat difficult. This was all at a time when Northern Ireland's unemployment rate averaged 19% as a result of the decline of traditional industries in Belfast.

Despite all this the greatest threat that the new political entity faced in its first few years was constitutional and came in the shape of the Boundary Commission. In the course of negotiations over the Anglo-Irish Treaty in 1921, which had created the Boundary Commission, Lloyd-George assured Craig that only minor territorial changes would take place whilst leading Michael Collins to believe that huge areas would change hands. It wasn't until 1925 that it was decided that no changes would be made and Northern Ireland would be left as it was.

The situation in Northern Ireland was not made any easier by the lack of experience of government ministers. Only Craig had had previous government experience, most of the rest of the posts were allocated as a reward for political service and not on any basis of suitability or fitness to perform their job. This was compounded by the fact that there had been no pre-planning for a Home Rule parliament in Northern Ireland.

Sometimes criticism of individual ministers for their uninspired style of government can be harsh, considering the atmosphere in which they tried to function when every policy or initiative was subject to accusations of sectarianism. One such example was Lord Londonderry's 1923 Education Act which made provision for the establishment of a non-sectarian, secular system of education. Ironically this came under attack from both the Catholic Church (as it took the education of Catholic children out of exclusively Catholic hands) and the Protestant community because it didn't make compulsory the teaching of a programme of Protestant Bible instruction by teachers.

With the Ulster Unionist party in permanent government and firmly in control of all state institutions, nationalists and Catholics took little part in the new Northern Ireland state. Nationalist leaders initially boycotted the new parliament, but did take their seats from 1925 in an attempt to provide the Catholic minority with some representation at Stormont. Their level of representation was, however, significantly reduced by the abolition of proportional representation for parliamentary elections in 1927. Electoral discrimination was to be one

of the biggest grievances of the nationalist community under the Stormont government.

Other, more day-to-day grievances were felt in the areas of employment - in both the public and private sectors, housing and policing. In all these areas Catholics felt that they were deliberately discriminated against by Protestants who, from their positions of power, tended to control allocation of housing and jobs. All this contributed to the mentality that Northern Ireland was a 'Protestant state for a Protestant people'.

Whilst at the time of partition in 1920, it had been envisaged by some that Northern Ireland and its southern neighbour might, at some time in the future, come together again, in actual fact the two jurisdictions and their people grew further apart. Partition became entrenched in the inter-war years, and was reinforced by the Southern Ireland's constitutional change in 1948, when it became a Republic. Essentially Northern Ireland over time developed and established a unique political identity, and the Republic of Ireland's leaders made little effort to understand it.

Throughout this period inter-communal relations in Northern Ireland were poor and the arrival of the "liberal" Unionist leader Captain Terence O'Neill as Prime Minister in 1963 was to bring matters to a head. On taking office, O'Neill stated that he planned to raise living standards, not just for Catholics, but across the working classes. This attracted fierce opposition; both from within O'Neill's own party, and from other unionists, in particular, Ian Paisley. Paisley's main aim was to keep Northern Ireland Protestant at all costs and he opposed O'Neill's reforms vigorously and vociferously, particularly those granting equality to Catholics and co-operation with the Republic of Ireland. Despite O'Neill's condemnation, Paisley commanded substantial support among working-class Protestants. His uncompromising politics provided a strong contrast to those of the upper-class patrician O'Neill. O'Neill's promised reforms were rewarded by the resumption of Stormont seats by the Nationalist Party, who had previously boycotted the Parliament, but many felt that his actual reforms did not go far enough, especially within the context of siting a new 'city' (Craigavon, named after James Craig) and a university (Coleraine, as opposed to Derry) in predominantly Protestant areas.

Civil Rights to Hunger Strikes

Organisations such as the Campaign for Social Justice and the Northern Ireland Civil Rights Association (NICRA) were formed to demand equal rights for Catholics in housing, employment and voting. A student march, associated with NICRA, from Belfast to Derry in January 1969 broke out into fierce rioting after it passed through predominantly loyalist areas and was attacked by a crowd of loyalists. In the aftermath of the march, widespread rioting broke out across Northern Ireland and the issue started to move away from that of civil rights towards that of religious and national identity.

By the time of O'Neill's resignation in April 1969 (he was succeeded by Major Chichester-Clark), limited reforms had been undertaken, but the RUC had banned all marches. Continued street violence led to the deployment of British troops in Derry and Belfast in August that year, initially to protect Catholic communities from sectarian attacks.

In 1971, amid further escalations of violence, internment (imprisonment without trial) was reintroduced to Northern Ireland by Unionist Prime Minister Brian Faulkner (who had succeeded Chichester-Clark), albeit with little if any success. Though banned, civil right marches continued, and on 30th January 1972, a civil rights march ended with the British army shooting dead 13 men in what have been seen as controversial circumstances during a march in Derry. The day has become universally known as "Bloody Sunday". Nationalist political passions reached a new pitch not only in Northern Ireland but in the South as well; the British Embassy in Dublin was burned down in protest at the killings. The rapidly deteriorating security situation caused the Stormont administration to be prorogued by British Prime Minister Edward Heath, and Direct Rule from London introduced, initially as a temporary measure.

The 1970s saw an unprecedented resurgence of paramilitary violence, from both republican and loyalist quarters. The chief protagonists were the Provisional IRA, who took their name from the old Irish Republican Army of the Irish Civil War. The IRA saw its support rise dramatically through the 1970s, especially after the British government's re-introduction of internment, and it began a campaign of violence aimed at making the administration of Northern Ireland unprofitable and unmanageable for the British government. They waged war on the economic life of Northern Ireland by bombing numerous commercial and administrative targets, and on the police and army security establishment through direct attacks on personnel. Much smaller, splinter groups such as the Irish National Liberation Army (INLA) were also formed.

On the loyalist side, the UVF (the name taken from Carson's 1914 volunteer army) had become a secretive group intent on illegal activities, and was proscribed in 1966. By the 1970s its membership had also risen dramatically, along with that of the much larger Ulster Defence Association (UDA). Loyalist paramilitary violence was sporadic, spontaneous and random, mainly taking the form of indiscriminate shooting of Catholics in retaliation for IRA attacks on police officers, British Army troops and Protestant civilians.

The stakes were raised in 1979 when, amongst other incidents Lord Mountbatten, a prominent member of the British royal family, and later eighteen British soldiers were murdered in two republican attacks. The subsequent security clampdown brought about the loss of special category (PoW) status in local prisons, which led republican prisoners to go on hunger strike. 10 IRA men starved themselves to death, including the leader of the hunger-strikers, Bobby Sands, who was elected to the Fermanagh/South Tyrone Westminster seat whilst on hunger strike. Their deaths led to further rioting in Northern Ireland and Dublin, symptomatic of continuing community polarisation. The long-term significance of the hunger strikes was the stimulus they gave to the development of Sinn Féin as a serious political force.

From Violence to Agreement?

Since the 1970s and the Sunningdale Agreement there have been many political initiatives aimed at finding a solution to the situation in Northern Ireland and these are outlined in further detail in Chapter 2. The long and rocky road that came to be known as the Northern Ireland peace process finally led to an agreement that most of the major political players approved of in 1998 with The Good Friday Agreement. Although inter-communal strife is still going on in many parts of Northern Ireland and sectarian murders and beatings are still a regular occurrence, life in the province has improved drastically under the paramilitary ceasefires. For the most part, ordinary people can go about their everyday life without constant fear for their safety and generally, Northern Ireland has prospered during peacetime. New buildings, shops, restaurants and other entertainment venues are appearing all over the province and the numbers of visitors is gradually increasing.

It is clear that there is still a long way to go, particularly in light of the current political crisis but it is accepted by many that the crucial constitutional issues relating to the status of Northern Ireland itself have been decided, for the short term at least. Nonetheless divisions nurtured over centuries remain deep-rooted and will not disappear easily. Loyalists unclaimed by paramilitary groups and republican splinter groups have not ceased violence; they are seen as a minority by both moderate and extreme parties, nationalist and unionist. Both sides have many issues that they feel are outstanding - there is a unionist perception that the IRA is not sincere about peace, and nationalists have questioned the validity of loyalist ceasefires in the face of continuing sectarian attacks.

The future, however, is not entirely without hope. Communities have been helped by a fall in unemployment, contributed to by economic optimism. despite setbacks the long term signs indicate a trend towards a more peaceful future.

The Place

Geographical Overview

Northern Ireland occupies 5461 square miles in the northeast of the island of Ireland, which itself lies on the extreme northwest of the European continent. Its area takes up around one sixth of the island, approximately the size of Connecticut or Yorkshire. On the east it is separated from Scotland by the North Channel and from England by the Irish Sea; to the west and south it borders the Republic of Ireland. Its greatest distance north-south measures 85 miles, east-west 111 miles.

Northern Ireland's landscape consists mainly of low hill country, although there are two significant mountain ranges: the Mournes, which extend from South Down to Strangford Lough in the east, and the Sperrins, reaching through the northwest boundaries of Northern Ireland. The highest point in Northern Ireland is one of the twelve peaks of the Mournes: Slieve Donard in Co Down, some 2796 ft above sea level. From the top of Slieve Donard the Isle of Man is visible and in favourable conditions, the

Northern Ireland: Counties, Roads and Rivers   *Ordance Survey Copyright*

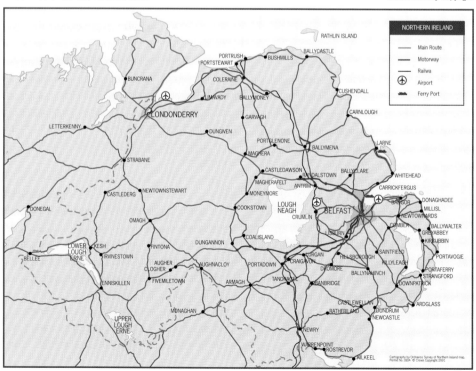

Scottish coast, Mount Snowdon in Wales and even the Cumbrian Hills of England may be seen. There is also a substantial tract of high land in Co Antrim known as the Antrim Plateau, or more commonly the 'Glens of Antrim'. In contrast, the lowest lying point in Northern Ireland is The Marsh, near Downpatrick, actually 1.3 ft below sea level.

There are also over 60 forests, including 9 forest parks, and a number of wooded areas. The southwest is

River Lagan, Belfast

mainly forested, with a number of small lakes and rivers which drain into Lough Erne. The lake, split into Upper and Lower Lough Erne, is a 50-mile waterway favoured by many for fishing and pleasure boating, particularly following the recent development of the Shannon-Erne waterway.

A basalt plateau extends throughout Northern Ireland, leading to brown earth soil that varies as a result of glacially transported material. This can appear as drumlins, smooth mounds that occur principally in parts of South Down and Armagh. Glaciation also created the area's principal valleys: the River Bann in the north, the Blackwater in the southwest and the Lagan in the east. These valleys have always been vital in providing routes through the heart of the North, and the waterways are still used commercially and for pleasure. Land between the estuary of the River Roe and the city of Derry was reclaimed from the sea in the nineteenth century for flax growing. As the land is below sea level, it is drained artificially and the estuary itself is now a nature reserve.

Lough Neagh is the largest freshwater lake on the whole island; the largest in the British Isles and one of the largest in Europe. It covers an area of 153 square miles out of Northern Ireland's total of 246 square miles of inland water and tideways. As well as providing all kinds of freshwater fish, the Lough is also the centre of a centuries-old eel fishery, which exports hundreds of tonnes of Ulster eels every year. The best view of Lough Neagh is generally available from a plane flying into Belfast International Airport: the surrounding land is very flat, making the Lough, despite its size, a somewhat hidden feature of Northern Ireland.

Farming land in Northern Ireland varies from the fertile arable expanses of North Down and South Antrim to the boggy low lying lands of the Fermanagh lakelands and the stony upland of mid Ulster and the Sperrins. Nonetheless there is sufficient quality land to support a major agricultural industry with the abundance of pasture giving dairy and livestock industries a competitive advantage.

Peat soils, historically the main source of fuel for peasant farmers, are a feature of the island and quite common in the North. Peat and turf are still cut extensively for fuel, although mainly for private domestic use as commercially they are not particularly significant. Few mineral resources are naturally present in Northern Ireland although gravel, clays, chalk and limestone provide the basis for the manufacture of lime, bricks and cement. Most other raw materials, such as oil and coal, are not rich in Northern Ireland and need to be imported. In fact Northern Ireland is at something of a competitive disadvantage in that it is entirely dependent on imported fuels to meet its energy requirements. The town of Coalisland is named after a vein of coal that, although present, has never been successfully mined. There is also a significant deposit of lignite on the western shores of Lough Neagh but this has yet to be proven commercially viable.

Northern Ireland's climate is temperate, although much affected by its maritime location. High winds are common, especially in the north and on the east coast, and south westerly winds tend to drive away clouds from the Atlantic. As a result, the weather in Northern Ireland can be fairly changeable, going from overcast to a blue sky in a short space of time. Rainfall varies from as little as 32.5 inches to 80 inches per year, generally increasing towards eastern areas. Spring is relatively dry; summer and winter are disproportionately wet. Winters are generally long because of Northern Ireland's location north and west, which also leads to shorter days in the winter months. Snow is not uncommon, but rarely settles and is seldom severe. However, summer days are also proportionately longer than average. Average temperatures range from 3.3 degrees centigrade in winter to 18 degrees in the summer, indicating few extremes of hot and cold. The mildness and humidity of Northern Ireland's climate, together with slow natural drainage, has given the area a reputation for lush green fields and constant rain, although conditions are generally quite pleasant.

Northern Ireland is also widely noted for its breathtaking scenery, including some 330 miles of coastal road. In fact, over 20% of the land has been designated as Areas of Outstanding Natural Beauty. This has been helped by low population density in many areas, leaving the countryside largely unspoilt. The generous natural landscape has also led to the growth of all kinds of outdoor pursuits. There are several championship standard golf courses, as well as opportunities for coarse fishing, as salmon and trout are plentiful in rivers. Watersports such as sailing and windsurfing are also popular, as are climbing, hiking and horse riding.

Area of Counties

Antrim	1176 sq miles
Armagh	513 sq miles
Down	982 sq miles
Fermanagh	715 sq miles
Londonderry	814 sq miles
Tyrone	1261 sq miles
Total	5461 sq miles

Mountains

Slieve Donard Co Down	2796 ft
Sawel Co Tyrone / Co Londonderry border	2240 ft
Cuilcagh Co Fermanagh	2188 ft
Slieve Gullion Co Armagh	1894 ft
Trostan Co Antrim	1817 ft

Lakes

Lough Neagh	153 sq miles
Lower Lough Erne	42 sq miles
Upper Lough Erne	13 sq miles

Rivers

Upper Bann: 47 miles from Mourne Mountains to Lough Neagh

Lower Bann: 38 miles from Lough Neagh to the Atlantic Ocean

Lagan: 32 miles from the Mournes to Belfast Lough

Counties

Northern Ireland is comprised of six of Ireland's 32 counties. Although often thought of as having some ancient tribal or cultural significance, the county divisions were entirely a British administrative creation in the 19th Century. The six counties of Northern Ireland each have their own unique image and characteristics and are described briefly below.

Antrim

Antrim occupies the north-east corner of Northern Ireland, stretching from Belfast in the south to the north coast. To the east is the Irish Sea, and Antrim's western boundary for the most part is Lough Neagh and the River Bann. It is Northern Ireland's second largest county by size. County Antrim is a mixture of urban centres including most of north and west Belfast, the towns of Ballymena, Larne, Carrickfergus, Ballymoney and Antrim town itself, and large rural stretches.

Antrim is possibly best known for its picturesque 'Glens', home to traditional rural lifestyles and splendid mountain scenery, and its rugged north coast where Northern Ireland's premier visitor attraction, the Giant's Causeway, is located.

Armagh

Armagh is Northern Ireland's smallest county, characterised by the large towns of Lurgan and Portadown (Craigavon) to the north, the ecclesiastical city of Armagh itself mid-county and drumlin country in the south.

Known in Ireland and worldwide as the 'Orchard County', Armagh has a major apple production and processing industry, famous for the local 'Bramley' cooking apple. The cathedral city itself, with its religious significance, is described below under 'cities'. The border areas have witnessed much of the anti-British violence carried out during the Troubles and the area of South Armagh, near the Irish border, earned the unfavourable tag of 'bandit country' during the 1970s and 1980s. However South Armagh offers fine scenery around Slieve Gullion and many interesting attractions for the visitor.

The county is currently enjoying the unprecedented status of being all-Ireland Gaelic football champions!

Londonderry

County Londonderry – the 'Oak Leaf' county - lies to the north west of Northern Ireland, and combines the major population centres of Derry city and Coleraine with numerous small towns and villages becoming ever more rural toward the south of the county. Northern Ireland's second largest mountain range, the Sperrins, runs through the heart of the county and 'Crossing the Sperrins', through the notorious 'Glenshane Pass', is a well known feature of any journey between Derry and Belfast. The county is defined geographically by four main river valleys: the Bann, the Roe, the Faughan and the Foyle.

Down

Like Antrim, County Down incorporates a major slice of Belfast – most of the south and east of the city. The other substantial towns in the county are Bangor and Newtownards in the north-east, Lisburn in the north-west, Banbridge and Ballynahinch in mid-county and Newcastle, Downpatrick and Newry in the south.

Down is home to the Mountains of Mourne, Northern Ireland's highest mountain range and source of the River Bann. It also encloses Northern Ireland's second largest inland waterway, Strangford Lough, which opens up to the Irish sea.

Down incorporates the industrial with the rural and with numerous attractive small towns such as Moira, Hillsborough and Castlewellan, and has a significant tourism industry centred around the popular tourist resorts of Newcastle and Bangor.

Fermanagh

Fermanagh is a predominantly rural county located to the south-west of Northern Ireland. It has by far the smallest population of any of the six counties and its main industries are agriculture and tourism. The tourism

industry is largely based around Fermanagh's two major internal waterways: Lower and Upper Lough Erne. These lakes are a major attraction to anglers and a centre for boating holidays. Fermanagh's main centre is the picturesque town of Enniskillen, the regional administrative centre which is built around a series of islands at the mouth of Lower Lough Erne. Other significant towns, providing employment and centres of population are Lisnaskea, in the south of the county and Irvinestown in the north.

Tyrone

Tyrone is Northern Ireland's largest county by size and stretches from Lough Neagh in the East to the border with Donegal in the West. There is no dominant town in the county, the four main ones being Strabane to the north west, Cookstown to the east, Omagh in the centre and Dungannon to the south. The main industry is agriculture although there is a spread of industry throughout the main towns. Tyrone, meaning Eoin's Land, is the ancient home of the O'Neill clan, once the dominant rulers of Ulster. The 'Red Hand' of Ulster remains the symbol of the county to this day. Tyrone's main rivers include the Ballinderry, the Owenreagh and Strule and are known to anglers for the quality of their fishing.

Cities in Northern Ireland

Northern Ireland now has five cities: Belfast, Derry, Armagh, Lisburn and Newry although these are quite different from each other in size and all are very small by global standards. Lisburn and Newry have just recently been awarded city status during the 2002 Golden Jubilee celebrations as part of a UK-wide initiative.

Belfast

The capital city of Northern Ireland, Belfast is also its administrative, industrial and commercial centre. It has a population of around 350,000 and enjoys an enviable setting, facing out to sea and cradled on all sides by ranges of hills and mountains. The name Belfast itself is derived from the Irish béal feirste. This literally means 'mouth of the river' and came from Belfast's position at the head of the River Lagan, which becomes Belfast Lough as it joins the Irish Sea. Originally a small town, Belfast saw its population increase significantly with the Industrial Revolution. In 1800 its population was around

20,000 but the enormous growth of the linen industry caused Belfast to expand rapidly. Rows of small terraced housing serve as a reminder of the thousands of mill and factory workers who moved from the countryside and settled in the city. In 1888, Belfast became a city by royal charter and by the end of the 19th century had overtaken Dublin in terms of its population. By the beginning of the Second World War, during which Belfast experienced serious bombing at the hands of German planes targeting its shipyards and engineering works, its population had exceeded 400,000.

The city also suffered heavily in economic and social terms during the 'Troubles', when it became a frequent target of paramilitary bombs. In recent years however it has enjoyed a major revival of cultural activities and a more positive atmosphere, with new hotels, restaurants and entertainment venues springing up all over the city. Currently Belfast is bidding for the title of European Capital of Culture 2008.

Belfast is also a district, in local Government terms, covering some 44 square miles (115 square km), taking in several smaller towns and villages around its limits. 2001 Census figures reveal the population of Belfast's electoral district to be 277,391, which demonstrates the extent to which life in Northern Ireland does indeed centre around its capital city.

Derry (Londonderry)

Derry, the 'Maiden City', is located on the river Foyle in the north west of Northern Ireland, and has a population of around 100,000. It is one of the oldest settlements on the island of Ireland, having traditionally been founded in 546 AD by St Columba. The name Derry comes from the Irish word Doire or Daire, meaning oak grove, in particular one surrounded by water or a peat bog. This was the case in Derry, the grove being on an island in the River Foyle. The water beside the island gradually dried out, leaving a boggy area that became known as the 'Bogside'. In the early seventeenth century, King James I gave the City of London responsibility for settling this area of Ireland. Derry was fortified in 1613 and renamed Londonderry by royal charter as part of the Plantation of Ulster. The debate over what the city should be called is a long-standing one with some people now adopting the phrase 'Stroke City' as a humourous and inoffensive option.

Although much smaller than Belfast and no bigger than a typical English town the inhabitants of Derry are very proud of their City status and their rich heritage. The defined area of Derry city itself is relatively small, only 3.4 square miles. Derry has never been a prosperous city, with unemployment continually above the Northern Ireland average. Traditionally it has had a particular problem with male unemployment as its well-established shirtmaking industry has tended to provide more jobs taken up by women. Poverty remains a problem in the city. In recent years, although the shirt factories have been closing there has been an influx of new engineering and high-tech investments in the city, and Derry has developed a new economic self-confidence. It is expected that initiatives such as re-locating public sector jobs to the city will help go some way towards alleviating unemployment.

Despite its image as a divided city Derry is developing a vibrant cultural life with its new Millennium Forum hosting many famous musicians and theatrical productions. Each October the entire city comes alive for the annual Halloween festival, when houses are decorated and people dress up to enjoy the festivities. Architecturally the city boasts the famous City Walls and the Guildhall, which are both must-see sights for any visitor. The emergence of new hotels, bars and restaurants have meant that Derry city has become more appealing as a place for people to visit as well as to live and work.

The Guildhall, Derry

Armagh

Armagh is similarly an historical city, first founded on the hill fort of Ard Mhacha in the 4th century AD. It has a population of less than 20,000 and barely merits inclusion in the top 10 of Northern Ireland's towns (by population). Important in terms of Ulster and Ireland as a whole, it is the ancient city of St Patrick. Both Church of Ireland and Catholic cathedrals in the city are named after the patron saint of Ireland and both churches' archbishops are based in the ecclesiastical city. Armagh city also boasts an observatory (founded in 1765) and planetarium. Of particular note is the fine Regency and Georgian architecture that is prominent around the City Centre in the area of the Mall.

The wider Armagh local Government district covers an area of 261 square miles, and, according to the 2001 Census figures has a population of 54,263 indicating low population density in what is a heavily rural area. The county of Armagh is known as the Orchard County; famous for fruit growing, in particular apples, although there are a number of light industrial centres as well.

Lisburn

Lisburn, some 8 miles southwest of Belfast and increasingly merging with the south western outskirts of the city, was a small village until plantation. The English government invited French Huguenots to settle there, who nurtured the growing linen industry by the introduction of new Dutch looms. Lisburn quickly became a major linen producer, although today this focus has progressed to synthetic fabrics. The River Lagan, which meets the sea in Belfast, runs through the centre of Lisburn and although the linen industry based around the river has declined, Lisburn remains an important centre for commerce and industry in Northern Ireland and is also a popular residential location, acting as a 'commuter town' for Belfast.

Newry

Newry is notable for having the first inland waterway in the British Isles, which contributed greatly to the town's prosperity in the nineteenth century. The canal had 14 locks and provided a means to export mainly linen and stone. By 1840 its importance had declined, however, and Newry town remained small in consequence. Its name is derived from the Gaelic for a yew tree, which was according to legend planted by St Patrick in the area.

Newry has experienced rapid growth in population and economic activity in recent years and today is a busy city benefiting from its close proximity to the border with the Republic of Ireland. The city itself is some forty miles south of Belfast and only sixty miles north of Dublin.

Towns in Northern Ireland

Many of Northern Ireland's towns date from the seventeenth century, when London companies formed the Honourable The Irish Society. They planned and built towns around a central meeting place, known as a diamond. Two streets would intersect the diamond and the town itself would be built on a grid pattern. These towns would usually include fortifications around the town's boundary, a market house and a planter's residence. Limavady and Coleraine in County Londonderry are good examples of 'plantation towns'.

Later, in the nineteenth century, smaller 'mill villages' such as Bessbrook in County Armagh, were planned around greens which may have been used as 'bleach greens' for bleaching linen. These villages and small towns were characterised by terraces of small, neat mill-workers houses, many of which have been modernised but are preserved in their original architectural form.

Other larger market towns tend to have a long, wide main street. For example, Cookstown in County Tyrone is known for its main street, 1.25 miles long and 130 ft wide. Lurgan in County Armagh is another example. Given the rural environment, there are many small market towns throughout the area. Northern Ireland also has an abundance of tiny villages and hamlets, especially in more remote areas. The smallest Irish description of a rural district is a 'townland' which could be as little as 300 acres. In 1846 Ordnance Survey recorded more than 60,000 of these townlands across the island of Ireland. In some parts of Northern Ireland, people are very proud of their townlands and actively try to preserve them by using them in preference to their official road or street name as part of their postal address.

During the seventeenth century plantation, the majority of place names all over Ireland were 'anglicised' by planters, from their original Gaelic Irish. Translation meant that many place names are remarkably similar, especially in terms of prefix; the basic difference being a spelling closer to the English phonetics of the original Gaelic name. Common examples include Bally-, from Baile, meaning town; and Drum- or Drom-, from droim, meaning ridge. Knock comes from the Irish word cnoc meaning hill, and carrick from the Irish carraig, meaning rock.

Hillsborough, County Down

The Bann river is often seen as a dividing line in Northern Ireland: the more prosperous east and the poorer, less populated west. Derry is unquestionably the major population centre of the West and local businesses often complain that Northern Ireland stops 'left of the Bann'. Most people live east of the Bann and few of the towns to the west have more than 10,000 inhabitants.

Northern Ireland's main towns (in terms of population based on 1991 census figures) are described briefly below:

Bangor (pop 52437)

Third in terms of population after Belfast and Derry, Bangor is a large town located on the affluent North Down coastline, some 16 miles east of Belfast. The town centre is very close to the sea front at the mouth of Belfast Lough. Although it is a commercial and administrative centre in its own right Bangor is also a residential location for many people whose employment is in Belfast. Bangor is a popular seaside tourist resort attracting many visitors, particularly to its splendid marina, during the summer months.

Ballymena (pop 28717)

Ballymena is also one of Northern Ireland's largest and busiest towns, and is the main administrative centre for the north east region of Northern Ireland. The town is home to some major manufacturing industries and also services a large and prosperous rural population, enjoying one of the lowest rates of unemployment in the North. Despite its prosperity, Ballymena's image has been under assault with the town being associated in recent years with acts of political extremism and hard drugs. Nonetheless the town is highly regarded in terms of the quality of its shops and its people maintain a reputation for friendliness and warmth.

Craigavon including, Lurgan (pop 21905) and Portadown (pop 21299).

Craigavon, Portadown and Lurgan are all part of a south west extension of the Lagan Valley and Belfast's industrial area. The central Craigavon area was originally designated a 'new town' in the late 1960s, hoping to create a new lifestyle in a modern environment with a fully integrated approach to planning. The town, named after unionist Prime Minister James Craig, later Lord Craigavon, was supposed to join together the established towns of Lurgan and Portadown (just 5 miles apart) and provide relief for the overcrowding experienced in Belfast at that time. However, people did not move to Craigavon in the numbers anticipated and, particularly in the 1970s, there was insufficient employment available for those who did. The result was surplus, unwanted public housing alongside economic deprivation. Its popularity did not reach expectations at the time of its creation, although more recently Craigavon is becoming a preferred location for Belfast-bound commuters.

The Craigavon area with its proximity to Lough Neagh and good communications infrastructure is developing a very positive lifestyle image built around recreation and leisure.

Coleraine (pop 20721)

Coleraine is in County Londonderry, although it is the main town on the north east coast of Northern Ireland, which mainly falls under County Antrim. The town is centred where Northern Ireland's biggest river, the Bann, joins the North Sea. It is a busy industrial centre and market town, as well as being a University town with a major campus located on its northern outskirts. Coleraine is a popular base for touring the north Antrim coast, and is close to two of Northern Ireland's most popular holiday resorts, Portrush and Portstewart.

Larne (pop 17575)

Larne is home to Northern Ireland's second most important port (only Belfast ranks above it), as well as a busy commercial centre. Situated about 20 miles north east of Belfast and sheltered by the Islandmagee headland, Larne is a busy ferryport, taking heavy volumes of passengers and cargo to the Scottish ports of Stranraer and Cairnryan. It is also home to some of Northern Ireland's busiest industries, with a narrow stretch of water separating it from the North's biggest power station, Ballylumford.

Omagh (pop 17280)

Omagh has seen significant growth as a result of increased administration in the western regions of Northern Ireland. In more recent times it experienced the worst single atrocity of the Northern Ireland troubles – a bomb in the town centre in August 1998 which killed 29 people. Omagh is a busy market town and its location in the rural centre of Northern Ireland means that it serves a substantial rural hinterland. Its people have earned extensive recognition for the dignified manner in which the community has rebuilt itself following the 1998 atrocity.

Strabane (pop 11981)

Strabane is situated on the border, some 20 miles south of Derry, and sits to the east of the River Foyle. Strabane has historically experienced some of the highest levels of unemployment in any of Northern Ireland's large towns. However, its heritage is rich, as Strabane was an important printing and publishing centre in the eighteenth century and the American Declaration of Independence was printed there.

Enniskillen (pop 11436)

Enniskillen is the unofficial capital of the Fermanagh lakelands, as well as being the administrative and commercial centre for the county. It is possibly Northern Ireland's most picturesque large town. With its island location and accompanying attractions Enniskillen is a popular tourist centre, particularly for boating and angling enthusiasts.

Dungannon (pop 9420)

Dungannon town is situated in the south of County Tyrone in the centre of Northern Ireland. Its Irish name is Dún Geanainn, meaning Gannon's fort. Today Dungannon is a market town, also hosting light industries including food processing, crystal and fabrics. Dungannon is the main commercial centre for the largely rural area of South Tyrone

Lough Erne, County Fermanagh

The People

Northern Ireland's "Troubles" are rooted in social and cultural differences that go back many hundreds of years and it is impossible to describe the people without reference to history and religion. The area has always had strong links with the western areas of Scotland as a consequence of its close proximity. English and Scottish settlers during the Plantation found that apart from their nationality, their Protestant faith marked them as separate from the native Irish. Unlike the Norman invaders of 1170, the English and Scottish planters of the 16th and 17th centuries resisted any integration of their culture into that of the native population. Over time they came to form the majority of the population in County Antrim, North Down and the Lagan Valley.

The Protestant planters of Ulster contributed greatly to the government's anglicisation of Ireland. They did this by translating place names from Irish, and establishing English over Gaelic as the official language. Scottish influence is especially striking in the regional accents and dialects of Northern Ireland. Areas with stronger Scottish links, such as the county of Antrim and parts of county Down, have discernible Scottish accents; indeed inhabitants of towns like Ballymena are often mistaken for Scots by visitors. Similarly, areas close to the border with the Republic of Ireland show southern characteristics in language, for example people from Derry and Donegal sound quite similar.

There is an uneven distribution of Protestant and Catholic communities throughout Northern Ireland. Protestants tended to settle in the northern and eastern areas, and many of those who did settle in western and border areas moved, or were driven away as a result of political violence. As a result Northern Ireland is strongly Catholic and Nationalist overall west of the Bann and overwhelmingly Protestant and Unionist to the east of the river.

Population
Size and Composition

The population of Northern Ireland on 30 June 2001 (estimated) was 1,689,319; overall, in the period 1991-2001, the population has increased by 5.1%. Every local government area in Northern Ireland saw its population increase over the past ten years, apart from Belfast City, which recorded a population decrease of 5.4%. The only growth in Belfast was in the number of 20-24 year olds which may indicate a growing student population. Banbridge, Carrickfergus and Ards experienced the greatest increases. There is a small (but growing) female majority of 42,000 which translates as a balance of 51% females to 49% males. Population by age and gender is set out in table 1.1.

Table 1.1 Northern Ireland Population by gender and age 2000			
Age Group	**Male**	**Female**	**Total**
Under16	209,150	198,831	407,981
16 and over	622,897	666,897	1,289,794
16-21	173,916	163,844	337,760
30-44	184,402	189,850	374,352
45-59 Female/ 45-64 Male	175,105	146,456	318,561
60 Female/ 65 Male & over	89,474	169,764	259,221
16 to 59 Female/ 45-64 Male	533,423	497,150	1,030,573
75 & over	35,085	64,090	99,175
Total: All Ages	832,047	865,728	1,697,775

Source NISRA

The three key determinants of population size are the birth rate, death rate and net inward or outward migration. Although Northern Ireland's birth rate has always outpaced the death rate, the natural growth in population has tended to be checked by a high degree of net outward migration. Birth rates are generally higher in the West and South of Northern Ireland than in the East and North, however the highest birth rate in Northern Ireland is in Magherafelt (16.9 per 1000 compared to Northern Ireland average of 13.6 per 1000). The lowest birth rate in Northern Ireland is in North Down.

Net outward migration from Northern Ireland was 214 in 1999-00 which represents a 90% fall from the previous year's figure of 2,844 and suggests a trend of falling outward migration. Early indications from the 2001 census, however suggest that this is not actually the case and that Northern Ireland in fact has a net emigration trend.

Population Density

The overall population density of Northern Ireland in 2000 was estimated at 125 persons per square kilometre. Population density also varies considerably across Northern Ireland tending to be at its lowest in the centre and west of the Province and higher in the east and in the hinterlands of the larger towns and cities. Local government districts with the highest population densities are Belfast, North Down and Carrickfergus, while Moyle, Fermanagh and Omagh have the lowest.

Another unusual dimension to the population distribution of Northern Ireland is that it is not overwhelmingly concentrated in cities and towns. Although the Greater Belfast area accounts for almost one third of the total population in Northern Ireland, most of the remaining inhabitants are to be found in numerous small towns, villages, hamlets and relatively remote rural locations. Two thirds of Northern Ireland's land mass is west of the River Bann, and there are virtually no towns of population greater than 15,000 people (excluding the City of Derry) in this area.

Life Expectancy and Population Growth

Birth rates in Northern Ireland are generally high by UK standards although the overall birth rate for the region has slowed down significantly in recent years.In 1971 there were 20.6 births per 1,000 population in Northern Ireland, falling to 17.6 in 1981, 16.2 in 1991 and down to 13.6 in 1999. 8% of all Northern Ireland births in 1999 were to mothers under the age of 20. Mothers aged 40 and over accounted for 2% of all births.

1999 saw death rates in Northern Ireland increase slightly, which is against the overall recent trend which has seen them gradually falling, reflecting the general tendency for people to live longer. Indeed life expectancy for children born in the period 1997-99 is calculated to be 80 (women) and 74 (men); the highest ever. Table 1.2 illustrates recent trends in births, deaths and life expectancy in Northern Ireland over the last 30 years.

Table 1.2 Birth Rate, Death Rate, Life Expectancy in Northern Ireland

Year	Births*	Deaths*	Life Expectancy**	
			Male	Female
1971	20.6	10.5	67.6	73.7
1981	17.6	10.5	69.2	75.6
1991	16.2	9.4	72.8	78.7
1999	13.6	9.3	74.3	79.6

* per 1000 population

** years

Source NISRA

Marriage rates in Northern Ireland have been falling steadily over the past 30 years. Whilst in 1971 there were 7.9 marriages per 1000 of population, the figure for 1999 has fallen to just 4.5. This is indicative of changing trends in society, whereby it has become increasingly common for people to live together without getting married. This is a trend which is, however, less prevalent in Northern Ireland than elsewhere in the United Kingdom. In Northern Ireland in the period 1996-1999 10% of people aged 16-59 were co-habiting outside marriage; the corresponding figure for the United Kingdom as a whole was 23%

It had been expected that the population of Northern Ireland would generally continue to increase gradually, however, the recently-released figures from the 2001 census show that this in actual fact may not be the case. As more detailed information is released it will become clearer as to the precise trends but is clear that Northern Ireland continues to have a high level of outward migration. This is especially true in relation to young people, many of whom leave the province to obtain their higher education in Britain or elsewhere and never return. Similarly many graduates and other young people feel obliged to leave Northern Ireland in order to find suitable employment. Another factor relating to migration, which is particularly relevant to Northern Ireland is political stability and in light of current developments, this is something which it will be difficult to predict reliably.

Table 1.3 Northern Ireland Population Projection to 2040 (thousands)

	2000	2005	2010	2015	
Males	832	850	865	880	
Females	866	877	888	899	
Total	1,698	1,727	1,753	1,778	
	2020	2026	2031	2036	2040
Males	891	899	898	890	881
Females	908	915	915	908	898
Total	1,800	1,814	1,812	1,798	1,779

Source NISRA

Population and Religion

One of the key insights into Northern Ireland – from a political perspective – is the changing religious composition of the population. Given that political affiliations correlate significantly with religious divisions, any changes in the relative numbers of the two communities are assumed to have political implications. In most other parts of the western world the religious breakdown of the population would only be of academic interest but in Northern Ireland it attracts much more attention for this reason.

Of considerable political significance is the perception that the birth rate in the Catholic community is traditionally much higher than in the Protestant community, adding weight to the majority community's fear that political power would shift from the declining Protestant majority to the growing Catholic minority. Over recent years both birth rates have slowed down and the gap has narrowed significantly.

Religious Affiliation

Northern Ireland is home to people from a variety of ethnic and religious backgrounds. However, most people in the region describe themselves in terms of the principal Christian denominations found throughout the English-speaking world: the Roman Catholic Church; the Church of Ireland (Anglican); the Presbyterian Church; or other, smaller Protestant denominations. In the Northern Ireland Census of population 1991, 38% of the population stated that they were Roman Catholic and 51% said that they were non-Catholic, of whom the vast majority were Protestant. Non-Christian religious groupings were numerically small and included 972 Muslims, 742 Hindus, 410 Jews, 319 Baha's and 270 Buddhists. Small groups of respondents who described themselves as agnostics, freethinkers and humanists were also counted as Non-Catholic. The 1991 Census was the first to give respondents the option of stating that they had no religious beliefs and 59,234 people (approximately 4% of the population) did so. 7% of respondents did not answer the religion question.

A continuous household survey conducted in 1993-94 and 1995-96 indicated that 42% of the NI population were Catholic and 54% were Protestant. There is much anticipation of the recent 2001 census data, which is likely to indicate that the gap between numbers of Protestants and Catholics has closed further, with Catholics expected to comprise around 45% of the population.

Northern Ireland has higher rates of church attendance than elsewhere in the United Kingdom and religion is, in its own right, important to the life of the area. Even people who have little formal religious commitment often have a social background which is linked to one or other of the two main religious communities. Frequently it is on this basis that they are perceived by others to belong to either the Protestant or Catholic community. The community to which a person belongs often influences many other aspects of their life: their national identity, language, the area in which they live, the school they or their children attend, the political party they support and even their name. Religious community background (rather than belief) as the principal source of social identity in Northern Ireland has been the subject of considerable academic attention.

Religious Segregation

Northern Ireland's 26 Local Government Districts (LGDs) vary in terms of the religious composition of respective populations. In 1991, the proportion of Protestants in each LGD population ranged from more than three-quarters in Carrickfergus and Castlereagh Borough Councils to around a fifth in Newry and Mourne District Council. Correspondingly, Carrickfergus has the lowest Catholic proportion (7%) and Newry and Mourne the highest (72%). In North Down, 9% of respondents stated that they had no religious beliefs, the highest proportion for any LGD.

For smaller geographical areas a high degree of residential segregation often exists between the Protestant and the Catholic communities in Northern Ireland. The 1991 Census was conducted by aggregating data from 3,729 Enumerating Districts (EDs), where each ED was a small homogeneous area containing around 150 households. In about half of Northern Ireland's EDs, the population was either more than 90% Protestant or more than 90% Catholic, while in a further 17% of EDs, one or other community accounted for between 80 and 90% of the population. This reflects the deep polarisation of the two communities in areas that at a higher level of analysis appear mixed.

Language and Identity

The Northern Ireland Social Attitudes Survey was first conducted in 1989. Focusing on a range of social and political issues, it collected the opinions of a representative sample of persons aged 18 or over who live in private households. In the 1995 survey, 63% of Catholic respondents described themselves as 'Irish' compared with 5% of Protestants. In contrast, 64% of Protestant respondents described themselves as 'British' compared with 11% of Catholics. The 1991 Census also contained a question on knowledge of the Irish language, which was to be answered in respect of the population aged three or over. Approximately one in ten people (89% of whom were Catholic) could speak, read or write Irish. In 1995-96, 1038 pupils in Northern Ireland, equating to 0.3% of all school enrolments, were taught through the medium of Irish.

Northern Ireland: Households

Household size

Households in Northern Ireland tend to be significantly larger than the average for the United Kingdom as a whole. The average Northern Ireland household comprised 3 persons in 1999-2000, whereas in Great Britain the average was closer to 2. In 1999, 29% of Northern Ireland households comprised four or more people compared with 21% in Great Britain. Northern Ireland's households have generally been larger than the UK average, partly because of the tendency for Northern Ireland families to have more children, and also the fact that the traditional extended family (including grandparents) has survived to a greater extent in Northern Ireland.

Single person households make up around 26% of Northern Ireland's total households compared to 29% in Great Britain. 22% of all Northern Ireland households consist of married or cohabiting couples with no children. At 30% it is significantly higher in Great Britain.

Although family sizes are higher in Northern Ireland, they have been coming down steadily in absolute terms. Higher expectations about living standards and changes to the structure of living costs has meant that many families on average incomes would struggle to maintain a desired standard of living for larger household sizes, i.e. with more than 2 or 3 children. Economic forces therefore, combined with social attitudinal change in relation to family planning have put downward pressure on family size. This trend has been apparent in both religious communities.

Table 1.4: Number of Persons in Household 1995-96 to 1999-2000

No of persons	Northern Ireland				Great Britain		
	95-96	96-97	98-99	99-00	95-96	96-97	98-99
1	25	25	25	25	28	27	29
2	27	27	30	30	35	34	36
3	17	16	16	15	16	16	15
4	16	17	16	15	15	15	14
5	9	9	8	8	5	5	5
>6	6	5	5	5	2	2	2
Average Household size	2.78	2.75	2.71	2.67	2.44	2.43	2.36

Source: NISRA; General Household Survey, Office for National Statistics

Household Income and Expenditure

In 1999-2000 62% of household income in Northern Ireland was derived from wages and salaries, 7% from self-employment and approximately 22% from social security benefits. Northern Ireland households derive almost twice as much of their income from state benefits compared with the UK as a whole.

In 1999-2000 the highest proportion of Northern Ireland weekly household expenditure was spent on food (21%), motoring (14%) and leisure services (11%). The biggest distinguishing factors between Northern Ireland and the UK as a whole was the extent to which a higher proportion of average weekly expenditure in Northern Ireland was on food, reflecting the overall lower average income. It is also notable that Northern Ireland households spend a significantly lower proportion of their income on housing than those in the rest of the UK - 9% compared with 16%.

Within Northern Ireland levels of household income and expenditure can vary with social class, housing classification and household composition. There is less variation in income and expenditure by geographical area, although there is an established trend for average incomes to be higher in the East than in the West.

Overall, although household income and expenditure in Northern Ireland is lower than the UK average it follows a similar pattern when analysed by household composition and tenure.

Table 1.5: Sources of household income, 1999-2000*

Wages and salaries	62	66
Self employment	7	10
Investments	2	5
Annuities and pensions	6	7
Social security benefit	22	12
Other	1	1
Average gross weekly household income	£358	£480

* as a % of average gross weekly household income

Source NISRA

Table 1.6: Type of Household 1995-96 to 1999-2000

Type of household	Northern Ireland			Great Britain		
	97-98	98-99	99-00	95-96	96-97	98-99
1 person only	26	25	26	28	27	29
2 or more adults	3	3	3	2	3	2
Married / Cohabiting couple:						
with dependent children	30	28	29	24	25	23
with non-dependent children only	7	8	7	6	6	6
no children	20	21	22	29	28	30
Lone parent:						
with dependent children	8	9	8	7	7	7
with non-dependent children only	4	5	4	3	3	3
Two or more families	1	1	1	1	1	1

Source: NISRA; General Household Survey, Office for National Statistics

CHAPTER 2

Government of Northern Ireland

Political History and Recent Developments 1920–1985

Introduction

Northern Ireland came into being with the enactment of the Government of Ireland Act on 23 December 1920. The Act created two new jurisdictions in Ireland each with their own parliament. The jurisdiction of the new Northern Ireland comprised the six North-eastern counties of Antrim, Armagh, Down, Fermanagh, Londonderry and Tyrone.

The Government of Ireland Act provided for a Northern Ireland Parliament consisting of two chambers. The first, a 52 member House of Commons, the second, a Senate, consisting of 26 members all elected by the lower chamber except for the two ex-officio seats held by the Lord Mayor of Belfast and the Mayor of Londonderry. Although Northern Ireland was given its own devolved government, Section 75 of the Government of Ireland Act 1920 specified that the supreme authority of the UK parliament would continue to apply.

In addition, to continue the formal presence of the monarch in the most peripheral region of the United Kingdom, the office of Governor of Northern Ireland was created under the Act. The executive powers of the new Northern Ireland Parliament were vested in the office of the Governor who replaced the previous Lord Lieutenant.

From the outset the powers of the new government were clearly defined. All powers relating to defence, armed forces and foreign policy were retained by Westminster and the powers of the Northern Government limited in relation to taxation, with Westminster reserving the power to raise income tax and customs and excise duties.

Although the legislation had anticipated the reunification of Ireland by agreement between the two parliaments facilitated by a new institution, the Council of Ireland, the institutions established by the provisions of the Government of Ireland Act were to last for over 50 years.

The First Northern Ireland Parliament

Following elections in May 1921 the first parliament of Northern Ireland opened on 7 June 1921 in the council chamber of Belfast City Hall, where a Unionist Party government headed by James Craig was sworn in.

The new government comprised seven departments

Parliament Buildings Stormont

headed by the Department of the Prime Minister, which maintained a coordinating role with Westminster and across the other local ministries.

The continuation of political conflict for several years following the 1921 Treaty of Independence in the south meant that the anticipated reunification of the two administrations, North and South, did not occur. Instead Northern Ireland drifted further from the Free State and did not participate in the proposed Council of Ireland or Boundary Commission. The institutions established under the first Craig Government continued relatively uninterrupted until the Second World War with Craig's Ulster Unionist party permanently in government.

Parity

Growing acceptance of the "principle of parity" in terms of the requirement to treat Northern Ireland citizens on the same basis as the Westminster government would treat citizens of Great Britain had developed throughout this period. However, despite the "principle of parity" successive governments held relative freedom in their management of the internal administration of the North and were able, amongst other initiatives, to introduce radical reform of the electoral system, effectively reinforcing the government's political control.

The establishment of the post-war Labour government at Westminster under the leadership of Clement Atlee had a radical agenda for social and economic reform, which unsettled the right-of-centre Unionist administration in Northern Ireland from the outset and brought the "principle of parity" into sharper focus.

In the post war period the financial relationship underpinning parity was extensively developed between London and Belfast. The establishment of parity in public services and taxation in 1946 consequently meant that the Northern Ireland budget had to be "cleared" in advance by the Treasury in London. Comprehensive National Insurance legislation passed in 1948 consolidated previously separated funds into a single fund for the United Kingdom guaranteeing equal benefits throughout the jurisdiction. This was followed in 1949 by further developments which saw national assistance, family allowances, pensions and health service provisions being put onto an equal footing with the UK coupled with the guarantee that where the cost of providing these services should be higher in Northern Ireland than in

Britain the UK government would fund 80 per cent of the surplus costs. Arguably this was the ancestry of the current system of financial management for Northern Ireland, now administered under the terms of the Barnett Formula.

The passing of the Public Health and Local Government Act of 1946 led to the creation of a new Ministry of Health and Local Government at Stormont with responsibility for rolling out the provisions for the Welfare state as envisaged by the Beveridge Report and originating from Westminster. Greater emphasis was placed on improving the housing stock and social housing was built largely at the expense of the Treasury to be administrated by Northern Ireland's local authorities.

Notwithstanding the absorption of Westminster's post-war reforms the institutions of government in Northern Ireland continued on into the 1960s where in the second-half of the decade opposition to the perceived inequities of single party dominated institutions intensified. In particular, political opposition crystallised in the institutional areas of:

- Housing;
- Electoral system: voting rights;
- Public appointments;
- Policing.

Direct Rule

Despite many reforms the political and security situation continued to deteriorate beyond the control of the Northern Ireland government to the extent that the Conservative government at Westminster led by Ted Heath was forced to suspend the Stormont parliament for one year to allow political negotiations on institutional reform to proceed. The consequent introduction of Direct Rule meant that Northern Ireland, for the first time since 1921, would be governed politically from Westminster. Although existing departmental and civil service structures would continue as normal.

Political Initiatives

Two years later inter-party negotiations brought about the Sunningdale Agreement and with the passing of the Northern Ireland Assembly Act 1973 a new set of governmental institutions, led by an Assembly elected by proportional representation with a 'power-sharing' Executive elected by the Assembly. The Northern Ireland Constitution Act 1973 reshuffled Northern Ireland's government departments in preparation for the new Executive.

Direct Rule

Following considerable political unrest, the Stormont government was prorogued in March 1972 and replaced with Direct Rule by the Temporary Provisions Act. The British Secretary of State for Northern Ireland, together with junior ministers through the Northern Ireland Office, took over the duties formerly carried out by the Northern Ireland parliament. Legislation pertaining to Northern Ireland was passed through Westminster in the form of Orders in Council, which could not be amended on the floor of the House of Commons. The first Secretary of State for Northern Ireland was William Whitelaw, a senior Conservative politician.

Political Initiatives: 'Sunningdale'

The British government attempted to introduce various initiatives aimed at establishing devolved administration for Northern Ireland after the prorogation of the Stormont administration. The first of these was the Sunningdale Agreement of 1973, which emerged following historic British and Irish Government negotiations alongside discussions involving the local political parties. A 78-seat assembly to be elected under proportional representation was proposed. This would establish a power-sharing executive, composed of unionist and nationalist parties. Of the many political parties in Northern Ireland, only three accepted: the Ulster Unionist Party (UUP), the Social Democratic and Labour Party (SDLP) and Alliance. The Executive was faced with severe pressure from loyalists who opposed power sharing. A general strike, organised by loyalists and supported by most unionists, brought Northern Ireland to a standstill and the Executive collapsed, replaced again by Direct Rule. Despite its failure, the Sunningdale Agreement had established the principle of power sharing in the context of future political initiatives.

Political Initiatives: 'Rolling Devolution'

In the early 1980s, Secretary of State James Prior proposed what became known as 'rolling devolution', the idea being that a Northern Ireland assembly would initially be given limited, consultative powers. These new powers could increase significantly as circumstances permitted, i.e. as a culture of power-sharing and cross-community co-operation evolved. 59 members were elected to a new assembly in October 1982, although the SDLP and Sinn Féin assembly members refused to participate in the new institution. The Ulster Unionists boycotted the assembly over security policy, so that the only full participants were the DUP and Alliance.

However, political opposition to 'Sunningdale' was intense and the agreement ultimately failed to capture the support of a majority of Unionists. A general strike brought about the collapse of the new Executive after only 5 months of a power-sharing administration. Direct Rule returned on 30 May 1974.

Despite numerous and varied political initiatives including attempts to create a gradual re-introduction of a local administration (rolling devolution) Direct Rule was to continue unabated for the next 25 years. This however did not stop the process of ongoing institutional reform.

From 1972 onwards Northern Ireland was governed by a Secretary of State, a full member of the British Cabinet who was assisted by several junior ministers, generally MPs from Britain. The Northern Ireland Office took over responsibility for the law and order functions of the Ministry of Home Affairs and reported to the Secretary of State on broad political matters.

In 1976 the Department of the Civil Service was separated out of the Department of Finance but re-attached in the form of the new Department of Finance and Personnel in 1982. Government departments were again re-formed to comprise six new departments. These were:

- Department of Economic Development;
- Department of the Environment;
- Department of Education;
- Department of Social Services;
- Department of Health;
- Department of Agriculture.

In addition, there was a radical reform of local government under the Local Government (Northern Ireland) Act of 1972 providing for the replacement of all previous local authorities with 26 new district councils. This reform coincided with the demise of Stormont and the introduction of Direct Rule and councils were given fewer powers than had previously been envisaged. District councils' responsibilities were confined to the relatively minor functions of street cleaning, refuse collection, cemeteries and leisure facilities. The main functions of health and education were operated by area Boards largely comprised of central government appointees. A new centralised housing authority, the Northern Ireland Housing Executive, assumed all previous local authority-housing duties.

The Anglo-Irish Agreement

Further close co-operation at British-Irish Government level culminated in the Anglo-Irish Agreement. The signing of this Agreement in 1985 proved highly unacceptable to unionists, who resigned their Westminster seats in protest, boycotted district councils and generally made it clear that they would not allow the Republic of Ireland any role as of right in Northern Ireland. Their use of the Assembly to criticise the Anglo-Irish Agreement eventually led to the dissolution of the Assembly by the British government.

The Anglo-Irish Agreement established an Intergovernmental Conference and permanent secretariat at Maryfield, on the outskirts of Belfast. In effect the British government, led by Prime Minister Margaret Thatcher, had acknowledged the right of the Republic of Ireland to consultation over the future of Northern Ireland. The British government also asserted that it had no selfish or strategic interest in Northern Ireland and reaffirmed that the North could only rejoin the Republic of Ireland if a majority of Northern Ireland people consented.

The Anglo-Irish Agreement

The next major political development was the Anglo-Irish Agreement signed on 15 November 1985 by the British and Irish governments, which in an all-round constitutional package gave the Irish Republic a formal, albeit consultative, role in the government of Northern Ireland.

The formal establishment of an Irish governmental physical presence in Belfast and the involvement of Dublin ministers in a consultative role across a range of policy areas in Northern Ireland created fierce resentment in the Unionist community. Unionist politicians were united in opposition to an Agreement, which they felt had, unjustly, been formulated without their input and imposed without their consent, and employed protests, resignations and other tactics in a major campaign to thwart it.

Political Development and New Structures of Government 1986–1999

Despite much pessimism in the early years following the signing of the Anglo-Irish Agreement, the Northern Ireland parties continued in talks to break the deadlock. Unionists were motivated by a desire to reach an outcome that would create a locally devolved government and shift the trend away from Anglo-Irish joint administration. Nationalists buoyed by the backing of the Dublin government were also looking for a locally based government providing it offered the prospect of power sharing.

Peace Process

Hume-Adams Talks

Towards the end of the 1980s, John Hume (leader of the SDLP) engaged in talks with Gerry Adams (President of Sinn Féin), aimed at identifying the political circumstances in which the IRA could move from their military focused stance into the mainstream political arena. By 1993 the Hume-Adams talks had produced a series of documents and statements which were fed into continuing inter governmental discussions. Hume argued that if London stated it had no selfish desire to hold onto Northern Ireland then the IRA would have no reason to fight their "war".

Downing Street Declaration

Ongoing talks between the British and Irish governments were to culminate in the Downing Street Declaration of December 1993 in which, the British government acknowledged and accepted the principle of self-determination of the people in both parts of the island of Ireland, together with the principle of consent for any change being made. The Declaration reaffirmed that Britain had no selfish or strategic interest in Northern Ireland and it was hoped that this affirmation would facilitate an IRA ceasefire. Ceasefires were to follow, the IRA in August 1994, with the UVF and the UDA under the banner of the Combined Loyalist Military Command (CLMC) following in October.

Fresh Talks

July 1997 saw the election of a Labour government with a solid parliamentary majority, which enabled the new Prime Minster, Tony Blair, to inject fresh momentum into the peace process. Multi-party talks opened in September, following a three-strand formula. Strand one dealt with the internal administration of Northern Ireland; strand two considered the relationship between North and South, and strand three relations between London and Dublin: the East-West Dimension.

The Good Friday Agreement

Following considerable personal involvement by Prime Minister Tony Blair, Irish Taoiseach Bertie Ahern, American President Bill Clinton, and intensive discussions between the local political parties, the Belfast Agreement was signed on Good Friday, 10th April 1998. The majority of political parties supported the Agreement, notable exceptions being Ian Paisley's DUP and the smaller UKUP, both of whom refused to participate in the talks.

Essentially the Agreement was a balanced constitutional deal which recognised the need to examine institutions which would give expression to three sets of relationships: the two traditions in Northern Ireland; the two traditions in Ireland North and South; and the two nations Britain and Ireland (East and West).

Alongside the Belfast-based institutions there was to be a series of cross-border development bodies with representation from both sides reporting into a North-South Ministerial Council. In addition, there would be a British/Irish Council addressing issues on an East/West basis and a consultative Civic Forum reflective of sectoral and community interests outside of the party political system.

The proposed arrangements, which were voted through the London and Dublin parliaments and put to separate referenda in Northern Ireland and the Republic, created an elected Assembly in Northern Ireland with a power-sharing Executive. There would be an increase in the number of government departments along with a unique joint Office of the First and Deputy First Minister.

The new departments were:
- Office of the First and Deputy First Minister (OFMDFM)
- Department of Agriculture and Rural Development (DARD)
- Department of Culture, Arts and Leisure (DCAL)
- Department of Education (DENI)
- Department of Enterprise, Trade and Investment (DETI)

- Department of the Environment (DOE)
- Department of Finance and Personnel (DFP)
- Department of Health, Social Services and Public Safety (DHSSPS)
- Department of Further Education, Training and Employment (DFETE)
- Department of Regional Development (DRD)
- Department of Social Development (DSD).

(Details of each department are set out in Chapter 4.)

Following approval by the Westminster parliament of the Northern Ireland (Elections) Act 1998, for the holding of Assembly elections on 25 June 1998, the Act also provided for the Assembly to meet in 'shadow' mode, as set out in the 'Validation, Implementation and Review' section of the Agreement, pending the coming into effect of the substantive powers of the new institutions provided for in the Northern Ireland Act 1998.

The election results of 25 June 1998 were as follows:

Party		Seats
UUP	Ulster Unionist Party	28
SDLP	Social Democratic and Labour Party	24
DUP	Democratic Unionist Party	20
SF	Sinn Fein	18
All	The Alliance Party	6
UKUP	United Kingdom Unionist Party	5
PUP	Progressive Unionist Party	2
NIWC	Northern Ireland Women's Coalition	2
Others		3

On 1 July 1998 the Assembly met for the first time with Lord Alderdice as initial presiding officer. David Trimble MP, leader of the Ulster Unionist Party was elected as First Minister-designate and Séamus Mallon MP deputy leader of the Social Democratic and Labour Party as Deputy First Minister-designate.

The Northern Ireland Act 1998 gave force of law to the Agreement. Under the terms of the Act most of the provisions came into force on the 'appointed day' under section 3 including the North-South Ministerial Council, the British-Irish Council and the British-Irish Intergovernmental Council and the first six implementation bodies; at the same time the British and Irish constitutional changes came into effect.

Review of the Agreement

However, despite the election of an Assembly there were significant political obstacles to the formation of a devolved Government. In the light of the deadlock the Secretary of State Mo Mowlam announced that a review of the implementation of the Agreement would begin, in accordance with paragraph 4 of its Implementation, Validation and Review section. The Northern Ireland Bill was not withdrawn.

The Prime Minister and Taoiseach considered the scope of the Review and were joined by Senator George Mitchell, who had been Chairman of the 'Talks', and invited him to act as facilitator in the process. He began preliminary discussions with the parties immediately. The Prime Minister and Taoiseach made clear that the review would be limited in focus to determining how to carry forward matters relating to inclusive devolution and decommissioning.

The Review continued for almost double the length of time Senator Mitchell originally anticipated spending in Northern Ireland. During the Review a new Secretary of State for Northern Ireland, Peter Mandelson was appointed.

From 15 November 1999 a carefully planned series of statements indicated that the Review had produced consensus on the issues of the formation of an inclusive Executive and the decommissioning of weapons, enabling the necessary actions leading to devolution.

Devolution

Power was finally devolved to the Assembly and its Executive Committee on 2 December 1999. The Assembly succeeded in electing a cross community 12 strong Executive Committee using the d'Hondt system and assigning Ministers to their new Departments.

Despite the devolution of most of the day to day activities and powers of government to the new Assembly, and the establishment of North-South Bodies Northern Ireland continued to operate unambiguously as part of the United Kingdom. Northern Ireland would continue to have representation at Westminster and significant governmental powers would remain with Westminster for the foreseeable future.

The Government and Institutions of Northern Ireland

From the establishment of its own devolved parliament in 1921 until 1972 legislation for Northern Ireland was made in the form of acts of parliament. Following the suspension of the parliament in 1972 direct rule from Westminster was reintroduced.

Since 1972 there have been three devolved assemblies, 1974, 1982–86 and the current assembly established in 1998 under the terms of the Northern Ireland Act 1998. The Assembly of 1974 had legislative powers; the Assembly of 1982–86 had no legislative powers.

Prior to devolution on the 2 December 1999 the Northern Ireland Assembly had no legislative powers, however, following devolution legislative powers were transferred from Westminster and executive power to the power-sharing executive.

Northern Ireland Legislative Practice Before Devolution in 1999

Since 1972 the vast bulk of Northern Ireland's primary legislation has been carried into effect by means of Orders in Council and direct rule continued by order for one year at a time. From the late seventies certain acts relating to Great Britain have contained clauses known as "parity orders", enabling the same legislation to be issued for Northern Ireland.

Northern Ireland Act 1998

The Good Friday Agreement has seen the reestablishment of a Northern Ireland Assembly implemented by the Northern Ireland Act 1998. In elections using proportional representation the existing eighteen Westminster constituencies elected one hundred and eight members to the new Assembly. When the Assembly first met on 1 July 1998 it held no legislative powers until devolution on 2 December 1999. Following devolution a range of legislative powers were transferred from Westminster to the Assembly and executive power to the power-sharing Executive.

The terms of the Northern Ireland Act 1998 provide for the establishment of a legislative assembly and the creation of an Executive with a First Minister, Deputy First Minister and ten Ministers appointed under the d'Hondt procedure. The establishment of new institutions such as the North South Ministerial Council were also provided for under the Act. Areas devolved to the Assembly and Executive include health, education, social services, economic development, and agriculture, broadly corresponding with those areas devolved to the Welsh Assembly and Scottish Parliament.

Excepted and Reserved Matters

The Secretary of State retains certain clearly defined powers. These include constitutional and security matters relating to Northern Ireland, policing and relationships with the European Union, and are not devolved matters under the terms of the Northern Ireland Act 1998. Under the terms of the Northern Ireland Act 1998 Westminster continues to legislate in non-devolved or excepted matters in the form of Orders in Council, Acts and Statutory Instruments. Reserved matters including criminal law and civil defence may eventually be transferred to the Northern Ireland legislature. However, excepted matters will remain permanently with Westminster.

The table below sets out the main areas of government which remain "reserved" or "excepted".

Reserved	Excepted	Transferred
Policing	Elections	All matters
Security	Europe	not excepted
Prisons	Peace and	or reserved
Criminal Justice	Reconciliation	
Income Tax	Foreign Policy	
National Insurance		
Regulation of		
Telecommunications		
and Broadcasting		

The Northern Ireland Assembly

The Northern Ireland Assembly
Parliament Buildings, Stormont Estate
Belfast BT4 3XX
Tel: 028 9052 1862
Fax: 028 9052 1959

The Northern Ireland Assembly was established as part of the Good Friday Agreement, following its endorsement by simultaneous referenda in Northern Ireland and the Republic of Ireland. It is composed of 108 elected members: 6 elected, using proportional representation, from each of the 18 Westminster constituencies. There are 12 Executive Ministers, including the First Minister and Deputy First Minister who share a unique joint department, the Office of the First Minister and Deputy First Minister.

The legislative Assembly has full legislative and executive authority to make laws and take decisions on the functions of the 10 new Departments. Whilst certain functions remain reserved, the Assembly may legislate on these areas with the approval of the Secretary of State for Northern Ireland, and under the overall control of the Westminster Parliament.

An individual member, committee or Minister may initiate legislation. Voting is by simple majority unless cross-community support is required. A petition of 30 concerned members can trigger such a voting procedure.

In these cases, parallel consent or a weighted majority of 60% of those members present and voting, is required.

Ministerial departments and membership of their respective committees have been allocated according to a system of proportional representation ensuring that parties are given ministerial posts, committee chairs and committee seats in proportion to the number of Assembly members returned.

Much of the internal work of the Assembly and its Committees is governed by Standing Orders (produced mainly by the Assembly Procedures Committee).

Principal Officers and Officials of the Northern Ireland Assembly

The Speaker	The Lord Alderdice
Deputy Speakers	Donovan McClelland, Jim Wilson, Jane Morrice
Speaker's Private Secretary	Georgina Campbell
Speaker's Counsel	Nicolas Hanna QC

The Speaker is the Presiding Officer elected to the Northern Ireland Assembly under Section 39 of the Northern Ireland Act 1998 and provided for under Standing Order 1. The ruling of the Speaker is final on all questions of matter and procedure in the Assembly.

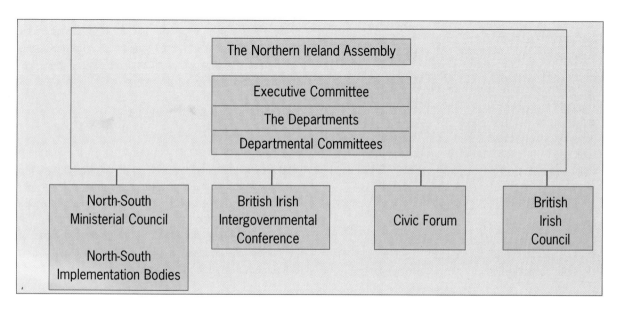

The Speaker's Office

The function of the Speaker's Office is to provide support to the Speaker in the execution of his duties, which include, amongst others:

- Presiding over plenary sessions of the Assembly;
- Scrutinising legislation at pre introduction and final stages;
- Nomination of members to various bodies, e.g. the Senate of the University of Ulster.

Office of the Clerk and Records of the Assembly

The Clerk notes all proceedings of the Assembly and the minutes of proceedings having been perused and signed by the Speaker, are printed and constitute the Journal of the Proceedings of the Assembly.

The Clerk is the custodian of all Journals of Proceedings, records and other documents belonging to the Assembly.

Office of the Assembly Commission

The Commission is the body corporate of the Northern Ireland Assembly and has responsibility under paragraph 40(4) of the Northern Ireland Act 1998 to provide the Assembly, or ensure that the Assembly is provided with, the property, staff and services required for the Assembly to carry out its work.

Principal Officers	
Clerk to the Assembly	Arthur Moir
Deputy Clerk to the Assembly	Joe Reynolds
Private Secretary to the Clerk	Shane McAteer
Deputy Chief Executive	Tom Evans
Clerk Assistant	Nuala Dunwoody
Editor of Debates	Simon Burrowes
Keeper of the House	Agnes Peacocke
Director of Research and Information	Allan Black
Director of Finance and Personnel	Fiona Hamill
Principal Clerk Bill Office	Martin Wilson
Principal Clerk Business Office	Alan Rogers
Principal Clerk of Committees	Debbie Pritchard
	John Torney
Principal Clerk	Alan Patterson
Examiner of Statutory Rules	Gordon Nabney
Comptroller and Auditor General	John Dowdall
Assembly Ombudsman	Tom Frawley

In addition to the Permanent Secretaries, the civil service through the provision of clerks and administrative support staff supports the work of the Northern Ireland Assembly. Clerks play a key role in the legislative process within the Assembly including the operation of the Committees and the management of the business of the House.

The Assembly Commission is responsible for providing and maintaining the property, services and staff required for the purposes of the Assembly.

The current members of the Northern Ireland Assembly Commission are:

- Lord Alderdice: Chairperson;
- Eileen Bell (Alliance);
- Rev Robert Coulter (UUP);
- John Fee (SDLP);
- Dr Dara O'Hagan (SF);
- Jim Wells (DUP).

Their task is to represent the interests of the Assembly and its 108 elected Members. Some of the responsibilities of the Assembly Commission are as follows:

- Agreement of room allocation for individual Assembly Members, Assembly parties, Committee Chairpersons, Ministers and the Assembly's own staff as well as office accommodation, press and visitors' facilities;
- Ensuring that the public has ready access to the public areas within Parliament Buildings;
- Arranging of all the services required to support the work of the Assembly e.g. the Office of the Official Report, Members' Services;
- Determining staffing levels and carrying out recruitment competitions to obtain the complement of staff required to support the Assembly.

The Office of the Clerk to the Northern Ireland Assembly

The function of the Office of the Clerk to the Northern Ireland Assembly is to provide a central policy and management function and to offer a range of corporate services to the Assembly. The Office also provides support services for the Clerk and Chief Executive, the Deputy Chief Executive, the Deputy Clerk, the Head of Legal Services and the Examiner of Statutory Rules. The Office comprises the following functional areas:

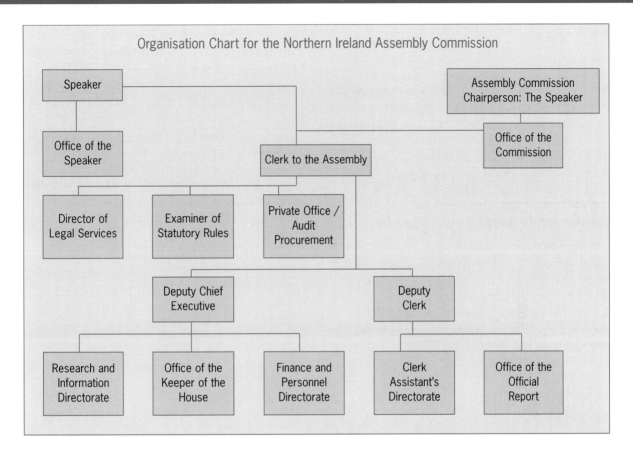

Organisation Chart for the Northern Ireland Assembly Commission

- Private office;
- Internal audit;
- Procurement office;
- Legal services;
- Examiner of statutory rules.

Clerk Assistant's Directorate

The function of the Clerk Assistant's Directorate is to meet the needs of Members and Committees when carrying out Assembly business, to establish a team of trained staff and maintain a programme of continuous staff training and development and to maximise resources within its budget. The Directorate is organised into three offices:

- The Bill Office;
- The Business Office;
- The Committee Office.

Office of the Official Report (Hansard)

The Function of the Office of the Official Report is to produce the Official Report of all sittings of the Assembly, including details of debates, resolutions, Questions, Votes and appropriate Committee sessions. The Hansard report, which is available to the public, lists the names of all the Members, reports what they say and records all the Assembly's decisions.

Keeper of the House Directorate

The function of the Keeper of the House Directorate is to deliver the best possible service to Members, the public and all those who work in or visit Parliament Buildings. Key areas of work include events, support services, works, health and safety and security. This is managed by the:

- Events Co-ordination Office;
- Facilities Branch;
- Works Branch;
- Health and Safety Branch;
- Security Branch.

Research and Information Directorate

The function of the Research and Information Directorate is to source, process, transform and communicate information for and within the Assembly and to ensure that its business is open to public interest and scrutiny. The Directorate comprises three functional units:
- Research and Library Services;
- Information Office;
- Information Systems Office.

Finance and Personnel Directorate

The function of the Finance and Personnel Directorate is to provide personnel support for Members and the Secretariat from recruitment to pensions and including financial and accounting systems and the provision of stationery, filing systems and reprographic services. The Directorate has four units:
- Personnel Office;
- Finance Office;
- Recruitment Office;
- Registry.

Elected Members of the Assembly

The table below summarises the outcome of the 1998 Northern Ireland Assembly elections.

Overall Assembly Election Results by Party (June 1998)			
Party	**1st pref votes**	**% total vote**	**Seats**
SDLP	177,963	22.0	24
UUP	172,225	21.3	28
DUP	146,989	18.1	20
Sinn Féin	142,858	17.6	18
Alliance	52,636	6.5	6
UKUP*	36,541	4.5	5
Ind Unionist**	23,127	2.9	3
PUP	20,634	2.6	2
NIWC	13,019	1.6	2
UDP	8,651	1.1	0
Others	15,674	1.8	0
Total	**810,317**	**100**	**108**

* 4 members of the UKUP resigned in January 1999 and formed the Northern Ireland Unionist Party. One member of the NIUP resigned in December 1999 and became an Independent Unionist.

** All 3 members formed the United Unionist Assembly Party (UUAP) in September 1998. Their leader, Denis Watson, later joined the DUP.

Northern Ireland Assembly

Assembly Members by Party Affiliation (September 2002)

Ulster Unionist Party

Dr Ian Adamson	Belfast East
Billy Armstrong	Mid Ulster
Roy Beggs	East Antrim
Billy Bell	Lagan Valley
Dr Esmond Birnie	Belfast South
Joan Carson	Fermanagh and South Tyrone
Fred Cobain	Belfast North
Rev Robert Coulter	North Antrim
Ivan Davis	Lagan Valley
Reg Empey	Belfast East
Sam Foster	Fermanagh and South Tyrone
John Gorman	North Down
Tom Hamilton*	Strangford
Derek Hussey	West Tyrone
Danny Kennedy	Newry and Armagh
James Leslie	North Antrim
David McClarty	East Londonderry
Alan McFarland	North Down
Michael McGimpsey	Belfast South
Dermot Nesbitt	South Down
Ken Robinson	East Antrim
George Savage	Upper Bann
Duncan Shipley-Dalton	South Antrim
John Taylor	Strangford
David Trimble	Upper Bann
Jim Wilson	South Antrim

* Replaced Tom Benson

Social Democratic and Labour Party

Alex Attwood	Belfast West
PJ Bradley	South Down
Joe Byrne	West Tyrone
Annie Courtney*	Foyle
Michael Coyle†	East Londonderry
John Dallat	East Londonderry
Mark Durkan	Foyle
Dr Sean Farren	North Antrim
John Fee	Newry and Armagh
Tommy Gallagher	Fermanagh and South Tyrone
Carmel Hanna	Belfast South
Denis Haughey	Mid Ulster
Dr Joe Hendron	Belfast West
Patricia Lewsley	Lagan Valley
Donovan McClelland	South Antrim
Dr Alasdair McDonnell	Belfast South
Eddie McGrady	South Down
Eugene McMenamin	West Tyrone
Alban Maginnis	Belfast North

Séamus Mallon	Newry and Armagh
Danny O'Connor	East Antrim
Eamonn O'Neill	South Down
Bríd Rodgers	Upper Bann
John Tierney	Foyle

* Replaced John Hume
† Replaced Arthur Doherty

Democratic Unionist Party

Paul Berry	Newry and Armagh
Gregory Campbell	East Londonderry
Mervyn Carrick	Upper Bann
Wilson Clyde	South Antrim
Nigel Dodds	Belfast North
Oliver Gibson	West Tyrone
William Hay	Foyle
David Hilditch	East Antrim
Roger Hutchinson*	East Antrim
Gardiner Kane	North Antrim
Rev William McCrea	Mid Ulster
Maurice Morrow	Fermanagh and South Tyrone
Rev Ian Paisley	North Antrim
Ian Paisley Jr	North Antrim
Edwin Poots	Lagan Valley
Iris Robinson	Strangford
Mark Robinson	Belfast South
Peter Robinson	Belfast East
Jim Shannon	Strangford
Peter Weir†	North Down
Jim Wells	South Down
Sammy Wilson	Belfast East

*elected as an Independent, but has since joined the DUP
†elected for the UUP but became a member of the DUP on 30th April 2002

Sinn Féin

Gerry Adams	Belfast West
Bairbre de Brún	Belfast West
Pat Doherty	West Tyrone
Michelle Gildernew	Fermanagh and South Tyrone
Gerry Kelly	Belfast North
John Kelly	Mid Ulster
Alex Maskey	Belfast West
Barry McElduff	West Tyrone
Martin McGuinness	Mid Ulster
Gerry McHugh	Fermanagh and South Tyrone
Mitchel McLaughlin	Foyle
Patrick McNamee	Newry and Armagh

Francie Molloy   Mid Ulster
Conor Murphy   Newry and Armagh
Mick Murphy   South Down
Mary Nelis   Foyle
Dr Dara O'Hagan   Upper Bann
Sue Ramsey   Belfast West

Alliance Party

Lord Alderdice   Belfast East
Eileen Bell   North Down
Seamus Close   Lagan Valley
David Ford   South Antrim
Kieran McCarthy   Strangford
Sean Neeson   East Antrim

Northern Ireland Unionist Party

Norman Boyd   South Antrim
Patrick Roche   Lagan Valley
Cedric Wilson   Strangford

Progressive Unionist Party

David Ervine   Belfast East
Billy Hutchinson   Belfast North

Northern Ireland Women's Coalition

Prof Monica McWilliams   Belfast South
Jane Morrice   North Down

United Kingdom Unionist Party

Robert McCartney   North Down

United Unionist Assembly Party

Fraser Agnew   Belfast North
Boyd Douglas   East Londonderry
Denis Watson*   Upper Bann

* in July 2002 a member of the DUP Assembly Party, but has not accepted the Assembly party whip. Officially still a member of the UUAP Assembly group.

Independent Unionist

Pauline Armitage* East Londonderry

* Elected as Ulster Unionist but expelled from the party 9 November 2001

Parliament Buildings Stormont

Assembly Members by Constituency (September 2002)

Belfast East

Ian Adamson (UUP)
Lord John Alderdice (All)
Reg Empey (UUP)
David Ervine (PUP)
Peter Robinson (DUP)
Sammy Wilson (DUP)

Belfast North

Fraser Agnew (UUAP)
Fred Cobain (UUP)
Nigel Dodds (DUP)
Billy Hutchinson (PUP)
Gerry Kelly (SF)
Alban Maginness (SDLP)

Belfast South

Esmond Birnie (UUP)
Carmel Hanna (SDLP)
Mark Robinson (DUP)
Alasdair McDonnell (SDLP)
Michael McGimpsey (UUP)
Monica McWilliams (NIWC)

Belfast West

Gerry Adams (SF)
Alex Attwood (SDLP)
Bairbre de Brún (SF)
Joe Hendron (SDLP)
Alex Maskey (SF)
Sue Ramsey (SF)

East Antrim

Roy Beggs Jr (UUP)
David Hilditch (DUP)
Sean Neeson (All)
Roger Hutchinson (Ind U)
Danny O'Connor (SDLP)
Ken Robinson (UUP)

East Londonderry

Pauline Armitage (Ind U)
Gregory Campbell (DUP)
John Dallat (SDLP)
Arthur Doherty (SDLP)
Boyd Douglas (Ind U)
David McClarty (UUP)

Fermanagh and South Tyrone

Joan Carson (UUP)
Sam Foster (UUP)
Tommy Gallagher (SDLP)
Michelle Gildernew (SF)
Gerry McHugh (SF)
Maurice Morrow (DUP)

Foyle

Annie Courtney (SDLP)
Mark Durkan (SDLP)
William Hay (DUP)
Mitchel McLaughlin (SF)
Mary Nelis (SF)
John Tierney (SDLP)

Lagan Valley

Billy Bell (UUP)
Seamus Close (All)
Ivan Davis (UUP)
Patricia Lewsley (SDLP)
Edwin Poots (DUP)
Patrick Roche (NIUP)

Mid Ulster

Rev Willie McCrea (DUP)
Martin McGuinness (SF)
Denis Haughey (SDLP)
Francie Molloy (SF)
John Kelly (SF)
Billy Armstrong (UUP)

Newry and Armagh

Paul Berry (DUP)
John Fee (SDLP)
Danny Kennedy (UUP)
Séamus Mallon (SDLP)
Conor Murphy (SF)
Pat McNamee (SF)

North Antrim

Rev Robert Coulter (UUP)
Sean Farren (SDLP)
Gardiner Kane (DUP)
James Leslie (UUP)
Rev Ian Paisley (DUP)
Ian Paisley Jr (DUP)

North Down

Eileen Bell (All)
John Gorman (UUP)
Robert McCartney (UKUP)
Alan McFarland (UUP)
Jane Morrice (NIWC)
Peter Weir (DUP)

South Antrim

Norman Boyd (NIUP)
Wilson Clyde (DUP)
David Ford (All)
Donovan McClelland (SDLP)
Duncan Shipley-Dalton (UUP)
Jim Wilson (UUP)

South Down

PJ Bradley (SDLP)
Eddie McGrady (SDLP)
Mick Murphy (SF)
Dermot Nesbitt (UUP)
Eamonn O'Neill (SDLP)
Jim Wells (DUP)

Strangford

Tom Hamilton (UUP)
Kieran McCarthy (All)
Iris Robinson (DUP)
Jim Shannon (DUP)
John Taylor (UUP)
Cedric Wilson (NIUP)

Upper Bann

David Trimble (UUP)
Bríd Rodgers (SDLP)
Denis Watson (DUP)
Dara O'Hagan (SF)
Mervyn Carrick (DUP)
George Savage (UUP)

West Tyrone

Oliver Gibson (DUP)
Pat Doherty (SF)
Joe Byrne (SDLP)
Barry McElduff (SF)
Derek Hussey (UUP)
Eugene McMenamin (SDLP)

A–Z of Assembly Members with Contact Details

Adams, Gerry MP

Party: Sinn Féin
Constituency: Belfast West

Assembly Office: Parliament Buildings,
Stormont Estate, Belfast, BT4 3XX

Tel: 028 9052 1144
Fax: 028 9052 1474

Constituency Office:
51-55 Falls Road,
Belfast, BT12 4PD

Tel: 028 9022 3000
Fax: 028 9022 5553

Adamson, Dr Ian

Party: Ulster Unionist
Constituency: Belfast East

Assembly Office: Parliament Buildings,
Stormont Estate, Belfast, BT4 3XX

Tel: 028 9052 1529
Fax: 028 9052 1760

Agnew, Fraser

Party: United Unionist Assembly
Constituency: Belfast North

Assembly Office: Parliament Buildings,
Stormont Estate, Belfast, BT4 3XX

Tel: 028 9052 1033
Fax: 028 9052 1032

Alderdice, John
(Lord Alderdice)

Party: Alliance
Constituency: Belfast East

Assembly Office: The Speaker's Office, Parliament Buildings,
Stormont Estate, Belfast, BT4 3XX

Tel: 028 9052 1130
Fax: 028 9052 1959

Private Secretary:
Ms Georgina Campbell
Tel: 028 9052 1181

Constituency Office:
44a Newtownards Road,
Belfast, BT4

Tel: 028 9073 8703
Fax: 028 9073 9318

Armitage, Pauline

Party: Independent Unionist
Constituency: East Londonderry

Assembly Office: Parliament Buildings,
Stormont Estate, Belfast, BT4 3XX

Tel: 028 9052 1912
Fax: 028 9052 1764

Constituency Office:
12 Dunmore Street, BT52 3RN
Tel: 028 7035 3811

Armstrong, Billy

Party: Ulster Unionist
Constituency: Mid Ulster

Assembly Office: Parliament Buildings, Stormont Estate, Belfast, BT4 3XX

Tel: 028 9052 0305
Fax: 028 9052 0302
Website: www.billyarmstrong.co.uk

Constituency Office: Prospect House, Coagh Road, Stewartstown Dungannon, Co Tyrone, BT71 5JH

Tel: 028 8773 8641/
028 8773 8462
Fax: 028 8773 8844

Personal Asst: Ms Sandra Overend

Attwood, Alex

Party: SDLP
Constituency: Belfast West

Assembly Office: Parliament Buildings,
Stormont Estate, Belfast, BT4 3XX

Tel: 028 9052 0375
Fax: 028 9052 0377

Constituency Office:

60 Andersonstown Road, Belfast
BT11 9AN

Tel: 028 9080 7808
Fax: 028 9080 7370

Personal Asst: Mrs Veronica Mullan

Beggs, Roy MLA

Party: Ulster Unionist
Constituency: East Antrim

Assembly Office: Parliament Buildings,
Stormont Estate, Belfast, BT4 3XX

Tel: 028 9052 1546
Fax: 028 9052 1556

Researcher: Mr Andrew Wilson

Constituency Office:
East Antrim Ulster Unionist,
Advice Centre, 32c North Street,
Carrickfergus, BT38 7AQ

Tel: 028 9336 2995
Fax: 028 9336 8048

Secretary: Miss Sarah Clarke

Bell, Billy

Party: Ulster Unionist
Constituency: Lagan Valley

Assembly Office: Room 307,
Parliament Buildings, Stormont
Estate, Belfast, BT4 3XX

Tel: 028 9052 1344
Fax: 028 9052 1756

Constituency Office:
2 Sackville Street, Lisburn,
Co Antrim, BT27 4AB

Tel: 028 9262 9171
Fax: 028 9260 5672

PA/Researcher: Ms Julie-Anne Bell

Bell, Eileen

Party: Alliance
Constituency: North Down

Assembly Office: Parliament Buildings, Stormont Estate,

Belfast, BT4 3XX

Tel: 028 9052 0352
Fax: 028 9052 1654

Assistant: Mr Derek Bell
Secretary: Mrs Rosemary Nickell

Constituency Office: 5 Central
Avenue, Bangor, BT20 3AF

Tel: 028 9147 9717
Fax: 028 9145 5995

Berry, Paul

Party: Democratic Unionist
Constituency: Newry and Armagh

Assembly Office: Parliament
Buildings,
Stormont Estate, Belfast, BT4 3XX

Tel: 028 9052 1191
Fax: 028 9052 1832

Constituency Office: 78 Market
Street, Tandragee, Co Armagh,
BT62 2BP

Secretary: Ms Kathryn Elliott
Office Asst: Mr Gareth Wilson

Tel: 028 3884 1668
Fax: 028 3884 9166

Birnie, Dr Esmond

Party: Ulster Unionist
Constituency: Belfast South

Assembly Office: Parliament
Buildings,
Stormont Estate, Belfast, BT4 3XX

Tel: 028 9052 0304
Fax: 028 9052 1560
Research Asst: Mr Alex Kane

Constituency Office: 117 Cregagh
Road, Belfast, BT6 0LA

Tel: 028 9087 2794
Fax: 028 9029 1149

Boyd, Norman

Party: Northern Ireland Unionist
Constituency: South Antrim

Assembly Office: Parliament
Buildings,
Stormont Estate, Belfast, BT4 3XX

Tel: 028 9052 1733
Fax: 028 9052 1754

Constituency Office: 38 Main
Street, Ballyclare, Co Antrim, BT39
9AA

Tel: 028 9334 9132
Fax: 028 9334 9128

Bradley, PJ

Party: SDLP
Constituency: South Down

Assembly Office: Parliament
Buildings,
Stormont Estate, Belfast, BT4 3XX

Tel: 028 9052 0344
Fax: 028 9052 0342
Website: www.pjbradley.com

Assistant: Mrs Sinead Challinor

Constituency Office:
2 East Street, Warrenpoint,
Newry, Co Down, BT34 3JE

Tel: 028 4177 2228
Fax: 028 4177 2229

Byrne, Joe

Party: SDLP
Constituency: West Tyrone

Assembly Office: Parliament
Buildings,
Stormont Estate, Belfast, BT4 3XX

Tel: 028 9052 0326
Fax: 028 9052 0327

Constituency Office: 9B Dromore
Road, Omagh, Co Tyrone, BT78
1QZ

Tel: 028 8225 0060
Fax: 028 8225 0065
Email: joebyrne@sdlp.com

Campbell, Gregory MP

Party: Democratic Unionist
Constituency: East Londonderry

Assembly Office: Parliament
Buildings, Stormont Estate,

Belfast, BT4 3XX

Tel: 028 9052 1106
Fax: 028 9052 1839

Constituency Office:
25 Bushmills Road, Coleraine,
Co Derry, BT52 2BP

Tel: 028 7032 7327
Fax: 028 7032 7328

Carrick, Mervyn

Party: Democratic Unionist
Constituency: Upper Bann

Assembly Office: Parliament
Buildings,
Stormont Estate, Belfast, BT4 3XX

Telephone: 028 9052 1193
Fax: 028 9052 1834

Constituency Office:
15A Mandeville Street, Portadown,
Co Armagh, BT67 2PB

Tel: 028 3833 5965
Fax: 028 3833 5977

Assistant: Mrs Ruth Allen

Carson, Joan

Party: Ulster Unionist
Constituency: Fermanagh and South
Tyrone

Assembly Office: Parliament
Buildings,
Stormont Estate, Belfast, BT4 3XX

Tel: 028 9052 1557
Fax: 028 9052 1766

Constituency Office: 115 Moy Road,
Dungannon, BT71 7DX

Tel: 028 8778 4285
Fax: 028 8778 4285

PA: Mr Ivor Whitten
Asst PA: Mr Kenneth Donaldson

Close, Seamus

Party: Alliance
Constituency: Lagan Valley

Assembly Office: Parliament
Buildings,
Stormont Estate, Belfast, BT4 3XX

Tel: 028 9052 0353
Fax: 028 9052 1650

Constituency Office: 123 Moira
Road, Lisburn, BT28 1RJ

Tel: 028 9267 0639
Fax: 028 9266 6803

Clyde, Wilson

Party: Democratic Unionist
Constituency: South Antrim

Assembly Office: Parliament
Buildings,
Stormont Estate, Belfast, BT4 3XX

Tel: 028 9052 1111
Fax: 028 9052 1822

Assembly Asst: Mr Hubert Nicholl
Tel: 028 9447 2274
Fax: 028 9446 9011

Constituency Office: 69 Church
Street, Antrim, BT41 4BG

Tel: 028 9446 2280
Fax: 028 9446 9001

Assistant: Mr Jack McClay

Cobain, Fred

Party: Ulster Unionist
Constituency: Belfast North

Assembly Office: Parliament
Buildings,
Stormont Estate, Belfast, BT4 3XX

Constituency Office:
921 Crumlin Road, BT14 8AB

Tel: 028 9072 9400
Fax: 028 9071 8834

Coulter, Rev Robert

Party: Ulster Unionist
Constituency: North Antrim

Tel: 028 9052 1246
Fax: 028 9052 1741

Courtney, Annie

Party: SDLP
Constituency: Foyle

Assembly Office: Parliament

Buildings,
Stormont Estate, Belfast, BT4 3XX

Constituency Office:
Suite 5, Spencer House,
Waterside, Derry, BT47 6AA

Tel: 028 7131 3831
Fax: 028 7128 0221

Dallat, John

Party: SDLP
Constituency: East Londonderry

Assembly Office: Parliament
Buildings,
Stormont Estate, Belfast, BT4 3XX

Telephone: 028 9052 0347
Fax: 028 9052 0345

Constituency Office:
11 Bridge Street, Kilrea,
Co Londonderry, BT51 5RR

Tel: 028 2954 1798

Davis, Ivan

Party: Ulster Unionist
Constituency: Lagan Valley

Assembly Office: Parliament
Buildings,
Stormont Estate, Belfast, BT4 3XX

Tel: 028 9052 1029
Fax: 028 9052 1027
Secretary: Mrs Allyson Morrow

Constituency Office:
2 Sackville Street, Lisburn,
Co Antrim, BT27 4AB

Tel: 028 9266 7699

de Brún, Bairbre

Party: Sinn Féin
Constituency: Belfast West

Assembly Office: Parliament
Buildings,
Stormont Estate, Belfast, BT4 3XX

Tel: 028 9052 1675
Fax: 028 9052 1673

Constituency Rep: Mr John Leathem

Constituency Office: 53 Falls Road,
Belfast, BT12 4PD

Tel: 028 9022 3000
Fax: 028 9022 0045

Dodds, Nigel MP

Party: Democratic Unionist
Constituency: Belfast North

Assembly Office: Parliament
Buildings,
Stormont Estate, Belfast, BT4 3XX

Tel: 028 9052 1101
Fax: 028 9052 1750

Constituency Office: 210 Shore
Road, Belfast, BT15 3QB

Tel: 028 9077 4774
Fax: 028 9077 7685

Constituency Asst: Mr Andrew
Hunter
Secretary: Mrs Yvonne Sloan

Doherty, Arthur*

Party: SDLP
Constituency: East Londonderry

Assembly Office: Parliament
Buildings,
Stormont Estate, Belfast, BT4 3XX

Tel: 028 9052 0350
Fax: 028 9052 0348

Constituency Office:
59 Catherine Street, Limavady,
Co Londonderry, BT49 9DA

Tel: 028 7776 9790
Fax: 028 7776 6475

(*Replaced by Michael Coyle
following resignation)

Doherty, Pat MP

Party: Sinn Féin
Constituency: West Tyrone

Assembly Office: Parliament
Buildings,
Stormont Estate, Belfast, BT4 3XX

Tel: 028 9052 0323
Fax: 028 9052 1722

Constituency Office: 1 Melvin Road, Strabane, Co Tyrone, BT82 9PP

Tel: 028 7188 6464
Fax: 028 7188 6466

PA: Mrs Michelle McDermott

Douglas, Boyd

Party: United Unionist Assembly
Constituency: East Londonderry

Assembly Office: Parliament Buildings,
Stormont Estate, Belfast, BT4 3XX

Tel: 028 9052 1141
Fax: 028 9052 1465

Constituency Office:
279 Drumrane Road, Dungiven,
Co Londonderry, BT47 4NL

Tel: 028 7774 1630
Fax: 028 7774 0030

Researcher: Mr Mark Gibson
Secretary: Mrs K Douglas

Durkan, Mark

Party: SDLP
Constituency: Foyle

Assembly Office: Parliament Buildings,
Stormont Estate, Belfast, BT4 3XX

Tel: 028 9052 1691
Fax: 028 9052 1688

Constituency Office: 7B Messines Terrace, Racecourse Road, Derry, BT48 7QZ

Tel: 028 7136 0700
Fax: 028 7136 0808

Secretary: Ms Carol Ryan
Asst Secretary: Ms Jackie Durkan

Empey, Sir Reg

Party: Ulster Unionist
Constituency: Belfast East

Assembly Office: Parliament Buildings,
Stormont Estate, Belfast, BT4 3XX

Tel: 028 9052 1335
Fax: 028 9052 1761

Constituency Office: 4a Belmont Road, Belfast,BT4 2AN

Tel: 028 9065 8217
Fax: 028 9047 1161

Ervine, David

Party: Progressive Unionist
Constituency: Belfast East

Assembly Office: Parliament Buildings, Stormont Estate, Belfast, BT4 3XX

Tel: 028 9052 1469
Fax: 028 9052 1468

Constituency Office:
299 Newtownards Road,
Belfast, BT4 1AG

Tel: 028 9022 5040
Fax: 028 9022 5041

Farren, Dr Sean

Party: SDLP
Constituency: North Antrim

Assembly Office: Parliament Buildings,
Stormont Estate, Belfast, BT4 3XX

Tel: 028 9052 1708
Fax: 028 9052 1706

Constituency Office:
Bryan House, 16-18 Bryan Street,
Ballymena, Co Antrim

Tel: 028 7083 3042
Fax: 028 7083 4152

Assistant: Mrs Patricia Farren
Constituency Assts:
Mr Joe Montgomery

Fee, John

Party: SDLP
Constituency: Newry and Armagh

Assembly Office: Parliament Buildings,
Stormont Estate, Belfast, BT4 3XX

Tel: 028 9052 0378

Fax: 028 9052 0381

Constituency Office: 2 Bridge Street, Newry, Co Down, BT35 8AE

Tel: 028 3025 2999
Fax: 028 3026 7828

Ford, David

Party: Alliance
Constituency: South Antrim

Assembly Office: Parliament Buildings,
Stormont Estate, Belfast, BT4 3XX

Tel: 028 9052 1139
Fax: 028 9052 1313

Constituency Office: 23a Ballyclare Road, Newtownabbbey, Co Antrim, BT36 5EX

Tel: 028 9084 0930

Foster, Sam

Party: Ulster Unionist
Constituency: Fermanagh and South Tyrone

Assembly Office: Parliament Buildings,
Stormont Estate, Belfast, BT4 3XX

Tel: 028 9052 1355
Fax: 028 9052 1856

Constituency Office:1 Regal Pass, Enniskillen, Co Fermanagh, BT74 7NT
  Tel: 028 6632 2028
  Fax: 028 6632 2678

Gallagher, Tommy

Party: SDLP
Constituency: Fermanagh and South Tyrone

Assembly Office: Parliament Buildings,
Stormont Estate, Belfast, BT4 3XX

Tel: 028 9052 1702
Fax: 028 9052 1701

Constituency Office: 39 Darling Street, Enniskillen, BT74 7DP

Tel: 028 6634 2848
Fax: 028 6634 2838

Gibson, Oliver

Party: Democratic Unionist
Constituency: West Tyrone

Assembly Office: Parliament Buildings,
Stormont Estate, Belfast, BT4 3XX

Tel: 028 9052 1102
Fax: 028 9052 1811

Constituency Office: 12 Main Street, Beragh, Omagh, Co Tyrone, BT79 05Y

Tel: 028 8075 7000
Fax: 028 8075 8024

Secretary: Mrs Audrey McKenzie

Gildernew, Michelle MP

Party: Sinn Féin
Constituency: Fermanagh and South Tyrone

Assembly Office: Parliament Buildings,
Stormont Estate, Belfast, BT4 3XX

Telephone: 028 9052 1627
Fax: 028 9052 1625

Constituency Office: 60 Irish Street, Dungannon, Co Tyrone, BT70 1DQ

Tel: 028 8772 2776
Fax: 028 8772 2776

Gorman, Sir John

Party: Ulster Unionist
Constituency: North Down

Assembly Office: Parliament Buildings,
Stormont Estate, Belfast, BT4 3XX

Tel: 028 9052 0306
Fax: 028 9052 1543

Hamilton, Tom

Party: Ulster Unionist
Constituency: Strangford

Assembly Office: Parliament Buildings,
Stormont Estate, Belfast, BT4 3XX

Tel: 028 9052 0307
Fax: 028 9052 1017

Hanna, Carmel

Party: SDLP
Constituency: Belfast South

Assembly Office: Parliament Buildings,
Stormont Estate, Belfast, BT4 3XX

Tel: 028 9052 0369
Fax: 028 9052 0367

Political Asst: Ms Aine O'Keeffe

Constituency Office: 17 Elmwood Mews, Belfast, BT9 6BD

Tel: 028 9068 3535
Fax: 028 9068 3503

Office Admin: Nuala McAleenan

Haughey, Denis

Party: SDLP
Constituency: Mid Ulster

Assembly Office: Parliament Buildings,
Stormont Estate, Belfast, BT4 3XX

Tel: 028 9052 1684
Fax: 028 9052 1685

Private Secretary: Mr Stephen Cowan

Constituency Office:
54A William Street, Cookstown, Co Tyrone, BT80 8NB

Tel: 028 8676 3349
Fax: 028 8676 9187

Constituency Asst: Mr Peter Cassidy

Hay, William

Party: Democratic Unionist
Constituency: Foyle

Assembly Office: Parliament Buildings,
Stormont Estate, Belfast, BT4 3XX

Tel: 028 9052 1107
Fax: 028 9052 1815

Constituency Office:
9 Ebrington Terrace, Waterside, Londonderry, BT47 1JS

Tel: 028 7134 6271
Fax: 028 7132 9550

Personal Asst: Mr William Irwin

Hendron, Dr Joe

Party: SDLP
Constituency: Belfast West

Assembly Office: Parliament Buildings,
Stormont Estate, Belfast, BT4 3XX

Tel: 028 9052 1681
Fax: 028 9052 1679

Constituency Office:
60 Springfield Road, Belfast, BT12 7AH

Tel: 028 9023 6278
Fax: 028 9023 3033

Hilditch, David

Party: Democratic Unionist
Constituency: East Antrim

Assembly Office: Parliament Buildings,
Stormont Estate, Belfast, BT4 3XX

Tel: 028 9052 1115
Fax: 028 9052 1842

Constituency Office: 22 High Street, Carrickfergus, BT38 7AA

Tel: 028 9332 9980
Fax: 028 9332 9979

Researcher: Mr William Ashe

Hussey, Derek

Party: Ulster Unionist
Constituency: West Tyrone

Assembly Office: Parliament Buildings,
Stormont Estate, Belfast, BT4 3XX

Tel: 028 9052 1247
Fax: 028 9052 1741

Constituency Office: 48 Main Street, Castlederg, Co Tyrone, BT81 7AT

Tel: 028 8167 9299
Fax: 028 8167 9298

Hutchinson, Billy

Party: Progressive Unionist
Constituency: Belfast North

Assembly Office: Parliament Buildings,
Stormont Estate, Belfast, BT4 3XX

Tel: 028 9021 1299
Fax: 028 9052 1311

Constituency Office: 135 Shore Road, Belfast, BT15 3PN

Tel: 028 9077 2307
Fax: 028 9077 0060

Hutchinson, Roger

Party: Democratic Unionist
Constituency: East Antrim

Assembly Office: Parliament Buildings,
Stormont Estate, Belfast, BT4 3XX

Tel: 028 9052 1743
Fax: 028 9052 1752

Constituency Office: 38B Point Street, Larne, Co Antrim, BT40 1HY

Tel: 028 2827 9369
Fax: 028 2827 3035

Kane, Gardiner

Party: Democratic Unionist
Constituency: North Antrim

Assembly Office: Parliament Buildings,
Stormont Estate, Belfast, BT4 3XX

Tel: 028 9052 1108
Fax: 028 9052 1817

Constituency Office: 142a Main Street, Bushmills
Co Antrim, BT57 8QE

Tel: 028 2073 0373
Fax: 028 2073 1303

Kelly, Gerry

Party: Sinn Féin
Constituency: Belfast North

Assembly Office: Parliament Buildings,
Stormont Estate, Belfast, BT4 3XX

Tel: 028 9052 0359
Fax: 028 9052 0337

Constituency Office:
291 Antrim Road, BT15 2G2

Tel: 028 9074 0817
Fax: 028 9074 0814

Kelly, John

Party: Sinn Féin
Constituency: Mid Ulster

Assembly Office: Parliament Buildings,
Stormont Estate, Belfast, BT4 3XX

Tel: 028 9052 1633
Fax: 028 9052 1631

Kennedy, Danny

Party: Ulster Unionist
Constituency: Newry and Armagh

Assembly Office: Parliament Buildings,
Stormont Estate, Belfast, BT4 3XX

Tel: 028 9052 1336
Fax: 028 9052 1757

Constituency Office: 3 Mallview Terrace, Armagh, BT61 9AN

Tel: 028 3751 1655
Fax: 028 3751 1771

Political Secretary: Mrs Olive Whitten

Leslie, James

Party: Ulster Unionist
Constituency: North Antrim

Assembly Office: Parliament Buildings,
Stormont Estate, Belfast, BT4 3XX

Tel: 028 9052 1850
Fax: 028 9052 1536

Constituency Office:
30a Ballymoney Street,
Ballymena, Co Antrim, BT43 6AL

Tel: 028 2564 2262
Fax: 028 2564 2264

Lewsley, Patricia

Party: SDLP
Constituency: Lagan Valley

Assembly Office: Parliament Buildings,
Stormont Estate, Belfast, BT4 3XX

Tel: 028 9052 0331
Fax: 028 9052 0332

PA: Mrs Frances Murphy

Constituency Office: 34 Alina Gardens, Dunmurry, Belfast, BT17 0QJ

Tel: 028 9029 0846
Fax: 028 9266 9976

Administrator: Miss Tara Lewsley

Maginness, Alban

Party: SDLP
Constituency: Belfast North

Assembly Office: Parliament Buildings,
Stormont Estate, Belfast, BT4 3XX

Telephone: 028 90521703

Constituency Office: 228 Antrim Road, Belfast, BT15 2AN

Tel: 028 9022 0520
Fax: 028 9022 0522

Mallon, Séamus MP

Party: SDLP
Constituency: Newry and Armagh

Assembly Office: Parliament Buildings,
Stormont Estate, Belfast, BT4 3XX

Tel: 028 9052 1319
Fax: 028 9052 1329

Constituency Office: 2 Bridge Street, Newry, Co Down, BT35 8AE

Tel: 028 3026 7933
Fax: 028 3026 7828

Maskey, Alex

Party: Sinn Féin
Constituency: Belfast West

Assembly Office: Parliament Buildings,
Stormont Estate, Belfast, BT4 3XX

Tel: 028 9052 1224
Fax: 028 9052 1241

McCarthy, Kieran

Party: Alliance
Constituency: Strangford

Assembly Office: Parliament Buildings,
Stormont Estate, Belfast, BT4 3XX

Tel: 028 9052 0351
Fax: 028 9052 1651

PA: Mr Peter Copeland

Constituency Office: 7 Main Street,
Kircubbin, Co Down, BT22 2SS

Tel: 028 4273 8221
Fax: 028 4273 9023

McCartney, Robert

Party: UK Unionist
Constituency: North Down

Assembly Office: Parliament Buildings,
Stormont Estate, Belfast, BT4 3XX

Tel: 028 9052 1482
Fax: 028 9052 1483

Researcher: Mr John Cobain
Secretary: Mrs Anne Moore

McClarty, David

Party: Ulster Unionist
Constituency: East Londonderry

Assembly Office: Parliament Buildings,
Stormont Estate, Belfast, BT4 3XX

Tel: 028 9052 0310
Fax: 028 9052 0309

Constituency Office: 12 Dunmore Street, Coleraine, Co Londonderry

Tel: 028 7032 7294
Secretary: Mrs Patricia Fitzsimmons

McClelland, Donovan

Party: SDLP
Constituency: South Antrim

Assembly Office: Parliament Buildings,
Stormont Estate, Belfast, BT4 3XX

Telephone: 028 9052 1693
Fax: 028 9052 1694

McCrea, Rev William

Party: Democratic Unionist
Constituency: Mid Ulster

Assembly Office: Parliament Buildings,
Stormont Estate, Belfast, BT4 3XX

Tel: 028 9052 0462
Fax: 028 9052 1289

Constituency Office: 10 Highfield Road, Magherafelt, Co Londonderry, BT45 5JD

Tel: 028 7963 2664
Fax: 028 7930 0701

Secretary: Mr Ian McCrea

McDonnell, Dr Alasdair

Party: SDLP
Constituency: Belfast South

Assembly Office: Parliament Buildings,
Stormont Estate, Belfast, BT4 3XX

Tel: 028 9052 0338
Fax: 028 9052 0329

Constituency Office: 150 Ormeau Road, Belfast, BT7 2SL

Tel: 028 9024 2474
Fax: 028 9043 9935

Constituency Staff: Miss Sinead Murphy

McElduff, Barry

Party: Sinn Féin
Constituency: West Tyrone

Assembly Office: Parliament Buildings,
Stormont Estate, Belfast, BT4 3XX

Tel: 028 9052 1624
Fax: 028 90521622

Constituency Office: 4-5 James St, Omagh, Co Tyrone, BT78 1DH

Tel: 028 8076 1744
Fax: 028 8076 1727

McFarland, Alan

Party: Ulster Unionist
Constituency: North Down

Assembly Office: Parliament Buildings,
Stormont Estate, Belfast, BT4 3XX

Tel: 028 9052 1528
Fax: 028 9052 1768

Constituency Office: 77A High Street, Bangor, Co Down, BT20 5BD

Tel: 028 9147 0300
Fax: 028 9147 0301

McGimpsey, Michael

Party: Ulster Unionist
Constituency: Belfast South

Assembly Office: Parliament Buildings,
Stormont Estate, Belfast, BT4 3XX

Tel: 028 9052 1361
Fax: 028 9052 1852

Constituency Office: Unit 2, 127-145 Sandy Row, Belfast, BT12 5ET

Tel: 028 9024 5801
Fax: 028 9024 5801

PA/Researcher: Ms Michelle Bostock

McGrady, Eddie MP

Party: SDLP
Constituency: South Down

Assembly Office: Parliament Buildings, Stormont Estate, Belfast, BT4 3XX

Tel: 028 9052 1288
Fax: 028 9052 1545

Secretaries: Ms Margaret Ritchie
Researchers: Mrs Amanda Lavery,
Ms Theresa Doran

Constituency Office: 32 Saul Street,
Downpatrick, Co Down, BT30 6NQ

Tel: 028 4461 2882
Fax: 028 4461 9574

McGuinness, Martin MP

Party: Sinn Féin
Constituency: Mid Ulster

Assembly Office: Parliament
Buildings,
Stormont Estate, Belfast, BT4 3XX

Tel: 028 9052 0369
Fax: 028 9052 0360

Constituency Office: 32 Burn Road,
Cookstown, Co Tyrone, BT80 8DN

Tel: 028 8676 5850
Fax: 028 8676 6734

PA: Mr Oliver Molloy

McHugh, Gerry

Party: Sinn Féin
Constituency: Fermanagh and South
Tyrone

Assembly Office: Parliament
Buildings,
Stormont Estate, Belfast, BT4 3XX

Tel: 028 9052 1621
Fax: 028 9052 1619

Constituency Office:
7 Market Square, Enniskillen

Tel: 028 6632 8214
Fax: 028 6632 9915

McLaughlin, Mitchel

Party: Sinn Féin
Constituency: Foyle

Assembly Office: Parliament
Buildings,
Stormont Estate, Belfast, BT4 3XX

Tel: 028 9052 1603
Fax: 028 9052 1601

Constituency Office: 15 Cable
Street, Bogside, Derry, BT48 9HF

Tel: 028 7130 9264
Fax: 028 7130 8781

Manager: Mr Gerry MagLochlainn

McMenamin, Eugene

Party: SDLP
Constituency: West Tyrone

Assembly Office: Parliament
Buildings,
Stormont Estate, Belfast, BT4 3XX

Tel: 028 9052 0324
Fax: 028 9052 1354

Constituency Office:
33a Abercorn Square, Strabane, Co
Tyrone, BT82 8AQ

Tel: 028 7188 6633
Fax: 028 7188 6233

PA: Mrs Kathleen McMenamin
Secretary: Mrs Terri Quigley

McNamee, Patrick

Party: Sinn Féin
Constituency: Newry and Armagh

Assembly Office: Parliament
Buildings,
Stormont Estate, Belfast, BT4 3XX

Telephone: 028 9052 0355
Fax: 028 9052 03546

Constituency Office: 38 Irish Street,
Armagh, BT61 7EP

Tel: 028 3751 1797
Fax: 028 3751 8493

Assistant: Mrs Patricia O'Rawe

McWilliams, Monica

Party: NIWC
Constituency: Belfast South

Assembly Office: Parliament
Buildings,
Stormont Estate, Belfast, BT4 3XX

Tel: 028 9052 1463
Fax: 028 9052 1461

Co-ordinator: Ms Ann McCann

Constituency Office: 50 University
Street, Belfast, BT7 1HB

Tel: 028 9023 3100
Fax: 028 9024 0021

Communications: Ms Chris
McCartney

Molloy, Francis

Party: Sinn Féin
Constituency: Mid Ulster

Assembly Office: Parliament
Buildings,
Stormont Estate, Belfast, BT4 3XX

Tel: 028 9052 0463
Fax: 028 9052 0365

Constituency Office: 7-9 The
Square, Coalisland, Co Tyrone,
BT71 4LN

Tel: 028 8774 8689
Fax: 028 8774 6903

Assistant: Mrs Michelle O'Neill

Morrice, Jane

Party: NIWC
Constituency: North Down

Assembly Office: Parliament
Buildings,
Stormont Estate, Belfast, BT4 3XX

Tel: 028 9052 1297

Constituency Office:
108 Dufferin Ave
Bangor, BT20 3AY

Tel: 028 9147 0739
Fax: 028 9066 0424

Morrow, Maurice

Party: Democratic Unionist
Constituency: Fermanagh and South
Tyrone

Assembly Office: Parliament
Buildings,
Stormont Estate, Belfast, BT4 3XX

Tel: 028 9052 1296
Fax: 028 9052 1295

Constituency Office: 626 Scotch
Street, Dungannon, BT70 1BJ

Tel: 028 8775 2799

Murphy, Conor

Party: Sinn Féin
Constituency: Newry and Armagh

Assembly Office: Parliament
Buildings, Stormont Estate, Belfast,
BT4 3XX

Tel: 028 9052 1630
Fax: 028 9052 1628

Constituency Office: 4 Maryville,
Main Street, Camlough, Newry, Co
Down, BT35 7JQ

Tel: 028 3083 9470
Fax: 028 3083 9423

Murphy, Mick

Party: Sinn Féin
Constituency: South Down

Assembly Office: Parliament
Buildings,
Stormont Estate, Belfast, BT4 3XX

Tel: 028 9052 1618
Fax: 028 9052 1616

Neeson, Sean

Party: Alliance
Constituency: East Antrim

Assembly Office: Parliament
Buildings,
Stormont Estate, Belfast, BT4 3XX

Tel: 028 9052 1314
Fax: 028 9052 1313

Constituency Office:
North Street, Carickfergus,
BT38 7AQ

Tel: 028 9335 0286

Nelis, Mary

Party: Sinn Féin
Constituency: Foyle

Assembly Office: Parliament
Buildings,
Stormont Estate, Belfast, BT4 3XX

Tel: 028 9052 0322
Fax: 028 9052 1721

Nesbitt, Dermot

Party: Ulster Unionist
Constituency: South Down

Assembly Office: Room 279,
Parliament Buildings, Stormont
Estate, Belfast, BT4 3XX

Tel: 028 9052 1444
Fax: 028 9052 1419

PA: Mr Philip Robinson

Constituency Office: 19 Causeway
Road, Newcastle, BT33 0DL

Tel: 028 4372 4400
Fax: 028 4372 5116

O'Connor, Danny

Party: SDLP
Constituency: East Antrim

Assembly Office: Parliament
Buildings,
Stormont Estate, Belfast, BT4 3XX

Tel: 028 9052 0372
Fax: 028 9052 0374

Constituency Office: 55c Main
Street, Larne, BT40 1JE

Tel: 028 2827 0033
Fax: 028 2827 0077

O'Hagan, Dr Dara

Party: Sinn Féin
Constituency: Upper Bann

Assembly Office: Parliament
Buildings,
Stormont Estate, Belfast, BT4 3XX

Tel: 028 9052 1671
Fax: 028 9052 1672

Constituency Office: 77 North
Street, Lurgan
Co Armagh, BT67 9AH

Tel: 028 3834 9675
Fax: 028 3832 2610

O'Neill, Eamonn

Party: SDLP
Constituency: South Down

Assembly Office: Room 216,
Parliament Buildings, Stormont
Estate, Belfast, BT4 3XX

Tel: 028 9052 0461
Fax: 028 9052 1015

Constituency Office: 60 Main
Street, Castlewellan
Co Down BT31 9DJ

Tel: 028 4377 8833
Fax: 028 4377 8844

Researcher: Miss Ciara O'Neill

Paisley, Dr Ian MP MEP

Party: Democratic Unionist
Constituency: North Antrim

Assembly Office: Parliament
Buildings,
Stormont Estate, Belfast, BT4 3XX

Constituency Office: 256 Ravenhill
Road, Belfast, BT6 8GJ

Tel: 028 9045 8900/4255
Fax: 028 9045 7783

Secretary: Mrs Sharon Leslie
Researcher: Mr Tom Gilmore

Paisley, Ian Jnr

Party: Democratic Unionist
Constituency: North Antrim

Assembly Office: Parliament
Buildings, Stormont Estate
Belfast, BT4 3XX

Tel: 028 9045 4255
Fax: 028 9045 7783

Researcher: Mr Mervin Storey
Constituency Office: 46 Hill Street,
Ballymena, BT43 6BH

Tel: 028 2564 1421
Fax: 028 2564 1421

Receptionist/Sec: Mrs Beth Baird

Poots, Edwin

Party: Democratic Unionist
Constituency: Lagan Valley

Assembly Office: Parliament
Buildings,
Stormont Estate, Belfast, BT4 3XX

Tel: 028 9052 1114
Fax: 028 9052 1824

Constituency Office: 46 Bachelors
Walk, Lisburn, Co Antrim, BT28
1XN

Tel: 028 9260 3003
Fax: 028 9262 7994

Personal Secretary: Mrs Mabel
Hanna

Ramsey, Sue

Party: Sinn Féin
Constituency: Belfast West

Assembly Office: Parliament
Buildings,
Stormont Estate, Belfast, BT4 3XX

Constituency Office: 222
Stewartstown Road, BT17 0DZ

Tel: 028 9061 1176
Fax: 028 9061 1237

Robinson, Iris MP

Party: Democratic Unionist
Constituency: Strangford

Assembly Office: Room 345,
Parliament Buildings, Stormont
Estate, Belfast, BT4 3XX

Tel: 028 9052 1103
Fax: 028 9052 1813

PA: Jonathon Robinson

Constituency Office: 2B James
Street, Newtownards, BT23 4DY

Tel: 028 9182 7701
Fax: 028 9182 7703

Secretaries: Mrs Jacqui Louden,
Mrs Alice Rahilly

Robinson, Ken

Party: Ulster Unionist
Constituency: East Antrim

Assembly Office: Parliament
Buildings,
Stormont Estate, Belfast, BT4 3XX

Tel: 028 9052 1881
Fax: 028 9052 1925

Secretary: Mrs Louisa Robinson

Constituency Office: 32c North
Street, Carrickfergus, Co Antrim,
BT38 7AQ

Tel: 028 9336 2995
Fax: 028 9336 8048

Robinson, Mark

Party: Democratic Unionist
Constituency: Belfast South

Assembly Office: Room 353,
Parliament Buildings, Stormont
Estate, Belfast, BT4 3XX

Tel: 028 9052 1129
Fax: 028 9052 1829

Researcher: Miss Julie Oswald

Constituency Office: 215a Lisburn
Road, Belfast, BT9 7EJ

Tel: 028 9022 5969
Fax: 028 9022 5905

Assistant: Mrs Anne McCormick

Robinson, Peter MP

Party: Democratic Unionist
Constituency: Belfast East

Assembly Office: Room 208,
Parliament Buildings, Stormont
Estate, Belfast, BT4 3XX

Tel: 028 9052 1049
Fax: 028 9052 1337

Private Secretary: Mr Gareth
Robinson

Constituency Office: Strandtown
Hall, 96 Belmont Avenue, Belfast,

BT4 3DE

Tel: 028 9047 3111
Fax: 028 9047 1797

Secretary: Mrs Margaret Kingham
Assistant/Sec: Mrs Wilhelmina Reid

Roche, Patrick

Party: Northern Ireland Unionist
Constituency: Lagan Valley

Assembly Office: Parliament
Buildings,
Stormont Estate, Belfast, BT4 3XX

Tel: 028 9052 1994
Fax: 028 9052 1848

Constituency Office: 64 Antrim
Road, Lisburn, BT28 1OD

Tel: 028 9267 4100
Fax: 028 9267 4104

Rodgers, Bríd

Party: SDLP
Constituency: Upper Bann

Assembly Office: Parliament
Buildings,
Stormont Estate, Belfast, BT4 3XX

Constituency Office: 41 North
Street, Lurgan, Co Armagh, BT67
9AG

Tel: 028 3832 2140
Fax: 028 3831 6996

Secretary: Ms Teresa Higgins

Savage, George

Party: Ulster Unionist
Constituency: Upper Bann

Assembly Office: Parliament
Buildings,
Stormont Estate, Belfast, BT4 3XX

Constituency Office: 22 Newry
Street, Banbridge, BT32 3JZ

Tel: 028 3888 1448
Fax: 028 3882 0401

Shannon, Jim

Party: Democratic Unionist
Constituency: Strangford

Assembly Office: Parliament Buildings,
Stormont Estate, Belfast, BT4 3XX

Tel: 028 9052 1128
Fax: 028 9052 1828

Constituency Office: DUP Advice
Centre, 34a Francis Street,
Newtownards, Co Down, BT23 7DN

Tel: 028 9182 7990
Fax: 028 9182 7991

Shipley-Dalton, Duncan

Party: Ulster Unionist
Constituency: South Antrim

Assembly Office: Parliament Buildings,
Stormont Estate, Belfast, BT4 3XX

Tel: 028 9052 0317
Fax: 028 9052 0315

Constituency Office: 19A Fountain
St, Antrim, BT41 4BB

Taylor, Rt Hon John

Party: Ulster Unionist
Constituency: Strangford

Assembly Office: Parliament Buildings,
Stormont Estate, Belfast, BT4 3XX

Tel: 028 9052 1803
Facsimile 028 9052 1581

Constituency Office: 6 William
Street, Newtownards, BT23 4AE

Tel: 028 9181 4123
Fax: 028 9181 4123

Tierney, John

Party: SDLP
Constituency: Foyle

Assembly Office: Parliament
Buildings, Stormont Estate, Belfast,
BT4 3XX

Constituency Office: 5 Bayview

Terrace, Derry, BT48 7EE

Tel: 028 7136 2631
Fax: 028 7136 3423

Trimble, Rt Hon David MP

Party: Ulster Unionist
Constituency: Upper Bann

Assembly Office: Parliament Buildings,
Stormont Estate, Belfast, BT4 3XX

Tel: 028 9052 1013

Constituency Office: 2 Queen
Street, Lurgan, Co Armagh, BT66
8BQ

Tel: 028 3832 8088
Fax: 028 3832 2343

Watson, Denis

Party: United Unionist Assembly
Constituency: Upper Bann

Assembly Office: Parliament Buildings,
Stormont Estate, Belfast, BT4 3XX

Tel: 028 9052 1923
Fax: 028 9052 1068

Weir, Peter

Party: Democratic Unionist
Constituency: North Down

Assembly Office: Parliament
Buildings, Stormont Estate, Belfast,
BT4 3XX

Tel: 028 9052 0320
Fax: 028 9052 0319

PA: Dr Philip Weir

Constituency Office: 77A High
Street, Bangor, Co Down, BT20
5BD

Tel: 028 9147 0300

Office Manager: Mr James
McKerrow

Wells, Jim

Party: Democratic Unionist
Constituency: South Down

Assembly Office: Parliament
Buildings, Stormont Estate, Belfast,
BT4 3XX

Tel: 028 9052 1110
Fax: 028 9052 1820

Constituency Office: 2 Belfast Road
Ballynahinch, BT24 8DZ

Tel: 028 9756 4200
Fax: 028 9756 4200

Wilson, Cedric

Party: Northern Ireland Unionist
Constituency: Strangford

Assembly Office: Parliament
Buildings,
Stormont Estate, Belfast, BT4 3XX

Tel: 028 9052 1294
Fax: 028 9052 1293

Constituency Office: 2B Ann Street,
Newtownards, Co Down, BT23 7AB

Tel: 028 9181 0484

Wilson, Jim

Party: Ulster Unionist
Constituency: South Antrim

Assembly Office: Parliament
Buildings,
Stormont Estate, Belfast, BT4 3XX

Tel: 028 9052 1292
Fax: 028 9052 1291

Constituency Office: 3a Rashee
Road, Ballyclare, Co Antrim, BT39
9HJ

Tel: 028 9332 4461
Fax: 028 9332 4462

Wilson, Sammy

Party: Democratic Unionist
Constituency: Belfast East

Assembly Office: Parliament
Buildings, Stormont Estate, Belfast,
BT4 3XX

Tel: 028 9052 1192
Fax: 0289052 1834

The Executive

Strand 2 of the Good Friday Agreement provided for executive authority to be discharged on behalf of the Assembly by a First Minister, Deputy First Minister and up to ten ministers with departmental responsibilities. The First and Deputy First Minister are elected on a cross community basis and following their election the posts of Ministers allocated to parties on the basis of the d'Hondt system by reference to the number of seats each party has in the Assembly. The Ministers constitute an Executive Committee convened and presided over by the First and Deputy First Minister.

Ten departmental ministers were also appointed with responsibility for the new Northern Ireland departments. Together these ministers make up the Executive Committee of twelve. The Executive Committee with departmental responsibilities (at time of going to print) is set out below. The DUP have a policy of rotating ministerial post holders.

Arrangements to ensure decisions are taken on a cross community basis are:

- Either parallel consent, i.e. a majority of those members present and voting, including a majority of the unionist and nationalist designations present and voting;
- Or a weighted majority (60 per cent) of members present and voting, including at least 40 per cent of each of the nationalist and unionist delegations present and voting.

Key decisions requiring cross-community support will be designated in advance, including election of the Chair of the Assembly, the First Minister and Deputy First Minister, standing orders and budget allocations. In other cases, such decisions could be triggered by a Petition of Concern brought by a significant minority of Assembly Members (30/108).

The duties defined for the First Minister and the Deputy First Minister include dealing with and coordinating the work of the Executive Committee and the response of the Northern Ireland Executive to external relationships.

The Executive Committee

The Executive Committee, effectively Northern Ireland's Cabinet, provides a forum for the discussion of issues which cut across the responsibilities of two or more Ministers, prioritising executive and legislative proposals and recommending a common position where necessary in dealing with external relationships.

On a yearly basis the Executive Committee agrees a programme incorporating an agreed budget linked to policies and priorities, subject to approval by the Assembly, following scrutiny in Committee.

A party may decline the opportunity to nominate a person to serve as a Minister or subsequently change its nominee. All Northern Ireland Departments are headed by

Executive Committee prior to suspension in October 2002

David Trimble — First Minister		Mark Durkan — Deputy First Minister		
Brid Rodgers Minister for Agriculture and Rural Development	**Michael McGimpsey** Minister for Culture, Arts and Leisure	**Martin McGuinness** Minister for Education	**Sir Reg Empey** Minister for Enterprise, Trade and Investment	**Dermot Nesbitt** Minister for the Environment
Sean Farren Minister for Finance and Personnel	**Bairbre de Bruin** Minister for Health, Social Services and Public Safety	**Carmel Hanna** Minister for Employment and Learning	**Peter Robinson** Minister for Regional Development	**Nigel Dodds** Minister for Social Development

a Minister who liaises with their respective statutory Committee.

As a condition of appointment Ministers must affirm the pledge of office undertaking to discharge effectively and in good faith all the responsibilities attaching to their office. Ministers hold full executive authority in their respective areas of responsibility within any broad programme agreed by the Executive Committee and endorsed by the Assembly as a whole.

The Northern Ireland Executive is a body unique in the multi party membership of its composition in contrast to the one party representation in the British Cabinet. Against the background of conflict and dissension, which have divided local parties over traditional issues, the realisation of a Programme for Government is regarded as an important milestone.

First Minster David Trimble MP MLA and Deputy First Minster Mark Durkan MLA

The First Minister and Deputy First Minister

The Assembly originally elected, on a cross community basis, a First Minister, David Trimble, leader of the largest party in the Assembly, the Ulster Unionist Party (UUP) and a Deputy First Minister, Séamus Mallon of the second largest party, the SDLP. David Trimble later resigned as a protest against the lack of progress on decommissioning of paramilitary weapons, and was replaced temporarily by Reg Empey, the Minister for Enterprise, Trade and Development. Séamus Mallon remained as Deputy First Minister but was replaced by Mark Durkan prior to suspension.

The First and Deputy First Minister must stand for election as a pair of candidates, one from each of the two traditions, and must be elected by the Assembly as a pair. The First Minister and Deputy First Minister must be

elected within six weeks following the election of the Assembly. Together they must have the support of an absolute majority of the Assembly, plus a majority of nationalist and a majority of unionist members. If there is an absence of a viable option for the election of First Minister or Deputy First Minister, another Minister may hold the position as acting First or Deputy First Minister for a period of six weeks.

Junior Ministers

In the Northern Ireland Executive there were two junior ministers in OFMDFM, Denis Haughey and James Leslie.

Programme for Government

It was agreed in the Good Friday Agreement that in order to create effective government for Northern Ireland:

"The Executive Committee will seek to agree each year, and review as necessary a programme incorporating an agreed budget linked to policies and programmes, subject to approval by the Assembly, after scrutiny in Assembly Committees, on a cross-community basis".

The Programme for Government is the administration's core policy document providing a strategic overview of the planned work of the Executive and demonstrating how policies and programmes delivered by different departments and agencies may be combined to achieve agreed priorities. The Programme for Government may be best described as an amalgamation of departmental business plans into the overall corporate plan. The Programme for Government is essentially a rolling three-year plan, updated each year in line with annual spending plans.

The First Minister and Deputy First Minister hold responsibility for setting the overall priorities for government through the Programme for Government. Ministers are expected to adhere to these priorities.

The Programme and Budget are closely linked. Programme priorities identified in the Programme for Government are reflected in the budget prepared by the Finance Minister and drive decisions on the allocation of financial resources. Executive Programme Funds (EPFs) are being used to promote a more coherent approach to policy and programme development. These separately ring fenced funds were created by the Executive to assist the development of new policies, services, programmes and projects of major importance, which will contribute towards delivering progress.

Four important areas have been identified for greater emphasis within the Programme for Government:

- Investment in infrastructure;
- Improved service delivery;
- Tackling social exclusion, in particular poverty;
- Partnership.

Five key priorities for ministers, their departments and related agencies were identified in the Programme for Government:

- Growing as a community;
- Working for a healthier people;
- Investing in education and skills;
- Securing a competitive economy;
- Developing North/South, East/West and international relations.

Cross cutting policy development themes are emphasised within the Programme for Government. Themes applicable for cross cutting measures include: promoting equality of opportunity and good relations; promoting sustainable living; and developing as a region.

Within the Programme for Government specific actions have been identified in support of the priorities. Public Service Agreements (PSAs) have been introduced for all departments. These set out the key outcomes and outputs that will be delivered by each department with the resources they have available.

An Annual Report, the first published in July 2002 provides an overview of the performance of the Executive and each of the departments in achieving the targets set in the Programme for Government.

Service Delivery Agreements (SDAs) have also been introduced for each department in relation to their Public Service Agreement setting out the actions to be taken by the department to deliver its targets and raise service standards.

The Barnett Formula

The Barnett Formula is used to determine the resources available for the devolved administrations in Scotland, Wales and Northern Ireland. Subject to the agreement of the Assembly, the Executive has full discretion under the Treasury's Funding Policy in the allocation of resources under the Northern Ireland Executive Departmental Expenditure Limit to meet local requirements.

The Northern Ireland Executive has expressed concerns about the Barnett Formula, which broadly measures spending per person taking little account of relative need. These concerns have been addressed to the Treasury and may eventually lead to a review of the formula.

The July 2002 Comprehensive Spending Review allocated an additional 3.9 per cent real increase in public expenditure in Northern Ireland over the period 2003/04 to 2005/06.

The Reinvestment and Reform Initiative

The Reinvestment and Reform Initiative was announced by the First and Deputy First Ministers on the 2 May 2002 as an innovative approach for the provision of substantial investment in the modernisation and improvement of infrastructure, progression of sustainable economic and social improvements and the delivery of better public services.

Under a favourable borrowing environment the Reinvestment and Reform Initiative will provide significantly increased funds to meet requirements for capital investment in health, education and transport, far in excess of the resources available under traditional means of funding. Latest estimates of the gap between what is sustainable under the current budget and actual capital investment requirements stand at £6 billion over the next ten years.

Initially, the Reinvestment and Reform Initiative is expected to provide a £200 million capital injection in the next two years of which £125 million will be a loan from the Treasury, repayable from existing regional rate income and £75 million from Executive resources. New borrowing powers providing the option of using additional revenue sources to lever in low cost borrowing which would accelerate the pace of infrastructure investment will be available from 2004–05.

The Executive planned to create a new organisation in the form of a strategic investment body, to ensure that infrastructure is planned at a strategic level, resources maximised and existing programmes complemented.

The funds available under its Reinvestment and Reform initiative will allow the Executive discretion to vary its spending powers, and by borrowing from the Treasury at advantageous interest rates, set the pace of investment programmes in a manner previously unknown, without the need to operate solely within the confines of the allocations under the Barnett Formula.

Departmental and Other Assembly Committees

A detailed explanation of the Committee system and description of Committee memberships follows below:
The Committees along with the Executive were suspended in October 2002 and when reinstated it is posible that they will have changed.

Introduction

The executive structures envisaged in the Good Friday Agreement have the effect of creating a strong inclusive government but no formal opposition. The architects of the Agreement therefore saw the need to create a strong committee system where elected members would play a robust formal role in interfacing with the Executive.

Paragraph 9 of Strand One of the Good Friday Agreement sets out the formal powers of the Committees, which include a "scrutiny, policy development, and consultation role with respect to the Department with which each is associated". The Committees also play a role in the "initiation of legislation", a significant and considerable power to vest in a legislative committee. However, to date the main focus of Committee work has been driven by the Executive Programme, although in terms of reporting and the breadth of their inquiries they have shown a readiness to take the initiative on certain issues.

Scrutiny Role of Committees

Whilst Statutory Committees have powers of inquiry and reporting they also hold an important role within the legislative process which involves taking the committee stage of primary legislation issuing from the associated department and examining the ensuing statutory instruments.

The Committee produces a report, following the 30-day period allowed for the committee stage.

In effect the committees act as a democratic check and balance on the power of Ministers and the Executive in the absence of an "opposition" as is traditionally understood within the UK Westminster model.

Whilst committees do have the power to propose their own legislation, this has yet to occur as the Executive Programme for Government has largely determined their workload.

The ability of committees to effectively scrutinise and hold the Executive to account is hampered by the inclusive nature of the Executive, on which all but the smallest parties and those who do not wish to participate are represented, and the fact that the majority of seats on each committee are held by the larger parties who also hold the majority of Executive positions.

Statutory Committees (Departmental Committees)

The Assembly has 10 Statutory Committees with a Chair and a Deputy Chair elected using the proportional d'Hondt system. In essence d'Hondt is a voting system used to allocate Ministerial or Committee positions based on party political strength. Similarly Chairmanships, Vice Chairmanships and Membership of Committees are allocated in broad proportion to party strengths in the Assembly.

There are no co-opted members on to any of the committees, whether Statutory, Standing or Ad Hoc. However, Statutory Committees do appoint specialist advisors where they deem it appropriate to the conduct of an inquiry.

Statutory Committees enjoy the power "to consider and advise on departmental budgets and annual plans in the context of the overall budget allocation". The procedure for processing the budget requires each of the Statutory Committees, through dialogue with their respective Ministers, to examine and scrutinise departmental allocations in line with the Programme for Government and to submit their views to the Finance and Personnel Committee who interpret and draw together the respective views. These are then submitted to the Department of Finance and Personnel, enabling the Minister to bring forward a revised budget for consideration.

Membership of Statutory Committees

Seats on Statutory Committees consisting of 11 members should reflect the diversity of political parties represented within the Assembly. Seats on Statutory Committees should be allocated to ensure that a majority of seats on each committee are allocated to a party with a majority within the Assembly. The number of seats allocated to each party should be proportionate to its membership of the Assembly.

The Business Committee holds responsibility for the allocation of seats to individual members or the parties subject to approval by the Assembly.

The quorum for the Statutory Committees is set at five. Simple majority passes votes by a show of hands. The duration of the Committee is the life of the Assembly unless otherwise determined by the Assembly.

Statutory or Departmental Committees of the Assembly

The ten departmental committees are listed below, with details of support staff.

Agriculture and Rural Development Committee

Chair	Rev Ian Paisley (DUP)
Vice-chair	George Savage (UUP)
Members	David Ford (ALL)
	Gardiner Kane (DUP)
	Ian Paisley Jnr (DUP)
	Pat Doherty (SF)
	Gerry McHugh (SF)
	Billy Armstrong (UUP)
	Boyd Douglas (UUAP)
	P J Bradley (SDLP)
	John Dallat (SDLP)
Principal Clerk	John Torney
Committee Clerk	Paul Moore
Tel	028 9052 1784
Fax	028 90521939
E mail	committee.agriculture@niassembly.gov.uk
Executive Support	Rosemary Barclay
Committee Assistant	Kyran Hewitt

Education Committee

Chair	Danny Kennedy (UUP)
Vice-chair	Sammy Wilson (DUP)
Members	Eileen Bell (All)
	Oliver Gibson (DUP)
	Mitchel McLaughlin (SF)
	Gerry Mc Hugh (SF)
	John Fee (SDLP)
	Tommy Gallagher (SDLP)
	Alban Maginness (SDLP)
	Tom Hamilton (UUP)
	Ken Robinson (UUP)
Principal Clerk	John Torney
Committee Clerk	Christine Darragh
Tel	028 9052 1629
Fax	028 9052 1371
E mail	committee.education@niassembly.gov.uk
Assistant Clerk	Julie McMurray
Executive Support	Joanne Adair
Committee Assistant	Collette Angelone

Culture, Arts and Leisure Committee

Chair	Eamonn O'Neill (SDLP)
Vice-chair	John Kelly (SF)
Members	Kieran McCarthy (All)
	Jim Shannon (DUP)
	David Hilditch (DUP)
	Mick Murphy (SF)
	Eugene McMenamin (SDLP)
	Ian Adamson (UUP)
	Ivan Davis (UUP)
	Jim Wilson (UUP)
	Fraser Agnew (UUAP)
Principal Clerk	John Torney
Committee Clerk	Loretta Gordon
Tel	028 9052 1574
Fax	028 9052 1063
E mail	committee.culture@niassembly.gov.uk
Assistant Clerk	Linda Gregg
Executive Support	Mairead Higgins
Committee Assistant	John McCourt

Enterprise, Trade and Investment Committee

Chair	Pat Doherty (SF)
Vice-chair	Sean Neeson (All)
Members	Wilson Clyde (DUP)
	Jim Wells (DUP)
	Jane Morrice (NIWC)
	Dara O'Hagan (SF)
	Eugene McMenamin (SDLP)
	John Fee (SDLP)
	Annie Courtney (SDLP)
	Alasdair McDonnell (SDLP)
	David McClarty (UUP)
	Billy Armstrong (UUP)
Principal Clerk	John Torney
Committee Clerk	Cathie White
Tel	028 9052 1230
Fax	028 9052 1063
E mail	committee.enterprise@niassembly.gov.uk
Assistant Clerk	John Nesbitt
Executive Support	Judith Presho
Committee Assistant	Derek Donaldson

Employment and Learning Committee

Chair	Dr Esmond Birnie (UUP)
Vice-chair	Mervyn Carrick (DUP)
Members	David Hilditch (DUP)
	Roger Hutchinson (DUP)
	Monica McWilliams (NIWC)
	Barry McElduff (SF)
	Michelle Gildernew (SF)
	John Dallat (SDLP)
	Ian Adamson (UUP)
	Joan Carson (UUP)
Principal Clerk	John Torney
Committee Clerk	Dr Andrew Peoples
Tel	028 9052 1272
Fax	028 9052 1433
E mail	committee.hfete@niassembly.gov.uk
Assistant Clerk	Colin Jones
Executive Support	Anne Colville
Committee Assistant	Catherine McGrattan

Environment Committee

Chair	Rev Willie McCrea (DUP)
Vice-chair	Patricia Lewsley (SDLP)
Members	David Ford (All)
	Edwin Poots (DUP)
	Francis Molloy (SF)
	Mary Nellis (SF)
	David McClarty (UUP)
	Joan Carson (UUP)
	William Armstrong (UUP)
	Denis Watson (UUAP)
Principal Clerk	John Torney
Committee Clerk	John Simmons
Tel	028 9052 1271
Fax	028 9052 0343
E mail	committee.environment@niassembly.gov.uk
Assistant Clerk	Jim Beatty
Executive Support	Jim Nulty
Committee Assistant	Mary Devine

Finance and Personnel Committee

Chair	Francis Molloy (SF)
Vice-chair	Roy Beggs (UUP)
Members	Seamus Close (All)
	Maurice Morrow (DUP)
	Roger Hutchinson (DUP)
	Alex Maskey (SF)
	Alex Attwood (SDLP)
	Patricia Lewsley (SDLP)
	William Bell (UUP)
	Derek Hussey (UUP)
	Peter Weir (DUP)
Principal Clerk	Martin Wilson
Committee Clerk	Alan Patterson
Tel	028 9052 1785
Fax	028 9052 1939
E mail	committee.finance@niassembly.gov.uk
Executive Support	Edel Gillen
Committee Assistant	Sharon Bowman

Health, Social Services and Public Safety Committee

Chair	Dr Joe Hendron (SDLP)
Vice-chair	Tommy Gallagher (SDLP)
Members	Paul Berry (DUP)
	Iris Robinson MP (DUP)
	Monica McWilliams (NIWC)
	John Kelly (SF)
	Sue Ramsey (SF)
	Annie Courtney (SDLP)
	Pauline Armitage (Ind U)
	Rev Robert Coulter (UUP)
	Tom Hamilton (UUP)
Principal Clerk	John Torney
Committee Clerk	Peter Hughes
Tel	028 9052 1786
Fax	028 9052 1939
E mail	committee.hssps@niassembly.gov.uk
Assistant Clerk	Dermot Harkin
Executive Support	Valerie Artt
Committee Assistant	Kerry McFerran

Regional Development Committee

Chair	Alban Maginness (SDLP)
Vice-chair	Alan McFarland (UUP)
Members	William Hay (DUP)
	Mark Robinson (DUP)
	Roger Hutchinson (DUP)
	David Ervine (PUP)
	Pat McNamee (SF)
	Joe Byrne (SDLP)
	Derek Hussey (UUP)
	George Savage (UUP)
	P J Bradley (SDLP)
Principal Clerk	John Torney
Committee Clerk	Liam Barr
Tel	028 9052 1281
Fax	028 9052 0343
E mail	committee.regiondevel@niassembly.gov.uk
Assistant Clerk	Seamus Fay
Executive Support	Neill Currie
Committee Assistant	Sharon Young

Social Development Committee

Chair	Fred Cobain (UUP)
Vice-chair	Gerry Kelly (SF)
Members	Mark Robinson (DUP)
	Sammy Wilson (DUP)
	Billy Hutchinson (PUP)
	Mary Nellis (SF)
	Danny O'Connor (SDLP)
	Eamonn O'Neill (SDLP)
	John Tierney (SDLP)
	Sir John Gorman (UUP)
	Tom Hamilton (UUP)
Principal Clerk	Stephen Graham
Tel	028 9052 1887
Fax	028 9052 1939
E mail	committee.socdev@niassembly.gov.uk
Committee Clerk	Keith Barker
Assistant Clerk	Liam Hart
Executive Support	Victoria Surplus

Northern Ireland Executive

Non-Statutory Committees

Standing Committees and Ad Hoc Committees are the two types of non-statutory committee in the Assembly.

Standing Committees

Standing Committees are permanent Assembly Committees whose chair and deputy chair are filled utilising the same procedures for Statutory Committees as described above and detailed in Standing Order 46. However the process for nomination of chairs and deputies to Statutory and Non Statutory Committees should be separate and distinct.

In respect to other matters such as quorum and nomination of members the same procedures apply as those for Statutory Committees.

The Assembly has established a number of committees, which take care of the many aspects of running a legislative forum. These are:

- The Business Committee;
- Procedures Committee;
- Committee of the Centre;
- Public Accounts Committee;
- Committee on Standards and Privilege;
- Audit Committee.

Business Committee

The Business Committee chaired by the Speaker discusses forthcoming business and makes arrangements for the business of the Assembly. The Committee consists of thirteen members, with two members appointed to act as Chair in the absence of the Speaker. Each party delegation is entitled to cast the number of votes equivalent to the number of members who adhere to the Whip of that party. The Business Committee also determines the dates of Recess.

Procedures Committee

The Committee on Procedures is a Standing Committee of the Northern Ireland Assembly established in accordance with paragraph 10 of Strand One of the Belfast Agreement and under Assembly Standing Orders 49 and 53. The Committee has 11 members including a Chairperson and Deputy Chairperson and a quorum of five. The Committee has the power to:

- Consider and review on an ongoing basis the Standing Orders and procedures of the Assembly;

- Initiate enquiries and publish reports;
- Update the Standing Orders of the Assembly for punctuation and grammar;
- Annually republish Standing Orders.

Committee of the Centre

The Committee of the Centre, established to scrutinise the Office of the First Minister and Deputy First Minister under Standing Order 54, although it is restricted by its remit to only some of the functions of the OFMDFM.

Standing Order 54 states that the Committee of the Centre is to examine and report on the following functions carried out in the OFMDFM.

- Economic Policy Unit (other than the Programme of Government);
- Equality Unit;
- Civic Forum;

Business Committee

Chairman	The Lord Alderdice (Speaker)	
Members	Ian Paisley Jnr	DUP
	Kieran McCarthy	DUP
	Billy Hutchinson	PUP
	Prof Monica McWilliams	NIWC
	John Tierney	SDLP
	PJ Bradley	SDLP
	Sue Ramsey	SF
	Conor Murphy	SF
	David McClarty	UUP
	Ivan Davis	UUAP
	Denis Watson	UUAP
Clerk	Alan Rogers	
Tel:	028 9052 1919	

Procedures Committee

Chairman	Conor Murphy	SF
Deputy Chair	Duncan Shipley-Dalton	UUP
Members	Nigel Dodds	DUP
	Ian Paisley Jr	DUP
	Pat McNamee	SF
	Alex Attwood	SDLP
	Alban Maginness	SDLP
	Ivan Davis	UUP
	David McClarty	UUP
	Fraser Agnew	UUAP
	Roger Hutchinson	DUP
Clerk	Ciaran McGarrity	
Tel:	028 9052 1475	

Committee of the Centre

Chairman	Edwin Poots	DUP
Deputy Chair	Oliver Gibson	DUP
Members	Jim Shannon	DUP
	David Ervine	PUP
	Eileen Bell	All
	Barry McElduff	SF
	Pat McNamee	SF
	Dr Dara O'Hagan	SF
	Annie Courtney	SDLP
	Patricia Lewsley	SDLP
	Dr Alasdair McDonnell	SDLP
	Eugene McMenamin	SDLP
	Roy Beggs Jr	UUP
	Dr Esmond Birnie	UUP
	Danny Kennedy	UUP
	Duncan Shipley-Dalton	UUP
	Ken Robinson	UUP
Clerk	Hugh Farren, Tel: 028 9052 1360	
	Stella McArdle, Tel: 028 9052 1821	

The Public Accounts Committee

Chairman	William Bell	UUP
Deputy Chair	Conor Murphy	SF
Members	Seamus Close	All
	Mervyn Carrick	DUP
	David Hilditch	DUP
	Jane Morrice	NIWC
	John Dallat	SDLP
	Danny O'Connor	SDLP
	Donovan McClelland	SDLP
	Pauline Armitage	Ind U
	Roy Beggs Jr	UUP
Clerk	Michael Rickard	
Tel:	028 9052 1785	

Committee on Standards and Privileges

Chairman	Donovan McClelland	SDLP
Deputy Chair	Derek Hussey	UUP
Members	Kieran McCarthy	All
	Paul Berry	DUP
	Jim Wells	DUP
	Mick Murphy	SF
	Dr Dara O'Hagan	SF
	Danny O'Connor	SDLP
	Dr Ian Adamson	UUP
	Sir John Gorman	UUP
Clerk	Alan Rogers	
Tel:	028 9052 1858	

- European Affairs and International Matters;
- Community Relations;
- Public Appointments Policy;
- Freedom of Information;
- Victims;
- Nolan Standards;
- Public Service Office;
- Emergency Planning;
- Women's Issues.

The Committee consists of 17 members and has the power to send for persons and papers as required in conjunction with their role in the legislative process. The Committee of the Centre has replaced the Standing Committees on Human Rights and Community Relations, European Affairs and Equality.

The Public Accounts Committee

The role of the Public Accounts Committee is "to consider accounts, and reports on accounts laid before the Assembly" and is in effect the "financial watchdog" of the Assembly. The Committee has the power to send for persons, papers and records and neither the Chair nor the Deputy Chairperson of the Committee shall be a member of the same political party as the Minister of Finance and Personnel or of any Junior Minister appointed to the Department of Finance and Personnel.

Committee on Standards and Privileges

The role of the Committee on Standards and Privileges is to:

- Consider specific matters relating to privilege referred to it by the Assembly;
- Oversee the work of the Assembly Clerk on Standards;
- Examine the arrangements for the compilation, maintenance and accessibility of the Register of Members Interests and any other registers of interest established by the Assembly and from time to time the form and content of those registers;
- Consider any matter relating to the conduct of Members, including specific complaints in relation to alleged breaches of any code of conduct to which the Assembly has agreed and which have been drawn to the Committee's attention;
- Recommend modifications to the Code of

Conduct;

- Make a report to the Assembly on any matter falling within Standing Order 51.

The Committee has the power to send for persons, papers and records that are relevant to its enquiries. An Assembly Commissioner for Standards will carry out an investigation into any matter referred to him by the Assembly Clerk of Standards and will report to the Committee on Standards and Privileges, however, his report may not include any recommendations for any sanction or penalty to be imposed upon any Members of the Assembly.

Whilst exercising his duties in relation to the role of Assembly Commissioner for Standards, he will not be subject to the direction or control of the Assembly.

Audit Committee

The Audit Committee is governed by procedures set out in Standing Order 53. Under the terms of the order no more than one member of the Committee may simultaneously be a member of the Public Accounts Committee.

The Audit Committee has a membership of five and quorum of two.

Ad Hoc Committees

Ad Hoc Committees are established to deal with specific time-bounded terms of reference that the Assembly may set. Their role is often to consider a piece of draft legislation and produce a written report. Five such committees have been established to date:

Flags (NI) Order 2000
Reported on 16 October 2000

Financial Investigation (NI) Order
Reported on 6 February 2001

Life Sentences (NI) Order 2001
Reported 12 March 2001

Proceeds of Crime Bill
Reported 28 May 2001

Criminal Injuries Compensation Order and Scheme
Reported 27 November 2001

Sub Committees

Each Committee has the authority to establish sub Committees, however, unless approved by the Business Committee, no Committee may have more than one sub Committee in operation at any one time.

Sub Committees may be appointed to consider specific, time-bounded matters within the terms of reference set by the parent Committee, once these matters have been resolved the sub Committee will report to the Parent Committee and be dissolved.

Each sub Committee should reflect the party strengths in the Assembly as far as possible and the parent Committee will determine the quorum for the sub Committee.

Audit Committee

Chairman	John Dallat	SDLP
Deputy Chair	Billy Hutchinson	PUP
Members	Derek Hussey	UUP
	Gerry McHugh	SF
	Mark Robinson	DUP
Clerk	Tony Logue	
Tel:	028 9052 1263	

Other Institutions of the Good Friday Agreement

Introduction

The Good Friday Agreement has radically transformed British and Irish government institutional and constitutional relationships with Northern Ireland. Under the terms of the Agreement both Governments made significant constitutional and legislative changes altering their expressions of sovereignty over Northern Ireland. Following the agreement of the Republic of Ireland to amend Articles 2 and 3 of the Irish Constitution, the British Government repealed the Government of Ireland Act 1920. These changes became effective with the enactment of the Northern Ireland Act 1998, which became law on 19 September 1998, implementing the Good Friday Agreement.

New Structures

To reflect the changed expressions of British and Irish sovereignty over Northern Ireland, new institutions were created. These were the:

- North South Ministerial Council;
- North South Implementation Bodies;
- British Irish Council;
- British Irish Intergovernmental Conference.

The North South Ministerial Council

The North South Ministerial Council (NSMC) was established on 2 December 1999, under the terms of the Good Friday Agreement and is the lead institution in developing all aspects of North South co-operation, bringing together Ministers from Northern Ireland and the Irish Government. The role of the Council is to develop consultation, co-operation and action on all-island and cross-border matters of mutual interest. It also provides leadership and direction for the six North South implementation bodies.

The North South Ministerial Council provided for in

NSMC Joint Secretariat	
39 Abbey Street	
Armagh BT61 7EB	
Northern Ireland Joint Secretary:	Peter Smyth
Tel:	028 3751 5002
Irish Joint Secretary:	Tim O'Connor
Tel:	028 3751 5001

Strand Two of the Good Friday Agreement meets in plenary format twice a year with Northern Ireland represented by the First and Deputy First Minister and relevant ministers and the Irish government by the Taoiseach and relevant ministers. Smaller groups meet on a "regular and frequent" basis to discuss specific cross-border issues with each side represented by the appropriate minister. The Council may also meet to resolve disagreements and discuss common issues and concerns. Agendas for all meetings are settled by prior agreement.

Both sides must abide by "the rules for democratic authority and accountability in force in the Northern Ireland Assembly and the Oireachtas respectively". The Agreement obliges all relevant government Ministers in the Assembly and Oireachtas to participate in the Council.

Government ministers have considerable discretion but they remain accountable to their legislatures, the Assembly and the Oireachtas respectively. The First and Deputy First Minister have a duty to ensure "cross-community participation" on the Council.

The Council is supported by a Joint Secretariat in Armagh staffed by personnel from the OFMDFM and the Irish Civil service. Responsibility for arranging NSMC meetings in sectoral and plenary formats, arranging papers for the meetings and monitoring the work of the bodies rests with the Joint Secretariat.

North South Implementation Bodies

On 2 December 1999 under the aegis of the North South Ministerial Council, six North South Implementation Bodies, established between the British and Irish Governments came into being. These bodies exist to implement policies agreed by Ministers in the North South Ministerial Council and are expected to develop cross-border co-operation on practical matters of mutual concern.

The bodies operate under the North-South Ministerial Council (NSMC) and are funded from grants made by the relevant government departments, North and South. They are staffed by a combination of civil servants (either transferred or seconded from their parent Departments, North and South) and, increasingly beyond the initial period, directly recruited staff. With the agreement of the Northern Ireland Assembly and the Oireachtas it will be open to the North-South Ministerial Council to set up additional Implementation Bodies in the future.

The new bodies are:

- Waterways Ireland;
- The Food Safety Promotion Board;
- InterTradeIreland;
- The Special EU Programmes Body;
- The Foyle, Carlingford and Irish Lights Commission;
- The North South Language Body.

WATERWAYS IRELAND

Headquarters, 5-7 Belmore Street
Enniskillen, Co Fermanagh, BT74 6AA
Tel: + 44 (28) 6632 3004
Fax: + 44 (28) 6634 6237
Website: www.waterwaysireland.org
Email: information@waterwaysireland.org

Chief Executive Officer:
John Martin (pictured)
Directors:
Brian D'Arcy (Operations)
Colin Brownsmith (Finance and
Personnel)
Martin Dennany (Marketing and
Communications)
Nigel Russell (Technical Services)

Waterways Ireland is one of six North-South implementation
Bodies established under the British-Irish Agreement in 1999
and has responsibility for the management, maintenance,
development and restoration of Ireland's inland navigations,
principally for recreational purposes. The waterways under the
remit of the Body are:

The Royal Canal; The Grand Canal; The Barrow Navigation;
The Shannon Navigation; The Shannon-Erne Waterway;
The Erne Navigation; and The Lower Bann.

The headquarters for Waterways Ireland is in Enniskillen and
regional offices are located in Dublin, Scarriff and
Carrick-on-Shannon.

THE FOOD SAFETY PROMOTION BOARD

The Food Safety Promotion Board
7 Eastgate Avenue, Eastgate, Little Island, Cork
Tel: 00 353 21 2304 100
Fax: 00 353 21 2304 111
E-mail: info@fspb.org

Chief Executive: Martin Higgins

The Food Safety Promotion Board is principally charged with
promoting food safety – through public campaigns,
conferences, training and advising professionals and the
general public. It is also involved in supporting North-South
scientific co-operation, and links between institutions working
in the field of food safety – laboratories, statutory food safety
enforcement agencies, and international and domestic research
bodies.

InterTradeIreland
Old Gasworks Business Park
Kilmorey Street
Newry BT34 2DE
Tel: (028) 3083 4100
Responsible for North/South trade and business development
via a range of programmes
Chief Executive: Liam Nellis

SPECIAL EU PROGRAMMES BODY

Special EU Programmes Body (SEUPB)
Headquarters: EU House, 6 Cromac Place
Belfast BT7 2JB
Tel: +44 (0) 28 9026 6660
Fax: +44 (0) 28 9026 6661
Website:www.seupb.org
Email: info@seupb.org

Chief Executive: John McKinney

The SEUPB is one of the six cross border bodies established
under the Belfast Agreement and is the Managing Authority for
the EU Programme for Peace and Reconciliation in Northern
Ireland and the Border Region of Ireland and INTERREG IIIA.

LEADING THE RESURGENCE OF THE ULSTER-SCOTS LANGUAGE AND CULTURE

Ulster-Scots is the fastest growing cultural movement in Europe.

Ulster-Scots is recognised as a European Regional Language by the
UK Government for the purposes of the European Charter
on Regional or Minority Languages.

The Ulster-Scots Agency is actively helping Ulster-Scots celebrate
and develop their language, culture and identity.

If you would like more information on the Agency's work, or would be interested
in applying for a cultural development grant,
please contact the Agency on 028 (048) 90231113, email: info@ulsterscotsagency.org.uk
or write to The Ulster-Scots Agency, Franklin House, 10-12 Brunswick Street, Belfast, BT2 7GE

*The Ulster-Scots Agency/Tha Boord o Ulstèr-Scotch is part of the
North/South Language Implementation Body*

Tha Boord o **Ulstèr**-Scotch
Ulster-**Scots** Agency

Leid
Language   Fiddle playing
Dancing   Lear   Education
History
Highland Pipes
Fowkgates   Pageantry   Poetry
Culture   Forstannin
Folklore   Awareness

The Foyle, Carlingford and Irish Lights Commission
22 Victoria Road, Waterside, Londonderry
Tel: 028 7134 2100
Fax: 028 7134 2720
Website: www.loughs-agency.org
E-mail: general@loughs-agency.org
Chief Executive: Derick Anderson

The Foyle, Carlingford and Irish Lights Commission – at present one Agency has been established (Loughs Agency). A second Agency (Lights Agency) will be established once the appropriate legislation is in place

The North-South Language Body (including Irish Language and Ulster-Scots Agencies)

The Language Body is a single body reporting to the North-South Ministerial Council, but composed of two separate and largely autonomous agencies: the Irish Language Agency, Foras na Gaeilge, and the Ulster-Scots Agency, Tha Boord o Ulster-Scotch.   Each of these agencies has a separate board, which together constitutes the Board of the North South Language Body.

FORAS NA GAEILGE

Foras na Gaeilge

7 Cearnóg Mhuirfean
Baile Átha Cliath 2
Teil: (00353 1) 639 8400
1850 325 325
Tuaisceart:0845 309 8142
Facs: (00353 1) 639 8401
Eolas@forasnagaeilge.ie
www.forasnagaeilge.ie

Cathaoirleach: Maighréad Uí Mháirtín

Bunaíodh Foras na Gaeilge ar 2 Nollaig 1999 faoin Acht um Chomhaontú na Breataine - na hÉireann agus is í an príomhaidhm atá ag an bhForas ná an Ghaeilge a chur chun cinn ar fud oileán na hÉireann. Chomh maith le cúramaí Bhord na Gaeilge, tugadh réimse leathan feidhmeanna breise don Fhoras chun chur lena éifeacht i gcur chun cinn na Gaeilge. Mar shampla i gcúrsaí oideachais agus téarmaíochta tugadh na feidhmeanna

a bhí ag an nGúm agus na feidhmeanna a bhí ag an gCoiste Téarmaíochta don Fhoras. Is iad na príomhchúrmaí ata ag an bhForas ná:
• an Ghaeilge a chur chun cinn;
• úsáid na Gaeilge a éascú agus a spreagadh sa chaint agus sa scríbhneoireacht sa saol poiblí agus sa saol príobháideach sa Deisceart agus, i gcomhthéasc Chuid 111 den Chairt Eorpach do Theangacha Réigiúnacha nó Mionlaigh, i dTuaisceart Éireann mar a mbeidh éileamh cuí ann;
• comhairle a thabhairt don dá lucht riaracháin, do chomhlachtaí poiblí, agus do ghrúpaí eile san earnáil phríobháideach agus dheonach;
• tionscadail tacaíochta a ghabháil de láimh, agus cúnamh deontais a thabhairt do chomhlachtaí agus do ghrúpaí de réir mar a mheasfar is gá;
• taighde, feachtais tionscnaimh, agus caidreamh poiblí agus caidreamh leis na meáin, a ghabháil de láimh;
• téarmaíocht agus foclóirí a fhorbairt;
• tacú le hoideachas trí mheán na Gaeilge agus le múineadh na Gaeilge.

Foras na Gaeilge was established on 2 December 1999 under the terms of the British-Irish Agreement Act, and the main objective of the Foras is to promote the Irish language on the island of Ireland. As well as taking over the functions of Bord na Gaeilge, a wide range of extra functions were given to the Foras to add to its effectiveness in the promotion of the Irish language. For example in the area of education and terminology the Foras took over the functions of an Gúm and the functions of an Coiste Téarmaíochta.

The main functions of the Foras are:
• promotion of the Irish language;
• facilitating and encouraging its use in speech and writing in public and private life in the South and, in the context of part III of the European Charter for Regional or Minority Languages, in Northern Ireland where there is appropriate demand;
• advising both administrations, public bodies and other groups in the private and voluntary sectors;
• undertaking supportive projects, and grant-aiding bodies and groups as considered necessary;
• undertaking research, promotional campaigns, and public and media relations;
• developing terminology and dictionaries;
• supporting Irish-medium education and the teaching of Irish.

When you're fighting an invisible enemy, knowledge is your best defence

Food safety demands constant publicity and awareness, which is where **safefood** comes in, filling the knowledge gap with vital safety information. **safefood** acts as a knowledge and resource centre in the full time promotion of food hygiene and nutrition messages on the island of Ireland. **safefood** works within the following areas:

• **Food safety promotion** among the general public and through the schools systems, through campaigns to increase awareness of safety and also to educate the public on nutrition.

• **Research into food safety. safefood** is responsible for setting research priorities into nationwide safety issues as well as commissioning and funding this research.

• **Alerts.** When vital safety information must quickly be made public **safefood** works with the relevant agencies to ensure that the facts are made available.

• **Foodborne disease surveillance. safefood** acts alongside other agencies, analysing and publishing relevant data as well as facilitating an information exchange between the various concerned parties.

• **Laboratory forum. safefood** works with a variety of laboratories, coordinating a knowledge pool of disease surveillance and testing methods.

For information contact: **safefood**, 7 Eastgate Avenue, Eastgate, Little Island, Co. Cork
e-mail :info@safefoodonline.com
Tel : 00353 21 2304100   Fax: 00353 21 2304111

Tha Boord o Ulster Scotch: The Ulster Scots Agency

The Ulster Scots Agency, Tha Boord o Ulster Scotch is the new body responsible for the promotion of the Ulster Scots language and culture on the island of Ireland. It is part of the North South language implementation body that was set up under the Belfast Agreement.

The Ulster Scots Agency Board consists of eight members, four from Northern Ireland and four from the South. The Agency is responsible to the North South Ministerial Council, and in particular to the two ministers, in the Northern Ireland Assembly and Dail Eireann, whose remits include language and culture. The Agency will advise administrations, public bodies and other groups in the private and voluntary sectors. It will be involved in undertaking supportive projects, and grant aiding bodies and groups; undertaking research and promotional campaigns; public and media relations; developing terminology, dictionaries and literature. It will also support Ulster Scots language developments.

Other Areas Identified for North South Co-operation

In addition to the six Implementation Bodies a further six areas have initially been identified for co-operation between existing government departments and other bodies, North and South. The North South Ministerial Council is responsible for taking forward:

Transport : Strategic planning and development of cross-border co-operation on transport matters.

Agriculture: Discussion of Common Agricultural Policy (CAP) issues, animal and plant health policy and research and rural development

Education: Education for children with special needs (e.g. autism, dyslexia), educational underachievement, teacher qualifications, and school, youth and teacher exchanges on a cross-border basis;

Health: Accident and emergency planning, emergency services, co-operation on high technology equipment, cancer research and health promotion. The Council in the health and food safety sector considers matters for co-operation in Health as well as considering matters relating to the Food Safety Promotion Board;

Environment: Research into environmental protection, water quality management and waste management in a cross-border context.

LOUGHS AGENCY

Foyle Carlingford and Irish lights Commission (FCILC)
Loughs Agency Headquarters
22 Victoria Road
Londonderry
BT47 2AB
Email: general@loughs-agency.org
Tel: 0044 (0)28 7134 2100
Fax: 0044 (0)28 7134 2720

Carlingford Regional Office
Old Quay Lane
Carlingford
Co Louth
Email: Carlingford@loughs-agency.org
Tel/Fax: 00353 (0)42 9383888

Chief Executive: Derick Anderson (pictured)
Senior Policy Officer: John Pollock
Chief Inspector: Stanley Thorpe
Biologist: Patrick Boylan

FCILC Board
Peter Savage (Chair)
Lord Cooke of Islandreagh (Vice Chair)
Jack Allen
Keith Anderson
Dick Blakiston-Houston
Francis Feely
Pat Griffin
Siobhan Logue
Joseph Martin
Arthur Morgan
Andrew Ward

MISSION
The Loughs Agency aims to provide sustainable social, economic and environmental benefits through the effective conservation, management, promotion and development of the fisheries and marine resources of the Foyle and Carlingford Areas.

Tourism: A limited company publicly-owned by Bord Fáilte Eireann and the Northern Ireland Tourist Board markets the island of Ireland overseas as a tourism destination. The new Company, Tourism Ireland Limited, operates under the overall policy direction of the North South Ministerial Council. It does not however lead to a diminution in the role of the two separate tourism agencies Bord Failte and the Northern Ireland Tourist Board.

TOURISM IRELAND

Tourism Ireland Ltd
5th Floor, Bishop's Square
Redmond's Hill, Dublin 2
Tel: (00 353 1) 476 3400
Fax: (00 353 1) 476 3666

Tourism Ireland Ltd
2 Beresford Road, Coleraine, BT52 1GE
Tel: (028) 7035 9200
Fax: (028) 7032 6932

Chief Executive Officer:
Paul O'Toole (pictured)

Tourism Ireland is responsible for marketing the entire island of Ireland overseas as a tourism destination. Established under the framework of the Belfast Agreement of Good Friday 1998, the company's mandate is to increase tourism to the island of Ireland and to support Northern Ireland in realising its tourism potential.

To fulfil these roles, the company employs a wide range of marketing tools including an extensive suite of branded literature available in nine languages, direct marketing and advertising (television and press). The company also has an online presence, with local language Tourism Ireland websites. Tourism Ireland acts as an agent for Bord Fáilte and the Northern Ireland Tourist Board in implementing the international element of their product and regional marketing programmes.

British Irish Institutions

The British Irish Council

The British Irish Council was established to 'promote the harmonies and mutually beneficial development of relationships among the peoples of the United Kingdom and Ireland'. It is made up of representatives of the British and Irish Governments, of the devolved institutions in Northern Ireland, Scotland, Wales, the Isle of Man and the Channel Islands.

The British Irish Council will exchange information, discuss, consult and use best endeavours to reach agreement on matters of mutual interest, East and West.

The Council has decided as a priority to examine and develop policies for co-operation on drugs, social exclusion, the environment and transport. Other areas for discussion will include agriculture, tourism, health, education, approaches to EU issues, links between cities, towns and local districts, sporting activity and minority and lesser-used languages.

British-Irish Intergovernmental Conference

The British-Irish Intergovernmental Conference was designed to replace the Anglo-Irish Intergovernmental Council and the Intergovernmental Conference established under the 1985 Anglo-Irish Agreement. It comprises, primarily representation of the UK Government at Westminster and the Irish Government in Dublin. It will promote bilateral co-operation on matters of

---

The British Irish Council

UK Joint Secretary:	Donal Henderson
Tel:	020 7270 5913
Joint Secretary:	Susan Conlon
Tel:	00353 1 4082843

Civic Forum Secretariat

The Arches Centre
11–13 Bloomfield Avenue
Belfast BT5 5HD

Tel:	028 90 52 8841
Fax:	028 90 52 8833
E-mail:	secretariat@civicforum-ni.org
Website:	www.civicforum-ni.org
Chairman:	Chris Gibson OBE

Membership of the Civic Forum

Agriculture and Fisheries

Alan McCulla	CEO Anglo-Irish Fish Producers Association
Aidan McNamee JP	Member of the Ulster Farmers Union Council

Arts and Sport

Elizabeth Bicker	Chair of Belfast Music Society
Gordon Woods	Former Director of Art and Design Education UUC
Dawson Stelfox	Architect with Consarc Design Group
Jim McKeever	Member of Sports Council

Business

Frank Bryan	Deputy President Belfast Junior Chamber of Commerce
Peter Donaldson	Managing Director of Kilco Group
Clare Gibson	Former MD of Abbey Training Services
Bryan Johnston	Retired
Patrick Mahony	Stockbroker, Edward Jones
Gwen Savage	Retired Director of Gwen Savage and Co Ltd
Colin Shillington	Partner in Solutions Together

Churches

Daphne Gilmour	Elder and Session Clerk of Presbyterian Church
George Glenn	Chief Executive of Churches in Co-operation
Eileen Gallagher	Head of Religious Studies St Michael's College
Louise Warde Hunter	Director of Belfast Common Purpose
Pater David McConaghie	Elim Minister Founder of Caleb Foundation

Community Relations

Roisin McGlone	Director Springfield Inter Community Development Project
David Porter	Director Evangelical Contribution on NI (ECONI)

Culture

Doug Elliot	MD of Ormeau Gas Works
David White	Tutor in cultural diversity and race awareness
Gordon Lucy	Director of the Ulster Society
Donncha MacNiallais	Irish Language Resource Centre (An Gaeleras)

Education

Carmel McKinney	Chair of Belfast Education and Library Board
Jeanette Chapman	Education Adviser, CCMS

Trade Union

Pauline Buchanan	Resigned October 2000
Inez McCormack	Regional Secretary of UNISON and President of ICTU
Richard Jay	Senior Lecturer in Politics QUB AUT Rep
Keith Cradden	Member of Derry District Partnership Board
Susan Bustard	Irish Bank Officials Association
Kevin Cooper	National Executive Council of the NUJ
Mick O'Reilly	Regional Secretary of ATGWU

Victims

Alan McBride	Youth Worker WAVE Trauma Centre
Patricia MacBride	Manager of the Bloody Sunday Centre, Derry

Voluntary and Community

Paddy Joe McClean	Member of Age Concern NI Executive
Eamonn Keeenan	Training and Research Officer NIACRO
Avril Watson	Director of Law Centre NI
Kevin McLaughlin	Member of Human Rights Commission
Patrick Yu	Executive Director of NI Council for Ethnic Minorities
Kevin Daly	Chair of Mid-Ulster Carers Group
Avery Bowser	Child Witness Development Officer NSPCC
Brian Dougherty	Independent Member of the Police Board
Ryan Williams	Business in the Community
Eithne McNulty	Workers Educational Association
James Orr	Wildfowl and Wetlands Trust Castle Espie
Duane Farrell	National Youth Council of Ireland
Annabel Weldon	Director of Money and Relationship Counselling
Brian Symington	Royal National Institute for the Deaf
Janet Muller	Director of POBAL
Josephine Whatmough	Retired Adviser to National Trust
Emma McDowell	Secretary of Belfast Carers National Association
Lynn Carvill	Co-ordinator of the Organisation of the Unemployed

First Minister

Gary McMichael	Former leader of the UDP
Betty McClurg	Chair of Craigavon Hospitals Trust
Richard Monteith	Solicitor

Deputy First Minister

Brian O'Reilly	Regional President of Saint Vincent de Paul
Sharon Haughey	Student, University of Ulster

mutual interest between the British and Irish Governments, including, in particular, issues in relation to Northern Ireland, when the locally elected Northern Ireland Ministers will also attend meetings.

Joint Ministerial Committee on Devolution

A Joint Ministerial Committee on Devolution has been established to enable Ministers from the devolved governments of Scotland, Wales and Northern Ireland to take forward joint action.

The role of the Committee is to examine non-devolved matters, which may conflict with responsibilities devolved in the regions.

Joint Ministerial Committees have been created on the Knowledge Economy, Health and Poverty. Ministers also engage in less formal meetings to discuss matters such as housing, agriculture and the environment.

There are also plans to form the following committees:

- Minecor Committee (Ministerial Committee on European Co-ordination) to present public policy of all UK regions towards Europe;
- Sports Cabinet;
- Creative industry taskforce;
- Drugs task force;
- Agriculture Ministers Committee.

The Prime Minister of the United Kingdom is the Chair of the Joint Ministerial Committee on Devolution. Meetings are attended by the Secretaries of State for Scotland, Wales and Northern Ireland and may be located anywhere in the UK. Whilst the agenda and location are made public the content of these meetings are confidential.

A secretariat comprising staff from the UK cabinet office and staff from each of the devolved regions in the UK supports the work of the committee.

The Civic Forum

The Civic Forum is a consultative body, with no formal legislative or governmental powers consisting of 60 members plus a Chair of the voluntary, business, agriculture, trade union, education, culture, community relations, fisheries sectors, of whom 3 members are appointed by the First and Deputy First Minister each. Members are appointed for a three-year term.

The inaugural Chairman of the Civic Forum is Chris Gibson a former chair of the Northern Ireland branch of the Confederation of British Industry (CBI), retired Chief Executive of Golden Vale Ltd and Chair of the Irish Centre for Ecumenics and of the Centre for Cross-Border Studies in Armagh.

Members of the Civic Forum contribute on a voluntary basis and the role of the Forum is to "articulate the views of society to ensure those policies and programmes that are developed by the government address the needs and aspirations of a modern civilised and inclusive society".

The first meeting of the Civic Forum was held in plenary on 9 October 2000. Meetings are held in plenary every two months; standing committees, project groups and working groups have been established to carry forward the programme of work. These groups meet monthly or more regularly as required.

Reports from the Forum's standing committees, project teams and ad hoc working groups are received in plenary, where key issues are debated and the policies and procedures of the Forum agreed.

Work of the Civic Forum

Functions of the Civic Forum

- Serve civic society;
- Provide advice to and consultation with the Northern Ireland Assembly;
- Make a distinctive and challenging contribution o social, economic, cultural and environmental matters affecting Northern Ireland;
- Act as an interface between policy makers and civic society;
- Create a receptive space for voices that often go unheard;
- Promote and respect human rights, equality and diversity;
- Promote sustainable investment in and development of society.

The Civic Forum work programme comprises three strands:

- Responding to major government consultation exercises;
- Research and analysis of key social, economic and cultural issues;
- Business Improvement measures.

In the period since its establishment the Civic Forum has

made submissions in a diverse range of areas.

In January 2001 the Forum made a substantive submission on the first draft of the Programme for Government (PfG). The Forum also submitted its views on the draft of the second PfG during the consultation phase.

Other submissions made by the Forum include, "Investing for Health", The Review of Post Primary Education, Priorities for Social Inclusion, the Role of the Commissioner for Children.

Work on two consultation papers, Employability and Long Term Unemployment, and the draft Bill of Rights were completed during October and November 2001.

The Forum has also commented upon a working paper produced by the Community Relations Unit of the Office of the First Minister and Deputy First Minister as part of its review of Community Relations Policy and has also submitted a response to the Review of the Parades Commission.

The Forum is also undertaking its own consultation exercise in a number of areas:

- Life long learning; and entrepreneurship and creativity. Developing an understanding of the needs, interests and concerns of the educationally disadvantaged;
- Combating poverty. Defining poverty in Northern Ireland terms, examining policy initiatives such as New TSN, Promoting Social Inclusion and other European initiatives;
- Towards a plural society. Development of the theme of inclusiveness in the context of wider society in line with four themes of: culture, citizenship, reconciliation and community relations;
- Creating a Sustainable Northern Ireland. The Group aims to develop debate on various aspects of Sustainable Development to raise awareness within the Forum and wider civic society.

North South Consultative Forum

Although not as yet formed, the Belfast Agreement specifically provided for the possibility of establishing an equivalent of the Civic Forum, structured on an all Island basis. Supporters of the concept, particularly in the voluntary and community sector, see considerable benefits in such an institution although the Republic of Ireland does not at present have a direct "mirror" institution to Northern Ireland's Civic Forum from which to draw the Southern membership of the new body.

CHAPTER 3

Electoral System, Political Parties and Election Results

Electoral System, Political Parties and Election Results

Introduction

The legislative and institutional framework of the electoral system for Northern Ireland is unique in a number of aspects within the UK. All elections and electoral matters, including the franchise and electoral registration are in the terms of the Northern Ireland Constitution Act 1973, and the Northern Ireland Act 1998, excepted matters, and therefore remain the responsibility of the Government at Westminster regardless of devolution.

Four types of election are held in Northern Ireland:
- Local government;
- Northern Ireland Assembly;
- Westminster parliament;
- European parliament.

Proportional representation, the single transferable vote (STV), is used for all elections except Westminster where, in keeping with the rest of the UK, simple plurality, the 'first past the post' system is applied. Although arguably less democratic than STV, 'first past the post' has continued to be favoured by successive governments as this electoral approach provides a successful UK government with a substantial majority of seats on around 45 per cent of the popular vote.

The Office of the Chief Electoral Officer

The Chief Electoral Officer position is unique to Northern Ireland and is appointed by the Secretary of State for Northern Ireland under section 14 of the Electoral Law Act (Northern Ireland). He is an independent officer responsible for the conduct of all elections in Northern Ireland. The Chief Electoral Officer has no direct counterpart in Great Britain, where electoral registration and the conduct of all elections are primarily the responsibility of local authorities.

The Chief Electoral Officer is the registration and returning officer for each parliamentary constituency in Northern Ireland, and the returning officer for European parliamentary elections, Assembly elections and district council elections. He is responsible for the preparation of polling station schemes, the maintenance of election equipment and all other administrative matters relating to elections in Northern Ireland.

The Chief Electoral Officer has a small number of Deputy Electoral Officers and Assistant Electoral Officers to assist him, primarily in the compilation of the electoral register and related duties, but they also act as Deputy Returning Officers, except for local government elections where the Clerk of the particular council is the ex-officio Returning Officer but acts under the control and supervision of the Chief Electoral Officer.

Electoral Fraud

Over a long period, but increasingly in recent years, there have been many allegations of various kinds of electoral fraud, the most common being 'vote stealing' by impersonation. Although the electoral authorities have failed to find evidence of systematic or wide ranging electoral fraud taking place, Northern Ireland elections now operate under tight regulations governing identification at the polling station.

Northern Ireland Elections

Northern Ireland is unique within the United Kingdom in that it conducts all its elections, except those to the Westminster parliament, by proportional representation.

Westminster Parliament Elections

Elections for members of the Westminster parliament are conducted on a first past the post system in line with the rest of the United Kingdom and currently Northern Ireland returns 18 MPs, one for each of its parliamentary constituencies.

In Northern Ireland the law governing Westminster parliamentary elections is the Representation of the People Act 1983 as amended. The most recent amendments were made to the 1983 Act by the Representation of the People Act 2000. This was enacted to give effect to the recommendations contained in the Official Report of the Working Group on Electoral Procedures, dated 19 October 2000 chaired by the then Home Office Minister George Howarth MP.

The number of Westminster constituencies is determined by the Boundary Commission for Northern Ireland, constituted by the Parliamentary Constituencies Act 1986, as amended and extended by the Boundary Commission Act 1992. The Commission is an entirely independent body which is required to make periodical reports and to submit these to the Secretary of State not less than 8 or more than 12 years from the submission of the last report. The Commission completed its last review and reported in 1995 and therefore its next report must be submitted between 2003 and 2007.

European Parliament Elections

European parliamentary elections are currently conducted using the Single Transferable Vote (STV) system of proportional representation. For the purposes of these elections the whole of Northern Ireland is treated as one constituency, returning three MEPs every five years. Consequently there is no necessity for a Boundary Commission to review electoral boundaries for these elections.

The European Parliamentary Elections Act 1999, which substantially amended the European Parliamentary Elections Act 1978, governs the electoral provisions for election to the European parliament.

There are 626 members from 15 member states elected to the European parliament. Population size determines the numbers of members returned from each state and at present 87 UK members, including three from Northern Ireland are returned to the parliament.

The Treaty of Nice has however, extended the limit on members to 732 in consideration of the planned enlargement of the Union. A new distribution of seats in anticipation of the expected growth of the Assembly to as many as 27 member states applicable from the next European elections in 2004 has also been included under the terms of the Treaty. Existing member states will see their share of seats fall from 626 to 535 and in the UK the number of seats will fall from 87 to 72 under the new distribution, effective from the European parliament elections in 2009.

Grouping	Number of MEPs
European Peoples Party (Christian Democrats and European Democrats)	232
European Socialists	180
European Liberal, Democrat and Reform Party	51
Greens/European Free Alliance	48
Confederal Group of the European Left/ Nordic Green Left	42
Union for a Europe of Nations	30
Group for a Europe of Democracies and Diversities	16
Technical Group of Independent Members	18

Members of the European parliament attach themselves to ideological political rather than national groupings of which there are eight:

Nine MEPs, including Northern Ireland's Ian Paisley, have chosen not to align themselves with one of the above groups.

The European parliament elects a President and 14 Vice Presidents who serve two and a half year terms of office and constitute the Bureau of Parliament.

The Bureau of Parliament and leaders of each of the political groups constitute the Conference of Presidents. There is further detailed information about the European Union in the context of Northern Ireland in Chapter Ten.

Local Government Elections

Elections to the twenty-six district councils of Northern Ireland are also conducted by STV. Each local government area is divided into a number of wards, which are then grouped together for the purposes of STV into District Electoral Areas. Each District Electoral Area returns a number of councillors. Belfast has 9 Electoral Areas, but most other councils have between three and five. Councillors are elected using the Single Transferable Vote (STV), a type of proportional representation used in these elections since 1973.

The number and boundaries of each local government area (the area controlled by a district council), and ward boundaries, are determined by the Local Government Boundaries Commissioner. The District Electoral Areas Commissioner determines the grouping of wards. Both these Commissioners are entirely independent and submit recommendations to the Government every 10–15 years.

Local government elections are held every four years in Northern Ireland, the last taking place on 7 June 2001. Details of the election results are set out later in this chapter.

Northern Ireland Assembly Elections

The 108 member Northern Ireland Assembly was elected on 25 June 1998 using the single transferable vote system of proportional representation. Six members were returned from each of the 18 parliamentary constituencies.

The Ulster Unionist Party won 28 seats, the Social Democratic Labour Party 24, Democratic Unionist Party 20, Sinn Fein 18, Alliance 6, United Kingdom Unionist

Party 5, Progressive Unionist Party 2, Northern Ireland Women's Coalition 2 and Independent anti agreement Unionists 3. Elections to the Assembly take place every four years with the next election scheduled for 1 May 2003.

The Secretary of State for Northern Ireland is directly responsible for the law governing elections to the Northern Ireland Assembly, the primary legislation in these cases being the Electoral Law Act (Northern Ireland) 1962 and currently the Northern Ireland (Elections) Act 1998 and the Northern Ireland Act 1998.

Electoral Systems

Proportional Representation Single Transferable Vote (STV)

A number of proportional representation alternatives exist to the first past the post electoral model, which seek to ensure a direct, and close correlation between total votes cast for each party and the number of seats won. The first past the post system, properly referred to as simple plurality, is the one that is least connected to the principle of proportional representation.

The single transferable vote system (STV), used for local, European and Northern Ireland Assembly elections under the Northern Ireland Act 1998 is based on multi member constituencies in which voter preferences for candidates are expressed in numerical order. Voters rank candidates in order of preference (1 for their most preferred candidate, 2 for their second choice, etc). A quota is calculated by dividing the number of votes cast plus one by the number of seats available plus one. If a candidate has enough votes to reach the quota, he or she is elected. If the candidate has more votes than the quota, the surplus votes are taken and redistributed proportionately according to the voter's next choice. The candidate with the least number of votes is eliminated, and their votes redistributed in the same way. The process continues until all available seats have been filled.

The d'Hondt Mechanism

Proportional representation has a role beyond the election of Members in the Northern Ireland Assembly. The d'Hondt system of proportional representation is the designated method for the assignment of committee chairmanships and the appointment of Ministers in the Assembly. The d'Hondt mechanism has its origins in

Belgium where it was first applied in 1889 between the Flemings and Walloons to ensure representation for whichever ethnic group was in a minority

The formulae to allocate seats under the mechanism were also devised by a Belgian, H.R. Droop who produced the procedure for establishing the quota in multi member constituencies. Victor d'Hondt devised what is technically known as the "largest average" formula for allocating seats in an assembly.

The d'Hondt system takes the number of seats obtained by each party and divides them by one, two, three, four, etc. The ministries are then given to the parties with the twelve largest quotients ranked from the largest to the smallest quotient.

Although, the majority party is favoured under d'Hondt the advantage is that minority interests also gain representation, a critical factor for the success of the new Assembly and power sharing in the Northern Ireland Executive. However it does make it unlikely that significantly smaller parties such as the PUP or NIWC would be able to obtain a ministry under this system.

The use of d'Hondt leads to a number of potential scenarios regarding the balance of power in the Executive.

First-past-the-post (Simple Plurality)

First-past-the-post, is used throughout the UK for local (except in Northern Ireland) and general elections. Each constituency returns a single winner, the candidate with the most votes. The winner does not require a majority of votes cast, merely more votes than the closest rival.

First past the post is particularly disproportionate in its translation of votes into seats and this has a number of highly significant ramifications with regard to the composition and operation of parliament and political leadership.

The first-past-the-post system has generally delivered stability in the UK in that the leading party even though it achieves less than 50 per cent share of vote can gain a comfortable majority of seats in parliament. In Northern Ireland this less representative system has occasioned considerable "tactical voting" where people will often vote for a candidate who would not be their first choice in an STV election in order to defeat a candidate to whom they are strongly opposed.

Northern Ireland Political Parties

Northern Ireland has around 25 registered political parties although throughout the last 20 years electoral politics have been dominated by 4 or 5 major parties. The minor parties comprise in the main fringe unionist parties and socialist groups, along with a number of sectional interests.

There are two large unionist parties: the Ulster Unionist Party (UUP) and the Democratic Unionist Party (DUP). Two main parties also represent the nationalist community: the Social Democratic and Labour Party (SDLP) and Sinn Féin. In some sense there is symmetry between these alignments, with the UUP and SDLP appealing increasingly to middle-class and middle-ground unionists and nationalists respectively. The more aggressive and uncompromising DUP and Sinn Féin tend to attract more support among the working classes and young voters. The fifth biggest group, the Alliance Party, straddles the two political communities, although its support base has been severely eroded in recent years. The table right lists the political parties currently registered in Northern Ireland.

Independents do not constitute a single political party. Candidates who are not part of a registered political party in Northern Ireland must, under electoral law, describe themselves as 'Independent' on the ballot paper.

Political Parties Religious/Ethnic Spectrum

As a consequence of historical political divisions it is very difficult to attempt to show Northern Ireland parties on a traditional left-right spectrum. The parties themselves place tremendous emphasis on the constitutional issue of Northern Ireland in their manifestoes, leaving more traditional economic and social issues aside as secondary considerations. Some politicians would contend that their ideologies and policies exist, but are overshadowed by 'sectarian politics', and that most people in Northern Ireland tend to vote according to religion and nationality, leaving less 'demand' for other policies.

Pro/Anti Agreement Spectrum

The UUP is broadly pro-Agreement, but has a significant anti-Agreement faction, which has been gaining in strength. All of the nationalist parties represented in the Northern Ireland Assembly are pro-Agreement. The anti-

Registered Political Parties in Northern Ireland

UUP	Ulster Unionist Party
SDLP	Social Democratic and Labour Party
DUP	Democratic Unionist Party
SF	Sinn Féin
All	Alliance
PUP	Progressive Unionist Party
NIWC	Northern Ireland Women's Coalition
UKUP	United Kingdom Unionist Party
UUAP	United Unionist Assembly Party
Cons	Conservative Party of Northern Ireland
NIUP	Northern Ireland Unionist Party
WP	Workers' Party
CC	Community Candidate
NRA	Newtownabbey Ratepayers Association
UTW	Ulster Third Way
Ind	Independent
VFY	Vote for Yourself Party
Green	Green Party of Northern Ireland
NLP	Natural Law Party
United	United Unionist Party
Lab	Labour Party of Northern Ireland
Energy	Energy 106
Soc	Socialist Party of Northern Ireland
Comm	Communist Party of Northern Ireland

Religious/Ethnic Distribution of Parties

Catholic/Nationalist: SDLP, SF, WP
Centre Other: Alliance, NIWC
Protestant/Unionist: UUP, DUP, PUP, NIUP, UKUP, UUAP

Pro-Agreement:

UUP, SDLP, SF, NIWC, Alliance, PUP, WP

Anti-Agreement:

DUP, UKUP, NIUP, UUAP

Agreement grouping within the Assembly consists of the DUP and several smaller unionist parties.

Main Political Parties in Northern Ireland

Ulster Unionist Party (UUP)

Cunningham House, 429 Holywood Road,
Belfast BT4 2LN
Tel: (028) 9076 5500
Fax: (028) 9076 9419
Website: www.uup.org
E-mail: uup@uup.org

Leader:	David Trimble MP MLA
Deputy:	John Taylor
Secretary:	Jack Allen
Chairperson:	James Cooper
President:	Rev Martyn Smyth MP
Contact:	General Secretary

The Ulster Unionist Party is the oldest and largest political party in Northern Ireland. Its central cause is the maintenance of Northern Ireland's position within the UK and the legitimacy of Northern Ireland as a distinct political, economic and cultural entity. While supportive of the co-operative relationships with the Irish Republic, the Ulster Unionist party prefers cross border matters to be considered within the economic rather than political arena.

Formal links are retained with the Orange Order, which enjoys voting rights within the party.

UUP Leadership

David Trimble, MP for the Upper Bann constituency was elected leader of the Ulster Unionist party in 1995. Throughout his career David Trimble has moved along the spectrum of Unionism from an uncompromising member of the hard-line loyalist Vanguard movement in the 1970s, to a more pragmatic leader supporting the Good Friday Agreement and acceptance of limited cross border bodies. In 1998 he and John Hume, then leader of the SDLP shared the Nobel Peace Prize for their efforts in securing the Agreement. More recently he has faced an increasing challenge to his leadership from the anti-agreement wing of the UUP.

Social Democratic and Labour Party (SDLP)

121 Ormeau Road, Belfast, BT7 1SH
Tel: (028) 9024 7700
Fax: (028) 9023 6699
Website: www.sdlp.ie
E-mail: sdlp@indigo.ie

Leader:	Mark Durkan MLA
Deputy:	Brid Rodgers MLA
Secretary:	Gerry Cosgrove
Chairperson:	Alex Attwood MLA
Contact:	Party HQ

For the past 30 years, the SDLP had been recognised as the main nationalist party attracting the majority of the Catholic vote. However, in the 2001 Westminster and local elections Sinn Féin increased its electoral support significantly, challenging the position of the SDLP as the leading nationalist party.

Founded in 1970 by seven individuals including John Hume and the socialist Gerry Fitt following the civil rights agitation, the SDLP sought to replace the old Nationalist party with a more dynamic version of politics.

The SDLP supports the principle of Irish unity advocating the achievement of this through constitutional political means and the principle of consent of the majority rather than violence or insurrection.

SDLP Leadership

Mark Durkan has assumed two of the largest roles in Northern Ireland politics. He stood unopposed as leader of the SDLP and was elected Deputy First Minister on 6 November 2001. Previously Mark Durkan was Chairperson of the SDLP from 1990–1995 and a Member of the Forum for Peace and Reconciliation from 1994 until 1996 when he was elected to the Northern Ireland Forum for Political Dialogue. Durkan was also one of the SDLP's chief negotiators at the inter-party talks leading to the Good Friday Agreement and Director of the referendum campaign. Widely regarded as being the principal author of the Good Friday Agreement, he now faces the challenge of securing the leading position of the SDLP.

Democratic Unionist Party (DUP)

91 Dundela Avenue, Belfast, BT4 3BU

Tel: (028) 9047 1155
Fax: (028) 9052 1289
E-mail: info@dup.org.uk
Website: www.dup.org.uk

Leader:	Rev Ian Paisley MP MEP MLA
Deputy:	Peter Robinson MP MLA
Secretary:	Nigel Dodds MP MLA
Chairperson:	Maurice Morrow MLA
President:	Jim McClure
Contact:	Allan Ewart

The DUP is staunchly anti agreement, in contrast to the Ulster Unionists although sharing their core beliefs. Founded in 1971 by the Rev Ian Paisley, replacing his Protestant Unionist Party the party is popularised by its slogan of "no surrender" and hard line stance on the constitutional status of Northern Ireland as part of the UK and resistance towards any form of co-operation with the Irish Republic.

The DUP stands behind the UUP in terms of vote share amongst Unionists, but the party's success in European elections reflects the popularity of its veteran leader, Rev Ian Paisley. The party currently holds five Westminster seats and 22 Assembly seats. The DUP is entitled to two ministerial posts within the Executive, but as a feature of its policy of opposition, it has rotated these posts among its members.

Despite its opposition to the Agreement, and public stance of non-cooperation with Sinn Féin, the DUP had accepted its Ministerial positions and participated in the cross party committees.

DUP Leadership

Ian Paisley is the leader of the DUP, MP for north Antrim since 1970 and a popular MEP since 1979. Unyielding in his opposition to republicanism, he is vociferously critical of the peace process and involvement of the Ulster Unionist party. As leader of the Free Presbyterian Church Dr Paisley is a staunch opponent of ecumenism and his attitude to the Roman Catholic faith draws much criticism from his opponents who regards his stance as sectarian.

Sinn Féin (SF)

51/55 Falls Road, Belfast, BT12 4PD

Tel: (028) 9022 3000
Fax: (028) 9022 3001
Website: www.sinnfein.ie
E-mail: sinnfein@iol.ie

President:	Gerry Adams MP MLA
Deputy:	Pat Doherty MP MLA
Secretary:	Lucilita Bhreatnach
Chairperson:	Mitchel McLaughlin MLA
Contact:	Party Headquarters

Representing republicanism within the Northern Ireland political spectrum, Sinn Féin's share of the Catholic/nationalist vote has continued to rise, attracting more first preference votes than the SDLP in the 2001 Westminster and local government elections.

Sinn Féin dates its all-island origins from the independence movement that gathered momentum at the end of World War I in 1918. Linked with the Provisional IRA, Sinn Féin followed a policy of abstentionism in politics until the 1980s. A significant shift in party policy occurred in 1998 when members voted to change the party's constitution and allowed elected party representatives to take their seats in a devolved Northern Ireland Assembly. Whilst Unionist scepticism remains about the durability of Sinn Féin's commitment to the peace process, recent movement on decommissioning by the IRA has helped demonstrate the party's continued commitment to constitutional politics.

Sinn Féin's four MPs have not taken their seats in Westminster because of their refusal to take the oath of allegiance to the British monarch. Sinn Féin also has five seats in Dail Eireann.

Sinn Féin Leadership

Gerry Adams, President of Sinn Féin since 1990, has been credited with the transformation of Sinn Féin from a political vehicle representing the aims of the IRA to a sophisticated well-organised political party. An MP for West Belfast from 1982 to 1992 and again from 1997, he acknowledged as early as 1980 that Republican aims were unlikely to be satisfied through military means alone.

The Alliance Party of Northern Ireland

88 University Street, Belfast, BT7 1HE

Tel: (028) 9032 4274
Fax: (028) 9033 3147
Website: www.allianceparty.org
E-mail: alliance@allianceparty.org

Leader: David Ford MLA
Deputy: Eileen Bell MLA
Secretary: Stephen Farry
Chairperson: Jayne Dunlop
Contact: Stephen Farry

The Alliance Party describes itself as a non-sectarian political group, dedicated to co-operation between all the people of Northern Ireland. The party was formed in 1970 to give political expression to those who felt that nationalist and unionist political parties did not reflect their views. Alliance draws its members from all religious and political perspectives.

Six members in the Assembly and forty councillors in local government represent the Alliance Party. Alliance, unlike the majority of other parties in the Northern Ireland political arena does not adopt a unionist or nationalist perspective to their politics. The party's members of the new Assembly have designated themselves as "centre" working to promote liberal, anti-sectarian politics.

Alliance Party Leadership

John Alderdice, now Lord Alderdice and Speaker in the Northern Ireland Assembly led the party from 1989–1998. The party is now led by David Ford a member of Antrim Borough Council since 1993 and elected Assembly Member for South Antrim. He was elected leader of the Alliance party in October 2001, following roles as Party General Secretary from 1990–1998 and Chief Whip.

Progressive Unionist Party (PUP)

182 Shankill Road, Belfast, BT13 2BH

Tel: (028) 9032 6233
Fax: (028) 9024 9602
E-mail: central@pup-ni.org
Website: www.pup.org

Leader: David Ervine MLA
Secretary: Colin Robinson
Chairperson: Dawn Purvis
Contact: Eileen Ward

Formed in 1997, the Progressive Unionist Party seeks to represent loyalist working class voters and is linked to the paramilitary UVF. The party has adopted a pro agreement stance believing that there must be "sharing of responsibility" between Unionists and Nationalists, whilst maintaining their firm belief in the Union with Great Britain. The party has two members in the Assembly, David Ervine and Billy Hutchinson and holds four local councillor positions.

PUP Leadership

David Ervine, a Member of the Assembly and a Belfast City Councillor leads the party. While arguing in favour of compromise with nationalists, he is opposed to a United Ireland and believes the loyalist ceasefire depends on the continued security of Northern Ireland within the UK.

Northern Ireland Women's Coalition (NIWC)

50 University Street, Belfast, BT7 1HB

Tel: (028) 9023 3100
Fax: (028) 9024 0021
E-mail: niwc@iol.ie
Website: www.niwc.org

Leader: Monica McWilliams MLA
Chairperson: Helen Crickard
Contact: Elizabeth Byrne McCullough

 The Northern Ireland Women's Coalition, which is strongly pro-Agreement, was established in 1996 with the aim of putting forward an agenda of "reconciliation through dialogue, accommodation and inclusion" and ensuring that women were represented in the Forum talks on the future of Northern Ireland. Monica McWilliams, leader, and Jane Morrice represent the party in the Assembly.

United Kingdom Unionist Party (UKUP)

Room 214, Parliament Buildings, Stormont
Belfast BT4 3XX

Tel: (028) 9052 1482
Fax: (028) 9052 1483
E-mail: info@robertmccartney.org
Website: www.robertmccartney.org

Leader: Robert McCartney MLA

Founded by Robert McCartney in 1996 the UKUP campaigned for a No vote in the Referendum, and returned 5 members to the new Assembly in 1998. In January 1999, internal differences led to 4 members resigning from the party, leaving the UKUP with Robert McCartney as its sole representative in the Assembly.

Northern Ireland Unionist Party (NIUP)

Room 358 Parliament Buildings, Stormont
Belfast, BT4 3XX

Tel: (028) 9052 1901
Fax: (028) 9052 1845
E-mail: info@niup.org
Website: www.niup.org

Leader: Cedric Wilson MLA

Following the resignation of four Assembly members from the UKUP the NIUP was formed on the 5 January 1999. The Northern Ireland Unionist Party is pro union and anti agreement. The party is led by Cedric Wilson and has three elected representatives in the Assembly, Norman Boyd, Patrick Roche and Cedric Wilson.

Workers' Party

6 Springfield Road, Belfast BT12 7AG

Tel: (028) 9032 8663
Fax: (028) 9033 3475
Website: www.workers-party.org
E-mail: info@workers-party.org

Party Presdient: Sean Garland

The Workers' Party has republican origins and is strongly socialist. Formed after a split within Sinn Féin in the 1970s it proceeded to adopt a Marxist ideology. The party suffered a split in 1992. The Workers' Party has seen its share of the vote decrease substantially in recent elections, and currently has no political representation at any level.

Conservative Party of Northern Ireland

176 Kings Road, Belfast, BT7 7EN

A small number of Conservative Councillors have been elected in North Down, but the party remains an insubstantial force in Northern Ireland.

Green Party

62 Haypark Avenue, Belfast, BT7 3FE

Tel: (028) 9029 3362
Fax: (028) 9029 3362
Website: www.belfast.co.uk/nigreens
E-mail:nigreens@belfast.co.uk

Leaders: Andrew Frew and Malachy McAnespie

The Green Party has contested Northern Ireland elections since 1990, albeit with very little success. Despite running candidates in most elections, the party remains among the smallest in Northern Ireland, campaigning on ecological and environmental issues.

Natural Law Party

The Natural Law Party has the undistinguished record of coming last in almost every election it has contested since its launch in 1992, although it has fielded candidates in virtually every election.

Electoral Results and Analysis

Northern Ireland has had 16 elections in the last 20 years, and despite their plentiful nature each has been vigorously contested and generated keen interest in the community. Whilst voting patterns have shown strong adherence to traditional allegiances, the longer-term trend would suggest that nationalist parties are gaining ground on their unionist counterparts and centre parties are finding it difficult to hold their votes against more uncompromising rivals in both communities.

An interesting development within the electoral landscape has been the emerging struggle for dominance not only between, but also within the two religio-political groupings, i.e. between UUP and DUP, SDLP and Sinn Féin.

The table below shows each party's electoral results for all major elections since 1982. This includes elections to the various political initiatives such as the Assembly of 1982 and the Forum of 1996. It excludes by-elections, including the multiple by-elections of 1986, as they are not as significant in terms of long-term trends.

Results for all elections since 1982 (except by-elections)
(percentage share of vote by party)

	UUP	DUP	SDLP	SF	All	WP	PUP	NIWC	UKUP	Other
1982	29.7	23.0	18.8	10.1	9.3	2.7	–	–	–	6.4
1983	34.0	20.0	18.0	13.4	8.0	1.9	–	–	–	4.7
1984	21.5	33.6	22.1	13.3	5.0	1.3	–	–	–	3.2
1985	29.5	24.3	17.8	11.8	7.1	1.6	–	–	–	7.9
1987	37.8	11.7	21.1	11.4	10.0	2.6	0.9	–	–	4.5
1989	31.3	17.7	21.0	11.2	6.9	2.1	–	–	–	9.8
1989 E	22.2	30.0	25.5	9.2	5.2	1.0	–	–	–	6.9
1992	34.5	13.1	23.5	10.0	8.7	0.5	–	–	–	9.7
1993	29.4	17.3	22.0	12.4	7.6	–	–	–	–	11.3
1994	23.8	29.2	28.9	9.9	4.1	0.5	–	–	–	3.6
1996	24.2	18.8	21.4	15.5	6.5	–	3.5	1.0	3.6	5.5
1997	32.7	13.6	24.1	16.1	8.0	0.3	1.4	0.4	1.6	1.8
1997 L	27.9	15.6	20.6	16.9	6.6	0.4	2.2	0.5	0.5	8.8
1998	21.3	18.1	22.0	17.6	6.5	0.2	2.6	1.6	4.5	5.6
1999	17.6	28.4	28.1	17.3	2.1	–	3.3	–	3.0	0.2
2001	26.8	22.5	21.0	21.7	3.6	0.3	0.6	0.4	1.7	1.4
2001 L	22.9	21.4	19.4	20.6	5.1	0.2	1.6	0.4	0.6	7.8

Key:

1982	Northern Ireland Assembly		**1993**	Local Government
1983	UK Government		**1994**	European
1984	European		**1996**	Northern Ireland Forum (for Peace Talks)
1985	Local Government		**1997**	UK Government
1987	UK Government		**1998**	Northern Ireland Assembly
1989	Local Government		**1999**	European
1989 E	European		**2001**	UK Government
1992	UK Government		**2001 L**	Local Government

Northern Ireland Westminster Elections

Northern Ireland currently returns 18 MPs to Westminster in a general election (out of a total of 635). From its conception in the Government of Ireland Act, 1920, until 1983 it had just 12 MPs. In 1983 the number of MPs was reconsidered by the Boundary Commission, five extra seats were created, and contested for the first time in the June 1983 general election. In 1995, the Boundary Commission examined the situation again and created a further seat for Northern Ireland, bringing the total to eighteen for the election of May 1997. Revision of constituency boundaries and electorate is generally undertaken every 10–12 years.

Northern Ireland's MPs until recently were somewhat of an anomaly within the British political system. During the existence of the Stormont government, Northern Ireland MPs were not allowed to rise in Westminster matters that came under the remit of the Stormont government, a convention that was strongly criticised by many. Legislation passed in Westminster has tended to exclude Northern Ireland, which has had its own customised version of each Westminster Act. This has resulted in Northern Ireland legislation differing from the rest of the UK, perhaps most notably in recent years, the Provision of Abortion Act, which at present is in effect everywhere in the UK except Northern Ireland.

The Belfast Agreement and the establishment of the new Northern Ireland Assembly will undoubtedly have an effect on the role of Westminster MPs. Now that Northern Ireland has its own devolved government, the role of elected representatives in Westminster will probably become more specialised and focused and less linked to constituency casework.

The principal parties in Northern Ireland can be seen in the table below. The Ulster Unionists, the SDLP, the DUP, the Alliance Party and Sinn Féin have tended to dominate Westminster elections. However, the Alliance Party is the only one of the five never to have won a Westminster seat, despite capturing up to 12 per cent of the total vote on occasions.

The table of seats gained, shown below, reflects the two-party battle within unionism and the similar contest between the two nationalist parties. In 1992 the Ulster Unionists and SDLP enjoyed the majority of votes from their respective communities, but by 2001 the DUP and Sinn Féin had caught up, Sinn Féin overtaking the SDLP for the first time. Smaller parties usually suffer under the first-past-the-post electoral system in Westminster elections, although the figures have previously shown one or two seats going to independents (nationalist or unionist), and unionist breakaway parties such as James Kilfedder's Ulster Popular Unionist Party from 1983 to 1992, and Robert McCartney's United Kingdom Unionist Party in 1997.

The influence of 'electoral pacts' between unionist parties is also highly significant. In areas with a large nationalist minority, the UUP and DUP have often agreed that one of their candidates stand down, to allow a straight run for a single unionist candidate and avoid losing the seat to nationalists by splitting the unionist majority. Conversely, the SDLP and Sinn Féin have not entered into such agreements, even where the arithmetic suggested that a single nationalist candidate could comfortably win a seat.

Set out below is the historical electoral performance of Northern Ireland's political parties in Westminster election from 1979–2001 in terms of share of popular vote and number of seats won.

Westminster MPs as elected in 2001

Constituency	Name	Party
Belfast East	Peter Robinson	DUP
Belfast North	Nigel Dodds	DUP
Belfast South	Rev Martin Smyth	UUP
Belfast West	Gerry Adams	SF
East Antrim	Roy Beggs	UUP
East Londonderry	Gregory Campbell	DUP
Fermanagh & South Tyrone	Michelle Gildernew	SF
Foyle	John Hume	SDLP
Lagan Valley	Jeffrey Donaldson	UUP
Mid Ulster	Martin McGuinness	SF
Newry and Armagh	Séamus Mallon	SDLP
North Antrim	Rev Ian Paisley	DUP
South Antrim	David Burnside	UUP
North Down	Sylvia Hermon	UUP
South Down	Eddie McGrady	SDLP
Strangford	Iris Robinson	DUP
Upper Bann	David Trimble	UUP
West Tyrone	Pat Doherty	SF

Seats by Party

Party	Seats	Party	Seats
UUP	6	SF	4
DUP	5	SDLP	3

Northern Ireland Westminster Elections 1979–2001

Parties' % share of vote

Party	1979	1983	1987	1992	1997	2001
UUP	36.6	34.0	37.8	34.5	32.7	26.8
SDLP	18.2	17.9	21.1	23.5	24.1	21.0
DUP	10.2	20.0	11.7	13.1	13.6	22.5
SF		13.4	11.4	10.0	16.1	21.7
All	11.9	8.0	10.0	8.7	8.0	3.6
WP		2.0	2.6	0.5	0.3	0.3
PUP					1.4	0.6
NIWC					0.4	0.4
UKUP					1.6	1.7
Others	23.1	4.7	5.4	9.7	1.8	1.4
Turnout %	**68.4**	**73.3**	**67.4**	**69.7**	**67.1**	**68.0**

Parties' Share of Seats

Party	1979	1983	1987	1992	1997	2001
UUP	5	11	9	10	10	6
SDLP	1	1	3	4	3	3
DUP	3	3	3	2	2	5
SF		1	1		2	4
All						
Ind. Unionist	1					
UUUP	1					
Ind. Nationalist	1					
UPUP		1	1	1		
UKUP					1	
Total	**12**	**17**	**17**	**17**	**18**	**18**

Houses of Parliament, Westminster

The 2001 UK Westminster Government General Election

Electorate 1,191,070 Total Votes Polled 810,381
Turnout 68.0% Spoiled Votes 7,074

Results by Constituency

A map of the Westminster constituency boundaries is shown on page 97 below.

Belfast East

Name	Party	Votes	% Total vote
Peter Robinson*	DUP	15,667	42.5
Tim Lemon	UUP	8,550	23.2
David Alderdice	All	5,832	15.8
David Ervine	PUP	3,669	10.0
Joseph O'Donnell	SF	1,237	3.4
Ciara Farren	SDLP	888	2.4
Terry Dick	Cons	800	2.2
Joseph Bell	WP	123	0.3
Rainbow George Weiss	VFY	71	0.2

*Sitting MP

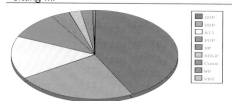

Electorate	58,455
Turnout	63.4%
Total Valid Vote	36,829
DUP Majority	7,117

East Belfast held by Peter Robinson of the DUP since 1979 has a substantial unionist majority. Robinson's nearest rivals were the UUP and Alliance, although the DUP majority was well over six and a half thousand votes.

Belfast North

Name	Party	Votes	% Total vote
Nigel Dodds	DUP	16,718	40.8
Gerry Kelly	SF	10,331	25.2
Alban Maginness	SDLP	8,592	21.0
Cecil Walker*	UUP	4,904	12.0
Marcella Delaney	WP	253	0.7
Rainbow George Weiss	VFY	134	0.3

*Sitting MP

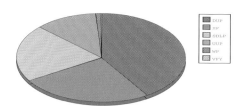

Electorate	60,941
Turnout	67.8%
Total Valid Vote	40,932
DUP Majority	6,387

North Belfast is one of the most deeply divided areas in Northern Ireland, and this is reflected in its elections. Cecil Walker held the seat for the Ulster Unionist Party since 1983, unopposed by candidates from the other Unionist parties until the 2001 election when Nigel Dodds of the DUP ran in direct competition. Nigel Dodds won two fifths of the vote, beating Walker into 4th place, behind both the SDLP and Sinn Féin.

Belfast South

Name	Party	Votes	% Total vote
Martin Smyth*	UUP	17,008	44.8
Alasdair McDonnell	SDLP	11,609	30.6
Monica McWilliams	NIWC	2,968	7.8
Alex Maskey	SF	2,894	7.6
Geraldine Rice	All	2,042	5.4
Dawn Purvis	PUP	1,112	2.9
Patrick Lynch	WP	204	0.6
Rainbow George Weiss	VFY	115	0.3

*Sitting MP

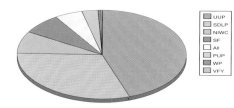

Electorate	59,436
Turnout	64.3%
Total Valid Vote	37,952
UUP majority	5,399

The Ulster Unionist Party candidate Martin Smyth retained South Belfast. Smyth's closest rival was the SDLP's Dr Alasdair McDonnell.

Monica McWilliams of the Northern Ireland Women's Coalition, fighting only the party's second general election, polled in third position.

Belfast West

Name	Party	Votes	% Total vote
Gerry Adams*	SF	27,096	66.1
Alex Attwood	SDLP	7,754	18.9
Eric Smyth	DUP	2,641	6.4
Chris McGimpsey	UUP	2,541	6.2
John Lowry	WP	736	1.8
David Kerr	UTW	116	0.3
Rainbow George Weiss	VFY	98	0.2

Sitting MP

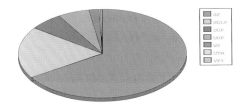

Electorate	59,617
Turnout	69.9%
Total Valid Vote	40,982
SF Majority	19,342

This constituency has a very strong Catholic and nationalist majority, although it includes much of the loyalist Shankill Road within its boundaries. Gerry Fitt, one of the founders and former leader of the SDLP, held Belfast West from 1966 to 1983.

By 1983 Fitt had resigned from the SDLP, and Gerry Adams of Sinn Fein won the seat. Although Dr Joe Hendron of the SDLP won the seat in 1992, Adams was successful in both 1997 and 2001.

East Antrim

Name	Party	Votes	% Total vote
Roy Beggs*	UUP	13,101	36.4
Sammy Wilson	DUP	12,973	36.0
John Matthews	All	4,483	12.5
Danny O'Connor	SDLP	2,641	7.4
Robert Mason	Ind	1,092	3.0
Janette Graffin	SF	903	2.5
Alan Greer	Cons	807	2.2

Sitting MP

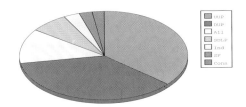

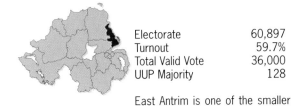

Electorate	60,897
Turnout	59.7%
Total Valid Vote	36,000
UUP Majority	128

East Antrim is one of the smaller constituencies and has an overwhelming unionist majority. Since its establishment by the Boundary Commission in 1983 Roy Beggs of the UUP has held the seat with increasingly strong opposition coming from the DUP.

East Londonderry

Name	Party	Votes	% Total vote
Gregory Campbell	DUP	12,813	32.1
Willie Ross*	UUP	10,912	27.4
John Dallat	SDLP	8,298	20.8
Francie Brolly	SF	6,221	15.6
Yvonne Boyle	All	1,625	4.1

Sitting MP

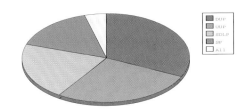

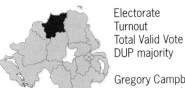

Electorate	60,215
Turnout	66.9%
Total Valid Vote	39,869
DUP majority	1,901

Gregory Campbell of the DUP took the East Londonderry seat from Willie Ross of the UUP who had held it with a majority of 4,000. The loss of this seat for the UUP was unexpected not least because of the hard-line anti-Agreement and anti-Trimble stance of the incumbent MP.

Fermanagh and South Tyrone

Name	Party	Votes	% Total vote
Michelle Gildernew	SF	17,739	34.1
James Cooper	UUP	17,686	34.0
Tommy Gallagher	SDLP	9,706	18.7
Jim Dixon	Ind	6,843	13.2
*Sitting MP			

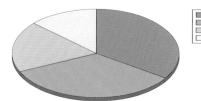

Electorate	66,640
Turnout	79.0%
Total Valid Vote	51,974
SF majority	53

Ulster Unionist Ken Maginnis had held Fermanagh South Tyrone since 1983 but his decision not to stand for re-election in 2001 and the entry of independent unionist Jim Dixon enabled Michelle Gildernew of Sinn Féin to win the seat narrowly from the UUP.

Foyle

Name	Party	Votes	% Total vote
John Hume*	SDLP	24,538	50.2
Mitchel McLaughlin	SF	12,988	26.6
William Hay	DUP	7,414	15.2
Andrew Davidson	UUP	3,360	6.9
Colm Cavanagh	All	579	1.1
*Sitting MP			

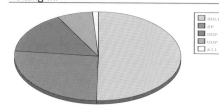

Electorate	70,943
Turnout	69.6%
Total Valid Vote	48,879
SDLP majority	11,550

John Hume, former leader of the SDLP has held the constituency since its creation in 1983. Despite big swings elsewhere from SDLP to Sinn Féin, the seat was retained by the SDLP with a comfortable majority of 11,550. Foyle was possibly the only nationalist constituency where Sinn Féin did not gain significant ground on the SDLP.

Lagan Valley

Name	Party	Votes	% Total vote
Jeffrey Donaldson*	UUP	25,966	56.5
Seamus Close	All	7,624	16.6
Edwin Poots	DUP	6,164	13.4
Patricia Lewsley	SDLP	3,462	7.6
Paul Butler	SF	2,725	5.9
*Sitting MP			

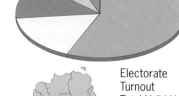

Electorate	72,671
Turnout	63.6%
Total Valid Vote	45,941
UUP majority	18,342

Jeffrey Donaldson has held Lagan Valley since 1997, when he replaced the retiring UUP leader, Jim Molyneaux. Donaldson won over 50 per cent of the vote in 2001, with his nearest rival, Alliance's Seamus Close, 18,000 votes behind.

Mid Ulster

Name	Party	Votes	% Total vote
Martin McGuinness*	SF	25,502	51.1
Ian McCrea	DUP	15,549	31.1
Eilish Haughey	SDLP	8,376	16.8
Francie Donnelly	WP	509	1.0

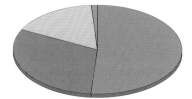

Electorate	61,390
Turnout	82.1%
Total Valid Vote	49,936
SF majority	9,953

Martin McGuinness retained Mid-Ulster for Sinn Féin, increasing his majority from 1,900 to almost 10,000 votes.

The SDLP continued to drop behind the two leading parties in an area with very high turnout.

Newry and Armagh

Name	Party	Votes	% Total vote
Séamus Mallon*	SDLP	20,784	37.4
Conor Murphy	SF	17,209	30.9
Paul Berry	DUP	10,795	19.4
Sylvia McRoberts	UUP	6,833	12.3
*Sitting MP			

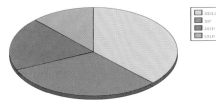

Electorate	72,466
Turnout	77.6%
Total Valid Vote	55,621
SDLP majority	3,575

The SDLP Deputy Leader Seamus Mallon retained Newry and Armagh, with a much-reduced majority of 3,500 votes over Sinn Fein's Conor Murphy.

The DUP decided to run a candidate, contrary to their previous tactic of allowing the UUP to present a single unionist. Paul Berry, at 10,795 votes, pushed the UUP's Sylvia McRoberts into 4th place.

North Antrim

Name	Party	Votes	% Total vote
Ian Paisley*	DUP	24,539	49.9
Lexie Scott	UUP	10,315	21.0
Sean Farren	SDLP	8,283	16.8
John Kelly	SF	4,822	9.8
Jayne Dunlop	All	1,258	2.5
*Sitting MP			

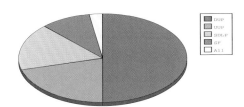

Electorate	74,451
Turnout	66.6%
Total Valid Vote	49,217
DUP Majority	14,224

North Antrim is the stronghold of the DUP leader, Ian Paisley since he first won the seat in 1970 with the UUP coming consistently second. The constituency has a substantial unionist majority.

North Down

Name	Party	Votes	% Total vote
Sylvia Hermon	UUP	20,833	56.0
Robert McCartney*	UKUP	13,509	36.3
Marietta Farrell	SDLP	1,275	3.4
Julian Robertson	Cons	815	2.2
Chris Carter	UIV	444	1.2
Eamon McConvey	SF	313	0.9

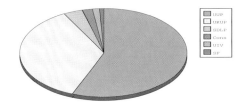

Electorate	63,212
Turnout	59.1%
Total Valid Vote	37,189
UUP Majority	7,324

North Down had not been held by any of the main political parties for over 20 years, Independent Unionist James Kilfedder holding the seat throughout the 70's and 80's succeeded by another Independent Unionist, Robert McCartney in 1995.

McCartney had held the North Down seat since the by-election in 1995. In 2001 the Alliance party withdrew in support of the pro-Agreement UUP candidate, Lady Sylvia Hermon. Its support proved crucial to the UUP. Sylvia Hermon took North Down with a majority of 7,324.

South Antrim

Name	Party	Votes	% Total vote
David Burnside	UUP	16,366	37.1
Willie McCrea*	DUP	15,355	34.8
Sean McKee	SDLP	5,336	12.1
Martin Meehan	SF	4,160	9.4
David Ford	All	1,969	4.4
Norman Boyd	NIUP	972	2.2
*Sitting MP			

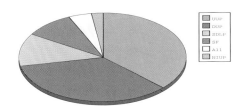

Electorate	70,651
Turnout	62.5%
Total Valid Vote	44,158
UUP Majority	1,011

Clifford Forsythe of the Ulster Unionists held this seat from 1983 until his death in April 2000.

In the 2000 by-election Willie McCrea of the DUP won the seat with a majority of 822 votes. However, the situation was reversed in 2001, when Burnside won the seat back for the UUP by just over 1,000 votes.

South Down

Name	Party	Votes	% Total vote
Eddie McGrady*	SDLP	24,136	46.4
Mick Murphy	SF	10,278	19.7
Dermot Nesbitt	UUP	9,173	17.6
Jim Wells	DUP	7,802	15.0
Betty Campbell	All	685	1.3

*Sitting MP

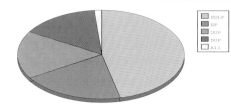

Electorate	73,519
Turnout	71.6%
Total Valid Vote	52,074
SDLP Majority	13,858

Eddie McGrady of the SDLP has held South Down since 1987, when he displaced Enoch Powell of the UUP by just over 700 votes. Since then, McGrady has increased his majority to almost 14,000 votes in 2001.

Strangford

Name	Party	Votes	% Total vote
Iris Robinson	DUP	18,532	42.8
David McNarry	UUP	17,422	40.3
Kieran McCarthy	All	2,902	6.7
Danny McCarthy	SDLP	2,646	6.1
Liam Johnson	SF	930	2.2
Cedric Wilson	NIUP	822	1.9

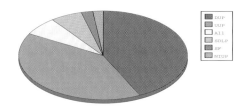

Electorate	72,192
Turnout	60.2%
Total Valid Vote	43,254
DUP majority	1,110

The contest for the Strangford seat, vacated by the UUP's John Taylor was close with David McNarry coming within 1,100 votes of retaining the seat for the UUP. Iris Robinson, DUP, was the eventual winner.

Upper Bann

Name	Party	Votes	% Total vote
David Trimble*	UUP	17,095	33.5
David Simpson	DUP	15,037	29.5
Dara O'Hagan	SF	10,771	21.1
Dolores Kelly	SDLP	7,607	14.9
Tom French	WP	527	1.0

*Sitting MP

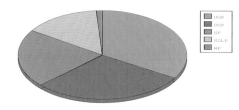

Electorate	72,574
Turnout	70.8%
Total Valid Vote	51,037
UUP majority	2,058

Until 2001 the UUP leader, David Trimble, had comfortably held Upper Bann. In 1997 Trimble enjoyed a majority of over 9,000 votes, with the two nationalist candidates placed between himself and the DUP. In 2001, however, the DUP's David Simpson came within 2,000 votes of winning the seat and causing a major upset.

In the absence of SDLP candidate Bríd Rodgers, the Sinn Féin vote increased significantly, largely at the expense of the SDLP.

West Tyrone

Name	Party	Votes	% Total vote
Pat Doherty	SF	19,814	40.8
Willie Thompson*	UUP	14,774	30.4
Bríd Rodgers	SDLP	13,942	28.8
Electorate	60,739	Turnout	80.6%
Total Valid Vote	48,530	SF majority	5,040

In West Tyrone Pat Doherty of Sinn Féin beat the UUP's Willie Thompson by a majority of over 5,000 votes. The SDLP had hoped to achieve success in this constituency by fielding Bríd Rodgers away from her usual Upper Bann constituency, however this tactic proved unsuccessful.

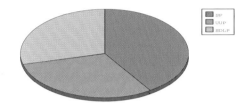

SF
UUP
SDLP

Westminster Constituencies (Also used for Assembly Elections)

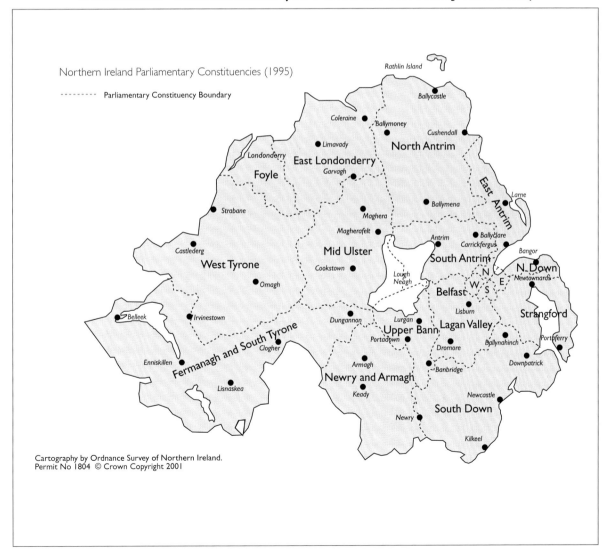

Northern Ireland Parliamentary Constituencies (1995)

- - - - - - - - Parliamentary Constituency Boundary

Cartography by Ordnance Survey of Northern Ireland.
Permit No 1804 © Crown Copyright 2001

Northern Ireland Assembly Elections, June 1998

Over the years Northern Ireland has elected a number of different local 'assemblies'. Most of these were associated with various initiatives by UK governments to establish a form of devolved administration in Northern Ireland. Given that these initiatives varied in scope and context the results are not readily comparable with the recently elected legislative assembly.

Elections were contested for the new Northern Ireland Assembly on Thursday 25 June 1998. The 18 Westminster constituencies were used, each to return 6 Assembly members. The electoral system used was a form of proportional representation, the Single Transferable Vote (STV).

The result suggested a 70% pro-Agreement majority, against a 30% anti-Agreement minority spearheaded by the DUP. In reality however the result was possibly somewhat closer. A number of elected members in David Trimble's ostensibly pro-Agreement Ulster Unionist Party were either actually personally against the Agreement, or had not fallen decisively on either side of the argument. At the outset this did not matter greatly, as there was a pro-Agreement majority within both of the unionist and nationalist camps: as required to make the institutions workable.

However, over time there has undoubtedly been an erosion of the pro-Agreement majority within unionism and in particular, within the Ulster Unionist Party.

Overall Results By Party

Party	Name	Seats	% of Seats
UUP	Ulster Unionist Party	28	25.9
SDLP	Social Democratic and Labour Party	24	22.2
DUP	Democratic Unionist Party	20	18.5
SF	Sinn Féin	18	16.7
All	Alliance Party	6	5.5
UKUP	United Kingdom Unionist Party*	5	4.6
PUP	Progressive Unionist Party	2	1.9
NIWC	Northern Ireland Women's Coalition	2	1.9
Ind	Independents**	3	2.8
Total		**108**	**100**

* 4 members of the UKUP resigned in January 1999 and formed the Northern Ireland Unionist Party. One member of the NIUP resigned in December 1999 and became an Independent Unionist.

** All 3 members formed the United Unionist Assembly Party (UUAP) in September 1998. Their leader, Denis Watson, later joined the DUP.

Results by Constituency

Details of the Assembly election results are set out below. They are organised by Westminster constituency, and include results for every candidate, as well as details of turnout, quota and count elected.

Belfast East

Electorate	60,562	Total Vote	39,593
Quota	5,657	Turnout	66.0%

Party	Candidates	% Vote	Seats
DUP	3	30.9	2
UUP	3	24.3	2
All	2	18.0	1
PUP	2	13.6	1
UKUP	1	3.4	
SDLP	1	2.6	
Others	8	7.2	
Total	**20**	**100.0**	**6**

Candidate	Party	1st Pref Votes	Elected
Peter Robinson	DUP	11,219	1st Count
John Alderdice	All	6,144	1st Count
Reg Empey	UUP	5,158	12th Count
David Ervine	PUP	5,114	7th Count
Ian Adamson	UUP	3,447	15th Count
Denny Vitty	UKUP	1,362	–
Peter Jones	SDLP	1,025	–
Jim Rogers	UUP	1,015	–
Richard Good	All	1,000	–
Joe Donnell	SF	917	–
Pearl Sagar	NIWC	711	–
Sammy Wilson	DUP	633	12th Count
Robert Girvan	UDP	516	–
John Norris	DUP	373	–
David Bleakley	Lab	369	–
Dawn Purvis	PUP	271	–
Lesley Donaldson	Cons	203	–
Joe Bell	WP	79	–
David Collins	NLP	22	–
John Lawrence	Ind	15	–

Belfast North

Electorate	62,541	Total Vote	41,125
Quota	5,876	Turnout	67.3%

Party	Candidates	% Vote	Seats
SF	2	21.3	1
DUP	2	21.3	1
SDLP	2	21.1	1
UUP	2	10.9	1
PUP	1	9.1	1
All	1	3.1	
UU	1	7.2	1
Others	7	6.0	
Total	**18**	**100.0**	**6**

Candidate	Party	1st Pref Votes	Elected
Nigel Dodds	DUP	7,476	1st Count
Alban Maginness	SDLP	6,196	1st Count
Gerry Kelly	SF	5,610	10th Count
Billy Hutchinson	PUP	3,751	11th Count
Martina McIlkenny	SF	3,165	–
Fraser Agnew	UU	2,976	11th Count
Martin Morgan	SDLP	2,465	–
Fred Cobain	UUP	2,415	11th Count
David Browne	UUP	2,064	–
Eric Smyth	DUP	1,288	–
Glyn Roberts	All	1,267	–
John White	UDP	911	–
Stephen Cooper	UKUP	748	–
Peter Emerson	Green	257	–
Sam McAughtrey	Lab	255	–
Steven Doran	WP	155	–
Kevin Blair	NLP	76	–
Dolores Quinn	Ind	50	–

Belfast South

Electorate	61,209	Total Vote	40,724
Quota	5,818	Turnout	67.4%

Party	Candidates	% Vote	Seats
UUP	3	23.4	2
SDLP	2	21.7	2
DUP	2	13.0	1
All	1	10.0	
NIWC	1	9.6	1
SF	1	6.4	
PUP	1	5.2	
Others	8	10.7	
Total	**19**	**100.0**	**6**

Candidate	Party	1st Pref Votes	Elected
Alasdair McDonnell	SDLP	4,956	6th Count
Michael McGimpsey	UUP	4,938	5th Count
Steve McBride	All	4,086	–
Monica McWilliams	NIWC	3,912	10th Count
Carmel Hanna	SDLP	3,882	10th Count
Esmond Birnie	UUP	2,875	8th Count
Mark Robinson	DUP	2,872	8th Count
Sean Hayes	SF	2,605	–
Myreve Chambers	DUP	2,449	–
Ernie Purvis	PUP	2,112	–
David Adams	UDP	1,745	–
Jim Clarke	UUP	1,720	–
Grant Dillon	UKUP	1,496	–
William Dixon	Ind	437	–
Boyd Black	Lab	231	–
Paddy Lynn	WP	176	–
Roger Lomas	Cons	97	–
James Anderson	NLP	73	–
Niall Cusack	Lab	62	–

Belfast West

Electorate	60,669	Total Vote	41,794
Quota	5,971	Turnout	70.5%

Party	Candidates	% Vote	Seats
SF	5	59.0	4
SDLP	2	24.8	2
PUP	1	5.2	
UUP	1	3.9	
DUP	1	3.2	
Others	5	3.8	
Total	**15**	**100.0**	**6**

Candidate	Party	1st Pref Votes	Elected
Gerry Adams	SF	9,078	1st Count
Joe Hendron	SDLP	6,140	1st Count
Bairbre de Brún	SF	4,711	9th Count
Alex Maskey	SF	4,330	10th Count
Alex Attwood	SDLP	4,280	10th Count
Sue Ramsey	SF	3,946	6th Count
Michael Ferguson	SF	2,585	–
Hugh Smyth	PUP	2,180	–
Chris McGimpsey	UUP	1,640	–
Margaret Ferris	DUP	1,345	–
Thomas Dalzell-Sheridan	UKUP	666	–
John Lowry	WP	607	–
Dan McGuinness	All	129	–
Michael Kennedy	NLP	29	–
Mary Cahillane	Soc	128	–

East Antrim

Electorate	59,313	Total Vote	35,610
Quota	5,088	Turnout	60.9

Party	Candidates	% Vote	Seats
UUP	3	29.6	2
All	2	20.1	1
DUP	2	22.1	1
SDLP	1	6.0	1
SF	1	2.1	
UKUP	1	8.0	1
PUP	1	4.0	
Other	5	8.1	
Total	**16**	**100.0**	**6**

Candidate	Party	1st Pref Votes	Elected
Roy Beggs Jr	UUP	5,764	1st Count
Sean Neeson	All	5,247	1st Count
David Hilditch	DUP	4,876	8th Count
Jack McKee	DUP	3,013	–
Roger Hutchinson	UKUP	2,866	13th Count
May Steele	UUP	2,399	–
Ken Robinson	UUP	2,384	13th Count
Danny O'Connor	SDLP	2,106	13th Count
Stewart Dickson	All	1,921	–
James Brown	Ind	1,571	–
William Greer	PUP	1,432	–
Chrissy McAuley	SF	746	–
Tommy Kirkham	UDP	596	–
Robert Lindsay Mason	Ind	424	–
Terence Dick	Cons	233	–
James Barr McKissock	NLP	32	–

East Londonderry

Electorate	59,370	Total Vote	39,564
Quota	5,653	Turnout	67.7%

Party	Candidates	% Vote	Seats
UUP	3	25.2	2
SDLP	2	23.7	2
DUP	2	23.7	1
SF	2	9.8	
Ind	1	9.6	1
Others	6	8.0	
Total	**15**	**100.0**	**6**

Candidate	Party	1st Pref Votes	Elected
Gregory Campbell	DUP	6,099	1st Count
David McClarty	UUP	5,108	5th Count
John Dallat	SDLP	4,760	6th Count
Arthur Doherty*	SDLP	4,606	8th Count
Boyd Douglas	Ind	3,811	9th Count
Pauline Armitage	UUP	3,315	9th Count
David Nicholl	UDP	3,280	–
Malachy O'Kane	SF	2,521	–
Barbara Dempsey	All	2,395	–
Robert McPherson	UUP	1,531	–
John McIlhenny	SF	1,339	–
David Gilmour	PUP	582	–
George Robinson	DUP	171	–
Maura McCann	NLP	46	–

Arthur Doherty resigned and was replaced by Michael Coyle with effect from 1 September 2002.

Fermanagh and South Tyrone

Electorate	65,383	Total Vote	51,043
Quota	7,292	Turnout	77.4%

Party	Candidates	% Vote	Seats
SF	3	26.9	2
UUP	3	24.6	2
SDLP	2	21.6	1
DUP	2	13.9	1
All	1	1.2	
Others	3	11.8	
Total	**14**	**100.0**	**6**

Candidate	Party	1st Pref Votes	Elected
Tommy Gallagher	SDLP	8,135	1st Count
Sam Foster	UUP	5,589	5th Count
Gerry McHugh	SF	5,459	7th Count
Michelle Gildernew	SF	4,703	9th Count
Joan Carson	UUP	4,400	10th Count
Jim Dixon	UKUP	4,262	–
Maurice Morrow	DUP	3,987	10th Count
Pat Treanor	SF	3,552	–
Bert Johnston	DUP	3,095	–
Olive Mullen	SDLP	2,872	–
Bertie Kerr	UUP	2,583	–
Marie Crawley	NIWC	1,729	–
Stephen Farry	All	614	–
Simeon Gillan	NLP	63	–

Foyle

Electorate	68,888	Total Vote	48,794
Quota	6,971	Turnout	72.0 %

Party	Candidates	% Vote	Seats
SDLP	4	47.8	3
SF	4	26.0	2
DUP	1	12.5	1
UUP	1	9.6	
Others	5	4.1	
Total	**15**	**100.0**	**6**

Candidate	Party	1st Pref Votes	Elected
John Hume*	SDLP	12,581	1st Count
William Hay	DUP	6,112	8th Count
Mitchel McLaughlin	SF	5,341	5th Count
Jack Allen	UUP	4,669	–
Mark Durkan	SDLP	4,423	6th Count
John Tierney	SDLP	3,778	7th Count
Mary Nelis	SF	3,464	8th Count
Annie Courtney	SDLP	2,560	–
Gearoid O hEara	SF	2,531	–
Lynn Fleming	SF	1,360	–
Colm Cavanagh	All	1,058	–
Ken Adams	Lab	345	–
Brian Gurney	PUP	287	–
Peter MacKenzie	Green	253	–
Donn Brennan	NLP	32	–

* John Hume (SDLP) resigned with effect from 1 December 2000. Annie Courtney (SDLP), who took the seat on 11 December 2000, replaced him.

Lagan Valley

Electorate	71,661	Total Vote	46,510
Quota	6,645	Turnout	65.7 %

Party	Candidates	% Vote	Seats
UUP	4	30.8	2
DUP	2	18.0	1
All	1	14.6	1
UKUP	1	11.5	1
SF	1	4.3	
SDLP	1	8.7	1
UDP	1	8.0	
Others	4	4.1	
Total	**15**	**100.0**	**6**

Candidate	Party	1st Pref Votes	Elected
Seamus Close	All	6,788	1st Count
Billy Bell	UUP	5,965	5th Count
Patrick Roche	UKUP	5,361	9th Count
Edwin Poots	DUP	5,239	7th Count
Patricia Lewsley	SDLP	4,039	9th Count
Ivan Davis	UUP	3,927	9th Count
Gary McMichael	UDP	3,725	–
David Campbell	UUP	3,158	–
Cecil Calvert	DUP	3,111	–
Paul Butler	SF	2,000	–
Ken Hull	UUP	1,289	–
Annie Campbell	NIWC	955	–
William Bleakes	Cons	702	–
Frances McCarthy	WP	208	–
John Cairns	NLP	43	–

Mid Ulster

Electorate	59,991	Total Vote	49,798
Quota	7,115	Turnout	84.4%

Party	Candidates	% Vote	Seats
SF	3	40.8	3
SDLP	2	22.2	1
DUP	2	21.4	1
UUP	2	13.9	1
All	1	1.0	
Others	3	0.7	
Total	**13**	**100.0**	**6**

Candidate	Party	1st Pref Votes	Elected
Rev William McCrea	DUP	10,339	1st Count
Martin McGuinness	SF	8,703	1st Count
Denis Haughey	SDLP	6,410	6th Count
Francis Molloy	SF	6,008	6th Count
John Kelly	SF	5,594	6th Count
Patsy McGlone	SDLP	4,666	–
Billy Armstrong	UUP	4,498	6th Count
John Junkin	UUP	2,440	–
Yvonne Boyle	All	497	–
Paul McLean	DUP	307	–
Francie Donnelly	WP	207	–
Harry Hutchinson	Soc	91	–
Mary Daly	NLP	38	–

Newry and Armagh

Electorate	71,553	Total Vote	54,136
Quota	7,734	Turnout	77.3%

Party	Candidates	% Vote	Seats
SDLP	3	35.0	2
SF	3	26.0	2
UUP	2	18.1	1
DUP	1	13.3	1
Others	5	7.6	
Total	**14**	**100.0**	**6**

Candidate	Party	1st Pref Votes	Elected
Séamus Mallon	SDLP	13,582	1st Count
Paul Berry	DUP	7,214	4th Count
Danny Kennedy	UUP	5,495	6th Count
Conor Murphy	SF	4,839	8th Count
Davy Hyland	SF	4,643	–
Pat McNamee	SF	4,570	8th Count
Jim Speers	UUP	4,324	–
John Fee	SDLP	3,166	8th Count
Frank Feeley	SDLP	2,205	–
Mary Allen	Ind	1,227	–
Kate Fearon	NIWC	1,138	–
William Fraser	Ind	933	–
Pete Whitcroft	All	777	–
David Evans	NLP	23	–

North Antrim

Electorate	73,247	Total Vote	49,697
Quota	7,100	Turnout	69.0 %

Party	Candidates	% Vote	Seats
UUP	3	22.3	2
SDLP	2	16.9	1
SF	2	8.1	
DUP	3	37.6	3
All	1	4.6	
Other	7	10.5	
Total	**18**	**100.0**	**6**

Candidate	Party	1st Pref Votes	Elected
Rev Ian Paisley	DUP	10,590	1st Count
Sean Farren	SDLP	6,433	6th Count
Rev Robert Coulter	UUP	5,407	10th Count
Ian Paisley Jr	DUP	4,459	2nd Count
Gardiner Kane	DUP	3,638	12th Count
James Leslie	UUP	3,458	12th Count
William Wright	Ind	3,297	–
Jayne Dunlop	All	2,282	–
Patricia Campbell	UUP	2,199	–
James McCarry	SF	2,024	–
Joe Cahill	SF	2,021	–
Malachy McCamphill	SDLP	1,982	–
Richard Rodgers	PUP	641	–
Oliver McMullan	Ind	478	–
Maurice McAllister	UDP	400	–
Chris McCaughan	Ind	194	–
John Wright	NLP	156	–
Thomas Palmer	Ind	38	–

North Down

Electorate	62,942	Total Vote	37,313
Quota	5,331	Turnout	60.2 %

Party	Candidates	% Vote	Seats
UUP	3	32.6	3
UKUP	2	22.4	1
All	2	14.4	1
DUP	2	6.9	
SDLP	1	5.5	
NIWC	1	4.8	1
Others	8	13.4	
Total	**19**	**100.0**	**6**

Candidate	Party	1st Pref Votes	Elected
Robert McCartney	UKUP	8,188	1st Count
John Gorman	UUP	4,719	6th Count
Alan McFarland	UUP	4,653	6th Count
Eileen Bell	All	3,669	9th Count
Peter Weir	UUP	2,775	12th Count
Marietta Farrell	SDLP	2,048	–
Jane Morrice	NIWC	1,808	12th Count
Gavin Walker	All	1,699	–
Alan Graham	DUP	1,558	–
Alan Chambers	Ind	1,382	–
Stewart Currie	PUP	1,376	–
Brian Wilson	Ind	1,327	–
St Clair McAlister	DUP	1,013	–

Leonard Fee	Cons	337	–
Tom Lindsay	UDP	265	–
Vanessa Baird-Gunning	Lab	212	–
Elizabeth Roche	UKUP	173	–
Christopher Carter	UIV	72	–
Andrea Gribben	NLP	39	–

South Antrim

Electorate	69,426	Total Vote	43,991
Quota	6,285	Turnout	63.2 %

Party	Candidates	% Vote	Seats
UUP	3	30.0	2
DUP	2	20.1	1
UKUP	1	9.9	1
SDLP	2	17.7	1
All	1	8.6	1
SF	1	7.3	
PUP	1	3.5	
NIWC	1	2.5	
Others	2	0.4	
Total	**14**	**100.0**	**6**

Candidate	Party	1st Pref Votes	Elected
Jim Wilson	UUP	6,691	1st Count
Wilson Clyde	DUP	6,034	6th Count
Norman Boyd	UKUP	4,360	7th Count
Donovan McClelland	SDLP	4,309	8th Count
Duncan Shipley-Dalton	UUP	4,147	9th Count
David Ford	All	3,778	10th Count
Tommy Burns	SDLP	3,474	–
Martin Meehan	SF	3,226	–
Stuart Deignan	DUP	2,816	–
Norman Hunter	UUP	2,337	–
Ken Wilkinson	PUP	1,546	–
Joan Cosgrove	NIWC	1,108	–
Oliver Frawley	Lab	137	–
George Stidolph	NLP	28	–

South Down

Electorate	71,000	Total Vote	51,353
Quota	7,337	Turnout	73.7%

Party	Candidates	% Vote	Seats
SDLP	4	45.3	3
SF	2	15.1	1
UUP	2	14.5	1
DUP	1	9.4	1
UKUP	1	5.0	
NIWC	1	3.2	
Others	6	7.5	
Total	**17**	**100.0**	**6**

Candidate	Party	1st Pref Votes	Elected
Eddie McGrady	SDLP	10,373	1st Count
Mick Murphy	SF	6,251	6th Count
P J Bradley	SDLP	5,571	10th Count
Dermot Nesbitt	UUP	5,480	8th Count
Jim Wells	DUP	4,826	11th Count
Hugh Carr	SDLP	3,731	–
Eamon O'Neill	SDLP	3,582	11th Count

Frederick Wharton	UKUP	2,576	–
Norman Hanna	UUP	1,939	–
Anne Carr	NIWC	1,658	–
George Graham	Ind	1,562	–
Garret O'Fachtna	SF	1,520	–
Anne-Marie Cunningham	AI	1,502	–
Malachi Curran	Lab	498	–
Desmond O'Hagan	WP	130	–
Patrick O'Connor	Ind	121	–
Thomas Mullins	NLP	33	–

Strangford

Electorate	70,868	Total Vote	42,922
Quota	6,132	Turnout	61.9%

Party	Candidates	% Vote	Seats
UUP	5	34.4	2
DUP	3	27.7	2
All	2	12.2	1
SDLP	2	9.0	
UKUP	1	7.2	1
Others	10	9.5	
Total	**22**	**100.0**	**6**

Candidate	Party	1st Pref Votes	Elected
Iris Robinson	DUP	9,479	1st Count
John Taylor	UUP	9,203	1st Count
Cedric Wilson	UKUP	3,078	18th Count
Kieran McCarthy	All	2,947	17th Count
Peter Osborne	All	2,269	–
John Beattie	Ind	2,247	–
Danny McCarthy	SDLP	1,982	–
Brian Hanvey	SDLP	1,883	–
Thomas Benson*	UUP	1,623	17th Count
Jim Shannon	DUP	1,415	18th Count
Ricky Johnston	PUP	1,342	–
David McNarry	UUP	1,073	–
Tommy Jeffers	DUP	1,007	–
Wilbert Magill	Ind	951	–
Tom Hamilton	UUP	615	–
Paddy McGreevy	SF	614	–
Blakely McNally	UDP	322	–
Thomas Beattie	Cons	263	–
Agnes Orr	Ind	201	–
Andrew Frew	Green	200	–
Jonathan Stewart	Lab	181	–
Sarah Mullins	NLP	27	–

*died on 24 Dec 2000; Tom Hamilton (UUP) replaced him on 17 Jan 2001.

Upper Bann

Electorate	70,852	Total Vote	50,399
Quota	7,200	Turnout	72.3%

Party	Candidates	% Vote	Seats
UUP	4	28.9	2
SDLP	2	23.7	1
DUP	2	15.5	1
SF	2	14.3	1
UUU	1	9.6	1
All	1	3.1	
Others	6	4.9	
Total	**18**	**100.0**	**6**

Candidate	Party	1st Pref Votes	Elected
David Trimble	UUP	12,338	1st Count
Bríd Rodgers	SDLP	9,260	1st Count
Denis Watson	UUAP	4,855	14th Count
Dara O'Hagan	SF	4,301	10th Count
Mervyn Carrick	DUP	4,177	13th Count
Ms Ruth Allen	DUP	3,635	–
Francie Murray	SF	2,915	–
Mel Byrne	SDLP	2,687	–
Frank McQuaid	All	1,556	–
David Vance	UKUP	1,405	–
Sam Gardiner	UUP	1,097	–
George Savage	UUP	669	14th Count
Mark Neale	UUP	455	–
Alan Evans	Lab	439	–
Tom French	WP	270	–
Kenny McClinton	Ind	207	–
Brian Silcock	Ind	101	–
Jack Lyons	NLP	32	–

West Tyrone

Electorate	59,081	Total Vote	45,951
Quota	6,565	Turnout	79.4 %

Party	Candidates	% Vote	Seats
SF	3	34.1	2
SDLP	3	25.7	2
DUP	1	17.4	1
UUP	2	15.8	1
Others	6	7.0	
Total	**15**	**100.0**	**6**

Candidate	Party	1st Pref Votes	Elected
Oliver Gibson	DUP	8,015	1st Count
Pat Doherty	SF	7,027	1st Count
Joe Byrne	SDLP	6,495	4th Count
Barry McElduff	SF	4,963	9th Count
Derek Hussey	UUP	4,622	8th Count
Seamus Devine	SF	3,676	–
Eugene McMenamin	SDLP	3,548	9th Count
Alastair Patterson	UUP	2,615	–
Pat McDonnell	SDLP	1,772	–
Paddy McGowan	Ind	1,269	–
Ann Gormley	All	1,011	–
Johnny McLaughlin	Soc	570	–
Laurence O'Kane	Ind	171	–
Tommy Owens	WP	157	–
Robert Johnstone	NLP	40	–

Local Government Elections

Since Northern Ireland's local government structure was reformed in 1973 there have been 8 local government elections across the 26 Local Government Districts (LGDs). Results for the main parties have tended to correspond with overall performance in other elections although independents have featured more strongly.

Turnout for local elections is generally around 50–60 per cent, which is significantly lower than UK government elections, and also lower than the Assembly elections in 1998. This is probably reflective of the fact that the responsibilities of local authorities include areas such as waste disposal, cemeteries and parks, which although vital in everyday life, go largely unnoticed in comparison with mainstream political issues. Nevertheless the parties and candidates fiercely contest the elections, although issues raised at the hustings are matters over which they actually have little authority.

However, turnout for the 2001 local government election, at 66 per cent, was significantly higher than usual. This was largely due to the fact that Westminster elections were held on the same day.

The tables below show summary results for all local government elections since 1985.

2001 Local Government Election

Turnout: 66%

	Votes	% votes	seats	% seats
UUP	181336	22.9	154	26.5
DUP	169477	21.4	131	20.1
SDLP	153424	19.4	117	22.5
SF	163269	20.7	108	18.5
All	40443	5.1	28	4.8
PUP	12661	1.6	4	0.7
Others	70247	8.9	40	6.9
Total	**790857**	**100**	**582**	**100**

1997 Local Government Election

Turnout: 53.6%

	Votes	% votes	seats	% seats
UUP	176239	27.9	185	31.9
DUP	98686	15.6	91	15.6
SDLP	130417	20.6	120	20.6
SF	106938	16.9	74	12.7
All	41421	6.6	41	7
PUP	13744	2.2	6	1
UDP	6244	1	4	0.7
Others	58508	9.2	61	10.5
Total	**632197**	**100**	**582**	**100**

1993 Local Government Election

Turnout: 56.6%

	Votes	% votes	seats	% seats
UUP	184608	29.4	197	33.8
DUP	108863	17.3	103	17.7
SDLP	138619	22	127	21.8
SF	78092	12.4	51	8.8
All	47649	7.6	44	7.6
Others	71275	11.3	60	10.3
Total	**629106**	**100**	**582**	**100**

1989 Local Government Election

Turnout 56.1%

	Votes	% votes	seats	% seats
UUP	193(028)	31.3	194	34.9
DUP	109332	17.7	110	19.8
SDLP	129557	21	121	21.8
SF	69032	11.2	43	7.7
All	42659	6.9	38	6.8
WP	13078	2.1	4	0.7
Others	60523	9.8	46	8.3
Total	**617209**	**100**	**566**	**100**

1985 Local Government Election

Turnout: 60.1%

	Votes	% votes	seats	% seats
UUP	188497	29.5	190	33.6
DUP	155297	24.3	142	25.1
SDLP	113967	17.8	101	17.8
SF	75686	11.8	59	10.4
All	45394	7.1	34	6
WP	10276	1.6	4	0.7
Others	50505	7.9	36	6.4
Total	**639622**	**100**	**566**	**100**

2001 Local Government Elections: Detailed Results

Results are arranged by council, and within each council, by ward. Each ward lists the electorate, the total number of valid votes cast, and the quota for each ward and the turnout for each ward. Every candidate who stood for election is listed, along with his or her party, the number of first-preference votes, and if successful, the count on which they were elected.

Antrim Borough Council

Antrim Borough Council has a total of 19 councillors and 3 wards as follows:

Antrim North West	5 seats
Antrim South East	7 seats
Antrim Town	7 seats

Summary of council

Electorate 32430   Valid Vote 20238   Turnout 62.4%

Party	% Vote	Seats
UUP	33	7
SDLP	21	5
DUP	23	5
SF	13	2
All	6	0
Others	4	0
Total	100	19

Antrim North West (5 seats)

Electorate	8544	Valid Vote	5820
Quota	971	Turnout	69.4%

Party	Candidates	% Vote	Seats
UUP	2	18.2	1
SDLP	2	30.4	2
DUP	1	18.1	1
SF	2	23.9	1
All	1	2.3	
NIUP	1	7.1	
Total	109	100	5

Candidate	Party	1st Pref Votes	Elected
Wilson Clyde	DUP	1053	1st Count
Michael Donoghue	All	133	
Brian Johnston	NIUP	413	
Bobby Loughran	SDLP	1093	1st Count
Joseph McCavana	SF	384	
Donovan McClelland	SDLP	678	5th Count
Martin Meehan	SF	1007	1st Count
Stephen Nicholl	UUP	430	8th Count
Avril Swann	UUP	629	

Antrim South East (7 seats)

Electorate	12770	Valid Vote	8060
Quota	1008	Turnout	64.7%

Party	Candidates	% Vote	Seats
UUP	4	40.4	3
SDLP	2	15.4	1
DUP	2	23.4	2
SF	1	8.7	1
All	1	7.2	
CC	1	4.9	
Total	11	100	7

Candidate	Party	1st Pref Votes	Elected
Thomas Burns	SDLP	1072	1st Count
Samuel Dunlop	DUP	1367	1st Count
William Harkness	DUP	525	9th Count
Sean Mallon	SDLP	168	
Allison McCartney	All	578	
Michael McGivern	Ind	393	
Martin McManus	SF	703	9th Count
Mervyn Rea	UUP	1042	1st Count
Roderick Swann	UUP	213	
Roy Thompson	UUP	1062	1st Count
Edgar Wallace	UUP	937	7th Count

Antrim Town (7 seats)

Electorate	11616	Valid Vote	6358
Quota	795	Turnout	56.4%

Party	Candidates	% Vote	Seats
UUP	4	37.6	3
SDLP	2	19.5	2
DUP	3	25.6	2
SF	1	7.8	
All	1	6.4	
PUP	1	3.1	
Total	12	100	7

Candidate	Party	1st Pref Votes	Elected
Adrian Cochrane-Watson	UUP	632	4th Count
Brian Graham	DUP	516	6th Count
Aine Gribbon	SF	495	
Oran Keenan	SDLP	611	9th Count
Paddy Marks	UUP	1116	1st Count
Jack McClay	DUP	366	
Sean McKee	SDLP	632	9th Count
Paul Michael	UUP	470	6th Count
Drew Ritchie	UUP	268	
John Smyth	DUP	749	3rd Count
Peter Whitcroft	All	406	
Ken Wilkinson	PUP	197	

Ards Borough Council

Ards Borough Council has a total of 23 councillors and 4 wards as follows:

Ards East	6 seats
Ards Peninsula	5 seats
Ards West	6 seats
Newtownards	6 seats

Summary of council

Electorate 38416 Valid Vote 21954 Turnout 57.1%

NB: The above figures do not include Ards East Ward because, there only being 6 candidates, no election took place.

Party	% Vote	Seats
UUP	32	8
SDLP	4	9
DUP	37	1
SF	0	0
All	17	4
Others	10	1
Total	**100**	**23**

Newtownards (6 seats)

Electorate	12965	Valid Vote	7050
Quota	1008	Turnout	56.1%

Party	Candidates	% Vote	Seats
UUP	1	33.3	2
DUP	3	37.5	2
All	1	12.2	1
Ind	2	17.0	1
Total	**7**	**100**	**6**

Candidate	Party	1st Pref Votes	Elected
George Ennis	DUP	1608	1st Count
Thomas Hamilton	UUP	1288	1st Count
Hamilton Lawther	DUP	363	5th Count
Wilbert Magill	Ind	889	2nd Count
Bobby McBride	DUP	671	
Alan McDowell	All	859	3rd Count
Nancy Orr	Ind	312	
David Smyth	UUP	1060	1st Count

Ards West (6 seats)

Electorate	13602	Valid Vote	8030
Quota	1148	Turnout	60.7%

Party	Candidates	% Vote	Seats
UUP	3	42.2	2
DUP	3	36.9	3
All	2	18.5	1
Cons	1	2.4	
Total	**9**	**100**	**6**

Candidate	Party	1st Pref Votes	Elected
Christopher Connolly	Cons	190	
Kathleen Coulter	All	732	
Margaret Craig	DUP	1230	1st Count
Robert Gibson	UUP	2454	1st Count
David Gilmore	DUP	693	6th Count
Jim McBriar	All	756	6th Count
William Montgomery	DUP	1039	6th Count
Philip Smith	UUP	625	2nd Count
Arthur Spence	UUP	311	

Ards Peninsula (5 seats)

Electorate	11849	Valid Vote	6874
Quota	1146	Turnout	59.8%

Party	Candidates	% Vote	Seats
UUP	2	17.9	1
SDLP	1	12.5	1
DUP	2	36.8	2
All	2	19.2	1
Ind	3	13.6	
Total	**10**	**100**	**5**

Candidate	Party	1st Pref Votes	Elected
Ronnie Ambrose	Ind	255	
Joseph Boyle	Ind	526	
Angus Carson	UUP	710	8th Count
Paul Carson	UUP	520	
Robert Drysdale	DUP	705	2nd Count
Danny McCarthy	SDLP	860	7th Count
Kieran McCarthy	All	1286	1st Count
James McMullan	Ind	153	
Stephen McSherry	All	35	
Jim Shannon	DUP	1824	1st Count

Ards East

There was no election in Ards East because six candidates stood for the six seats. Therefore, all candidates were automatically re-elected:

Linda Cleland	All	Ronnie Ferguson	UUP
George Gregory	DUP	Jeff Magill	UUP
John Shields	UUP	Terence Williams	DUP

Armagh City and District Council

Armagh City and District Council has a total of 22 councillors and 4 wards as follows:

Armagh City	6 seats
Crossmore	5 seats
Cusher	6 seats
The Orchard	5 seats

Summary of council

Electorate 38911   Valid Vote 29962   Turnout 77.0%

Party	% Vote	Seats
UUP	26	7
SDLP	24	6
DUP	26	4
SF	21	5
All	0	0
Others	3	0
Total	**100**	**22**

Armagh City (6 seats)

Electorate	10014	Valid Vote	7438
Quota	1063	Turnout	76.0%

Party	Candidates	% Vote	Seats
UUP	2	18.8	1
SDLP	4	29.1	2
DUP	1	11.6	1
SF	2	29.1	2
Ind	1	8.6	
NIWC	1	2.8	
Total	**11**	**100**	**6**

Candidate	Party	1st Pref Votes	Elected
Pat Brannigan	SDLP	1013	4th Count
Mealla Bratton	SDLP	325	
Anna Brolly	SDLP	370	10th Count
Michael Carson	SDLP	456	
Margaret Connolly	NIWC	209	
Freda Donnelly	DUP	861	8th Count
Gordon Frazer	UUP	528	
Pat McNamee	SF	1261	1st Count
Sylvia McRoberts	UUP	868	7th Count
John Nixon	Ind	646	
Cathy Rafferty	SF	901	3rd Count

Cusher Ward (6 seats)

Electorate	11175	Valid Vote	8588
Quota	1227	Turnout	78.1%

Party	Candidates	% Vote	Seats
UUP	4	34.6	3
SDLP	1	11.6	1
DUP	3	44.7	2
SF	1	6.9	
Ind	1	2.2	
Total	**10**	**100**	**6**

Candidate	Party	1st Pref Votes	Elected
Paul Berry	DUP	3549	1st Count
Heather Black	DUP	185	2nd Count
Tom Canavan	SDLP	1001	7th Count
Jimmy Clayton	UUP	679	7th Count
Derrick Matthews	Ind	186	
Sharon McClelland	UUP	367	
Noel Sheridan	SF	591	
Eric Speers	UUP	1202	2nd Count
Mervyn Spratt	DUP	103	
Robert Turner	UUP	725	7th Count

Crossmore (5 seats)

Electorate	8488	Valid Vote	6758
Quota	1127	Turnout	81.1%

Party	Candidates	% Vote	Seats
UUP	1	13.7	1
SDLP	4	39.9	2
DUP	1	13.8	
SF	2	32.6	2
Total	**8**	**100**	**5**

Candidate	Party	1st Pref Votes	Elected
Noel Berry	DUP	930	
Evelyn Corry	UUP	927	7th Count
Brian Cunningham	SF	1336	1st Count
Tommy Kavanagh	SDLP	989	3rd Count
Jim Lennon	SDLP	554	
Joe McGleenan	SDLP	452	
James McKernan	SDLP	703	5th Count
Pat O'Rawe	SF	867	6th Count

The Orchard (5 seats)

Electorate	9234	Valid Vote	7178
Quota	1197	Turnout	79.0%

Party	Candidates	% Vote	Seats
UUP	3	34.3	2
SDLP	2	20.2	1
DUP	2	28.5	1
SF	1	17.0	1
Total	**8**	**100**	**5**

Candidate	Party	1st Pref Votes	Elected
John Campbell	SDLP	796	5th Count
Paul Corrigan	SF	1221	1st Count
Brian Hutchinson	DUP	1363	1st Count
William Irwin	DUP	686	
Eamon McNeill	SDLP	651	
Charles Rollston	UUP	645	5th Count
Jim Speers	UUP	1324	1st Count
Olive Whitten	UUP	492	

Jane Dunlop	All	317	
Simon Hamilton	DUP	411	
Gerard Magee	SF	382	
William McElfatrick	UUP	242	
Joseph McKernan	UUP	613	8th Count
Maurice Mills	DUP	625	9th Count
William Parkhill	PUP	30	
Gillian Scott	UUP	532	
Audrey Wales	Ind	263	
William Wright	Ind	553	9th Count

Ballymena Borough Council

Ballymena Borough Council has 24 councillors and 4 wards as follows:

Ballymena North	7 seats
Ballymena South	7 seats
Bannside	5 seats
Braid	5 seats

Summary of council

Electorate 43948   Valid Vote 28833   Turnout 65.6%

Party	% Vote	Seats
UUP	27	7
SDLP	16	4
DUP	45	11
SF	1	0
All	1	0
Others	10	2
Total	**100**	**24**

Ballymena North (7 seats)

Electorate 12286   Valid Vote 7742
Quota 968   Turnout 63.0%

Party	Candidates	% Vote	Seats
UUP	4	24.8	2
SDLP	1	13.8	1
DUP	3	27.8	2
SF	1	4.9	
All	1	4.1	
Ind	3	24.2	2
PUP	1	0.4	
Total	**14**	**100**	**7**

Candidate	Party	1st Pref Votes	Elected
James Alexander	DUP	1110	1st Count
James Henry	Ind	1060	1st Count
PJ McAvoy	SDLP	1071	1st Count
James Armstrong	UUP	533	9th Count

Ballymena South (7 seats)

Electorate 11772   Valid Vote 7007
Quota 877   Turnout 60.0%

Party	Candidates	% Vote	Seats
UUP	2	22.1	2
SDLP	1	17.3	1
DUP	5	55.8	4
PUP	2	1.4	
Ind	1	3.4	
Total	**11**	**100**	**7**

Candidate	Party	1st Pref Votes	Elected
Elizabeth Adger	DUP	1061	1st Count
Peter Brown	UUP	459	9th Count
Martin Clarke	DUP	793	5th Count
James Currie	UUP	1092	1st Count
William McCaughey	PUP	51	
William Moore	DUP	285	
Hubert Nicholl	DUP	755	6th Count
Declan O'Loan	SDLP	1212	1st Count
Jean Rainey	PUP	43	
David Tweed	DUP	1018	1st Count
David Warwick	Ind	241	

Bannside (5 seats)

Electorate 10493   Valid Vote 7460
Quota 1244   Turnout 72.0%

Party	Candidates	% Vote	Seats
UUP	2	24.0	1
SDLP	2	17.6	1
DUP	4	55.2	3
NIUP	1	2.5	
PUP	1	0.7	
Total	**10**	**100**	**5**

Candidate	Party	1st Pref Votes	Elected
Samuel Gaston	DUP	890	6th Count
Roy Gillespie	DUP	1427	1st Count
Seamus Laverty	SDLP	938	4th Count
Kenneth McCaughey	PUP	53	
Samuel McClean	UUP	727	

William McNeilly	UUP	1060	5th Count
Joseph Montgomery	SDLP	375	
Thomas Nicholl	DUP	962	6th Count
Norman Sloan	NIUP	186	
William Wilkinson	DUP	842	

Braid (5 seats)

Electorate	9397	Valid Vote	6624
Quota	1105	Turnout	71.4%

Party	Candidates	% Vote	Seats
UUP	3	40.3	2
SDLP	1	17.5	1
DUP	3	41.8	2
PUP	1	0.4	
Total	8	100	5

Candidate	Party	1st Pref Votes	Elected
Desmond Armstrong	UUP	815	
David Clyde	UUP	961	6th Count
Margaret Gribben	SDLP	1158	1st Count
Robert Hamilton	PUP	29	
Samuel Hanna	DUP	1242	1st Count
Robert Osborne	DUP	707	
Lexie Scott	UUP	893	6th Count
Robin Stirling	DUP	819	4th Count

Ballymoney Borough Council

Ballymoney Borough Council has a total of 16 councillors and 3 wards as follows:

Ballymoney Town	5 seats
Bann Valley	6 seats
Bushvale	5 seats

Summary of council

Electorate 19277   Valid Vote 12558   Turnout 65.1%

Party	% Vote	Seats
UUP	24	5
SDLP	18	2
DUP	42	8
SF	11	1
All	0	0
Others	5	0
Total	100%	16

Ballymoney Town (6 seats)

Electorate	6187	Valid Vote	3733
Quota	623	Turnout	61.5%

Party	Candidates	% Vote	Seats
UUP	3	26.9	2
SDLP	1	12.3	0
DUP	3	44.2	3
Ind	3	16.6	
Total	10	100	5

Candidate	Party	1st Pref Votes	Elected
Jeffrey Balmer	Ind	125	
Cecil Cousley	DUP	788	1st Count
William Johnston	UUP	257	
Anne Logan	Ind	119	
Justin McCamphill	SDLP	459	
Thomas McKeown	UUP	396	3rd Count
James Simpson	UUP	351	5th Count
Ian Stevenson	DUP	433	4th Count
Robert Storey	DUP	429	4th Count
Jim Wright	Ind	376	

Bann Valley (6 seats)

Electorate	7451	Valid Vote	5220
Quota	746	Turnout	71.7%

Party	Candidates	% Vote	Seats
UUP	2	18.6	1
SDLP	2	20.1	1
DUP	3	39.7	3
SF	1	21.5	1
Total	8	100	6

Candidate	Party	1st Pref Votes	Elected
John Finlay	DUP	859	1st Count
Joseph Gaston	UUP	711	3rd Count
Robert Halliday	DUP	675	4th Count
Malachy McCamphill	SDLP	663	2nd Count
Philip McGuigan	SF	1123	1st Count
Paddy O'Kane	SDLP	388	
John Watt	UUP	261	
Robert Wilson	DUP	540	5th Count

Bushvale (5 seats)

Electorate	5706	Valid Vote	3605
Quota	601	Turnout	63.2%

Party	Candidates	% Vote	Seats
UUP	2	27.8	2
SDLP	2	19.4	1
DUP	2	44.0	2
SF	1	8.8	
Total	7	100	5

Candidate	Party	1st Pref Votes	Elected
Frank Campbell	DUP	589	2nd Count
Harry Connolly	SDLP	548	3rd Count
Bill Kennedy	DUP	997	1st Count
William Logan	UUP	457	3rd Count
Francis McCluskey	SDLP	151	
Sean McErlain	SF	318	
John Ramsay	UUP	545	3rd Count

Banbridge District Council

Banbridge District Council has 17 councillors and 3 wards as follows:

Banbridge Town	6 seats
Dromore	5 seats
Knockiveagh	6 seats

Summary of council

Electorate 30293   Valid Vote 20568   Turnout 67.9%

Party	% Vote	Seats
UUP	37	7
SDLP	19	3
DUP	28	5
SF	4	0
All	2	1
Others	10	1
Total	**100**	**17**

Banbridge Town (6 seats)

Electorate   10939   Valid Vote   7054
Quota   1008   Turnout   65.6%

Party	Candidates	% Vote	Seats
UUP	3	41.4	3
SDLP	1	19.9	1
DUP	2	20.9	1
UKUP	1	5.5	
All	1	6.0	1
Ind	1	6.3	
Total	**9**	**100**	**6**

Candidate	Party	1st Pref Votes	Elected
Joan Baird	UUP	1979	1st Count
Derek Bell	UUP	458	2nd Count
Ian Burns	UUP	485	6th Count
Frank Downey	Ind	448	
Kyle Ferguson	DUP	697	
David Hudson	UKUP	389	
Pat McAleenan	SDLP	1404	1st Count
Jim McElroy	DUP	774	6th Count
Frank McQuaid	All	420	5th Count

Dromore (5 seats)

Electorate   9149   Valid Vote   6129
Quota   1022   Turnout   68.1%

Party	Candidates	% Vote	Seats
UUP	2	29.2	2
SDLP	1	19.6	1
DUP	2	39.3	2
NIUP	1	0.7	
Ind	1	11.2	
Total	**7**	**100**	**5**

Candidate	Party	1st Pref Votes	Elected
Nora Beare	UUP	896	3rd Count
David Herron	DUP	1032	1st Count
Thompson Howe	Ind	685	
William Martin	UUP	894	3rd Count
Cassie McDermott	SDLP	1202	1st Count
Joe McIlwaine	NIUP	45	
Paul Rankin	DUP	1375	1st Count

Knockiveagh (6 seats)

Electorate   9937   Valid Vote   7385
Quota   1056   Turnout   75.4%

Party	Candidates	% Vote	Seats
UUP	3	31.2	2
SDLP	1	18.3	1
DUP	2	24.6	2
SF	1	10.2	
UKUP	1	5.3	
Ind	1	10.4	1
Total	**9**	**100**	**6**

Candidate	Party	1st Pref Votes	Elected
Stephen Briggs	UKUP	387	
Violet Cromie	UUP	486	
Brendan Curran	SF	755	
Seamus Doyle	SDLP	1351	1st Count
John Hanna	UUP	617	5th Count
Stephen Herron	DUP	735	5th Count
John Ingram	UUP	1202	1st Count
Malachy McCartan	Ind	768	5th Count
Wilfred McFadden	DUP	1084	6th Count

Belfast City Council

Belfast City Council has 51 councillors and 9 wards as follows:

Balmoral	6 seats
Castle	6 seats
Court	5 seats
Lower Falls	5 seats
Upper Falls	5 seats
Laganbank	5 seats
Oldpark	6 seats
Pottinger	6 seats
Victoria	7 seats

Summary of council

Electorate 167869   Valid Vote 122188   Turnout 72.8%

Party	% Vote	Seats
UUP	18	11
SDLP	17	9
DUP	18	10
SF	28	14
All	7	3
Others	12	4
Total	**100**	**51**

Court (5 seats)

Electorate	15674	Valid Vote	9752
Quota	1626	Turnout	64.3%

Party	Candidates	% Vote	Seats
UUP	2	23.1	1
DUP	2	34.1	2
SF	1	2.7	
UDP	1	17.8	1
UTW	1	0.3	
PUP	2	22.0	1
Total	**9**	**100**	**5**

Candidate	Party	1st Pref Votes	Elected
Fred Cobain	UUP	722	
Mick Conlon	SF	269	
David Kerr	UTW	28	
Frank McCoubrey	UDP	1732	1st Count
Chris McGimpsey	UUP	1527	1st Count
Elaine McMillen	DUP	720	5th Count
William Smyth	PUP	813	
Eric Smyth	DUP	2605	1st Count
Hugh Smyth	PUP	1336	5th Count

Laganbank (5 seats)

Electorate	17799	Valid Vote	10832
Quota	1806	Turnout	62.7%

Party	Candidates	% Vote	Seats
UUP	2	26.2	2
SDLP	2	28.8	2
DUP	1	8.1	
SF	1	16.2	1
All	1	7.6	
PUP	1	2.6	
Ind	2	2.5	
NIWC	1	6.5	
WP	1	1.5	
Total	**12**	**100**	**5**

Candidate	Party	1st Pref Votes	Elected
Jim Clarke	UUP	819	7th Count
Andrew Frew	Ind	141	
Mark Long	All	825	
Patrick Lynn	WP	158	
Patrick McCarthy	SDLP	1511	6th Count
Michael McGimpsey	UUP	2019	1st Count
Alex Maskey	SF	1748	5th Count
Anne Monaghan	NIWC	703	
Barbara Muldoon	Ind	128	
Peter O'Reilly	SDLP	1612	5th Count
Dawn Purvis	PUP	286	
Richard Scott	DUP	882	

Castle (6 seats)

Electorate	21068	Valid Vote	14132
Quota	2019	Turnout	68.8%

Party	Candidates	% Vote	Seats
UUP	1	11.0	1
SDLP	2	27.8	2
DUP	2	33.3	2
SF	1	14.1	1
All	1	6.9	
PUP	1	2.5	
Ind	2	2.0	
WP	1	0.6	
NIWC	1	1.8	
Total	**12**	**100**	**6**

Candidate	Party	1st Pref Votes	Elected
Alexander Blair	Ind	109	
David Browne	UUP	1550	8th Count
Elizabeth Byrne-McCullough	NIWC	253	
Thomas Campbell	All	984	

Janet Carson	PUP	352	
Patrick Convery	SDLP	1403	8th Count
Ian Crozier	DUP	759	2nd Count
Marcella Delaney	WP	84	
Nigel Dodds	DUP	3949	1st Count
Danny Lavery	SF	1991	3rd Count
Alban Maginness	SDLP	2520	1st Count
David Mahood	Ind	178	

Balmoral (6 seats)

Electorate	20958	Valid Vote	13614
Quota	1945	Turnout	66.2%

Party	Candidates	% Vote	Seats
UUP	2	19.7	1
SDLP	2	29.9	2
DUP	2	25.0	2
SF	1	9.9	
All	1	12.4	1
PUP	1	3.1	
Total	**9**	**100**	**6**

Candidate	Party	1st Pref Votes	Elected
Margaret Crooks	UUP	2276	1st Count
Thomas Ekin	All	1684	4th Count
Carmel Hanna	SDLP	3077	1st Count
John Hiddleston	UUP	411	
Stephen Long	SF	1349	
Catherine Molloy	SDLP	987	3rd Count
Thomas Morrow	PUP	421	
Ruth Patterson	DUP	1377	4th Count
Robert Stoker	DUP	2032	1st Count

Upper Falls (5 seats)

Electorate	22107	Valid Vote	15358
Quota	2560	Turnout	72.2%

Party	Candidates	% Vote	Seats
SDLP	2	28.5	1
SF	4	68.3	4
All	1	0.9	
NIWC	1	2.3	
Total	**8**	**100**	**5**

Candidate	Party	1st Pref Votes	Elected
Alex Attwood	SDLP	3260	1st Count
Mary Ayres	All	136	
Michael Browne	SF	2469	3rd Count
Mary Catney	NIWC	365	
Brian Heading	SDLP	1112	
Paul Maskey	SF	3349	1st Count
Chrissie McAuley	SF	1801	4th Count
Gerard O'Neill	SF	2866	1st Count

Lower Falls (5 seats)

Electorate	18349	Valid Vote	12648
Quota	2109	Turnout	72.1%

Party	Candidates	% Vote	Seats
SDLP	1	15.9	1
SF	5	80.2	4
WP	1	3.9	
Total	**7**	**100**	**5**

Candidate	Party	1st Pref Votes	Elected
Marie Cush	SF	2230	1st Count
Tom Hartley	SF	2351	1st Count
John Lowry	WP	488	
Fra McCann	SF	2399	1st Count
Sean McKnight	SF	1247	
Marie Moore	SF	1917	5th Count
Margaret Walsh	SDLP	2016	2nd Count

Oldpark (6 seats)

Electorate	23866	Valid Vote	15975
Quota	2283	Turnout	69.8%

Party	Candidates	% Vote	Seats
UUP	1	7.0	
SDLP	2	19.1	1
DUP	1	14.9	1
SF	4	46.8	3
All	1	1.0	
PUP	1	9.5	1
Ind	2	1.7	
Total	**12**	**100**	**6**

Candidate	Party	1st Pref Votes	Elected
James Bates	Ind	209	
Gerard Brophy	SF	2755	1st Count
Joleen Connolly	SDLP	1114	
Rene Greig	Ind	59	
William Hutchinson	PUP	1516	6th Count
Nelson McCausland	DUP	2392	1st Count
Margaret McClenaghan	SF	2467	1st Count
Thomas McCullough	All	160	
Martin Morgan	SDLP	1932	1st Count
Eoin O'Broin	SF	957	8th Count
Fred Proctor	UUP	1116	
Kathy Stanton	SF	1298	

Victoria (7 seats)

Electorate	28160	Valid Vote	16909	
Quota	2114	Turnout	62.0%	

Party	Candidates	% Vote	Seats
UUP	3	36.6	3
SDLP	1	1.8	
DUP	3	28.1	2
Cons	1	1.4	
All	2	22.8	2
PUP	1	4.1	
Ind	4	5.2	
Total	**15**	**100**	**7**

Candidate	Party	1st Pref Votes	Elected
Ian Adamson	UUP	3286	1st Count
David Alderdice	All	3119	1st Count
Wallace Browne	DUP	2492	1st Count
Alan Crowe	UUP	582	8th Count
Danny Dow	Ind	746	
Ciara Farren	SDLP	305	
Peter Gray	Cons	239	
Billy Hands	Ind	15	
Lawrence John	Ind	11	
Naomi Long	All	729	9th Count
Margaret McKenzie	DUP	783	
Robert Moorhead	PUP	697	
Robin Newton	DUP	1469	9th Count
Jim Rogers	UUP	2322	1st Count
Sammy Walker	Ind	114	

Pottinger

Electorate	21854	Valid Vote	12968	
Quota	1853	Turnout	61.4%	

Party	Candidates	% Vote	Seats
UUP	2	28.2	2
SDLP	1	3.5	
DUP	3	36.2	2
SF	1	9.7	1
All	1	5.3	
PUP	2	13.2	1
Ind	1	1.7	
UKUP	1	0.6	
WP	1	1.0	
Cons	1	0.6	
Total	**14**	**100**	**6**

Candidate	Party	1st Pref Votes	Elected
Joseph Bell	WP	129	
John Bushell	Ind	218	
Mary Campbell	DUP	577	
Margaret Clarke	UUP	559	10th Count
Jason Docherty	Cons	66	

Reg Empey	UUP	3097	1st Count
David Ervine	PUP	1582	3rd Count
David Fairfield	UKUP	74	
Mervyn Jones	All	693	
Joseph O'Donnell	SF	1264	10th Count
Robin Stewart	PUP	127	
Harry Toan	DUP	205	10th Count
Leo van Es	SDLP	459	
Sammy Wilson	DUP	3918	1st Count

Carrickfergus Borough Council

Carrickfergus Borough Council has a total of 17 councillors and 3 wards as follows:

Carrick Castle	5 seats
Kilroot	6 seats
Knockagh Monument	6 seats

Summary of council

Electorate 27257 Valid Vote 15418 Turnout 56.6%

Party	% Vote	Seats
UUP	24	4
SDLP	0	0
DUP	32	6
SF	0	0
All	24	5
Others	20	2
Total	**100%**	**17**

Carrick Castle (5 seats)

Electorate	6542	Valid Vote	3583	
Quota	598	Turnout	54.8%	

Party	Candidates	% Vote	Seats
UUP	1	12.1	1
DUP	2	31.4	2
PUP	1	7.3	
Ind	3	27.6	1
All	2	21.6	1
Total	**9**	**100**	**5**

Candidate	Party	1st Pref Votes	Elected
David Beck	PUP	259	
William Cameron	Ind	303	
Darin Ferguson	UUP	435	6th Count
William Hamilton	Ind	552	4th Count
Margaret Hawkins	All	112	
David Hilditch	DUP	996	1st Count
Patricia McKinney	DUP	130	6th Count
Sean Neeson	All	662	1st Count
Nicholas Wady	Ind	134	

Kilroot (6 seats)

Electorate	10903	Valid Vote	6184	
Quota	884	Turnout	58.1%	

Party	Candidates	% Vote	Seats
UUP	1	17.7	1
DUP	2	30.0	2
All	2	24.1	2
Ind	2	28.2	1
Total	**7**	**100**	**6**

Candidate	Party	1st Pref Votes	Elected
William Ashe	DUP	1425	1st Count
James Brown	Ind	1275	1st Count
Robert Cavan	All	684	4th Count
Terence Clements	DUP	430	2nd Count
Janet Crampsey	All	807	3rd Count
Sam Crowe	Ind	470	
Eric Ferguson	UUP	1093	1st Count

Knockagh Monument (6 seats)

Electorate	9812	Valid Vote	5651	
Quota	808	Turnout	59.0%	

Party	Candidates	% Vote	Seats
UUP	2	38.9	2
DUP	2	34.0	2
PUP	1	2.9	
All	2	24.2	2
Total	**7**	**100**	**6**

Candidate	Party	1st Pref Votes	Elected
May Beattie	DUP	1420	1st Count
Roy Beggs	UUP	1575	1st Count
Stewart Dickson	All	1165	1st Count
Carolyn Howarth	PUP	166	
James McClurg	DUP	501	3rd Count
Noreen McIlwrath	All	199	6th Count
Gwen Wilson	UUP	625	2nd Count

Castlereagh Borough Council

Castlereagh Borough Council has a total of 23 councillors and 4 wards as follows:

Castlereagh Central	6 seats
Castlereagh East	7 seats
Castlereagh South	5 seats
Castlereagh West	5 seats

Summary of council

Electorate   48943 Valid Vote 30682   Turnout 62.7%

Party	% Vote	Seats
UUP	22	5
SDLP	11	2
DUP	39	10
SF	2	0
All	15	4
Others	11	2
Total	**100**	**23**

Castlereagh East (7 seats)

Electorate	15245	Valid Vote	9159	
Quota	1145	Turnout	62.0%	

Party	Candidates	% Vote	Seats
UUP	1	20.5	1
DUP	5	50.2	5
PUP	1	5.1	
Ind	2	9.8	
All	2	14.4	1
Total	**11**	**100**	**7**

Candidate	Party	1st Pref Votes	Elected
William Abraham	Ind	245	
David Drysdale	UUP	1879	1st Count
Claire Ennis	DUP	204	7th Count
Francis Gallagher	Ind	650	7th Count
Sandy Geddis	DUP	92	
Gillian Graham	All	400	
Richard Johnston	PUP	466	
Kim Morton	DUP	120	7th Count
Peter Osborne	All	923	3rd Count
Iris Robinson	DUP	4093	1st Count
Jim White	DUP	87	5th Count

Castlereagh South (5 seats)

Electorate	12212	Valid Vote	7992	
Quota	1333	Turnout	66.8%	

Party	Candidates	% Vote	Seats
UUP	2	27.0	2
SDLP	2	23.6	1
DUP	2	26.3	1
SF	1	5.0	
All	2	17.5	1
Cons	1	0.6	
Total	**10**	**100**	**5**

Candidate	Party	1st Pref Votes	Elected
John Beattie	DUP	1590	1st Count
Christine Copeland	SDLP	949	
Brian Hanvey	SDLP	940	9th Count
Michael Henderson	UUP	1725	1st Count
Roger Lomas	Cons	52	
Sean Hayes	SF	396	
Margaret Marshall	All	381	
Barbara McBurney	UUP	431	7th Count
Andrew Ramsey	DUP	509	
Geraldine Rice	All	1019	6th Count

Castlereagh West (5 seats)

Electorate	10958	Valid Vote	6830
Quota	1139	Turnout	64.0%

Party	Candidates	% Vote	Seats
UUP	1	25.3	1
SDLP	1	17.5	1
DUP	3	29.4	2
SF	1	2.3	
All	1	16.6	1
PUP	1	4.4	
NIWC	1	4.5	
Total	**9**	**100**	**5**

Candidate	Party	1st Pref Votes	Elected
Eileen Cairnduff	NIWC	306	
Sara Duncan	All	1130	2nd Count
Frederick Ferguson	PUP	301	
Cecil Hall	UUP	1728	1st Count
Rosaleen Hughes	SDLP	1196	1st Count
Sean Montgomery	SF	158	
Simon Robinson	DUP	1858	1st Count
Vivienne Stephenson	DUP	61	6th Count
Charles Tosh	DUP	92	

Castlereagh Central (6 seats)

Electorate	10528	Valid Vote	6701
Quota	958	Turnout	65.9%

Party	Candidates	% Vote	Seats
UUP	1	15.4	1
SDLP	1	6.4	
DUP	4	50.4	3
UKUP	1	4.3	
All	1	11.5	1
PUP	1	7.5	1
Ind	1	3.3	
Cons	1	1.2	
Total	**11**	**100**	**6**

Candidate	Party	1st Pref Votes	Elected
Joanne Bunting	DUP	302	2nd Count
Alan Carson	Ind	219	
Michael Copeland	UUP	1032	1st Count
Terence Dick	Cons	82	
Grant Dillon	UKUP	289	
John Dunn	DUP	74	
Michael Long	All	769	2nd Count
Sean Mullan	SDLP	427	
John Norris	DUP	161	2nd Count
Peter Robinson	DUP	2841	1st Count
Thomas Sandford	PUP	505	2nd Count

Coleraine Borough Council

Coleraine Borough Council has a total of 22 councillors and 4 wards as follows:

Bann	6 seats
Coleraine Central	6 seats
Coleraine East	5 seats
The Skerries	5 seats

Summary of council

Electorate 39018   Valid Vote 24495   Turnout 62.8%

Party	% Vote	Seats
UUP	36	10
SDLP	20	4
DUP	28	7
SF	0	0
All	6	0
Others	10	1
Total	100	22

Coleraine East (5 seats)

Electorate	8415	Valid Vote	4753
Quota	793	Turnout	57.8%

Party	Candidates	% Vote	Seats
UUP	2	26.7	2
SDLP	1	7.7	
DUP	3	44.2	3
All	1	5.8	
PUP	1	3.1	
Ind	3	12.5	
Total	**11**	**100**	**5**

Candidate	Party	1st Pref Votes	Elected
Toye Black	UUP	808	1st Count
Maurice Bradley	DUP	1389	1st Count
Alistair Crawford	Ind	149	
William Creelman	DUP	596	2nd Count
Phyllis Fielding	DUP	118	9th Count
David Gilmour	PUP	146	
Thomas Houston	Ind	319	
Martin Hunter	Ind	126	
Paddy McGowan	All	274	
Robert McPherson	UUP	460	8th Count
John Montgomery	SDLP	368	

Bann (6 seats)

Electorate	10232	Valid Vote	7383
Quota	1055	Turnout	73.7%

Party	Candidates	% Vote	Seats
UUP	3	34.0	3
SDLP	2	30.5	2
DUP	2	20.0	1
Ind	2	13.9	
All	1	1.6	
Total	**10**	**100**	**6**

Candidate	Party	1st Pref Votes	Elected
Robert Bolton	Ind	514	
Yvonne Boyle	All	116	
Olive Church	UUP	986	5th Count
John Dallat	SDLP	1714	1st Count
William King	UUP	821	6th Count
Reginald McAuley	Ind	512	
Adrian McQuillan	DUP	1216	1st Count
Eamon Mullan	SDLP	535	2nd Count
Hazel Sommers	DUP	265	
James Watt	UUP	704	6th Count

Coleraine Central (6 seats)

Electorate	11571	Valid Vote	6993
Quota	1000	Turnout	61.6%

Party	Candidates	% Vote	Seats
UUP	3	44.7	3
SDLP	1	17.6	1
DUP	2	30.4	2
All	1	7.3	
Total	**7**	**100**	**6**

Candidate	Party	1st Pref Votes	Elected
David Barbour	UUP	717	3rd Count
Timothy Deans	DUP	699	2nd Count
Elizabeth Johnston	UUP	1016	1st Count
David McClarty	UUP	1395	1st Count
James McClure	DUP	1426	1st Count
Gerry McLaughlin	SDLP	1232	1st Count
Eamon O'Hara	All	508	

The Skerries (5 seats)

Electorate	8800	Valid Vote	5366
Quota	895	Turnout	61.9%

Party	Candidates	% Vote	Seats
UUP	3	35.5	2
SDLP	1	18.4	1
DUP	2	19.3	1
All	1	12.7	
Ind	1	14.1	1
Total	**8**	**100**	**5**

Candidate	Party	1st Pref Votes	Elected
Christine Alexander	Ind	757	5th Count
Pauline Armitage	UUP	729	5th Count
Barbara Dempsey	All	681	
Alexander Gilkinson	DUP	359	
Norman Hillis	UUP	625	4th Count
Samuel Kane	UUP	552	
Billy Leonard	SDLP	988	1st Count
Desmond Stewart	DUP	675	2nd Count

Cookstown District Council

Cookstown District Council has a total of 16 councillors and 3 wards as follows:

Ballinderry	6 seats
Cookstown Central	5 seats
Drum Manor	5 seats

Summary of council

Electorate 23065 Valid Vote 18726   Turnout 81.2%

Party	% Vote	Seats
UUP	21	3
SDLP	24	4
DUP	18	2
SF	33	6
All	0	0
Others	4	1
Total	**100**	**16**

Cookstown Central (5 seats)

Electorate	7503	Valid Vote	5656
Quota	943	Turnout	77.0%

Party	Candidates	% Vote	Seats
UUP	2	27.6	1
SDLP	2	19.8	1
DUP	2	20.9	1
SF	2	31.7	2
Total	**8**	**100**	**5**

Candidate	Party	1st Pref Votes	Elected
Seamus Campbell	SF	364	6th Count
Peter Cassidy	SDLP	792	5th Count
Albert Crawford	UUP	238	
Hugh Davidson	DUP	120	
Eddie Espie	SDLP	328	
Ian McCrea	DUP	1064	1st Count
John McNamee	SF	1427	1st Count
Trevor Wilson	UUP	1323	1st Count

Ballinderry (6 seats)

Electorate	8938	Valid Vote	7421
Quota	1061	Turnout	84.8%

Party	Candidates	% Vote	Seats
UUP	2	17.2	1
SDLP	2	32.5	2
DUP	2	20.3	1
SF	2	30.0	2
Total	**8**	**100**	**6**

Candidate	Party	1st Pref Votes	Elected
Mary Baker	SDLP	641	2nd Count
Walter Greer	UUP	946	5th Count
Pearse McAleer	SF	1567	1st Count
Samuel McCartney	DUP	537	
Anne McCrea	DUP	969	5th Count
William McCollum	UUP	334	
Patsy McGlone	SDLP	1771	1st Count
Michael McIvor	SF	656	3rd Count

Drum Manor (5 seats)

Electorate	6624	Valid Vote	5649
Quota	942	Turnout	86.6%

Party	Candidates	% Vote	Seats
UUP	1	19.8	1
SDLP	1	15.6	1
DUP	1	13.4	
SF	2	39.0	2
Ind	1	12.2	1
Total	**6**	**100**	**5**

Candidate	Party	1st Pref Votes	Elected
Sam Glasgow	UUP	1118	1st Count
Dessie Grimes	SF	1233	1st Count
Maureen Lees	DUP	756	
James McGarvey	SDLP	884	2nd Count
Oliver Molloy	SF	969	1st Count
Sam Parke	Ind	689	5th Count

Craigavon Borough Council

Craigavon Borough Council has 26 councillors and 4 wards as follows:

Central	7 seats
Loughside	5 seats
Lurgan	7 seats
Portadown	7 seats

Summary of council

Electorate 56717 Valid Vote 39645 Turnout 69.9%

Party	% Vote	Seats
UUP	28	8
SDLP	20	7
DUP	23	6
SF	21	4
All	2	0
Others	6	1
Total	**100**	**26**

Central (7 seats)

Electorate	15747	Valid Vote	10633
Quota	1330	Turnout	67.5%

Party	Candidates	% Vote	Seats
UUP	4	29.5	2
SDLP	2	16.4	2
DUP	3	24.3	2
SF	2	16.9	1
All	1	3.6	
WP	1	1.2	
Ind	2	7.2	
Total	**15**	**100**	**7**

Candidate	Party	1st Pref Votes	Elected
David Calvert	Ind	761	
Kieran Corr	SDLP	745	Elected*
Frederick Crowe	UUP	802	9th Count
Alan Evans	Ind	96	
Tom French	WP	132	
Sean Hagan	All	379	
Audrey Lindsay	UUP	250	
Patricia Mallon	SDLP	996	7th Count
Samuel McCammick	UUP	396	
Francis Murray	SF	1198	6th Count
Robert Smith	DUP	810	Elected*
Woolsey Smith	DUP	1060	10th Count
Peter Toland	SF	602	
Kenneth Twyble	UUP	1694	1st Count
Denis Watson	DUP	712	

* Elected without reaching quota

Loughside (5 seats)

Electorate	12545	Valid Vote	8851
Quota	1476	Turnout	72.6%

Party	Candidates	% Vote	Seats
UUP	1	4.9	
SDLP	4	47.2	3
DUP	1	2.9	
SF	3	45.0	2
Total	**9**	**100**	**5**

Candidate	Party	1st Pref Votes	Elected
Alexander Dougan	DUP	261	
Dolores Kelly	SDLP	2022	1st Count
William Lindsay	UUP	433	
Maurice Magill	SF	1131	2nd Count
Mary McAlinden	SDLP	735	2nd Count
Kieran McGeown	SDLP	360	
Sean McKavanagh	SDLP	1055	2nd Count
John O'Dowd	SF	1971	1st Count
Mairead O'Dowd	SF	883	

Lurgan (7 seats)

Electorate	14911	Valid Vote	10510
Quota	1314	Turnout	72.1%

Party	Candidates	% Vote	Seats
UUP	5	47.1	4
SDLP	1	7.6	1
DUP	2	33.3	2
SF	1	6.9	
Ind	1	1.2	
UKUP	1	3.9	
Total	**11**	**100**	**7**

Candidate	Party	1st Pref Votes	Elected
Jonathan Bell	DUP	1942	1st Count
Sydney Cairns	UUP	749	5th Count
Meta Crozier	UUP	965	3rd Count
Samuel Gardiner	UUP	1728	1st Count
William Grafton	Ind	130	
Mary McNally	SDLP	801	5th Count
Stephen Moutray	DUP	1555	1st Count
Matthew Rooney	SF	719	
George Savage	UUP	1237	2nd Count
William Tate	UUP	276	
David Vance	UKUP	408	

Portadown (7 seats)

Electorate	13514	Valid Vote	9651
Quota	1207	Turnout	73.2%

Party	Candidates	% Vote	Seats
UUP	4	26.9	2
SDLP	1	12.8	1
DUP	3	27.3	2
SF	2	20.2	1
All	1	2.8	
Ind	1	10.0	1
Total	**12**	**100**	**7**

Candidate	Party	1st Pref Votes	Elected
Sydney Anderson	UUP	883	8th Count
Alan Carson	DUP	213	9th Count
Ignatius Fox	SDLP	1233	1st Count
George Hatch	UUP	872	8th Count
Davy Jones	Ind	971	8th Count
Brian McKeown	SF	1348	1st Count
Noel Mercer	SF	604	
Mark Neale	UUP	462	
William Ramsey	All	266	
David Simpson	DUP	2352	1st Count
John Tate	DUP	67	
David Thompson	UUP	380	

Derry City Council

Derry City Council has 30 councillors and 5 wards as follows:

Cityside	5 seats
Northland	7 seats
Rural	6 seats
Shantallow	5 seats
Waterside	7 seats

Summary of council

Electorate 71476 Valid Vote 48045 Turnout 67.2%

Party	% Vote	Seats
UUP	6	2
SDLP	43	14
DUP	14	4
SF	30	10
All	1	0
Others	6	0
Total	**100**	**30**

Shantallow (5 seats)

Electorate	15381	Valid Vote	10228
Quota	1705	Turnout	68.6%

Party	Candidates	% Vote	Seats
SDLP	4	56.1	3
SF	4	38.6	2
Ind	1	5.3	
Total	**9**	**100**	**5**

Candidate	Party	1st Pref Votes	Elected
Mary Bradley	SDLP	2304	1st Count
Shaun Gallagher	SDLP	1287	3rd Count
Oliver Green	SF	1084	
Tony Hassan	SF	1237	4th Count
Charles McDaid	Ind	542	
Josephine McGinty	SF	384	
William O'Connell	SDLP	1135	5th Count
Ciaran O'Doherty	SDLP	1017	
Gearoid O'hEara	SF	1238	4th Count

Rural (6 seats)

Electorate	14409	Valid Vote	9829
Quota	1405	Turnout	69.0%

Party	Candidates	% Vote	Seats
UUP	2	16.6	1
SDLP	3	39.9	3
DUP	2	24.3	1
SF	2	16.5	1
All	1	1.7	
Total	**10**	**100**	**6**

Candidate	Party	1st Pref Votes	Elected
Thomas Conway	SDLP	1274	4th Count
Annie Courtney	SDLP	1444	1st Count
Andrew Davidson	UUP	1074	6th Count
Paul Fleming	SF	943	7th Count
Ernest Hamilton	UUP	554	
William Hay	DUP	1511	1st Count
Bill Irwin	DUP	879	
Brian Kelly	All	166	
James Kelly	SF	677	
Jim McKeever	SDLP	796	10th Count
Brenda Stevenson	SDLP	511	

City Side (5 seats)

Electorate	9244	Valid Vote	6627
Quota	1105	Turnout	75.0%

Party	Candidates	% Vote	Seats
SDLP	3	45.5	2
SF	4	51.1	3
Ind	1	3.4	
Total	**8**	**100**	**5**

Candidate	Party	1st Pref Votes	Elected
Jim Anderson	SF	989	5th Count
Liam Boyle	SDLP	629	
James Clifford	SDLP	1176	1st Count
Cathal Crumley	SF	1093	1st Count
Seana Deery	Ind	228	
Donncha MacNiallais	SF	618	
Barney O'Hagan	SF	684	6th Count
Pat Ramsey	SDLP	1210	1st Count

Waterside (7 seats)

Electorate	15882	Valid Vote	10354
Quota	1295	Turnout	66.6%

Party	Candidates	% Vote	Seats
UUP	3	13.9	1
SDLP	2	20.7	2
DUP	4	43.3	3
SF	2	12.7	1
All	1	2.6	
PUP	1	1.5	
Ind	2	5.3	
Total	**15**	**100**	**7**

Candidate	Party	1st Pref Votes	Elected
Colm Cavanagh	All	270	
Gregory Campbell	DUP	1887	1st Count
Mildred Garfield	DUP	710	11th Count
Joe Millar	DUP	1218	2nd Count
Drew Thompson	DUP	669	
Jim Guy	Ind	484	
William Webster	Ind	63	
Catherine Cooke	PUP	153	
Gerard Diver	SDLP	1330	1st Count
Anne-Marie McDaid	SDLP	817	11th Count
Lynn Fleming	SF	974	8th Count
Francis O'Deorain	SF	338	
Mary Hamilton	UUP	982	9th Count
Gordon Hill	UUP	98	
James McCorkill	UUP	361	

Northland (7 seats)

Electorate	16402	Valid Vote	11007
Quota	1376	Turnout	69.1%

Party	Candidates	% Vote	Seats
SDLP	5	54.0	4
SF	4	39.0	3
Ind	4	7.0	
Total	**13**	**100**	**7**

Candidate	Party	1st Pref Votes	Elected
Daniel Bradley	Ind	82	
Colm Bryce	Ind	274	
Catherine Harper	Ind	14	
William Temple	Ind	407	
Sean Carr	SDLP	1157	5th Count
John Kerr	SDLP	1248	3rd Count
Joseph McClintock	SDLP	922	
Kathleen McCloskey	SDLP	1528	1st Count
Helen Quigley	SDLP	1087	5th Count
Maeve McLaughlin	SF	1240	4th Count
Gerry MagLochlainn	SF	938	
Mary Nelis	SF	980	4th Count
William Page	SF	1130	5th Count

Down District Council

Down District Council has 23 councillors and 4 wards as follows:

Ballynahinch	5 seats
Downpatrick	7 seats
Newcastle	6 seats
Rowallane	5 seats

Summary of council

Electorate	44909	Valid Vote 29883	Turnout 66.5%

Party	% Vote	Seats
UUP	22	6
SDLP	41	10
DUP	14	2
SF	17	4
All	0	0
Others	6	1
Total	**100**	**23**

Ballynahinch (5 seats)

Electorate	9997	Valid Vote	6868
Quota	1145	Turnout	70.1%

Party	Candidates	% Vote	Seats
UUP	3	24.0	1
SDLP	3	39.4	2
DUP	3	23.0	1
SF	1	13.6	1
Total	**10**	**100**	**5**

Candidate	Party	1st Pref Votes	Elected
William Alexander	DUP	593	
Harvey Bicker	UUP	790	6th Count
Francis Braniff	SF	937	6th Count
Francis Casement	SDLP	592	
John Cochrane	UUP	674	
Ann McAleenan	SDLP	962	3rd Count
Alan McIlroy	DUP	126	
John Reid	UUP	182	
Patrick Toman	SDLP	1150	1st Count
Jim Wells	DUP	862	5th Count

Rowallane (5 seats)

Electorate	10464	Valid Vote	6857
Quota	1143	Turnout	66.9%

Party	Candidates	% Vote	Seats
UUP	3	41.8	3
SDLP	2	25.1	1
DUP	2	26.2	1
SF	1	4.4	
Ind	1	2.5	
Total	**9**	**100**	**5**

Candidate	Party	1st Pref Votes	Elected
Robert Burgess	UUP	1113	3rd Count
Albert Colmer	UUP	1027	5th Count
William Dick	DUP	1198	1st Count
Anthony Lacken	SF	304	
James Marks	Ind	169	
Edward Rea	UUP	728	6th Count
Margaret Ritchie	SDLP	1440	1st Count
Kathleen Stockton	SDLP	279	
William Walker	DUP	599	

Downpatrick (7 seats)

Electorate	13109	Valid Vote	8428
Quota	1054	Turnout	66.1%

Party	Candidates	% Vote	Seats
UUP	1	9.3	1
SDLP	6	52.7	4
DUP	1	2.4	
SF	2	21.1	1
Ind	3	13.1	1
WP	1	1.4	
Total	**14**	**100**	**7**

Candidate	Party	1st Pref Votes	Elected
Raymond Blaney	Ind	835	9th Count
Peter Craig	SDLP	1077	1st Count
Dermot Curran	SDLP	1024	1st Count
John Doris	SDLP	852	7th Count
John Foster	DUP	203	
Helen Honeyman	Ind	101	
John Irvine	SDLP	233	
Liam Johnston	SF	633	
Gerry Mahon	SDLP	404	
Eamonn McConvey	SF	1147	1st Count
Jack McIlheron	UUP	782	9th Count
Patrick O'Connor	Ind	173	
Des O'Hagan	WP	115	
Ann Trainor	SDLP	849	7th Count

Newcastle (6 seats)

Electorate	11339	Valid Vote	7730
Quota	1105	Turnout	69.9%

Party	Candidates	% Vote	Seats
UUP	1	15.7	1
SDLP	4	44.6	3
DUP	1	9.0	
SF	2	27.6	2
Ind	1	3.1	
Total	**9**	**100**	**6**

Candidate	Party	1st Pref Votes	Elected
Willie Clarke	SF	1163	1st Count
Gerry Douglas	UUP	1211	1st Count
Peter Fitzpatrick	SDLP	700	3rd Count
David McAllister	Ind	243	
Francis McDowell	SF	972	4th Count
Charles McGrath	SDLP	438	
Carmel O'Boyle	SDLP	1000	3rd Count
Eamonn O'Neill	SDLP	1308	1st Count
Stanley Priestley	DUP	695	

Dungannon and South Tyrone Borough Council

Dungannon and South Tyrone Borough Council has a total of 22 councillors and 3 wards as follows:

Blackwater	5 seats
Clogher Valley	5 seats
Dungannon Town	6 seats
Torrent	6 seats

Summary of council

Electorate 34985 Valid Vote 27994 Turnout 80.0%

Party	% Vote	Seats
UUP	23	6
SDLP	17	4
DUP	18	3
SF	36	8
All	0	0
Others	6	1
Total	**100**	**22**

Torrent (6 seats)

Electorate	10314	Valid Vote	8390
Quota	1199	Turnout	83.0%

Party	Candidates	% Vote	Seats
UUP	1	10.8	1
SDLP	1	15.2	1
DUP	1	3.6	
SF	4	55.6	3
Ind	1	14.8	1
Total	**8**	**100**	**6**

Candidate	Party	1st Pref Votes	Elected
Norman Badger	UUP	910	5th Count
Jim Canning	Ind	1244	1st Count
Jim Cavanagh	SDLP	1274	1st Count
Desmond Donnelly	SF	944	6th Count
Brendan Doris	SF	985	
Michael Gillespie	SF	1336	1st Count
Robert McFarland	DUP	304	
Francis Molloy	SF	1393	1st Count

Blackwater (5 seats)

Electorate	8102	Valid Vote	6678
Quota	1114	Turnout	83.7%

Party	Candidates	% Vote	Seats
UUP	3	31.6	2
SDLP	1	14.2	1
DUP	2	29.6	1
SF	2	22.6	1
Total	**8**	**100**	**5**

Candidate	Party	1st Pref Votes	Elected
David Brady	UUP	669	
Roger Burton	DUP	991	7th Count
Patsy Daly	SDLP	948	3rd Count
James Ewing	DUP	985	
Phelim Gildernew	SF	1032	2nd Count
William Hamilton	UUP	775	6th Count
Derek Irwin	UUP	801	7th Count
Dominic Molloy	SF	477	

Clogher Valley (5 seats)

Electorate	7827	Valid Vote	6487
Quota	1082	Turnout	84.5%

Party	Candidates	% Vote	Seats
UUP	2	25.1	1
SDLP	2	23.0	1
DUP	2	21.7	1
SF	2	30.2	2
Total	**8**	**100**	**5**

Candidate	Party	1st Pref Votes	Elected
Donald Beatty	UUP	681	
Seamus Flanagan	SF	1159	1st Count
Anthony McGonnell	SDLP	1150	1st Count
Sean McGuigan	SF	799	6th Count
Johnston McIlwrath	DUP	816	4th Count
Robert Mulligan	UUP	951	5th Count
Thomas Murphy	SDLP	342	
David Robinson	DUP	589	

Dungannon Town (6 seats)

Electorate	8742	Valid Vote	6439
Quota	920	Turnout	74.7%

Party	Candidates	% Vote	Seats
UUP	2	24.8	2
SDLP	1	17.2	1
DUP	2	19.2	1
SF	2	30.3	2
Ind	1	8.5	
Total	**8**	**100**	**6**

Candidate	Party	1st Pref Votes	Elected
Walter Cuddy	UUP	853	5th Count
Gerry Cullen	Ind	549	
Vincent Currie	SDLP	1110	1st Count
Derek Greenaway	DUP	363	
John McLarnon	SF	1138	7th Count
Ken Maginnis	UUP	740	1st Count
Barry Monteith	SF	813	2nd Count
Maurice Morrow	DUP	873	4th Count

Fermanagh District Council

Fermanagh District Council has a total of 23 councillors in 4 wards as follows:

Enniskillen	7 seats
Erne East	6 seats
Erne North	5 seats
Erne West	5 seats

Summary of council

Electorate	42002	Valid Vote	32187	Turnout	76.6%

Party	% Vote	Seats
UUP	31	7
SDLP	19	4
DUP	12	2
SF	33	9
All	0	0
Others	5	1
Total	**100**	**23**

Erne East (6 seats)

Electorate	10700	Valid Vote	8678
Quota	1240	Turnout	82.6%

Party	Candidates	% Vote	Seats
UUP	2	27.0	2
SDLP	1	14.9	1
DUP	1	9.3	
SF	3	42.3	3
Ind	1	6.5	
Total	**8**	**100**	**6**

Candidate	Party	1st Pref Votes	Elected
Harold Andrews	UUP	1348	1st Count
Ruth Lynch	SF	1428	1st Count
Brian McCaffrey	SF	1191	2nd Count
Michael Phillips	Ind	559	
Fergus McQuillan	SDLP	1293	1st Count
Cecil Noble	UUP	998	Elected*
Tomas O'Reilly	SF	1050	4th Count
Paul Robinson	DUP	811	

* Elected without reaching quota

Enniskillen (7 seats)

Electorate	13326	Valid Vote	9540
Quota	1193	Turnout	73.5%

Party	Candidates	% Vote	Seats
UUP	4	33.4	2
SDLP	2	17.8	1
DUP	2	12.6	1
SF	2	25.3	2
UKUP	1	1.9	
Ind	1	9.0	1
Total	**12**	**100**	**7**

Candidate	Party	1st Pref Votes	Elected
Frank Britton	SDLP	934	6th Count
Joe Dodds	DUP	1096	4th Count
Samuel Dunne	DUP	105	
Raymond Ferguson	UUP	1486	1st Count
Eamonn Flanagan	SDLP	766	
Patrick Gilgunn	SF	1070	3rd Count
Robert Irvine	UUP	709	8th Count
Basil Johnston	UUP	589	
Davy Kettyles	Ind	861	7th Count
Alan Madill	UKUP	182	
Gerry McHugh	SF	1339	1st Count
Barbara Stuart	UUP	403	

Erne West (5 seats)

Electorate	9196	Valid Vote	7299
Quota	1217	Turnout	81.2%

Party	Candidates	% Vote	Seats
UUP	2	24.8	1
SDLP	1	21.6	1
DUP	1	5.4	
SF	3	48.2	3
Total	**7**	**100**	**5**

Candidate	Party	1st Pref Votes	Elected
David Black	DUP	392	
Pat Cox	SF	1266	1st Count
Wilson Elliott	UUP	981	Elected*
Gerry Gallagher	SDLP	1578	1st Count
Stephen Huggett	SF	1111	Elected*
Robin Martin	SF	1139	Elected*
Derrick Nixon	UUP	832	

*Elected without reaching quota

Erne North (5 seats)

Electorate	8880	Valid Vote	6670
Quota	1112	Turnout	76.6%

Party	Candidates	% Vote	Seats
UUP	3	38.5	2
SDLP	2	21.6	1
DUP	3	22.2	1
SF	1	17.7	1
Total	**9**	**100**	**5**

Candidate	Party	1st Pref Votes	Elected
Joe Cassidy	SF	1181	1st Count
Julie Dervan	SDLP	568	
Tom Elliott	UUP	1030	2nd Count
Billy Gilmore	DUP	277	
Bert Johnston	DUP	1113	1st Count
Bertie Kerr	UUP	854	Elected*
Caldwell McClaughry	UUP	685	
John O'Kane	SDLP	871	3rd Count
Billy Simpson	DUP	91	

*Elected without reaching quota

Larne Borough Council

Larne Borough Council has a total of 15 councillors and 3 wards as follows:

Coast Road	5 seats
Larne Lough	5 seats
Larne Town	5 seats

Summary of council

Electorate 23136 Valid Vote 13819   Turnout 59.7%

Party	% Vote	Seats
UUP	29	4
SDLP	10	2
DUP	29	5
SF	4	0
All	14	2
Others	14	2
Total	**100**	**15**

Larne Lough (5 seats)

Electorate	8552	Valid Vote	5079
Quota	847	Turnout	61.2%

Party	Candidates	% Vote	Seats
UUP	3	38.4	2
DUP	2	35.5	2
All	1	23.1	1
Ind	1	3.0	
Total	**7**	**100**	**5**

Candidate	Party	1st Pref Votes	Elected
Roy Beggs	UUP	1248	1st Count
David Fleck	UUP	374	5th Count
John Hall	UUP	329	
John Mathews	All	1171	1st Count
Bobby McKee	DUP	1341	1st Count
Gregg McKeen	DUP	492	2nd Count
William Small	Ind	151	

Larne Town (5 seats)

Electorate	7463	Valid Vote	4435
Quota	740	Turnout	60.6%

Party	Candidates	% Vote	Seats
UUP	2	22.3	1
SDLP	1	12.9	1
DUP	2	21.2	1
SF	1	4.3	
PUP	1	2.4	
All	1	5.4	
Ind	4	31.5	2
Total	**12**	**100**	**5**

Candidate	Party	1st Pref Votes	Elected
William Adams	Ind	327	
William Adamson	PUP	107	
John Anderson	Ind	292	
Roy Craig	Ind	390	10th Count
James Dunn	UUP	804	2nd Count
Janette Graffin	SF	191	
Alastair Holden	DUP	165	
Robert Lyndsay Mason	Ind	389	10th Count
Jack McKee	DUP	776	2nd Count
Margaret Richmond	All	239	
Andrew Wilson	UUP	185	
Martin Wilson	SDLP	570	8th Count

Coast Road (5 seats)

Electorate	7121	Valid Vote	4305
Quota	718	Turnout	61.8%

Party	Candidates	% Vote	Seats
UUP	2	24.3	1
SDLP	1	17.4	1
DUP	2	28.8	2
SF	1	7.1	
All	1	13.7	1
Ind	1	8.7	
Total	**8**	**100**	**5**

Candidate	Party	1st Pref Votes	Elected
William Cunning	Ind	379	
Joan Drummond	UUP	614	5th Count
Winston Fulton	DUP	753	2nd Count
Martin Graffin	SF	305	
Geraldine Mulvenna	All	589	5th Count
Daniel O'Connor	SDLP	750	2nd Count
Rachel Rea	DUP	485	6th Count
Thomas Robinson	UUP	430	

Limavady Borough Council

Limavady Borough Council has a total of 15 councillors and 3 wards as follows:

Bellarena	5 seats
Benbradagh	5 seats
Limavady Town	5 seats

Summary of council

Electorate   21283   Valid Vote 15216   Turnout 71.5%

Party	% Vote	Seats
UUP	15	3
SDLP	29	4
DUP	18	2
SF	25	4
All	0	0
Others	13	2
Total	**100**	**15**

Limavady Town (5 seats)

Electorate	6877	Valid Vote	4720
Quota	787	Turnout	69.5%

Party	Candidates	% Vote	Seats
UUP	3	21.1	2
SDLP	2	22.7	1
DUP	1	30.3	1
SF	1	8.9	
Ind	1	13.6	1
UUAP	1	3.4	
Total	**9**	**100**	**5**

Candidate	Party	1st Pref Votes	Elected
Brian Brown	Ind	642	5th Count
Jack Dolan	UUP	383	4th Count
William Kennedy	UUP	241	
John Kerr	SDLP	530	
Dessie Lowry	SDLP	542	5th Count
Malachy O'Kane	SF	419	
John Rankin	UUP	372	4th Count
George Robinson	DUP	1430	1st Count
Alister Smyth	UUAP	161	

Benbradagh (5 seats)

Electorate	6750	Valid Vote	5037
Quota	840	Turnout	76.3%

Party	Candidates	% Vote	Seats
SDLP	2	21.0	1
SF	3	50.3	3
DUP	1	5.1	
UUAP	2	23.6	1
Total	**8**	**100**	**5**

Candidate	Party	1st Pref Votes	Elected
Anne Brolly	SF	1056	1st Count
Francis Brolly	SF	917	1st Count
Michael Coyle	SDLP	559	6th Count
Marion Donaghy	SF	559	6th Count
Boyd Douglas	UUAP	748	3rd Count
Mark Gibson	UUAP	442	
Gerard Lynch	SDLP	497	
John Murray	DUP	259	

Bellarena (5 seats)

Electorate	7656	Valid Vote	5459
Quota	910	Turnout	72.2%

Party	Candidates	% Vote	Seats
UUP	2	24.7	1
SDLP	3	41.2	2
DUP	1	18.8	1
SF	1	15.3	1
Total	**7**	**100**	**5**

Candidate	Party	1st Pref Votes	Elected
Michael Cartan	SDLP	845	1st Count
Joseph Cubitt	DUP	1027	3rd Count
Martin McGuigan	SF	833	3rd Count
John McKinney	SDLP	685	
Gerard Mullan	SDLP	721	3rd Count
William Smyth	UUP	641	
Edwin Stevenson	UUP	707	5th Count

Lisburn City Council

Lisburn City Council has 30 councillors and 5 wards as follows:

Downshire	5 seats
Dunmurry Cross	7 seats
Killultagh	5 seats
Lisburn Town North	7 seats
Lisburn Town South	6 seats

Summary of council

Electorate 75619   Valid Vote 46759   Turnout 61.8%

Party	% Vote	Seats
UUP	35	13
SDLP	9	3
DUP	20	5
SF	16	4
All	11	3
Others	9	2
Total	**100**	**30**

Lisburn Town North (7 seats)

Electorate	17506	Valid Vote	10773
Quota	1347	Turnout	62.5%

Party	Candidates	% Vote	Seats
UUP	3	44.0	3
DUP	2	17.1	1
SF	1	4.2	1
All	1	17.7	1
Ind	3	11.7	1
UDP	1	5.3	
Total	**11**	**100**	**7**

Candidate	Party	1st Pref Votes	Elected
David Adams	UDP	577	
David Archer	UUP	1619	1st Count
James Armstrong	SF	451	
William Beattie	Ind	423	
David Craig	DUP	1036	7th Count
Ronnie Crawford	Ind	711	7th Count
Adrian Creighton	Ind	123	
William Watson	UUP	1190	3rd Count
William Leathem	DUP	808	
William Lewis	UUP	1183	4th Count
Trevor Lunn	All	1903	1st Count
Lorraine Martin	UUP	749	7th Count

Lisburn Town South (6 seats)

Electorate	12339	Valid Vote	7053
Quota	1008	Turnout	58.8%

Party	Candidates	% Vote	Seats
UUP	5	47.3	3
DUP	2	19.9	1
SF	1	3.5	
All	1	21.2	1
UDP	1	7.2	1
NIUP	1	0.9	
Total	**11**	**100**	**6**

Candidate	Party	1st Pref Votes	Elected
David Archer	UUP	721	7th Count
Seamus Close	All	1495	1st Count
Ivan David	UUP	1521	1st Count
Francis Kerr	SF	245	
Margaret Little	UUP	253	
Joe Lockhart	UUP	592	8th Count
Tom Mateer	UUP	246	
Gary McMichael	UDP	509	Elected*
Paul Porter	DUP	1061	1st Count
Allen Russell	DUP	346	
Gary Teeney	NIUP	64	

*Elected without reaching quota

Downshire (5 seats)

Electorate	12983	Valid Vote	8483
Quota	1414	Turnout	66.3%

Party	Candidates	% Vote	Seats
UUP	3	43.7	3
DUP	2	31.1	1
SF	1	1.3	
All	1	14.1	1
Ind	1	7.2	
Cons	1	2.6	
Total	**9**	**100**	**5**

Candidate	Party	1st Pref Votes	Elected
James Baird	UUP	1507	1st Count
William Bleakes	Ind	609	
Elizabeth Campbell	All	1201	4th Count
Allan Ewart	DUP	632	
William Falloon	UUP	1007	Elected*
Joanne Johnston	Cons	217	
Cara McCann	SF	111	
Edwin Poots	DUP	2006	1st Count
William Ward	UUP	1193	4th Count

*Elected without reaching quota

Dunmurry Cross (7 seats)

Electorate	18673	Valid Vote	11591
Quota	1449	Turnout	64.4%

Party	Candidates	% Vote	Seats
UUP	1	13.4	1
SDLP	2	23.0	2
DUP	1	7.8	
SF	5	53.9	4
Green	1	1.9	
Total	**10**	**100**	**7**

Candidate	Party	1st Pref Votes	Elected
William Bell	UUP	1550	1st Count
Paul Butler	SF	2061	1st Count
Michael Ferguson	SF	1549	1st Count
Paul Flynn	SF	422	
Patricia Lewsley	SDLP	2029	1st Count
Malachy McAnespie	Green	218	
Billy McDonnell	SDLP	640	6th Count
Stephen Moore	DUP	910	
Sue Ramsey	SF	1219	6th Count
Veronica Willis	SF	993	6th Count

Killultagh (5 seats)

Electorate	14118	Valid Vote	8859
Quota	1477	Turnout	63.9%

Party	Candidates	% Vote	Seats
UUP	3	35.2	2
SDLP	1	14.9	1
DUP	2	29.9	2
SF	1	5.2	
All	2	6.4	
Ind	1	3.7	
Cons	1	4.7	
Total	**11**	**100**	**5**

Candidate	Party	1st Pref Votes	Elected
Cecil Calvert	DUP	1382	7th Count
Jim Dillon	UUP	1923	1st Count
Alison Gawith	All	439	
Owen Gawith	All	131	
Ita Gray	SF	457	
Neil Johnston	Cons	419	
Samuel Johnston	UUP	537	Elected*
Peter O'Hagan	SDLP	1318	5th Count
Gordon Ross	Ind	332	
James Tinsey	DUP	1263	Elected*
Ken Watson	UUP	658	

*Elected without reaching quota

Magherafelt District Council

Magherafelt District Council has 16 councillors and 3 wards as follows:

Magherafelt Town	6 seats
Moyola	5 seats
Sperrin	5 seats

Summary of council

Electorate   28033   Valid Vote 22453   Turnout 80.1%

Party	% Vote	Seats
UUP	10	2
SDLP	20	3
DUP	21	3
SF	44	7
All	0	0
Others	5	1
Total	**100**	**16**

Magherafelt Town (6 seats)

Electorate   10509   Valid Vote   8026
Quota   1147   Turnout   77.6%

Party	Candidates	% Vote	Seats
UUP	1	13.7	1
SDLP	2	21.0	1
DUP	2	30.6	2
SF	2	34.7	2
Total	**7**	**100**	**6**

Candidate	Party	1st Pref Votes	Elected
John Kelly	SF	1700	1st Count
Joseph McBride	SDLP	990	4th Count
Rev William McCrea	DUP	2255	1st Count
Paul McClean	DUP	197	2nd Count
Seamus O'Brien	SF	1085	3rd Count
George Shiels	UUP	1103	2nd Count
Frances Symington	SDLP	696	

Sperrin (5 seats)

Electorate   8941   Valid Vote   7478
Quota   1247   Turnout   85.3%

Party	Candidates	% Vote	Seats
SDLP	2	22.5	1
DUP	1	9.7	
SF	3	56.0	3
Ind	1	10.4	1
WP	1	1.4	
Total	**8**	**100**	**5**

Candidate	Party	1st Pref Votes	Elected
Francis Donnelly	WP	104	
Patrick Groogan	SF	1651	1st Count
John Kerr	SF	1206	2nd Count
Kathleen Lagan	SDLP	1136	4th Count
Francis McKendry	SDLP	551	
Rodney Mitchell	DUP	723	
Robert Montgomery	Ind	776	Elected*
Hugh Mullan	SF	1331	1st Count

*Elected without reaching quota

Moyola (5 seats)

Electorate   8583   Valid Vote   6949
Quota   1159   Turnout   82.8%

Party	Candidates	% Vote	Seats
UUP	1	17.8	1
SDLP	2	15.8	1
DUP	2	20.9	1
SF	2	42.5	2
Ind	1	3.0	
Total	**8**	**100**	**5**

Candidate	Party	1st Pref Votes	Elected
Thomas Catherwood	DUP	1023	4th Count
Elizabeth Forde	DUP	430	
Oliver Hughes	SF	1578	1st Count
Naaman Hutchinson	Ind	210	
John Junkin	UUP	1237	1st Count
Patrick McErlean	SDLP	713	3rd Count
James O'Neill	SF	1375	1st Count
Elizabeth Foster	SDLP	383	

Moyle District Council

Moyle District Council has 15 councillors and 3 wards as follows:

Ballycastle	5 seats
Giant's Causeway	5 seats
The Glens	5 seats

Summary of council

Electorate   11272   Valid Vote 7251   Turnout 64.3%

Party	% Vote	Seats
UUP	14	3
SDLP	23	4
DUP	21	3
SF	10	1
All	0	0
Others	32	4
Total	**100**	**15**

The Glens (5 seats)

Electorate   4037   Valid Vote   2750
Quota   459   Turnout   69.4%

127

Party	Candidates	% Vote	Seats
SDLP	3	29.8	2
SF	2	14.4	1
DUP	1	7.0	
Ind	4	48.8	2
Total	10	100	5

Candidate	Party	1st Pref Votes	Elected
Christine Blaney	SDLP	281	Elected *
Monica Digney	SF	216	Elected *
Anne McAuley	SF	178	
James McAuley	Ind	77	
Catherine McCambridge	SDLP	348	6th Count
James McCarry	Ind	279	
Randal McDonnell	Ind	316	6th Count
Archie McIntosh	SDLP	190	
Evelyn Robinson	DUP	194	
Oliver McMullan	Ind	671	1st Count

* Elected without reaching the quota

Ballycastle (5 seats)

Electorate	4122	Valid Vote	2434
Quota	406	Turnout	61.3%

Party	Candidates	% Vote	Seats
UUP	1	15.6	1
SDLP	2	32.2	2
DUP	1	14.2	1
SF	1	12.2	
Ind	4	25.8	1
Total	9	100	5

Candidate	Party	1st Pref Votes	Elected
Madeline Black	SDLP	429	1st Count
Seamus Blaney	Ind	197	Elected *
Anna Edwards	Ind	40	
Helen Harding	UUP	379	4th Count
Gardiner Kane	DUP	345	Elected *
Liam McBride	Ind	202	
Chris McCaughan	Ind	189	
Michael Molloy	SDLP	357	4th Count
Charlie Neill	SF	296	

* Elected without reaching the quota

Giant's Causeway (5 seats)

Electorate	3123	Valid Vote	2067
Quota	345	Turnout	67.7%

Party	Candidates	% Vote	Seats
UUP	2	30.0	2
SDLP	1	3.7	
DUP	3	47.5	2
Ind	2	18.8	1
Total	8	100	5

Candidate	Party	1st Pref Votes	Elected
Robert Chestnutt	DUP	228	
William Graham	UUP	398	1st Count
George Hartin	DUP	258	5th Count
David McAllister	DUP	495	1st Count
Price McConaghy	Ind	367	1st Count
Moira McGouran	SDLP	76	
Robert McIlroy	UUP	223	5th Count
Thomas Palmer	Ind	22	

Newry and Mourne District Council

Newry and Mourne District Council has 30 councillors and 5 wards as follows:

Crotlieve	7 seats
The Fews	6 seats
The Mournes	5 seats
Newry Town	7 seats
Slieve Gullion	5 seats

Summary of council

Electorate   61864   Valid Vote 45566   Turnout 73.7%

Party	% Vote	Seats
UUP	13	4
SDLP	36	10
DUP	6	1
SF	39	13
All	0	0
Others	6	2
Total	100	30

The Fews (6 seats)

Electorate	11457	Valid Vote	8890
Quota	1271	Turnout	79.6%

Party	Candidates	% Vote	Seats
UUP	2	22.0	2
SDLP	3	28.6	1
DUP	1	7.8	
SF	3	41.6	3
Total	9	100	6

Candidate	Party	1st Pref Votes	Elected
Craig Baxter	DUP	693	
John Feehan	SDLP	1071	2nd Count
Danny Kennedy	UUP	1231	3rd Count
Brendan Lewis	SF	1172	6th Count
Jimmy McCreesh	SF	1279	1st Count
Pat McGinn	SF	1243	2nd Count
Andy Moffett	UUP	727	4th Count
Angela Savage	SDLP	595	
Charlie Smyth	SDLP	879	

The Mournes (5 seats)

Electorate	10440	Valid Vote	7686
Quota	1282	Turnout	75.2%

Party	Candidates	% Vote	Seats
UUP	2	30.7	2
SDLP	2	27.0	1
DUP	2	25.4	1
SF	1	16.9	1
Total	7	100	5

Candidate	Party	1st Pref Votes	Elected
William Burns	DUP	1845	1st Count
Linda Burns	DUP	110	
Michael Cole	SDLP	1205	4th Count
Martin Cunningham	SF	1291	1st Count
Marian Fitzpatrick	SDLP	872	
Isaac Hanna	UUP	1178	2nd Count
Henry Reilly	UUP	1185	2nd Count

Slieve Gullion (5 seats)

Electorate	10524	Valid Vote	8168
Quota	1362	Turnout	80.2%

Party	Candidates	% Vote	Seats
SDLP	3	31.9	2
SF	4	68.1	3
Total	7	100	5

Candidate	Party	1st Pref Votes	Elected
Colman Burns	SF	1431	1st Count
John Fee	SDLP	1195	5th Count
Terry Hearty	SF	1283	3rd Count
Packie McDonald	SF	1415	1st Count
Mary McKeown	SDLP	568	
Elena Martin	SF	1436	1st Count
Pat Toner	SDLP	840	

Crotlieve (7 seats)

Electorate	15786	Valid Vote	11291
Quota	1412	Turnout	73.6%

Party	Candidates	% Vote	Seats
UUP	1	6.2	
SDLP	5	51.0	4
DUP	1	2.4	
SF	3	26.4	2
Ind	2	14.0	1
Total	12	100	7

Candidate	Party	1st Pref Votes	Elected
PJ Bradley	SDLP	2103	1st Count
Hugh Carr	SDLP	1189	2nd Count
Michael Carr	SDLP	714	8th Count
John McConnell	UUP	697	
Ruth McConnell	DUP	274	
Brendan Murney	SDLP	576	
Mick Murphy	SF	1743	1st Count
Ciaran Mussen	Ind	834	
Eamonn O'Connor	SF	428	
Josephine O'Hare	SDLP	1175	3rd Count
Michael Ruane	SF	807	8th Count
Anthony Williamson	Ind	751	8th Count

Newry Town (7 seats)

Electorate	13657	Valid Vote	9531
Quota	1192	Turnout	71.7%

Party	Candidates	% Vote	Seats
UUP	1	7.6	
SDLP	4	33.6	3
SF	4	45.5	3
Ind	2	13.3	1
Total	11	100	7

Candidate	Party	1st Pref Votes	Elected
Charlie Casey	SF	1119	6th Count
Brendan Curran	SF	1025	6th Count
Frank Feeley	SDLP	940	3rd Count
Davy Hyland	SF	1213	1st Count
John McArdle	SDLP	811	6th Count
Billy McCaigue	UUP	727	
Pat McElroy	SDLP	950	3rd Count
Peter McEvoy	SDLP	503	
Conor Murphy	SF	984	
Declan O'Callaghan	Ind	109	
Jack Patterson	Ind	1150	2nd Count

Newtownabbey Borough Council

Newtownabbey Borough Council has 25 councillors and 4 wards as follows:

Antrim Line	7 seats
Ballyclare	5 seats
Macedon	6 seats
University	7 seats

Summary of council

Electorate	58535	Valid Vote	35035	Turnout	59.9%

Party	% Vote	Seats
UUP	29	9
SDLP	6	2
DUP	27	8
SF	5	1
All	8	1
Others	25	4
Total	**100**	**25**

Antrim Line (7 seats)

Electorate	16969	Valid Vote	10467
Quota	1309	Turnout	63.2%

Party	Candidates	% Vote	Seats
UUP	3	27.2	2
SDLP	2	19.3	2
DUP	3	22.2	2
SF	2	13.3	1
All	1	5.2	
NIWC	1	2.9	
NIUP	1	4.0	
Ind	2	5.9	
Total	**15**	**100**	**7**

Candidate	Party	1st Pref Votes	Elected
James Beckett	Ind	228	
John Blair	Ind	389	
Norman Boyd	NIUP	418	
Joan Cosgrove	NIWC	299	
Janet Crilly	UUP	1704	1st Count
Nigel Hamilton	DUP	1350	1st Count
Ivan Hunter	UUP	607	8th Count
Arthur Kell	UUP	536	
Noreen McClelland	SDLP	887	10th Count
Tommy McTeague	SDLP	1128	10th Count
Briege Meehan	SF	754	10th Count
Liz Snoddy	DUP	337	
Arthur Templeton	DUP	640	10th Count
Pam Tilson	All	547	
Roisin McGurk	SF	643	

University (7 seats)

Electorate	16785	Valid Vote	9996
Quota	1250	Turnout	60.6%

Party	Candidates	% Vote	Seats
UUP	3	33.6	3
DUP	2	22.7	2
PUP	1	8.1	
NIUP	1	5.0	
CC	1	4.5	
UUAP	2	13.0	1
All	1	13.1	1
Total	**11**	**100**	**7**

Candidate	Party	1st Pref Votes	Elected
Fraser Agnew	UUAP	828	9th Count
Alister Bell	CC	447	
Billy Boyd	NIUP	504	
Lynn Frazer	All	1313	3rd Count
Barbara Gilliland	UUP	1351	3rd Count
Billy Greer	PUP	811	
Roger Hutchinson	DUP	1791	3rd Count
John Mann	DUP	479	9th Count
Ken Robinson	UUP	1535	3rd Count
John Scott	UUAP	469	
Vi Scott	UUP	468	9th Count

Ballyclare (5 seats)

Electorate	12666	Valid Vote	7548
Quota	1259	Turnout	61.1%

Party	Candidates	% Vote	Seats
UUP	4	42.8	3
DUP	2	38.3	2
PUP	1	3.3	
All	1	10.1	
Cons	1	2.2	
CC	1	3.3	
Total	**10**	**100**	**5**

Candidate	Party	1st Pref Votes	Elected
James Bingham	UUP	1192	3rd Count
Paul Girvan	DUP	2583	1st Count
Alan Greer	Cons	169	
Pamela Hunter	DUP	308	2nd Count
Norman Lavery	PUP	249	
Patrick McCudden	All	761	
Vera McWilliams	UUP	1231	2nd Count
Sharon Parkes	CC	247	
Edward Turkington	UUP	541	7th Count
Peter Walker	UUP	267	

Macedon (6 seats)

Electorate	12115	Valid Vote	7024
Quota	1004	Turnout	60.1%

Party	Candidates	% Vote	Seats
UUP	1	11.1	1
DUP	2	27.3	2
SF	1	5.0	
PUP	1	5.7	
All	1	2.5	
Ind	4	36.9	2
CC	1	2.3	
NRA	1	9.2	1
Total	**12**	**100**	**6**

Candidate	Party	1st Pref Votes	Elected
Andy Beattie	Ind	276	
Michael Campbell	All	173	
William DeCourcy	DUP	1355	1st Count
Kenneth Hunter	DUP	563	6th Count
Dougie Jamison	PUP	398	
Bob Kidd	Ind	378	
Tommy Kirkham	Ind	611	8th Count
Mark Langhammer	Ind	1326	1st Count
Victor Robinson	CC	160	
Kevin Vernon	SF	350	
Dineen Walker	UUP	784	7th Count
Billy Webb	NRA	650	7th Count

North Down Borough Council

North Down Borough Council has 25 councillors and 4 wards as follows:

Abbey	6 seats
Ballyholme & Groomsport	7 seats
Bangor West	7 seats
Holywood	5 seats

Summary of council

Electorate   56614   Valid Vote 32497   Turnout 57.4%

Party	% Vote	Seats
UUP	27	8
SDLP	0	0
DUP	14	5
SF	0	0
All	18	5
Others	41	7
Total	**100**	**25**

Holywood Ward (5 seats)

Electorate	10063	Valid Vote	6125
Quota	1021	Turnout	62.1%

Party	Candidates	% Vote	Seats
UUP	2	30.0	2
DUP	1	15.0	1
PUP	1	2.0	
All	2	24.5	1
NIWC	1	8.3	
Ind	2	17.1	1
Cons	1	3.1	
Total	**10**	**100**	**5**

Candidate	Party	1st Pref Votes	Elected
Lindsay Cumming	Cons	188	
Gordon Dunne	DUP	916	4th Count

Candidate	Party	1st Pref Votes	Elected
Norma Heaton	NIWC	509	
Robert Irvine	Ind	232	
Ellie McKay	UUP	1346	1st Count
Susan O'Brien	All	1070	1st Count
Denis Ogborn	Ind	815	6th Count
Diana Peacock	UUP	491	6th Count
David Rose	PUP	122	
Larry Thompson	All	436	

Ballyholme & Groomsport (7 seats)

Electorate	17348	Valid Vote	1(028)7
Quota	1286	Turnout	60.4%

Party	Candidates	% Vote	Seats
UUP	3	23.7	2
DUP	1	11.3	1
PUP	1	0.9	
UKUP	2	8.1	
NIUP	1	1.4	
NIWC	1	6.4	1
All	2	12.4	1
Ind	3	35.8	2
Total	**14**	**100**	**7**

Candidate	Party	1st Pref Votes	Elected
Alan Chambers	Ind	2099	1st Count
Leslie Cree	UUP	1631	1st Count
Alexander Easton	DUP	1164	4th Count
Marsden Fitzsimons	All	939	8th Count
Arthur Gadd	UUP	202	
Henry Gordon	UKUP	571	
Ian Henry	UUP	601	9th Count
Brian Lacey	PUP	90	
Austen Lennon	Ind	1363	1st Count
Elizabeth Roche	NIUP	140	
Ernest Steele	Ind	218	
Joseph Teggart	UKUP	276	
Gavin Walker	All	336	
Patricia Wallace	NIWC	657	11th Count

Abbey (6 seats)

Electorate	13455	Valid Vote	6975
Quota	997	Turnout	53.7%

Party	Candidates	% Vote	Seats
UUP	2	30.0	2
DUP	2	22.4	2
PUP	1	6.0	
NIUP	1	0.7	
UKUP	1	13.1	1
All	1	17.1	1
Cons	1	2.7	
Ind	3	8.0	
Total	**12**	**100**	**6**

Candidate	Party	1st Pref Votes	Elected
Christopher Carter	Ind	175	
Ruby Cooling	DUP	1263	1st Count
Irene Cree	UUP	1246	1st Count
Stewart Currie	PUP	417	
Colin Dean	NIUP	48	
Roberta Dunlop	UUP	843	3rd Count
Stephen Farry	All	1195	1st Count
Lisa Fleming	Cons	191	
William Gordon	Ind	89	
Valerie Kinghan	UKUP	912	5th Count
Karl McLean	Ind	297	
John Montgomery	DUP	299	10th Count

Bangor West (7 seats)

Electorate	15748	Valid Vote	9110
Quota	1139	Turnout	59.2%

Party	Candidates	% Vote	Seats
UUP	3	27.7	2
DUP	1	10.9	1
PUP	1	5.9	
UKUP	2	14.0	1
Cons	1	1.9	
All	2	19.1	2
Ind	1	20.5	1
Total	**11**	**100**	**7**

Candidate	Party	1st Pref Votes	Elected
Roy Davies	UUP	796	7th Count
Alan Field	UKUP	599	
Alan Graham	DUP	989	6th Count
Tony Hill	All	630	7th Count
Bill Keery	UKUP	676	7th Count
James Rea	PUP	538	
Julian Robertson	Cons	172	
Marion Smith	UUP	1311	1st Count
Evan Ward	UUP	416	
Anne Wilson	All	1112	2nd Count
Brian Wilson	Ind	1871	1st Count

Omagh District Council

Omagh District Council has 21 councillors and 3 wards as follows:

Mid Tyrone	7 seats
Omagh Town	7 seats
West Tyrone	7 seats

Summary of council

Electorate   33462   Valid Vote 26634   Turnout 79.6%

Party	% Vote	Seats
UUP	16	3
SDLP	22	6
DUP	13	2
SF	40	8
All	0	0
Others	9	2
Total	**100**	**21**

Mid Tyrone (7 seats)

Electorate	11421	Valid Vote	9551
Quota	1194	Turnout	85.4%

Party	Candidates	% Vote	Seats
UUP	1	12.4	1
SDLP	2	20.8	2
DUP	1	10.3	4
SF	5	56.5	
Total	**9**	**100**	**7**

Candidate	Party	1st Pref Votes	Elected
John Clarke	SF	1446	1st Count
Damien Curran	SF	1244	1st Count
Barney McAleer	SF	917	2nd Count
Michael McAnespie	SF	995	2nd Count
Cathal McCrory	SF	791	
Samuel McFarland	DUP	984	
Gerry O'Doherty	SDLP	994	4th Count
Seamus Shields	SDLP	989	4th Count
Robert Wilson	UUP	1191	4th Count

Omagh Town (7 seats)

Electorate	11036	Valid Vote	7976
Quota	998	Turnout	74.3%

Party	Candidates	% Vote	Seats
UUP	2	14.6	1
SDLP	3	22.7	2
DUP	2	15.8	1
SF	2	23.6	1
Ind	3	23.2	2
Total	**12**	**100**	**7**

Candidate	Party	1st Pref Votes	Elected
John Anderson	UUP	552	
Sean Begley	SF	1123	1st Count
Joe Byrne	SDLP	1007	1st Count
Vincent Campbell	SDLP	178	
Josephine Deehan	SDLP	629	7th Count
Paddy Gallagher	SF	763	
Oliver Gibson	DUP	1087	1st Count
Thomas McCordick	DUP	171	

Patrick McGowan	Ind	1074	1st Count
Reuben McKelvey	UUP	614	4th Count
Johnny McLaughlin	Ind	759	5th Count
Kevin Taylor	Ind	19	

West Tyrone (7 seats)

Electorate	11005	Valid Vote	9107
Quota	1139	Turnout	84.4%

Party	Candidates	% Vote	Seats
UUP	2	19.8	1
SDLP	2	22.5	2
DUP	2	14.8	1
SF	4	38.4	3
WP	1	2.3	
Ind	1	2.2	
Total	**12**	**100**	**7**

Candidate	Party	1st Pref Votes	Elected
Thomas Buchanon	DUP	1093	4th Count
Stephen Harpur	DUP	257	
Peter Kelly	SF	839	6th Count
Damien McCrossan	SF	614	
Patrick McDonnell	SDLP	1372	1st Count
Barry McElduff	SF	1276	1st Count
Gerry McMenamin	Ind	202	
Liam McQuaid	SDLP	679	7th Count
Tommy Owens	WP	211	
George Rainey	UUP	1135	3rd Count
David Sterritt	UUP	666	
Patrick Watters	SF	763	7th Count

Strabane District Council

Strabane District Council has 16 councillors and 3 wards as follows:

Derg	5 seats
Glenelly	5 seats
Mourne	6 seats

Summary of council

Electorate 27312 Valid Vote 24162 Turnout 78.5%

Party	% Vote	Seats
UUP	17	2
SDLP	19	4
DUP	19	3
SF	40	7
All	0	0
Others	5	0
Total	**100**	**16**

Derg (5 seats)

Electorate	8455	Valid Vote	6800
Quota	1134	Turnout	82.0%

Party	Candidates	% Vote	Seats
UUP	2	24.6	1
SDLP	1	11.3	1
DUP	2	21.5	1
SF	3	42.5	2
Total	**8**	**100**	**5**

Candidate	Party	1st Pref Votes	Elected
Kathleen Allison	DUP	672	
Gerard Foley	SF	651	
Derek Hussey	UUP	1110	3rd Count
Thomas Kerrigan	DUP	793	6th Count
Eamonn McGarvey	SF	910	5th Count
Charlie McHugh	SF	1331	1st Count
Bernadette McNamee	SDLP	768	Elected*
Edward Tuner	UUP	565	

*Elected without reaching quota

Glenelly (5 seats)

Electorate	7867	Valid Vote	6328
Quota	1055	Turnout	82.1%

Party	Candidates	% Vote	Seats
UUP	2	23.1	1
SDLP	1	17.9	1
DUP	2	34.6	2
SF	2	24.4	1
Total	**7**	**100**	**5**

Candidate	Party	1st Pref Votes	Elected
Allan Bresland	DUP	1313	1st Count
Martin Conway	SF	603	
Robert Craig	UUP	585	
John Donnell	DUP	879	2nd Count
James Emery	UUP	876	5th Count
Tom McBride	SDLP	1133	1st Count
Claire McGill	SF	939	6th Count

Mourne (6 seats)

Electorate	10990	Valid Vote	8334
Quota	1191	Turnout	77.6%

Party	Candidates	% Vote	Seats
UUP	1	5.3	
SDLP	3	27.1	2
DUP	1	4.9	
SF	4	50.3	4
Ind	2	12.4	
Total	**11**	**100**	**6**

Candidate	Party	1st Pref Votes	Elected
Ivan Barr	SF	1262	1st Count
Ann Bell	SDLP	438	8th Count
Daniel Breslin	SF	628	8th Count
Kathleen Craig	DUP	408	
Paul Gallagher	Ind	445	
Fred Hanry	SDLP	284	
Sam Martin	UUP	439	
Brian McMahon	SF	977	7th Count
Eugene McMenamin	SDLP	1538	1st Count
Jarlath McNulty	SF	1326	1st Count
James O'Kane	Ind	589	

European Parliament Elections

Members of the European Parliament

The European Parliament is composed of members from each of the fifteen member states in broad proportion to their population. The Parliament shares legislative and budgetary authority with the European Council and exercises democratic and political supervision over the other institutions.

The UK has an entitlement of 87 European Parliament seats. Of this, Northern Ireland returns 3 MEPs by an election held every 5 years. In this case Northern Ireland is a single constituency, and the three European MPs are elected by proportional representations, the Single Transferable Vote (STV). The current MEPs, returned in June 1999, are:

Ian Paisley MP MLA

Party: DUP
European Political Group
Non-attached

Constituency Contact:
Rhonda Paisley
256 Ravenhill Road
Belfast
BT6 8GJ

Tel: (028) 9045 4255
Fax: (028) 9045 7783
Brussels Contact:
European Parliament
Rue Wiertz
B–1047 Brussels, Belgium
Tel: + 32 2 284 5410
Fax: + 32 2 284 9410

John Hume MP

Party: SDLP
European Political Group
Party of European Socialists

Constituency Contact:
Ronan McCay
5 Bayview Terrace
Derry
BT48 7EE

Brussels Contact: Tom Lyne
European Parliament
Rue Wiertz
B–1047 Brussels, Belgium
Tel: + 32 2 284 5190
Fax: + 32 2 284 9190

Jim Nicholson

Party UUP
European Political Group
European People's Party and European
Democrats

Constituency Contact:
429 Holywood Road,
Belfast
BT4 2LN
Tel: (028) 9076 5500
Fax: (028) 9024 6738

Brussels Contact:
European Parliament
Rue Wiertz
B–1047 Brussels, Belgium
Tel: + 32 2 284 5933
Fax: + 32 2 284 9933

European Parliament Election Results for Northern Ireland

In the European election of June 1999, the Northern Ireland electorate returned the following candidates:

Ian Paisley	DUP	28.4 % of vote	Elected 1st count
John Hume	SDLP	28.1 % of vote	Elected 1st count
Jim Nicholson	UUP	17.6 % of vote	Elected 3rd count

Turnout, although higher in 1999 than in the previous election in 1994, was 57.7%, significantly lower than both Westminster and Assembly elections in Northern Ireland. European elections in this area are generally fought hard by the DUP and SDLP who since 1979 have very successfully fielded their party leaders in the election.

The European election in June 1999 was significant in that Ian Paisley called on voters to treat it as a rerun of the Belfast Agreement referendum, in which he claimed that a majority of unionists had actually voted against the Agreement. Once again, Paisley topped the poll, just beating John Hume of the SDLP, although the DUP vote actually decreased from previous European elections. Paisley's vote was broadly in line with the proportion of 'no' votes in the Agreement referendum. The SDLP's vote had been increasing, but was checked by the strength of nationalists voting for Sinn Féin's Mitchel McLaughlin. That party's share of the vote nearly doubled, but despite this it failed to displace the UUP as the third winner.

The dominance of Northern Ireland's three largest political parties is clearly demonstrated in the table above. The DUP candidate, Dr Ian Paisley, has consistently topped the poll since the first election in 1979, with John Hume's SDLP comfortably in second place. The only battle is for third place, with Sinn Féin chasing the UUP in the most recent election. It should be noted however that turnout is traditionally relatively low in European elections.

Party % of Total 1st Preference Vote for European Elections					
Party	**1979**	**1984**	**1989**	**1994**	**1999**
UUP	11.9	21.5	22.2	23.8	17.6
SDLP	24.6	22.1	25.5	28.9	28.1
DUP	29.8	33.6	29.9	29.2	28.4
Sinn Féin		13.3	9.1	9.9	17.3
Alliance	6.8	5.0	5.2	4.1	2.1

Details of the earlier European Parliamentary Elections are set out below.

1979 European Election

Electorate	1,029,490	Total Valid Vote	572,239
Quota	143,060	Turnout	55.6%

Name	Party	1st Pref Votes	% Total Vote	Count Elected
Rev I Paisley	DUP	170,688	29.8	1st
J Hume	SDLP	140,622	24.6	3rd
J Taylor	UUP	68,185	11.9	6th
H West	UUP	56,984	10.0	
O Napier	All	39,026	6.8	
J Kilfedder	Ind U	38,198	6.7	
B McAliskey	Ind	33,969	5.9	
D Bleakley	Utd.Community	9,383	1.6	
P Devlin	ULP	6,122	1.1	
E Cummings	UPNI	3,712	0.6	
B Brennan	Rep C	3,258	0.6	
F Donnelly	Rep C	1,160	0.2	
J Murray	U. Lib	932	0.2	

ULP:	United Labour Party
UPNI:	Unionist Party of Northern Ireland
Rep C:	Republican Clubs
U. Lib:	Ulster Liberal Party

1984 European Election

Electorate	1,065,363	Total Valid Vote	685,317
Quota	171,330	Turnout	65.4%

Name	Party	1st Pref Votes	% Total Vote	Count Elected
Rev I Paisley	DUP	230,251	33.6	1st
J Hume	SDLP	151,399	22.1	4th
J Taylor	UUP	147,169	21.5	2nd
D Morrison	SF	91,476	13.3	
D Cook	All	34,046	5.0	
J Kilfedder	UPUP	20,092	2.9	
S Lynch	WP	8,712	1.3	
C McGuigan	Ecology	2,172	0.3	

1989 European Election

Electorate	1,106,852	Total Valid Vote	534,811
Quota	133,703	Turnout	48.3%

Name	Party	1st Pref Votes	% Total Vote	Count Elected
Rev I Paisley	DUP	160,110	29.9	1st
J Hume	SDLP	136,335	25.5	1st
J Nicholson	UUP	118,785	22.2	2nd
D Morrison	SF	48,914	9.1	
J Alderdice	All	27,905	5.2	
A Kennedy	Cons	25,789	4.8	
M Samuel	GP	6,569	1.2	
S Lynch	WP	5,590	1.0	
M Langhammer	LRG	3,540	0.7	
B Caul	Lab '87	1,274	0.2	

GP:	Green Party
LRG:	Labour Representation Group
Lab '87:	Labour '87

1994 European Election

Electorate	1,162,344	Total Valid Vote	559,867
Quota	139,967	Turnout	49.4%

Name	Party	1st Pref Votes	% Total Vote	Count Elected
Rev I Paisley	DUP	163,246	29.2	1st
J Hume	SDLP	161,992	28.9	1st
J Nicholson	UUP	133,459	23.8	2nd
M Clark-Glass	All	23,157	4.1	
T Hartley	SF	21,273	3.8	
A McGuinness	SF	17,195	3.1	
F Molloy	SF	16,747	3.0	
Rev H Ross	UIM	7,858	1.4	
Myrtle Boal	Cons	5,583	1.0	
J Lowry	WP	2,543	0.5	
N Cusack	Lab	2,464	0.4	
J Anderson	NLP	1,418	0.2	
J Campion	Peace	1,088	0.2	
D Kerr	Ind Ulst.	571	0.1	
S Thompson	NLP	454	0.1	
M Kennedy	NLP	419	0.1	
R Mooney	Con. Ind	400	0.1	

Lab:	Labour Party
Peace:	Peace Coalition
Ind Ulst:	Independent Ulster
Con. Ind:	Constitutional Independent

1999 European Election

Electorate	1,190,160	Total Valid Vote	678,809
Quota	169,703	Turnout	57.7%

Name	Party	1st Pref Votes	% Total Vote	Count Elected
Rev I Paisley	DUP	192,762	28.4	1st
J Hume	SDLP	190,731	28.1	1st
J Nicholson	UUP	119,507	17.6	3rd
M McLaughlin	SF	117,643	17.3	
D Ervine	PUP	22,494	3.3	
R McCartney	UKUP	20,283	3.0	
S Neeson	All	14,391	2.1	
J Anderson	NLP	998	0.2	

CHAPTER 4

The NIO and Northern Ireland Government Departments

The NIO and Northern Ireland Government Departments

Note: At the time of going to print the operation of the Northern Ireland Assembly has been suspended. However this chapter describes the processes of both Direct Rule and devolved government in anticipation - given that the Belfast Agreement itself has not been suspended - that at some point there will be a restoration of devolved administration.

The Role of Westminster in Northern Ireland

This section sets out how the United Kingdom Institutions of government at Westminster impact on Northern Ireland and how powers are divided between the UK government, through the Secretary of State for Northern Ireland and the Northern Ireland Office on one hand, and the devolved administration on the other.

From the establishment of its own devolved parliament in 1921 until 1972 legislation for Northern Ireland was made in the form of Acts of Parliament. Following the suspension of the parliament in 1972 direct rule from Westminster was reintroduced.

Since 1972 there have been three devolved assemblies, 1974, 1982-86 and the current assembly established in 1998 under the terms of the Northern Ireland Act 1998. The Assembly of 1974 and the present Assembly were given legislative powers; the Assembly of 1982-86 had no legislative powers.

Prior to devolution on the 2 December 1999 the Northern Ireland Assembly had no legislative powers, however, following devolution legislative powers were transferred from Westminster and executive power to the power-sharing executive.

Northern Ireland Act 1998

The Belfast Agreement saw the reestablishment of a Northern Ireland Assembly implemented by the Northern Ireland Act 1998. In elections using proportional representation the existing eighteen Westminster constituencies elected one hundred and eight members to the new Assembly. The terms of the Northern Ireland Act 1998 provided for the establishment of a legislative assembly and the creation of an Executive with a First Minister, Deputy First Minister and ten ministers appointed under the d'Hondt procedure. The establishment of new institutions such as the North South Ministerial Council were also provided for under the Act. Areas devolved to the Assembly and Executive include education, social services, the arts and agriculture, broadly corresponding with those areas devolved to the Welsh Assembly and Scottish Parliament. For more detailed information on excepted and reserved matters, refer to Chapter 2 Government of Northern Ireland.

Northern Ireland Elected Representation at Westminster

Whilst Northern Ireland currently returns 18 MPs to Westminster, in the past it had a disproportionately lower representation. From the enactment of the Government of Ireland Act 1920 until 1983 it had a representation of 12 MPs. However, the Boundary Commission in 1983 reconsidered the level of representation in Westminster. Five extra seats were created, and contested for the first time in the June 1983 general election. In 1995, the Boundary Commission examined the situation again and created a further seat bringing the total to eighteen for the May 1997 election. A revision of constituency boundaries and electorate is undertaken every 10-12 years. In addition to its MPs, Northern Ireland also has significant representation in the House of Lords.

Westminster MPs as Elected in 2001		
Constituency	Name	Party
Belfast East	Peter Robinson	DUP
Belfast North	Nigel Dodds	DUP
Belfast South	Rev Martin Smyth	UUP
Belfast West	Gerry Adams	SF
East Antrim	Roy Beggs	UUP
Londonderry East	Gregory Campbell	DUP
Fermanagh & South Tyrone	Michelle Gildernew	SF
Foyle	John Hume	SDLP
Lagan Valley	Jeffrey Donaldson	UUP
Mid Ulster	Martin McGuinness	SF
Newry and Armagh	Séamus Mallon	SDLP
North Antrim	Rev Ian Paisley	DUP
North Down	Sylvia Hermon	UUP
South Antrim	David Burnside	UUP
South Down	Eddie McGrady	SDLP
Strangford	Iris Robinson	DUP
Upper Bann	David Trimble	UUP
West Tyrone	Pat Doherty	SF

Westminster MPs by Party (2002)	
Party	Seats
UUP	6
DUP	5
SDLP	3
SF	4
Total	18

Membership of the Northern Ireland Affairs Select Committee (2002)

Member	Party	Constituency
Adrian Bailey	Lab	West Bromwich West
Harry Barnes	Lab	North East Derbyshire
Henry Bellingham	Cons	North West Norfolk
Roy Beggs	UUP	East Antrim
Tony Clarke	Lab	Northampton South
Stephen McCabe	Lab	Birmingham, Hall Green
Eddie McGrady	SDLP	South Down
Stephen Pound	Lab	Ealing North
Peter Robinson	DUP	Belfast East
Martin Smyth	UUP	Belfast South
Mark Tami	Lab	Alyn & Deeside
Bill Tynan	Lab	Hamilton South
Michael Mates(Chair)	Cons	East Hampshire

Committee Clerk: Dr C Ward
Northern Ireland Affairs Committee
House of Commons
London SW1A 0AA
Tel: 020 7219 2172
Fax: 020 7219 0580
E-mail: northircom@parliament.uk

Northern Ireland Business at Westminster

The right to debate matters pertaining to Northern Ireland and legislate in those areas not devolved to the Northern Ireland Assembly is retained by Westminster.

Northern Ireland business in the Commons is conducted in a number of ways:

• For Primary legislation, through the full Westminster legislative process;
• Through the Northern Ireland Grand Committee;
• Through the Northern Ireland Affairs Select Committee;
• Through Questions addressed to the Secretary of State for Northern Ireland.

Northern Ireland Affairs Select Committee

The Northern Ireland Affairs Select Committee was first proposed in 1990 and then established in 1994 to examine the expenditure, policy and administration of the Northern Ireland Office and the administration of the Crown Solicitor's Office. It has the power to send for persons, papers and records. The committee has investigated areas such as employment, electricity prices, education, BSE and the security forces in Northern Ireland. It produces detailed reports and recommendations on these matters following an extensive process of "taking of evidence" from interested parties on any given issue. The committee has a maximum of thirteen members with a quorum of four.

Michael Mates MP, Chairman
Northern Ireland Affairs Committee

The Northern Ireland Office

The Northern Ireland Office (NIO) is a government department, established in 1972 when amid considerable unrest the powers of the Northern Ireland parliament at Stormont were transferred to the Secretary of State for Northern Ireland. Its role is to provide support for the Secretary of State and to work closely with UK departments and the Northern Ireland Assembly, to advise, offer guidance and ensure effective consultation between the UK and the Northern Ireland devolved administration.

Northern Ireland Office

Castle Buildings
Stormont Estate
Belfast
BT4 3ST
Tel: (028) 9052 0700

11 Millbank
London
SW1P 4PN
Tel: (010) 7210 3000
Website: www.nio.gov.uk

Secretary of State

The Secretary of State for Northern Ireland, presently Paul Murphy, a member of the UK Cabinet, heads the Northern Ireland Office (NIO). Until the restoration of direct rule on the 15 October 2002 the Secretary of State was assisted by two junior ministers, Jane Kennedy, Minister of State at the NIO with responsibility for Security, Policing and Prisons and Des Browne, Parliamentary Under Secretary of State with responsibility for Criminal Justice, Victims and Human Rights. Under direct rule Ian Pearson and Angela Smith now also assist the Secretary of State.

The Role of the Secretary of State for Northern Ireland Post Devolution

With effect from 2 December 1999, ministerial functions in regard to devolved matters in Northern Ireland were transferred to the Northern Ireland Assembly and its Executive. Under devolution the Secretary of State continued to represent Northern Ireland interests within

Northern Ireland Secretaries of State since 1972

Name	Party	Date
Paul Murphy	Labour	2002 -
John Reid	Labour	2000 - 2002
Peter Mandelson	Labour	1999 - 2000
Mo Mowlam	Labour	1997 - 1999
Patrick Mayhew	Conservative	1992 - 1997
Peter Brooke	Conservative	1989 - 1992
Tom King	Conservative	1985 - 1989
Douglas Hurd	Conservative	1984 - 1985
James Prior	Conservative	1981 - 1984
Humphrey Atkins	Conservative	1979 - 1981
Roy Mason	Labour	1976 - 1979
Merlyn Rees	Labour	1974 - 1976
Francis Pym	Conservative	1973 - 1974
William Whitelaw	Conservative	1972 - 1973

the Cabinet. Provision for consultation, co-operation and exchanges of information in relation to the interests of the devolved administration in the policies of the UK government are provided for by the Memorandum of Understanding and associated system of concordats between the Northern Ireland Office and the Northern Ireland Executive Committee.

Excepted matters as set out in Schedule 2 to the Northern Ireland Act 1998 cover areas of national responsibility, which it is envisaged, will always remain the responsibility of the UK parliament. Reserved matters set out in Schedule 3 of the Act are also matters of national policy, although the Assembly may make provision for dealing with them, subject to the consent of the Secretary of State and parliamentary control. Some reserved matters, policing, security, prisons, and criminal justice currently remain within the responsibility of the Secretary of State. It is envisaged within the terms of the Good Friday Agreement that these matters will be transferred to the administration in Northern Ireland. Transferred matters - which are all matters that are not excepted or reserved - fall within the responsibility of the devolved administration, the NI Assembly.

A fundamental government power, the power to levy taxation remains a reserved matter. The Northern Ireland Finance Minister is therefore quite constrained in determining the size of the budget of the Northern Ireland government and more involved in the simpler matter of how the public expenditure budget is allocated amongst the various departments.

Following devolution the Secretary of State retains responsibility for a wide range of excepted and reserved matters including:

- Security and public order: armed forces and security policy in Northern Ireland;
- Policing: responsibility for policing policy and implementation of policing reform;
- Prisons: responsibility for prisons policy and management of Prison Service;
- Criminal justice: offenders and courts policy;
- Elections: operating Northern Ireland's electoral system.

In addition to representing Northern Ireland interests in all matters in Cabinet, in major financial matters he has responsibility for advising the Chancellor, particularly where the Assembly bids for additional funding. There are other excepted and reserved matters, which continue to be the responsibility of the Lord Chancellor in Northern Ireland, such as judicial appointments and matters relating to the courts.

The Secretary of State has statutory responsibility for giving consent to Assembly Bills where these impact on reserved matters other than incidentally and for forwarding all Assembly bills for Royal Assent. Should the Secretary of State consider a bill to be incompatible with international obligations, defence, national security or public order he may choose not to submit it for Royal Assent.

In relation to reserved or excepted matters, UK departments have certain responsibilities extending to Northern Ireland; to consider their impact on transferred matters, and also to ensure that UK policies will work effectively.

In the conduct of its duties the Northern Ireland Office also operates a number of Executive Agencies across a range of activities.

Public Expenditure

The Northern Ireland Office currently employs approximately 4000 staff, over half of whom are prison warders or auxiliaries. The total estimated running cost provision for the department in 2000-2001 was £226 million.

The Northern Ireland Office Spending Programme provided for expenditure of around £1 billion in 2000-2001 on the police, the prison service, the payment of criminal damage and injuries compensation, the probation service, criminal justice, including juvenile detention centres and after-care, grants to voluntary bodies concerned with the rehabilitation of offenders, crime prevention and victim support, elections, security, including services in support of the security forces, legal and forensic services, European Union peace and reconciliation projects, the Northern Ireland Human Rights Commission, the Equality Commission for Northern Ireland, Information Service and central (Northern Ireland Office) administration. It also provides for the costs of The Saville enquiry into Bloody Sunday.

Principle Responsibilities of the Northern Ireland Office

Security in Northern Ireland

The government has expressed its desire to achieve a return to normal security and policing arrangements, with the army assuming a peacetime role within Northern Ireland, the removal of military bases and barriers, a reduction in troop levels and a cessation of emergency legislation. However, the threat of further terrorist activity and concern for public safety will determine the rate at which this objective may be achieved.

In September 2000 the army had published its long-term vision for its presence in Northern Ireland, which envisages a "peacetime garrison of around 8,000 full time soldiers based in no more than 20 sites".

Victims Liaison Unit

The Victim's Liaison Unit was established in the Northern Ireland Office as a response to the report compiled by Sir Kenneth Bloomfield "We Will Remember Them". Following devolution many of the issues facing victims became the responsibility of the new administration. In response a Victims Unit was set up in the Office of the First Minister and Deputy First Minister.

However, it was also necessary to retain the Victims Liaison Unit within the NIO as many victims' issues fell within the reserved and excepted matters, which had not been devolved.

Responsibilities of the NIO's Victims Liaison Unit:

Support for Ministers in the NIO;
Provision of core funding to victims' support groups;
Management and provision of grant aid to the Northern Ireland Memorial Fund;
Ensuring victims' issues are dealt with in the reserved and excepted fields in Northern Ireland particularly in areas such as compensation, criminal justice, security and dealing with the "disappeared";
Articulating the case for victims in the reserved and excepted fields.

Responsibilities of the OFMDFM's Victims Unit:

Support for Ministers in the devolved administration;
Development of a suitable programme under PEACE II to address victims' needs;
Development of a separate programme of activities designed to meet the strategic needs of victims;
Ensuring the needs of victims are addressed in the devolved administration including management of an interdepartmental working group on victims' issues;
Ensuring that the commitments on victims contained in the Programme for Government are met;
Articulating the case for victims within the devolved assembly.

Both organisations have responsibility for:

Improving the capacity and professionalism of victims' organisations and introducing core values and standards for groups to adhere to;
Implementing the findings of the Bloomfield report;
Building networks for victims and victims' organisations to share experience and best practice.

To date the government has committed over £18.25 million to support measures for victims of the Troubles, which include the establishment of a regional family trauma centre, an educational bursary scheme, the establishment of the Northern Ireland Memorial Fund, a review of criminal injuries compensation and funding for groups working with victims.

The present minister with responsibility for victims is Mr Des Browne.

The Compensation Agency

The Agency formed on the 1 April 1992 administers three statutory compensation schemes on behalf of the Secretary of State for Northern Ireland: the Criminal Injuries and Criminal Damage Compensation Schemes and compensation under the Terrorism Act 2000.

The Compensation Agency

Royston House
34 Upper Queen Street
Belfast
BT1 6FD
Tel: 028 9024 9944
Fax: 028 9024 6956
Web: www.nics.gov.uk/co
Email: comp-agency@nics.gov.uk

Prisons Administration

The Northern Ireland Prison Service includes three prisons and a young offenders centre.

Northern Ireland Prison Service

Dundonald House
Upper Newtownards Road
Belfast
BT4 3SU
Tel: 028 9052 2922
Fax: 028 9052 5160
Web: www.niprisonservice.gov.uk
Email: info@niprisionservice.gov.uk
Director General: Peter Russell

The Prison Population (October 2002)

Establishment	Sentenced	Awaiting Trial	Total
Maghaberry	268	289	557
Magilligan	316	0	316
Hydebank YOC	72	91	163
Total	656	380	1036

The bulk of the prison population in Northern Ireland is now made up of people convicted of non-terrorist related offences.

Life Sentence Prisoners

As of 1st February 2002 there were 85 life sentence prisoners including 3 prisoners detained at the Secretary of State's pleasure. Since 1981 special arrangements have been in place for the release on licence of life sentence prisoners and under these arrangements 457 prisoners have been released to date.

The power to release a life sentence prisoner rests with the Secretary of State, after consultation with the Lord Chief Justice of Northern Ireland and the trial judge. The non-statutory Life Sentence Review Board formally advises the Secretary of State on the release of such prisoners. The average length of sentence served by a life sentence prisoner is 15 years.

Accelerated Release Prisoners

Under the terms of the Good Friday Agreement, the Northern Ireland (Sentences) Act was introduced in July 1998. Prisoners convicted of offences attracting a sentence of five years or more became eligible to apply for early release from the Independent Sentence Review Commission. The first releases under this scheme came on 11th September 1998. The releases to date are as follows:

Loyalist	194
Republican	241
Non-Aligned	12
Total	447

The Probation Board for Northern Ireland

The Probation Board for Northern Ireland

80-90 North Street
Belfast
BT1 1LD
Tel: 028 9026 2400
Fax: 028 9026 2472
Chairman: Brian Rowntree
Chief Executive: Oliver Brannigan

The Probation Board for Northern Ireland is an executive non-departmental body financed by grant in aid by the Northern Ireland Office, established by the Probation Board (NI) Order 1982.

The remit of the Board is the establishment and maintenance of an adequate and efficient probation service with responsibility for the development of the service in line with government policy.

The main Board undertakes: the supply of information to the courts through pre sentence reports, the supervision of offenders subject to community disposals and the provision of social welfare services in prisons. Initiatives aimed to support the supervision of offenders in the community are also supported by the Board.

The Secretary of State for Northern Ireland has overall responsibility for appointments to the Board.

Members of The Probation Board for Northern Ireland

Julian Crozier	Bernadette Grant
Robert Hanna	Janine Hillen
Pat Killen	Robert Mullan
Maura McCann	Francesca Reid
Geraldine Rice	Brian Stuart
Eileen Bell	Mary Clarke-Glass
Denis Moloney	Aidan Sherrard
Neil Boyle	Mairead Gilheaney

Policing in Northern Ireland

Policing and security have been a source of great political and social division in Northern Ireland. With over 3,000 civilians, including hundreds of security force personnel and members of government killed throughout the past thirty years of the "Troubles", policing and the role of the Police Service in Northern Ireland remains an emotive issue within all sections of the community. Recent reforms under 'Patten', the launch of the PSNI and controversial unresolved matters such as alleged security force collusion have continued to maintain the high priority of policing on the general political agenda.

Review of Policing in Northern Ireland

Given the divisive nature of policing in Northern Ireland it was not dealt with in detail under the terms of the Good Friday Agreement. Instead the Agreement promised a subsequent detailed review of policing. The Review Group on Policing, the Independent Commission on Policing in Northern Ireland, was set up shortly after the signing of the Agreement under the chairmanship of current EU Commissioner and former Conservative Minister Chris Patten.

The Patten Report

The "Patten" Report recommended radical reform of the Royal Ulster Constabulary including:

* A change of name, uniform, insignia;
* Structural Reforms;
* Creation of a democratically accountable, powerful Police Board to whom the Chief Constable would report;
* Quotas for recruitment to make the Service more representative of the community;
* Establishment of a Police Ombudsman for independent investigation of complaints.

Policing in Northern Ireland is governed by the "tripartite structure" involving the Secretary of State for Northern Ireland, the Policing Board and the Chief Constable. The Police (NI) Act 2000 details the provisions for this arrangement, which substantially implements the recommendations of the Patten Commission and

establishes the duty of the Chief Constable to exercise his functions to provide for the efficiency of the service and the conduct of policing in an impartial manner.

As policing is a reserved matter, not yet devolved to the Northern Ireland Assembly, the Secretary of State sets the statutory framework for policing and is empowered to set long term political objectives. His role encompasses obtaining and providing the annual police grant and approving the appointment of senior police officers. He is responsible for making the regulations which set out the terms and conditions of service of police officers and may regulate on the emblems and flags of the police service; he appoints the Independent Members of the Policing Board, the Oversight Commissioner, Inspectors of Constabulary to inspect the police service and is involved in the selection of the Police Ombudsman.

The Secretary of State may issue Codes of Practice to the Policing Board and has issued a code on the appointment of independent members to District Policing Partnerships and may also issue guidance on the use of public order equipment. He also carries responsibility for issues concerning national security.

The Westminster government remains committed to devolving responsibility for policing and justice functions once the devolved institutions are operating effectively. The target for devolving these responsibilities to the Assembly was originally scheduled for May 2003 following the Assembly elections and rests on the implementation of the Criminal Justice Review and further progress on implementation of the Patten report.

Police Service Restructuring

In addition to the change of name to the Police Service of Northern Ireland, the force has been restructured. Twenty-nine new District Command Units (DCUs) have been created. Twenty-five of these match the boundaries of District Council areas outside Belfast. For administrative and logistical reasons Belfast City Council area has been split into four DCUs - North, South, East and West.

The development of DCUs is in line with the RUC's own 'Fundamental Review of Policing' published in 1996 and was one of the central recommendations in the Patten Report, i.e. that policing should be delivered with and for the community.

The new structure devolves all decision-making about resources, personnel, services and budgets to local District Commanders.

The policing reforms are designed in order to allow all communities within Northern Ireland to support a new beginning in policing. It remains to be seen if this goal can be achieved given the package of changes are criticised for being either too radical or for not being radical enough.

NORTHERN IRELAND POLICING BOARD

Northern Ireland Policing Board
Waterside Tower
31 Clarendon Road
Clarendon Dock
Belfast
BT1 3BG
Tel: 028 9040 8500
Fax: 028 9040 8525
E-mail: information@nipolicingboard.org.uk
Web: www.nipolicingboard.org.uk

Chief Executive: Robert McCann

The Northern Ireland Policing Board was created on 4 November 2001 and is tasked with securing the maintenance, effectiveness and efficiency of the Police Service of Northern Ireland. It draws its legislative power from the Police (Northern Ireland) Act 2000. Its key responsibility is to hold the Chief Constable to account for his actions and those of his staff - this means that the Chief Constable is answerable to the Board on any aspect of policing in Northern Ireland. The Policing Board has 19 members in total, including the Chairman and Vice-Chairman. 10 members are members of the Northern Ireland Assembly; 9 are Independent members appointed by the Secretary of State for Northern Ireland.

The Policing Board

The establishment of the Policing Board under the terms of the Police (NI) Act 2000 which replaces the Police Authority is comprised of 10 democratically elected Assembly Members chosen by the parties and 9 independent members appointed by the Secretary of State on the basis of their skills and experience.

The UUP, DUP, and SDLP are represented on the Policing Board; Sinn Fein has not taken up its invitation to nominate members.

The Policing Board has responsibility for the accountability of the police and monitoring and evaluating the service provided. The powers of the Board include:

- Ensuring the efficiency and effectiveness of the service;
- Setting objectives and performance targets for the annual Policing Plan published by the Board;
- Monitoring the performance of the Chief Constable against the plan;
- Monitoring the human rights performance of the service;
- Maintaining the knowledge of the Board in relation to patterns of recruitment and assessment of the effectiveness of recruitment procedures;
- Assessing the effectiveness of the new police code of ethics;
- Assessing public satisfaction with police and district policing partnerships;
- Requiring the Chief Constable to report on any matter connected with policing and the option to establish an inquiry;
- Determining the policing budget;
- Appointing senior officers subject to approval of the Secretary of state;
- Making arrangements to secure the economy, efficiency and effectiveness of the Board and police service;
- Production of an annual report.

The Board in fulfilling its function is required to give consideration to the principle that policing should be impartial and to the overall policing plan.

Policing Board Members (October 2002)	
Desmond Rea	Chairman
Denis Bradley	Vice-Chairman
Alex Attwood	MLA SDLP
Viscount Brookeborough	UUP
Joe Byrne	MLA SDLP
Fred Cobain	MLA UUP
Brian Dougherty	
Barry Gilligan	
William Hay	MLA DUP
Tom Kelly	
Lord Kilclooney	MLA UUP
Sam Foster	MLA UUP
Pauline McCabe	
Alan McFarland	MLA UUP
Eddie McGrady	MLA SDLP
Rosaleen Moore	
Ian Paisley (Junior)	MLA DUP
Suneil Sharma	
Sammy Wilson	MLA DUP

Police Powers

In the exercise of their powers the police are responsible to the law primarily under the terms of PACE 1989 (The Police and Criminal Evidence (NI) Order 1989) and the Code under it. Their powers to combat terrorism arise under the Terrorism Act 2000 and the associated Code. The police may seek support from the armed forces when facing major terrorist or public order issues.

The general duties of officers are set out in the Police (Northern Ireland) Act 2000 to: protect life and property, preserve order, prevent crime and bring offenders to justice. In the discharge of their duties officers are guided by a code of ethics and must seek to co-operate and aim to secure the support of the local community.

POLICING *with the* COMMUNITY

Working with your community to make it a safer place

The Police Service of Northern Ireland is committed to meeting the challenges of change and to working with the community to tackle crime, protect human rights and improve the quality of life for everyone. For further information log on to **www.psni.police.uk**.

A Professional Progressive Police Service

The Chief Constable

The Chief Constable has responsibility for the operational direction and control of the police service with managerial responsibility for the police and other staff of the service and the use of resources. Hugh Orde has been appointed as the new Chief Constable of the Police Service of Northern Ireland.

Under the terms of the Police (NI) Act 2000 the Chief Constable is required to:

• Produce a draft of the policing plan detailing how he intends to police Northern Ireland in line with priorities set by the Secretary of State and the Policing Board. The Policing Board approves and publishes this plan before the commencement of each financial year;

• Ensure that district Commanders produce local policing plans, which are consistent with the annual plan after consultation with the local District Policing Partnership;

• Bring to the attention of all officers the terms of the new declaration (or oath);

• Draft an action plan for increasing the number of women in the Police Service should the Board require;

• Provide guidance to officers on the registration of notifiable memberships (memberships of an organisation which might be regarded as affecting the ability of an officer to discharge his duties effectively and impartially);

• Ensure that officers read and understand the code of ethics;

• Report on any matter connected with policing to the Board. The Chief Constable may "appeal" against such a request to the Secretary of State in specific grounds as set out in the Act;

• Produce and publish an annual report.

Policing Resources

Overall financial responsibility for police resources rests with the Policing Board however, day-to-day management with the exception of the purchase of land is delegated to the Chief Constable who has responsibility for the delivery of the policing service. £660 million was granted for policing by the Secretary of State at the commencement of the financial year, staff costs accounting for £470 million and £2.5 million for the running costs of the Policing Board. A further £10 million has been made available to meet additional policing costs.

PSNI Staff Complement (June 2002)	
Chief Constable	1
Deputy Chief Constable	2
Assistant Chief Constable	9
Chief Superintendent	40
Superintendent	161
Chief Inspector	168
Inspector	490
Sergeant	1414
Constable	6243
Total Regular Officers	8488
Full Time Reserve	3202
Part Time Reserve	1765

The recruitment campaign for the new Police Service of Northern Ireland under the 50:50 procedures set out in the 2000 Act utilised an independent recruitment agency and assessment. Applicants are tested to gain entry to a merit pool and the 50:50 rule of Catholic and non-Catholic is applied. The first set of recruits for the PSNI commenced training on 4 November 2001 and further training and recruitment exercises are ongoing.

Under the terms of the 2000 Act the Oversight Commissioner is responsible for overseeing the implementation of the changes in policing arrangements and structures recommended in the Patten report. Tom Constantine was appointed as the Oversight Commissioner on 31st May 2000. Following political difficulties between the parties a second revised Implementation plan on the Report by the Independent Commission on Policing for Northern Ireland "The Community and the Police Service" published in August 2001 set out the work required, lead responsibility, and timescale for implementation of each recommendation. A comprehensive account of the progress made in the implementation of the Patten proposals is given and updated timescales and targets are also included.

The Implementation Plan stated that a review to report on the new policing arrangements was to commence in March 2002 on the basis of the experience gained during the first year of the operation of the Policing Board with a report expected by October 2002. A number of areas where the Government intends to amend legislation following the review have been indicated in the updated Implementation Plan.

POLICE OMBUDSMAN

Police Ombudsman for Northern Ireland
New Cathedral Buildings
St Anne's Square
11 Church Street
BELFAST
BT1 1PG

Tel: 028 9082 8600 / 0845 601 2931
Fax: 028 9082 8659
Email: info@policeombudsman.org
Website: www.policeombudman.org

Police Ombudsman: Mrs Nuala O'Loan

The office of the Police Ombudsman for Northern Ireland provides an independent system for the investigation of complaints against police officers, including those which allege that the conduct of a police officer may have caused death or serious injury. The Police Ombudsman can react to incidents- even if no individual complaint has been made -if she believes it is in the public interest to do so.

The Role of the Police Ombudsman

The role of the Ombudsman's office is to provide an impartial police complaints system for the police and civilians under the terms of the Police (NI) Act 1998.

The current ombudsman is Nuala O'Loan. The role of the Police Ombudsman includes the following:

- Receives complaints;
- Deals with complaints about how the police behave when they are doing their job. Complaints may involve allegations of criminal behaviour by a police officer, or allegations that the police officer broke the police code of conduct;
- Decides how to deal with complaints;
- Decides the outcome of complaints;
- Monitors trends and patterns in complaints.

The Police Ombudsman may investigate a matter if there is reason to think that a police officer may have committed a criminal offence or broken the police code of conduct.

Forensic Science Agency

The Forensic Science Agency of Northern Ireland provides scientific advice and support to enhance the delivery of justice.

The Forensic Science Agency of Northern Ireland

151 Belfast Road
Carrickfergus
BT38 8PL
Tel: 028 90 36 1888
Fax: 028 90 36 1900
Web: www.fsani.org.uk

Chief Executive: Dr Richard Adams

Administration of Justice

The Role of the Court Service

> **The Northern Ireland Court Service**
>
> Windsor House
> 9-15 Bedford Street
> Belfast
> BT2 7LT
> Tel: 028 9032 8594
> Fax: 028 9032 8494
> Web: www.courtsni.gov.uk

The Court Service was established by the Judicature (Northern Ireland) Act 1978 as "a unified and distinct Civil Service of the Crown" and is a department of the Lord Chancellor, currently Lord Irvine. The functions of the Court Service as defined by statute are:

- To facilitate the conduct of the business of the Supreme Court, county courts, magistrates courts and coroners courts;
- To give effect to judgements to which the Judgements Enforcement (Northern Ireland) Order 1981 applies;
- To discharge such other functions as are conferred on or transferred to it.

The Lord Chancellor holds responsibility for a wide range of functions affecting the administration of justice in Northern Ireland and has the leading role in appointments to judicial, quasi-judicial offices and Queen's Counsel. He holds ministerial responsibility for legal aid, matters affecting the provision of legal services to the public, and determining the statutory framework for the structure, jurisdiction and operation of the courts in Northern Ireland. The role of the Court Service is to support the Lord Chancellor in the discharge of these responsibilities.

Organisational Structure of the Court Service

The Court Service is led by a Director General, David Lavery, who is Head of Department, Principal Accounting Officer and Accountant General of the Supreme Court of Judicature of Northern Ireland, reporting directly to the Lord Chancellor and supported by three directors, each with responsibility for a division within the Court Service. The three divisions are:

- Operations;
- Policy and Legislation;
- Corporate Services.

Alan Hunter has been appointed as director with responsibility for Legal Aid.

Operations Division

The Operations Division led by George Keatley is responsible for:

- Delivering operational functions associated with the administration of the courts ranging from issuing originating processes to the implementation of court decisions;
- Administering the Fixed Penalty Office;
- Enforcing court judgements under the Judgements Enforcement (Northern Ireland) Order 1981;
- Providing administrative support to the Social Security and Child Support Commissioners, the Pensions Appeals Tribunals and the Tribunal established under section 91 of the Northern Ireland Act 1998;
- Meeting the standards laid down in the Courts Charter for Northern Ireland.

Policy and Legislation Division

The Policy and Legislation Division, which is led by Laurene McAlpine, undertakes central government functions in support of the Lord Chancellor's ministerial responsibilities including:
- Determining the policy and legislative framework within which the courts will operate;
- Carrying out on behalf of the Lord Chancellor the functions of the Central Authority under the European and Hague Conventions on Child Abduction;
- Providing legal advice to the Court Service and HM Coroners on the complete range of executive functions;
- Developing legal aid policy;
- Monitoring expenditure on legal aid and its associated administration;
- Providing the Secretariat to Court Rules Committees, the Judicial Studies Board for Northern Ireland, the Lay Panel Training Committee and the Lord Chancellor's Legal Advisory Committee.

Corporate Services Division

Frank Duffy leads the Corporate Services Division. The division has responsibility for:

- Providing a range of services in support of other divisions and the judiciary, including personnel and training, resource management, procurement, including capital projects and information technology;

- Supporting judicial appointments, including advisory committees;
- Providing an internal audit function;
- Managing funds lodged in court on behalf of adults and minors.

The Court Structure in Northern Ireland

The House of Lords

Final court of Appeal in the UK

Hears appeals on points of law in cases of major importance

The Court of Appeal

Hears appeals on points of law in criminal and civil cases from all courts

---

The High Court

Hears complex or important civil cases in three divisions and also appeals from County Courts

Queen's Bench Division   **Chancery Division**   **Family Division**

County Courts including Family Care Centres (7 Divisions)

Hears a wide range of civil actions from Magistrates' Courts

Small Claims Courts

Hears consumer claims and minor civil cases

The Crown Court

Hears all serious criminal cases

Magistrates' Courts (including Juvenvile Courts and Family Proceedings Courts)
(21 Petty Sessions Districts)

Conducts preliminary hearings in more serious criminal cases, cases involving juveniles and some civil and domestic cases, including family proceedings

Coroners' Courts

Investigates the circumstances of sudden, violent or unnatural deaths

The Enforcement of Judgements Office

Enforces money and other judgements

A new multi court complex has been completed on Belfast's Laganside. The complex comprises Crown, county and magistrates courts and their administration. A new headquarters for the Bar Council and the Department of the Director of Public Prosecutions is currently under construction on a site adjacent to the Royal Courts of Justice in Belfast.

Policy and Legislative Programme

The Court Service aims to provide policy advice and deliver an agreed programme of legislation including court rules involving the formulation of non executive policy, including civil and criminal policy, advice on such policy to ministers and on the general administration of justice. The Court Service also advises the Chancellor on a breadth of judicial and public appointments and the operation of recruitment and selection procedures.

The Northern Ireland Judiciary

The role of the Court Service is to ensure the efficient and effective disposal of court business and support the Judiciary. The relationship between the Judiciary and the Courts Service is crucial in the administration of the courts and tribunals. However, whilst close co-operation is required it is imperative that the independence of the judiciary is maintained.

Full and Part Time Judiciary

Supreme Court	
Lord Chief Justice	1
Lord Justices of Appeal	3
High Court Judges	7
Masters	7
Principal Secretary and Legal Secretary to the Lord Chief Justice	1
Official Solicitor	1
County Courts	
County Court Judges	14
District Judges	4
Magistrates Courts	
Resident Magistrates	17
Chief Social Security and Child Support Commissioner	1
Social Security and Child Support Commissioner	1
Coroner	1

Appointments to the Judiciary

Recommendations to the Lord Chancellor are made by Advisory Committees on the appointment of Justices of the Peace, Lay Panel Members and General Commissioners of Income Tax. The manager of the Judicial Appointments Branch performs the role of Assistant Secretary of Commissions (Northern Ireland) to each Committee.

Criminal Justice Review

The Good Friday Agreement committed the British government to establishing a wide-ranging review of criminal justice through a mechanism with an independent element. The Agreement indicated that the criminal justice system should be fair and impartial, responsive to the community and encouraging of its involvement, have the confidence of all parts of the community and deliver justice efficiently and effectively.

The Director General of the Court Service represented the Lord Chancellor on the Criminal Justice Review Group, which was chaired by a senior official of the Northern Ireland Office, including a representative of the Attorney General together with a number of independent assessors.

The report of the Criminal Justice Review Group published in March 2000 was welcomed by the British and Irish Governments, which considered that its early and effective implementation would make a positive contribution to the overall implementation of the Good Friday Agreement.

The Legal Profession in Northern Ireland

The legal profession in Northern Ireland is composed of two separate and complementary branches:
- Barristers;
- Solicitors.

Differences in the services each provide are reflected by the differences in their training and organisation. Solicitors provide the first point of contact for those seeking legal advice and in many cases such as conveyancing, making wills or matrimonial matters may be the only contact necessary. However a barrister may be required to advise or represent a client in court. Contact in the first instance is usually through the client's solicitor rather than directly with the client, this is thought to aid the maintenance of impartiality.

Should a case proceed, the solicitor may undertake the preparatory work however, barristers with their experience of litigation and knowledge of the procedures of the court and judiciary will focus on the presentation of the matter. The client and solicitor meet as and if required by the nature of the case.

In November 2002 there were 552 barristers in independent practice in Northern Ireland. There are 67 Queen's Counsel, barristers who have earned a high reputation and are appointed by the Queen on the recommendation of the Lord Chancellor as senior advocates and advisers. The title does not imply an association with the State.

Barristers who are not Queen's Counsel are called Junior Counsel. This term is misleading since many members of the Junior Bar are experienced barristers with considerable expertise.

The Executive Council and the Bar Council

The Executive Council is involved with the education and fees of students; calling counsel to the Bar although the call to the Bar is performed by the Lord Chief Justice on the invitation of the Benchers; administration of the Bar Library, to which all practising members of the Bar belong and liaising with corresponding bodies in other countries. The Bar Council is responsible for the maintenance of the standards, honour and independence of the Bar and, through its Professional Conduct Committee, receives and investigates complaints against members of the Bar in their professional capacity.

The General Council of the Bar
in Northern Ireland

Royal Courts of Justice
Belfast
BT1 3JP
Tel: 028 9024 1523
Fax: 028 9023 1850

THE LAW SOCIETY NORTHERN IRELAND

Law Society Northern Ireland
Law Society House
98 Victoria Street
Belfast BT1 3JZ
Web: www.lawsoc-ni.org
Tel: (028) 9023 1614
Fax: (028) 9023 2606

In 1992 a Royal Charter was granted to solicitors in Northern Ireland to permit the setting up of the Incorporated Law Society of Northern Ireland. Under the Solicitors (Northern Ireland) Order of 1976, the Law Society acts as the regulatory authority governing the education, accounts, discipline and professional conduct of solicitors in order to maintain the independence, ethical standards, professional competence and quality of services offered to the public.

The Society operates through an elected Council which is served by numerous Standing and Special Committees, all comprising practising solicitors. It takes an active interest in all issues connected with law and order and the administration of justice.

Legal Aid Administration

The Law Society of Northern Ireland holds statutory responsibility for the civil legal aid scheme and administers criminal legal aid on behalf of the Lord Chancellor. The Legal Aid department is managed by the Legal Aid Committee of the Law Society composed of solicitors and barristers, one of whom is appointed by the Lord Chancellor. Financial memoranda and management statements govern relationships between the Law Society, its Legal Aid committee and department and the Court Service. The Court Service facilitates the administration of legal aid by the Legal Aid department.

hello

how can we help you?

Would you like to know more about the Orange network in your area?
Do you have any comments or questions about our existing transmitter sites
or our future coverage plans? If so, we would like to hear from you.

You can contact Orange in Northern Ireland at the following address:

Orange PCS Ltd
Quay Gate House
15 Scrabo Street
Belfast BT5 4BD
Tel: 028 9073 6600
Fax: 028 9073 6601
Email: jonathan.rose@orange.co.uk

A Freephone information line is also available on:
0800 783 5021

www.orange.co.uk

Northern Ireland's Government Departments

Although Northern Ireland had its own devolved government from the foundation of the state in 1920 until 1972, for most of the last 30 years the province has been governed directly from Westminster. However, since the passing of the 1998 Northern Ireland Act a devolved government was restored featuring a power sharing Executive and eleven new government departments.

Local ministers up to the time of the suspension of the Assembly in October 2002 headed the departments.

First Minister	David Trimble
Deputy First Minister	Mark Durkan
Dept of Agriculture and Rural Development	Brid Rodgers
Dept of Culture, Arts and Leisure	Michael McGimpsey
Dept of Education	Martin McGuinness
Dept for Employment and Learning	Carmel Hanna
Dept of Enterprise, Trade and Investment	Reg Empey
Dept of the Environment	Dermot Nesbitt
Dept of Finance and Personnel	Sean Farren
Dept of Health, Social Services and Public Safety	Bairbre de Brun
Dept for Regional Development	Peter Robinson
Dept for Social Development	Nigel Dodds

Following the suspension of the Northern Ireland Assembly, ministers from Westminster, who operate under the authority of the Northern Ireland Office, replaced local ministers representing the ten departments on the Northern Ireland Executive.

Northern Ireland Office Team

Secretary of State	Paul Murphy MP
Minister of State	Jane Kennedy MP
Parliamentary Under Secretary	Des Browne MP
Parliamentary Under Secretary	Ian Pearson MP
Parliamentary Under Secretary	Angela Smith MP

Four ministers support the Northern Ireland Office headed by the Secretary of State Paul Murphy and together they are responsible for the governance of Northern Ireland and the management of the ten departments whilst direct rule is in place.

Following the introduction of direct rule, the ministerial portfolios were allocated as follows:

Minister of State Jane Kennedy MP retained her existing NIO responsibilities for security and prisons and assumed responsibility for the Department of Education, and the Department of Employment and Learning.

Parliamentary Under Secretary of State Des Browne MP retained his existing NIO responsibilities as minister for victims and assumed responsibility for the Department of Social Development, the Department of Health, Social Services and Public Safety, Equality, Human Rights and Community Relations.

Newly appointed Parliamentary Under Secretary of State Ian Pearson MP assumed ministerial responsibility for the Department of Finance and Personnel, the Department of Enterprise, Trade and Investment, the Department of Agriculture and Rural Development, the Economic Policy Unit and Europe.

Newly appointed Parliamentary Under Secretary of State Angela Smith MP assumed responsibility for the Department of the Environment, the Department for Regional Development and the Department of Culture, Arts and Leisure.

Details of the Northern Ireland Departments are set out over.

Office of the First Minister and Deputy First Minister

Parliament Buildings, Stormont, Belfast BT4 3XX
Tel: 028 9052 8400
Fax: 028 9052 1283
Web: www.ni.gov.uk

Direct Rule Ministers: Ian Pearson, Angela Smith

Head of the Civil Service: Nigel Hamilton,Tel: 028 9037 8133

Second Permanent Secretary: Will Haire, Tel: 028 9037 8143

The Office of the First Minister and Deputy First Minister was established as a department on 1 December 1999 following the devolution of power to Northern Ireland.

The work of the department revolves around three interrelated roles:
* To support the work of the Executive;
* To undertake the departmental functions allocated to the First Minister and Deputy First Minister; and
* To provide a service to the other government departments.

The Office of First and Deputy First Minister (OFMDFM) is a new concept among the power sharing institutions established under the Good Friday Agreement. Essentially it is intended to be a joint department where the leaders of the two 'blocs' of government manage the overall government agenda and incorporate policy units, which cover sensitive central government functions. Now operated by the Northern Ireland Office, UUP leader David Trimble and SDLP leader Mark Durkan previously led OFMDFM. The "joint " nature of the department effectively prevents government policy from developing except by agreement and depends on a degree of goodwill between the main political players in government in order to operate effectively.

Areas of Responsibility

Brussels Office;
Central Emergency Planning Unit;
Central IT Unit for Northern Ireland;
Children and Young Peoples Unit;
Civic Forum Secretariat;
Community Relations Unit;
Economic Policy Unit;
Equality Unit;
Executive Information Service;
Executive Secretariat;

Honours;
Human Rights;
Machinery of Government;
North/South Ministerial Council;
Northern Ireland Bureau in Washington;
Public Appointments;
Public Service Reform Unit;
Review of Public Administration;
Secretariat for Commissioner
  for Public Appointments;
Victims Unit

Office of The First Minister and Deputy First Minister Structure

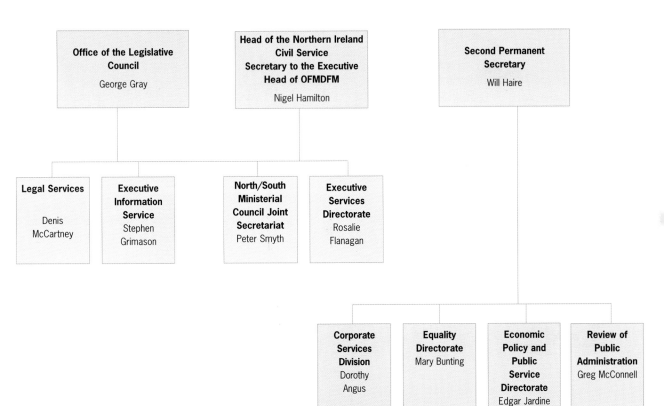

Equality Directorate

Director: Mary Bunting
Tel: 028 9052 2857
Fax: 028 9052 0761
E-mail:
mary.bunting@ofmdfmni.gov.uk

Equality and Social Need Division

Head of Division: Gerry Mulligan
Tel: 028 9052 3148
Fax: 028 9052 8300
E-mail:
gerry.mulligan@ofmdfmni.gov.uk

The New TSN Unit

Contact: Harriet Ferguson
Tel: 028 9052 2048
Fax: 028 9052 3323
E-mail:
harriet.ferguson@ofmdfmni.gov.uk

Section 75 Statutory Duty Unit

Contact: Ray Morrison
Tel: 028 9052 3140
Fax: 028 9052 3272
E-mail:
ray.morrison@ofmdfmni.gov.uk

Race Equality Unit

Contact: Ken Fraser
Tel: 028 9052 2615
Fax: 028 9052 3323
E-mail: ken.fraser@ofmdfmni.gov.uk

Gender Equality Unit

Contact: Hilary Harbinson
Tel: 028 9052 8194
Fax: 028 9052 3323
E-mail:
hilary.harbinson@ofmdfmni.gov.uk

Research Branch

Contact: Dr Stephen Donnelly
Tel: 028 9052 3284
Fax: 028 9052 3272
E-mail:
stephen.donnelly@ofmdfmni.gov.uk

Community Relations, Human Rights and Victims Division

Head of Division: Chris Stewart
Tel: 028 9052 8351
Fax: 028 9052 8474
E-mail:
chris.stewart@ofmdfmni.gov.uk

Community Relations Unit

Contact: Denis Ritchie
Tel: 028 9052 3460
Fax: 028 9052 2229
E-mail:
denis.ritchie@ofmdfmni.gov.uk

Human Rights Unit

Contact: Chris Stewart
Tel: 028 9052 8351
Fax: 028 9052 8874
E-mail:
chris.stewart@ofmdfmni.gov.uk

Victims Unit

Contact: Fergus Devitt
Tel: 028 9052 3167
Fax: 028 9052 8354
E-mail:
fergus.devitt@ofmdfmni.gov.uk

Children and Young People's Unit

Contact: Heather Stevens
Tel: 028 9052 3118
Fax: 028 9052 8275
E-mail:
heather.stephens@ofmdfm.gov.uk

Anti-Discrimination Division

Head of Division: Patricia McAuley
Tel: 028 9052 3156
Fax: 028 9052 8300
E-mail:
patricia.mcauley@ofmdfmni.gov.uk

Single Equality Bill

Contact: Ivan Millen
Tel: 028 9052 3365
Fax: 028 9052 3272
E-mail: ivan.millen@ofmdfmni.gov.uk

Race, Fair Employment and Disability Discrimination

Contact: Ken Walker
Tel: 028 9052 3158
Fax: 028 9052 3272
E-mail: ken.walker@ofmdfmni.gov.uk

Sex and Sexual Orientation Discrimination and Equal Pay

Director: Drew Haire
Tel: 028 9052 0088
Fax: 028 9052 3272
E-mail: drew.haire@ofmdfmni.gov.uk

Oversight of Equality Commission

Director: Drew Haire
Tel: 028 9052 0088
Fax: 028 9052 3272
E-mail: drew.haire@ofmdfmni.gov.uk

North Belfast Community Action Unit

Head of Unit: Evelyn Cummins
Tel: 028 9072 6014
Fax: 028 9072 6102
E-mail:
evelyn.cummins@ofmdfm.gov.uk

The North Belfast Community Action Unit is part of the Office of the First Minister and Deputy First Minister

but also reports to the Department for Social Development. The Unit is guided by a steering group of officials from both these departments and has responsibility for developing a long term strategy; encouraging partnerships; building community capacity; and addressing interface issues in North Belfast.

Executive and Corporate Services Directorate

Director: Rosalie Flanagan
Tel: 028 9037 8123
Fax: 028 9037 8035
E-mail:
rosalie.flanagan@ofmdfmni.gov.uk

Executive Secretariat
(Including NSMC, BIC and Civic Forum Liaison)

Head of Division: Stewart Johnston
Tel: 028 9037 8149
Fax: 028 9037 8035
E-mail:
stewart.johnston@ofmdfmni.gov.uk

Contact: Gail McKibbin
Tel: 028 9037 2514
Fax: 028 9037 8427
E-mail:
gail.mckibbin@ofmdfmni.gov.uk

Machinery of Government Division

Head of Division: Linda Devlin
Tel: 028 9037 8157
Fax: 028 9037 8221
E-mail:
linda.devlin@ofmdfmni.gov.uk

Machinery of Government Division essentially performs an internal support function within the Northern Ireland administration. It operates at the interface of the OFMDFM and other government departments and the Northern Ireland Assembly, co-ordinating and monitoring flows of information and providing guidance on a range of activities.

Contact: Tom Watson
Tel: 028 9037 8159
Fax: 028 90378221
E-mail:
tom.watson@ofmdfmni.gov.uk

Reserved and Excepted Matters

Contact: Tom Watson
Tel: 028 9037 8159
Fax: 028 9037 8221
E-mail:
tom.watson@ofmdfmni.gov.uk

Contact: Jim Hamilton
Tel: 028 9037 8158
Fax: 028 9037 8221
E-mail: jim.hamilton@ofmdfm.gov.uk

Assembly Section

Contact: Dr Deirdre Griffith
Tel: 028 9037 8162
Fax: 028 9037 8221
E-mail:
deirdre.griffith@ofmdfmni.gov.uk

Contact: Geoff Beattie
Tel: 028 9037 8161
Fax: 028 9037 8221
E-mail:
geoff.beattie@ofmdfm.gov.uk

Legislation Progress Unit

Contact: Jim Hamilton
Tel: 028 9037 8158
Fax: 028 9037 8221
E-mail:
jim.hamilton@ofmdfmni.gov.uk

The functions of the Legislation Progress Unit are to manage, co-ordinate and monitor Northern Ireland legislation from the Northern Ireland Departments.

Corporate Services Division

Head of Division: Dorothy Angus
Tel: 028 9052 8153
Fax: 028 9052 0748
E-mail:
dorothy.angus@ofmdfmni.gov.uk

Finance

Contact: Audrey Playfair
Tel: 028 9052 3440
Fax: 028 9052 8135
E-mail:
audrey.playfair@ofmdfmni.gov.uk

Personnel and Office Services

Contact: Liz Elliott
Tel: 028 9052 2119
Fax: 028 9052 2339
E-mail: liz.elliott@ofmdfmni.gov.uk

Information Technology

Contact: Robert Fee
Tel: 028 9052 2670
Fax: 028 9052 3452
E-mail: robert.fee@ofmdfmni.gov.uk

Knowledge Network Team

Contact: Robert Fee
Tel: 028 9052 2670
Fax: 028 9052 3452
E-mail: robert.fee@ofmdfmni.gov.uk

Central Management Branch

Contact: Geoffrey Simpson
Tel: 028 9052 3245
Fax: 028 9052 2933
E-mail: geoffrey.simpson@ofmdfm

Central Appointments Unit (CAU)

Contact: Geoffrey Simpson
Tel: 028 9052 3245
Fax: 028 9052 8125
E-mail:geoffrey.simpson@ofmdfm

Honours

Contact: Gary Smith
Tel: 028 9052 8162
Fax: 028 9052 8200
E-mail: gary.smith@ofmdfmni.gov.uk

Central Emergency Planning Unit (CEPU)

Contact: Bill Clements
Tel: 028 9052 8860
Fax: 028 9052 8875
E-mail:
bill.clements@ofmdfmni.gov.uk

The Northern Ireland Bureau, Washington

Contact: Danny McNeill, Director
Tel: 001 202 367 0461
Fax: 001 202 367 0468
E-mail: dmcneill@nibureau.com

Deputy Director/First Secretary:
Michael Gould
Tel: 011 202 367 0462
Fax: 001 202 367 0468
E-mail: m.gould@nibureau.com
Web: www.nibureau.com

The Northern Ireland Bureau acts as a focal point for Northern Ireland Affairs in the US and represents the interests of the Executive and the Northern Ireland Assembly with the legislative and Executive branches of the US government in Washington. Beyond that, however, it also has a remit to explore with relevant State governments the possibilities for developing co-operative linkages with organisational counterparts in Northern Ireland.

Economic Policy Unit and Public Service Directorate

Director: Edgar Jardine
Tel: 028 9052 8505
Fax: 028 9052 2262
E-mail:
edgar.jardine@ofmdfmni.gov.uk

Economic Policy Unit

Head of Division: Eugene Rooney
Tel: 028 9052 3198
Fax: 028 9052 2262
E-mail:
eugene.rooney@ofmdfmni.gov.uk

The role of the Economic Policy Unit is to support the First Minister and Deputy First Minister, and through them the Executive Committee as a whole, in their strategic role and responsibilities for the formulation, co-ordination and management of the policies of the Administration.

Economic Policy and Effectiveness

Contact: Michael Brennan
Tel: 028 9052 2428
Fax: 028 9052 2552
E-mail:
michael.brennan@ofmdfmni.gov.uk

Policy Innovation Unit

Contact: Colin Jack
Tel: 028 9052 8439
Fax: 028 9252 2552
E-mail: colin.jack@ofmdfmni.gov.uk

Reinvestment and Reform Initiative

Contact: Alan Maitland
Tel: 028 9052 8251
Fax: 028 9052 2552
E-mail:
alan.maitland@ofmdfmni.gov.uk

Programme for Government and Financial Resources

Programme for Government and PSAs

Contact: Katrina Godfrey
Tel: 028 9052 2516
Fax: 028 9052 2552
E-mail:
katrina.godfrey@ofmdfmni.gov.uk

Finance Issues

Contact: John McKenna
Tel: 028 9052 2742
Fax: 028 9052 2552
E-mail:
john.mckenna@ofmdfmni.gov.uk

Review of Public Administration

Chief Operating Officer:
Greg McConnell
Tel: 028 9037 8156
Fax: 028 9037 8227
E-mail:
greg.mcconnell@rpani.gov.uk

Deputy Chief Operating Officer: Neill Jackson
Tel: 028 9037 8153
Fax: 028 9037 8227
E-mail: neill.jackson@rpani.gov.uk

Project Officers
Joan Cassells
Tel: 028 9037 8201
Fax: 028 9037 8222
E-mail: joan.cassells@ofmdfmni.gov.uk

Debbie Donnelly
Tel: 028 9037 8212
Fax: 028 9037 8222
E-mail:
debbie.donnelly@rpani.gov.uk

Mary McCullough
Tel: 028 9037 8045
Fax: 028 9037 8222
E-mail:
mary.mccullough@rpani.gov.uk

Hugh McPolland
Tel: 028 9037 8228
Fax: 028 9037 8222
E-mail:
hugh.mcpolland@rpani.gov.uk

Public Service Reform Unit

Head of Division: Peter May
Tel: 028 9052 8389
Fax: 028 9052 2262
E-mail: peter.may@ofmdfmni.gov.uk

Continuous Improvement of Public Services

Contact: Gerry O'Neill
Tel: 028 9052 6108
Fax: 028 9052 6107
E-mail:
gerry.oneill@ofmdfmni.gov.uk

Investors in People (IIP) Standard

Contact: Gerry O'Neill
Tel: 028 9052 6108
Fax: 028 9052 6107
E-mail:
gerry.oneill@ofmdfmni.gov.uk

Policy on Agencies and Non-departmental Public Bodies

Contact: Sharon Henderson
Tel: 028 9052 6657
Fax: 028 9052 6107
E-mail:
sharon.henderson@ofmdfmni.gov.uk

Contact: Cecil Millar
Tel: 028 9052 6109
Fax: 028 9052 6107
E-mail: cecil.millar@ofmdfmni.gov.uk

Strategy and European Affairs Division

Head of Division: Peter May

Tel: 028 9052 8389
Fax: 028 9052 2262
E-mail: peter.may@ofmdfmni.gov.uk

The Division deals with European policy and co-ordination issues and Measure 4.1 of the Peace II Programme. It also deals with a range of important strategic issues likely to come before the Executive.

European Policy Issues
Contact: Julie Mapstone
Tel: 028 9052 3105
Fax: 028 9052 2552
E-mail:
julie.mapstone@ofmdfmni.gov.uk

Measure 4.1 and Interface with NI EU Interests

Contact: Paul Geddis
Tel: 028 9052 8445
Fax: 028 9052 2552
E-mail:
paul.geddis@ofmdfmni.gov.uk

Office of the Northern Ireland Executive in Brussels

Head of Division: Tony Canavan
Tel: 00332 290 1335
Fax: 00332 290 1333
E-mail:
tony.canavan@ofmdfmni.gov.uk

The office provides the focal point for developing and progressing the Executive's policy approach to Europe. Its role is:

• Monitoring the development by EU institutions of policies relevant to Northern Ireland and providing up to date information to Ministers and Departments;
• Ensuring that NI interests are fully represented in policy developments by EU institutions;
• Raising the positive profile of Northern Ireland among European policy makers and opinion formers;
• Promoting inter-regional links between Northern Ireland and other parts of Europe.

Central Information Technology Unit (Northern Ireland)

Head of Division: Des Vincent
Tel: 028 9052 7426
Fax: 028 9052 7235
E-mail:
des.vincent@ofmdfmni.gov.uk

The Central Information Technology Unit (Northern Ireland) was established in April 1997 with a remit to drive forward the use of Information & Communication Technologies in the Northern Ireland Civil Service to:

• Improve the quality of service to the customer (citizen or business);
• Reduce the cost of service delivery.

e-Government Policy, and Modernising Law for the Information Age

Contact: Ray Wright

Tel: 028 9052 7688
Fax: 028 9052 7235
E-mail: ray.wright@ofmdfmni.gov.uk

Contact: John McKernan
Tel: 028 9052 7313
Fax: 028 9052 7235
E-mail:
john.mckernan@ofmdfmni.gov.uk

e-Government Strategy and Collaborative Projects

Contact: John Price
Tel: 028 9052 7405
Fax: 028 9052 7235
E-mail: john.price@ofmdfmni.gov.uk

Executive Information Service

Director: Stephen Grimason
Tel: 028 9037 8101
Fax: 028 9037 8013
E-mail:
stephen.grimason@ofmdfm.gov.uk
Deputy Director: John McKervill
Tel: 028 9052 2615
Fax: 028 9052 2996
E-mail:
john.mckervill@ofmdfmni.gov.uk

The Executive Information Service (EIS), provides the full range of news and public relations services to ministers and their departments. It seeks to present policy and activity of the Northern Ireland Administration. The central unit of EIS is based in Castle Buildings with staff out posted to provide an information service in each department.

Public Relations Unit

Contact: Lorna Armstrong
Tel: 028 9037 8112
Fax: 028 9037 8020
E-mail:
lorna.armstrong@ofmdfmni.gov.uk

Press Office

Contact: Don McAleer
Tel: 028 9037 8105
Fax: 028 9037 8016
E-mail:
don.mcaleer@ofmdfmni.gov.uk

Contact: Paul Pringle
Tel: 028 9037 8106
Fax: 028 9037 8016
E-mail:
paul.pringle@ofmdfmni.gov.uk

Co-ordination and Planning

Contact: Don McAleer
Tel: 028 9037 8105
Fax: 028 9037 8016
E-mail:
don.mcaleer@ofmdfmni.gov.uk

Press officers assigned to other
Ministers

Department of Agriculture and Rural Development

Contact: Bernie McCusker
Tel: 028 9052 4619
Fax: 028 9052 5003
E-mail:
bernadette.mccusker@dardni.gov.uk

Department of Culture, Arts and Leisure

Contact: Brian Kirk
Tel: 028 9025 8901
Fax: 028 9025 8906
E-mail: biran.kirk@dcalni.gov.uk

Department of Education

Contact: Jill Garrett

Tel: 028 9127 9356
Fax: 028 9127 9271
E-mail: jill.garrett@deni.gov.uk

Department of Enterprise, Trade and Investment

Contact: Jill Heron
Tel: 028 9052 9201
Fax: 028 9052 9546
E-mail: jill.heron@detni.gov.uk

Department of the Environment

Contact: Philip Maguire
Tel: 028 9054 0013
Fax: 028 9054 0029
E-mail: philip.maguire@doeni.gov.uk

Department of Finance and Personnel

Contact: Colin Ross
Tel: 028 9052 7375
Fax: 028 9052 7419
E-mail: colin.ross@dfpni.gov.uk

Department of Health, Social Services and Public Safety

Contact: Jim Hamilton
Tel: 028 9052 0636
Fax: 028 9052 0572
E-mail:
jim.hamilton@dhsspsni.gov.uk

Department for Employment and Learning

Contact: Gwyn Treharne
Tel: 028 9025 7790
Fax: 028 9025 7795
E-mail:
gwyn.treharne@dhfeteni.gov.uk

Department for Regional Development

Contact: Eamon Deeny
Tel: 028 9054 0004
Fax: 028 9054 1199
E-mail: eamon.deeny@drdni.gov.uk

Department for Social Development

Contact: Colm Shannon
Tel: 028 9056 9211

Fax: 028 9056 9269
E-mail: colm.shannon@dsdni.gov.uk

The North/South Ministerial Council Joint Secretariat

Joint Secretary: North:
Dr Peter Smyth
Tel: 028 3751 5004
Fax: 028 3751 1406
Web:
www.northsouthministerialcouncil.org

North/South Ministerial Council
Joint Secretariat, 39 Abbey Street
Armagh BT61 7EB

Contact: Pat Donaghy
Tel: 028 3751 5008
Fax: 028 3751 1406
E-mail: pat.donaghy@ofmdfmni.gov.uk

Contact: Basil Davidson
Tel: 028 3751 3036
Fax: 028 3751 1406
E-mail: basil.davidson@ofmdfmni.gov.uk

Office of the Legislative Counsel

Head of Directorate: George Gray
Tel: 028 9052 1307
Fax: 028 9052 1306
E-mail:
george.gray@ofmdfmni.gov.uk

Legal Services Directorate

Director: Denis McCartney
Tel: 028 9037 8125
Fax: 028 9037 8037
E-mail:
irena.elliott@ofmdfmni.gov.uk

Contact: Caroline Webb
Tel: 028 9037 8126
Fax: 028 9037 8037
E-mail:
caroline.webb@ofmdfmni.gov.uk

I'M RUNNING BETTER,

BREATHING EASIER

AND SAVING A FORTUNE.

I'M SO GLAD I KICKED THE HABIT.

Nigel Rowden, Fleet Manager, Thales Group.

Department of Agriculture and Rural Development

Dundonald House
Upper Newtownards Road
Belfast
BT4 3SB
Tel: 028 9052 4999
Fax: 028 9052 5003
Web: www.dard.gov.uk

Direct Rule Minister: Ian Pearson

Permanent Secretary: Peter Small
Tel: 028 9052 4613

The Department of Agriculture and Rural Development (DARD) aims to promote sustainable economic growth and the development of the countryside in Northern Ireland. The department assists the competitive development of the agri-food, fishing and forestry sectors of the Northern Ireland economy having regard for the needs of consumers, the welfare of animals and the conservation and enhancement of the environment.

DARD has responsibility for food, farming and environmental policy, as well as development of the agricultural, forestry and fishing industries in Northern Ireland. It provides a business development service for farmers, and a veterinary service with administration of animal health and welfare. It is responsible to the Department of the Environment, Food and Rural Affairs (DEFRA) in Great Britain, for the administration in Northern Ireland of schemes affecting the whole of the United Kingdom. The department also oversees the application of European Union agricultural policy to Northern Ireland.

The Department was given considerable recognition for the professional manner in which it handled the foot-and-mouth animal health crisis.

Department of Agriculture and Rural Development Structure

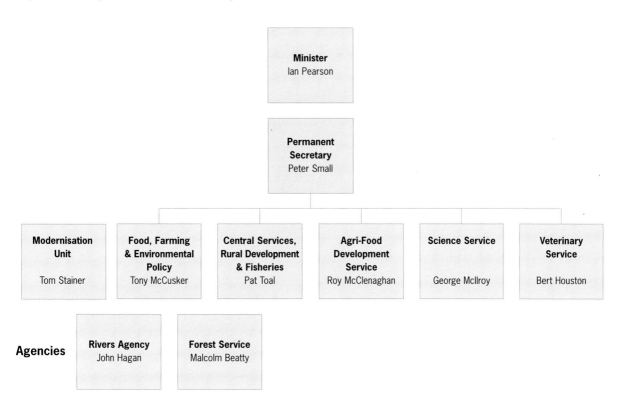

Food, Farming and Environmental Policy

Under Secretary: Tony McCusker

Animal Health and Welfare and Farm Policy

Assistant Secretary: L McKibben

Animal Health and International Trade
Principal: D G Kerr

Disease Control
Principal: C McMaster

TSE Division
Principal: K Davey

Farm Policy
Principal: J Cassells

Environmental and Food Policy

Assistant Secretary: D Small

Environmental Policy Division
Principal: J B McKee

Food Policy Division
Principal: P Scott

Grants & Subsidies

Assistant Secretary: R Jordan

Grants & Subsidies (Policy) Division
Principal: M B Thompson

Grants & Subsidies (Payments) Division
Principal: B Glendinning

Grant & Subsidies (Inspection) Division
Principal: W J McWhirter

Economics & Statistics
Assistant Secretary: S A McBurney

Senior Principal: Vacant

Principals: I Hunter, A G S Crawford, S A E Magee, N Fulton

Central Services, Rural Development & Fisheries

Under Secretary: Pat Toal

Personnel and Business Support

Assistant Secretary: P McCloy

Personnel Management Division
Principal: R J Campton

Personnel Services Division
Principal: E Dickson

Business Support Division
Principal: G Hill

Information, Estates and Office Services

Senior Principal: J E Long

Information Services Division
Principal: G Cromey

Offices Services and Estate Management, Typing Service
Deputy Principal: M Moore

Co-ordination

Assistant Secretary: P Keegan

Press Office
Principal: B McCusker

Co-Ordination Division
Principal: E Gallagher

Rural Proofing
Principal: M McLernon

Rural Development

Assistant Secretary:
G L T McWhinney

Rural Development (Central Unit)
Principal: A P Morton

Area Co-ordinator (North)
Principal: J McLernon

Area Co-ordinator (South)
Principal: V McKevitt

Area Co-ordinator (West)
Principal: S Nugent

Finance

Assistant Secretary: G Lavery

Finance Division
Principal: T F Bryans

Resource Control Division
Principal: J F Ditchfield

Internal Audit
Principal: S McGuinness

Financial Reporting Division
Principal: E Gaw

Fisheries

Assistant Secretary: N Cormick

Principal: A Dorbie

Sea Fisheries
Principal: E Sung

Chief Fisheries Officer
Principal: M McCaughan

Modernisation Unit

Assistant Secretary: T Stainer
Principals: B Stuart, H Hagan

Agri-Food Development Service

Under Secretary: Roy McClenaghan,
Chief Agriculture Officer

Food Service

Head of Food Service
Senior Deputy Chief Agriculture Officer: Dr J G S Speers

Food Education Division, Loughry College:
Dr W M A Mullan

Food Technology Division, Loughry College:
D Legge

Supply and Packaging Division, Loughry College:
D McDowell

Business Opportunities Service

Deputy Chief Agriculture Officer:
D G O'Neill

Quality Assurance Division:
W Weatherup

Supply Chain Development:
A MCKeown

Rural Enterprise Division:
T C Turney

Agriculture & Horticulture Service

Head of Agriculture & Horticulture Service Senior Deputy Chief Agriculture Officer: J Fay

Technology & Business Division, Beef and Sheep, Greenmount College:
J Herron

Higher Education Division:
Dr S J Kennedy

Further Education Division:
H Jones

Education Development Division, Greenmount College:
P McGurnaghan

Technology & Business Division, Crops and Horticulture, Greenmount College:
S Millar

Technology & Business Division, Dairy and Pigs, Greenmount College:
I McCluggage

Enniskillen College:
S McAlinney

Technical Support Division

Head of Technical Support:
Ian Titterington

Organisation and Staff Development Division: Dr F N J Long

Countryside Management:
H I Gracey

Education and Finance Division:
P Rooney

Information and Promotions Division: P B Niblock

Peace II Co-ordination Division:
TB Morrison

Science Service

Under Secretary: Dr G McIlroy

Administration
Senior Principal Scientific Officer:
Dr R J Boyd

Biometrics
Senior Principal Scientific Officer:
Dr E A Goodall

Food, Agricultural & Environmental Sciences

Deputy Chief Scientific Officer: Dr S Neill

Food Science
Senior Principal Scientific Officers:
Prof A Gilmour, Dr L J Farmer

Agricultural & Environmental Sciences
Senior Principal Scientific Officers:
Dr S I Heaney, Dr R J Stevens, Prof C E Gibson, Dr S Mayne (Acting)

Applied Plant Service and Agri-food Economics

Deputy Chief Scientific Officer: Prof R J Marks

Applied Plant Science
Senior Principal Scientific Officers:
Dr M S Camlin, Dr S H S Sharma

Agri-food Economics Unit
Deputy Chief Agricultural Economist:
Dr J Davis

Veterinary Sciences

Deputy Chief Scientific Officer:
Prof W A Ellis (Acting)

Deputy Chief Veterinary Research Officer:
Vacant

Senior Veterinary Research Officers:
Dr T D G Bryson, Dr S Kennedy,

Veterinary Service

Under Secretary: Bert Houston

Formulation of National & International Policy

Deputy Chief Veterinary Officer:
Colin Hart (Acting)

Veterinary Public Health Policy
Senior Principal Veterinary Officer
Robert Huey

Trade, Residues and Medicine
Divisional Veterinary Officer:
Paul Pollard

Transmissible Spongiform Encephalopathy -Meat inc. by products
Divisional Veterinary Officer:
John O'Neill

Meat Hygiene
Divisional Veterinary Officer:
Jean Wales

Zoonoses
Divisional Veterinary Officer:
Barbara Cooper

Cattle and Sheep Identification, Registration and Movement
Divisional Veterinary Officer:
David Cassells

Epizootic Section
Senior Principal Veterinary Officer:
Cyril Rutledge

Scrapie, Northern Ireland Scrapie Plan, Animal Protein
Divisional Veterinary Officer:
Sandra Dunbar

BSE, Transmissible Spongiform Encephalopathy

Divisional Veterinary Officer:
George Byrne

Epizootic Disease, Artificial
Insemination
Divisional Veterinary Officer:
Michael Hatch

Welfare/AD including Welfare of
Animals, Slaughter or Killing
Divisional Veterinary Officer:
Fiona Murdock

Enzootic Section
Senior Principal Veterinary Officer:
Owen Denny

Bovine Tuberculosis
Divisional Veterinary Officer:
Paddy McGuckian

Brucellosis-Routine
Divisional Veterinary Officer:
Roy Watt

Brucellosis- New Initiatives
David Irwin

Epidemiology
Divisional Veterinary Officer:
Darrell Abernethy

Enforcement
Divisional Veterinary Officer:
Vacant

Implementation of Policy and Staffing

Deputy Chief Veterinary Officer
M Geddis (Acting)

Northern Region

Senior Principal Veterinary Officer
B McCartan

Ballymena DVO
Divisional Veterinary Officer:
M Sherrey

Coleraine DVO
Divisional Veterinary Officer:
J Breen

Larne DVO
Divisional Veterinary Officer:
D Marshall

Omagh DVO
Divisional Veterinary Officer:
L Rutlege

Londonderry DVO
Divisional Veterinary Officer:
R W Kirke

APHIS Development (Animal and
Public Health Information System)
Divisional Veterinary Officer:
D Torrens

Southern Region

Senior Principal Veterinary Officer
Divisional Veterinary Officer:
M Steel

Armagh DVO
Divisional Veterinary Officer:
J Gillespie

J Dungannon DVO
Divisional Veterinary Officer:
I McKeown

Enniskillen DVO
Divisional Veterinary Officer:
D W Brown

Newry DVO
Divisional Veterinary Officer:
R Harwood

Newtownards DVO
Divisional Veterinary Officer:
P Price

Veterinary Public Health -

Implementation
Senior Principal Veterinary Officer:
R O'Flaherty

Meat North
Divisional   Veterinary   Oficer:
T Coulter

Meat South
Divisional   Veterinary   Officer:
P Treanor

Portal Inspectorate, Management of
College Veterinary Oficers
Divisional Veterinary Officer: J Guy

Corporate Services Division
Principal Officer: A Ralston

Forest Service

Forest Service of Northern Ireland
Dundonald House
Upper Newtownards Road
Belfast
BT4 3SB
Tel: 028 9052 4480
Fax: 028 9052 4570
Web: www.drdni.gov.uk/forestry
Chief Executive: Malcolm Beatty

Corporate Services Director:
T C McCully
Functions: Corporate Services,
Estates & Technical Services,
Drawing Office, Graphic Design,
Personnel, Finance, Accounts,
Marketing, Administration &
Purchasing.

Operations

Director: J J O'Boyle
Functions: Establishment,
Maintenance, Recreation, Nurseries,
Private Forestry & Acquisitions,
Deputise for CEO, Compile &
Control Operational Budget,

Co-ordinate all Operational Programmes, Harvesting, Marketing & Engineering.

Policy and Standards

Director: P Hunter-Blair
Functions: Policy, Training, Safety & Development, Research, Forest Practice, Education, Private Woodlands, Plant Health & Conservation.

Rivers Agency

Rivers Agency
Hydebank
4 Hospital Road
Belfast
BT8 8JP
Tel: 028 9025 3355
Fax: 028 9025 3455

Chief Executive: John Hagan

Corporate Services

Director of Corporate Services: J S Allister
Functions: Finance, Personnel, Legislation, Corporate Planning, Efficiency Plants, Annual Reports, Human Resource Development

Operations

Director of Operations: M Hamilton
Functions: Operational Management, Design, Health and Safety, Environment, Plant Unit, Emergency Planning

Principal Engineers: P Aldridge, A Kirkwood, P McCrudden

Development

Director of Development: F R White
Functions: Capital Works Programme, Construction Procurement, Hydrometrics, Asset Management, Planning Advice, Information Technology, Professional Standards

Principal Engineers: J Clarke, S Dawson, P Mehaffey, J Nicholson

Department of Culture, Arts and Leisure

Interpoint
20-24 York Street
Belfast
BT15 1AQ
Tel: 028 9025 8825
Fax: 028 9025 8906
Web: www.dcalni.gov.uk

Direct Rule Minister: Angela Smith MP
Permanent Secretary: Dr Aideen McGinley OBE
Tel: 028 9025 8814
Deputy Secretary: Carol Moore
Tel: 028 9025 8848

Private Office
Private Secretary: Julie Childs
Tel: 028 9025 8807

Press Office
Principal Information Officer: Brian Kirk
Tel: 028 9025 8900

The Department of Culture, Arts and Leisure (DCAL), was formed from an amalgamation of agencies and functions previously associated with DANI, DENI and DoE. Its chief aim is to promote individual, social and economic development. This is to be achieved principally by maximising participation in a wide range of cultural, arts and leisure activities including sports.

DCAL has responsibilities for libraries and museums, with the aim of increasing public interaction in these areas and improving facilities and services available. It also aims to encourage public participation in the areas of sport and the arts, again by increasing opportunities for participation.

DCAL oversees the Public Records Office of Northern Ireland (PRONI) and Ordnance Survey of Northern Ireland (OSNI), both executive agencies established to provide information and other resources to the public.

DCAL has direct involvement in two cross-border implementation bodies: the North/South Language body, which incorporates boards for the development of Irish and Ulster-Scots, and Waterways Ireland. Through these the Department seeks to maximise the benefits of cross-border co-operation on areas of mutual interest.

Department of Culture, Arts and Leisure Structure

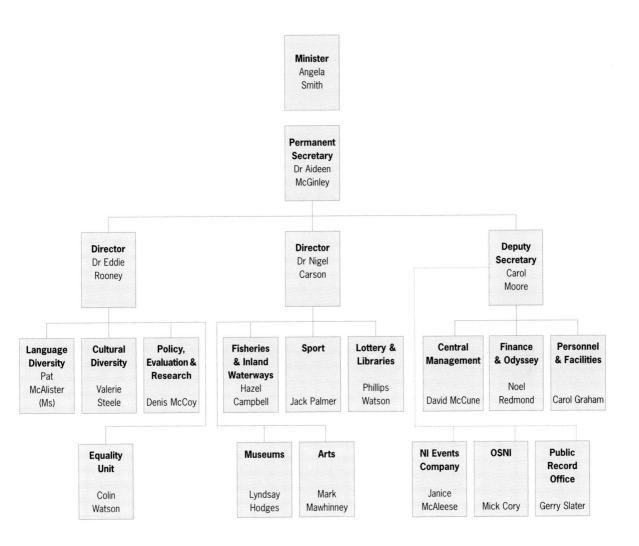

Policy, Research and Cultural/Linguistic Diversity

Director: Dr Eddie Rooney

Linguistic Diversity
Head of Department: Pat McAlister (Ms)

Cultural Diversity
Head of Department: Valerie Steele

Policy, Evaluation & Research
Head of Department: Denis McCoy

Equality Unit
Head of Department: Colin Watson

Arts, Inland Waterways/Fisheries, Libraries, Museums and Sport

Director: Nigel Carson

Fisheries & Inland Waterways
Head of Department: Hazel Campbell

Sport
Head of Department: Jack Palmer

Libraries & Lottery
Head of Department: Philips Wilson

Arts
Head of Department:
Mark Mawhinney

Museums
Head of Department:
Lyndsay Hodges

Corporate Services and Agencies

Deputy Secretary: Carol Moore

Central Management Unit
Head of Department: David McClure

Finance and Odyssey
Head of Department:
Noel Redmond

Personnel & Facilities Management
Head of Department: Carol Graham

Northern Ireland Events Company
Chief Executive: Janice McAleese

Ordnance Survey of Northern Ireland,
Chief Executive: Mick Cory

Public Record Office of Northern Ireland
Chief Executive: Dr Gerry Slater

Departmental Agencies

Public Record Office of Northern Ireland
66 Balmoral Avenue
Belfast
BT9 6NY
Tel: 028 9025 5905
Fax: 028 9025 5999
Web: www.proni.nics.gov.uk
E-mail: proni@dcalni.gov.uk

Chief Executive: Dr Gerry Slater

Head of Access: Aileen McClintock
Head of Acquisition:
Dr David Lammey
Head of Corporate Services:
Tom Robinson
Head of Reader Services:
Valerie Adams

ORDNANCE SURVEY OF NORTHERN IRELAND

Colby House, Stranmillis Court, Belfast, BT9 5BJ

Tel: 028 9025 5755
Fax: 028 9025 5700
Web: www.osni.gov.uk

Chief Executive: Mick Cory
Director of Corporate Services: Grace Nesbitt
Director of Operations/Strategy: Trevor Steenson
Director of Business Development: Stan Brown
Customer Services Manager: Marty McVeigh

Ordnance Survey of Northern Ireland (OSNI), the official mapping agency, employs about 180 staff, the majority at its headquarters at Colby House, Stranmillis, and over 60 field surveyors operating from regional offices

throughout the Province. Following devolution, OSNI was transferred to the Department of Culture, Arts and Leisure.

OSNI is responsible for the mapping infrastructure of Northern Ireland and its principal objective is to maintain an accurate, comprehensive and up-to-date digital topographical framework from which a range of digital products, from small to large scale, which underpin customers' Geographical Information Systems (GIS) are derived, as well as a range of paper maps for planning, tourism and leisure.

Ordnance Survey of Northern Ireland, Colby House, Stranmillis Court, Belfast BT9 5BJ. Tel 028 9025 5786
Fax 028 9025 5700   e-mail: osni@osni.gov.uk   www: http://www.osni.gov.uk   © Crown Copyright 2002

Department of Education

Rathgael House
Balloo Road
Bangor
Co Down
BT19 7PR
Tel: 028 9127 9279
Fax: 028 9127 9100
Web: www.deni.gov.uk

Direct Rule Minister: Jane Kennedy

Permanent Secretary: Gerry McGinn
Tel: 028 9127 9309
Deputy Secretary: Stephen Peover
Tel: 028 9127 9313

The Department of Education has responsibility for aspects of education relating to schools and the Youth Service. This includes policy, legislation and resource issues for both areas.

In regard to the Education Service, the Department of Education has responsibility for strategic planning and accounting for public expenditure. The Department manages the funding and administration of schools. It monitors schools' effectiveness, and oversees school planning and provision. The Department also has an inspectorate, and makes appointments to the five Education and Library Boards.

The Department develops policy regarding schools curriculum, and the assessment of pupils, including examinations. It oversees transfer procedures and school enrolment, and provides special education services and pupil support.

The Department of Education also has responsibility for community relations among young people, which is part of its overall youth services remit. The Department provides a comprehensive youth service, and supports many associated organisations.

(The priorities in education in Northern Ireland are discussed in further detail in Chapter 7.)

Department of Education Structure

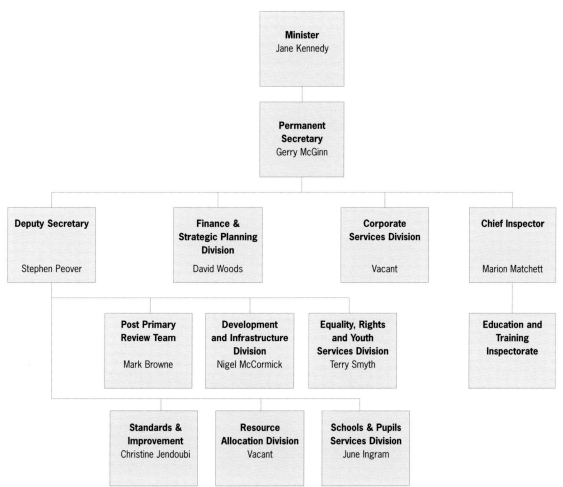

Education and Training Inspectorate

Chief Inspector: Marion Matchett

Policy, Planning and Improvement

Assistant Chief Inspector:
Stanley Goudie

Special Education, Alternative
Provision; Youth and Community;
Culture, Arts and Leisure

Assistant Chief Inspector:
Paul McAllister

Post-16 Education including Schools,
Further Education, Training, Higher
Education and Teacher Education

Assistant Chief Inspector:
Mr Vivian McIver

Pre-16 Education, including pre-school,
primary and post-primary

Assistant Chief Inspector:
Loretto Watson

Inspection Services Branch (ISB)

Deputy Principal: Jenny McIlwain

Standards and Improvement Division

Head of Division: Christine Jendoubi

Qualifications and Business/Education
Links Branch

Principal: Vacancy
Deputy Principal: David Mann
Functions:
Examinations/Qualifications, 14-19
Issues, Key Stage 4

Flexibility Pilot Scheme

6th Form Provision/Careers Education, School Information and Prospectus Regulations, School/Industry Links, Northern Ireland Business Education Partnership

Curriculum and Assessment Branch

Principal: Alastair Bradley
Deputy Principal: Ashley Waterworth
Functions: CCEA, Curriculum 4-16, Assessment 4-14, Target-setting

School Improvement Branch

Principal: Peter Lowry
Deputy Principal: David McMullan
Functions: School Improvement and Support Programmes

Teacher Education Branch

Principal: Vacant
Deputy Principal: Ron Armstrong
Functions: General Teaching Council, Initial/ In Service Teacher Education, Education Technology

Finance and Strategic Planning Division

Head of Division: David Woods

Financial Planning Branch

Principal: Brian Morrow
Deputy Principal: Ivy Nelson
Functions: Public Expenditure Planning, Budgeting and Monitoring, Resource Budgeting, Main and Supplementary Estimates.

Accounts Branch

Principal: Ronnie McQuitty
Deputy Principal: Jason Hayes
Functions: Payment Processing, Appropriation Accounts, Resource Accounts, Accountability Issues.

Internal Audit Unit

Principal: Vacant
Deputy Principal: Alistair McIlroy
Deputy Principal: Brendan McLernon
Functions: Internal Audit and monitoring of systems of Internal control.

Economic Advisory Unit

Principal Economist: Mike Archer
Deputy Economists:
Rodney Smith
M McGibbon
Function: Economic advice on policy issues, advice on value for money of projects and in relation to specific issues.

Strategy Management Unit

Principal: Vacant
Deputy Principal: Vacant
Function: To promote the arrangements for strategic and business planning both in the department and in relation to the main education partners. To co-ordinate the Programme for Government and Public Service Agreement and Service Delivery Agreement targets.

Corporate Services Division

Head of Division: Vacant

Business Development Unit

Principal: Mary Cunningham
BDU: Deputy Principal: Ken Reid
Functions: Staff development
ISU: SSA: Billy Girvan, Mary Cromey
Functions: Information systems development and support

Freedom of Information

Principal: Tom Orr

Machinery of Government Branch

Principal: Dave Brittain
Deputy principal: Trevor Brant
Functions: Co-ordination of business and development of relations with NI Assembly/Westminster, Legislation, Greening Government, Central Bureau

Personnel Services Branch

Principal: Paul Cartwright
Deputy Principal: Donal Moran
Functions: Accommodation, Support Services, Health and Safety, Equal Opportunities
Deputy Principal: Mary Donnelly
Functions: Personnel and Pay, Staff Welfare Service

Information Services

Principal: Jill Garrett
Deputy Information Officer: Anne Martin
Functions: Organising Press Conferences, In-house magazine, Preparing Press Releases and Statements, Media Monitoring, Media Queries.

Statistics and Research Branch

Principal: Dr Ivor Johnston
Deputy Principal: Patricia Wyers, Martin Thompson, Jonathan Crook
Functions: Research, Statistical Series, Analysis.

Equality, Rights and Youth Service Division

Head of Division: Terry Smyth

Equality, Rights and Social Inclusion Branch

Principal: Gillian Ardis
Deputy Principal: Elaine McFeeters
Function: New TSN, Human Rights, Racial Awareness, Special Education Needs, Disability Legislation; Equality Scheme

Youth Service Branch

Principal: David McClarin
Deputy Principal: Ivan Houston
Functions: Policy for Youth Service, Youth Council for Northern Ireland, Capital grants to recognised voluntary organisation, Grants for Training of Youth Workers.

Community Relations Branch

Deputy Principal: Phyllis Richardson
Functions: Schools Community Relations Programme, Youth Service Community Relations Support Scheme, Community Relations Core Funding Scheme, Cultural Traditions Programme

Pupil Support Branch

Principal: Mary Potter
Deputy Principal: Jackie Simpson
Deputy Principal: Brian White

Deputy Principal: Philip Melarkey
Function: Issues affecting children and young people at risk of underachievement in education. Promoting social inclusion and tackling disadvantage

Schools and Pupil Services Division

Head of Division: June Ingram

School Administration Branch

Principal: Brian Hill
Deputy Principal: Gary Montgomery
Functions: Home to school transport, school meals service, funding and administration of CCMS.

Deputy Principal: Dominic McCullough
Functions: General administration and school management issues.

Open Enrolment and Transfer Procedure Branch

Principal: John Leonard
Deputy Principal: Vacant
Functions: Open Enrolment Policy and Legislation Administration, Transfer/Selection Policy and Research Project, Class Sizes (KS1) Policy and Legislation, Implementation.

School Education Branch

Principal: Irene Murphy
Deputy Principal: Susan Carnson
Deputy Principal: Tommy Mitchell
Functions: School Finance
Deputy Principal: Garth Manderson
Functions: Special educational needs policy, legislation, codes of practice

Development and Infrastructure Division

Head of Division: Nigel McCormick

Buildings Branch

Principal: Sean Johnston
Deputy Principal: Derek Patterson
Functions: Finance and Energy Efficiency Section
Deputy Principal: Brian Miller
Functions: School Projects Section (including Education Reform)

Development Branch

Principal: Vacant
Deputy Principal: Jacqui Loughrey
Functions: Economic Appraisals, Development Proposals and Capital Priorities in respect of Secondary, Grammar Schools, Pre-school Expansion Programmes SEELB/BELB/WELB
Deputy Principal: Roy Newell
Functions: Economic Appraisals, Development Proposals and Capital Priorities in respect of Primary, Special, Nursery, Pre-school Expansion Prog SELB/NEELB
Deputy Principal: (Acting) Eric Mayne
Function: Estates management project

PPP Unit
Principal: Paddy McNally
Deputy Principals:
Pamela McCormick;
Michael Stewart
Functions: Policy and Development of PPP in Education; General PPP guidance.

Deputy Principal: John Williamson
Functions: To develop, update and implement strategy in relation to

schools estate. Departmental oversight of classroom 2000 issues

School Policy Branch

Principal: Stephen Sandford
Deputy Principal:
Bruce Fitzsimmons
Functions: Pre-school Education Expansion Programme

Deputy Principal: Linda Martin
Functions: Policy on Provision of Integrated Education, Irish Medium Education, Funding of NICIE and Comhairle na Gaelscolaiochta, Registration of Independent schools.

Special Funding Initiatives Unit

Deputy Principal: Richard Hodgett
Deputy Principal: Dave Bradley
Functions: Peace II funding, Building Sustainable Prosperity Programme (BSP), Belfast Regeneration Initiative, Londonderry Regeneration Initiative

Resource Allocation Division

Head of Division: Vacant

Teacher Negotiating Committee Branch

Principal: Ted McGuigan
Deputy Principal: John McClure
Functions: Teachers' salaries and conditions of service,

Teachers' Pay and Administration and Teachers' Pensions Branches

Principal: Mervyn Gregg
Deputy Principal: (Acting) Brian Quinn
Functions: Teachers' Pay and Administration

Deputy Principal: Esterina Large
Functions: Teachers' Pensions

Deputy Principal: Celine Elliott (Acting)
Functions: Computer System Project Manager

School Finance Branch

Principal: John Caldwell
Deputy Principal: Peter O'Neill
Functions: Recurrent funding of voluntary, grammar and grant maintained integrated schools.
Deputy Principal: Alan Bell
Deputy Principal: Gareth Manderson
Functions: School finance, LMS schemes

Area Board Resource Allocation and Monitoring Branch (ABRAM)

Principal: Eric McCloy
Deputy Principal: Frank Ferguson
Functions: Resource Distribution to ELB's, budgeting control and monitoring, ELB personnel and accountability issues

Special Funding Initiatives Unit

Deputy Principal: Richard Hodgett
Deputy Principal: Dave Bradley
Functions: Peace II funding, Building Sustainable Prosperity Programme (BSP), Belfast Regeneration Initiative, Londonderry Regeneration Initiative

Post-Primary Review Team

Head of Division: Dr Mark Browne
Principal: Leslie Ashe
Principal: Des Whyte
Deputy Principal: Roberta Sterling
Deputy Principal: Jacqui McLaughlin
Functions: Review of post primary education including transfer from primary to post primary schools

Department for Employment and Learning

Adelaide House
Adelaide Street
Belfast
BT2 8FD
Tel: 028 9025 7777
Fax: 028 9025 7778
Web: www.del.gov.uk

Direct Rule Minister: Jane Kennedy
Permanent Secretary: Alan Shannon
Tel: 028 9025 7834

Private Office:
Private Secretary: Chris McConkey
Tel: 028 9025 7887

The Department for Employment and Learning (DEL) is responsible for the development of policy for, and the planning, funding and administration of further and higher education, with advice from the Northern Ireland Higher Education Council and the Further Education Consultative Committee. It is also responsible for policy in respect of student loans and awards (mandatory, discretionary and postgraduate) and for the payment of postgraduate awards.

DEL's key objective is to develop a culture of lifelong learning and to promote wider access to, and greater participation in, further and higher education, particularly from groups previously underrepresented. It aims to improve quality and performance in the higher and further education sectors, and to enhance the contribution of these sectors to the regional economy.

The department has assumed the responsibilities of the former Training and Employment Agency. In this respect DEL's aim is to assist economic development and help people find sustainable employment through training and employment services. DEL also deals with the processing of Northern Ireland employment and industrial relations legislation, and has responsibility for matters relating to the Labour Relations Agency.

(Further information on Higher Education and Training in Northern Ireland is set out in chapter 7.)

Department of Employment and Learning Structure

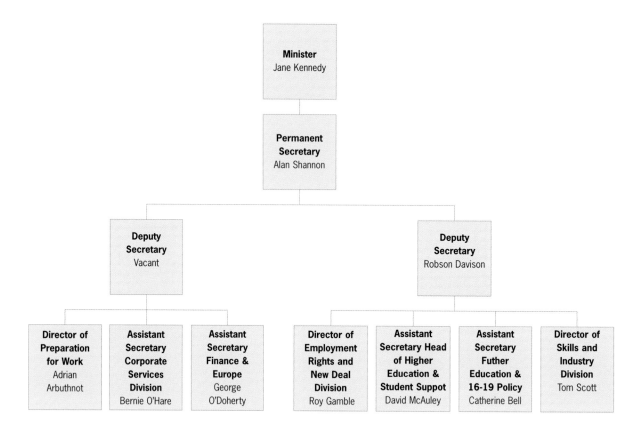

Skills and Industry Division

Head of Division: Tom Scott

Management Development
Head of Unit: Tom Hunter

Sectoral Development
Head of Unit: Jim Hanna

Supplier Services
Head of Unit: Tommy McVeigh

Training Programmes/IFI
Head of Unit: Richard Kenny

Training Services
Head of Unit: Francis Creagh
(Acting)

Preparation for Work Division

Head of Division: Adrian Arbuthnot

Eastern Region
Regional Manager: Kieran Brazier

Western Region
Regional Manager: Daragh Shields

Employment and Policy
Head of Unit: Jim Wilkinson

New Deal Policy
Head of Unit: Martin Caher

Disablement Advisory Service
Head of Unit: John Campbell

Partnership Team
Head of Unit: Martin Boyd (Acting)

Regional Operations Support
Head of Unit: Peter Poland

Employment Programmes
Head of Unit: Liz Young

Employment Assessment Unit
Head of Unit: Joe Carleton

Business Change Team
Head of Unit: Siobhan Logue

Employment Rights Division

Head of Division: Roy Gamble

Employment Rights (1)
Head of Unit: Tim Devine

Employment Rights (2)
Head of Unit: Vacant

Bill Team

Head of Unit: William Caldwell

Office of Industrial Tribunals and Fair
Employment Tribunals

Head of Unit: Ann Loney

Deputy Secretary: Robson Davison

Finance & European Division

Head of Division: George O'Doherty

Finance (1)
Head of Unit: Denis Lowry

Finance (2)
Head of Unit: Jim Russell

European Policy Unit
Head of Unit: Raymond Little

European Unit
Head of Unit: John Neill

Higher Education & Student Support Division

Head of Division: David McAuley

Student Support
Head of Unit: Gerry Rogan

Higher Education Finance
Head of Unit: Geoff Harrison

Higher Education Policy
Head of Unit: Sean McGarry

Tertiary Education Economic Unit
Head of Unit: Dr Linda Bradley

Tertiary Education Statistics and Research
Head of Unit: Victor Dukelow

Research and Evaluation
Head of Unit: Terry Morahan

Life Long Learning Division

Head of Division: Catherine Bell

Further Education Accountability
Deputy Head of Division:
Dr Roy Graham

Further Education Finance
Head of Unit: Rose Morrow

Further Education Capital Development
Head of Unit: Tom Redmond

Further Education Policy and Strategic Development
Head of Unit: Sheena Mairs

Learndirect
Head of Unit: Jan Harvey (Acting)

Qualifications and Learning Policy
Head of Unit: Deirdre McGill

Corporate Services Division
Head of Division: Bernie O'Hare

Personnel
Head of Unit: Judith Shaw

CIS
Head of Unit: Mervyn Langtry

Central Policy and Planning
Head of Unit: Daryl Young

Media and Marketing Unit
Head of Unit: Gywn Treharne

Department of Enterprise, Trade and Investment

Netherleigh House
Massey Avenue
Belfast
BT4 2JP
Tel: 028 9052 9900
Fax: 028 9052 9550
Web: www.detini.gov.uk

Direct Rule Minister: Ian Pearson
Permanent Secretary: Bruce Robinson
Tel: 028 9052 9441
Private Office
Private Secretary: Michael Harris
Tel: 028 9052 9208

The Department of Enterprise, Trade and Investment (DETI) is responsible for providing an appropriate framework for strengthening economic development in Northern Ireland. Its key objective is to promote employment and investment for sustainable economic growth and the improvement of competitiveness in business and industry.

DETI is the department responsible for the development agency Invest Northern Ireland. Invest Northern Ireland is the new agency incorporating the former IDB, IRTU, LEDU, and NITB agencies.

DETI also provides regulatory services covering companies and energy, and manages the Minerals and Petroleum Unit. The department also deals with consumer affairs, the Health and Safety Executive and the Employment Medical Advisory Service and the Northern Ireland Tourist Board.

Department of Enterprise, Trade and Investment Structure

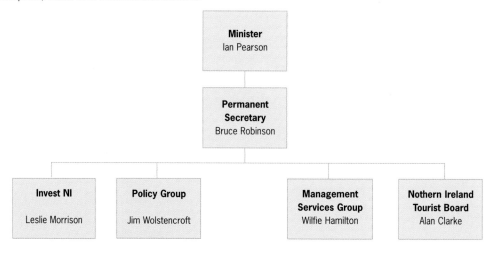

182

Policy Group

(Acting) Director: Jim Wolstencroft

Strategic Policy
Head of Division: Mike Warnock

Strategic Review Unit
Principal: Rosemary Crawford

Longer Term Policy Initiatives
Principal: Jenny Pyper

Economics
Principal: Robert Clulow

Planning Unit
Principal: Mark Pinkerton

Invest Northern Ireland Support Unit
Principal: Gerry McGeown

Policy Evaluation & Organisation Change Division

Head of Division: Malcolm Bryan

Statistics
Principal: Joanne McCutcheon

Tourism Policy
Principal: David Carson

Equality Issues/ Human Rights/ State Aids
Principal: Mike Maxwell

Trade Development
Principal: Ashley Ray

Energy Division

Head of Division: Jim McKeown

Gas Regulation
Principal: Jack Beattie

Electricity Regulation
Principal: Damian McAuley

Economic Infrastructure

Head of Division: Vacant

Minerals
Principal: Peter Taggart

Telecoms
Principal: Anne Conaty

Renewables (Wind Power etc)
Principal: David Stanley

Emergency Planning
Principal: Vacant

Management Services Group

Director: Wilfie Hamilton
Tel: 028 9052 9203

Business Regulation Division
Head of Division: Mike Bohill

Private Office
Principal: John Hinds

Companies Registration
Principal: Jackie Johnston

Insolvency Service
Director: Reg Nesbitt
Principals: Joe Hasan, Leslie Grimley

Trading Standards
Principal: David Livingstone

Social Economy
Principal: Vacant

Personnel Division
Head of Division: Steve Hare

Personnel
Principal: Alan Lamont

ISU and Services
Principal: Joe O'Hare

Personnel Development
Principal: Paula McCeary

E Government
Principal: Tom Kennedy

Information Technology
Head of Division: Pat Cunningham

Finance and EU Division

Head of Division: Neil Lavery

Finance Branch and Accounts Branch
Principal: Errol Crooks

Resource Accounting
Principal: Rodney Brown

Invest Northern Ireland Accounts Project
Principal: Charlie Doly

Internal Audit
Principal: Alan Magee

European Programme
Principal: Howard Keery

Communication Division

Head of Division: Fiona Hepper

Press Office
Principal Information Officer:
Jill Heron

Private Office/Central Management/Assembly Section/Legislative Monitoring
Principal: Jim Hinds

Departmental Agencies

Invest Northern Ireland
64 Chichester Street
Belfast
BT1 4JX
Tel: 028 9023 9090
Fax: 028 9054 5000
www.investni.com

Chief Executive: Leslie Morrison
Managing Directors: Chris Buckland
Leslie Ross, Terri Scott,
Tracy Meharg

Further details of the organisation structure and activities of Invest Northern Ireland are detailed in Chapter 9, A Guide to Doing Business.

Northern Ireland Tourist Board
St Anne's Quarter
North Street
Belfast
BT1 1NB
Tel: 028 9023 1221
Fax: 028 90240 960
Web:
www.discovernorthernireland.com
Chief Executive: Alan Clarke

Department of the Environment

Clarence Court
10-18 Adelaide Street
Belfast
BT2 8GB
Tel: 028 9054 0540
Fax: 028 9054 0024
Web: www.doeni.gov.uk

Direct Rule Minister: Angela Smith
Acting Permanent Secretary: Felix Dillon
Tel: 028 9054 0002

Private Office
Private Secretary: Julian Smyth
Tel: 028 9054 1166

The Department of the Environment has a number of strategic objectives relating to the conservation, protection and improvement of the natural and built environment. It is also charged with promoting a system of local government that meets the needs of ratepayers and citizens.

The Department has responsibility for planning policy in Northern Ireland, as well as the promotion of sustainable development. As part of this the Department of the Environment oversees the Driver and Vehicle Testing Agency, which checks the safety and roadworthiness of road vehicles, including their impact on the environment. The Department also oversees the Driver and Vehicle Licensing Agency.

The Department of the Environment has a central role in protecting wildlife and the countryside, including pollution and waste management. The Department's Environment and Heritage Services has an important role in enhancing the natural and built environment.

The Department also has responsibility for the promotion of road safety, both by publicity campaigns and direct action.

Department of the Environment Structure

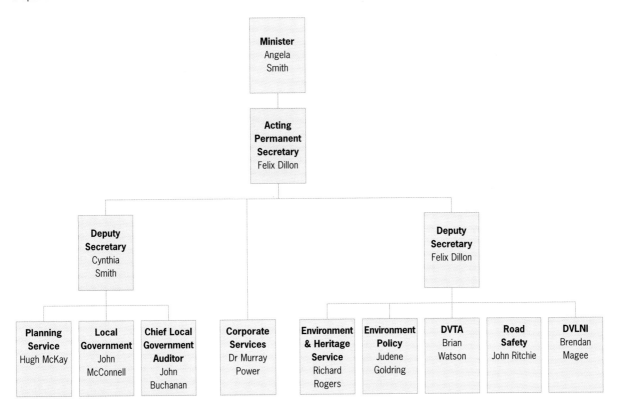

Corporate Services

Director: Dr Murray Power

Planning and Local Government

Deputy Secretary: Cynthia Smith

Local Government Audit

Chief Local Government Auditor:
John Buchanan

Local Government Policy

Director of Local Government:
John McConnell

Principals: David Barr,
Marie Finnegan

Planning Service

Clarence Court
10-18 Adelaide Street
Belfast
BT2 8GB
Tel: 028 9054 0540
Fax: 028 9054 0665

Chief Executive: Hugh McKay

Director of Corporate Services:
Ian Maye

Director of Professional Services:
Vacant

Professional Services Manager:
Hilary Heslip

Regional Offices

Ballymena
County Hall
182 Galgorm Hall
Ballymena
BT42 1QF
Tel: 028 2565 3333
Fax: 028 2566 2127
Acting Divisional Planning Manager:
Clifford McIlwaine

Belfast
Bedford House
16-22 Bedford Street
Belfast
BT2 7FD
Tel: 028 9025 2800
Fax: 028 9025 2828
Divisional Planning Manager:
David Carroll

Coleraine
County Hall
Castlerock Road
Coleraine
BT51 3HS
Tel: 028 7034 1300
Fax: 028 7034 1434
Divisional Planning Manager:
Jim Cavalleros

Craigavon
Marlborough House
Central Way
Craigavon
BT64 1AD
Tel: 028 3834 1144
Fax: 028 3834 1065
Divisional Planning Manager:
Patrick McBride

Downpatrick
Rathkeltair House
Market Street
Downpatrick
BT30 6EA
Tel: 028 4461 2211
Fax: 028 4461 8196
Divisional Planning Manager:
Tom Clarke

Enniskillen
County Buildings
15 East Bridge Street
Enniskillen
BT74 7BW
Tel: 028 6634 6555
Fax: 028 6634 6550
Divisional Planning Manager:
Brian Hughes

Londonderry
Orchard House
40 Foyle Street
Londonderry
BT48 6AT
Tel: 028 7131 9900
Fax: 028 7131 9777
Divisional Planning Manager:
Jim Cavalleros

Omagh
County Hall
Drumragh Avenue
Omagh
BT79 7AE
Tel: 028 8225 4000
Fax: 028 8225 4009
Divisional Planning Manager: Brian
Hughes

Road Safety, DVTA, DVLNI, Environment and Heritage

Deputy Secretary: Felix Dillon
Tel: 028 9054 1178

Road Safety Division
Director: John Ritchie
Principal: David Walker

Environment Policy Division
Director: Judena Goldring
Deputy Director: Norman Simmons

Water Framework Directive
Mark Livingstone

Ambient Air and Noise Quality
Helen Anderson

NSMC/BIC:
Liz Benson

Water Quality
Principal: Sheila Rodgers

Climate Change, Transboundary Air
Pollution & Radioactivity
Principal: Roger Lightbody

Natural and Built Environment
Principal: Brian Murphy

Integrated Pollution Prevention &
Control
Principal: Sandy Truesdale

Environmental Issues
Acting Principal: Chris Savage

Environment and Heritage Service
Commonwealth House
35 Castle Street
Belfast
BT1 1GU
Tel: 028 9025 1477
Fax: 028 9054 6660
Web: www.nics.gov.uk/ehs

Chief Executive: Richard Rogers

Built Heritage
Director: Vacant

Environmental Protection
Director: Roy Ramsey

Natural Heritage
Director: John Faulkner

Driver and Vehicle Licensing Northern
Ireland (DVLNI)
County Hall
Castlerock Road
Coleraine
Co Londonderry
BT51 3TA
Tel: 028 7034 1249
Fax: 028 7034 1424
Web: www.doeni.gov.uk/dvlni/

Chief Executive: Brendan Magee
Driver Licensing and Corporate
Services
Director: George Dillon

Road and Transport Licensing:
Director: Stewart Martin
Tel: 028 9025 4101

Driver and Vehicle Testing Agency
(DVTA)
Balmoral Road
Belfast
BT12 6QL
Tel: 028 9068 1831
Fax: 028 9066 5520
Web: www.nics.gov.uk/dvta

Chief Executive: Brian Watson

Department of Finance and Personnel

Rathgael House, Balloo Road
Bangor, Co Down BT19 7NA
Tel: 028 9127 9279
Fax: 028 9185 8104
Web: www: nics.gov.uk

Direct Rule Minister: Ian Pearson
Permanent Secretary: Pat Carvill
Tel: 028 9185 8174
Second Permanent Secretary: Andrew McCormick
Tel: 028 9052 7437

Private Office
Private Secretary: Maurice Rooney
Tel: 028 90 52 9140

The Department of Finance and Personnel, or DFP, has a wide range of functions, many of which are carried out centrally either by the department directly or through an agency on behalf of the Northern Ireland Civil Service (NICS) as a whole.

DFP is responsible for public expenditure, including the formulation of an annual budget. It seeks to secure appropriate funding from various sources, including the European Union. It is also responsible for personnel, which translates as the general management of the Civil Services (including the areas of policy, pay, recruitment and security). The Department is also responsible for the area of law reform and the provision of legal services to other Northern Ireland departments.

The department provides procurement services for goods, services and works to the Northern Ireland government departments and their associated public bodies. It is also responsible for the development of procurement policy for the Northern Ireland Civil Service and the dissemination of best practice and provides a single point of contact for advice on procurement matters.
It provides a valuation service to the public sector, and through the Rate Collection Agency (RCA), collects rates in Northern Ireland. The Department is also responsible for the Land Registers of Northern Ireland, and also provides a range of design, maintenance and advisory services on construction matters to the Northern Ireland public sector.

DFP oversees the work of NISRA, the Northern Ireland Statistical Research Agency, which provides a service to support the development, monitoring and evaluation of social and economic policy, as well as providing information to the general public, and organising the Census of Population.

Department of Finance and Personnel Structure

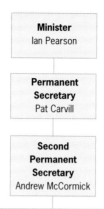

Minister
Ian Pearson

Permanent Secretary
Pat Carvill

Second Permanent Secretary
Andrew McCormick

Departmental Solicitor's Office	Office of Law Reform	Central Finance	Central Personnel Group	Corporate Services	Central Procurement
Robin Cole	Gareth Johnston	Leo O'Reilly David Thomson	Linda Brown	David Ferguson	John McMillen

Agencies

Business Development Service	Northern Ireland Statistics and Research Agency	Rate Collection Agency	Land Registers of Northern Ireland	Valuation & Lands Agency
Derek Orr	Norman Caven	Arthur Scott	Patricia Montgomery	Nigel Woods

Departmental Solicitor's Office
Head of Legal Services: Robin Cole

Office of Law Reform
Director: Gareth Johnston

Central Finance Group
Director: Leo O'Reilly

Director of Supply: David Thomson

European Division (Division of Central Finance Unit)
Assistant Secretary: Bill Pauley

Central Personnel Group
Director: Linda Brown

Corporate Services Division
Director: David Ferguson

Central Procurement
Churchill House
20-34 Victoria Square
Belfast BT1 4QW
Tel: 028 9025 0283
Fax: 028 9025 0333

Director: John McMillen

Business Development Service
Craigantlet Buildings
Stoney Road
Belfast
BT4 3SX
Tel: 028 9052 0444
Fax: 028 9052 7270
Acting Chief Executive: Derek Orr

Northern Ireland Statistics & Research Agency
McAuley House
2-14 Castle Street
Belfast
BT1 1SA
Tel: 028 9034 8100
www.nisra.gov.uk
Chief Executive: Norman Caven

Rate Collection Agency
Oxford House
49-55 Chichester Street
Belfast
BT1 4HH

Tel: 028 9052 2252
Fax: 028 9052 2113
Web: www.nics.gov.uk/rca
Chief Executive: Arthur Scott

Land Registers of Northern Ireland
Lincoln Building
27-45 Great Victoria Street
Belfast
BT2 7SL
Tel: 028 9025 1515
Fax: 028 9025 1550

Chief Executive:
Patricia Montgomery

Valuation and Lands Agency
Queen's Court
56-66 Upper Queen Street
Belfast
BT1 6FD
Tel: 028 9025 0700
Fax: 028 9054 3750
Chief Executive: Nigel Woods

Department of Health, Social Services and Public Safety

Castle Buildings
Stormont Estate
Upper Newtownards Road
Belfast
BT4 3SJ
Tel: 028 9052 0500
Fax: 028 9025 0572
Web: www.dhsspsni.gov.uk

Direct Rule Minister: Des Browne
Permanent Secretary: Clive Gowdy
Tel: 028 9052 0559

Private Office
Private Secretary: Emer McLarkey
Tel: 028 9052 0642

The Department of Health, Social Services and Public Safety (DHSSPS) administers the business of health, personal social services, public health and public safety. It has as its overall aim the improvement in health and social wellbeing of the people of Northern Ireland. This is realised through a 5-year corporate planning cycle that sets out the overall mission, criteria for success, corporate values, aims and measurable targets and objectives.

The department is broadly divided into three sections: Health and Personal Social Services, which includes policy and legislation for healthcare and social services; Public Health, responsible for promoting public health and wellbeing; and Public Safety, responsible for the Fire Authority, food safety and emergency planning. DHSSPS has responsibility for setting the strategic direction and overseeing the delivery of the health and personal social services, as well as the promotion of voluntary activity and community development in the health sector.

DHSSPS also has responsibility for public safety, which includes the provision of ambulance and fire services. It seeks to ensure that the health and social services and the fire services are prepared to deal effectively with all incidents.

Department of Health, Social Services and Public Safety Structure

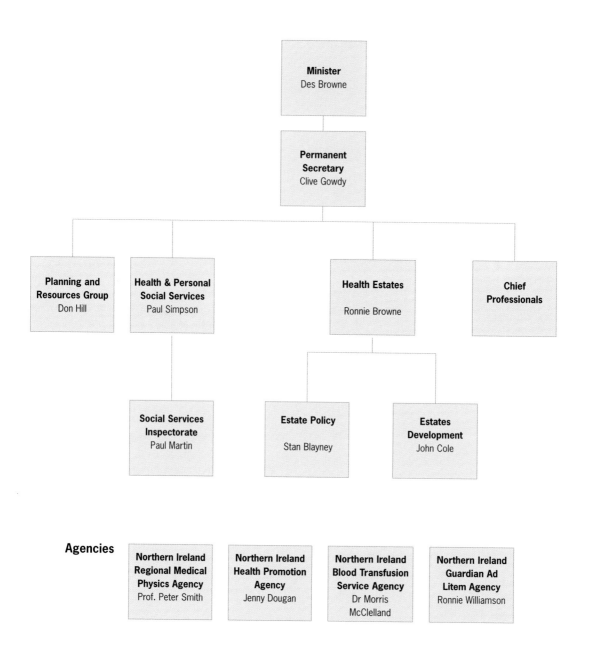

Minister
Des Browne

Permanent Secretary
Clive Gowdy

Planning and Resources Group
Don Hill

Health & Personal Social Services
Paul Simpson

Health Estates
Ronnie Browne

Chief Professionals

Social Services Inspectorate
Paul Martin

Estate Policy
Stan Blayney

Estates Development
John Cole

Agencies

Northern Ireland Regional Medical Physics Agency
Prof. Peter Smith

Northern Ireland Health Promotion Agency
Jenny Dougan

Northern Ireland Blood Transfusion Service Agency
Dr Morris McClelland

Northern Ireland Guardian Ad Litem Agency
Ronnie Williamson

Chief Professional Officers

Chief Medical Officer
Dr Henrietta Campbell
Tel: 028 9052 0563

Chief Dental Officer
Doreen Wilson
Tel: 028 9052 2940

Chief Nursing Officer
Judith Hill
Tel: 028 9052 0562

Chief Pharmaceutical Officer
Dr Norman Morrow
Tel: 028 9052 3279

Chief Environmental Officer
Nigel McMahon
Tel: 028 9052 0552

Health and Personal Social Service Management Group

Deputy Secretary
Paul Simpson
Tel: 028 9052 2667

Social Services Inspectorate
Chief Inspector: Paul Martin
Tel: 028 9052 0561

Human Resources

Director: David Bingham

Children and Community Care
Director: Leslie Frew

Secondary Care
Director: Brian Grzymek

Primary Care
Director: Jim Livingstone

Planning & Performance Management
Director: John McGrath

Planning and Resources Group

Deputy Secretary: Don Hill

Personnel & Corporate Services
Director: Paul Conliffe

Professional Technology & Information Systems
Director: Garry Williams

Finance
Director: Andrew Hamilton

Public Safety, Strategic Planning and Information and Analysis Unit
Director: Denis McMahon

Health Estates Agency

Stoney Road
Dundonald
Belfast
BT16 1US
Tel: 028 9052 0025
Fax: 028 9052 3900
Web: www.dhsspsni.gov.uk/hea

Chief Executive: Ronnie Browne

Estates Development
Director: John Cole

Estates Policy
Director: Stan Blayney

Departmental Agencies

Northern Ireland Guardian Ad Litem Agency
Centre House
79 Chichester Street
Belfast
BT1 4JE
Tel: 028 9031 6650
Fax: 028 9031 9811

Chief Executive: Ronnie Williamson

Northern Ireland Health Promotion Agency
18 Ormeau Avenue
Belfast
BT2 8HS
Tel: 028 9031 1611
Fax: 028 9031 1711
Web:
www.healthpromotionagency.org.uk

Chief Executive: Jenny Dougan

Northern Ireland Blood Transfusion Agency
Belfast City Hospital Complex
Lisburn Road
Belfast
BT9 7TS
Tel: 028 9032 1414
Fax: 028 9043 9017
Web: www.nibts.org

Chief Executive: Morris McClelland

Northern Ireland Regional Medical Physics Agency
Musgrave and Clarke House
Royal Hospitals Site
Grosvenor Road
BT12 6BA
Tel: 028 9034 6488
Fax:
Chief Executive: Professor Peter Smith

Department for Regional Development

Clarence Court
10-18 Adelaide Street
Belfast
BT2 8GB
Tel: 028 9054 0540
Fax: 028 9054 0024
Web: www.drdni.gov.uk

Direct Rule Minister: Angela Smith

Permanent Secretary: Stephen Quinn
Tel: 028 9054 1175

Private Office
Private Secretary (Acting): Stewart Mathews
Tel: 028 9054 0105

Principal Information Officer: Eamon Deeny
Tel: 028 9054 0817

The Department for Regional Development (DRD) is charged with strategic and transport planning in Northern Ireland. It is responsible for the provision and maintenance of roads, water and sewage services. The Department also develops policy relating to public transport, including rail, bus, ports and airports. Much of DRD's operational work is carried out by its two executive agencies: the Roads Service and the Water Service.

The department has recently published a ten-year development strategy, "Shaping Our Future" which has created considerable interest in future infrastructural development priorities. A big issue facing the Minister and Department is the possible introduction of a charging structure for water.

Department for Regional Development Structure

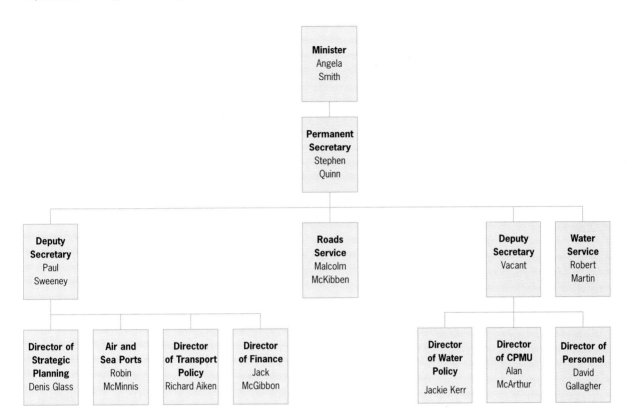

Strategic Planning, Transport and Finance

Deputy Secretary: Paul Sweeney

Air and Sea Ports
Director: Robin McMinnis

Transport Policy
Policy Director: Richard Aiken

Finance
Director: Jack McGibbon

Regional Planning Strategy
Director: Billy Gamble

Strategic Planning
Director: Dennis Glass

Regional Transport Strategy
(Acting) Aileen Gault

Roads Management Services, Personnel and Water

Deputy Secretary (Acting):
Paul Sweeney

Personnel
Director: David Gallagher

Central Policy Unit
Director: Alan McArthur

Water Policy
Director: Jackie Kerr

ROADS SERVICE

ROADS Service

Clarence Court
10-18 Adelaide Street
Belfast
BT2 8GB
Telephone: (028) 9054 0540
Fax: (028) 9054 0024
E-mail: roads@drdni.gov.uk
Web: www.drdni.gov.uk/roads

Chief Executive:
Malcolm McKibbin

Director of Corporate Services:
Jim Carlisle
Director of Engineering: Geoff Allister
Director of Network Services: David Orr
Director of Finance: John McNeill

Head of Roads Service Consultancy:
Derick McCandless
Head of Roads Service Direct:
Ken Hutton (Acting)
Head of Strategic Planning:
Peter McWilliams
Head of Transportation: Denis O'Hagan

Roads Service is responsible for just over 24,800 kilometres of public roads together with about 8,000 kilometres of footways, 6,000 bridges, 240,000 street lights, and 370 public car parks. It has a staff complement of 2,156 and an overall budget of £191.1 million. The Agency's main functions are to make sure that:
• the public road network is managed and maintained;
• the public road network is developed to improve road safety and traffic management;
• measures are taken to implement the Department's sustainable transportation policy; and
• all its activities are carried out in a fair and equitable way.

Regional Offices

Eastern Division
Hydebank
4 Hospital Road
Belfast
BT8 8JL
Telephone: 028 9025 3000
Fax: 028 9025 3220
E-mail: roads.eastern@drdni.gov.uk
Divisional Manager: Joe Drew
Deputy Divisional Manager:
Tom McCourt

Northern Division
County Hall
Castlerock Road
Coleraine
BT51 3HS
Telephone: 028 7034 1300
Fax: 028 7034 1430
E-mail: roads.northern@drdni.gov.uk
Divisional Manager: Andrew Murray

Southern Division
Marlborough House
Central Way
Craigavon
BT64 1AD
Telephone: 028 3834 1144
Fax: 028 3834 1867
E-mail: roads.southern@drdni.gov.uk
Divisional Manager: John White

Western Division
County Hall
Drumragh Avenue
Omagh
BT79 7AF
Telephone: 028 8225 4111
Fax: 028 8225 4010
E-mail: roads.western@drdni.gov.uk
Divisional Manager: Pat Doherty

Water Service

Northland House
3 Frederick Street
Belfast
BT1 2NR
Tel: 028 9024 4711
Fax: 028 9035 4888

Chief Executive: Robert Martin
Director of Corporate Services:
Robin Mussen
Acting Director of Development:
Robert White
Director of Finance: David Carson
Director of Operations: John Kelly
Technical Director: Harry Thompson

Regional Offices
Eastern Division
34 College Street
Belfast
BT1 6DR
Tel: 028 9032 8161
Fax: 028 9035 4828

Northern Division
Academy House
121a Broughshane Street
Ballymena
BT43 6BA
Tel: 028 2565 3655
Fax: 028 2566 3131

Southern Division
Marlborough House
Central Way
Craigavon
BT64 1AD
Tel: 028 3834 1100
Fax: 028 3832 0555

Western Division
Belt Road
Altnagelvin
Londonderry
BT47 2LL
Tel: 028 7131 2221
Fax: 028 7131 0330

Department for Social Development

Churchill House
Victoria Square
Belfast
BT1 4SD
Tel: 028 9056 9100
Fax: 028 9056 9240
Web: www.dsdni.gov.uk

Direct Rule Minister: Des Browne

Permanent Secretary: John Hunter
Tel: 028 9056 9203
Private Office
Private Secretary: Beverley Bigger
Tel: 028 9056 9216

The Department for Social Development (DSD) brings together areas of work from both the former Department of Health and Social Services and the Department of the Environment. It administers the social security, child support and pension schemes and associated appeals services.

DSD is responsible for housing policy and urban regeneration and community development, along with social and charities legislation and the voluntary activity unit.

The department sponsors a number of non-departmental public bodies. These include the Northern Ireland Housing Executive (NIHE), Laganside Corporation and several advisory and tribunal bodies.

The Department for Social Development's mission is to promote individual and community wellbeing through integrated social and economic action. Many of its policies impact on health, particularly housing. It interacts with many of the poorest in society, and has responsibility for improving housing, delivering social security benefits, providing child support services and developing community infrastructure. A key element of current DSD strategies is to provide, through the Northern Ireland Housing Executive and Housing Associations, high quality affordable social housing for those on low incomes and in greatest need.

Department for Social Development Structure

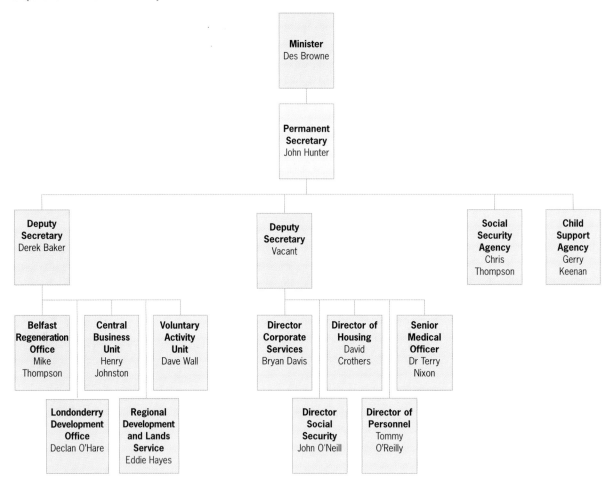

Resources Housing and Social Security Group

Deputy Secretary: Vacant
Tel: 028 9056 9205

Corporate Services Division
Director: Bryan Davis
Tel: 028 9056 9104

Finance
Principal: Brendan Devlin
Tel: 028 9056 9358

Office of the Permanent Secretary
Principal: George Davidson
Tel: 028 9056 9200

Information Office
Principal: Colm Shannon
Tel: 028 9056 9211

Statistics
Principal: Dr Chris Morris
Tel: 028 9052 2280

Economics
Principal: Noel McNally
Tel: 028 9055 1953

Equality & Corporate Planning Unit
Principal: Robert Breakey
Tel: 028 9056 9161

Decision Making & Appeals Service
Deputy Principal: John McMullan
Tel: 028 9054 3628

Personnel Division

Director: Tommy O'Reilly
Tel: 028 9056 9130

Establishment Officer
Rosaleen Carlin
Tel: 028 9022 4009

ADSO/Emergency Planning
Deputy Principal: Blair White
Senior Medical Officer:
Dr Terry Nixon
Tel: 028 9056 9376

Housing Division

Director David Crothers
Tel: 028 9054 1004

Housing Management
Principal: George Davidson
Tel: 028 9054 1167

Housing Finance
Principal: Michael Sands
Tel: 028 9054 4170

Housing Associations Branch
Principal: Billy Graham
Tel: 028 9056 8382

Housing Policy (NIHE & Energy)
Principal: (acting on rotation)
Jerome Burns
Tel: 028 9054 0789

Housing Policy (Housing Assoc,
Co-Ownership, Private Rented
Sector)
Principal: (acting on rotation)
Jerome Burns
Tel: 028 9054 1131

Housing Bill
Principal: Scott Carson
Tel: 028 9054 0046

Urban Regeneration and Community
Development Division

Deputy Secretary: Derek Baker
Tel: 028 9056 2006

Belfast Regeneration Office
Director: Mike Thompson
Tel: 028 9025 1973

Central Business Unit
Director: Henry Johnston
Tel: 028 9056 9262

Londonderry Development Office
Director: Declan O'Hare
Tel: 028 7131 9782

Regional Development Office
Director: Eddie Hayes
Tel: 028 9025 1901

Voluntary and Community Unit
Director: Dave Wall
Tel: 028 9056 9304

Departmental Agencies

Social Security Agency

Social Security Agency (Northern
Ireland)
Churchill House
Victoria Square
Belfast
BT1 4SS
Tel: 028 9056 9100
Fax: 028 9056 9178
Web: www.nics.gov.uk/ssa

Chief Executive: Chris Thompson

Personnel and Planning Directorate

Personnel Director: Tommy O'Reilly
Tel: 028 9056 9130

Personnel Officer: Vacant
Tel: 028 9056 9100

Personnel Branch
Senior Manager: P Magee
Tel: 028 9056 9457

Support Services
Senior Manager: N Walker
Tel:028 9052 2871

Welfare Reforms Accommodation
Senior Manager: J Hatchell
Tel: 028 903970

Welfare Reforms
Senior Manager: M Frampton
Tel: 028 9056 9445

Training and Development Unit
Principal: Andrew Bell
Tel: 028 9054 3624

Chief Executive's Office
Principal: John Johnston
Tel: 028 9056 9101

Communications Unit
Deputy Principal: Martin McDermott
Tel: 028 9056 9335

Benefit Security Directorate

Director: John Nevin
Tel: 028 9056 9131

Strategic Development Unit
Principal: Peter Crossley
Tel: 028 7036 1085

Benefit Investigation Services
Principal: Rene Murray
Tel: 028 9054 4604

Risk Management Unit
Principal: P Crossley
Tel: 028 7036 1085

Monitoring Advice and Guidance
Principal: L Bell
Tel: 028 9056 9198

Welfare Reforms
Principal: J O'Neill
Tel: 028 9037 6088

Business Development Directorate

Director: David McCurry
Tel: 028 9056 9132

Service Delivery
Principal: Tony McKenna
Tel: 028 9056 9126

IS/IT Unit
Principal: Johnny Graham
Tel: 028 9054 4627

Active Modern Service
Principal: Sean Johnston
Tel: 028 9056 9177

Belfast Benefit Centre
Principal: Eoin Neeson
Tel: 028 9023 1846

Finance and Support Unit

Director: John Deery
Tel: 028 9056 9129

Agency Resources Branch
Principal: Damian Prince
Tel: 028 9069605

Finance Support Branch
Principal: Alan Harvey
Tel: 028 9052 2007

Agency Audit Unit
Principal: Donald Heaney
Tel: 028 9025 2642

Support Services
Principal: Noel Walker
Tel: 028 9052 2871

Commercial Services Branch
Principal: Michael Broy
Tel: 028 9052 0084

Operations Directorate

Director: Barney McGahan
Tel: 028 9056 9128

Network Support Branch
Principal: Mickey Kelly
Tel: 028 9052 2149

Family and Disability Benefits
Principal: Colin McRoberts
Tel: 028 9033 6940

Incapacity Benefits & Pensions
Principal: John Turkington
Tel: 028 9033 6942

Success Impact Unit, New Deal, Child Benefit Project, New Tax Credit
Principal: R Mathews
Tel: 028 9037 6020

Belfast North & East Antrim
Principal: Jim Harvey
Tel: 028 9054 3265

Belfast West & Lisburn
Principal: Tom Wilson
Tel: 028 9054 2830

North District
Principal: Mervyn Hogg
Tel: 028 7046 1011

South District
Principal: Angela Clarke
Tel: 028 8773 3314

East Down District
Principal: J Sinnamon
Tel: 028 9054 5664

West District
Principal: Brian Doherty
Tel: 028 7131 9543

Child Support Agency

Chief Executive: Gerry Keenan
Tel: 028 9089 6805

Operations Division

Director: John Canavan
Tel: 028 9089 6840

New Client Teams
Principal: Michael Donnelly
Tel: 028 9047 6240

NI Operations, Centre & Field
Principal: Rory Murphy
Tel: 028 9089 6855

Maintenance Assessment & Fraud
Principal: Mervyn Adair
Tel: 028 9089 6955

Debt & Accounts
Principal: Catherine McCallum
Tel: 028 9047 6002

Business Development
Principal: Mary Quinn
Tel: 028 9089 6843

Eastern Business Unit
Principal: Stephen Smith
Tel: 028 9089 6810

Resources Division

Personnel
Principal: Jayne Forster
Tel: 028 9089 6820

Finance
Principal: Stephen Boyd
Tel: 028 9089 6789

Government Executive Agencies and Public Bodies

Some of the main categories of government agencies are set out below:

Non-Departmental Public Bodies

These are neither government departments nor parts of a department, but have a role in the process of government. There are three kinds of non-departmental public bodies: executive bodies, advisory bodies and tribunals, whose functions are essentially judicial.

Executive Bodies

Executive bodies are public organisations whose duties include executive, administrative, regulatory or commercial functions. Operating within broad policy guidelines set by departmental ministers they are to varying degrees independent of government in the execution of their day-to-day responsibilities, employ their own staff and have their own budget.

Next Steps Agencies

The Next Steps initiative, which commenced in 1988, saw the transformation of the basic structure of the civil service. The development of Next Steps agencies represents the delivery of services by satellites, which although outside government departments remain within a framework of central policy control.

The introduction of Next Steps agencies has acted as a catalyst for major managerial and structural change coupled with improvements in service delivery by the civil service, greater visibility of senior civil servants and increased accountability, emphasising the distinction between the policy making and policy execution functions of government.

Northern Ireland Next Steps Agencies

Business Development Service
Compensation Agency
Construction Service
Driver and Vehicle Licensing Northern Ireland
Driver and Vehicle Testing Agency
Environment and Heritage Service
Forensic Science Agency of Northern Ireland
Forest Service of Northern Ireland
Health Estates
Land Registers of Northern Ireland
Employment Service
Northern Ireland Child Support Agency
Northern Ireland Prison Service
Northern Ireland Statistics and Research Agency
Ordnance Survey of Northern Ireland
Planning Service
Procurement Service
Public Record Office of Northern Ireland
Rate Collection Agency
Rivers Agency
Roads Service
Social Security Agency Northern Ireland
Valuation and Lands Agency
Water Service

QUANGOs

The system of QUANGOs (an acronym for quasi autonomous non governmental organisations) has attracted much criticism because nearly all of the members are appointed rather than elected. The question of democratic accountability and the future evolution of administrative structures in Northern Ireland is the subject of a major government Review of Public Administration.

Executive Agencies:

A-Z Listing

Business Development Service
Craigantlet Buildings
Stoney Road
Belfast
BT4 3SX
Tel: 028 9052 0444
Fax: 028 9052 7270
Acting Chief Executive: Derek Orr

Relevant Department: Department of
Finance and Personnel

The Compensation Agency
Royston House
34 Upper Queen Street
Belfast
BT1 6FD
Tel: 028 9024 9944
Fax: 028 9024 6956
Chief Executive: Frank Brannigan

Relevant Department: Northern
Ireland Office

Driver and Vehicle Licensing Agency (DVLA)
County Hall
Castlerock Road
Coleraine
BT51 3TA
Tel: 028 7034 1461
Fax: 028 7034 1422
Chief Executive: Brendan Magee

Relevant Department: Department of
the Environment

Driver and Vehicle Testing Agency (DVTA)
Balmoral Road
Belfast
BT12 6QL
Tel: 028 9068 1831
Fax: 028 9066 5520
Web: www.doeni.gov.uk/dvta

Chief Executive: Stanley Duncan

Relevant Department: Department of
the Environment

Environment and Heritage Service
Commonwealth House
35 Castle Street
Belfast
BT1 1GU
Tel: 028 9025 1477
Fax: 028 9054 6660
Web: www.nics.gov.uk/ehs
Chief Executive: Richard Rodgers

Relevant Department: Department
of the Environment

Forensic Science Agency of Northern Ireland
151 Belfast Road
Carrickfergus
BT38 8PL
Tel: 028 9036 1888
Fax: 028 9036 1900
Web: www.fsani.org.uk
Chief Executive: Dr Richard Adams

Relevant Department: Northern
Ireland Office

Forest Service of Northern Ireland
Forest Service Headquarters
Dundonald House
Upper Newtownards Road
Belfast
BT4 3SB
Tel: 028 9052 4480
Fax: 028 9052 4570
Web: www.drdni.gov.uk/forestry
Chief Executive: Malcolm Beatty

Relevant Department: Department
of Agriculture and Rural
Development

Health Estates
Stoney Road
Dundonald

Belfast BT16 1US
Tel: 028 9052 0025
Fax: 028 9052 3900
Web: www.dhssni.gov.uk/hpss/hea
Chief Executive: Ronnie Browne

Relevant Department: Department of
Health, Social Services and Public
Safety

Invest Northern Ireland
64 Chichester Street
Belfast
BT1 4JX
Tel: 028 9023 9090
Fax: 028 9054 5000
Web: www.investni.com
Chief Executive: Leslie Morrison

Land Registers of Northern Ireland
Lincoln Building
27-45 Great Victoria St
Belfast
BT2 7SL
Tel: 028 9025 1515
Fax: 028 9025 1550
Web: www.lrni.gov.uk
Chief Executive:
Patricia Montgomery

Relevant Department: Department of
Finance and Personnel

Northern Ireland Blood Transfusion Agency
Belfast City Hospital Complex
Lisburn Road
Belfast
BT9 7TS
Tel: 028 9032 1414
Fax: 028 9043 9017
Web: www.nibts.org
Chief Executive: Morris McClelland

Relevant Department: Department
of Health, Social Services and
Public Safety

Northern Ireland Child Support Agency (CSA)
Great Northern Tower
17 Great Victoria Street
Belfast
BT2 7AD
Tel: 028 9089 6666
Fax: 028 9089 6777
Web: www.dhssni.gov.uk/child-support
Chief Executive: Gerry Keenan

Relevant Department: Department for Social Development

Northern Ireland Guardian Ad Litem Agency
Centre House
79 Chichester Street
Belfast
BT1 4JE
Tel: 028 9031 6550
Fax: 028 9031 9811
Executive Director:
Ronnie Williamson

Relevant Department: Department of Health, Social Services and Public Safety

Northern Ireland Health Promotion Agency
18 Ormeau Avenue
Belfast
BT2 8HS
Tel: 028 9031 1611
Fax: 028 9031 1711
Web:
www.healthpromotionagency.org.uk
Chief Executive: Brian Gaffney

Relevant Department: Department of Health, Social Services and Public Safety

Northern Ireland Prison Service
Dundonald House
Upper Newtownards Road
Belfast
BT4 3SU
Tel: 028 9052 0700
Fax: 028 9052 5375
Director General: Peter Russell

Relevant Department: Northern Ireland Office

Northern Ireland Statistics and Research Agency (NISRA)
McAuley House
201 Castle Street
Belfast
BT1 1SA
Tel: 028 9034 8100
Fax: 028 9034 8161
Web: www.nisra.gov.uk
Acting Chief Executive:
Dr Norman Caven

Relevant Department: Department of Finance and Personnel

Ordnance Survey of Northern Ireland (OSNI)
Colby House
Stranmillis Court
Belfast
BT9 8BJ
Tel: 028 9025 5755
Fax: 028 9025 5735
Web: www.osni.gov.uk
Chief Executive: Mick Cory

Relevant Department: Department of Culture, Arts and Leisure

Planning Service
Clarence Court
10-18 Adelaide Street
Belfast
BT2 8GB
Tel: 028 9054 0540
Fax: 028 9054 0665

Web: www.doeni.gov.uk/planning/
Chief Executive: Hugh McKay

Relevant Department: Department of the Environment

Public Record Office of Northern Ireland (PRONI)
66 Balmoral Avenue
Belfast
BT9 6NY
Tel: 028 9025 1318
Fax: 028 9025 5999
Web: www.proni.nics.gov.uk
Chief Executive: Gerry Slater

Relevant Department: Department of Culture, Arts and Leisure

Rate Collection Agency (RCA)
Oxford House
49-55 Chichester Street
Belfast
BT1 4HH
Tel: 028 9025 2252
Fax: 028 9025 2113
Web: www.nics.gov.uk/rca
Chief Executive: Arthur Scott

Relevant Department: Department of Finance and Personnel

Rivers Agency
Hydebank
4 Hospital Road
Belfast
BT8 8JP
Tel: 028 9025 3355
Fax: 028 9025 3455
Chief Executive: John Hagan

Relevant Department: Department of Agriculture and Rural Development

Roads Service

Clarence Court
10-18 Adelaide Street
Belfast
BT2 8GB
Tel: 028 9054 0540
Fax: 028 9054 0024
Web: www.drdni.gov.uk/roads
Chief Executive:
Dr Malcolm McKibben

Relevant Department: Department
for Regional Development

Social Security Agency (Northern Ireland)

Churchill House
Victoria Square
Belfast
BT1 4SS
Tel: 028 9056 9100
Fax: 028 9056 9178
Web: www.nics.gov.uk/ssa
Chief Executive: Chris Thompson

Relevant Department: Department
for Social Development

Valuation and Lands Agency

Queen's Court
56-66 Upper Queen Street
Belfast
BT1 6FD
Tel: 028 9025 0700
Fax: 028 9054 3750
Chief Executive: Nigel Woods

Relevant Department: Department
of Finance and Personnel

Water Service

Northland House
3 Frederick Street
Belfast
BT1 2NR
Tel: 028 9024 4711
Fax: 028 9035 4888
Chief Executive: Robert Martin

Relevant Department: Department
for Regional Development

Public Bodies: A-Z Listing

Appeals Service Northern Ireland

Cleaver House
3 Donegall Square North
Belfast
BT1 5GA
Tel: 028 9051 8518
Fax: 028 9051 8516
Head of Local Operations:
Tracey McCloskey

Relevant Department: Department
for Social Development

Arts Council of Northern Ireland

77 Malone Rd
Belfast
BT9 6AQ
Tel: 028 9038 5200
Fax: 028 9066 1715
Web: www.artscouncil-ni.org
Chief Executive: Roisin McDonagh

Lottery Department
Tel: 028 9025 8825
Fax: 028 9025 8906

Relevant Department: Department
of Culture, Arts and Leisure

Boards of Visitors and Visiting Committees Secretariat

Prison Service
Room 20A
Stormont Annexe
Stormont Estate
Belfast
BT3 2ST
Tel: 028 9052 5477
Fax: 028 9052 4843

Relevant Department:
Northern Ireland Office

BELFAST CITY CENTRE MANAGMENT Co.

BELFAST
City Centre Management

Belfast City Centre Management Co.
Second Floor, Sinclair House
95/101 Royal Avenue
Belfast
BT1 1FE

Tel: (028) 9024 2111
Fax: (028) 9023 0809
email: info@belfastcentre.com
Website: www.belfastcentre.com

Joanne Jennings
City Centre Manager

BCCM was set up in January 2000 as a
Company Limited by Guarantee, jointly
core funded by BCC and BRO to
provide a bridge between central and
local government and the private sector,
and to promote a cleaner, safer, more
attractive and more accessible city
centre.

In April 2002 BCCM joined a Strategic
Alliance with the Belfast Chamber of
Trade and Commerce, which has
enabled us to develop as the only
business lobby specifically focused on
Belfast with a strong relationship with
Belfast City Council and other public
sector services.

This strong relationship means that we
in conjunction with city centre
businesses can shape the future
development of Belfast.

Belfast Harbour Commissioners
Harbour Office
Corporation Square
Belfast
BT1 3PB

Chief Executive: Gordon Irwin
Principal Activity: Harbour Authority
Tel: 028 9055 4422
Fax: 028 9055 4411

E-mail: info@belfast-harbour.co.uk
Website: www.belfast-harbour.co.uk

Boundary Commission for Northern Ireland
c/o Northern Ireland Office
Millbank
London
SW1P 4QE
Tel: 0207 210 6569
Fax: 0207 210 6537
Commission Secretary:
Linda Rogers

Relevant Department: Northern Ireland Office

Charities Advisory Committee
4th Floor
Churchill House
Victoria Square
Belfast
BT1 4QW
Tel: 028 9056 9650
Fax: 028 9056 9654
Secretary: Trevor Campbell

Relevant Department: Department for Social Development

Construction Industry Training Board
17 Dundrod Road
Crumlin
Co Antrim
BT29 4SR
Tel: 028 9082 5466
Fax: 028 9082 5693

Web: www.citbni.org.uk
Chief Executive: Allan McMullen

Relevant Department: Department of Employment and Learning

Council for Catholic Maintained Schools (CCMS)
160 High Street
Holywood
Co Down
BT18 9HT
Tel: 028 9042 6972
Fax: 028 9042 4255
Chief Executive: Donal Flanagan

Relevant Department: Department of Education

Council for Nature Conservation and the Countryside
5-33 Hill Street
Belfast
BT1 2LA
Tel: 028 9054 3076
Fax: 028 9054 3076

Relevant Department: Department of the Environment

Disability Living Allowance Advisory Board for Northern Ireland
Castle Court
Belfast
BT1 1DS
Tel: 028 9033 6916
Fax: 028 9054 2112

Relevant Department: Department for Social Development

Distinction and Meritorious Service Awards Committee
Room 4A
Dundonald House
Upper Newtownards Road
Belfast
BT4 3SF
Tel: 028 9052 4243

Fax: 028 9052 4437
Web: www.dmsac.org.uk

Relevant Department: Department for Health, Social Services and Public Safety

Drainage Council for Northern Ireland
C/o Rivers Agency
Hydebank
4 Hospital Road
Belfast
BT8 8JP
Tel: 028 9025 3355
Fax: 028 9025 3455

Relevant Department: Department of Agriculture and Rural Development

Education and Library Boards

Relevant Department: Department of Education
For more information see Chapter 7: Education and Training in Northern Ireland

Belfast Education and Library Board
40 Academy Street
Belfast
BT1 2NQ
Tel: 028 9056 4000
Fax: 028 9033 1714
Chief Executive: David Cargo

North Eastern Education and Library Board
County Hall
182 Galgorm Road
Ballymena
BT42 1HN
Tel: 028 2565 3333
Fax: 028 2564 6071
Chief Executive: Gordon Topping

South Eastern Education and Library
Board

Grahamsbridge Road
Dundonald
Belfast
BT16 2HS
Tel: 028 9056 6200
Fax: 028 9056 6266
Chief Executive: Jackie Fitzsimons

Southern Education and Library Board

3 Charlemont Place
The Mall
Armagh
BT61 9AX
Tel: 028 3751 2200
Fax: 028 3751 2490
Web: www.selb.org
Chief Executive: Helen McClenaghan

Western Education and Library Board

1 Hospital Road
Omagh
Co Tyrone
BT79 0AW
Tel: 028 8241 1411
Fax: 028 8241 1400
Web: www.welbni.org
Chief Executive: Joseph Martin

Enterprise Ulster

The Close
Ravenhill Reach
Belfast
BT6 8RB
Tel: 028 9073 6400
Fax: 028 9073 6404
Web: www.enterpriseulster.co.uk
Chief Executive: Joe Eagleson

Relevant Department: Department
for Employment and Learning

Equality Commission for Northern
Ireland

Equality House
7-9 Shaftesbury Square
Belfast BT2 7DP

Tel: 028 9050 0600
Fax: 028 9031 1554
Web: www.equalityni.org
Chief Executive: Evelyn Collins

Relevant Department: Office of the
First Minister and Deputy First
Minister

Fire Authority for Northern Ireland

Brigade HQ
1 Seymour Street
Lisburn
BT27 4SX
Tel: 028 9266 4221
Fax: 028 9267 7402
Acting Chairman: Pat Bradley

Relevant Department: Department
of Health, Social Services and
Public Safety

Fisheries Conservancy Board for
Northern Ireland

1 Mahon Road
Portadown
Craigavon
BT62 3EE
Tel: 028 3833 4666
Fax: 028 3833 8912
Chief Executive: Karen Simpson

Relevant Department: Department
of Culture, Arts and Leisure

General Consumer Council for
Northern Ireland

Elizabeth House
116 Holywood Rd
Belfast
BT4 1NY
Tel: 028 9067 2488
Fax: 028 9065 7701
Director: Maeve Bell

Relevant Department: Department
of Enterprise, Trade and Investment

Health and Safety Executive for
Northern Ireland

83 Ladas Drive
Belfast
BT6 9FR
Tel: 028 9024 3249
Fax: 028 9024 3249
Web: www.hse-ni.org.uk
Chief Executive: Jim Keyes

Relevant Department: Department
of Enterprise, Trade and Investment

Historic Buildings Council

5-33 Hill Street
Belfast
BT1 2LA
Tel: 028 9054 3050
Fax: 028 9054 3076

Relevant Department: Department
of the Environment

Historic Monuments Council

5-33 Hill Street
Belfast
BT1 2LA
Tel: 028 9054 3050
Fax: 028 9054 3076

Relevant Department: Department
of the Environment

Juvenile Justice Board

Rathgael Centre
169 Rathgael Road
Bangor
BT19 1TA
Tel: 028 9145 4276
Fax: 028 9127 1579

Relevant Department: Northern
Ireland Office

LABOUR RELATIONS AGENCY

Labour Relations Agency
Head Office
2-8 Gordon Street
BELFAST BT1 2LG
Tel: (028) 9032 1442
Fax: (028) 9033 0827

Regional Office
1-3 Guildhall Street
LONDONDERRY BT48 6BJ
Tel: (028) 7126 9639
Fax: (028) 7126 7729
e-mail: info@lra.org.uk
website: www.lra.org.uk

Chief Executive:
William Patterson

Established in 1976 as an independent NDPB, the Labour Relations Agency promotes the improvement of employment relations in Northern Ireland. Agency services include:

- impartial advice on employment relations;
- comprehensive conciliation, mediation and arbitration facilities;
- preparation of codes of practice;
- provision of information notes;
- talks on employment rights and practices;
- workshops on the preparation of employment documents;

- general enquiry service;
- employment relations research.

Our clients can be employers, employers' associations, trades unions workers and other organizations or individuals who require assistance on employment practices and employment relations.

Laganside Corporation
Clarendon Building
15 Clarendon Road
Belfast
BT1 3BG
Tel: 028 9032 8507
Fax: 028 9033 2141
Web: www.laganside.com
Chief Executive: Kyle Alexander

Relevant Department: Department of Social Development

Law Reform Advisory Committee for Northern Ireland
Lancashire House
5 Linenhall Street
Belfast
BT2 8AA
Tel: 028 9054 2900
Fax: 028 9054 2909

Relevant Department: Department of Finance and Personnel

Legal Aid Advisory Committee for Northern Ireland
Northern Ireland Court Service
Windsor House
9-15 Bedford Street
Belfast
BT2 7LT
Tel: 028 9032 8594
Fax: 028 9032 1758

Relevant Department: Department of Finance and Personnel

Livestock and Meat Commission for Northern Ireland
Lissue House
31 Ballinderry Road
Lisburn
BT28 2SL
Tel: 028 9263 3000
Fax: 028 9263 3001
Web: www.lmcni.com
Chief Executive: David Rutledge

Relevant Department: Department of Agriculture and Rural Development

Local Government Staff Commission
Commission House
18-22 Gordon Street
Belfast
BT1 2LG
Tel: 028 9031 3200
Fax: 028 9031 3151
Web: www.lgsc.org.uk
Chief Executive: Adrian Kerr

Relevant Department: Department of the Environment

Mental Health Commission for Northern Ireland
Elizabeth House
118 Holywood Road
Belfast
BT4 1NY
Tel: 028 9065 1157
Fax: 028 9047 1180
Chief Executive: Francis Walsh

Relevant Department: Department of Health, Social Services and Public Safety

Mental Health Review Tribunal for Northern Ireland

Room 105
Dundonald House
Upper Newtownards Road
Belfast
BT4 3SF
Tel: 028 9048 5550
Fax: 028 9052 4615

Relevant Department: Department of Health, Social Services and Public Safety

National Board for Nursing, Midwifery and Health Visiting for Northern Ireland

Centre House
79 Chichester Street
Belfast
BT1 4JE
Tel: 028 9023 8152
Fax: 028 9033 3298
Chief Executive: Paddy Blaney

Relevant Department: Department of Health, Social Services and Public Safety

National Museum and Galleries of Northern Ireland

Botanic Gardens
Belfast
BT9 5AB
Tel: 028 9038 3000
Fax: 028 9038 3003
Chief Executive Officer:
Mike Houlihan

Relevant Department: Department of Culture, Arts and Leisure

Northern Ireland Advisory Committee on Telecommunications (NIACT)

Chamber of Commerce
22 Great Victoria Street
Belfast
Bt2 7QA
Tel: 028 9024 2631
Fax: 028 9024 7024

Web: www.acts.org.uk
Director: Frank Hewitt

NICO

"NI Tradeable Services Exporter of the Year 2001"

64 Chichester Street
Belfast
BTI 4JX
Web : www.nico.org.uk
Tel : (028) 9054 4902
Fax : (028) 9054 4900

Chief Executive : Rupert Haydock

NI-CO was established in 1992 to market the skills and expertise of the Northern Ireland public, private and voluntary sectors overseas. To date NI-CO has delivered more than 100 projects in over 36 different countries worldwide.

Northern Ireland Building Regulations Advisory Committee

Construction Service
Churchill House
Victoria Square
Belfast
BT1 4QW
Tel: 028 9025 0433
Fax: 028 9025 0225

Relevant Department: Department of Finance and Personnel

Northern Ireland Central Services Agency for Health and Personal Social Services

25 Adelaide Street
Belfast
BT2 8FH
Tel: 028 9032 4431
Fax: 028 9023 2304
Chief Executive: Stephen Hodkinson

Relevant Department: Department of Health, Social Services and Public Safety

Northern Ireland Community Relations Council

6 Murray St
Belfast
BT1 6DN
Tel: 028 9022 7500
Fax: 028 9022 7551
Chief Executive: Dr Duncan Morrow

Northern Ireland Council for the Curriculum, Examinations and Assessment (CCEA)

Clarendon Dock
29 Clarendon Road
Belfast
BT1 3BG
Tel: 028 9026 1200
Fax: 028 9026 1234
Chief Executive: Gavin Boyd

Relevant Department: Department of Education

Northern Ireland Council for Postgraduate Medical and Dental Education

5 Annadale Avenue
Belfast
BT7 3JH
Tel: 028 9049 2731
Fax: 028 9064 2279
Chief Executive: Jack McCluggage

Relevant Department: Department of Health, Social Services and Public Safety

Northern Ireland Economic Council

Pearl Assurance House
1-3 Donegall Square East
Belfast
BT1 5HB
Tel: 028 9023 2125
Fax: 028 9033 1250
Web: www.niec.org.uk
Director: Michael Brennan

Relevant Department: Department
of Finance and Personnel

Northern Ireland Fishery Harbour
Authority

3 St Patrick's Avenue
Downpatrick
Co Down
BT30 6DW
Tel: 028 4461 3844
Fax: 028 4461 7128
Chairman: Robert Ferris

Relevant Department: Department
of Agriculture and Rural
Development

Northern Ireland Housing Executive

The Housing Centre
2 Adelaide Street
Belfast
BT2 8PB
Tel: 028 9024 0588
Fax: 028 9043 9803
Web: www.nihe.gov.uk
Chief Executive: Paddy McIntyre

Relevant Department: Department
for Social Development

Northern Ireland Human Rights
Commission

Temple Court
39 North Street
Belfast
BT1 1NA
Tel: 028 9024 3987
Fax: 028 9024 7844
Web: www.nihrc.org

Chief Commissioner:
Prof Brice Dickson
Chief Executive: Paddy Sloan

Northern Ireland Industrial Court

Room 203
Adelaide House
39-49 Adelaide Street
Belfast
BT2 8FD
Tel: 028 9025 7675
Fax: 028 9025 7555

Relevant Department: Department
of Employment and Learning

Northern Ireland Local Government
Officers' Superannuation Committee

Templeton House
411 Holywood Road
Belfast
BT4 2LP
Tel: 028 9076 8025
Fax: 028 9076 8790

Relevant Department: Department
of the Environment

Northern Ireland Museums Council

66 Donegall Pass
Belfast
BT7 1BU
Tel: 028 9055 0215
Fax: 028 9055 0216
Web: www.nimc.co.uk
Director: Chris Bailey

Relevant Department: Department
of Culture, Arts and Leisure

Northern Ireland Review Body
(Operator and Vehicle Licensing)

c/o 148-158 Corporation Street
Belfast
BT1 3DH
Tel: 028 9025 4100
Fax: 028 9025 4086

Relevant Department: Department
of the Environment

Northern Ireland Social Care Council

Room 422
Dundonald House
Upper Newtownards Road
Belfast
BT4 3SF
Tel: 028 9041 7600
Fax: 028 9052 4369
Chairman: Dr Jeremy Harbison

Northern Ireland Tourist Board

St Anne's Court
59 North Street
Belfast
BT1 1NB
Tel: 028 9023 1211
Fax: 028 9024 0960
Web: www.nitb.com
Chief Executive: Alan Clarke

Relevant Department: Department
of Enterprise, Trade and Investment

Northern Ireland Transport Holding
Company

Chamber of Commerce House
22 Great Victoria Street
Belfast
BT2 7LX
Tel: 028 9024 3456
Fax: 028 9033 3845
Chief Executive: Ted Hesketh

Relevant Department: Department
for Regional Development

The Office of Electricity and Gas
Regulation (OFREG)

Brookmount Buildings
42 Fountain St
Belfast
BT1 5EE
Tel: 08457 660456
Fax: 028 9031 1740
Director General: Douglas McIldoon

Parliamentary Ombudsman for Northern Ireland and Northern Ireland Commissioner for Complaints
33 Wellington Place
Belfast
BT1 6HN
Tel: 028 9023 3821
Web: www.ni-ombudsman.org.uk
Ombudsman: Tom Frawley

Planning Appeals Commission
Park House
87-91 Great Victoria Street
Belfast
BT2 7AG
Tel: 028 9024 4710
Fax: 028 9031 2536
Web: www.pacni.gov.uk
Chief Commissioner: John Warke

Relevant Department: OFMDFM

Police Ombudsman for Northern Ireland
New Cathedral Buildings
St Anne's Square
Church Street
Belfast
BT1 1PG
Tel: 028 9082 8600

Police Ombudsman: Nuala O'Loan

Probation Board for Northern Ireland
80-90 North Street
Belfast
BT1 1LD
Tel: 028 9026 2400
Fax: 028 9026 2472

Relevant Department: The Northern Ireland Office

Rent Assessment Panel
Clarence Court
10-18 Adelaide Street
Belfast

BT2 8GB
Tel: 028 9054 0540
Fax: 028 9054 1117

Relevant Department: Department for Social Development

Road Safety Council of Northern Ireland
117 Lisburn Road
Belfast
BT9 7BS
Tel: 028 9066 9453
Fax: 028 9066 1959

Sports Council for Northern Ireland
House of Sport
Upper Malone Road
Belfast
BT9 5LA
Tel: 028 9038 1222
Fax: 028 9068 2757
Web: www.sportscouncil-ni.org.uk
Chief Executive: Eamonn McCartan

Relevant Department: Department of Culture, Arts and Leisure

Staff Commission for Education and Library Boards
Forestview
Purdy's Lane
Belfast
BT8 7AR
Tel: 028 9049 1461
Fax: 028 9049 1744

Relevant Department: Department of Education

Trading Standards Service
Belfast:
176 Newtownbreda Rd, BT8 6QS
Tel: 028 9025 3900

Londonderry
Asylum Road, BT48 7EA
Tel: 028 7131 9548

Armagh:
Alexander Road, BT61 7JF
Tel: 028 3752 9834

Enniskillen:
Queen Elizabeth Road, BT74 7JH
Tel: 028 6634 3222

Ballymena:
121a Broughshane St, BT43 6BA
Tel: 028 2566 4720

Ulster Supported Employment Limited
182-188 Cambrai Street
Belfast
BT13 3JH
Tel: 028 9035 6600
Fax: 028 9035 6611
Web: www.usel.co.uk
Chief Executive: Mitchell Wylie

Relevant Department: Department for Employment and Learning

Water Council (Northern Ireland)
Clarence Court
10-18 Adelaide Street
Belfast
BT2 8GB
Tel: 028 9054 0540
Fax: 028 9054 1156

Relevant Department: Department for Regional Development

Youth Council for Northern Ireland
Forestview
Purdy's Lane
Belfast
BT8 7AR
Tel: 028 9064 3882
Fax: 028 9064 3874
Web: www.youthcouncil-ni.org.uk
Chief Executive: David Guilfoyle

Relevant Department: Department of Education

CHAPTER 5

Local Government and Administration in Northern Ireland

Local Government and Administration in Northern Ireland

Introduction

Along with Westminster and the Stormont Executive, Northern Ireland has a third tier of government, in the form of its 26 councils, which are involved in policy and decision-making at a local level.   These 26 Local Government Districts (LGDs) are subdivided into a number of wards, usually between three and five (although Belfast has nine).   Each of these wards returns a number of councillors who collectively comprise the council and act as a single-tier local authority. Local government elections are held once every four years, with councillors elected by proportional representation. The last local government elections were held on the same day as the last General Election, 7 June 2001.

A Local Government District may be a borough, city or district council.   Belfast, Derry, Armagh, Lisburn and Newry all have city councils (although Armagh is officially a 'City and District' Council); the other 21 are either borough or district councils.   A mayor and deputy mayor head city and borough councils, while chairpersons head district councils, the office-bearers in both cases being elected at the council's Annual General Meeting. Details of the current holders of these positions are included later in this chapter. The mayor or chairperson of the council has a high profile within the council area, performing ceremonial duties and often playing a key role in promoting the area and welcoming visiting dignitaries.

Councils vary considerably in size, with Belfast being the largest by far, followed by Derry, Lisburn, Craigavon and Newtownabbey. In contrast, Moyle, Limavady and Magherafelt are among the smallest.

Northern Ireland's present system of local government dates from the 1970s. In the context of the civil rights movement and continuing general upheaval it was decided to reorganise the administration of key services at local level, and examine the geographical boundaries of local authorities.   In response to the Macrory Report, the Local Government (Northern Ireland) Act 1972 sought to address claims of political bias in many areas of service provision. It produced a significant change in the roles and responsibilities of councils, most notably a diminution in their control of education and health care.   Housing provision had already been transferred to a newly appointed housing authority, the Northern Ireland Housing Executive, in 1970. Education,

libraries and health were to be administered by area boards of appointed members, not directly accountable to councils. Local authorities retained responsibility for refuse collection, leisure and recreation facilities, building control, cemeteries and tourist amenities while nominating a number of members to the appointed health and education and library boards.

Local authorities also retained a consultative role in matters such as planning, roads and housing, and were encouraged to offer leadership and support to local economic development.

Local Government Services

The main functions of local councils in Northern Ireland can generally be grouped together under the following headings:

Technical Services

The typical functions of a council's Technical Services department include:
- Cleansing   (household waste collections, trade waste collections, street cleaning);
- Parks (developing and maintaining the council's parks, other green areas and for planting and flower displays in towns and villages);
- Building maintenance: handling building control applications to ensure that building regulations are adhered to during construction by carrying out regular inspections;
- Street naming;
- Providing technical advice to the council e.g. in the area of energy management.

Leisure Services

The typical functions of a council's Leisure Services department include:
- Leisure centres and the management of sports facilities;
- Tourism development, including Tourist Information Centres and the management of council-owned recreation and visitor attractions;
- Community development and community relations;
- Development of sports and the arts.

Lisburn City Council Offices

211

Environmental Health

Environmental Health Officers are responsible for the following areas:

- Pollution control (air pollution, noise complaints, public health nuisances);
- Health and safety;
- Consumer protection;
- Food control and hygiene (food sampling, bacteriological and chemical water sampling).

Administration

Administration departments provide a range of administrative and legal services to councils, including:

- The Inspector's Office, which has responsibility for dog control, litter control, petroleum licensing, and entertainment licensing, street trading licensing and the issue of amusement permits;
- The Registrar who registers births, deaths and marriages;
- Discharging the Council's duty to assert, protect and keep open public rights of way;
- Managing burials.

Corporate Services

Corporate Services departments typically have responsibility for the council's financial accounts, remittance advice, payment of invoices, and salaries. Corporate Services may often include the Human Resources and Information Technology departments.

Economic Development

In recent years local authorities have increased their workload in the area of local economic development with many councils now employing an Economic Development Officer whose remit includes the promotion of local economic development by encouraging and supporting local enterprise and attracting overseas companies to invest in their area.

Miscellaneous

Councils also have a limited legislative role within their district. They have authority to introduce byelaws regarding matters such as playing fields and dog control.

Councils and Consultation

Councils do not operate in isolation but work with other public bodies and have an input in the decisions, which these organisations make. Below are examples of the type of consultation which councils engage in.

The Department of the Environment must consult with the local council on:

- Applications for planning approval and on the Area Plan which is produced for its area;
- Roads and car parks in the area to ensure that the views of as many local residents are obtained as possible;
- Water and sewerage to ensure the area's requirements are met;
- Environmental issues, listed buildings and Areas of Special Scientific Interest.

The Northern Ireland Housing Executive ascertains the views of councils on proposed housing developments. The Department of Health, Social Services and Public Safety and individual Health Boards and Trusts seek councils' comments and views on health provision in their area. Central government also seeks the views of councils on new legislation.

A Changing Role

With twenty-six local councils in Northern Ireland, local government is a sizeable employer, with over 9,000 employees. The expansion of local government in recent years has seen their role encompass areas such as economic development, tourism, community development/relations and the arts.

In addition to these functions, the Northern Ireland Office has requested councils to develop Community Safety Strategies to enhance the safety of local communities in their area. Under this initiative local councils will work with the police in areas such as drug and alcohol abuse, the provision of youth clubs and other social issues, with the objective of reducing the potential for crime. Local councils also play a role in the new police partnership boards, separate from the district partnership boards, involving a partnership approach with the police at local level.

Local councils play a central role in dispensing the EU Special Peace and Reconciliation Funds. Local Strategy Partnerships were formed (LSPs) and their role and remit will continue to develop under the auspices of Peace II.

Further explanation of the Peace II initiative is to be found in Chapter 10, The European Union and Economic Support Initiatives in Northern Ireland.

Local councils are also under pressure in a number of environmental areas particularly with waste management and diminishing landfill capacity. Ever more stringent environmental legislation will continue to add to these pressures.

Public Administration: The Future

The devolution of additional powers to the Northern Ireland Assembly may eventually translate into an extension of responsibilities for local authorities. A Review of Public Administration, under the auspices of the Office of the First Minister and Deputy First Minister (OFMDFM) is currently in progress, the first stage of which was launched on 12 February 2002.

Best Value

Although local council spending accounts for only three per cent of the public purse, there has been pressure to improve the efficiency of this spending. Over the past decade local government as part of a central government efficiency drive, has been required to move from automatic municipal provision of services to a process of compulsory competitive tendering (CCT). As a result many services are now outsourced to the private sector.

The CCT process has largely been replaced by a new regime called 'best value'. This regime has the objective of focusing local government on providing better value in its services to ratepayers. Under the 'best value' initiative, local councils take a 'bottom-up' approach to reviewing services and divide up the full range of services for review individually over a five-year period. However, with only one section of the organisation undergoing review at any one time it can be difficult to achieve optimal reform.

In 2001 the Minister for the Environment introduced a Best Value bill. The bill was loosely based on England's Local Government Act 1999 which introduced best value in England. Many local councillors saw the bill as being too prescriptive and there was unease about the inspection process, which was to be undertaken by the existing local government auditor. With many MLAs also being local councillors there was significant interest in the bill. The Environment Committee eventually rejected the bill and a vote in the Assembly against the bill saw the Environment Minister being forced withdraw it.

Best Value Initiative

Best value is a new regime aimed at improving the quality of local government services. It was introduced by the UK government as a replacement for the competitive tendering (CCT) regime. Under best value local councils are required to apply the so-called 'four Cs' to all their services: challenge, consult, compare and compete. Regular inspections of services are carried out to ensure that best value is being achieved. Each council is given a star rating depending on their performance.

Challenge

This involves challenging the way councils have traditionally approached their services. Councils have to consider whether they really require certain services and identify customer need for each activity. The auditor assesses whether councils have been genuinely self-critical by checking that challenges have not just been raised, but acted upon with evidence of changes.

Consult

Councils have to provide evidence that they have consulted ratepayers and key local stakeholders as part of their best value reviews. They must also monitor levels of customer satisfaction with services.

Compare

Councils are required to benchmark their services against other councils and private sector providers. They must compare their performance against national best value performance indicators and implement an improvement plan aimed at raising their performance.

Compete

This is the part of the best value initiative that resembles the old CCT regime. Councils have to show that in-house services are the most cost effective by subjecting them to external competition. If in-house services are more expensive the council may switch to an external service provider.

How Local Councils Function

Although there are contrasts between the councils they do adhere to a similar organisational structure. Local councils conduct their activities through a council of all members, aided by a number of committees made up of smaller groups of members. The council and committees work in close co-operation with the senior officers, who are employed by the council and head the various functions of the council.

A typical local authority management team consists of:

- The Chief Executive and Clerk;
- Director of Technical Services;
- Chief Environmental Health Officer;
- Chief Building Control Officer;
- Director of Leisure Services;
- Director of Development;
- Director of Administration or Corporate Services.

The actual structure varies between councils depending on the size of the council. Some functions, such as environmental health and building control, follow a 'group' structure whereby a 'Group Officer' is responsible for the function amongst a group of adjacent councils.

The Committee System

Although the decision-making process takes place in the council chamber, the local council system operates by delegating its work to series of committees; these committees fall into three broad categories:

- **Central committees**, which take an overall view of policies and the allocation of resources. These include committees such as the Finance and General Purposes or Policy and Resources Committee;
- **Functional committees** responsible for groups of related services or main council functions, such as Recreation and Leisure Services, Environmental Health, Technical Services;
- **Joint committees** with other district councils, in areas such as tourism where there is an obvious overlap with adjacent council areas.

The council may also appoint sub-committees or working parties to carry out specific tasks. Such committees usually operate for a short period and are most effective when tasked to complete a specified project within a defined timeframe.

Elections for the various offices such as chairman and mayor and the determination of membership of the various committees for the coming year are held at the annual meeting. The appointment of the committee chairmen is usually left until the committee has its first meeting. The size of each of the committees varies from council to council, some committees contain all the elected representatives as members and others are made up of a selected number of the full list of members. Some of the smaller councils do not have a formal committee system and transact all their business in full council meetings.

Although much of the work of the council is carried out in committees, the full council remains in control. It is normal practice for each committee to report to the full council each month with committee reports forming part of the agenda. Full council meetings tend to be more formal than committee meetings. The most common method of reporting committee business to the council is simply by submitting the minutes of each meeting to the council for scrutiny or approval where required. In this way the council can inform itself of the action taken by the committee under delegated powers or can deal with recommendations which need council approval.

Council Funding

Councils receive funding from a number of sources:

Rates

Rates paid on domestic and commercial premises form a large part of a council's revenue. Certain premises do not pay rates at the full value and farmland has no rateable value. Rates vary significantly between different local government districts and are shown in the table later in this chapter.

Central Grant

Rates on property are supplemented by a grant from central government.

Other sources

Councils also generate income from other activities, such as leisure centres, pitches and halls.

Rates, the general grant and the other sources of income are used to meet a council's revenue expenditure required to cover the day-to-day running of services provided such as refuse collection.

Money spent on long term or major projects, such as new buildings (leisure centres, offices etc) or the purchase of heavy plant or machinery i.e. capital expenditure is financed by alternative means. As these facilities will benefit residents in the future, it is viewed as unfair to expect them to be paid for entirely by the people paying rates at any one period in time. Therefore in order to spread the cost evenly, councils undertake loans to finance capital expenditure. In this way, those using a facility some years after its construction will still pay towards its provision. Government grants of up to 75 per cent are available to fund capital expenditure for recreation, tourism and community projects. Capital income may also be generated by the disposal of capital assets no longer required by the council, e.g. disused buildings or vehicles.

Payments to Councillors

There are four allowances which may be payable to councillors:

Basic Allowance:

Payable to all councillors in recognition of their time and expense commitment and is intended to cover incidental costs. The basic allowance is £2,500 per councillor per annum.

Attendance Allowance:

Payable for those approved duties included in a council's scheme of allowances. A £20 flat rate, regardless of the number of meetings in any 24-hour period.

Special Responsibility Allowance:

Payable for those special responsibilities included in a council's scheme of allowances, within maximum levels determined by the Department of the Environment.

Travel and Subsistence Allowance:

These allowances compensate councillors for expenditure necessarily incurred when performing an approved duty.

District Rate Services

Council Responsible For:

Refuse Collection and Disposal
Recycling and Waste Management
Civic Amenity Provision
Grounds Maintenance
Street Cleansing
Cemeteries
Public Conveniences
Food Safety
Health and Safety
Environmental Protection
Consumer Protection
Environmental Improvement
Estates Management
Building Design and Maintenance
Building Control-Inspection and Regulation of New Construction
Dog Control
Enforcement Byelaws Litter etc
Sundry Licensing
Sports and Leisure Services
Forum Leisure Complex
Sports and Recreational Facilities
Parks, Open Spaces, Playgrounds
Community Centres
Tourism
Arts, Heritage and Cultural Facilities

Other Services

Economic Development
Registration of Births, Deaths and Marriages
Community Development
Community Safety
Sports Development
Summer Schemes
Regional Rate Services

Council Not Responsible For:

Education	Water
Personal Social Services	Sewerage
Roads	Libraries
Public Housing	Planning
Fire Service	Street Lighting
Police Service	Collection of Rates
Trading Standards	Transport
Drainage	

District Rate By Council 2002/2003

The figures below are the District Rate multiplier which when multiplied by the N.A.V or rateable value of a property will give an approximation of the rates bill due for a property.

Council Area	Domestic	Non-Domestic (Commercial)
Antrim	2.4572	0.5075
Ards	2.5421	0.4972
Armagh	2.7037	0.5292
Ballymena	2.3732	0.4946
Ballymoney	2.4397	0.5167
Banbridge	2.5389	0.5250
Belfast	2.7118	0.5245
Carrickfergus	2.5158	0.5329
Castlereagh	2.3144	0.4734
Coleraine	2.3997	0.4966
Cookstown	2.4525	0.4813
Craigavon	2.5549	0.5370
Downpatrick	2.6004	0.5101
Dungannon	2.3935	0.4713
Fermanagh	2.3387	0.4613
Larne	2.6638	0.5159
Limavady	2.4933	0.4953
Lisburn	2.4570	0.4923
Derry	2.6957	0.5336
Magherafelt	2.3381	0.4735
Moyle	2.6632	0.5473
Newry	2.7147	0.5333
Newtownabbey	2.6065	0.5470
North Down	2.5706	0.4827
Omagh	2.6457	0.5012
Strabane	2.5163	0.4962

Source: Rate Collection Agency

The Department of the Environment has issued guidelines for the allowances system for local councillors: "Guidance on Councillors' Allowances, Tax and Social Security Benefits, September 1998".

Rates

Rates bills consist of two distinct elements, the regional rate and the district rate.

Regional Rates

Since devolution, regional rates are determined annually by the Executive and approved by the Assembly. The level of revenue required is calculated by reference to the level of spending needed for public services, balanced by

Domestic Regional Rate 2002/2003	132.47 pence in the £
Business Regional Rate 2002/2003	31.42 pence in the £

an evaluation of what may be considered an acceptable rates burden. Thus the regional rate is essentially a contribution to public expenditure mirroring the Council Tax in England, Scotland and Wales.

Domestic water and sewerage services are no longer partly funded by the regional rate, as was the case prior to 1 April 1999, but are now a call on the public expenditure provision available within the Northern Ireland Executive's Departmental Expenditure Limit. Non-domestic water charges provide some £40 million per annum towards the costs of the services.

District Rates

District rates are struck independently of the regional rate, and determined by the respective local councils and are calculated to provide funding for local council services. A major new pressure facing councils over the next decade is the funding of waste management. Approximately 65 per cent of a district council's income is met by the district rates and other sources of income are the General Exchequer Grant (12 per cent), specific grants, fees and charges (23 per cent). District rates are struck each year at levels that take account of the other sources of income.

Local Government Organisations

Northern Ireland Local Government Association

123 York Street, Phillip House, Belfast BT15 1AB
Tel: 028 9024 9286
Fax: 028 9023 3328
Chief Executive: Heather Moorhead
Development Officer: Karen McCarbery
Communications Officer: James Lavery
Policy Officer: Damian McGinn
President: Cllr Mrs E Johnston (Coleraine) UUP
Vice Presidents: Cllr P McGlone (Cookstown) SDLP
                  Cllr M Mills (Ballymena) DUP
                  Cllr F Molloy (Dungannon) SF

The Northern Ireland Local Government Association is a newly formed organisation in November 2001 with all 26 councils participating and all major parties involved at Senior Officer and Executive levels, which has assumed a similar role to its predecessor, the Association of Local Authorities for Northern Ireland (ALANI), as a representative body for local government in Northern Ireland.

Key Points

- Executive committee comprised of 32 councillors plus 3 advisors (Mr R Gilmore, Mr M Rankin, Mr M McGuckin)
- SOLACE acts as an advisory group;
- Appointments must be made to outside bodies by Executive Committee using the d'Hondt system.

Local Government Staff Commission

Local Government Staff Commission for Northern Ireland
Commission House, 18–22 Gordon Street
Belfast BT1 2LG
Tel: 028 9031 3200
Fax: 028 9031 3151
E-mail: info@lgsc.org.uk
Chief Executive: Adrian E Kerr

This is an Executive Non Departmental Public Body (NDPB) established under the Local Government Act (NI) 1972 for the purpose of exercising general oversight of matters connected with the recruitment, training and terms and conditions of employment of officers of district councils and of making recommendation to councils on such matters. This purpose has been extended under subsequent legislation to include the Northern Ireland Housing Executive and to "monitor the fair employment practices of councils and their compliance with statutory requirements in relation to fair employment".

SOLACE

SOLACE is the Society of Local Authority Chief Executives and Senior Managers. It is the representative body for senior strategic managers working in local government and provides professional development for its members.

Chairperson: Robert Gilmore
Banbridge District Council
Tel: 028 4066 0600

Secretary: Norman Dunn
Newtownabbey Borough Council
Tel: 028 9034 0000

Guide to the 26 Local Councils

A brief summary of each local authority is set out below in alphabetical order. Each summary contains details of the membership of the council and its working committees along with principle characteristics of the area served. The summaries also set out the main points of contact for the various council services.

Guide to Council Committees

In order to optimise space the titles of Council Committees have been abbreviated. The key to the abbreviations is as follows:

Abbreviation	Committee Title
A21	Agenda 21
BC & PW	Building Control and Public Works
BVal	Best Value
Cen Serv	Central Services
City Der	City of Derry Airport
City Mktg	City Marketing
CLS	Client Services
Comm	Community
Comm & Leis	Community and Leisure Services
Cons	Consultative
Corp	Corporate Services
CTS	Contract Services
Cult	Cultural
Dev	Development
Dev & Leis	Development and Leisure
Dist Dev	District Development
Econ Dev	Economic Development
Env Ctrl	Environmental Control
Env Hlth	Environmental Health
Env Serv	Environmental Services
Exec	Executive
Fin	Finance
Gen Pur	General Purposes
Hlth	Health
Mon	Monitoring
Pers	Personnel
Plan	Planning
Pol	Policy
Pol Res/Serv	Policy Resources and Services
PSL	Public Services Liaison
Pub Serv	Public Services
Rec	Recreation
Res	Resources
Serv	Services
Stf & Pol	Staff & Policy
Stat	Statutory
Stgy	Strategy
Tech	Technical
TP	Town Planning
Tour	Tourism

ANTRIM BOROUGH COUNCIL

Area: 421 km²   Population: 51,000

The Steeple, Antrim BT41 1BJ
Tel: 028 9446 3113
Fax: 028 9446 4469
E-mail: contact@antrim.gov.uk
Web: www.antrim.gov.uk

The main population centres in Antrim borough include Antrim town itself, Crumlin, Randalstown and Templepatrick.   The borough covers an area of 220 square miles and is the third fastest growing local government district in Northern Ireland, with one of the lowest unemployment rates of all 26 District Council areas in Northern Ireland.

Antrim town has a long industrial past and was a centre for man-made fibres and is the home of several large indigenous companies, including construction company Mivan Construction which operates internationally.

Elected Members

Mayor: Mervyn Rea (UUP)   Deputy Mayor: Bobby Loughran (SDLP)
Council Committee Membership

Councillor	Party	Dev & Leisure	Env Serv	P S L	Stgy & Res
Thomas Burns	SDLP	•	•	•	•
Wilson Clyde	DUP			•	
Adrian Cochrane-Watson	UUP	•	•	•	
Samuel Dunlop	DUP	•	•	•	•
Brian Graham	DUP	•	•	•	
William Harkness	DUP	•	•	•	
Oran Keenan	SDLP	•	•	•	•
Bobby Loughran	SDLP	•	•	•	•
Paddy Marks	UUP	•	•	•	•
Donovan McClelland	SDLP			•	
Martin McManus	SF	•	•	•	•
Martin Meehan	SF		•	•	
Paul Michael	UUP	•		•	•
Stephen Nicholl	UUP	•		•	
Mervyn Rea	UUP	•	•	•	
Drew Ritchie	UUP	•		•	
John Smyth	DUP			•	•
Roy Thompson	UUP		•	•	
Edgar Wallace	UUP		•	•	•

• Member

Senior Officers

Chief Executive	Samuel Magee	samuel.magee@antrim.gov.uk
Corporate Services	Neill Cauwood	neill.cauwood@antrim.gov.uk
Development and Leisure	Philip Lucas	philip.lucas@antrim.gov.uk
Environmental Services	John Quinn	john.quinn@antrim.gov.uk

Council Contact Details

Corporate Services

Chief Executive's Office	028 9446 3113
Administration	028 9446 3113
Finance	028 9446 3113
Human Resources	028 9446 3113
Public Relations	028 9448 1303
Registration of Births, Deaths & Marriages	028 9446 3113

Environmental Services

Building Control	028 9448 1321
Dog Control	028 9448 1319
Environmental Health	028 9448 1319
Parks	028 9446 3113
Recycling	028 9446 3113
Refuse Collection	028 9448 1308
Waste Management	028 9448 1308

Development & Leisure Services

Arts, Heritage & Culture	028 9442 8000
Countryside Recreation	028 9446 3113
Economic Development & Tourism	028 9448 1318
Events & Festivals	028 9446 3113
Sport & Recreation	028 9446 3113

ARDS BOROUGH COUNCIL

Area: 363 km²   Population: 71,000

Council Offices, 2 Church Street, Newtownards BT23 4AP

Tel: 028 9182 4000
Fax: 028 9181 9628
E-mail: ards@ards-council.gov.uk
Web: www.ards-council.gov.uk

Although the town of Newtownards dominates Ards Borough Council, the borough covers a much larger area, including the Ards Peninsula, which encloses Strangford Lough. Other main population centres include the coastal towns of Portaferry and Greyabbey. Ards enjoys an enviable location, just a few miles from Belfast city, but on the shores of Strangford Lough. The town of Newtownards is an administrative and commercial centre for the southeast region of Northern Ireland, and a busy retailing location. Tourism is very important to the area, notably Strangford Lough, which is designated as an Area of Outstanding Natural Beauty. The area has a mix of industries including food processing and a wide range of manufacturing plants, from engineering to textiles.

Elected Members

Mayor: Jeff Magill (UUP) Deputy Mayor: Jim McBriar (All)

Council Committee Membership

Councillor	Party	Pol & Res	Coun Serv	Econ Dev	Hlth & Soc Serv	Bor Dev
Angus Carson	UUP	•	•	•	•	•
Linda Cleland	All	•	•			•
Margaret Craig	DUP	•	•	•		•
Robin Drysdale	DUP	•	•	•		•
George Ennis	DUP	C	•	•		•
Ronnie Ferguson	UUP	•	•			•
Robert Gibson	UUP	•	•	•	•	•
David Gilmore	DUP	•	•	•		•
Hamilton Gregory	DUP	•	•	•		C
Thomas Hamilton	UUP	VC	•			VC
Hamilton Lawther	DUP	•	•			•
Jeff Magill	UUP	•	•	•	•	•
Wilbert Magill	Ind	•	•			•
Jim McBriar	All	•	C	•		•
Alan McDowell	All	•	•	C	•	•
Danny McCarthy	SDLP	•	•			•
Kieran McCarthy	All	•	•			•
William Montgomery	DUP	•	•			•
Jim Shannon	DUP	•	•			•
John Shields	UUP	•	•			•
Philip Smith	UUP	•	VC	•		•
David Smyth	UUP	•	•		•	•
Terence Williams	DUP	•	•	VC	•	•

• Member   C Chair   VC Vice-chair (Chair and Vice-Chair not yet appointed in Health & Social Services Committee)

Senior Officers

Chief Executive	David Fallows	david.fallows@ards-council.gov.uk
Administration	Ashley Boreland	ashley.boreland@ards-council.gov.uk
Corporate Services	David Clarke	david.clarke@ards-council.gov.uk
Development	Derek McCallan	derek.mccallan@ards-council.gov.uk
Environmental Health	John Rea	john.rea@ards-council.gov.uk
Leisure Services	John McKnight	john.mcknight@ards-council.gov.uk
Technical Services	Archie Walls	archie.walls@ards-council.gov.uk
Borough Inspector	Richard Brittain	richard.brittain@ards-council.gov.uk

Council Contact Details

Chief Executive's Office	028 9182 4017

Corporate Services	
Accounts	028 9182 4006

Development	
Economic Development	028 9182 4025
Tourism	028 9182 6846

Environmental Health	
Public Health	028 9182 4056
Pest Control	028 9182 4059

Technical Services	
Building Control	028 9182 4033
Refuse Collection	028 9182 4014

ARMAGH CITY AND DISTRICT COUNCIL

Area: 673 km^2 Population: 54,900

Palace Demesne, Armagh BT60 4EL
Tel: 028 3752 9600
Fax: 028 3752 9601
E-mail: info@armagh.gov.uk
Web: www.armagh.gov.uk

Armagh lies 40 miles south of Belfast in the south east of Northern Ireland. The main population centres in Armagh District include Armagh city, Markethill, Keady, Tandragee and Loughgall. For almost 4,000 years, Armagh has been at the centre of Irish legend and folklore as the seat of kings and the site chosen by St Patrick to become the centre of the Christian religion in his era. The city is the ecclesiastical capital of Ireland with both Church of Ireland and Roman Catholic cathedrals.

Although Armagh city is the main centre of population the council area is mostly rural with agriculture forming a large part of economic activity. The county of Armagh is known as the 'orchard county', reflecting the importance of the local Bramley apple industry. The area has also significant light manufacturing activity, which is dominated by the textile and clothing sector.

Elected Members

Mayor: Anna Brolly (SDLP)   Deputy Mayor: Eric Speers (UUP)

Council Committee Membership

Councillor	Pty	Env. Hlth & Rec	Regen & Devt	Res	Scrutiny & BVal	PSL	Exec
Paul Berry	DUP	•				C	•
Heather Black	DUP		•	•	VC	•	
Pat Brannigan	SDLP		•	•	C	•	•
Anna Brolly	SDLP					•	
John Campbell	SDLP	•			•	VC	
Tom Canavan	SDLP	VC	•			•	
Jimmy Clayton	UUP		•		•	•	
Paul Corrigan	SF	•			•	•	
Evelyn Corry	UUP			•		•	
Brian Cunningham	SF		•	VC		•	
Freda Donnelly	DUP				•	•	
Brian Hutchinson	DUP	•	•	•		•	•
Tommy Kavanagh	SDLP	•	•			•	
James McKernan	SDLP	•		•		•	
Pat McNamee	SF				•	•	
Sylvia McRoberts	UUP		•			•	
Pat O'Rawe	SF	C		•		•	•
Cathy Rafferty	SF		•			•	
Charles Rollston	UUP	VC			•	•	
Eric Speers	UUP	•		•		•	
Jim Speers	UUP		C			•	•
Robert Turner	UUP	•		C		•	•

• Member   C Chair   VC Vice-chair   Executive Committee does not elect a Vice-chair

Senior Officers

Chief Executive	Victor Brownlees	v.brownlees@armagh.gov.uk
Development	Sharon O'Gorman	s.ogorman@armagh.gov.uk
Corporate Services	David McCammick	d.mccammick@armagh.gov.uk
Environmental Services	John Briggs	j.briggs@armagh.gov.uk

Council Contact Details

Corporate Administrative Services 028 3752 9605
Personnel Management/Training
Legal and Insurance, ICT, Property

Clerk & Chief Executive Secretariat 028 3752 9603
Servicing of Council & Committee Meetings
Mayor Secretariat
Visions Project

Member Services   028 3752 9649

Registration of Births, Deaths and Marriages   028 3752 9615

Financial Services   028 3752 9619
Purchasing/Auditing
Rates, Budgets & Financial Regulations

Regeneration and Development   028 3752 9642
Local Economic Development
Rural Development
Urban Regeneration
Tourism Development

Environmental Health & District Services   028 3752 9626
Food Safety and Inspection
Health and Safety at Work
Pollution Control
Environmental Co-ordination
Waste Management/Litter/Recycling
Dog Control

Operational Services   028 3752 9624
Refuse Collection/Street Cleansing

BALLYMENA BOROUGH COUNCIL

Area: 630km²   Population: 59,000

Ardeevin, 80 Galgorm Road,
Ballymena BT42 1AB
Tel: 028 2566 0300
Fax: 028 2566 0400
Email: info@ballymena.gov.uk
Web: www.ballymena.gov.uk

Ballymena Borough Council is located in one of Northern Ireland's most fertile and prosperous farming regions. It is 27 miles north of Belfast and 22 miles from the Port of Larne. The present borough of Ballymena was created in 1973 by the merging of the former borough with the surrounding rural hinterland of the former Ballymena Rural District Council. The borough with the town of Ballymena as its centre covers 200 square miles. Ballymena is the regional administrative centre for many organisations in the northeastern part of Northern Ireland.

Ballymena town is the foremost retail centre for the region with a good representation of the main high street chains. Other population centres include the smaller towns and villages of Kells, Cullybackey, Portglenone, Broughshane and Ahoghill. Farming and agri-food industries play a major role in the borough's economy. The borough is also the home of Gallaher Tobacco Company and Michelin Tyres.

Elected Members

Mayor: Hubert Nicholl (DUP) Deputy Mayor: Roy Gillespie (DUP)

Council Committee Membership

Councillor	Party	Pers. Policy & Eqty	Devt & Leis	A21	Env	Fin, Est & Info Comms Tech	Pub. Health Liaison
Elizabeth Adger	DUP	•	•		•	•	•
James Alexander	DUP	•	•		•	C	•
Neil Armstrong	UUP	•	•		•	•	•
Peter Brown	UUP	•	•		•	•	•
Martin Clarke	DUP	•	•		•	•	•
James Currie	UUP	•	C	•	•	•	•
David Clyde	UUP	•	•	•	•	•	•
Samuel Gaston	DUP	•	•		•	•	•
Roy Gillespie	DUP	•	•	•	•	•	•
Margaret Gribben	SDLP	•	•	•	•	•	•
Samuel Hanna	DUP	•	•	•	•	•	•
James Henry	Ind	•	•		•	•	•
Seamus Laverty	SDLP	•	•		•	•	•
PJ McAvoy	SDLP	•	•	•	•	•	•
Joseph McKernan	UUP	•	•	C	•	•	•
William McNeilly	UUP	•	•		•	•	•
Maurice Mills	DUP	C	•	•	•	•	•
Thomas Nicholl	DUP	•	•	•	•	•	•
Hubert Nicholl	DUP	•	•	•	•	•	•
Declan O'Loan	SDLP	•	•		•	•	•
Lexie Scott	UUP	•	•		•	•	•
Robin Stirling	DUP	•	•	•	•	•	•
David Tweed	DUP		•		•	•	•
William Wright	Ind	•	•	•	•	•	•

• Member   C Chair Committees do not have Vice-chairs. Other Chairmen elected Sept. 2002.

Senior Officers

Chief Executive	Mervyn Rankin	mervyn.rankin@ballymena.gov.uk
Economic Devt Officer	Aidan Donnelly	aidan.donnelly@ballymena.gov.uk
Building Control	Maurice Watterson	maurice.watterson@ballymena.gov.uk
Devt & Leisure Svcs	Ronald McBride	ronald.mcbride@ballymena.gov.uk
Environmental Health	Alex Kinghorn	alex.kinghorn@ballymena.gov.uk
Financial and IT Svcs	Victor Benson	victor.benson@ballymena.gov.uk
Personnel Services	Rodger McKnight	rodger.mcknight@ballymena.gov.uk

Council Contact Details

Council Head Office – Ardeevin	**028 2566 0300**
Arts/Cultural Activities	
Building Control	
Community Relations	
Community Services	
Consumer Protection	
Direct Services Organisation	
Dog/Litter Control	
Economic Development	
Environmental Improvements	
Food Control	
Noise/Air Pollution Control	
Recreations, Leisure Facilities, Parks, Open Spaces	
Registration Births, Deaths, Marriages	
Refuse Collection/Disposal	
Street Cleaning	
Tourism	
Postal Numbering	

Cemeteries

Ballymena Cemetery	028 2565 6026

Community Centres

Ahoghill Community Centre	028 2587 8198
Ballee Community Centre	028 2563 1350
Ballykeel 2000 Community Centre	028 2563 8129
Broughshane Community Centre	028 2586 1621
Cullybackey Community Centre	028 2588 1295
Dunclug Community Centre	028 2563 0050
Gracehill/Galgorm Community Centre	028 2564 0526
Harryville Community Centre	028 2564 2281
Kells & Connor Community Centre	028 2589 2627
Portglenone Community Centre	028 2582 1912

Museums

Arthur Cottage (Seasonal)	028 2588 0781
Ballymena Museum	028 2564 2166

Ballymena Council has placed an increasing emphasis on its leisure and environmental facilities. The Borough is host to a major environmental project - the £10 million ECOS Centre - built on the banks of the River Braid. The project incorporates numerous interactive features, generates its own power from solar and biomass energy and provides attractive conference and visitor facilities.

BALLYMONEY BOROUGH COUNCIL

Area: 416 km^2 Population: 26,000

Borough Offices
Riada House, 14 Charles Street, Ballymoney BT53 6DZ
Tel: 028 2766 2280
Fax: 028 2766 5150
Email: info@ballymoney.gov.uk
Web: www.ballymoney.gov.uk

Ballymoney Borough Council is one of the smallest local authorities accounting for 3 per cent of Northern Ireland's land mass. The borough is bordered to the west by the Lower River Bann, to the north and east by the Coleraine and Moyle councils and to the south by Ballymena. Approximately one third of the borough's 26,000 inhabitants live in or near the town of Ballymoney, which is the administrative, commercial and educational centre for the area.

Elected Members

Mayor:	Frank Campbell (DUP)
Deputy Mayor:	Cecil Cousley (DUP)

Council Committee Membership

Councillor	Party	Dev	Leisure & Amenities	Finance & General Purposes	Health & Env	BVal
Frank Campbell	DUP	•	•	•	•	•
Harry Connolly	SDLP		•			
Cecil Cousley	DUP	•	•	•	•	•
John Finlay	DUP	•	•	•		•
Joseph Gaston	UUP		•	•	•	
Robert Halliday	DUP		•		•	
Bill Kennedy	DUP	•	•	•	•	•
William Logan	UUP		•	•	•	•
Malachy McCamphill	SDLP	•	•			•
Philip McGuigan	SF				•	•
Thomas McKeown	UUP	•				
John Ramsay	UUP	•			•	•
James Simpson	UUP	•		•		
Ian Stevenson	DUP	•		•	•	
Mervyn Storey	DUP	•		•		
Robert Wilson	DUP		•	•	•	

• Member

Senior Officers

Chief Executive	John Dempsey	john.dempsey@ballymoney.gov.uk
Building Control	Joe Martin	joe.martin@ballymoney.gov.uk
Finance and Administrative Services	Iris McCleery	iris.mccleery@ballymoney.gov.uk
Health and Environmental Services	John Michael	john.michael@ballymoney.gov.uk
Leisure and Amenities	John Paul	john.paul@ballymoney.gov.uk

BANBRIDGE DISTRICT COUNCIL

Area: 451 km^2 Population: 40,000

Civic Building, Downshire Road, Banbridge BT32 3JY
Tel: 028 4066 0600
Fax: 028 4066 0601
E-mail: info@banbridgedc.gov.uk
Web: www.banbridgedc.gov.uk

Banbridge district is situated on the north west of County Down on the main Belfast to Dublin road. Its main population centre is Banbridge town itself, which as its name suggests, was established around a major crossing of the river Bann. Banbridge has long been associated with the linen industry (and subsequently textiles) and agriculture for its economic activity. Agriculture remains important for the area and other activity revolves around small manufacturing companies and public sector employment.

Elected Members

Chairman: David Herron (DUP)   Vice-Chairman: Seamus Doyle (SDLP)

Council Committee Membership

Councillor	Party	PSL	Leis & Dev	Env Serv	Pol & Res	Hlth Care
Joan Baird	UUP	•		•	•	C
Nora Beare	UUP	•	•	•		•
Derick Bell	UUP	•	•		•	
Ian Burns	UUP	VC	•	•		•
Seamus Doyle	SDLP	•	VC		•	
John Hanna	UUP	•	C		•	
David Herron	DUP	C	•		•	•
Stephen Herron	DUP	•		•	•	
John Ingram	UUP	•	•	•		
William Martin	UUP	•	•	VC	•	
Pat McAleenan	SDLP	•	•	•		•
Malachy McCartan	Ind	•	•	•		
Cassie McDermott	SDLP	•		C	•	•
Jim McElroy	DUP	•		•	•	•
Wilfred McFadden	DUP	•	•		C	VC
Frank McQuaid	All	•		•	VC	
Paul Rankin	DUP	•	•	•		

Senior Officers

Chief Executive	Robert Gilmore	robert.gilmore@banbridgedc.gov.uk
Corporate Services	Pat Cumiskey	pat.cumiskey@banbridgedc.gov.uk
Development	Liam Hannaway	liam.hannaway@banbridgedc.gov.uk
Environmental Services	Ken Forbes	ken.forbes@banbridgedc.gov.uk
Leisure Services	Mike Reith	mike.reith@banbridgedc.gov.uk
Technical Services	Ken Forbes	ken.forbes@banbridgedc.gov.uk

Ballymena

for business, for leisure, for value!

eisure contact:
28 25 638494
mail: ballymenatic@hotmail.com

rts & Events contact:
28 25 660441
mail: Rosalind.Lowry@ballymena.gov.uk

For a Conference Pack contact:
ecos millennium environmental centre
Kernohans Lane, Broughshane Road, Ballymena
Conferences: 028 25 664404
Email: info@ecoscentre.com
Website: www.ecoscentre.com

A MILLENNIUM PROJECT
SUPPORTED BY FUNDS
FROM THE NATIONAL LOTTERY

BELFAST CITY COUNCIL

Development Department

Development Department
Belfast City Council
Cecil Ward Building
4-10 Linenhall Street
Belfast BT2 8BP
Tel: (028) 9032 0202
Fax: (028) 9027 0496
Website: www.development.belfastcity.gov.uk
Email:development@belfastcity.gov.uk

Formed in April 1999 Belfast City Council's Development Department was set up as a ground-breaking initiative to give leadership to the city's sustainable regeneration. To achieve this vision the department works across a wide range of inter-related areas that include economic development, culture and heritage, tourism development, events, project management, estates management, procurement and planning advice. This unique combination of expertise provides a fertile environment for establishing new ways of working and thinking about the development of Belfast and allows the council to work strategically with partner organisations throughout the city. The department is led by its Director, Marie-Thérèse McGivern

Belfast City Council is by far the largest local authority in Northern Ireland, covering the centre of Belfast and much of the city's suburbs and employing over 2,000 people. The Council is based at Belfast City Hall, an impressive Georgian building at the very centre of the city. The city has a long tradition of manufacturing with its shipbuilding, engineering and textile factories. Its main manufacturing base has always been in the east of the city, around Harland and Wolff shipyard and Bombardier Aerospace aircraft plant but both these industries have experienced difficulties and job cuts in more recent times. Under the Council's stewardship the City boasts many fine amenities including numerous attractive parks and walkways, which have given many inner-city areas a new lease of life. The Council is also at the forefront of economic regeneration and kickstarts local business development via its First Stop Shop.

Council Contact Details

Arts and Heritage Unit	028 9027 0461
Building Control 24 hour Helpline	028 9023 6672
Building Control Technical Helpline	028 9027 0432
Building Control Licensing	028 9027 0287
Build Control Operations	028 9027 0285

(North & West Belfast)

Build Control Operations	028 9027 0290

(South & East Belfast)

Business Improvement Section	028 9027 0279
Chief Executive's Department	028 9027 0462
City Hall	028 9032 0202
City Hall (after hours)	028 9027 0275
Client Services Department	028 9032 0202
Committee Services	028 9027 0465
Community Development	028 9027 0463
Community/Leisure Services Section	028 9032 0202
Complaints Central Helpline	028 9027 0270
Conservation & Education Unit	028 9066 2259
Consumer Advice Centre	028 9032 8260
Contract Services Department	028 9032 0202
Economic Development Unit	028 9027 0482
Events Co-ordinator (Parks & Amenities)	028 9027 0467
Financial Services Section	028 9032 0202
First Stop Shop – Business Enquiry Service	028 9027 8399
Food Safety Division	028 9027 0468
Forest of Belfast Officer (Parks & Amenities)	028 9027 0350
Grounds Maintenance Head Office	028 9037 3031
Health & Environmental Services Dept	028 9032 0202
Health & Environmental (Emergency)	078 5049 9622
Home Safety Division	028 9027 0469
Human Resource Section	028 9032 0202
Information Services Belfast	028 9024 4832
Lord Mayor's Unit	028 9027 0215
Personnel	028 9032 0202
Pollution Control	028 9027 0428
Press and Media	028 9027 0221
Recycling	028 9027 0230
Refuse Collection (Commercial/Trade Accounts)	028 9027 0298
Refuse Collection (Commercial/Trade Operations)	028 9032 3190
Refuse Collection (Domestic)	028 9027 0230
Registration of Births, Deaths & Marriages	028 9027 0274
Tourism Unit	028 9027 0426
Waste Disposal Industrial/Hazardous/Special Waste	028 9032 0202
Waste Management (Complaints/Enquiries)	028 9027 0297

Elected Members

Lord Mayor: Alex Maskey (SF)

Council Committee Membership

Councillor	Party	Policy & Resources	Client Services	Contract Services	Development	Health & Environmental Services	Town Planning
Ian Adamson	UUP				•		•
David Alderdice	All	•				•	
Alex Attwood	SDLP		•				
Gerald Brophy	SF	•	•	•		•	
David Browne	UUP	•		C			•
Michael Browne	SF	•	•		•		
Wallace Browne	DUP		C	•		•	
Jim Clarke	UUP	•		•		VC	
Margaret Clarke	UUP		•	•		•	
Patrick Convery	SDLP		•			•	
Margaret Crooks	UUP	•	•			•	
Alan Crowe	UUP				•	•	
Ian Crozier	DUP	•		•	•		
Máire Cush	SF			•		•	
Nigel Dodds	DUP	•				•	
Thomas Ekin	All	•		•	•		
Reg Empey	UUP				•		•
David Ervine	PUP		•				
Carmel Hanna	SDLP	•				•	
Tom Hartley	SF	•					
Billy Hutchinson	PUP				•		•
Danny Lavery	SF	•			•		C
Naomi Long	All		•				•
Alban Maginness	SDLP			•			•
Alex Maskey	SF		•		•		
Paul Maskey	SF			•			
Chrissie McAuley	SF			•	C		
Fra McCann	SF	•	VC			•	
Patrick McCarthy	SDLP			•	•		•
Nelson McCausland	DUP			•	•		
Margaret McClenaghan	SF		•				•
Frank McCoubrey	Ind		•	•			
Chris McGimpsey	UUP	C	•	•		•	
Michael McGimpsey	UUP				•		•
Elaine McMillen	DUP			•		•	•
Catherine Molloy	SDLP				•		•
Marie Moore	SF			•		•	•
Martin Morgan	SDLP	VC		•		•	
Robin Newton	DUP	•			VC		
Eoin O'Broin	SF				•	•	
Joseph O'Donnell	SF		•		•		•
Gerard O'Neill	SF			VC			•
Peter O'Reilly	SDLP	•			•	C	
Ruth Patterson	DUP					•	•
Jim Rodgers	UUP						
Eric Smyth	DUP	•	•				•
Hugh Smyth	PUP	•				•	•
Robert Stoker	UUP		•		•		
Harry Toan	DUP		•	•			
Margaret Walsh	SDLP	•	•				•
Sammy Wilson	DUP				•		VC

• Member   C Chair   VC Vice-chair

Senior Officers

Chief Executive	Peter McNaney	mcnaneyp@belfastcity.gov.uk
Assistant Chief Executive	Robert Wilson	wilsonr@belfastcity.gov.uk
Client Services	Mervyn Elder	elderm@belfastcity.gov.uk
Development	Marie-Thérèse McGivern	mcgivernmt@belfastcity.gov.uk
Head of Economic Initiatives	Shirley McCay	mccays@belfastcity.gov.uk
Contract Services	Heather Louden	loudenh@belfastcity.gov.uk
Corporate Services	Trevor Salmon	salmont@belfastcity.gov.uk
Health and Environmental Services	William Francey	franceyw@belfastcity.gov.uk

CARRICKFERGUS BOROUGH COUNCIL

Area: 81 km^2 Population: 38,000

Town Hall
Joymount
Carrickfergus
BT38 7DL

Tel: 028 9335 1604
Fax: 028 9336 6676
E-mail: info@carrickfergus.org
Web: www.carrickfergus.org

The borough of Carrickfergus is located on the northern shore of Belfast Lough, stretching from Greenisland in the southwest to Whitehead in the east. Carrickfergus Castle has guarded Belfast Lough since the 12th century when the town was more important than Belfast. The landscape is a low-lying coastal strip where the main population centres are located. Further inland the ground rises indicating the southern most reaches of the Antrim plateau.

The town was once the home of a number of large man-made fibre plants, which closed down in the early 1980s. The factories that these companies left behind were converted to house local small and medium-sized enterprises (SMEs). Carrickfergus has also seen the recent development of its sea front with large retail, office and residential developments.

Council Contact Details

Town Hall	028 9335 1604
Administration Department	
Building Regulations	
Dangerous Structures	
Dog Licensing / Control	
Entertainments / Petroleum	
Licensing	
Finance Department	
Food Safety	
Litter ControlNoise / Air Pollution	
Property Certificates	
Registration of Births, Deaths and Marriages	
Town Clerk	

Heritage Centre	028 9336 6455
Community Relations	
Knight Ride	
Recreation Department	
Access to the Countryside	

Leisure Centre	028 9335 1711
Playing Field Bookings	
Andrew Jackson Centre	028 9336 6455
Carrickfergus Marina	028 9336 6666

Sullatober Depot	028 9335 1192
Bulky Waste Pickup	
Civic Amenity Area	
Street Cleansing	
Waste / Bin Collection	

Elected Members

Mayor:	Eric Ferguson (UUP)
Deputy Mayor:	May Beattie (DUP)

Council Committee Membership

Councillor	Party	Econ Dev	Rec	Env	Tech Serv	Fin & Gen Pur
William Ashe	DUP	C	•	•	•	•
May Beattie	DUP	•	•	•	•	•
Roy Beggs	UUP	•	•	VC	•	•
James Brown	Ind	•	•	•	•	
Robert Cavan	All	•	•	•	•	•
Terence Clements	DUP	•	C	•	•	•
Janet Crampsey	All	•	•	•	•	•
Stewart Dickson	All	•	•	•	•	C
Darin Ferguson	UUP	•	VC	•	•	•
Eric Ferguson	UUP	•	•	•	•	•
William Hamilton	Ind	VC	•	•	•	•
David Hilditch	DUP	•	•	•	C	•
James McClurg	DUP	•	•	•	•	VC
Noreen McIlwrath	All	•	•	•	•	•
Patricia McKinney	DUP	•	•	C	•	•
Sean Neeson	All	•	•	•	•	•
Gwen Wilson	UUP	•	•	•	VC	•

• Member   C Chair   VC Vice-chair

Senior Officers

Chief Executive	Alan Cardwell	info@carrickfergus.org
Acting Deputy Town Clerk	Alan Phair	aphair.tourism@carrickfergus.org
Building Control	Stephen Johnston	sjohnston.buildcon@carrickfergus.org
Environmental Services	Alan Barkley	abarkley.envhealth@carrickfergus.org
Finance	John McClimonds	jmcclimonds.finance@carrickfergus.org
Recreation	Norman Houston	nhouston.tourism@carrickfergus.org

CASTLEREAGH BOROUGH COUNCIL

Area: 85 km^2 Population: 67,000

Civic & Administrative Offices, Bradford Court
Upper Galwally, Belfast BT8 6RB
Tel: 028 9049 4500
Fax: 028 9049 4515
Website: www.castlereagh.gov.uk
E-mail: council@castlereagh.gov.uk

Castlereagh Borough Council covers much of the southern and eastern outskirts of Belfast, including the suburbs of Newtownbreda, Knock and Stormont, as well as the satellite towns of Carryduff and Comber. The borough has a strong engineering manufacturing base. Building on the success of the Dundonald Ice Bowl complex the council has initiated a major leisure development park.

Elected Members

Mayor: John Norris (DUP)
Deputy Mayor: Michael Copeland (UUP)

Council Committee Membership

Councillor	Party	Plan	Hlth	Leis	Tech Serv	Civic	Cen Serv
John Beattie	DUP	VC	•	•	•		VC
Joanne Bunting	DUP	•				•	•
Michael Copeland	UUP	•	•			•	•
David Drysdale	UUP	•		C			•
Sara Duncan	All	•			VC		•
Claire Ennis	DUP	•	•	•	•		
Francis Gallagher	Ind	•	•	•			
Cecil Hall	PUP	C			C		•
Brian Hanvey	SDLP	•	•	•			•
Michael Henderson	UUP	•		•	•	•	•
Rosaleen Hughes	SDLP	•	VC		•		
Michael Long	All	•	•			•	
Barbara McBurney	UUP	•	•	•	•	VC	•
Kim Morton	DUP	•	•	•	•	•	•
John Norris	DUP	•	•	•		C	•
Peter Osborne	All	•		VC			•
Geraldine Rice	All	•	C	•	•	•	
Iris Robinson	DUP	•		•			
Peter Robinson	DUP	•				•	•
Mark Robinson	DUP	•			•	•	C
Thomas Sandford	PUP	•			•	•	
Vivienne Stevenson	DUP	•	•	•	•		•
Jim White	DUP	•			•		•

• Member   C Chair   VC Vice-chair 2002/03

Senior Officers

Chief Executive	Adrian Donaldson	adriandonaldson@castlereagh.gov.uk
Economic Development	Alastair Higgins	alastairhiggins@castlereagh.gov.uk
Admin and Civic Services	Joan McCoy	joanmccoy@castlereagh.gov.uk

Council Contact Details

Headquarters	028 9049 4500
Lagan Valley Regional Park	028 9049 1922
Activity Centre, Ballybeen	028 9048 3905
Community Centres	
Ballyoran Centre	028 9041 0822
Belvoir Activity Centre	028 9064 2174
Castlereagh	028 9070 4251
Cregagh	028 9079 5848
Dungoyne	028 9048 7300
Tullycarnet	028 9048 1816
Parks and Playing Fields	
Henry Jones Memorial	028 9079 6711
Moat Park Playing Fields	028 9048 2209
Hydebank	028 9064 9647
Tullycarnet Park	028 9048 4099
Recreation Department	
Dundonald Ice Bowl	028 9048 2611
Lough Moss Centre	028 9081 4844
The Robinson Centre	028 9070 3948
Registrar of Births, Deaths and Marriages	028 9079 8405

COLERAINE BOROUGH COUNCIL

Coleraine Borough Council
66 Portstewart Road
Coleraine
BT52 1EY
Tel: (028) 7034 7034
Fax: (028) 7034 7026
Email: townclerk@colerainebc.gov.uk

Wavell Moore
Town Clerk and Chief Executive

The Borough of Coleraine is situated on Northern Ireland's spectacular north coast and covers an area of more than 180 square miles of dramatic coastal scenery and rich countryside interspersed with a number of bustling towns and quiet villages.

Coleraine Borough Council serves a population of over 56,000 which is supplemented substantially during the busy tourism season by the many visitors to the region.

Coleraine is also a university town, being home to the headquarters campus of Ireland's largest university, the University of Ulster.

Coleraine Council endeavours to progressively develop the borough by both the direct delivery of top-quality local services and a strong series of partnerships involving public, private, voluntary and community interests.

In addition to being the main town serving the North Coast tourism industry Coleraine is increasingly a centre for high-tech industry. The Council's economic development department has developed a new biotechnology centre in the Borough.

Elected Members

Mayor:	Olive Church (UUP)
Deputy Mayor:	Gerry McLaughlin (SDLP)

Council Committee Membership

Councillor	Party	Leisure	Planning	Policy
Christine Alexander	Ind	•	•	
Pauline Armitage	Ind	•	•	•
David Barbour	UUP	•	•	•
Toye Black	UUP	•	•	•
Maurice Bradley	DUP	•	•	C
Olive Church	UUP	•	C	•
William Creelman	DUP	•	•	•
John Dallat	SDLP	•	•	•
Timothy Deans	DUP	•	•	•
Phyllis Fielding	DUP	•	•	•
Norman Hillis	UUP	•	•	•
Elizabeth Johnston	UUP	•	•	•
William King	UUP	•	•	•
Billy Leonard	SDLP	•	•	•
David McClarty	UUP	•	•	•
James McClure	DUP	VC	•	•
Gerry McLaughlin	SDLP	•	VC	•
Adrian McQuillan	DUP	•	•	•
Robert McPherson	UUP	C	•	•
Eamon Mullan	SDLP	•	•	•
Desmond Stewart	DUP	•	•	•
James Watt	UUP	•	•	VC

• *Member*   C *Chair*   VC *Vice-chair*

Senior Officers

Chief Executive	Wavell Moore	townclerk@colerainebc.gov.uk
Corporate Services	David Bell	corporate@colerainebc.gov.uk
Environmental Health	George Montgomery	eh@colerainebc.gov.uk

Council Contact Details

Town Clerk & Chief Executive	028 7034 7034
Registration of Births	
Deaths & Marriages	028 7034 7021
Community Relations	028 7034 7044
Rural Development	028 7034 7045
Tourism & Marketing	028 7034 7044
Environmental Health Department	028 7034 7171
Buildings Regulations	028 7034 7253
Refuse Collection	028 7034 7272
Leisure Services	028 7034 7234
Arts/Events/Entertainment	028 7034 7234
Town Halls	
Coleraine Town Hall	028 7034 2850
Kilrea Town Hall	028 2974 0630
Portstewart Town Hall	028 7083 6986

COOKSTOWN DISTRICT COUNCIL

Area: 514 km²   Population: 32,000

12 Burn Road, Cookstown, BT80 8DT
Tel: 028 8676 2205
Fax: 028 8676 4360
Web: www.cookstown.gov.uk
E-mail: info@cookstown.gov.uk

Situated in the heart of Northern Ireland Cookstown District Council is one of the smaller districts in terms of population. The principal population centre is Cookstown itself. The area has a significant traditional manufacturing base, which is particularly strong in food processing. Manufacturing employs nearly a quarter of the local work force with agriculture being the other major employer. Central to the Council's local economic development plan is the development of the tourism sector.

Council Contact Details

Services	028 8676 2205
Building Control	
Development Department	
Environmental Health	
Finance / Personnel	
Operational Services	
Registration of Births, Deaths and Marriage	

Cookstown Leisure Centre	028 8676 3853
Dog Warden	028 8676 2205
The Burnavon (Arts Centre)	028 8676 9949
Tourist Information	028 8676 6727
Waste Disposal Site	028 8676 1153
After Hours Emergencies	028 8676 2205

Elected Members

Chairman:	Patsy McGlone (SDLP)
Vice-Chairman:	Trevor Wilson (UUP)

Council Committee Membership

Councillor	Party	Pol Res & Serv	Dev	Stat
Mary Baker	SDLP	•	•	•
Seamus Campbell	SF	•	•	•
Peter Cassidy	SDLP	•	•	•
Sam Glasgow	UUP	•	•	•
Walter Greer	UUP	C	•	•
Dessie Grimes	SF	•	•	•
Pearse McAleer	SF	•	•	•
Anne McCrea	DUP	•	•	•
Ian McCrea	DUP	•	•	•
James McGarvey	SDLP	•	VC	•
Patsy McGlone	SDLP	•	•	C
Michael McIvor	SF	•	•	•
John McNamee	SF	•	C	•
Oliver Molloy	SF	VC	•	•
Sam Parke	Ind	•	•	
Trevor Wilson	UUP	•	•	VC

• *Member   C Chair   VC Vice-chair*

Senior Officers

Chief Executive	Michael McGuckin	mjm@cookstown.gov.uk
Building Control	Trevor McAdoo	trevor.mcadoo@cookstown.gov.uk
Development	Fiona McKeown	fionamckeown@cookstown.gov.uk

CRAIGAVON BOROUGH COUNCIL

CRAIGAVON
Borough Council

Craigavon Borough Council
Civic Centre
Lakeview Road
Craigavon BT64 1AL
Tel: (028) 3831 2400
Fax: (028) 3831 2444
Website: www.craigavon.gov.uk

Chief Executive
Trevor Reaney

Craigavon Borough Council spends £15 million providing over 80 different services for the 80,000 people who live in Craigavon.

As well as providing some key services Council Officers and Members are continuously improving and developing services and leadership skills in working with local people to improve our quality of life, develop pride in our community and help shape our future.

Council also represents and lobbies government and other bodies to acquire benefits for the borough through a consultative and representative role; helps attract investment for further developments throughout the borough and enables other organisations to do likewise.

Craigavon is one of Northern Ireland's larger Councils incorporating the mature larger towns of Lurgan and Portadown, the new 'City' developments in between as well as a number of attractive villages sprinkled around the borough. Craigavon, given its strategic location where the Upper Bann joins Lough Neagh, and its first-class communications infrastructure is becoming an increasingly popular 'lifestyle' and recreational hub.

Elected Members

Mayor:	Jonathan Bell (DUP)
Deputy Mayor:	Sydney Anderson (UUP)

Council Committee Membership

Councillor	Party	Dev	Env Serv	Lei Serv	Pol & Res	PSL
Sydney Anderson	UUP		•		VC	
Jonathan Bell	DUP	•	•	•	C	•
Sydney Cairns	UUP			•		
Alan Carson	DUP			•		•
Kieran Corr	SDLP			•	•	•
Frederick Crowe	UUP	VC	•		•	•
Meta Crozier	UUP	•		C	•	•
Ignatius Fox	SDLP	•		•		
Samuel Gardiner	UUP	•	C	•	•	•
Arnold Hatch	UUP	•	•		•	C
Davy Jones	Ind			•		VC
Dolores Kelly	SDLP	•	•		•	•
Maurice Magill	SF	•	•			•
Patricia Mallon	SDLP	•	•			•
Mary McAlinden	SDLP	•		•		•
Sean McKavanagh	SDLP		•	•	•	
Brian McKeown	SF	•		•		•
Stephen Moutray	DUP	•	VC	•		•
Francis Murray	SF			•		•
John O'Dowd	SF	•		•	•	•
George Savage	UUP			•		
Thomas Simpson	DUP	C	•			•
Robert Smith	DUP	•	•	•		•
Kenneth Twyble	UUP		•	•	•	•

• *Member*　C *Chair*　VC *Vice-chair*

Senior Officers

Chief Executive	Trevor Reaney	trevor.reaney@craigavon.co.uk
Building Control	Robert Colvin	robert.colvin@craigavon.gov.uk
Development	Francis Rock	francis.rock@craigavon.gov.uk
Environmental Health	Colin Kerr	colin.kerr@craigavon.gov.uk
Environmental Services	Lorraine Crawford	lorraine.crawford@craigavon.gov.uk

Council Contact Details

Administration	028 3831 2461
Building Control, Craigavon	028 3831 2500
Chief Executive	028 3831 2402
Development	028 3831 2581
Environmental Health	028 3831 2521
Leisure Services	028 3831 2400
Technical Services	028 3831 2538
Refuse Collection	028 3831 9031

DERRY CITY COUNCIL

Area: 381 km²   Population: 107,000

98 Strand Road, Derry BT48 6DQ
Tel: 028 7136 5151
Fax: 028 7126 5448
Web: www.derrycity.gov.uk
E-mail: townclerk@derrycity.gov.uk

Derry is one of the oldest inhabited places in Ireland. The city is the largest centre of population outside Belfast with 107,000 inhabitants in the area (85,000 of which live in the urban area). The area has a relatively youthful population with almost half less than 25 years of age.

The city's hinterland includes the neighbouring districts of Strabane, Limavady and parts of Donegal. The City of Derry Airport is the main regional airport for the north west of the island, providing scheduled services to Glasgow, Manchester, London and Dublin. The Port of Londonderry is the UK's most westerly port and is of strategic importance to the north west of the island.

The area is the host to three educational institutions: the North West Institute of Further and Higher Education (NWIFHE), the University of Ulster at Magee and Queen's University at Altnagelvin. The local economy has traditionally had a strong manufacturing base, which has been dominated by textiles and clothing in the past. This has changed in recent times with diversification into chemicals and computer products.

Council Contact Details

Airport (City of Derry)	028 7181 0784
Building Control	028 7137 6521
Council Offices	028 7136 5151
Derry Visitor & Convention Bureau	028 7137 7577
Economic Development Section	028 7137 6532
Environmental Health	028 7136 5151
Marketing/Communications/PR	028 7137 6504
Registration of Births	
Deaths & Marriages	028 7126 8439
Tourist Information Centre	028 7126 7284

Elected Members

Mayor:	Kathleen McCloskey (SDLP)
Deputy Mayor:	Mary Hamilton (UUP)

Council Committee Membership

Councillor	Party	Plan	Rec & Leis	Env Serv	City Mark	Pol Res	City Der
Peter Anderson	SF	•	•	•	•	•	•
Mary Bradley	SDLP	•	•	•			
Gregory Campbell	DUP	•			•		
Sean Carr	SDLP	•	•				
Jim Clifford	SDLP	•	•	•			
Thomas Conway	SDLP	•		•	•		
Annie Courtney	SDLP	•			•		•
Cathal Crumley	SF	•			•		•
Andrew Davidson	UUP	•			•	•	•
Gerard Diver	SDLP	•			•	•	•
Lynn Fleming	SF	•	•				•
Paul Fleming	SF	•	•	•			
Shaun Gallagher	SDLP	•		C	•		
Mildred Garfield	DUP	•	•	•	•	•	C
Ernest Hamilton	UUP	•		•			
Tony Hassan	SF	•		•			
William Hay	DUP	•	•	•			•
John Kerr	SDLP	•	C			•	•
Gerry MacLochlainn	SF	•				•	
Kathleen McCloskey	SDLP	•				C	
Marie McDaid	SDLP	•	•				
Jim McKeever	SDLP	•			•	•	
Maeve McLaughlin	SF	•		•			
Joe Miller	DUP	•	•				
William O'Connell	SDLP	C			•	•	•
Barney O'Hagan	SF	•			•		•
Gearoid O'hEara	SF	•			C	•	
William Page	SF	•		•	•		
Helen Quigley	SDLP	•			•		
Pat Ramsey	SDLP	•			•		

• Member   C Chair   Committees do not have Vice-chairs

Senior Officers

Chief Executive	Cathal Logue	townclerk@derrycity.gov.uk
Building Control	Robert White	rwhite@derrycity.gov.uk
City Management	Gerry Henry	gerry.henry@derrycity.gov.uk
Environmental Health	John Meehan	meehan@derrycity.gov.uk
Recreation and Leisure	Jim Sanderson	jim.sanderson@derrycity.gov.uk
City Treasurer	Joseph Campbell	joe.campbell@derrycity.gov.uk
City Secretary and Solicitor	Damien McMahon	legal@derrycity.gov.uk

DOWN DISTRICT COUNCIL

Area: 649 km²   Population: 64,000

24 Strangford Road, Downpatrick, BT30 6SR
Tel: 028 4461 0800
Fax: 028 4461 0801
Web: www.downdc.gov.uk
E-mail: council@downdc.gov.uk

Down district covers a large geographical area, including the Mourne mountains, Northern Ireland's highest mountain range. The district's main population centres include the historic town of Downpatrick and the popular seaside resort of Newcastle. Agriculture and tourism contribute significantly to the local economy, and Kilkeel is one of Northern Ireland's main fishing ports. Economic development efforts centre on bringing inward investment to the new Down Business Park just outside Downpatrick.

Elected Members

Chairman:	Harvey Bicker (UUP)
Vice-Chairman:	Peter Craig (SDLP)

Council Committee Membership

Councillor	Party	Health	Pol & Res	Corp Services	Rec & Tech Serv	Cult & Econ Dev
Harvey Bicker	UUP	•				
Raymond Blaney	Ind	•	•			
Francis Braniff	SF	•			•	
Robert Burgess	UUP	•		VC		•
Willie Clarke	SF	•		C	•	
Albert Colmer	UUP	•	•	•	•	
Peter Craig	SDLP	•			C	
Dermot Curran	SDLP	•		•		C
William Dick	DUP	•	•		•	
John Doris	SDLP	•	•			•
Gerry Douglas	UUP	•	C	•		
Peter Fitzpatrick	SDLP	•		•		•
Anne McAleenan	SDLP	•	•	•		
Eamonn McConvey	SF	•	•		•	
Francis McDowell	SF	•				
Jack McIlheron	UUP	C			•	
Carmel O'Boyle	SDLP	•		•	VC	
Eamonn O'Neill	SDLP	•	VC			
Edward Rea	UUP	•		•	•	
Margaret Ritchie	SDLP	•		•	•	
Patrick Toman	SDLP	•			•	VC
Anne Trainor	SDLP	VC		•		
Jim Wells	DUP	•				

• *Member*   C *Chair*   VC *Vice-chair*

Senior Officers

Chief Executive	John McGrillen	chief.exec@downdc.gov.uk
Cultural & Economic Dev	Sharon O'Connor	sharon.oconnor@downdc.gov.uk
Director of Corp Services	Norman Stewart	norman.stewart@downdc.gov.uk
Recreational and Tech Serv	Frank Cunningham	frank.cunningham@downdc.gov.uk
Building Control	John Durnigan	john.durnigan@downdc.gov.uk

Council Contact Details

Environmental Health	028 4461 0824
Building Control	028 4461 0829
Births, Deaths and Marriages	028 4461 0825
Client Services	028 4461 0819
Economic Development	028 4461 0850
Tourist Information Downpatrick	028 4461 2233
Tourist Information Newcastle	028 4372 2222

DUNGANNON AND SOUTH TYRONE BOROUGH COUNCIL

Area: 772 km²   Population: 48,000

Circular Road, Dungannon, BT71 6DT,
Tel: 028 8772 0300
Fax: 028 8772 0368
Web: www.dungannon.gov.uk
E-mail: reception@infodungannon.gov.uk

The district covers 772 square kilometres situated to the west of Lough Neagh and stretches up the Clogher Valley towards the Sperrin mountains. The area has a population of 48,000, which is relatively young with around 40 per cent being under 25 years old. Agriculture is very important to the local economy and although it accounts for less than five per cent of the work force it accounts for nearly half of all the businesses in the area.

Council Contact Details

Council Offices	028 8772 0300
Building Control	028 8772 0329
Environmental Health	028 8772 0367
Technical Services	028 8772 6859
Economic Development	028 8772 0310
Leisure Centre	028 8772 0370
Killymaddy Tourist Information	028 8776 7327

Elected Members

Mayor:	Jim Cavanagh (SDLP)
Deputy Mayor:	Barry Monteith (SF)

Council Committee Membership

Councillor	Party	Dev	Public Serv	Corp Serv	Monitoring
Norman Badger	UUP	•	•	•	•
Roger Burton	DUP	•	•	•	VC
Jim Canning	Ind	•	•	•	
Jim Cavanagh	SDLP	•	•	•	
Walter Cuddy	UUP	•	•	C	
Vincent Currie	SDLP	•	•	•	
Patsy Daly	SDLP	•	•	•	•
Desmond Donnelly	SF	•	•	•	
Seamus Flanagan	SF	•	•	•	
Phelim Gildernew	SF	•	•	•	
Michael Gillespie	SF	•	•	•	
William Hamilton	UUP	•	VC	•	•
Derek Irwin	UUP	•	•	•	•
Anthony McGonnell	SDLP	•	•	•	
Sean McGuigan	SF	•	•	•	C
Johnston McIlwrath	DUP	•	C	•	
John McLarnon	SF	•	•	•	
Ken Maginnis	UUP	C	•	•	•
Francie Molloy	SF	•	•	•	•
Barry Monteith	SF	•	•	VC	•
Maurice Morrow	DUP	•	•	•	•
Robert Mulligan	UUP	VC	•	•	

• Member   C Chair   VC Vice-chair

Senior Officers

Chief Executive	William Beattie	gladys.smith@dungannon.gov.uk
Building Control	Jim McClelland	jim.mcclelland@dungannon.gov.uk
Development	Iain Frazer	iain.frazer@dungannon.gov.uk
Environmental Health	Alan Burke	alan.burke@dungannon.gov.uk
Finance	Maraid Canning	maraid.canning@dungannon.gov.uk
Human Resources	Brendan Currie	

FERMANAGH DISTRICT COUNCIL

Area: 1699 km²   Population: 58,000

Town Hall, Enniskillen, BT74 7BA
Tel: 028 6632 5050
Fax: 028 6634 2878
Web: www.fermanagh.gov.uk
E-mail: fdc@fermanagh.gov.uk

Located in the south west of Northern Ireland, Fermanagh District Council is unique as a local authority in Northern Ireland as its boundaries are also those of the County of Fermanagh. This helps create a strong sense of place and also means that Fermanagh District Council is the largest local government district, covering one eighth of Northern Ireland's land mass. The county covers 1699 square kilometres with a population of 58,000, three quarters of which live in rural areas. The main town in the county is Enniskillen. Tourism makes a significant contribution to the local economy, contributing nearly £20 million per annum. County Fermanagh is also known as Northern Ireland's lake district. The county suffers from being at the periphery of Northern Ireland and also from a low manufacturing base.

Elected Members

Chairman:	Fergus McQuillan (SDLP)
Vice-Chairman:	Harold Andrews (UUP)

Council Committee Membership

Councillor	Party	Env Serv	Planning	Policy & Res	Dev	Env Hlth
Harold Andrews	UUP	•	•	•	•	•
Frank Britton	SDLP	•	•		•	
Joe Cassidy	SF		•	•	•	
Pat Cox	SF		•		•	
Joe Dodds	DUP		•		•	•
Tom Elliott	UUP	•	•	•	•	
Wilson Elliott	UUP	•	•	•	•	
Raymond Ferguson	UUP		•	C	•	
Gerry Gallagher	SDLP	•	•	•	•	•
Patrick Gilgunn	SF	•	•		•	C
Stephen Huggett	SF	•	•	•	•	
Robert Irvine	UUP		•		•	•
Bert Johnston	DUP	•	•	•	•	
Davy Kettyles	Ind		•		•	•
Bertie Kerr	UUP	•	•	•	•	
Ruth Lynch	SF	•	•		•	
Robin Martin	SF	•	•	•	•	•
Brian McCaffrey	SF		•	•	•	•
Gerry McHugh	SF		•	•	•	
Fergus McQuillan	SDLP	•	•	•	•	•
Cecil Noble	UUP	C	•		•	•
John O'Kane	SDLP		C	•	•	
Thomas O'Reilly	SF	•	•		C	•

• Member   C Chair   Committees do not have Vice-chairs

Senior Officers

Chief Executive	Rodney Connor	rodney.connor@fermanagh.gov.uk
Building Control	Desmond Reid	desmond.reid@fermanagh.gov.uk
Development	Peter Thompson	peter.thompson@fermanagh.gov.uk
Environmental Health	Robert Forde	robert.forde@fermanagh.gov.uk
Environmental Services	Robert Gibson	robert.gibson@fermanagh.gov.uk
Finance	Brendan Hegarty	brendan.hegarty@fermanagh.gov.uk
Personnel	Tom McCabe	tom.mccabe@fermanagh.gov.uk
Technical Services	Gerry Knox	gerry.knox@fermanagh.gov.uk

LARNE BOROUGH COUNCIL

Area: 336 km²   Population: 31,000

Smiley Buildings, Victoria Road, Larne BT40 1RU
Tel: 028 2827 2313
Fax: 028 2826 0660
Web: www.larne.gov.uk
E-mail: admin@larne.gov.uk

The borough of Larne covers an area of 336 square kilometres and has a population of 31,000, nearly 20,000 of which live in the town of Larne. The borough lies on the east coast of Northern Ireland between the Glens of Antrim and the Antrim plateau. Larne is an important all-weather port with significant freight and passenger traffic all year round. There is also a strong manufacturing base in the borough with F G Wilson, now part of the Caterpillar Group, employing over 1300 people. The borough has also had a long association with the energy sector and is the home of Northern Ireland's largest power station.

Elected Members

Mayor: Bobby McKee (DUP)
Deputy Mayor: Daniel O'Connor (SDLP)

Council Committee Membership

Councillor	Party	Dev & Consul	Fin& Gen Pur	Tour, Leis & Com Serv	Works & Health
Roy Beggs	UUP	•	•	•	•
Roy Craig	Ind	•	•	C	•
Joan Drummond	UUP	•	•	•	VC
James Dunn	DUP	VC	C	•	•
David Fleck	UUP	•	•	•	•
Winston Fulton	DUP	•	•	•	•
Robert Lyndsay Mason	Ind	•	•	•	
Bobby McKee	DUP	C	•	•	•
Jack McKee	DUP	•	•	•	C
Greg McKeen	DUP	•	•	VC	•
John Matthews	All	•	VC	•	•
Geraldine Mulvenna	All	•	•	•	•
Daniel O'Connor	SDLP	•	•	•	•
Rachel Rea	DUP	•	•	•	•
Martin Wilson	SDLP	•	•	•	•

• *Member*   C *Chair*   VC *Vice-chair*

Senior Officers

Chief Executive	Colm McGarry	mcgarryc@larne.gov.uk
Economic Development	Ken Nelson	nelsonk@larne.gov.uk
Building Control	Mark Hamill	hamillm@larne.gov.uk
Corporate Services	Trevor Clarke	clarket@larne.gov.uk
Environmental Health	Morris Crum	crumm@larne.gov.uk
Finance	Helen Gault	gaulth@larne.gov.uk
Tourism & Community Dev	Herbie Francis	francish@larne.gov.uk

Council Contact Details

Building Control Service	028 2827 2313
Environmental Health	028 2827 2313
Council Depot	028 2826 2307
Larne Leisure Centre	028 2826 0478
Tourist Information Centre	028 2826 0088

LIMAVADY BOROUGH COUNCIL

Area: 586 km²   Population: 32,000

7 Connell Street, Limavady, BT49 0HA
Tel: 028 7772 2226
Fax: 028 7772 2010
Web: www.limavady.org
E-mail: john.stevenson@limavady.gov.uk

Limavady Borough Council is one of Northern Ireland's smallest local authorities, located to the north of County Derry. Limavady town is the main population centre, followed by Dungiven. The borough's main industries are agriculture, textiles and tourism. In addition to the existing industrial area at Aghanloo a new business park is being developed. Manufacturing accounts for nearly a quarter of all employment in the area and has been traditionally in the textiles sector. Tourism is based around the fine rural scenery of the Limavady area and has been boosted by continuous investment in quality hotel accommodation and leisure facilities.

Council Contact Details

Building Control	028 7776 0301
Economic Development Office	028 7776 0311
Environmental Health	028 7776 0302
Finance and Administration	028 7772 2226
Recreation & Tourism	028 7776 0304
Registration of Births	
Deaths & Marriages	028 7772 2226
Technical Services Department	028 7776 0305

Elected Members

Mayor:	George Robinson (DUP)
Deputy Mayor:	Anne Brolly (SF)

Council Committee Membership

Councillor	Party	Econ Dev	Fin & Gen Pur	Leis Ser	Plan & Dev Serv
Anne Brolly	SF	C	•	•	•
Francis Brolly	SF	•	•	C	•
Brian Brown	Ind	•	•	•	•
Michael Cartan	SDLP	•	C	•	•
Michael Coyle	SDLP	•	•	•	C
Leslie Cubitt	DUP	C	•	•	•
Jack Dolan	UUP	•	C	•	•
Marion Donaghy	SF	•	•	•	•
Boyd Douglas	UUAP	•	•	•	C
Dessie Lowry	SDLP	•	•	•	•
Martin McGuigan	SF	•	•	•	•
Gerard Mullan	SDLP	•	•	•	•
John Rankin	UUP	•	•	•	•
George Robinson	DUP	•	•	C	•
Edwin Stevenson	UUP	•	•	•	•

• Member   C Co-chair (Limavady has Co-chairs instead of Vice-chairs).

Senior Officers

Town Clerk and Chief Exec	John Stevenson	john.stevenson@limavady.gov.uk
Economic Development	Dermot McNally	dermot.mcnally@limavady.gov.uk
Building Control	Jim Mullan	jim.mullan@limavady.gov.uk
Environmental Health	Noel Crawford	noel.crawford@limavady.gov.uk
Finance and Administration	Eamon McCotter	eamon.mccotter@limavady.gov.uk
Recreation and Tourism	Sam McGregor	sam.mcgregor@limavady.gov.uk
Technical Services	Victor Wallace	victor.wallace@limavady.gov.uk

LISBURN CITY COUNCIL

Area: 447 km²   Population: 111,000

Lagan Valley Island, 1 The Island, Lisburn, BT27 4RL
Tel: 028 9250 9250
Fax: 028 9250 9208
Web: www.lisburn.gov.uk

Lisburn City Council covers 447 square kilometres of southwest Antrim and northwest Down stretching from Glenavy and Dundrod in the north to Dromore and Hillsborough in the south, and from Drumbo in the east to Moira in the west. Lisburn has a significant and growing industrial and commercial base.

Elected Members

Mayor:	Elizabeth Campbell (All)
Deputy Mayor:	William Bell (UUP)

Council Committee Membership

Councillor	Party	Plan	Leis Serv	Econ Dev	Env Serv	Corp Serv
David Archer	UUP	•	•			
T David Archer	UUP	•			C	
James Baird	UUP	•			•	
William Bell	UUP	•	•	•	•	•
Paul Butler	SF	•				•
Cecil Calvert	DUP	•	VC	•		
Elizabeth Campbell	All	•	•	•	•	•
Seamus Close	All	•	•			
David Craig	DUP	•	•			•
Ronnie Crawford	Ind	•		•		C
Ivan Davis	UUP	•	•			
Jim Dillon	UUP	•		VC		•
William Falloon	UUP	C		•	•	•
Michael Ferguson	SF	•		•	VC	
William Gardiner-Watson	UUP	•	•	C		
Samuel Johnston	UUP	•			•	
William Lewis	UUP	•	C	•		
Patricia Lewsley	SDLP	•			•	
Joe Lockhart	UUP	•			•	
Trevor Lunn	All	•		•		VC
Billy McDonnell	SDLP	•	•			
Gary McMichael	Ind	•	•			
Lorraine Martin	UUP	•				
Peter O'Hagan	SDLP	•		•		•
Edwin Poots	DUP	VC		•		•
Paul Porter	DUP	•			•	
Sue Ramsey	SF	•				
James Tinsley	DUP	•			•	
William Ward	UUP	•				•
Veronica Willis	SF	•	•			

• Member   C Chair   VC Vice-chair

Senior Officers

Chief Executive	Norman Davidson	norman.davidson@lisburn.gov.uk
Corporate Services	David Briggs	david.briggs@lisburn.gov.uk
Environmental Services	Colin McClintock	colin.mcclintock@lisburn.gov.uk
Leisure Services	Jim Rose	jim.rose@lisburn.gov.uk

Council Contact Details

Chief Executive's Department	028 9268 9016
Corporate Services Department	028 9260 7143
Central Services Depot	028 9267 3417
Civic Amenity Site	028 9030 8567

MAGHERAFELT DISTRICT COUNCIL

Area: 564 km²   Population: 39,000

Council Offices, 50 Ballyronan Road
Magherafelt BT45 6EN
Tel: 028 7939 7979
Fax: 028 7939 7980
Web: www.magherafelt.demon.co.uk
E-mail: mdc@magherafelt.demon.co.uk

Magherafelt is one of Northern Ireland's smallest local authorities by population. The town of Magherafelt is located in the centre of Northern Ireland and is the main administrative centre of the area. Agriculture is of vital importance to the local economy, and there is also a significant manufacturing base and a thriving construction sector.

Elected Members

Chairman:	Rev William McCrea (DUP)
Vice-Chairman:	John Kelly (SF)

Council Committee Membership

Councillor	Party	Rec & Tourism	General Pur & Finance
Thomas Catherwood	DUP		•
Patrick Groogan	SF		•
Oliver Hughes	SF		•
John Junkin	UUP		•
John Kelly	SF		
John Kerr	SF		•
Kathleen Lagan	SDLP		C
Joseph McBride	SDLP	•	
Paul McLean	DUP	C	
Rev William McCrea	DUP		
Patrick McErlean	SDLP		•
Robert Montgomery	Ind	•	
Hugh Mullan	SF	•	
Seamus O'Brien	SF	•	
James O'Neill	SF	•	
George Shiels	UUP	•	

• *Member*   C *Chair*

Senior Officials

Chief Executive	John McLaughlin	info@magherafelt.demon.co.uk
Economic Dev Officer	Michael Browne	info@magherafelt.demon.co.uk
Building Control	Ian Glendinning	info@magherafelt.demon.co.uk
Environmental Health	Clifford Burrows	magherafelt@ngs-councils.org.uk
Finance and Administration	JJ Tohill	info@magherafelt.gov.uk
Operations	Jackie Johnston	info@magherafelt.gov.uk

MOYLE DISTRICT COUNCIL

Area: 494 km²   Population: 15,000

Sheskburn House
7 Mary Street, Ballycastle BT54 6QH
Tel: 028 2076 2225
Fax: 028 2076 2515
Web: www.moyle-council.org
E-mail: info@moyle-council.org

Moyle District Council is Northern Ireland's smallest local authority, and despite having the world-famous Giant's Causeway as its main attraction, has a relatively low profile. The district covers the north east of County Antrim, embracing the 'Glens of Antrim'. The entire district is officially designated an Area of Outstanding Natural Beauty. Moyle's principal town is Ballycastle, which in itself is relatively small, and other centres include the villages of Bushmills, Cushendall and Cushendun. The main industries in the district are agriculture and tourism, although Bushmills also boasts the world's oldest licensed distillery.

Elected Members

Chairman:	William Graham (UUP)
Vice-Chairman:	Catherine McCambridge (SDLP)

Council Committee Membership

Councillor	Party	Councillor	Party
Madeline Black	SDLP	David McAllister	DUP
Christine Blaney	SDLP	Catherine McCambridge	SDLP
Seamus Blaney	Ind	Price McConaghy	Ind
Monica Digney	SF	Randal McDonnell	Ind
William Graham	UUP	Robert McIlroy	UUP
Helen Harding	UUP	Oliver McMullan	Ind
George Hartin	DUP	Michael Molloy	SDLP
Gardiner Kane	DUP		

Moyle District Council does not operate a committee system; all business is conducted at full council meetings.

Senior Officers

Chief Executive	Richard Lewis	rlewis@moyle-council.org
Administration and Finance	Moira Quinn	info@moyle-council.org
Building Control	David Kelly	info@moyle-council.org
Development	Esther Mulholland	dev@moyle-council.org
Technical Services	Tony Stuart	info@moyle-council.org
Tourism and Recreation	Kevin McGarry	ballycastle@nitic.net

NEWRY AND MOURNE CITY COUNCIL

Area: 898 km²   Population: 88,000

O'Hagan House, Monaghan Row
Newry BT35 8DJ
Tel: 028 3031 3031
Fax: 028 3031 3077
Web: www.newry.org/nmdc
E-mail: info@newryandmourne.gov.uk

Newry and Mourne lies in the south east of Northern Ireland, bordering on the Irish Republic, and contains portions of counties Down and Armagh.   The local administrative centre is Newry, now designated as a city. Newry has a long tradition of commerce and is strategically located 35 miles south of Belfast on the main Belfast to Dublin road.   As a result Newry benefits significantly from cross border trade.

Cross border trade is vital to the district, with the Irish Republic being the principal market for over 70 per cent of manufacturing companies in the Newry & Mourne area.

Council Contact Details

Administration/Equality/Personnel	028 3031 3031
Arts Centre	028 3026 6232
Building Control	028 3031 3000
Community Centres	
Barcroft	028 3026 7803
Bessbrook	028 3083 9666
Cloughreagh	028 3083 8454
Crossmalgen	028 3086 1949
Newtownhamilton	028 3087 8570
Forkhill	028 3088 8059
Annalong	028 4376 7116
Whitegates	028 3025 2121
District Development Department	028 3031 3233
Technical and Leisure Services	028 3031 3233
Environmental Health	028 3031 3100
Finance Department	028 3031 3031
Leisure Services	028 3026 7322
Newry Swimming Pool	028 3026 3481
Kilkeel Leisure Centre	028 4176 4666
Market Clerk's Office	028 3026 3004
Registrar of Births	
Deaths & Marriages	028 3031 3031

Elected Members

Chairman:	Frank Feeley (SDLP)
Vice Chairman:	Andy Moffett (UUP)

Council Committee Membership

Councillor	Party	Stf & Pol	BC & P W	Econ Dev	Env Cntrl	Com & Leis Serv	Dis Devt
PJ Bradley	SDLP						•
Colman Burns	SF		•				•
William Burns	DUP	•	•		•		•
Hugh Carr	SDLP	•			•		•
Michael Carr	SDLP		•	•		•	•
Charlie Casey	SF			•			•
Michael Cole	SDLP	•	•		VC	•	•
Martin Cunningham	SF		•				•
Brendan Curran	SF	•				•	•
John Fee	SDLP						•
John Feehan	SDLP	•			•	C	•
Frank Feeley	SDLP	VC	•	•			•
Isaac Hanna	UUP	•		•	•	•	C
Terry Hearty	SF		•				•
Davy Hyland	SF	C	•	•	•	•	•
Danny Kennedy	UUP	•					•
Breandan Lewis	SF	•		•	•		•
Elena Martin	SF	•	C			•	•
John McArdle	SDLP		VC		•		•
Jimmy McCreesh	SF			•			•
Packie McDonald	SF				•	VC	•
Pat McElroy	SDLP	•		C		•	•
Pat McGinn	SF	•			C	•	•
Andy Moffett	UUP	•		•	•	•	•
Mick Murphy	SF	•		•	•		•
Josephine O'Hare	SDLP			•	•	•	•
Jack Patterson	Ind	•	•		•	•	VC
Henry Reilly	UUP	•			•	•	•
Michael Ruane	SF	•				•	•
Anthony Williamson	Ind			VC			•

• Member   C Chair   VC Vice-chair

Senior Officers

Chief Executive	Thomas McCall
Enterprise Development	Jonathan McGilly
Administration	Edwin Curtis
Building Control	Fulton Somerville
District Development	Gerard McGivern
Environmental Health	Hugh O'Neill
Finance	Robert Dowey

NEWTOWNABBEY BOROUGH COUNCIL

Area: 151 km² Population: 81,000

Mossley Mill, Newtownabbey, BT36 5QA
Tel: 028 9034 0000
Fax: 028 9034 0200
Web: www.newtownabbey.gov.uk
E-mail: info@newtownabbey.gov.uk

Newtownabbey is situated directly north of Belfast and has benefited greatly from several large businesses relocating from Belfast city centre. Its close proximity to Northern Ireland's main airports and ports has made it an attractive location for inward investment. The borough hosts the University of Ulster campus at Jordanstown, which has strong links to local industry.

Elected Members

Mayor:	Paul Girvan (DUP)
Deputy Mayor:	Barbara Gilliland (UUP)

Council Committee Membership

Councillor	Party	Env & CTS	Dev	Corporate Services	Planning
Fraser Agnew	UUAP		C	•	•
James Bingham	UUP	•		•	C
Janet Crilly	UUP	•	•		•
William DeCourcy	DUP			•	•
Lynn Frazer	All	•	•		•
Barbara Gilliland	UUP	C	•		•
Paul Girvan	DUP	•	•		•
Nigel Hamilton	DUP		•	•	•
Ivan Hunter	UUP	VC	•		•
Kenneth Hunter	DUP	•		VC	•
Pamela Hunter	DUP	•	•	•	•
Roger Hutchinson	DUP		•	C	•
Tommy Kirkham	Ind		•	•	•
Mark Langhammer	Ind		•		•
John Mann	DUP		•	•	•
Briege Meehan	SF	•		•	•
Noreen McClelland	SDLP		•	•	•
Tommy McTeague	SDLP	•		•	•
Vera McWilliam	UUP	•	•	•	•
Ken Robinson	UUP	•	•	•	•
Vi Scott	UUP	•	•	•	•
Arthur Templeton	DUP		•	•	VC
Edward Turkington	UUP	VC	•		•
Dineen Walker	UUP		•	•	•
Billy Webb	NRA		•	•	•

• Member C Chair VC Vice-chair

Senior Officers

Chief Executive	Norman Dunn
Administration and HR	Neal Willis
Building Control	Stephen Montgomery
Contract Services	Hugh Kelly
Corporate Services	Mary Clare Deane
Development Services	Hilary Brady
Environmental Health	Sam Reid

Council Contact Details

Births, Deaths and Marriages	028 9034 0180
Building Control	028 9034 0140
Economic Development	028 9034 0072
Environmental Health	028 9034 0160
Refuse Collection	028 9034 0057
Tourist Information	028 9034 0000

NORTH DOWN BOROUGH COUNCIL

Area: 81 km² Population: 76,000

Town Hall, The Castle, Bangor, BT20 4BT
Tel: 028 9127 0371
Fax: 028 9127 1370
Web: www.northdown.co.uk
E-mail: enquiries@northdown.gov.uk

The borough of North Down extends along the southern shore of Belfast Lough from Holywood in the west, through Bangor, to Groomsport in the east. North Down is dominated in terms of population by the bustling town of Bangor, which is Northern Ireland's third largest town.

The borough has a thriving tourism sector and the traditional resort of Bangor is the only maritime resort on Belfast Lough. The retail sector is particularly strong in North Down and represents over 17 per cent of all registered businesses in the borough. North Down has a prosperous up-market image and a tradition of political support for independent candidates in elections.

Elected Members

Mayor:	Alan Graham (DUP)
Deputy Mayor:	Stephen Farry (All)

Council Committee Membership

Councillor	Party	Env & Ammen	Deput	Leis, Tour & Comm Dev	Plan & Pub Serv Liaison	Corp	Econ Dev
Alan Chambers	Ind		•	•	•	•	•
Ruby Cooling	DUP		•	•	•	•	•
Irene Cree	UUP		•	•	•	•	•
Leslie Cree	UUP	•	•		•	•	C
Roy Davies	UUP	•	•		•	•	•
Roberta Dunlop	UUP		•	•	•	•	•
Gordon Dunne	DUP		•	•	C	•	•
Alexander Easton	DUP		•	•	•	•	•
Stephen Farry	All	•	•		•	•	•
Marsden Fitzsimons	All		•	•	•	•	•
Alan Graham	DUP	•	•		•	•	•
Ian Henry	UUP		•	•	•	•	•
Tony Hill	All		•	•	•	•	•
Bill Keery	UKUP		•	•	•	•	•
Valerie Kinghan	UKUP	C	•		•	•	•
Austen Lennon	Ind		•	•	•	•	•
Ellie McKay	UUP	•	•		•	C	•
John Montgomery	DUP		•	•	•	•	•
Susan O'Brien	All	•	C		•	•	•
Denis Ogborn	Ind	•	•		•	•	•
Diana Peacock	UUP	•	•		•	•	•
Marion Smith	UUP		•	•	•	•	•
Patricia Wallace	NIWC	•	•		•	•	•
Anne Wilson	All		•	C	•	•	•
Brian Wilson	Ind	•	•	•	•	•	•

• Member   C Chair   Committees do not elect Vice-chairs

Senior Officers

Chief Executive	Trevor Polley	trevor.polley@northdown.gov.uk
Economic Development	Nick Rogers	nick.rogers@northdown.gov.uk
Amenities and Tech Serv	Jackie Snodden	jackie.snodden@northdown.gov.uk
Corporate Services	Ken Webb	ken.webb@northdown.gov.uk
Finance	Claire Escott	claire.escott@northdown.gov.uk
Leisure, Tourism & Com Serv	Stephen Reid	stephen.reid@northdown.gov.uk
Policy Unit	John Thompson	john.thompson@northdown.gov.uk
Environmental Services	Graham Yarr	graham.yarr@northdown.gov.uk

Council Contact Details

Building Control	028 9127 0371
Environmental Health	028 9127 0371
Registration of Births	
Deaths & Marriages	028 9127 0371

OMAGH DISTRICT COUNCIL

Area: 1130 km²   Population: 48,000

The Grange, Mountjoy Road, Omagh, BT79 7BL
Tel: 028 8224 5321
Fax: 028 8224 3888
Web: www.omagh.gov.uk
E-mail: info@omagh.gov.uk

Omagh district lies in the west of Northern Ireland, nestling at the foothills of the Sperrins. Omagh town, by far the largest population centre in the district, is also its county town and is the district's administrative and commercial centre.

Elected Members

Chairman:	Patrick McDonnell (SDLP)
Vice Chairman:	Michael McAnespie (SF)

Council Committee Membership

Councillor	Party	Policy & Resources	Envirn Services	Plan & Pub Serv Liaison	Devel
Sean Begley	SF	•	•	•	•
Thomas Buchanon	DUP	•	•	C	•
Joe Byrne	SDLP	•	•	•	•
Sean Clarke	SF	•	•	•	C
Damien Curran	SF	•	•	•	•
Josephine Deehan	SDLP	•	•	•	•
Oliver Gibson	DUP	•	•	•	•
Peter Kelly	SF	•	•	•	•
Barney McAleer	SF	•	•	•	•
Michael McAnespie	SF	•	•	•	•
Patrick McDonnell	SDLP	•	•	•	•
Barry McElduff	SF	•	•	•	•
Patrick McGowan	Ind	•	•	•	•
Reuben McKelvey	UUP	•	•	•	•
Johnny McLaughlin	Ind	•	•	•	•
Liam McQuaid	SDLP	•	C	•	•
Gerry O'Doherty	SDLP	C	•	•	•
Allan Rainey	UUP	•	•	•	•
Seamus Shields	SDLP	•	•	•	•
Patrick Watters	SF	•	•	•	•
Robert Wilson	UUP	•	•	•	•

• Member   C Chair   Committees do not elect Vice Chairs

Senior Staff

Chief Executive	Daniel McSorley	daniel.mcsorley@omagh.gov.uk
Building Control	Sean Kelly	sean.kelly@omagh.gov.uk
Client Services	Kevin O'Gara	kevin.ogara@omagh.gov.uk
Corporate Services	Elizabeth McSorley	elizabeth.mcsorley@omagh.gov.uk
Development	Vincent Brogan	vincent.brogan@omagh.gov.uk
Environmental Health	Gerry Harte	gerry.harte@omagh.gov.uk

STRABANE DISTRICT COUNCIL

47 Derry Road Strabane, BT82 8DY
Tele: 028 7138 2204
Fax: 028 7138 2264
Web: www.strabanedc.org.uk
E-mail: strabanedc@nics.gov.uk

Strabane District Council is one of the largest council areas in Northern Ireland. It is strategically located in the North West, with the City of Derry Airport less than 20 miles away. Its main town, Strabane, is an important gateway to Donegal. Strabane District has a strong tradition in textiles, agriculture and food processing and a growing tourism industry.

Philip Faithfull, BEd, FILAM, MIQA, MInstSRM
Clerk of Council &
Chief Executive
Strabane District Council

Philip Faithfull has over twenty years experience in local government and has been heavily involved with compulsory competitive tendering and best value. He has a particular interest in continuous improvement and quality.

Elected Members

Chairman:	Eugene McMenamin (SDLP)
Vice-Chairman:	Charlie McHugh (SF)

Council Committee Membership

Councillor	Party	Culture, Arts & Leis	Env	Econ Dev	Corporate and Regulatory Serv
Ivan Barr	SF	•	•	•	•
Ann Bell	SDLP	C	•	•	•
Allan Bresland	DUP	•	•	•	C
Daniel Breslin	SF	VC	•	•	•
John Donnell	DUP	•	•	•	•
James Emery	UUP	•	VC	VC	•
Derek Hussey	UUP	•	•	•	•
Thomas Kerrigan	DUP	•	•	•	•
Tom McBride	SDLP	•	•	C	•
Eamon McGarvey	SF	•	•	•	•
Claire McGill	SF	•	•	•	•
Charlie McHugh	SF	•	C	•	•
Brian McMahon	SF	•	•	•	VC
Eugene McMenamin	SDLP	•	•	•	•
Bernadette McNamee	SDLP	•	•	•	•
Jarlath McNulty	SF	•	•	•	•

• Member C Chair VC Vice-chair

Senior Officers

Chief Executive	Philip Faithfull	strabanedc@nics.gov.uk
Administration	Sharon Maxwell	strabanedc@nics.gov.uk
Building Control	John Stewart	strabanedc@nics.gov.uk
District Partnership	Patrick O'Doherty	strabanedc@nics.gov.uk
Environmental Health	Paddy Cosgrove	strabanedc@nics.gov.uk
Finance	Maureen Henebery	strabanedc@nics.gov.uk
Personnel	Paula Donnelly	strabanedc@nics.gov.uk
Recreation	Karen McFarland	strabanedc@nics.gov.uk
Technical Department	Malcolm Scott	strabanedc@nics.gov.uk
Economic Development	Geraldine Stafford	strabanedc@nics.gov.uk

CHAPTER 6

Health, Social Services and Housing in Northern Ireland

Overview of Health and Social Services in Northern Ireland

Introduction

Waiting lists, hospital bed shortages, cancelled operations and reports of patients on trolleys in hospital corridors have become a familiar element of daily news coverage in the UK and this is true also for Northern Ireland. However, alongside public concern about the state of the health service there has been a steady growth in public investment in health with further increases promised.

This chapter sets out the main structures for the provision of healthcare in Northern Ireland, the challenges facing the current system and provides a detailed insight into the government's plans for improvement in the provision of local health care services. It begins with a status take on health in Northern Ireland and an overview of some of the inequalities and problems.

Factors Determining Health in Northern Ireland

The social, cultural, economic and physical environment determines the extent to which a population experiences poor health and health inequalities. Many complex and interrelated factors have a role in determining health; these include:

- Disadvantage and social exclusion;
- Poverty;
- Unemployment;
- Low educational achievement;
- Poor social and community environment;
- Living conditions;
- Working conditions;
- The wider environment;
- Individual behaviour and lifestyle.

Disadvantage takes many forms all tending to concentrate on the same cohort of people, having a long-term detrimental effect on their health. Poverty is acknowledged as the greatest risk factor for health with recent research showing that 24 per cent of households in Northern Ireland live in poverty, a rise of 3 per cent since 1990. Over 40 per cent of single parents, 19 per cent of single pensioners and 18 per cent of couples with

children in Northern Ireland have been defined as as living in "absolute" poverty.

Unemployment is the link between poverty, social exclusion and poor mental and physical health. Whilst levels of unemployment in Northern Ireland have fallen sharply, halving since the early 1990s there are still approximately 300,000 economically inactive people of working age, representing an employment rate of 67.2 per cent compared to 75 per cent in Britain. This means that there are comparatively fewer people in work in Northern Ireland than in neighbouring countries.

Educational achievement is regarded as the vital factor in improving health and reducing inequalities in health, and there are strong links between levels of educational attainment and deprivation with the most deprived areas showing the lowest rates of educational achievement. According to the Department of Education almost a fifth of the workforce have no formal qualifications and 24 per cent of the population of Northern Ireland have literacy or numeracy problems compared to 21 per cent in England and 23 per cent in Scotland.

Homelessness is a major challenge to both physical and mental health. There were 14,164 homeless households in 2001–2002, a significant increase on the previous years figure of 12,694.

Housing condition is a major contributor to the quality of health. The most recent survey of housing stock in Northern Ireland by the Housing Executive showed a high level of unfitness including 14,000 tenants without central heating.

Issues in the wider environment also affect health and well being both directly and indirectly, including air and water quality.

Inequalities in Health in Northern Ireland

Despite improvements in the last century, in comparison to the rest of Europe Northern Ireland's health record remains consistently poor. Whilst life expectancy rates have improved significantly, Northern Ireland continues to lead the rankings in international league tables of the major diseases including cancer and coronary heart disease.

It is accepted that the level of socio-economic disadvantage experienced by an individual has a direct impact on their quality of health, increasing the likelihood of premature death, disability or illness. There is substantial evidence to suggest that inequalities in health in Northern Ireland are directly connected with deprivation, social class and geographic location. The gap between rich and poor has been widening faster and further in Northern Ireland than in Britain, and wealthier people can expect to live longer and are less likely to suffer ill health than those who are less affluent, as indicated in the table below.

Adults of working age in less wealthy areas are twice as likely to die prematurely than their wealthier counterparts. Not only are differences in health evident by social class and income, but also the differential between rich and poor in terms of health appears to be increasing in recent years. The health of people in the higher socio-economic groups appears to be improving, while that in the lower socio-economic groups is not.

The Department of Health, Social Services and Public Safety estimates that around 2,000 lives could be saved each year if these inequalities were tackled effectively.

However, affluence is not the only factor influencing health. As well as employment, marital and family difficulties can affect a person's wellbeing.

Other bad habits such as smoking, drinking, eating poorly and getting insufficient exercise have a role in the quality of our health and are a legacy of our cultural background.

In Northern Ireland historically high levels of unemployment, comparatively lower levels of income than those in the rest of the UK have driven socio-economic deprivation leading to increased levels of illness, placing greater demands on health and social services. Although the health of Northern Ireland's population is unquestionably better than it was a generation ago, the region suffers discernible differences when compared to other areas.

Data from the Department of Finance and Personnel suggests that Northern Ireland has a higher occurrence of disability amongst adults than the UK. Heart disease, cancer and respiratory disease account for 65 per cent of all adult deaths with suicides, accidents, strokes and other causes accounting for the remaining 35 per cent.

According to figures from the Department of Health, Social Services and Public Safety deaths from heart disease, stroke and other diseases of the circulatory system caused by smoking, unhealthy diet, raised blood pressure, diabetes and physical inactivity are major contributing factors to 40 per cent of all deaths in the province.

Cancer is the second most frequent cause of death in Northern Ireland; statistics show that:

- More than one-third of the population will suffer from a form of cancer during their lifetime;
- Men have a one in six chance and women a one in eight chance of dying from cancer before the age of 75;
- 800 people are killed by lung cancer each year and it accounts for one quarter of cancer deaths in the under 75s;
- Breast cancer accounts for one in three cancer cases amongst women.

Long standing illness is recognised as a general measure of poor health in the community. It was found in the 2000/01 Continuous Household Survey that 33 per cent of men and 36 per cent of women in Northern Ireland had a long-standing illness.

Increasingly the link between mental health and

Life Expectancy Rates in Northern Ireland

	1900	2002
Men	47	74.5
Women	47	79.6

Life Expectancy (years) by Deprivation Category (1991)

	Male	Female
Most Affluent	74.9	79.5
Affluent	73.5	78.9
Average	72.0	78.3
Deprived	70.6	77.2
Most Deprived	68.3	75.4

Source: Dr O'Reilly, Centre for Health and Social Care Research, Queen's University Belfast

Main Causes of Death and ill Health in Northern Ireland 2000

Coronary Heart Disease	22%
Respiratory Disease	20%
Stroke	10%
Cancer	24%
Accidents	2%
Suicide	1%
Other	21%

Source: NISRA/DHSSPS

emotional well-being and chronic physical disease is being accepted; people who are unemployed are twice as likely to experience a mental health problem than those in employment and 60 per cent of women in the lowest social class group are likely to experience a form of neurotic disorder in comparison to those in the professional group.

Statistics from the 2001 Health and Social Well Being Survey indicated that 21 per cent of the population aged 16+ considered themselves to be depressed and a similar percentage had a potential psychiatric disorder.

Suicide accounts for 1 per cent of deaths in Northern Ireland, one of the lowest rates in Europe, yet the trend is increasing with 163 registered deaths from suicide in 2000. It is estimated that 150 deaths and over 4,000 hospital admissions equating to 80,000 lost working days and a cost to the economy of £170 million are attributable to the effects of suicides and intentional self harm.

Domestic violence is the most common crime against women in Northern Ireland with 14,325 incidents reported between April 2000 to March 2001 and 1,176 sexual offences reported over the same period. It is acknowledged that the actual incidence of such violence and abuse is much higher than reported.

Accidents and road traffic incidents are a major cause of death in Northern Ireland claiming 616 lives in 2000. Home accidents account for 41 per cent of the total of all accidents and there is a significant statistical link between the nature of some accidents and socio-economic status. It is estimated that there are over 350 deaths and 150,000 injuries per annum equating to the loss of 180,000 working days and a cost to the economy of £370 million through accidental death and injury costs in Northern Ireland.

Children's Health

The differential in health status across social class can be seen in children from birth onwards. Babies in the lower socio-economic groups are more likely to have a low birth weight and die in infancy than the children of more affluent families. Infant mortality rates are nearly 50 per cent higher in the most deprived areas, compared to the least deprived. The proportion of children living in conditions of poverty is significantly higher, and over a quarter of children come from households dependent on Jobseeker's Allowance or Income Support.

Inequalities in health continue to be evident throughout childhood and in young adults. Rates of accidental injury and oral health provide clear examples of this. Accidents are a major cause of death and disability among children and young people. Children from less affluent areas are 15 times more likely to die in a house fire, 7 times more likely to die as a result of a road traffic accident, and 5 times more likely to be injured as pedestrians. These figures are of particular concern as the vast majority of accidents are preventable.

Although there has been a gradual improvement in oral health over the past 5 years, the most recent surveys indicate that the general level of oral health in Northern Ireland is still considerably worse than in Britain and the rest of Ireland, particularly amongst children. Oral health demonstrates a stark gradient across social class, with the most deprived children experiencing four times more tooth decay than the most affluent. Children in schools in the North and West of Belfast experience more tooth decay than those in other parts of the greater Belfast area. This is one of the reasons for the proposed introduction of fluoride to the water supply, although strong public opposition to the plan has meant that fluoridation of the water supply has not as yet occurred.

Teenage Parenthood

Northern Ireland has one of the highest rates of teenage pregnancy in Western Europe, as shown in the table overleaf.

Teenage parenthood is recognised as both a cause and a consequence of disadvantage. Evidence demonstrates that levels of teenage pregnancy correlate with those areas of high deprivation.

Percentage of all live births to mothers aged less than 20 years in various European Countries	
United Kingdom	6.9
Northern Ireland	6.4
Ireland	5.4
Austria	3.9
Finland	2.6
Denmark	1.8
Netherlands	1.3

Source: WHO (Europe)/NI percentage
derived from GRO (NI) statistics

Impact of Gender

The differences in men and women's health are striking, particularly once they reach middle and older age groups. Death rates are much higher in men in middle age and old age than in women in the same age groups, although this gap narrows in the over 80s. However, older women are far more likely than older men to report long-standing sickness and disability.

Ethnic Minorities

Ethnic groups also suffer from inequalities in health compounded by difficulties accessing services including health and social care, education and language support. Northern Ireland has a number of ethnic minorities, the largest of which is the Chinese community, with approximately 8000 people.

The Travelling Community is recognised as an ethnic group having poorer than average health status. Their life expectancy is 15 years less than that of a member of the settled community. Only one in ten of the Traveller population is over 40 years old and only one in one hundred over 65.

Infant mortality rates in travellers are three times higher than the general population.

Elderly People

People aged 65 and over account for 13 per cent of the population of Northern Ireland; by 2015 this figure is projected to rise to 16 per cent of the population. Smaller families, the growth of the number of women in the workplace and a more mobile population has resulted in an ageing population with rising rates of long-standing illness. It is acknowledged that there is a direct

relationship between low income among the elderly and reported levels of disability.

Disability

17 per cent of adults in Northern Ireland in comparison to 14 per cent in Britain have a disability. The violence of "the Troubles" resulting in many permanent injuries to victims is a significant factor in Northern Ireland's very high rate of disability. Lower income, social exclusion and limited access to services and transport are some of the challenges facing the disabled population.

Geographical Factors

Inequalities are also evident on comparison of geographical locations. About 2000 lives could be saved each year if those living in the council districts with the highest death rates had the health status of those in the districts with the lowest death rates. The electoral wards with the highest death rates are also those with the highest levels of deprivation. This correlation is particularly striking for deaths from coronary heart disease.

Smoking and Obesity

Smoking is recognised as the single greatest cause of premature death estimated to cause 2,800 deaths per annum. Compared to other members of the European Union Northern Ireland has the second highest percentage of 13 year olds reported to smoke daily and the fourth highest rate of 14 year olds.

Statistics show that although overall smoking rates have fallen over the last fifteen years, this has not occurred to the same extent among the less well off where the levels of smokers remain at their highest.

The figures show that among men in professional and managerial occupations, 15 per cent smoke compared with 42 per cent of those who are unskilled. For women the figures are 16 per cent and 38 per cent respectively. 24 per cent of employed men smoke compared to 49 per cent of unemployed men and 26 per cent of employed women smoke as opposed to 45 per cent who are unemployed.

Obesity is a growing healthcare challenge in Northern Ireland. Surveys show that obesity is an increasing trend with predictions showing that by 2010, 23 per cent of women and 22 per cent of men will be obese. The rate of obesity amongst children is also increasing. It is estimated that over 450 deaths per annum, 260,000 working days with a cost to the economy of £500 million are lost through the effects of obesity in Northern Ireland each year.

Alcohol and Drugs

Whilst the dangers associated with drug misuse have a higher profile, the level and effects of alcohol abuse in Northern Ireland is significant.

It is estimated that there are over 730 deaths per annum in Northern Ireland attributable to excess alcohol consumption. Statistics show that 82 per cent of men and 72 per cent of women are currently consumers of alcohol in Northern Ireland, and that 25 per cent of men and 14 per cent of women drink in excess of recommended limits.

Drug misuse is often associated with aspects of deprivation, and lack of educational and employment prospects with their resultant negative social consequences. Drug misuse is associated with crime, which has high costs for society affecting both victims and the community.

Drug misusers place additional burdens on the health, social services and social security systems. It is estimated that the costs of enforcement, prevention, treatment and rehabilitation are £8 million per annum whilst it is estimated that drug misuse results in additional costs of £300–500 million per annum to society in Northern Ireland.

Summary

In summary, the estimated total costs of preventable poor health are:

- £2 billion lost annually to the Northern Ireland economy;
- 6 million working days lost annually;
- 6,500 avoidable deaths annually;
- The loss of over 73,000 expected years of life annually.

However, in addition to the human costs associated with poor health, treatment of ill health has costly impacts for the health system and the general economy in Northern Ireland.

City Hospital, Belfast

Department of Health, Social Services and Public Safety

In Northern Ireland responsibility for health policy and provision falls under the Department of Health, Social Services and Public Safety (DHSSPS), established by the Departments (NI) Order 1999. The stated mission of the department is "to improve people's health and social well-being".

1000 staff are directly employed by the department, 2000 by the Fire Authority and over 40,000 other staff within the health and social services sector.

The Department's budget for the financial year 2002/2003 is around £2.5 billion. This income has been distributed as follows: £34 million or 1.3 per cent for departmental administration, £58m or 2.3 per cent to the Fire Authority (FANI) and £2,436 million or 96.4 per cent to Health and Personal Social Services (HPSS). This may be compared to the budgetary allocation for the department in 2000/2001 of £2.1 billion, with almost £2 billion going to the Health and Personal Social Services Programme, £51 million to the Fire Authority and £33 million for departmental administration.

The Department has three main areas of responsibility:

Health and Personal Social Services

Including policy and finance, legislation for hospitals, family practitioner services and community health and personal social services;

Public Health

Including policy, legislation and administrative action to promote and protect the health and well-being of the population; and

Public Safety

Including responsibility for the policy and legislation for the Fire Services and emergency planning.

For further detailed information about departmental organisation and personnel see Chapter 4 Government Departments and Agencies.

Resources and Investment

Resource Requirements 2003–04 of the Department of Health, Social Services and Public Safety

Latest budget figures from the Department of Health, Social Services and Public Safety indicate an opening requirement of around £2.7 billion including £75 million for capital purposes in 2003–04. Although this represents a continuation of the significant increases allocated to health in recent years, the department is targeting further real increases in funding in 2004/05 and 2005/06. The major issue currently facing the Department is the determination of a response to the Acute Hospitals Review, measures required to address capacity problems in the Acute sector, including winter pressures and waiting lists.

The Department of Health, Social Services and Public Safety has identified a high level of requirement in the provision of community care services, particularly regarding provision for the elderly and the needs of those with mental health problems or learning disabilities. It is envisaged that reform of the primary care sector through the establishment of Local Health and Social Care Groups will strategically complement the services offered by the hospital sector. An estimate of £46 million for goods and services has been made in the budget for 2003–04 to provide for rising drug costs and implications of the introduction of free nursing care. There are also significant provisions for increased pay and national insurance costs.

Although there is no guarantee of significant resources being available, the Department is seeking additional funding in the following areas:

Additional Funding Required	
	£m
Residential and Nursing Homes	37.0
Primary Care Infrastructure	7.7
New Services (Cancer, renal, cardiac)	9.0
Hospital Bed Capacity/Core Packages	13.0
Quality, Performance Measures	11.0
Investing in Health Strategy	18.5
Services for the Elderly	10.5
Mental Health Strategy	8.0
Learning Disability	8.0
Additional Capital Works	44.7

In addition to the additional funding sought, departmental strategies also identify other areas where additional resources are being targeted.

Investment in the Health Service of Northern Ireland

Under the Investing for Health Strategy the department as part of the PPP Forum has recently reviewed its estimate of the overall need to invest in the HPSS/Fire Authority estate to bring it up to modern standards. A £1.9 billion investment need over the next ten years mostly in the Acute sector has been identified.

A major investment package for the Health Service in Northern Ireland was announced by the Minister for Health, Social Services and Public Safety, on 3 July 2002. The £152.7 million investment was announced as a result of the Executive's Reinvestment and Reform Initiative. (Refer to Chapter 2 for further details).

Cancer Services

£59.5 million will be allocated for cancer services, primarily the new Cancer Centre at Belfast City Hospital, which is expected to be complete by 2005.

A custom built Chemotherapy Unit will be installed at Antrim Area Hospital to enable the hospital to fulfil its role as a Cancer Unit and a new CT scanner will be purchased for Belvoir Park Hospital.

Strategic Renewal

£20 million of investment has been announced for two acute sites, Altnagelvin Hospital and Daisy Hill Hospital.

Ambulance Service

£16.2 million has been allocated for investment in new infrastructure, a programme of fleet replacement and upgrading of essential medical equipment. 115 vehicles will be replaced and an additional 20 vehicles purchased which will operate under a centralised control centre.

Learning Disability

£11 million has been allocated to developing facilities at Muckamore Abbey Hospital and Stragreagh.

Additional Hospital Capacity

- 24 medical beds have been announced for Antrim Area Hospital;
- 35 additional beds at Craigavon Area Hospital;
- 42 additional beds at the Mater Hospital;
- A dedicated Day Procedure Unit at the Erne Hospital.

Renal Services

Dialysis stations will increase by 17 across the 4 HSS Board areas in 2002.

North and West Belfast

A £5.73 million funding package was announced for the North and West Belfast Trust to enable the development of four Health and Well Being Centres across the area. Funds were also made available for improvements at Holywell Hospital and critical infrastructure projects on the Royal Victoria Hospital and Belfast City Hospital.

Public Finance Initiative/Public-Private Partnership

The Public Finance Initiative (PFI), now known as Public-Private Partnership (PPP), was announced as a necessary and desirable way of raising finance for projects, by bringing private sector funding and skills to bear on long-term health infrastructural investment. Since its introduction in 1998, many schemes have been initiated using the PPP approach for funding. These have included management and disposal of clinical waste, equipment leasing and a new renal unit.

There is considerable public debate about the area of Public-Private Partnerships (PPPs), in no small part due to the perceived problems with privatisation in other areas. Opponents of PPP are concerned that private finance will put undue pressure on services to be profitable, rather than concentrate on serving the health needs of the population, and that services will suffer. A further criticism of PPP is that it is a very complex, drawn-out process which can cost the client more in the long term. However, advocates argue that it is vital to draw in private sector finance, as public money is not available in sufficient quantities. Nonetheless, public-private finance is still in relatively early development, and whilst the government is confident about the benefits it could bring, it remains to be seen how the policy will ultimately contribute long-term to health service provision in Northern Ireland.

Structure of the Department

The Department of Health, Social Services and Public Safety is structured into a number of groups and one Next Steps Agency.

There are five professional groups each led by a Chief Professional Officer. These are:

Public Health, Medical and Allied Group

The Public Health, Medical and Allied Group led by the Chief Medical Officer is responsible for business relating to public health, including the Investing for Health initiative; health protection; health promotion; and smoking, drugs and alcohol related strategies. The Group also provides medical services for the department, the Northern Ireland Civil Service and the Prison Service.

Social Services Inspectorate

Led by the Chief Inspector, the Social Services Inspectorate advises ministers, departments and government agencies on matters relating to social care. The Inspectorate is responsible for the completion of an annual inspection programme across a range of services and providers on behalf of the Department of Health, Social Services and Public Safety and the Northern Ireland Office. Policy development for social work, social care training and education, including postgraduate social work bursaries and other training support funding linked to the HPSS Training Strategy is the responsibility of the Social Services Inspectorate.

The Chief Inspector Paul Martin is supported by a team of inspectors and by the Social Services Analysis Branch. An Assistant Chief Inspector, Victor McElfatrick and two inspectors, assist him.

The aim of SSI is to work with others to ensure that social work and social care services are responsive to the needs of the population of Northern Ireland. Their role is to:

- Inspect social services provision and its organisation and management in order to promote quality standards, improve effectiveness and efficiency, and ensure the safety and well-being of service users;
- Provide professional advice and expertise to ministers, government departments and in the field on the formulation, implementation and review of social services and related health

policies, and the effective and efficient delivery of social services;
- Develop, promote and implement effective strategies for personal social services training and staff development; and
- Facilitate the conduct of business between the department and operators in the field.

The Chief Social Services Inspector answers directly to the minister. He provides advice on the quality of social work and social care services and the need for them. He reports on inspections to the minister and seeks approval for the publication of inspection reports. The Chief Inspector provides professional advice directly to ministers where he thinks this is necessary.

The Inspectorate works closely with all Directorates in the Health and Personal Social Services Management Group (HPSS Management Group) and the different Units within the Policy and Strategy Division including the Voluntary Activity Unit. The Inspectorate also provides an inspection and professional advice service to the Northern Ireland Office, which carries responsibility for the criminal justice system in Northern Ireland.

Inspections are conducted under statutory powers contained in the following enactments:
- Health and Personal Social Services (NI) Order 1972;
- The Adoption (NI) Order 1987;
- The Probation Board (Northern Ireland) 1982 as amended by the Criminal Justice (NI) Order 1991;
- The Registered Homes (NI) Order 1992;
- The Children (NI) Order 1995.

These powers give an effective base for inspecting a whole range of social work and social care services provided by Boards and Trusts, voluntary organisations and other agencies. The Chief Inspector, Assistant Chief Inspector and each of the Inspectors have the power to inspect social work and social care services.

The Central Personal Social Services Advisory Committee, established under the 1972 Health and Personal Social Services (Northern Ireland) Order oversees the inspection programme. This Committee is comprised of representatives from professional, voluntary and educational bodies and its role is to make proposals for inspection and endorse the inspection programme.

Nursing and Midwifery Advisory Group

The Group led by the Chief Nursing Officer is responsible for advising on all aspects of policy affecting nursing, midwifery, health visiting, education and services.

Dental Services Group

Led by the Chief Dental Officer, the Group provides advice on oral health, and delivers direct dental services to the Prisons and Young Offenders Centres. The Referral Dental Service also monitors treatment carried out by general dental practitioners.

Pharmaceutical Advice and Services Group

The Chief Pharmaceutical Officer is responsible for advising in regard to medicines and pharmaceutical services and has responsibility for medicines legislation relating to both human and veterinary medicines.

The two other groups are:

Planning and Resources Group

The group negotiates and manages financial resources, departmental staffing policy and resources, information and analysis and ICT support and development for the department and the health and social services bodies.

The Planning and Resources group also has responsibility for public safety policies, these include ambulance services, fire services and emergency planning, publication of the regional strategy for health and social well-being, and overall co-ordination of New TSN, Equality and Human Rights.

Health and Personal Social Services (HPSS) Management Group

The HPSS Management Group holds responsibility for policy development for a range of hospital, community health, primary care and social care programmes for the Health and Personal Social Services. Responsibilities include management of independent contractor services, managing the capital development programme; and the provision of strategic direction on human resources development.

The HPSS Management Group works closely with the four HPSS Boards, the Trusts, HSS Agencies, and four HSS Councils and is also responsible for setting annual targets and objectives for each of the HPSS boards, ensuring accountability for performance management.

Health Estates

Stoney Road, Dundonald, Belfast, BT16 1US
Tel: 028 9052 0025
Fax: 028 9052 3900
Web: www.dhsspsni.gov.uk

Chief Executive: Ronnie Brown

The Northern Ireland Health and Social Services Estates Agency, known as Health Estates is the Department's Next Steps Agency.

Established in October 1995 the Agency determines policy on estate issues relating to the delivery of health and social care.

The Agency provides advice, guidance and support strategically and operationally on estate matters and provides a range of executive consultancy services. The Agency also manages the contract for the treatment and disposal of all clinical waste.

Other Departmental Agencies and Organisations

Associated Bodies of the Department of Health, Social Services and Public Safety

Central Services Agency

25 Adelaide Street, Belfast, BT2 8FH
Tel: 028 9032 4431
Fax: 028 9023 2304

Chief Executive:	Stephen Hodkinson
Director of Finance and Administration:	P Gick
Director of Human Resources:	C MacAllister
Director of Family Practitioner Services:	P Shiels
Chairman:	Brian Carlin
Non Executive Director:	Barry Hession
Non Executive Director:	Peter Bloch
Non Executive Director:	Alan Cairns
Non Executive Director:	Sean Fulton

Established under the Health and Personal Social Services (Northern Ireland) Order 1972, the Central Services Agency supports HPSS in: Corporate Human Resource and Finance Services, Family Practitioner Services, Legal Services, Procurement, Regional Supplies, Research and Development, Fraud Investigation and NICARE, the health and social services unit working internationally.

Main divisions of the Central Services Agency are:

Regional Supplies Service (RSS)

RSS has no direct responsibility for patient care, but indirectly through the purchasing and supply of goods and services provides the infrastructure for the continued ability of the health service to deliver patient care. RSS includes the following divisions:

Regional Contracting Directorate

RSS is charged with the continued negotiation of regional contracts. The total value of regional contracts awarded for the region during 2001 was £33.7 million. These contracts include medical and non-medical supplies such as energy, consumables, services and fresh products.

Logistics

Customers of RSS purchased over £23 million from RSS Supplies and Distribution Services during 2001. RSS currently manages over 1.6 million product lines.

Purchasing

In 2001 RSS Purchasing Directorate actioned £133.5 million of Trust procurement activity.

Capital Projects Directorate

The Directorate is directly involved with specific customers in the equipping of major projects such as new theatres, intensive care units and out patient facilities.

Family Practitioner Services

The functions of the Family Practitioner Services Directorate are to pay community practitioners (General Medical Practitioners, General Dentist Practitioners, Chemist Contractors and Community Opthalmic Practitioners) on behalf of the Boards; to provide information derived mainly from the payment processes to Boards, the DHSS&PS and others; and to provide advice and services to practitioners in relation to payments and registration.

FPS also holds information on all payment data for approximately 20 per cent of HPSS expenditure, covering a range of activities from prescription to population data.

Research and Development Office

The remit of the Research and Development Office encompasses the research needs of the Department of Health, Social Services and Public Safety and all elements of the HPSS.

Directorate of Legal Services

The Directorate of Legal Services is a Business Unit of the Central Services Agency, which provides a range of legal services to the Northern Ireland Health and Social Services and is the largest provider of legal services to the HSS.

Other divisions within the Central Services Agency include:

- Nicare which provides a range of health, social care and social security programmes overseas;
- Human Resources Directorate;
- Counter Fraud Unit;
- Equality Unit;
- Directorate of Finance and Administration.

Occupational Health Service (OHS)

Musgrave Park Hospital
Stockman's Lane
Belfast, BT9 7JB
Tel: 028 9066 9501

The service provides comprehensive occupational health and medical advisory services to Northern Ireland government departments and agencies

The Northern Ireland Health Promotion Agency

18 Ormeau Avenue
Belfast BT2 8HS
Tel: 028 9031 1611
Fax: 028 9031 1711
Web: www.healthpromotionagency.org.uk

Chief Executive: Dr Brian Gaffney
Board Members: Alice Quinn   Evelyn Gilroy
               Fiona Bagnall   Anthony Harbinson
               Paul Burns   Dr David Higginson
               Una O'Kane   Liz Fiddis

The Health Promotion Agency provides a regional focus for health promotion. Its statutory functions include:

- Advising the Department on matters relating to health promotion:
- Undertaking health promotion activity;
- Planning and carrying out regional or local actions in co-operation with HSS Boards, District Councils, Education and Library Boards, voluntary organisations and other key interests;
- Sponsoring research and evaluation;
- Assisting the provision of training;
- Providing a regional centre for information and advice on health promotion;
- Making grants to and otherwise supporting voluntary organisations.

The Northern Ireland Blood Transfusion Service Agency

Belfast City Hospital Complex
Lisburn Road
Belfast BT9 7TS
Tel: 028 9032 1414
Fax: 028 9043 9017
Web: www.n-i.nhs.uk/niblood

Chief Executive: Dr Morris McClelland
Chairman: Dr Blakiston Houston

The Agency is responsible for the supply of blood and blood products and related clinical services.

The Northern Ireland Regional Medical Physics Agency

Musgrave and Clark House
Royal Hospital Site
Grosvenor Road
Belfast BT12 6BA
Tel: 028 9034 6488
Fax: 028 9031 3040

Chief Executive: Professor Peter Smith

The Agency provides scientific measurement and control of high technology equipment in the application of physics and engineering to health care provided by HPSS bodies.

The Northern Ireland Guardian Ad Litem Agency

Centre House, 79 Chichester Street
Belfast BT1 4JE
Tel: 028 90 9031 6550
Fax: 028 90 9031 9811

Chairman: Miss Mary Connolly
Chief Executive: Ronnie Williamson

The Northern Ireland Guardian Ad Litem Agency was established under the Health and Personal Social Services (Special Agencies) [NI] Order 1990. The Northern Ireland Guardian Ad Litem (Establishment and Constitution) Order [NI] 1995 commenced on 1 December 1995 making provision for the constitution of the Agency and appointment of the Agency Board.

The Agency established and maintains a panel of guardians appointed by the courts to safeguard the interests of children in proceedings specified under the Children (NI) Order 1987.

The Mental Health Commission for Northern Ireland
Elizabeth House, 118 Holywood Road
Belfast BT4 1NY
Tel: 028 9065 1157
Fax: 028 9047 1180

Chief Executive: Francis Walsh

The Mental Health Commission for Northern Ireland was established under the provisions of Part VI of the Mental Health (Northern Ireland) Order 1986. The Commission is an independent body whose role is to review the care and treatment of persons suffering from mental disorder. The Commission also has a duty to monitor the operation of the Order.

The Commission has a duty to ensure that no patient is either improperly detained or received into guardianship and that patients' rights are not infringed. The Commission visits and interviews patients and relatives in hospital and in the community and has the power to refer cases to the Mental Health Review Tribunal. The Commission has 15 members, including 5 lay people drawn from a cross section of relevant professions.

The Commission is staffed by members of the legal, medical, nursing, social work and psychology professions, who together with lay members are tasked with the duty to review the care and treatment for those suffering from mental disorder.

The Northern Ireland Council for Postgraduate Medical and Dental Education
5 Annadale Avenue
Belfast BT7 3JH
Tel: 028 9049 2731
Fax: 028 9064 2279

Chief Executive: Jack McCluggage

The core function of the Council is the provision and development of postgraduate and continuing medical and dental education within Northern Ireland. The Chief Executive/Postgraduate Dean supported by the Director of General Practice Education holds overall responsibility for this provision. The business of the Council falls largely into three functional areas: Hospital Medicine, General Practice and Dentistry.

Membership of the Northern Ireland Council for Postgraduate Medical and Dental Education

Chairman	Dr DAJ Keegan
Acting Vice Chairman	Dr JG Jenkins
Dean Medical Faculty QUB	Mr A Beard
	Mrs J Eve
	Prof R Hay
	Dr D Gilliland
NI Faculty of RCGPs	Dr C Kenny
	Dr A Little
Director Dentistry QUB	Prof P-J Lamey
Dental Co-ord Committee	Mr JH Gileece
	Mr R Kendrick
NHSSB	Dr S Kennedy
SHSSB	Dr PG Loughran
EHSSB	Dr C Beattie
WHSSB	Dr PB Devlin
Royal College of Physicians	Dr R Maw
Royal College of Surgeons	Mr BS Craig
Royal College of Pathologists	Dr GM McCusker
Royal College of Psychiatrists	Dr G McDonald
Royal College of Radiologists	Dr HK Wilson
Royal College of O&G	Dr MA Harper
Royal College of Anaesthetists	Dr P Elliott
Faculty of Public Health Medicine	Prof F Kee
Royal College of Paediatrics	Dr JG Jenkins

BMA NI	
General Practitioner Committee NI	Dr L Miller
NI Consultants and Specialists Committee	Dr DJ Conway
Hospital Junior Staff Committee	Dr P Maguire

Officers of the Council

Dr JR McCluggage	Chief Executive
Ms M Roberts	Administrative Director
Mr T Hutchinson	Financial Manager
Ms R Campbell	Training Manager
Mr IDF Saunders	Postgraduate Dental Dean
Mr K Alexander	Adviser in GDP
Mr J Farmer	Adviser in GDP
Mr DEB Mark	Associate Advisor in GDP
Mrs U McKeogh	Associate Advisor in GDP
Dr A McKnight	Director of Postgraduate General Practice Education
Dr M Crawford	Associate Adviser in Postgraduate General Practice Education
Dr T Bradley	Associate Adviser in Postgraduate General Practice Education
Dr D Gibson	Associate Adviser in Postgraduate General Practice Education
Dr I Taylor	Clinical Tutors Representative
Dr P Burnside	NI NACT Representative

The Council oversees the postgraduate and medical education of doctors and dentists and is responsible for the development and delivery of vocational training and continuing medical education for GPs and dentists.

The Fire Authority for Northern Ireland (FANI)
Brigade HQ, 1 Seymour Street
Lisburn BT27 4SX
Tel: 028 9266 4221
Fax: 028 9267 7402

Chief Executive:	John McClelland	
Board Members:	Mr W E Gaynor	Mr J A Kell
	Mr W Keys	Mr M Jones
	Mrs J Baird	Mr D Lavery
	Mrs R Craig	Mr J J McCosker
	Mrs P Kane	Mr F Proctor
	Miss A McLaughlin	Mr J Ross
	Dr S M M McRandal	Prof J T Shields
	Mr J Dillon	Mr E Smyth
	Mr A J Kane	

The Authority is responsible for the provision of regional fire services and ensuring their compliance with national fire cover standards and implementing the department's fire safety policy. The Northern Ireland Fire Brigade serves the 1.69 million people of Northern Ireland over 5,500 sq. miles.

The Fire Authority is composed of 17 members, appointed by the head of the Department of Health, Social Services and Public Safety. Belfast City Council appoints four and a further four are nominated by the Association of Local Authorities for Northern Ireland. The remaining nine members, including the Chairman and Vice Chairman are appointed in accordance with the procedures for the appointment of representatives to Non-Departmental Public Bodies.

The role of the Fire Authority is to determine detailed strategic policy for the Fire Brigade and it carries out an overseeing role via reports presented at monthly meetings.

The Fire Brigade is managed by its Chief Executive, the Chief Fire Officer assisted by three Assistant Chief Fire Officers and three senior non-uniformed members known collectively as the Principal Officers and Directors Group.

The Brigade is divided into four Operational Command Areas, with Brigade Headquarters situated in Lisburn, Co. Antrim. The Brigade is currently structured as follows (October 2002):

- 919 Whole time Fire-fighters;
- 980 Retained Fire-fighters;
- 12 Volunteer Fire-fighters;
- 59 Control Room Staff;
- 208 Support Staff;
- 53 Part time Caretakers.

These in turn serve to maintain 133 front line fire appliances operating from:
- 8 Whole time Fire Stations;
- 6 Whole time/Retained Fire Stations;
- 52 Retained Stations;
- 1 Volunteer Station.

The Northern Ireland Social Care Council (NISCC)
7th Floor Millennium House
19-25 Great Victoria Street
Belfast BT2 7AQ
Tel: 028 9041 7600
Fax: 028 9041 7601

Chairman: Dr Jeremy Harbison

The Northern Ireland Practice and Education Council for Nursing and Midwifery
Centre House
75 Chichester Street
Belfast
Tel: 028 90 238 152
Fax: 028 90 333 298

Chairman: Mrs Maureen Griffith
Chief Executive: Ms Paddie Blaney

Administration and Delivery of Healthcare Services

Structure of Health and Social Services in Northern Ireland

The Boards

Under DHSSPS are the four Health and Social Services Boards, the Western, Northern, Eastern and Southern Health and Social Services Boards, which act as agents of the department. The regional Boards carry out the bulk of all public expenditure on health in Northern Ireland.

Health Boards purchase healthcare services from Northern Ireland's Trusts and at local level from General Practitioner centres. There are 19 trusts of varying sizes the larger of which cover several major hospitals. General Practitioner centres may be large or small practices, which may chose to opt out of the NHS GP fund holder scheme.

Under the new plans announced in the (department's) Corporate Plan 2002/03–2004/05 and under the Investing for Health Strategy, Wellbeing Investment Plans (HWIP) are the new arrangements by which the four HSS Boards will try to secure effective health and social services for their local populations, improve health and social well being and reduce inequalities. These plans, which became effective in May 2002, are the key planning and accountability documents for the HPSS and consist of three main elements:

- HSS Boards' plans for commissioning services in their local areas;
- HSS Boards' plans to deliver on the Investing for Health Strategy of the department and reduce inequalities; and
- HSS Boards' plans to deliver on the major under-pinning themes of the Programme for Government.

The Health Well Being and Investment Plans will act as the single vehicle for all local HPSS planning. It is expected that health improvement planning will be done on a three year cycle rolling forward annually in the Health Well-Being and Investment Plan.

Investing for Health Partnerships

Each Health and Social Services Board will have responsibility for developing an Investing for Health Partnership in their area bringing together different organisations in partnership to ensure that actions to improve health are properly coordinated, and an action plan agreed to improve the health of the local population in line with the Investing for Health Strategy.

The purpose of the Partnerships is to identify opportunities to improve the health of the people in the area by addressing the social, cultural, economic and environmental determinants of health. The Partnerships will also seek to develop long term plans to meet the strategic aims of the department's Investing for Health Strategy and will be reflected in the annual Health and Well Being Investment Plans prepared annually by the Boards.

Members of these local partnerships will include representatives from voluntary, community and statutory organisations in the locality, including those from District Councils, the Housing Executive, Education and Library Boards and HSS Trusts. Where applicable members of the business community will also be invited to participate.

District Councils will have a key role in the Investing for Health Partnerships, presenting concerns particularly relevant to their locality and in respect to many of their statutory functions including environmental, health, consumer protection, building control, waste management, community services, and local economic development which have a direct bearing on health and the determinants of health.

The councils' participation in the Investing for Health Partnerships led by the Health Boards will also ensure that health issues are considered in local strategic planning processes and considered by other statutory bodies.

The Investing for Health Partnerships will run in parallel with existing networks such as Health Action Zones, Healthy Cities, Child Care Partnerships and Peace and Reconciliation Partnerships. Funding of £1.5 million from Executive Programme Funds has been made available for the establishment of the Partnerships. This funding will be available until March 2004.

The HSS Trusts

HSS Trusts have also been affected by the corporate plan, becoming accountable to the department in relation to the capital, income, workforce, estate and all other resources at their disposal and will be accountable for the effectiveness of their relationships with users, carers and the wider community. Each of the HSS Trusts is now expected to produce a Trust Delivery Plan (TDP) illustrating how the Trust intends to use their resources to deliver in line with planning goals set by the Minister for Health.

The Trusts will work in partnership with the Boards to implement the HWIPs and are required to produce an implementation plan, which will demonstrate:

- How the HWIP is to be effected within the Trust;
- Identify the consequences and risks to the Trust in relation to current and future clinical support services, funding sources both capital and revenue, costs, human resources, capital assets and information and management technology.

The Role of Trusts in Investing for Health

The Trusts will have a key role in developing the Investing for Health partnerships. Through their operational level links with voluntary and community groups they will facilitate initiatives at community level and maintain existing relationships with Agenda 21, Children's Services Committees, Health Action Zones, and Local Strategy Partnerships.

Local Health and Social Care Groups

New primary care arrangements were put in place in April 2002 following consultation on the proposals set out in the paper "Building the Way Forward in Primary Care". Under the new arrangements Local Health and Social Care Groups will be created to provide a framework to help primary care professionals work with others to improve health and well-being. It is hoped that this reorganisation of primary care will provide those involved with the delivery of primary care a broader perspective in assessing the needs of local communities and developing programmes aimed at promoting the health and well being of the local population and targeting health and social need.

Health and Social Services Councils

Health Councils were established in 1982 to shadow the areas covered by each of the Health Boards and report independently on the quality of healthcare delivery. The Councils regularly consult with the general public to monitor healthcare from the perspective of the consumer and make recommendations on how services might be improved.

Councils have an important role in representing their local area population and continuing to influence the policies of the Health Boards.

Councils will:

- Contribute to the development of HWIPs and closely monitor their outcomes;
- Report on the practical difference achieved by the HWIP from the perspective of the local population;
- Promote greater participation and involvement of the local community in the Investing for Health strategy.

Health and Social Services Boards (HSSBs)

Northern Ireland is served by 4 Health and Social Services Boards, each representing a geographical area and its population. The Boards were established under the Health and Personal Social Services (Northern Ireland) Order 1972 as amended by the Health and Personal Social Services (Northern Ireland) Order 1991. Originally the Boards had responsibility for all health and social services provided within their area, including hospitals, clinics, and social services centres. Towards the end of the 1980s central government initiated a series of reforms to the National Health Service (NHS), which affected the way services were provided in Britain and in Northern Ireland.

The Health and Social Services Boards work under government policies and guidelines, overseen by the Department for Health, Social Services and Public Safety. The role of the Boards is primarily to improve the health and wellbeing of the people who live in their area. This involves an assessment of the health and social services needed by local people, and arrangements for the provision of those services. Assessment takes place in consultation with 'stakeholders' in the health sector. Stakeholders include organisations and groups which have an interest in the health sector, and include elected representatives of local councils, professional organisations, voluntary groups, statutory bodies, HSS Trusts, primary healthcare professionals (such as GPs) and representatives of the local community.

From this consultation a plan is devised for the procurement of the services required. This is achieved by purchasing, or 'commissioning' health and social services, principally from 3 sources: Health and Social Services Trusts, voluntary organisations and private sector organisations. Boards negotiate Service Level Agreements with service providers, essentially contracts to provide services to patients.

Health and Social Services Boards are also required to evaluate all services provided, in order to ensure that they are meeting the needs of the population. This includes monitoring services provided in hospitals and in the community.

New primary care arrangements recently introduced by the then Minister for Health, Social Services and Public Safety, Bairbre de Brún meant the abolition of GP fund holding, to be replaced by Local Health and Social Care groups.

Health and Social Services Boards have responsibilities relating to the areas of family health and childcare. Boards manage the registration, inspection and monitoring of residential and nursing homes, including those for children and the elderly. They also have a role in overseeing arrangements for the delivery of health services to families by GPs, dentists, opticians and pharmacists.

Other services provided by Boards include the control of infectious diseases and the monitoring of the statutory functions delegated to Trusts.

Board Structure

Each Health and Social Services Board is composed of both executive and non-executive directors, and holds a public meeting every month. Geographical divisions between the Boards coincide with local government boundaries, so that each Board covers a number of local government districts. Each local authority nominates at least one representative to sit on the appropriate Board. Other members of the Boards are government nominees, as well as some senior executives employed by the Boards themselves.

Population breakdowns and other details of the HSSBs in Northern Ireland, are set out below.

The Eastern Board is by far the largest in terms of population, with almost two and a half times as many people as the smallest, the Western Board. The Southern Board is slightly bigger, but well behind the Northern Board, which itself is much smaller than the Eastern Board.

Royal Victoria Hospital, Belfast

Eastern Health and Social Services Board

Champion House, 12–22 Linenhall Street
Belfast BT2 8BS
Tel: 028 9032 1313
Fax: 028 9055 3680

The Eastern Health and Social Services Board (EHSSB) is the largest of the four Boards established in 1973. It serves a population of 667,000 (based on 2001 mid-year estimates), which is nearly half the population of Northern Ireland. The area covered includes the local government districts of Ards, Belfast, Castlereagh, Down, Lisburn and North Down.

Board Structure

The Board consists of non-executive Board members, executive Board members and a senior management team. A team of directors leads the Board:

Non-Executive Directors

Chairman: David Russell
              Edmund Johnston
              Professor Eithne McLaughlin
              Tony McMullan
              Mary Higgins
              Jim Stewart

Executive Directors

Chief Executive: Dr Paula Kilbane
Tel: 028 9032 1313   Fax: 028 9055 3625

Medical Director of Primary Care: Dr Stanton Adair
Tel: 028 9055 3782   Fax: 028 9055 3622

Director of Planning and Contracting: Anne Lynch
Tel: 028 9055 3900   Fax: 028 9055 3681

Director of Finance: Angela Paisley
Tel: 028 9055 3911   Fax: 028 9055 3621

Director of Social Services: John Richards
Tel: 028 9055 3964   Fax: 028 9055 3620

Director of Public Health: Dr David Stewart
Tel: 028 9055 3940   Fax: 028 9055 3682

Strategic Management Team

(Executive Board members are also on the Strategic Management Team).

Head of Corporate Services: Stephen Adams
Tel: 028 9055 3731   Fax: 028 9055 3680

Director of Pharmaceutical Services: Andreé McCollum
Tel: 028 9055 3793   Fax: 028 9055 3681

Head of Contracts: Colm McConville
Tel: 028 9055 3907   Fax: 028 9055 3681

Director of Dental Services: Will Maxwell
Tel: 028 9055 3780   Fax: 028 9055 3622

Director of Nursing Services: Mary Waddell
Tel: 028 9055 3739   Fax: 028 9055 3682

Expenditure

The Eastern Board spent approximately £698.2 million during the year ending 31 March 2001. The first table below indicates how the funding was broken down.

The Board spent £572m on Health and Personal Social Services Programmes of Care as shown below.

Expenditure		
	2000/ 2001 (£m)	**%**
Health care, personal social services and related services purchased	£572.1m	81.9%
Family Health Services	£113.8m	16.3%
Other	£12.2m	1.8%
Total	**£698.1**	**100%**

Source: Eastern HSSB

Eastern Board Expenditure By Programme of Care 2000/01

Programme of Care	**2000/2001 (£m)**	**%**
Physical Disability	£20m	3%
Health Promotion	£10m	2%
Primary Healthcare	£8m	1%
Acute Care	£226m	39%
Maternal and Child Health Care	£27m	5%
Family and Child Care	£44m	8%
Mental Health Care	£50m	9%
Learning Disability Care	£43m	8%
Elderly Care	£145m	25%
Total	**£573m**	**100%**

Source: Eastern HSSB

Purchase of Care by Provider		
	(£m)	**%**
Royal Group of Hospitals	£80.0m	14%
Belfast City Hospital	£63.2m	11%
Down Lisburn	£83.7m	15%
North & West Belfast Comm.	£83.7m	15%
NI Ambulance Service	£9.1m	2%
Ulster Community and Hospitals	£106.8m	18%
Greenpark	£20.1m	4%
South & East Belfast Community	£90.3m	15%
Mater Hospital	£15.6m	3%
Other Providers	£19.6m	3%
Total	**£573m**	**100%**

Source: Eastern HSSB

Main Providers of Health and Social Care 2000/2001

The main providers of care within the Eastern Health and Social Services Board's area are:

Acute Hospital Services

- Royal Hospitals HSS Trust
- Belfast City Hospital HSS Trust
- Mater Hospital HSS Trust
- Green Park Healthcare HSS Trust

Acute Hospitals and Community Health and Social Services

- Down Lisburn HSS Trust
- Ulster Community and Hospitals HSS Trust

Community Health and Social Services

- North and West Belfast HSS Trust
- South and East Belfast HSS Trust

Family Health Services

Within the Eastern Health and Social Services Board's area there are currently 146 medical practices, employing approximately 400 doctors. Around 70 per cent of these are fund-holding practices. Chemists, opticians and dentists also provide health services within the system.

Ambulance Services

Northern Ireland Ambulance Service
Headquarters, Knockbracken Healthcare Park
Saintfield Road
Belfast BT2 8SQ
Tel: 028 9040 0999
Fax: 028 9040 0900

Northern Health and Social Services Board

County Hall, 182 Galgorm Road
Ballymena BT42 1QB
Tel: 028 2565 3333
Fax: 028 2565 2311
Web: www.nhssb.n-i.nhs.co.uk

The Northern Health and Social Services Board serves the district council areas of Antrim, Ballymena, Ballymoney, Carrickfergus, Coleraine, Cookstown, Larne, Magherafelt, Moyle and Newtownabbey, which include around 428,000 people.

Board Structure

The Northern Board meets at 2.00pm on the third Thursday of each month. Mr J C Crutchley is the Board Secretary and Mrs C Reynolds, Corporate Business Manager.

Non-Executive Members

Chairman:	M Wood
	M E Mayrs
	T McKeown
	G B Owens
	R Milnes
	N J G Mulholland

Executive Members

Chief Executive: J S Macdonnell
Director of Finance: W Matthews
Director of Nursing &
Consumer Services: E McNair
Director of Public Health: Professor J D Watson
Director of Social Services: M Wilmot

Senior Management Team Members

Director, of Dental Services: A Millen
Director of Social Services: M Wilmont
Director, of Service, Performance
and Development: I Deboys
Director of Strategic Planning
and Commissioning: E McClean
Director of Pharmaceutical Services: Dr D Morrison
Director of Primary Care: W Boyd
Head of Information Services: M Sloan

Northern Board Expenditure

Area of Expenditure	(£m)	%
Purchase of Health and Social Care	£320.8m	82.7%
Family Health Services	£58.5m	15.1%
Board Administration and Commissioning Expenses	£5.9m	1.5%
Other	£2.8m	0.7%

Northern Health and Social

Expenditure by Programme of Care 2000/01

Programme of Care	(£m)	%
Acute Service	£137.9m	43%
Maternity and Child Health	£17.7m	5.5%
Family and Child Care	£18.1m	5.6%
Elderly Care	£73.2m	22.8%
Mental Health	£27.1m	8.5%
Learning Disability	£22.5m	7.0%
Physical and Sensory Disability	£9.5m	3.0%
Health Promotion and Disease Prevention	£5.5m	1.7%
Primary Health and Adult Community	£9.3m	2.9%

Northern Health and Social Services

Main Providers of Health and Social Care 2000/2001

Homefirst	£106.6m
United	£78.5m
Causeway	£63.3m
Royal	£24.1m
Belfast City	£14.8m
NI Ambulance	£5.6m
N&W Belfast	£5.5m
Green Park	£5.5m

Expenditure

The table above provides an analysis of the expenditure (£388.0 m) of the Board in 2000/01.

The largest single category of expenditure is the purchase of Health and Social Care.

Health and Social Services Trusts

The Northern Board covers three Health and Social Services Trusts:

Causeway Health and Social Services Trust

Providing both health and social care services in the local council areas of Ballymoney, Coleraine and Moyle

Homefirst Community Trust

Providing community health, mental health and social care services in the local council areas of Antrim, Ballymena, Carrickfergus, Cookstown, Larne, Magherafelt and Newtownabbey.

United Hospitals Trust

Provides services at Antrim, Braid Valley, Mid Ulster, Moyle and Whiteabbey hospitals.

Southern Health and Social Services Board

Tower Hill
Armagh BT61 9DR
Tel: 028 3741 4604
Fax: 028 3741 4550

The Southern Health and Social Services Board covers the District Council areas of Armagh, Banbridge, Craigavon, Dungannon and Newry and Mourne, which include around 312,000 people.

Board Structure

Chairman: William Gillespie

Non-Executive Directors

Sean Hogan	Philomena Hagan
John Brown	Patricia Moutray
Paul McCreesh	Susan Ingram

Executive Directors

Chief Executive:	Brendan Cunningham
Director of Public Health:	Dr Anne-Marie Telford
Director of Finance:	Sean McKeever
Director of Social Services:	Roy Blair
Director of Planning and Performance Management:	Colm Donaghy
Director of Primary Care:	Eddie Ritson

Southern Board Expenditure by Programme of Care 2000/01

Programme of Care	(£'000)	%
Acute	101,427	40.4
Maternal and Child Health	14,559	5.8
Family and Child care	12,296	4.9
Elderly Care	63,904	25.5
Mental Health	18,826	7.5
Learning Disability	19,826	7.9
Physical and Sensory Disability	8,190	3.2
Health Promotion	4,714	1.8
Primary Health and Adult community	7,035	2.8
Total	**250,781**	**100**

Source: Southern HSSB

Expenditure

In the year ending 31 March 2000, the Southern Board spent approximately £250 million on services.

Health and Social Services Trusts

The Southern Board has 4 Health and Social Services Trusts in its area:

- Armagh & Dugannon HSS Trust
- Newry & Mourne HSS Trust
- Craigavon Area Hospital Group Trust
- Craigavon/Banbridge Community Trust

Western Health and Social Services Board

15 Gransha Park
Clooney Road
Derry BT47 6FN
Tel: 028 7186 0086
Fax: 028 7186 0311

The Western Health and Social Services Board covers the District Council areas of Derry, Limavady, Strabane, Omagh and Fermanagh. The Board serves a population of 282,000 over an area of almost 5,000 sq kms from Limavady in the North to the Enniskillen area in the South. Population density is low, at around 58 persons per square kilometre.

Board Structure

Chairman: J Bradley

Non-Executive Directors

K Meehan	B Grant
E Turner	V Lusby
E Downey	R Williams

Executive Directors

Chief Executive:	S Lindsay
Director of Social Care:	D Burke
Director of Health Care/Chief Nurse:	M Bradley
Director of Finance and Information:	P McLaughlin

Expenditure

In the year up to 31 March 2001, the Board spent approximately £288 million on purchasing services, including £52 million spent on family health services and £59.3 million spent on the provision of family health services.

£198.8 million was spent with the HSS Trusts in the Western Board area. This figure includes expenditure on contracts with providers such as the Royal Group of Hospitals (£7.9 million), Green Park (£2.2 million) and Belfast City Hospital (£6.1 million).

The Central Services Agency makes payments on behalf of the Board to General Medical Practitioners, General Dental Practitioners and for Ophthalmic Services. Total expenditure on Family Health services in 2000/01 was £59.3 million.

The running costs of the Board attributable to the Board Administration and Commissioning and Registration and Inspection Unit were £4.7m, accounting for 1.6 per cent of the board's expenditure. The ceiling set by the department for administration costs was £5.7 million or 1.9 per cent. The savings in administration made by the Board of £1.04 million were applied directly towards patient and client care.

Western Board Expenditure By Programme of Care 2000/01

The Board provides services through its Programmes of Care. These programmes are detailed over, with a breakdown of funding within the Programmes.

Western Board Expenditure 2000/01

Trusts in Western Board Area	£000
Altnagelvin Hospital HSS Trust	53,234
Sperrin Lakeland HSS Trust	83,593
Foyle Community HSS Trust	61,993
Total	**198,820**

Trusts Outside Western Area & Other Expenditure	
N Ireland Ambulance Service	3,863
Other Providers	23,913
Other Contractual Liabilities	2,125
Total	**29,901**

Family Health Service	
General Medical Services	19,526
General Dental Services	8,573
Pharmaceutical Services	28,928
General Opthalmic Services	2,289
Total	**59,316**

Commissioning & Administration Expenditure	£000
Board Admin & Commissioning	4,431
Health & Social Services Council	94
Registration & Inspectin Unit	267
Other Services	1,424
Total	**6,216**
Total Expenditure	**293,901**

Programmes	Percentage of Total Expenditure (%)
Acute Hospital Services	39.7
Maternity and Child Care Services	5.5
Family and Child Care Services	7.2
Elderly Care Services	22.6
Mental Health Services	10.8
Services for People with a Learning Disability	5.9
Physical and Sensory Disability Services	3.1
Health promotion and Disease Prevention	1.7
Primary Health and Adult Community Services	3.5
	100%

Source: Western HSSB Annual Report

Altnagelvin Hospital, Derry

Health and Social Services Trusts

Details of Northern Ireland's Health and Social Services Trust (HSS Trusts) are set out below A–Z for ease of reference. The trusts are essentially providers of healthcare operating under contract to the regional Health and Social Services Boards, and are primarily appointed bodies.

Altnagelvin Hospitals Trust

Glenshane Road, Derry BT47 6SB
Tel: 028 7134 5171
Fax: 028 7161 1222

Chairman: Denis Desmond CBE
Chief Executive: Stella Burnside

The Trust was established in 1 April 1996. The Trusts facilities include:

- Altnagelvin Area Hospital;
- Ward 5, Waterside Hospital;
- Spruce House, Gransha Park.

The Trust provides a range of acute hospital services; Altanagelvin is the major district general hospital in the north-west and is the largest acute hospital in the north of Ireland, providing a designated cancer unit, and offering the most comprehensive and complex range of services of any hospital outside Belfast.

Board Members

Gerard Guckian	Non Executive Director
Columb Henry	Non Executive Director
Marlene Jefferson	Non Executive Director
Joan Casey	Non Executive Director
Neville Orr	Non Executive Director
Irene Duddy	Director of Nursing
Geoff Nesbitt	Medical Director
Raymond McCartney	Director of Business Services
Niall Smyth	Director of Finance

Acute Facilities within the Altnagelvin Hospitals Trust

Altnagelvin Area Hospital

Acute Hospital Services
450 Inpatient Beds
54 Day Case Beds

Ward 5, Waterside Hospital

Slow Stream Rehabilitation
18 Inpatient Beds

Spruce House, Gransha Park

Care of the Young Physically Disabled
17 In patient beds

Armagh and Dungannon HSS Trust

St Luke's Hospital, Armagh BT61 7NQ
Tel: 028 3752 2381
Fax: 028 3752 6302

Chairman: James Shaw
Chief Executive: Pauline Stanley

Armagh and Dungannon Health and Social Services Trust shares its service boundaries with those of Armagh City and District Council and Dungannon and South Tyrone Borough Council. The combined population of the two council areas is 102,000 and represents 33 per cent of the population in the Southern Health and Social Services Board. The Trust employs a total of 2,594 employees including 899 home helps.

Board Members

Eric Hamilton	Director of Social Services
John Mone	Director of Health Care Services and Nursing
Stephen McNally	Director of Finance
Dr Harold McNeill	Medical Director
Eric Barfoot	Non Executive Director
Roberta Brownlee	Non Executive Director
Deirdre I Dorman JP	Non Executive Director
W Oliver Ross	Non Executive Director
Patrick McCabe	Director of Planning and Performance Management
Kevin Toal	Director of Mental Health Services
Gordon Wells	Director of Personnel

Acute Facilities within the Armagh and Dungannon HSS Trust

- Millinure Hospital
- Armagh Community Hospital
- South Tyrone Hospital

Trust Staffing	
Nurses and MidWives	777
Admin and Clerical	325
Social work staff	204
Ancillary and General	176
Professional and Technical	141
Medical and Dental	49
Work and Maintenance	30
Home Helps	899

Trust Spending By Programme of Care 1999–2000		
Programme of Care	**(£'000)**	**%**
Acute Services	10,921	17%
Physical and Sensory Disability	2,595	4%
Learning Disability	10,947	17%
Mental Health	7,401	12%
Family and Child Care	3,246	5%
Maternity and Child Health	3,020	5%
Primary Health & Adult Community	1,073	2%
Health Promotion & Disease Prevention	1,503	2%
Elderly Care	22,344	36%

Belfast City Hospital HSS Trust

51 Lisburn Road, Belfast BT9 7AB
Tel: 028 9032 9241
Fax: 028 9032 6614

Chairman: Joan Ruddock OBE
Chief Executive: Quentin Coey

Board Members

WFI McKay	Deputy Chairman
V Fiddis	Non Executive Member
J R Hayes	Non Executive Member
R Huq	Non Executive Member
P Morgan	Non Executive Member
KJ Fullerton	Medical Director
J Copeland	Director of Finance
A McCabe	Director of Nursing
A Brown	Director of Operational Support
PA Haines	Director of Planning
MC Barkley	Director of Personnel

Causeway HSS Trust

80 Coleraine Road, Ballymoney BT53 6BP
Tel: 028 2766 6600
Fax: 028 2766 1201

Chairman: Jean Jefferson
Chief Executive: Norma Evans

Board Members

Jim Loughrey	Director of Child and Community Care Services
Neil Guckian	Director of Finance
Alan Braiden	Director of Acute Hospital Services
Wesley McGowan	Director of Medical Services
Linda Marshall	Director of Nursing and Quality
Jacinta Melaugh	Director of Human Resources
Nevin Oliver	Director of Business and Corporate Services
Windsor Murdock	GP Representative

Acute Facilities within the Causeway HSS Trust

- Causeway Hospital

Craigavon Area Hospital Group HSS Trust

68 Lurgan Road, Craigavon BT63 5QQ
Tel: 028 3833 4444
Fax: By department

Chairman: E McClurg
Chief Executive: J Templeton

During 2000/1 the Trust provided services to all four of the Northern Ireland Health and Social Services Boards. The SHSSB remains the main purchaser and user of Trust services. The Trust was also contracted to provide services to the patients of the 18 GP practices within the Southern Board area and to 30 GP practices outside the area.

Board Members

Dr W MCCaughey	Director of Medical Services/ Deputy Chief Executive
Dr NN Damani	Pathology and Laboratory Services
Dr SJ Hall	Radio Diagnosis and Imaging
Dr RJE Lee	Medicine
D Lowry	Obstetrics and Gynaecology
Dr I Orr	Anaesthesia and Theatres
WJI Stirling	Surgery
D Herron	Business Planning and Contracts
J Mone	Estates
J Austin	Nursing and Quality
M Richardson	Human Resources
LA Stead	Finance

Trust Staffing	
Admin and Clerical	404
Works and Maintenance	25
Ancillary and General	105
Nursing and Midwifery	1276
Social Work	11
Professional and Technical	358
Medical and Dental	251
Total	**2430**

Trust Spending By Programme of Care 1999–2000	
Programme of Care	**% of Trust Expenditure**
Learning Disability	10.6
Physical Disability	7.2
Health Promotion	3.7
Elderly	45.5
Primary Care	1.4
Maternal and Child Health	3.2
Child and Family Care	12.1
Mental Health	16.3

Acute Facilities within the Craigavon Area Hospital Group Trust

- South Tyrone Hospital
- Craigavon Area Hospital
- Lurgan Hospital
- Banbridge Polyclinic
- Daisy Hill Hospital
- Armagh Community Hospital

Craigavon and Banbridge Community HSS Trust

Bannvale House, 10 Moyallen Road, Gilford BT63 5JX
Tel: 028 3883 1983
Fax: 028 3883 1993

Chairman: David Cook
Chief Executive: Denis Preston

Established in April 1994, the Craigavon and Banbridge Community Health and Social Services Trust is responsible for the management of a range of community health and social care services and also for purchasing similar services from the independent and community/voluntary agencies.

The Trust covers a largely rural area, the principal towns of which are Banbridge, Lurgan and Portadown. The population of the Trust area is approximately 119,600 representing 38 per cent of the Southern Boards population.

In the 2000/01 period the Trust had an income of approximately £46.5m, 85 per cent of which was funded through a contract with the Southern Health and Social Services Board.

Board Members

John Farleigh	Non Executive Director
Cyril McElhinney	Non Executive Director
Louise Boyle	Director of Child and Family Care
Rosaleen Moore	Director of Mental Health and Disability
Stephen Best	Medical Director – Psychiatry
Mary McParland	Non Executive Director
Michael Morrow	Non Executive Director
Sean Wilson	Medical Director – General Practice
Martin Kelly	Director of Planning and Information
Kieran Donaghy	Director of Human Resources
Ronnie Crozier	Director of Finance
Roisin Burns	Director of Elderly and Primary Care
Roisin McDonagh	Non Executive Director

Down Lisburn HSS Trust

Lisburn Health Centre, 25 Linenhall Street
Lisburn BT28 1LU
Tel: 028 9266 5181
Fax: 028 9267 6026

Chairman: D Fitzsimmons
Chief Executive: J Compton

D Gorman (Vice Chair)	Non Executive Director
R Lavery	Non Executive Director
B McErlane	Non Executive Director
L Tavakoli	Non Executive Director
Donal Flanagan	Non Executive Director
P Simpson	Director of Finance
Kate Thompson	Executive Director for Social Work
A Finn	Executive Director for Nursing
Dr Harry Beers	Joint Medical Director

Acute Facilities within the Down Lisburn HSS Trust

- Downe Hospital
- Lagan Valley Hospital
- Downpatrick Maternity Hospital

Foyle HSS Trust

Riverview House, Abercorn Road, Derry BT48 6FB
Tel: 028 7126 6111
Fax: 028 7126 0806

Chairman: Anthony Jackson
Chief Executive: Elaine Way

Board Members

G Durkan	Non Executive Director
Anne-Marie Holmes	Non Executive Director
Dr Artie O'Hara	Medical Director
Joseph Doherty	Non Executive Director
Philip Babington	Non Executive Director
Bell Hogg	Non Executive Director

The total income of the Trust for 2000/01 was £78.4 million, including income from Westcare Business Services, legally part of Foyle HSS Trust which operates as a trading agency providing common support services to the Western Health and Social Services Board and to the Trusts in the Western Board area.

Programme of Care	£m	%
Maternity and Child Health	2.2	3.2
Family and Childcare	10.3	15.1
Older People	28.4	41.9
Mental Health	11.1	16.4
Learning Disability	8.6	12.7
Physical and Sensory Disability	3.7	5.4
Health Promotion	1.5	2.2
Primary Health	2.1	3.1
Sub Total	**67.9**	**100%**
Common Services to Other Trusts	6.2	
GP Support Services	0.8	
Capital Charges	3.5	

Source: Foyle Health & Social Services

Green Park HSS Trust

20 Stockmans Lane, Belfast BT9 7JB
Tel: 028 9066 9501
Fax: 028 9059 1501

Chairman: Ian Doherty
Chief Executive: Hilary Boyd

Board Members

Brian Sore	Director of Corporate Planning and Deputy Chief Executive
Dr Denis Connolly	Medical Director
Eleanor Hayes	Director of Patient Services
Therese McKernan	Director of Human Resources
Colin Cairns	Director of Support Services
Colin Bradley	Director of Finance
Jim Cooper	Non Executive Director
Alan Hannah	Non Executive Director
Jennifer Power	Non Executive Director
Mike Lewis	Non Executive Director
Margaret Shevlin	Non Executive Director

Acute Facilities within the Greenpark HSS Trust

- Musgrave Park Hospital
- Belvoir Park Hospital
- Forster Green Hospital

Homefirst Community HSS Trust

The Cottage, 5 Greenmount Avenue, Ballymena BT43 6DA
Tel: 028 2563 3700
Fax: 028 2563 3733

Chairman: William Boyd
Chief Executive: Christy Colhoun

Mater Infirmorum Hospital HSS Trust

45–51 Crumlin Road, Belfast BT14 6AB
Tel: 028 9080 2338
Fax: 028 9074 9784

Chairman: Lady McCollum
Chief Executive: Patricia Gordon

Board Members

GW Odling-Smee	Non Executive Director
Aidan A Canavan	Non Executive Director
Charles Jenkins	Non Executive Director
E Rosemary Dunlop	Non Executive Director
Barney McCaughey	Non Executive Director
Larry O'Neill	Director of Finance and Information
Dr J McLoughlin	Medical Director
Mary Hinds	Director of Nursing
Joan Pedan	Director of Corporate Development

Acute Facilities within the Mater Infirmorum Hospital HSS Trust

- Mater Infirmorum Hospital

Newry and Mourne HSS Trust

5 Downshire Place, Downshire Road, Newry BT34 1DZ
Tel: 028 3026 0505
Fax: 028 3026 9064

Chief Executive: Mr Eric Bowyer

The Newry and Mourne HSS Trust came into being on 1 April 1994 and provides a wide range of hospital community health and social services to the 86,000 population of the Newry and Mourne area.

During 2000/01 the Trust spent in excess of £58 million on the delivery of services. Over 1700 staff are employed by the Trust.

Board Members

M Dillon	Director of Finance and Planning
Dr P Loughran	Director of Acute Services
J O'Hagan	Director of Nursing and Community Health
J Flynn	Director of Social Services
E Cleland	Non Executive Director
L McArdel	Non Executive Director
D Farrell	Non Executive Director
P McCabe	Non Executive Director
Dr M Hollinger	Director of Community Medical and Preventative Services
L Cavan	Director of Professions Allied to Medicine
Dr A Mulholland	General Practitioner Advisor

Acute Facilities within the Newry and Mourne HSS Trust

- Daisy Hill Hospital

North West and Belfast HSS Trust

Glendinning House, 6 Murray Street, Belfast BT1 6DP
Tel: 028 9032 7156
Fax: 028 9082 1285

Chairperson: Patrick McCartin
Chief Executive: R G Black

The North and West Belfast HSS Trust provides a full range of community based health and social care services to 160,000 people, providing specialist services for people with learning disabilities at Muckamore Abbey Hospital. These services are provided to all four health and social services boards in Northern Ireland.

The Trust provides the Eastern Board with community nutrition and dietetic services, the child health information system, family planning services, services for people travelling abroad and services relating to sexual health and AIDS. The Trust operates from 50 locations and employs 3,500 people.

Board Members

Noel Rooney	Director of Operations/Social Work
Brenda Connolly	Director of Nursing
Peter Harvey	Director of Finance
Dr Caroline Marriott	Director of Medical Services (Hospitals)
Dr Robin McKee	Director of Medical Services (Community)
May Blood	Non Executive Director
Denis Power	Non Executive Director
Geraldine McAteer	Non Executive Director
Sarah Brennan	Non Executive Director
Aidrian Watson	Non Executive Director
Miriam Summerville	Director of Hospital Services
Paul Ryan	Director of Planning, Contracts and Information, Deputy Chief Executive
Eamonn Molloy	Director of Human Resources and Corporate Affairs

Acute Facilities within the North West and Belfast HSS Trust

- Muckamore Abbey

Northern Ireland Ambulance Service HSS Trust

Knockbracken Healthcare Park,
Saintfield Road
Belfast, BT8 8SG
Tel: 028 9040 0999
Fax: 028 9040 0900

Chairman: Doug Smyth
Chief Executive: Paul McCormick

Royal Group of Hospitals and Dental Hospital HSS Trust

Grosvenor Road, Belfast BT12 6BA
Tel: 028 9024 0503
Fax: 028 9024 0899

Chairman: Paul McWilliams OBE
Chief Executive: William McKee

Board Members

Dr McBride	Medical Director
Deirdre O'Brien	Director of Nursing and Patient Services
Sean Donaghy	Director of Finance
Hugh McCaughey	Director of Organisational Development
Monica Culvert	Non Executive Director
Anne Balmer	Non Executive Director
Frank Caddy	Non Executive Director
Cllr Tom Hartley	Non Executive Director
James O'Kane	Non Executive Director

Acute Facilities within the Royal Group of Hospitals and Dental Hospital HSS Trust

- The Royal Hospital

South and East Belfast HSS Trust

Knockbracken Healthcare Park, Saintfield Road
Belfast BT8 8BH
Tel: 028 9056 5656
Fax: 028 9056 5813

Chairman: Robin Harris
Chief Executive: Robert Ferguson

Board Members

Dr Paul Bell	Executive Chief of Medicine
Norman Carson	Executive Director of Finance
Hugh Connor	Executive Director of Social Work Head of Adult Services
Ray McGee	Executive Director of Nursing
John Veitch	Head of Children's Services
Dr Paul Bell	Head of Treatment Services
Dr Gillian Rankin	Head of Service Development
Stephen O'Brien	Head of Planning
Eddie Currie	Head of Operational Services
Vivienne Walker	Head of Human Resources

Acute Facilities within the South and East Belfast HSS Trust

- Acute Psychiatric at the Knockbracken Healthcare Centre Park

Sperrin Lakeland HSS Trust

Strathdene House, Tyrone and Fermanagh Hospital
Omagh, Co Tyrone BT79 0NS
Tel: 028 8283 5285
Fax: 028 8283 5286
E-mail: jhall@slt.n-i-nhs.uk

Chairman: Richard Scott
Chief Executive: Hugh Mills

Acute Facilities within the Sperrin Lakeland HSS Trust

- Erne Hospital
- Tyrone Country Hospital

Ulster Community and Hospitals Trust

39 Regent Street, Newtownards BT23 4AD
Tel: 028 9181 6666
Fax: 028 9182 0140

Chairman: Siobhan Grant
Chief Executive: Jim McCall

Acute Facilities within the Ulster Community and Hospitals Trust

- Ulster Hospital

United Hospitals HSS Trust

Bush House, 45 Bush Road, Antrim BT41 2QB
Tel: 028 9442 4673
Fax: 028 9442 4675

Chairman: Dr Harry McGuigan CBE
Chief Executive: Bernard Mitchell

Acute Facilities within the United Hospitals HSS Trust

- Antrim Hospital
- Whiteabbey Hospital
- Mid Ulster Hospital

Health and Social Services Councils

Northern Ireland has four Health and Social Services Councils; one shadowing each of the four Health and Social Services Boards. The Councils were established in 1991 under the provisions of the Health and Personal Social Services (Northern Ireland) Order 1991.

The principal function of each Council is to represent the interests of the general public in all areas of health and social services. This includes providing advice, information and support on a wide range of related issues, and guidance for those considering making a complaint about a service. Councils also work with local groups to monitor services, and to encourage people to put forward their opinions on health and social services, partly by carrying out surveys to gauge opinion. Councils represent the public in participating in consultations about health and social services, and acting to improve services. Finally, Councils visit health and social services facilities, to ensure that the public is being effectively provided for.

A Work Programme for each of the Councils is drawn up in conjunction with the Health Board being shadowed, and an annual report is published. The Councils are funded by their respective Boards but are autonomous. Councils have the right of consultation on developments and changes to services provided by Health and Social Services Boards, as well as the right to have formal meetings with Boards. They are also entitled to visit and inspect health and social service facilities.

Each Health and Social Services Council is composed of representatives from local councils, voluntary organisations and other interested groups. The Eastern Council has 30 members as the Eastern Board represents more people than any other Board. The Northern, Southern and Western Boards each have 24 members. A team of full-time staff support the councils.

Membership comprises approximately:
- 40 per cent district councillors;
- 30 per cent voluntary/community nominations;
- 30 per cent individuals with an interest in health and social care.

The Councils have a statutory duty to publish and distribute an annual report giving details of their performance during the preceding year.

The Councils must also adhere to a Code of Practice on Openness in the HPSS. Members must abide by a Code of Conduct, covering issues such as impartiality, financial accountability, confidentiality, non-discriminatory practices, casual gifts, hospitality and declaration of interests.

Each council maintains an up to date register of member's interests, which is open to the public for inspection. The Councils also have a procedure to enable members of the public to complain about them. The Ombudsman can ultimately investigate complaints about the Councils.

Details of each of the four Health and Social Services Councils follow.

Eastern Health and Social Services Council

19 Bedford Street, Belfast BT2 7EJ
Tel: 028 9032 1230
Fax: 028 9032 1750

Chairman: Brian Coulter

Board Members

Sandra Adams	Brian Henning
Eileen Askham	Brendan Henry
Cllr Gerald Brophy	James Hutchinson
Cllr Elizabeth Campbell	Cllr Joseph Lockhart
Cllr James Convery	Cllr Naomi Long
Cllr Alan Crowe	Brian Marshall
Cllr Dermot Curran	Sylvia McGarry
Monica Deasy	Patricia McMillan
Cllr Gordon Dunn	Cllr Christine Elaine McMillen
Cllr David Gilmore	George Monds
Cecil Graham	Cllr Marie Moore
Elizabeth Hamilton	Mary Muldoon
Dr Michael Harriott	Myrtle Neill
Kieran Harris	Muriel Patterson
Ald Michael Henderson	

Chief Officer: Jane Graham
Senior Managers: Raymond Newman, Brenda Devine
Research Officer: Geraldine Boyle

The Eastern Health and Social Services Council has 30 members in comparison to the 24 members of the other Councils. 12 members of the Eastern Council are elected representatives from city, district and borough councils. Voluntary and community groups or people in the community with an interest in health and social services nominate the other 18 members.

Northern Health and Social Services Council
8 Broadway Avenue, Ballymena BT43 7AA
Tel: 028 2565 5777
Fax: 028 2565 5112

Chairperson: Joe McFadden
Chief Officer: Noel Graham

Board Members

Beth Adger	Ballymena
Maureen Anderson	Larne
Mary Baker	Magherafelt
May Beattie	Carrickfergus
Pearse Boyle	Maghera
Annetta Crawford	Newtownabbey
Tom Creighton	Carrickfergus
Joan Drummond	Larne
Denise Hamill	Ballymena
Nigel Hamilton	Islandmagee
Irene Johnston	Coleraine
Liz Johnston	Coleraine
Robert Montgomery	Magherafelt
Catherine McCambridge	Ballycastle
Joe McFadden	Cushendun
Stephen Nicholl	Antrim
Mark Nolan	Larne
Ian Stevenson	Ballymoney

The total expenditure of the Northern Health and Social Services Council amounted to £171,258 to 31 March 2001.

The Northern Health and Social Services Council provides services to 430,500 people covering ten District and Borough Council areas of:

- Antrim
- Ballymena
- Magherafelt
- Cookstown
- Larne
- Carrickfergus
- Newtownabbey
- Coleraine
- Ballymoney
- Moyle

Southern Health and Social Services Council
Quaker Buildings, High Street, Lurgan BT66 8BB
Tel: 028 3834 9900
Fax: 028 3834 9858

Chairman   Roisin Foster
Vice-Chairman   Lynne Cairns

Board Members

Sydney Anderson	Brendan Montague
Patrick Brannigan	Peter Murray
Jim Cavanagh	John McArdle
John Coulter	Wilfred McFadden
Sue Cunningham	Adrian McKinney
Brendan Curran	Yvonne McKnight
Mary Ferris	Mary McNally
Isaac Hanna	Charles Rollston
Nazy Harris	David Simpson
Clive Henning	

The Southern Health and Social Services Council was established in 1991 as one of the four Health and Social Services Councils in Northern Ireland.

The Council is an independent consumer organisation, which has the legal right to:

- Be consulted by the Southern Health and Social Services Board on any major development in or changes to the service;
- Receive information from the Board about the planning and running of services;
- Visit health and social services facilities in the public sector.

The main role of the Council is to represent the views of the public, influence activities of the board in relation to the introduction of services, respond to Board proposals and recommend improvements to services where required. The Council is funded by the DHSSPS and held a budget of £185,000 for the year 2000–01. Eighty per cent of the budget is spent on salaries and premises.

Western Health and Social Services Council
'Hilltop', Tyrone and Fermanagh Hospital
Omagh, Co Tyrone, BT79 0NS
Tel: 028 8225 2555
Fax: 028 8225 2544

Chairman: Raymond Rogan
Vice-Chairman: M Reilly
Chief Officer: Stanley Millar

Board Members

P Brogan	Beragh
M Hamilton	Derry City Council
M Coyle	Dungiven (Council Representative)
M Devlin	Londonderry
H Andrews	Fermanagh
A Belle	Strabane
V Brown	Lisnaskea
M Burke	Derrylin
T Carlin	Londonderry
E Friel	Londonderry
P Galgunn	Enniskillen
J Kerr	Derry
I Maguire	Strabane
G McAleer	Omagh
P McGowan	Drumquin
R McKelvey	Omagh
W Page	Derry
M Robson	Derry
M Reilly	Enniskillen
M Trimble	Enniskillen
R Rogan	Londonderry

North/South, East/West and International Co-operation on Health

North/South

The Belfast Agreement introduced new arrangements for co-operation. The North South Ministerial Council provides a structure for ministers of all departments throughout Ireland to facilitate the exchange of information, discussion and consultation with a view to cooperating on matters of mutual interest. While agreement may be reached on the adoption of common policies in areas where there is a mutual cross-border and all-island benefit, decisions would be taken on implementation separately in each jurisdiction. Where appropriate, decisions on policies and action at an all-island and cross-border level would be implemented by the new cross-border implementation bodies.

Six cross-border implementation bodies have been established, including the Food Safety Promotion Board.

The Food Safety Promotion Board

The key function of the Food Safety Promotion Board is to ensure that producers, processors, distributors, caterers and the general public take responsibility for the provision of safe food. Other functions include promoting research in all aspects of food safety, dissemination of information on national and international food alerts, promotion of cross-border co-operation in the microbiological surveillance of food borne diseases, and promotion of scientific co-operation and linkages between laboratories under relevant EU directives. The Board also aims to develop a strategy for the island of Ireland for the delivery of specialised laboratory services.

The Board consults widely where appropriate and works closely with the Food Standards Agency in Northern Ireland, and the Food Safety Authority of Ireland (FSAI) in the South.

Practical North/South Co-operation under Health

The North South Ministerial Council (NSMC) identified health as one of the six additional areas for co-operation and collaboration. Five specific areas have been highlighted for co-operation under Health:
- Accident and emergency services;
- Planning for major emergencies;
- Co-operation on high technology equipment;

- Cancer research;
- Health promotion.

The NSMC agreed to share information and discuss opportunities for co-operation in relation to health promotion on an all Ireland basis, and to collaborate on public information campaigns, particularly major media campaigns. The NSMC also aims to share information on research and good practice for mutual benefit and examine the scope for research and public information and education in the areas of heart disease, cancer and smoking.

The Institute of Public Health in Ireland

The Institute of Public Health in Ireland, whose establishment predated the Belfast Agreement, works to promote North/South co-operation on public health in the following areas:

- Tackling health inequalities;
- Strengthening partnerships for health;
- Contributing to public health information and surveillance;
- Develop public health capacity and leadership;
- Networking internationally and nationally.

Under the remit of the Investing for Health strategy the Institute for Public Health will enhance its capacity to include the comparative monitoring of trends in health, the determinants of health, and health inequalities North and South, and relative to other EU countries, and highlighting new areas of concern as they emerge. The Institute advises on the methodology for health equity impact assessments, and disseminates information from international research and experience throughout Ireland.

There are plans for the department to undertake a study on the potential for, and barriers to, North/South co-operation for public health. This study will be undertaken in conjunction with the health departments North and South, involving community organisations, health service and other public sector organisations and professional groups.

European and International Programmes

European and international money has also been used to support cross-border programmes in the voluntary and community sector, for example in the area of early years and family support. It has been anticipated that there will

be scope for drawing on the new EU Peace Programme in particular for specified cross-border purposes over the coming five years. Another area to be addressed is the development of common data systems to allow meaningful comparisons to be made on a North/South basis.

East/West Co-operation in Health

The British-Irish Council provides a structure for co-operation between Britain and Ireland. It has identified a range of issues for co-operation, including social exclusion, drug misuse, the environment, transport and other issues in health and education.

A Concordat provides a more specific framework for co-operation between the Department of Health in England and departments concerned with health and social care in each of the devolved administrations. DHSSPS is also included in discussions, which feed in to the European Health Council.

There are a number of Joint Committees, which advise Health Departments such as the Joint Committee on Vaccination and Immunisation and the National Screening Committee.

Joint Ministerial Committee

There is a joint ministerial committee on health issues, providing an opportunity for the separate administrations to share information, experience and best practice on a wide range of policy issues. These include developing common measures of performance, learning from each other's experiences and sharing ideas on incentives.

Inter-Departmental Group on Tobacco

An interdepartmental group on tobacco was convened at the time of publication of the White Paper 'Smoking Kills' (December 1998). The membership of this group includes representatives from DHSSPS and the health departments in London, Edinburgh and Dublin. The purpose of the group is to provide strategic direction and share information on action against tobacco.

Anti-Drugs Co-ordination

Strong links exist between the devolved administrations and the Anti Drugs Co-ordination Unit in the Cabinet Office. There is frequent contact on a range of issues relating to drug misuse, including progress with the implementation of strategies for action.

Foods Standards Agency

The Food Standards Agency (FSA), operates in Northern Ireland and in Britain. It provides policy advice to Ministers on food safety, food standards and aspects of nutrition, and assists in the preparation of draft subordinate legislation. The Agency also provides representation in negotiations in the EU, and operates the Food Hazards Warning System. In addition, the Agency commissions research, and sets standards for enforcement of the legislation, monitoring performance of the enforcement authorities against these standards. It has the power to issue, refuse, revoke and suspend licences, approvals and authorisations. The Agency exercises its role in partnership with the Food Safety Promotion Board, so combining an East/West with a North/South dimension.

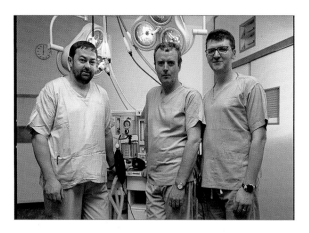

International Co-operation

Northern Ireland is one of the 51 members of the European Region of the World Health Organisation. The health policy framework for Europe, Health 21, sets 21 targets for health action, including closing the health gap between and with countries and multi Sectoral responsibility for health. World Health Organisation initiatives in Northern Ireland include:

- Healthy Cities;
- Health Promoting Schools;
- Health Promoting Hospitals.

The Health Promotion Agency has recently been designated as a collaborating centre for training and research in communications and information technology in Health promotion and disease prevention by the World Health Organisation.

Currently under development is a new EU Public Health Strategy and Action Plan and relationships are being developed with the National Cancer Institute in the United States with the objective of improving research and improving patient care. The Institute of Public Health in Ireland is working with leaders in Public Health in the US to develop a groundbreaking Creative Public Health Leadership course in Ireland.

Key Issues in Health in Northern Ireland

Investing for Health Initiative

The Investing for Health Initiative falls under "Working for a Healthier People" one of the Northern Ireland Executive's five overarching priorities in the Programme for Government. Investing for Health has been produced with the involvement of all the departments in the Executive through the Ministerial Group on Public Health and is complementary to the New Targeting Social Needs initiative and Equality Agenda.

The aim of the Investing for Health initiative is the development of a long term plan for the improvement of health care in Northern Ireland and by tackling the causes of poor health to individuals such as poor living conditions and social and economic disadvantage, thus pre empting the need for medical care. The Investing for Health initiative is an attempt by the department to shift the emphasis in healthcare from the treatment of ill health to its prevention by tackling the factors that adversely affect health.

The department has the lead responsibility for the Investing in Health framework including coordination at regional level. The main responsibilities of the department include:

- Providing guidance to the HPSS on the Investing for Health strategy and assisting with implementation;
- Co-ordinating the development and implementation of specific inter-agency strategies
- Preparation of public health legislation, including legislation to control tobacco advertising;
- Policy on and structural arrangements for health promotion monitoring and overseeing the performance of the Health and Social Services, including changes in the roles of Boards, Trusts and the Health Promotion Agency;
- Developing human resources policies for the HPSS to support Investing for Health;
- Implementing and developing its own Equality Scheme and New TSN Action Plan;
- Arranging for the introduction of new systems required to support the HPSS contribution to Investing for Health;

- Supporting regional voluntary organisations working for health improvement;
- Co-ordination of cross-border and international co-operation for health improvement;
- Policy on and structural arrangements for the control of communicable diseases, immunisation and screening.

Under the terms of the Investing for Health strategy the DHSSPS will undertake a review of the Public Health function in Northern Ireland. The aim of the review is to ensure that the department has all the components in place to respond to the health challenges facing Northern Ireland.

The Hayes Report; Hospital Rationalisation

With severe overcrowding in hospitals and a perceived inability on the part of the NHS to cope with a winter flu epidemic in 1999/2000, the Health Minister Bairbre de Brún announced a wide-ranging review of the health service in the region with a particular emphasis on acute services.

Dr Maurice Hayes

The issue of rationalisation of hospital services has been debated widely, many interpreting the terms as simply 'cutting back' on services. In August 2001 the report compiled by Chairman of the Acute Hospitals Review Group, Dr Maurice Hayes, was published, which made some far-reaching and controversial recommendations for change.

As a general finding, Dr Hayes reported that in the process of conducting a major consultation exercise all round Northern Ireland he had experienced considerable public dissatisfaction with the current provision of hospital services. Dr Hayes concluded that maintaining the status quo was therefore 'not an option'. The main recommendations of the report are set out below.

Acute Hospitals

Acute Hospitals are those capable of providing comprehensive accident and emergency services. Prior to devolution the Department of Health had been proposing to close seven of Northern Ireland's existing acute hospitals, centralising acute services to six main hospitals.

The original six to retain acute services were:

- Royal Victoria Hospital (RVH) Belfast
- City Hospital Belfast
- Ulster Hospital (Dundonald) Belfast
- Antrim Area Hospital Antrim
- Craigavon Area Hospital Craigavon
- Altnagelvin Derry

The Hayes report recommended that three more hospitals retain acute services, in addition to the six mentioned above. They were:

- Causeway Hospital Coleraine
- Daisy Hill Hospital Newry
- A New South West Hospital
  (to be built) Enniskillen

The hospitals that would lose their existing accident and emergency services would be:

- Mater Hospital Belfast
- Omagh Hospital Omagh
- Lagan Valley Lisburn
- Whiteabbey Newtownabbey
- and South Tyrone hospital, where the earlier decision had already been implemented.

In addition the Downe and Downpatrick hospitals would lose their maternity services. Inevitably, there were strong feelings about the downgrading of hospitals, and many critics argued that residents in areas served by them would be disadvantaged and possibly endangered by the reduction of services. Supporters of South Tyrone Hospital were particularly angry that the proposal was implemented so quickly in their area.

To compensate for the loss of acute services in some hospitals the Hayes report recommended that where possible a greater proportion of treatment should be delivered closer to patient's homes, either in health centres or in new local hospitals. The report did not recommend closing any hospitals, although this was of little compensation to those who perceived the loss of acute services at hospitals as a cost-cutting exercise that could have serious implications for the health of the local population.

Reorganisation of Health Service Structures

The Hayes report also made radical recommendations on the existing NHS structures in Northern Ireland.

It recommended that the four existing Health Boards be unified into one large single Board, and that the hospitals of Northern Ireland be further grouped into 3 'super' trusts, comprised as follows:

- **Greater Belfast**, including: RVH, City Hospital, Musgrave Park, Mater Hospital, Ulster Hospital, Whiteabbey Hospital, Lagan Valley, Downe Hospitals
- **Northern**, including: Altnagelvin, Antrim Hospital, Causeway, Coleraine
- **Southern**, including: Craigavon Area Hospital, Daisy Hill, 'New' South-West Hospital (Enniskillen)

Other Findings

Although proposing certain cutbacks as part of the overall package, the Hayes report also called for much higher numbers of professional staff, in particular aiming for an increase of 100 per cent in hospital consultants and a 25 per cent increase in the number of general practitioners.

A rotation system for doctors, between acute and local hospitals, was also recommended, as was a higher level of investment in the ambulance service.

If implemented its recommendations could take 15 years to fulfilment, with the new Trusts up and running by 2008.

As something of a "hot potato" politically, there has been limited government action on foot of the recommendations of the Hayes Report. It can be expected however that these recommendations will be engaged more fully by the minister responsible during 2003.

Private Healthcare

The NHS dominates healthcare in Northern Ireland although there is also a private sector presence in what is a growing health 'market'. The main players in the private market include BUPA, PPP, Norwich Union and WPA who all offer a range of different levels of private health insurance to individuals and to groups. For those who can afford it, private medical treatment guarantees immediate access to healthcare and it is this instant access rather than the actual treatment delivered that is often the key selling point. Medical insurance is also available, offering financial protection against illness and injury, although some people with poorer health, who are less affluent, are unable to afford it.

The main private sector hospital in Northern Ireland is the Ulster Independent Clinic in South Belfast, which, in addition to a wide range of healthcare treatment allows individuals (appropriately insured) to undergo operations without waiting and via their choice of surgeon.

NHS Consultants are free to operate a private practice as well as carry out their salaried NHS work. Many such consultants have private consulting rooms in their homes although some operate 'privately' within NHS facilities. A similar practice operates within dentistry; a dentist may offer the same service privately or on the NHS, with waiting times and costs differing greatly. Unlike the problems sometimes experienced in Britain, NHS dental services are widely available in Northern Ireland, although with long waiting times for NHS treatment, the private sector is growing.

This system has attracted much criticism on grounds of equity. It is argued that a two-tier health service is evolving with a high-quality instant service for those who can afford it and a lower quality service with long waiting lists for those who cannot. In addition, there are controversial regional disparities, whereby some treatments are available on the NHS (i.e. free) in some regions and not in others, which affects Northern Ireland adversely. An example is IVF (in-vitro fertilisation), a fertility treatment that is available on the NHS in various parts of the UK, but not in Northern Ireland. Northern Ireland tends to suffer from significantly less financial support for some treatments, which are not considered essential.

Ulster Independent Clinic
245 Stranmillis Road, Belfast
Tel: 028 9066 1212
Fax: 028 9038 1704

BUPA Health Screening Centre
14 Great Victoria Street, Belfast BT2 7BA
Tel: 028 90 232 723
Fax: 028 90 238 123

Complementary Medicine

Complementary medicine is a growing sector in Northern Ireland, including reflexology, Chinese medicine, homeopathy, acupuncture, chiropractic and hypnotherapy. These are not widely if at all available on the NHS, so patients have to pay for these types of health care.

Health Definitions

Acute Services/Secondary Care
Treatment and health care provided by hospitals

Acute Trusts
Trusts providing acute hospital care only

Community Care Services
Health or social care provided outside hospital

Community Trusts
Trusts providing Community Health and social services, but not acute hospital services

Primary Care
Health services provided by the GP, dentist, chemist, optician
Includes family and community health services and major components of social care delivered outside of hospitals, which may be accessed by an individual on their own behalf.

Social Care
Social care are services provided to help people cope with many types of personal hardship including:
• Physical or sensory disability;
• Protection of vulnerable children.

Hospitals and Hospices Listing

Hospitals A–Z

Albertbridge Road Day Hospital
225 Albertbridge Road, Belfast
Tel: 028 9045 6007
Fax: 028 9045 2638

Alexander Gardens Day Hospital
603 Antrim Road, Belfast BT15 4DR
Tel: 028 90802 171
Fax: 028 90802 176

Antrim Hospital
45 Bush Road, Antrim
Tel: 028 9442 4000
Fax: 028 9442 4654

Ards Community Hospital
Church Street, Newtownards BT23 4AS
Tel: 028 9181 2661
Fax: 028 9151 0113

Bangor Community Hospital
Castle Street, Bangor BT20 4TA
Tel: 028 9147 5100
Fax: 028 9147 5112

Belfast City Hospital
Lisburn Road, Belfast
Tel: 028 9032 9241
Fax: 028 9032 6614

Belvoir Park Hospital
Hospital Road, Belfast BT8 8JR
Tel: 028 9069 9069
Fax: 028 9069 9337

Braid Valley Hospital
Cushendall Road, Ballymena
Tel: 028 2563 5200
Fax: 028 2563 5237

Causeway Hospital
4 Newbridge Road, Coleraine
Tel: 028 7032 7032
Fax: 028 7034 6190

Craigavon Area Hospital
68 Lurgan Road, Portadown
Tel: 028 3833 4444
Fax: 028 3861 2471

Daisy Hill Hospital
5 Hospital Road, Newry
Tel: 028 3083 5000
Fax: 028 3025 0624

The Dental Hospital (RVH)
Grosvenor Road. Belfast
Tel: 028 9024 0503
Fax: 028 9043 8861

Downshire Hospital
Ardglass Road, Downpatrick
Tel: 028 4461 3311
Fax: 028 4461 2444

Downe Hospital
Pound Lane, Downpatrick
Tel: 028 4461 3311
Fax: 028 4461 5699

Erne Hospital
Cornagrade Road, Enniskillen
Tel: 028 6632 4711
Fax: 028 6638 2646

Forster Green Hospital
110 Saintfield Road, Belfast
Tel: 028 9079 3681
Fax: 028 9070 1526

Gransha Hospital
Clooney Road, Campsie, Londonderry
Tel: 028 7186 0261
Fax: 028 7186 5185

Holywell Hospital
60 Steeple Road, Antrim BT41 2RJ
Tel: 028 9446 5211
Fax: 028 9441 3190

Lagan Valley Hospital
Hillsborough Road, Lisburn
Tel: 028 9266 5141
Fax: 028 9266 6100

Lurgan Hospital
100 Sloan Street, Lurgan
Tel: 028 3832 3262
Fax: 028 3832 9483

Mater Infirmorum Hospital
47–51 Crumlin Road, Belfast
Tel: 028 90741 211
Fax: 028 90741 342

Mid Ulster Hospital
59 Hospital Road, Magherafelt
Tel: 028 7963 1031
Fax: 028 7963 3050

Mourne Hospital
Newry Street, Kilkeel
Tel: 028 4176 2235
Fax: 028 4176 9770

Moyle Hospital
Gloucester Ave, Larne BT40 1RP
Tel: 028 2827 5431
Fax: 028 2827 5346

Muckamore Abbey Hospital
1 Abbey Road, Muckamore, Antrim
Tel: 028 9446 3333
Fax: 028 9446 7730

Multiple Sclerosis Centre
Dalriada Hospital, 1a Coleraine Road,
Ballycastle BT54 6EY
Tel: 028 2076 3793
Fax: 028 2076 1501

Musgrave Park Hospital
Stockman's Lane, Belfast
Tel: 028 9066 9501
Fax: 028 9038 2008

Northwest Independent Hospital
Churchill House, Ballykelly, Limavady,
Co. Londonderry
Tel: 028 7776 3090
Fax: 028 7776 8306

Robinson Memorial Hospital
Newal Road, Ballymoney
Tel: 028 2766 0322
Fax: 028 2766 0326

Royal Belfast Hospital for Sick Children
184 Falls Road, Belfast BT12 6BA
Tel: 028 9024 0503
Fax: 028 9023 5340

Royal Maternity Hospital (RVH)
Grosvenor Road, Belfast BT12 6BA
Tel: 028 9024 0503
Fax: 028 9023 5256

Royal Victoria Hospital
Grosvenor Road, Belfast BT12 6BA
Tel: 028 9024 0503
Fax: 028 9023 5256

St Luke's Hospital
Loughall Road, Armagh
Tel: 028 3752 2381
Fax: 028 3752 6302

Shaftesbury Square Hospital
116–120 Great Victoria Street, Belfast
Tel: 028 9032 9808
Fax: 028 90321 2208

South Tyrone Hospital
Carland Road, Dungannon
Tel: 028 8772 2821
Fax: 028 8772 7332

Thompson House Hospital
19–21 Magheralave Road, Lisburn
Tel: 028 9266 5646
Fax: 028 9266 7681

Whiteabbey Hospital
Doagh Road, Newtownabbey,
Whiteabbey BT37 9RH
Tel: 028 9086 5181
Fax: 028 9036 5083

Hospices

Foyle Hospice
61 Culmore Road, Derry
Tel: 028 7135 1010
Fax: 028 7135 1011

Northern Ireland Hospice
74 Somerton Road, Belfast
Tel: 028 90 781 836
Fax: 028 90 370 585

Northern Ireland Hospice Children's Service
18 O'Neill Road, Belfast
Tel: 028 9077 7635
Fax: 028 9077 7144

Southern Area Hospice Services
St John's House, Courtenay Hill, Newry
Tel: 028 3026 7711
Fax: 028 3026 8492

Marie Curie Centre
Kensington Road, Belfast BT5 6NF
Tel: 028 9088 2000
Fax: 028 9088 2022

Housing in Northern Ireland

Overview

Until the reorganisation of local government in the early 1970s, responsibility for housing in Northern Ireland was held by local councils. In 1971 the Northern Ireland Housing Executive (NIHE) was created to take on this responsibility, under the then Department of the Environment. The NIHE was unique in that it was the UK's first comprehensive housing authority, with a wide range of powers and responsibilities beyond that of managing the public rented housing sector. The Department for Social Development has however, overall control over housing and housing policy, as outlined below.

Housing Market Analysis

The average price of houses in Northern Ireland across all types of property in 2002 was £95,000 compared with £47,661 in 1995 representing an increase of 99 per cent or 14 per cent per annum.

The highest percentage increases are in the terraced house market of 100 per cent over the five-year period from 1995 to 2000 and in the apartment market 125 per cent. Traditionally terraced housing has been the lowest cost sector offering an entry point into the private housing market in Northern Ireland; however, with price levels doubling from an average of £29.030 to £58,346 within a five-year period there are clearly implications for affordability.

With the average price of apartments increasing by 125 per cent since 1995 to reach an average price of £95,092 this sector is largely beyond the reach of first time buyers.

The semi detached housing market has risen in line with the overall market showing a 73 per cent increase over the five year period, although semi-detached bungalows have remained more affordable.

Affordability remains a critical issue when the 14 per cent increase in house prices per annum is compared with the average increase in incomes, which are increasing at a significantly lower rate of 4 per cent per annum. It is believed that the fundamental factor in maintaining affordability in Northern Ireland is low interest rates and the development of a flexible range of mortgage products. Thus, although housing prices have risen, monthly mortgage payments have not increased at the same rate. Whilst it is anticipated that interest rates will continue to remain at their current levels in the short to medium term, it is arguable that any significant rise in interest rates would have a severe impact on households in Northern Ireland triggering affordability problems.

Co-ownership Housing in Northern Ireland

Since the establishment of co-ownership, a concept where the mortgage burden can be lightened in exchange for equity, almost 16,000 properties have participated in the scheme with 12,000 having left. At the close of December 2000 4,236 properties remained in the scheme. In 1999/2000 587 new purchasers entered co-ownership and in 2000/2001 a further 510 entered co-ownership.

Although the scheme represents a significant initiative, co-ownership transactions represented less than 2 per cent of all housing transactions in 2000, reflecting the view of those in the housing industry that the scheme is not a major factor in the market.

Housing Policy

Under the Belfast Agreement responsibility for housing policy falls to the Housing Division within the Department for Social Development (DSD). The Division works closely with the Northern Ireland Housing Executive (NIHE) and the Registered Housing Associations (RHA). The Housing Division holds regulatory powers over these organisations, as well as overseeing that section of the private rented sector, which is controlled by the Rent (Northern Ireland) Order 1978. The Division also appoints the Board of the Northern Ireland Housing Executive and the Rent Assessment Panels.

The Housing Market in Northern Ireland				
	Dec 1990	**%**	**Dec 2000**	**%**
Owner Occupancy	347,000	60.9	442,000	68.2
NIHE	160,000	28.1	118,000	18.2
Housing Association	9,000	1.6	17,500	2.7
Private Rented	19,500	3.4	31,500	4.8
Vacant	34,500	6.1	39,500	6.1
Total	**570,000**		**648,500**	

Source: NIHE Housing Agenda 2002

Social Housing, Larne

For the financial year 2002/2003 the overall Housing budget will be around £612 million, obtained from rental income, capital receipts and government contribution. Within this total the Housing Executive's budget will be £537 million with around £73 million allocated to Housing Associations. An additional £35 million from private finance will supplement the social housing new build programme carried out by Housing Associations and the Co-Ownership Housing Association.

According to the Department for Social Development, new house prices fell throughout 2001, although remaining higher than in 2000. The price of a new NHBC (New Homes Building Council) registered house ranged from £57,000 to £188,000, with an average of £85,000. Flats and maisonettes were more expensive, averaging £97,000, reflecting the huge increase in 'luxury' apartments being built around Northern Ireland. The vast majority of new dwellings started were commissioned by the private sector, with over a third being detached.

The Northern Ireland Housing Executive

The Housing Centre
2 Adelaide Street, Belfast BT2 8PB
Tel: 028 9024 0588
Fax: 028 9031 8008

The Northern Ireland Housing Executive is a public body established under the Housing Executive (Northern Ireland) Act, 1971. Since then it has built over 80,000 new homes, housed more than 500,000 people, improved 350,000 homes in the private sector, and sold over 90,000 homes to sitting tenants.

Its primary responsibilities cover a wide range of issues relating to housing and its provision in Northern Ireland. The NIHE assesses housing conditions and requirements, and devises strategies to address them. It also seeks to improve the condition of housing stock where practical, and to demolish unfit housing. The NIHE manages its own housing stock and provides information and advice on housing issues. It works with the Housing Council, and with the 26 local district councils, and acts as the Home Energy Conservation Authority in Northern Ireland to encourage energy efficiency within the residential sector.

During 2001/02 the Housing Executive:
- Invested a net £240m in Northern Ireland;
- Approved over 10,000 grant applications in the private sector;
- Completed 2,495 major adaptations;
- Improved 1,997 Housing Executive homes;
- Carried out major repairs to over 23,000 Housing Executive homes;
- Paid £319m in Housing Benefits to public and private sector tenants.

Housing Board

Responsibility for general policy, management and operation of the Housing Executive lies with the Housing Board. The ten person Board, including chairman, Sid McDowell, meets every month and decides on all important matters affecting the Housing Executive including expenditure and new or revised policies. Seven members of the Board are appointed by the Minister responsible for housing, i.e. the Minister for Social Development, and the remaining three are nominated by the Northern Ireland Housing Council. At least one member must be female.

Members of the Board

Sid McDowell   Chairman
Jack Hood   Deputy Chairman
Anne Henderson
Kieran Brolly
Jane Jefferson
Brendan Mackin
Patsy McGlone
John Sheilds
Bobby McKee
Alistair Joynes

Chief Executive and Central Directors

The Chief Executive, Paddy McIntyre (pictured), is the accounting officer and chief officer in the Housing Executive and reports directly to the Board. He is responsible for setting the organisation's strategic direction and objectives and for ensuring performance is maintained.

The team of Central Directors report to the Chief Executive and as members of the Chief Executive's Management and Business Committees, decide on operational issues delegated by the Board as well as referring matters to it for approval. They are:

Arthur Halligan	Director of Finance
Colm McCaughley	Director of Client Services
Mike Shanks	Director of Development
Maureen Taggart	Director of Personnel and Management Services
Paul Brown	Director of Design Services
Imelda McGrath	Head of Information and Secretariat

The Structure of the Northern Ireland Housing Executive

The current structure of the Housing Executive is based on the following six divisions:

Corporate Services Division

The Director of Corporate Service Division is also the Deputy Chief Executive, presently Stewart Cuddy.

The division retains responsibility for strategic planning and research, information services and audit whilst taking responsibility for strategic relationships with housing associations and other private sector partners.

Housing and Regeneration

The division develops housing policy, landlord activity, commissioning and monitoring of physical projects including all regeneration activity.

Housing and regeneration is responsible for the management, maintenance and improvement of the Executive's 140,000 dwellings. Services are delivered to the public through a network of 37 local offices, including rent collection, maintenance, housing benefit, allocations, transfers and estate management.

District Managers report in turn to one of five Area managers. Schemes for the planned maintenance and improvement of dwellings are project managed by a province wide project services group. Building, maintenance and design standards are set by a technical standards group.

Design and Property Services

The division comprises all technical staff and is responsible for the design and delivery of physical programmes on site, as well as the management and operation of the private sector improvement grants function.

The division provides professional, technical and administrative support for the Housing Executive's programmes through five Practice Groups. Each Group operates as a business and has to compete with private sector consultants for Housing Executive work. The division also includes the Direct Labour Organisation.

Personnel and Management Services

This division maintains a range of support services:

Personnel:	covering training and development activities.
Facilities Services:	including purchasing, accommodation, health & safety, office services and security.
Legal Services:	providing legal advice to the Board and Directors.
Information Technology:	involved with the introduction and management of computerised systems.

Finance Division

The division provides support in relation to financial planning, financial accounting, management accounting and financial services.

Contact with Community Associations

The Housing Executive maintains regular contact with more than 500 community associations. This contact takes place at a local level with district officers, through local community associations and the District Consumer Panel. Contact at area level is with the Community Advisory Group and at central level, with the Central Community Advisory Group.

Northern Ireland Housing Council

The Housing Council was established by the Housing Executive Act (Northern Ireland) 1971. The Council is consulted by the Housing Executive and the DSD on all matters that affect housing policy in Northern Ireland. The Housing Executive meets once a month with the Housing Council, explaining operations and strategy. The Housing Council is made up of one representative from each of the 26 District Councils in Northern Ireland. There are three Housing Council members on the Board of the Housing Executive who are appointed for a one-year period.

Housing Executive Contact Details

Housing Executive Headquarters
The Housing Centre, 2 Adelaide Street,
Belfast BT2 8PB
Tel: 028 9024 0588

Area Offices

Belfast
32–36 Great Victoria Street
Belfast BT2 7BA
Tel: 028 9031 7000

Homeless Advice Centre
32–36 Great Victoria Street
Belfast BT2 7BA
Tel: 028 9031 7000

Private Sector

Housing Benefit
32–36 Great Victoria Street
Belfast BT2 7BA
Tel: 028 9031 7000

North East
Twickenham House, Mount Street,
Ballymena BT43 6BP
Tel: 028 2565 3399

South
Marlborough House, Central Way,
Craigavon BT64 1AJ
Tel: 028 3834 1188

South East
Strangford House, 28 Court Street
Newtownards BT23 7NX
Tel: 028 9182 0600

West
Richmond Chambers, The Diamond
Derry BT48 6QP
Tel: 028 7137 2000

District Offices

Antrim
48 High Street, Antrim BT41 4AN
Tel: 028 9442 8142

Armagh
48 Dobbin Street
Armagh BT61 7QQ
Tel: 028 3752 3379

Ballycastle
Fleming House, Coleraine Road,
Ballycastle BT54 6EY
Tel: 028 2076 2014

Ballymena
Twickenham House, Mount Street
Ballymena BT43 6BP
Tel: 028 2564 4211

Ballymoney
50–54 Main Street
Ballymoney BT53 6AL
Tel: 028 2766 3442

Banbridge
56 Bridge Street, Banbridge BT32 3JU
Tel: 028 4066 2721

Bangor
2 Alfred Street, Bangor BT20 5DH
Tel: 028 9127 0761

Belfast 1
9 Upper Queen Street, Belfast BT1 6FB
Tel: 028 9032 8282

Belfast 2
Laganview House, 95 Ann Street,
Belfast BT1 3HH
Tel: 028 9032 4558

Belfast 3
Murray House, Murray Street, Belfast
BT1 6DN
Tel: 028 9032 3642

Belfast 4
10–16 Hill Street, Belfast BT1 2LA
Tel: 028 9024 1525

Belfast 5
83–87 Shankill Road
Belfast BT13 1FD
Tel: 028 9032 9442

Belfast 6
1st Floor, Spencer House
71 Royal Avenue, Belfast BT1 1FE
Tel: 028 9032 6477

Belfast 7
90–106 Victoria Street
Belfast BT1 3GN
Tel: 028 9024 8312

Brownlow (Craigavon)
16 Legahory Centre
Craigavon BT65 5BE
Tel: 028 3834 4631

Carrickfergus
19 High Street
Carrickfergus BT38 7AN
Tel: 028 9335 1115

Castlereagh
30 Church Road
Dundonald BT16 2LN
Tel: 028 9048 5237

Coleraine
19 Abbey Street, Coleraine BT52 1DU
Tel: 028 7035 8111

Cookstown
15 Morgan's Hill Road
Cookstown BT80 8HA
Tel: 028 8676 2004

Dairy Farm
Stewartstown Road
Belfast BT17 0SB
Tel: 028 9061 1199

Downpatrick
51 John Street
Downpatrick BT30 6HS
Tel: 028 4461 3551

Dungannon
Ballygawley Road
Dungannon BT70 1EL
Tel: 028 8772 3000

Fermanagh
Riverview House
Head Street, Enniskillen BT74 7JT
Tel: 028 6632 5770

Larne
Sir Thomas Dixon Buildings
Victoria Road, Larne BT40 1RU
Tel: 028 2827 4426

Limavady
33 Catherine Street
Limavady BT49 9DA
Tel: 028 7776 2711

Lisburn
29 Antrim Street, Lisburn BT28 1AU
Telephone 028 9266 5222

Londonderry 1
Ulster Bank Chambers
Waterloo Place, Derry BT48 6BS
Tel: 028 7126 6227

Londonderry 2
2 Glendermott Road
Waterside, Derry BT47 1AU
Tel: 028 7131 1490

Londonderry 3
14 Collon Terrace, Derry BT48 7QP
Tel: 028 7137 3683

Lurgan
122 Hill Street, Lurgan BT66 6BU
Tel: 028 3832 6417

Magherafelt
3 Ballyronan Road
Magherafelt BT45 6BP
Tel: 028 7963 1121

Newry
35–45 Boat Street, Newry BT34 2DB
Tel: 028 3026 7331

Newtownabbey 1
Rantalard House, Rathcoole Drive
Rathcoole, Newtownabbey BT37 9AG
Tel: 028 9036 5911

Newtownabbey 2
2 Ballyearl Drive, New Mossley
Newtownabbey BT36 5XJ
Tel: 028 9084 3711

Newtownards
2 Frederick Street
Newtownards BT23 4LR
Tel: 028 9181 6979

Omagh
Riverston House, 7 Holmview Terrace
Omagh BT79 0AH
Tel: 028 8224 7701

Portadown
41 Thomas Street
Portadown BT62 3AF
Tel: 028 3836 1895

Strabane
48 Railway Road, Strabane BT82 8EH
Tel: 028 7138 2637

Home Improvement Grant Offices

Ballyclare
141 Hill Road, Ballyclare BT39 9DZ
Tel: 028 9335 2849

Ballymena
Twickenham House, Mount Street
Ballymena BT43 6BP
Tel: 028 2565 3399

Belfast
32–36 Great Victoria Street
Belfast BT2 7BA
Tel: 028 9031 7000

Craigavon
Marlborough House, Central Way
Craigavon BT64 1AJ
Tel: 028 3834 1188

Fermanagh
Riverview House, Head Street
Enniskillen BT74 7JT
Tel: 028 6632 5770

Lisburn
4 Graham Gardens
Lisburn BT28 1XE
Tel: 028 9266 5222

Londonderry
Richmond Chambers
The Diamond, Derry BT48 6QP
Tel: 028 7137 2000

Newry
35–45 Boat Street, Newry BT34 2DB
Tel: 028 3026 7331

Newtownards
Strangford House, 28 Court Street
Newtownards BT23 7NX
Telephone 028 9182 0600

Omagh
McAllister House
Woodside Avenue, Omagh BT79 7BP
Tel: 028 8224 6111

Housing in Multiple Occupation

32–36 Great Victoria Street
Belfast, BT2 7BA
Tel: 028 9031 7000

19 Abbey Street
Coleraine
BT52 1DU
Tel: 028 7035 8111

After Hours Homeless Service

Armagh
Tel: 028 3752 2381

Banbridge
Telephone 028 3833 4444

Belfast Inner & Greater
Tel: 028 9056 5444

Co Antrim
Tel: 028 9446 8833

Co Down (East, Mid & North)
Tel: 028 9056 5444

Coleraine
Tel: 028 9446 8833

Craigavon
Tel: 028 3833 4444

Derry
Tel: 028 7134 5171

Dungannon
Tel: 028 3752 2381

Enniskillen
Tel: 028 6632 4711

Magherafelt
Tel: 028 9446 8833

Newry & Mourne
Tel: 028 3083 5000

Omagh
Tel: 028 8224 5211

Housing Associations A–Z

Abbeyfield Housing Association
3 Grand Parade, Belfast BT5 5HG
Tel: 028 9040 2045
Fax: 028 9070 3776

Abode Housing Association
2a Wesley Court, Carrickfergus
Co. Antrim BT38 8HS
Tel: 028 9336 0973
Fax: 028 9336 1472
Chairman: W C Balmer

Ark Housing Association
9 Stranmillis Road, Belfast BT9 5AF
Tel: 028 9068 1808
Fax: 028 9066 4524
Chairman: Oliver Magill

Ballynafeigh Housing Association Ltd
70 Kimberly Street, Belfast   BT7 3DY
Tel: 028 9049 1569
Fax: 028 9064 3068

Belfast Community Housing Association Ltd
131 Ravenhill Road, Belfast BT6 8DR
Tel: 028 9045 7300
Fax: 028 9046 0788

BIH Housing Association Ltd
Russell Court, Claremont Street, Belfast BT9 6JX
Tel: 028 9032 0485
Fax: 028 9033 0402
Chairman: Nuala Lynch

Broadway Housing Association Ltd
Bedeque House, 3 Annesley Street, Belfast BT14 6AJ
Tel: 028 9074 2984

Choice Housing Association
95A Finaghy Road South, Belfast BT10 0BY
Tel: 028 9030 6920
Fax: 028 9030 6929

Clanmil Housing
Waring Street, Belfast BT1 2DX
Tel: 028 9087 6000
Fax: 028 9087 6001
Chairman: Derek Rankin
Chief Executive and Secretary: Clare McCarty

Connswater Housing Association Ltd
2 Severn Street, Belfast BT4 1FB
Tel: 028 9045 6596
Fax: 028 9046 6539

The Covenanter Residential Association Ltd
Cameron House, 98 Lisburn Road, Belfast BT9 6AG
Tel: 028 9066 4875

Donacloney Housing Association Ltd
38 Main Street, Donaghcloney, Craigavon BT66 7LR
Tel: 028 3888 1307
Fax: 028 3888 1307

Dungannon & District Housing Association Ltd
27 Market Square, Dungannon BT70 1JD
Tel: 028 8772 2121
Fax: 028 8775 3870

Filor Housing Association Ltd
282–290 Crumlin Road, Belfast BT14 7EE
Tel: 028 9035 1131
Fax: 028 9074 1755
President: Col Filor

Fold Housing Association
3 Redburn Square, Holywood BT18 9HZ
Tel: 028 9042 8314
Fax: 028 9042 8167
(see full listing on facing page)

Gosford Housing Association Armagh Ltd
6 Georges Street, Armagh BT60 1BY
Tel: 028 3752 8272
Fax: 028 3752 8272

Grove Housing Association Ltd
139 York Road, Belfast BT15 3GZ
Tel: 028 9074 0803
Fax: 028 9074 3520
Chairperson: Miss A Gibson

Habinteg Housing Association (Ulster) Ltd
Alex Moira House, 22 Hibernia Street, Holywood BT18 9JE
Tel: 028 9042 7211
Fax: 028 9042 8069
Chairman: John Cole

Hearth Housing Association
66 Donegal Pass, Belfast BT7 1BU
Tel: 028 9053 0121
Fax: 028 9053 0122
Chairman: Mrs K Latimer

FOLD HOUSING ASSOCIATION

working with people

Special Needs Housing

Fold Housing Association
3 Redburn Square
Holywood BT18 9HZ
Tel: 028 9042 8314
Fax: 028 9042 8167
Web: www.foldgroup.co.uk

Chairman: William Cameron OBE

**Chief Executive:
Brian Coulter**

FOLD, a non-profit body, has provided housing and care services since 1976. The FOLD Group consists of FOLD Housing Association, FOLD Trust and FOLD Help Limited.

FOLD manages 3,900 properties and employs 600 people delivering the following:

- Rented family housing.
- Tenanted Sheltered housing.
- Sheltered housing for lease/sale.
- Residential and Day Care.
- Home Improvement Services for elderly/ disabled.
- Community Alarms/assistive technology.
- 24-hours alarm monitoring for around 18,000 users.
- Special Needs Housing.

Larne & District Housing Association
Pound Green Court, St Johns Place, Larne BT40 1TB
Tel: 028 2826 7533

Millbern Trust
18 Hamel Court, Belfast BT6 9HX
Tel: 028 9079 5563
Fax: 028 9070 5758

CO-OWNERSHIP HOUSING

Co-Ownership
Housing

Northern Ireland Co-Ownership Housing Association Limited

Murray House, Murray Street
Belfast BT1 6DN
Tel: 028 9032 7276
Fax: 028 9033 0720
Web: www.co-ownership.org

Director: Kevin Butler

NICHA operates a form of Do It Yourself Shared Ownership (DIYSO) scheme called Co-Ownership throughout Northern Ireland. The scheme provides a low-cost route into home ownership for people who could not afford to buy a home of their own otherwise. Purchasers start with a 50%, 62.5% or 75% share in the property of their choice, and may increase their share at any time. Over 17,000 homes have been purchased through Co-Ownership to date.

Newington Housing Association (1975) Ltd
300 Limestone Road, Belfast BT15 3AR
Tel: 028 9074 4055
Chairperson: Mr P Privilege

North Belfast Mission Housing Society Ltd
17 Palmerston Road, Belfast BT4 1QA
Tel: 028 9336 3558
Fax: 028 9335 5319
Chairman: H S Hughes
Chief Executive: L McAdams

North & West Housing Ltd
18 Magazine Street, Derry BT48 6HH
Tel: 028 7126 3819
Fax: 028 7126 3362

Northern Ireland Federation of Housing Associations
38 Hill Street, Belfast BT1 2LB
Tel: 028 9023 0446
Fax: 028 9023 8057
NIFHA is the umbrella organisation for the Housing Association sector providing a range of representational and other services for its members.

OAKLEE HOUSING ASSOCIATION

Head Office
Leslie Morrell House
37-41 May Street
Belfast BT1 4DN
Tel: (028) 9044 1300
Fax: (028) 9044 1346
Web: www.oaklee.org.uk

Oaklee Housing Association provides quality, affordable housing and care services for older people, single persons and small households, family housing and supported housing for adults with special needs.

Open Door Housing Association (NI) Ltd
10–14 Commercial Court, Belfast BT1 2NB
Tel: 028 9024 3785
Fax: 028 9023 5336
Chairman: Paddy Gray

Presbyterian Housing Association (NI) Ltd
7a Weavers Court, Linfield Road, Belfast BT12 5GH
Tel: 028 9050 7755
Fax: 028 9050 7756
Chairman: Mr S W Parker

Rural Housing Association Ltd
Unit B11 Omagh Business Complex, Derry Road
Omagh BT78 5DY
Tel: 028 8224 6118
Fax: 028 8224 6120
Web: www.ruralhousing.co.uk/
Chairman: Mr A Kane
Chief Executive: Paddy McGurk

St Matthews Housing Association Ltd
58 Harper Street, Belfast BT5 4EN
Tel: 028 9045 1070

South Ulster Housing Association Ltd
20 Carleton Street, Portadown BT62 3EN
Tel: 028 3833 9795
Fax: 028 3835 0944

Strathfoyle Tenants Maintenance Ltd
34 Bawnmore Place, Strathfoyle, Derry BT47 1XP
Tel: 028 7186 0077
Fax: 028 7186 1444

Students Housing Association Co-op Ltd (SHAC)
29 Bedford Street, Belfast BT2 7EJ
Tel: 028 9024 6811
Fax: 028 9033 3724
Chairperson: Mark McClean

Triangle Housing Association Ltd
60 Eastermeade Gardens, Ballymoney BT53 6BD
Tel: 028 2766 6880
Fax: 028 2766 2994
Chairperson: Sheila Dwyer

Ulidia Housing Association Ltd
20 Derryvolgie Avenue, Belfast BT9 6FM
Tel: 028 9038 2288
Fax: 028 9038 2738
Chief Executive Officer: John Gartlan

Ulster Provident Housing Association
Carlisle Memorial Centre, 88 Clifton Street, Belfast BT13 1AB
Tel: 028 9031 1156

Woodvale & Shankill Housing Association Ltd
93 Woodvale Road, Belfast BT13 3BP
Tel: 028 9074 1618
Fax: 028 9074 7407

CHAPTER 7

Education and Training in Northern Ireland

Overview of the Northern Ireland Education System

Introduction

Children in Northern Ireland are legally obliged to attend school between the ages of 5 and 16. The system has three learning levels: primary, secondary and tertiary. In addition to this are pre-school/nursery and higher/adult education. Most children in Northern Ireland begin primary school at the age of 4. Primary education is geared toward completion of the UK Government's Key Stages 1 and 2, a curriculum designed to ensure basic standards of literacy and numeracy, as well as some initial science and possibly a foreign language. While in their last year at primary school, many pupils take what is known as the '11 plus' exam. This is a formal examination, the results of which for the most part determine the type of secondary school the child will attend.

According to their performance in the 11 plus, children progress to one of a variety of educational institutions. The most academically able children (according to the examination) for the most part attend a grammar school. These schools are generally focused towards academic results, normally A-levels, traditionally seen as the passport to a university place.

The majority of the remainder of children, i.e. those who do not attain a high enough grade in the examination, or those who do not sit it, attend comprehensive or secondary intermediate schools, which tend to be more vocational in their outlook. A smaller proportion of these pupils go on to attain A-levels and move onward to university, although many study for more vocational qualifications such as GNVQs.

Whilst different types of secondary school each have their own priorities, all are obliged to follow the curriculum formulated by the UK Department of Education. This tries to ensure that pupils leave school with certain basic levels of literacy and numeracy, as well as studying science and at least one foreign language.

A small percentage of children leave school with no qualifications, and some leave directly after taking their GCSE exams. However the majority stay on to undertake further qualifications. As well as secondary schools, many colleges of higher and further education offer both academic and vocational qualifications. Students can resit GCSEs and study for A-levels, BTECs, HNCs (Higher National Certificate) and HNDs (Higher National Diplomas) in a wide range of subjects. This can then lead to university, or alternatively provides a vocational qualification which is useful in the workplace.

As the needs of society change the education system seeks to be flexible and is currently supporting both the desire to increase availability of pre-school provision and encourage life-long learning. Alongside traditional, formal education there is also the Open University, offering part-time university education, and numerous colleges providing nighttime and daytime classes for part-time students. Despite this flexibility, however, there remain a number of perceived inequities in the system of education in Northern Ireland. Many educationalists regard the selection system as being more than unsatisfactory while others see the religious segregation of Northern Ireland's pupil population as being the fundamental weakness in the system. In addition there are concerns about pupil teacher ratios and the level of investment and resources allocated to education. Some of the principal issues facing the sector are discussed later in this chapter.

Structure of the Northern Ireland Education System

The structure of the education system in Northern Ireland is complex with ten Statutory Bodies involved in the management and administration of the system, including:

- The Department of Education;
- The Education and Library Boards (5);
- The Council for Catholic Maintained Schools;
- The Northern Ireland Council for the Curriculum, Examinations and Assessment (CCEA);
- The Staff Commission for the Education and Library Boards;
- The Youth Council for Northern Ireland.

There are also a number of voluntary bodies involved in the administration of the education system, including the Northern Ireland Council for Integrated Education, Comhairle na Gaelscolaiochta, (the council for Irish-medium schools) the Transferor Representatives Council which brings together representatives of the Transferor Churches (Church of Ireland, Presbyterian and Methodist); the Association of Governing Bodies which represents the voluntary grammar schools.

The roles and functions of these bodies are described in detail in the relevant sections below. However, there follows a brief overview of the main responsibilities of the Department, the Education and Library Boards (ELBs) and the Council for Catholic Maintained Schools (CCMS) to provide a context for the later material.

The Department of Education

The Department of Education is responsible for the central administration of education and related services in Northern Ireland. Its primary duties are to promote the education of young people in Northern Ireland and to secure the effective execution of its policy in relation to the provision of the education service. The structure, functions and senior personnel of the Department of Education are set out in detail in Chapter 4, Government Departments and Agencies.

Education and Library Boards

There are five Education and Library Boards (ELBs), which are the local education authorities and library authorities for their areas. ELBs have a statutory responsibility to ensure that there are sufficient schools of all kinds to meet the needs of their area; to provide all the finance for the schools under their management; and to equip, maintain and meet other running costs of maintained schools. ELB expenditure is funded at 100 per cent by the Department but the funding arrangements are necessarily complex:

- Expenditure provision for some services is determined centrally by the Department because such expenditure is demand determined or where there are specific initiatives targeted on specific schools across Northern Ireland;
- The bulk of ELB funding is through a Block Grant: ELBs have responsibility for considering the relative priority of different services in their areas and they reflect their views in financial schemes which are subject to Departmental approval;
- The total provision for block grant is distributed by the ELBs by an objective and open methodology (the Assessment of Relative Needs Exercise: ARNE);
- A wide range of need indicators are used in this formula with pupil population being the most important;
- Some 5 per cent of the total is distributed on the basis of the number of pupils in each area entitled to free school meals under Targeting Social Need (TSN).

Enrolments in Educational Institutions

Table 7.1 shows the current levels of educational provision in Northern Ireland in terms of numbers and categories of educational institution, along with associated student numbers.

Table 7.1: Educational Attendance by Type of Institution 2001		
Education Type	**Number**	**Number of Students**
NURSERY	95	11,931
PRE-SCHOOL*	305	3,957 (funded)
PRIMARY	902	174,481
SECONDARY (Excl Grammar)	166	92,979
GRAMMAR (Years 8-14)	72	62,574
SPECIAL	48	4,674
INDEPENDENT	27	1,255
HOSPITAL	3	171

Source: NISRA

*Pre-school = Voluntary and private pre-school centres

In addition there are 17 Further Education (FE) Colleges, and 2 Universities: the traditional red-brick Queen's University of Belfast, and the more recent University of Ulster, split between campuses at Jordanstown, Coleraine and Derry.

The number of students attending Northern Ireland's educational institutions has increased gradually, in most categories, in recent years as illustrated in table 7.2.

Although the increases in attendance in the primary and secondary sectors are largely a function of population growth, the recent rapid expansion of third level attendances reflects the policy continued by successive governments, of opening up third level opportunities to as many as possible.

Table 7.2: Schools - Number of Pupils

	1987/88	1990/91	1993/94	1996/97	1999/00	2000/01
Nursery						
- Full-time	2,677	2,702	2,839	2,983	3,277	3,304
- Part-time	2,170	2,224	2,434	2,513	2,675	2,661
Nursery classes (primary schools)						
- Full-time	1,838	1,729	1,747	1,901	2,629	3,225
- Part-time	530	838	853	1,125	1,418	2,741
Primary - Reception	1,868	2,084	2,394	2,499	2,318	1,963
Primary - Years 1-7	178,263	181,233	181,852	181,284	172,591	169,700
Grammar Preparatory - Reception	–	23	24	45	12	27
Grammar Preparatory - Years 1-7	3,815	3,641	3,633	3,354	3,011	2,791
Secondary (excluding Grammar)	92,534	86,667	89,167	90,746	92,603	92,979
Grammar - Years 8-14	52,466	54,479	59,097	61,997	62,361	62,574
Special Schools	3,811	3,983	4,392	4,680	4,688	4,674
Hospital Schools	245	234	191	178	173	171
Independent Schools	1,119	1,023	939	925	1,243	1,255
Total All Schools	**341,336**	**340,880**	**349,562**	**354,230**	**348,999**	**348,065**

Source: Department of Education

Table 7.3: Further Education Colleges

	1987/88	1990/91	1993/94	1996/97	1999/00	2000/01
All Vocational Students						
- Full-time	–	18,065	23,125	25,033	24,128	24,542
- Part-time	–	53,356	58,398	60,069	65,251	66,767
Students on non-vocational courses	51,178	53,505	46,680	59,087	66,732	N/A

Source: Department of Education

Table 7.4: Higher Education (NI Domiciled Students)

	1987/88	1990/91	1993/94	1996/97	1999/00	2000/01
Full-Time Undergraduates	20,640	24,617	31,331	34,940	38,414	39,133
Part-Time Undergraduates	4,801	5,949	7,276	15,079	18,618	19,137
Full-Time Post Graduates	1,722	2,186	2,871	3,382	3,524	3,627
Part-Time Post Graduates	2,574	3,485	4,620	5,650	5,625	5,036
Total	**29,737**	**36,237**	**46,098**	**59,051**	**66,181**	**66,933**

Source: Department of Education

Main Categories of School in Northern Ireland

There are a number of types of school in Northern Ireland, differing in the level of government control, as well as management structures. The main types are detailed below:

Controlled Schools

In terms of the religious divide in Northern Ireland's education system, controlled schools are essentially Protestant in terms of staffing, management and pupil intake. Controlled schools are managed by ELBs, who act as the employer, through Boards of Governors. Primary and secondary school Boards of Governors consist of representatives of transferors (mainly the Protestant Churches) along with representatives of parents, teachers and ELBs. Nursery, grammar and special school Boards of Governors consist of representatives of the latter three categories.

Maintained Schools

These schools are largely regarded as Catholic schools. Whilst they have a relatively close relationship with their local Education and Library Board, they are also aligned with the Council for Catholic Maintained Schools (CCMS), which is the employing authority for teaching staff. The ELB is the employing authority for non-teaching staff. In all non-Catholic maintained schools, the Board of Governors is the employing authority for all staff members. Maintained schools are able to exercise a somewhat greater degree of autonomy.

Voluntary Schools

Voluntary schools are quite independent of external control. Most voluntary schools are grammar schools with around 28,000 pupils under Catholic management, and around 20,000 pupils under Protestant management. There is also a large pre-school block of around 3,500 children, which operates with considerable autonomy.

Voluntary (Under Catholic Management)

This type of voluntary school is managed by Boards of Governors which consist of members nominated by trustees (mainly Roman Catholic), along with representatives of parents, teachers and ELBs. Voluntary schools vary in the rates of capital grant to which they are entitled, depending on the management structures they have adopted. A majority are entitled to capital grants at 100 per cent.

Voluntary (Under Other Management)

These are mainly voluntary grammar schools, managed by Boards of Governors which consist of persons appointed as provided in each school's scheme of management, along with representatives of parents and teachers and, in most cases, members appointed by the Department or ELBs. Voluntary Grammar schools have been funded directly by the Department but, under the 1998 Education Order, this responsibility is handed to ELBs.

Grant-Maintained Integrated Schools

In recent years a number of grant-maintained integrated schools have been established at primary and post-primary levels. Such schools have been funded directly by the Department but, under the 1998 Education Order, responsibility was passed to ELBs.

The practical operation of all schools has increasingly become a matter for Boards of Governors. They are responsible for the delivery of the curriculum, admission of pupils, and in the case of schools with delegated budgets, for the management of their own financial affairs, including staff matters.

Controlled Integrated Schools

Within the controlled sector there is a small but growing number of controlled integrated schools. Many of these have made a conscious decision to change over to integrated status.

Pre-School Education

Pre-school education is broken down into nursery and reception classes, provided by the state and by the independent sector. In recent years there has been much debate on the levels and funding of pre-school provision. In 1995/96 there were 10,785 children in funded places. Currently there are 17,878 children in funded places (11,931 in nursery classes, 1,990 in reception classes and 3,957 in voluntary/private pre-school education centres). This is a significant increase but may still leave as many as 7,000 children with no funded provision at all.

Table 7.5: Pre-School Education Places 2000/01								
Nursery Schools	Nursery Schools	Nursery Class in Primary Schools	Nursery Class in Primary Schools	Primary School Reception	Playgroup (funded places)	Day Nursery (funded places)	Other Provision (funded places)	Totals
Full-time	Part-time	Full-time	Part-time	Full-time	Part-time	Part-time	Part-time	
Controlled Schools								
1,897	2,455	1,801	1,512	686	–	–	–	8,351
Catholic Maintained Schools								
1,407	206	1,372	996	1,254	–	–	–	5,235
Other Maintained Schools								
–	–	26	–	4	–	–	–	30
Controlled Integrated Schools								
–	–	–	–	34	–	–	–	34
Grant Maintained Integrated Schools								
–	–	26	233	–	–	–	–	259
Voluntary Schools								
–	–	–	–	12	–	–	–	12
Voluntary Pre-School Centres								
–	–	–	–	–	3,461	–	12	3,473
Private Pre-School Centres								
–	–	–	–	–	306	178	–	484
Totals	3,304	2,661	3,225	2,741	1,990	3,767	178	12	17,878

Source: NISRA

Primary Education

Primary education is normally organised on the basis of a delivery period of seven years. Despite its informal appearance primary education is carefully structured against a detailed curriculum. Primary education is dominated by two categories of school: Controlled State Schools and Catholic Maintained Schools. Together they account for 95 per cent of all primary school enrolments. The remainder is accounted for by integrated primary schools.

Primary Curriculum

The Northern Ireland Curriculum, which was established by the Education Reform (Northern Ireland) Order 1989, set out the minimum educational entitlement for pupils aged 4 to 16 years. The Order was amended in 1993 and in 1996.

The 1989 Order requires schools to provided a curriculum for all pupils which:

- Promotes the spiritual, moral, cultural, intellectual and physical development of pupils at the school and thereby of society; and
- Prepares such pupils for the opportunities and experiences of adult life.

The Northern Ireland Curriculum was introduced on a phased basis from 1990. It was reviewed in 1994 and the revised Northern Ireland Curriculum was introduced in September 1996. It is currently being updated and the intended date for implementation is September 2002.

The curriculum is defined in terms of four key stages which cover the 12 years of compulsory schooling. Primary education incorporates Key Stages 1 and 2 as follows:

- Key Stage 1 covers school years 1-4 for pupils aged 4-8;
- Key Stage 2 covers school years 5-7 for pupils aged 8-11.

The Northern Ireland Curriculum does not constitute the whole curriculum for schools. Schools can develop additional curriculum elements to express their particular ethos and meet pupils' individual needs and circumstances.

Key Stages 1 and 2

The curriculum for Key Stages 1 and 2 includes:

- English;
- Mathematics;
- Science and Technology;
- History and Geography (known as the Environment and Society Area of Study);
- Art and Design, Music and Physical Education (known as the Creative and Expressive Area of Study);
- Religious Education;
- Irish, in Irish speaking schools only; and
- Four educational cross-curricular themes (Education for Mutual Understanding, Cultural Heritage, Health Education and Information Technology). The educational themes are not separate subjects but are woven through the main subjects of the curriculum.

Content

Each subject in the Northern Ireland Curriculum is defined within the Programmes of Study and Attainment Targets. There may be different numbers of Attainment Targets in each subject.

Programmes of Study

The Programmes of Study set out the opportunities which should be offered to all pupils, subject to their age and ability, in terms of the knowledge, skills and understanding at each key stage. Teachers use the programmes of study as a basis for planning schemes of work.

Attainment Targets

Attainment Targets define the expected standards of pupil performance in particular aspects of a subject in terms of Level Descriptions. These provide the basis for making judgements on pupils' attainment at the end of each key stage.

Level Descriptions

There are eight levels in each attainment target. For each level there is a Level Description indicating the type and range of attainment that a pupil working at that level should demonstrate. Teachers select the Level Description which best fits a pupil's performance over a period of time.

At the end of Key Stage 1, it is expected that the majority of pupils will be working at Level 2. At the end of Key Stage 2, it is expected that the majority of pupils will be working at either Level 3 or 4.

Secondary Education

Northern Ireland Curriculum

The Northern Ireland Curriculum, sets out the educational entitlement for pupils aged 11 to 16 years.

Second level education is defined as covering key stages 3 and 4 as follows:

- Key Stage 3, covers school years 8-10 for pupils aged 12-14;
- Key Stage 4, covers school years 11-12 for pupils aged 15-16.

The curricular requirements for Key Stages 3 and 4 are:

Key Stage 3

- English;
- Mathematics;
- Science, Technology and Design;
- History and Geography (known as the Environment and Society Area of Study);
- Art and Design, Music and Physical Education (known as the Creative and Expressive Area of Study);
- French or German or Italian or Spanish or Irish (known as the Modern Languages Area of Study);

- Religious Education;
- Six educational themes (Education for Mutual Understanding, Cultural Heritage, Health Education, Information Technology, Economic Awareness and Careers Education).

Key Stage 4

- English;
- Mathematics;
- Science;
- A course in one of History, Geography, Business Studies, Home Economics, Economics, Politics or an appropriate modular provision;
- Physical Education;
- Religious Education;
- An approved course in a modern language;and
- Six educational themes (Education for Mutual Understanding, Cultural Heritage, Health Education, Information Technology, Economic Awareness and Careers Education).

As with primary education the content of each subject in the Northern Ireland Curriculum at Key Stage 3 and 4 is defined in a Statutory Order and each Order consists of Programmes of Study and Attainment Targets.

At the end of Key Stage 3, it is expected that the majority of pupils will be working at either Level 5 or 6.

Table 7.6 outlines the main school types in the secondary sector. Broadly, there are four main categories of school - Catholic secondary and grammar and non-Catholic secondary and grammar.

Table 7.6: Northern Ireland Secondary Sector 2001	Pupils in non-grammar Secondary Schools	Pupils in Grammar Schools
Controlled Schools (non-grammar)	38,577	0
Controlled Schools (grammar)	0	14,691
Catholic Maintained Schools	45,382	0
Maintained Irish Medium Schools	332	0
Controlled Integrated Schools	1,935	0
Grant Maintained Integrated Schools	6,753	0
Voluntary Schools under Catholic Management	0	27,897
Voluntary Schools under other management	0	19,986
Totals		
1. Number of pupils	92,979	62,574
2. No.of pupils as %	59.8%	40.2%
Source: NISRA		

Third Level Education

In terms of institutions, tertiary level education in Northern Ireland consists of the two main universities (Queen's University, Belfast and the University of Ulster), two teacher-training colleges (St Mary's and Stranmillis) and 18 Further Education Colleges, including specialist centres for agriculture and catering. Several thousand people in Northern Ireland are also enrolled in the Open University. Participation in third-level education has grown steadily in recent years in Northern Ireland, across both the university and FE sectors, approximately doubling in number over a twenty-year period.

The number of students progressing to full-time undergraduate study has almost doubled since 1987. Additionally, the number of students availing of such study opportunities outside Northern Ireland has also doubled.

Details of Northern Ireland's two universities are set out overleaf, including faculty and departmental listings and names of senior university personnel.

QUEEN'S UNIVERSITY BELFAST

Queen's University Belfast
University Road
Belfast
BT7 1NN
Tel: (028) 9024 5133
Fax: (028) 9024 7895
Web: www.qub.ac.uk

As a top 20 UK university Queen's gives Northern Ireland an international profile through world-class research and teaching, making a major contribution to economic, social and cultural development.

Queen's is the longer established of Northern Ireland's two universities, founded in 1845 as Queen's College, part of the National University of Ireland. In 1908 Queen Victoria conferred university status on the college. The University offers a comprehensive range of courses across a number of faculties. Independent assessment of the teaching and research carried out at the University has placed it in the top 20 out of 170 colleges assessed in the UK. Queen's has a total of around 17,500 undergraduates and postgraduate students, plus a further 10,000 enrolled part-time students. Around 7,000 full-time and part-time students enrol each year and the university awards some 3,000 degrees and 1200 higher degrees annually.

Queen's University is one of Belfast's biggest employers, employing around 3,500 staff including 1,600 teaching and research staff.

Senior Officers of the University

Chancellor:	Senator George Mitchell
Pro-Chancellors:	Brenda McLaughlin
	Christopher Gibson
President and Vice Chancellor:	Professor George S Bain
Pro-Vice-Chancellors:	Professor Ken Brown (Academic Planning & Resources)
	Professor Robert J Crawford (Research and Development)
	Professor K L Bell (Students and Learning)
	Professor F G McCormac (Community and Communication)
Hon Treasurer:	Teresa Townsley
Registrar:	James P J O'Kane

Table 7.7: Staff Numbers 2001

Staff 2000/01	Full Time	Part Time
Academic	804	39
Academic Related	932	124
Clerical	463	181
Technical	298	31
Others	273	203
Total	**2770**	**578**

Academic Units

Faculty of Engineering
Schools: Aeronautical Engineering, Architecture, Chemical Engineering, Civil Engineering, Computer Science, Electrical and Electronic Engineering, Environmental Planning, Mechanical and Manufacturing Engineering, Northern Ireland Technology Centre.

Faculty of Medicine and Health Sciences
Schools: Dentistry, Medicine, Nursing and Midwifery, Medicine Research Office.

Faculty of Humanities
Schools: English, Classics and Ancient History, Languages, Literatures and Arts, Modern History, Music, Philosophical Studies, Anthropological Studies, Institutes: Irish Studies, Theology, Byzantine Studies.

Faculty of Legal, Social and Educational Sciences
Schools: Law, Management and Economics, Politics, Social Work, Sociology and Social Policy, Institutes: European Studies, Governance, Graduate School of Education, University Colleges: Stranmillis, Saint Mary's, Institute of Lifelong Learning, Armagh Outreach Campus.

Faculty of Science and Agriculture

Schools: Agriculture and Food Science, Archaeology and Palaeoecology, Biology and Biochemistry, Chemistry, Geography, Mathematics and Physics, Pharmacy, Psychology. Gibson Institute.

Academic Units outside the faculty structure

Centres: Migration Studies, Canadian Studies, Polymer Processing Research, QUESTOR Centre, Institute of Professional Legal Studies

Table 7.8: Student Numbers (QUB) 2000

	Undergraduates		Postgraduates		**Total**
	Full Time	Part Time	Full Time	Part Time	
Faculty of Engineering	2049	67	460	173	2749
Faculty of Humanities	1774	104	121	149	2148
Faculty of Legal, Social and Educational Sciences	2241	772	726	998	4737
Faculty of Medicine and Health Sciences	2547	1379	129	157	4212
Faculty of Science and Agriculture	2397	78	326	607	3408
Institute of Lifelong Learning	–	3659	1	10	3670
Academic General	46	15	21	39	121
Stranmillis University College	675	253	17	127	1072
St Mary's University College	631	83	13	154	881
Total	**12360**	**6410**	**1814**	**2414**	**22998**
Mature Students	15.5% of all Full Time Undergraduate students				
International Students	11.7% of all students				
Students with Special Needs	2.6% of all students				

The Quadrangle, Queen's University Belfast

University of Ulster

University of Ulster at Jordanstown

Shore Road
Newtownabbey
BT37 0QB
Tel: 028 9036 5131
Web: www.ulster.ac.uk

University of Ulster at Coleraine

Cromore Road
Coleraine
BT52 1SA
Tel: 028 7034 4141
Web: www.ulster.ac.uk

University of Ulster Magee College

College Avenue
Londonderry
BT48 7JL
Tel: 028 7137 1371
Web: www.ulster.ac.uk

University of Ulster at Belfast

York Street
Belfast
BT15 1ED
Tel: 028 9032 8515
Web: www.ulster.ac.uk

The University of Ulster's aim is to be an outstanding regional university with a national and international reputation for quality. The university makes a major contribution to the economic, social and cultural advancement of Northern Ireland as a region within a national and international context and plays a key role in attracting inward investment. The university has restructured at faculty and school level to reflect its new operating environment and changes in the world of work, in the economy and in the needs of society.

The university's course provision covers Arts, Business and Management, Engineering, Information Technology, Life and Health Sciences and Social Sciences. Courses have a strong vocational element and the majority include a period of industrial or professional placement. The university employs over 3500 staff, has an annual turnover in excess of £120 million and has embarked on a development programme of £200 million over the next 10 years.

Technology and knowledge transfer and commercial exploitation of ideas are promoted through a range of initiatives including the establishment of high technology campus incubators, its Science Research Parks, the Teaching Company Scheme and ongoing research and consultancy with business and industry.

The university is a major contributor to the R & D capacity within Northern Ireland in support of local business and industry.

Senior Officers of the University

President and Vice-Chancellor:	Professor Gerry McKenna
Pro-Vice-Chancellors:	Professor John Hughes
	Professor Jim Allen
	Professor Richard Barnett
	Professor Wallace Ewart
	Ann Tate
Director of Finance:	Michael Ryan
Acting Director of Human Resources:	Ronnie Magee
Director of Information Services:	Nigel McCartney
Director of Physical Resources:	Paddy Donnelly
Director of Planning and Governance Services:	Irene Aston
Director of Public Affairs:	Brendan Kelleher

Student Numbers

Tables 7.9 sets out total student population 1985/86 to 2000/01, whilst Table 7.10 shows Total Student Population by Faculty.

Table 7.9: Student Population by Campus

	1985/86	2000/01
Belfast		
- Full Time	540	911
- Part Time	133	126
- Sub Total	673	1037
Jordanstown		
- Full Time	4409	7287
- Part Time	2831	4950
- Sub Total	7240	12237
Coleraine		
- Full Time	2235	4104
- Part Time	329	864
- Sub Total	2564	4968
Magee		
- Full Time	276	1907
- Part Time	452	1024
- Sub Total	526	2931
Total All Campuses		
- Full Time	7460	14209
- Part Time	3745	6964
Total	**11205**	**21173**

Table 7.10: Total Student Population by Faculty 2000/01

Faculty	Full Time	Part Time	Total
Art & Design	2604	351	2955
Business & Management	3121	2940	6061
Engineering	1914	367	2281
Informatics	1817	466	2283
Science	1925	537	2462
Social & Health Sciences & Education	2828	2303	5131
Total	**14209**	**6964**	**21173**

Faculties and Departments

Faculty of Arts

Academy for Irish Cultural Heritages
Cultural Affairs
Institute of Ulster Scots Studies
School of Art and Design
School of History and International Affairs
School of Languages and Literature
School of Media and Performing Arts

Faculty of Business and Management

Northern Ireland Centre for Entrepreneurship
School of Accounting
School of Business Organisation and Management
School of Business, Retail and Financial Services
School of Hotel, Leisure and Tourism
School of International Business
School of Marketing, Entrepreneurship and Strategy
The Management Institute

Faculty of Engineering and Built Environment

School of Electrical and Mechanical Engineering
School of the Built Environment

Faculty of Informatics

School of Computing and Information Engineering
School of Computing and Intelligent Systems
School of Computing and Mathematics

Faculty of Life and Health Sciences

Faculty of Life and Health Sciences Virtual School
Institute of Postgraduate Medicine and Primary Care
School of Applied Medical Sciences and Sports Studies
School of Biological and Environmental Sciences
School of Biomedical Sciences
School of Nursing
School of Psychology
School of Rehabilitative Sciences

Faculty of Social Sciences

Research Graduate School (Social Sciences)
School of Communication
School of Economics and Politics
School of Education
School of Law
School of Policy Studies
School of Sociology and Applied Social Studies

The Open University

Established in 1971, the Open University is the UK's largest university, with over 200,000 full and part-time students. It is established throughout the UK and Ireland, and is ranked amongst the top UK universities for the quality of its teaching.

The Open University is unique within the UK in that it does not require any entry qualifications. Over 30% of students starting courses have qualifications below mainstream university requirements, but 70% of all students pass their courses each year. The majority of Open University students are part time, and although students can enter at the age of 18, two thirds are aged between 25 and 44.

Contact Details

The Open University's regional centre for Ireland is located in Belfast, providing student support and acting as the administrative headquarters for the region. It is led by Dr Rosemary Hamilton, Regional Director.

The Open University in Ireland
40 University Road
Belfast
BT7 1SU
Tel: 028 9024 5025
Fax: 028 9023 0565
Evening Advice: 0870 333 1444

The Centre is open: Monday to Friday 5pm to 9pm, Saturday 9am to 5 pm and Sunday 9 am to 1 pm

Teacher Training Colleges

Northern Ireland has two major centres for teacher training, St Mary's College and Stranmillis College. Both are University Colleges attached to Queen's University, Belfast.

ST MARY'S UNIVERSITY COLLEGE

St Mary's University College
191 Falls Road, Belfast BT12 6SE
Tel: 028 9032 7678
Fax: 028 9033 3719
Web: www.stmarys-belfast.ac.uk
Principal: Very Reverend Professor Martin O'Callaghan

St Mary's University College is undergoing an exciting transformation these days. The College has reached a new level of academic partnership with Queen's University as a School in the Faculty of Legal, Social and Educational Sciences. We are now offering degrees in both Teacher Education and Liberal Arts which are quality assured by the University. One of our goals is to expand student access . We are developing academic links and student exchanges with universities around the globe, and reinvigorating our commitment to be a key social resource for the local community. Our mission is to educate students in preparation for a lifetime of learning, leadership and service.

St Mary's University College is an independent Catholic institution although its degrees are validated through Queen's University Faculty of Legal, Social and Educational Sciences. Its primary task is the training and ongoing professional development of teachers in Catholic schools. The college currently has approximately 600 students and 62 lecturing staff.

Stranmillis University College

Stranmillis Road
Belfast
BT9 5DY
Tel: 028 9038 1271
Fax: 028 9066 4423
Web: www.stran.ac.uk
Principal: Professor Richard McMinn

Stranmillis College was founded in 1922 and has evolved into a multi-professional institution engaged not only in undergraduate and postgraduate teacher education but also the provision of pre-service and in-service training. The college, which has an enrolment of around 700 full-time students, offers a range of consultancy services to Northern Ireland schools, Education and Library Boards and other education agencies.

Further Education Sector

Northern Ireland has a network of 18 institutions of Further Education (with approximately 231 out centres) providing a range of courses of a technical or commercial nature as well as a wide range of general educational and recreational classes. Higher education courses have also been franchised from universities to colleges of further education. Part-time courses usually relate to employment and some apprentices are given day release to attend these courses. Colleges also provide courses of training for unemployed young people as part of the New Deal Programme.

The Department of Education directly funds further education colleges, whilst allowing institutions to become self-standing incorporated bodies.

Details of Northern Ireland's Further Education Colleges are set out below:

Castlereagh College of Further and Higher Education
Montgomery Road
Belfast BT9 6JD
Tel: 028 9079 7144
Fax: 028 9040 1820
College Director: Muriel Shankey

ARMAGH COLLEGE

Armagh College
College Hill
Armagh
BT61 7HN

Tel: (028) 3752 2205
Fax: (028) 3751 2845
email: enquiries@armaghcollege.ac.uk
Website: www.armaghcollege.ac.uk

Armagh College provides a range of high quality training programmes, which are tailored to meet your individual company needs. We offer a comprehensive list of programmes that will add value and increase your overall business performance. Areas covered include ICT, Management, Hospitality and Health and Safety to name a few.

Programmes can be delivered on your company premises or at the college, to suit your working schedule and are delivered Monday to Saturday.

For further information on the facilities and services we provide please contact: Sharon Williamson, Business Development Manager on (028) 3752 2205 or email: swilliamson@armaghcollege.ac.uk.

Causeway Institute of Further and Higher Education
Coleraine Road
Ballymoney BT53 6BT
Tel: 028 7035 4717
Fax: 028 7035 6377
College Director: Ian Williams

East Antrim Institute of Further
and Higher Education
400 Shore Road
Newtownabbey BT37 9RS
Tel: 028 9085 5000
Fax: 028 9086 2076
College Director: John Blayney

BELFAST INSTITUTE

The Gerald Moag Campus
125-153 Millfield
Belfast BT1 1HS
Tel: (028) 9026 5000
Fax: (028) 9026 5451
www.belfastinstitute.ac.uk

DIRECTOR:
Brian Turtle

Belfast Institute of Further and Higher Education is the largest educational establishment in Northern Ireland.

With over 44,000 enrolments, it is one of the largest providers of further and higher education in these islands.

The Institute delivers university degree and equivalent courses to nearly 5,000 students. Courses include Higher National Certificates and Diplomas, degrees, post-graduate qualifications and a range of professional awards.

Almost 20,000 students attend our 1,200 further education courses including National Vocational Qualifications, Advanced Vocational Certificates in Education, 'A' Levels and GCSEs, and a wide range of similar qualifications that can be matched to national award standards.

East Down Institute of Further and Higher Education
Market Street
Downpatrick
Co Down BT30 6ND
Tel: 028 4461 5815
Fax: 028 4461 5817
College Director: T L Place

East Tyrone Institute of Further Education
Circular Road
Dungannon
Co Tyrone BT71 6BQ
Tel: 028 8772 2323
Fax: 028 8775 2018
College Director: T Dardis

Fermanagh College
1 Dublin Road
Enniskillen BT74 6AE
Tel: 028 6632 2431
Fax: 028 6632 6357
College Director: Brian Rouse

Limavady College of Further Education
Main Street
Limavady BT49 0EX
Tel: 028 7776 2334
Fax: 028 7776 1018
College Director: Dr A Heaslett

Lisburn College of Further and Higher Education
Castle Street
Lisburn BT27 4SU
Tel: 028 9267 7225
Fax: 028 9267 7291
College Director: A J McReynolds

Loughry College: The Food Centre
Cookstown
Co Tyrone BT80 9AA
Tel: 028 8676 8100
Fax: 028 8676 1043
College Director: Dr J Speers

Newry and Kilkeel Institute of Further and Higher Education
Patrick Street
Newry
Co Down BT35 8DN
Tel: 028 3026 1071
Fax: 028 3025 9679
College Director: R J Mullan

North Down and Ards Institute
Castle Park Road
Bangor
Co Down BT20 4TF
Tel: 028 9127 6600
Fax: 028 9127 6601

North East Institute of
Further and Higher Education
Magherafelt Site
22 Moneymore Road
Magherafelt
BT45 6AE
Tel: 028 7963 2462
Fax: 028 7963 3501
College Director: Dr S M Owen Jones

Northern Ireland Hotel and
Catering College
Ballywillan Road
Portrush
Co Antrim BT56 8JL
Tel: 028 7082 3768
Fax: 028 7082 4733
College Director: Lucia Campbell

North West Institute of Further and
Higher Education
Strand Road
Londonderry BT48 7BY
Tel: 028 7126 6711
Fax: 028 7126 0520
College Director: P Gallagher

Omagh College of Further Education
2 Mountjoy Road
Omagh BT79 7AH
Tel: 028 8224 5433
Fax: 028 8224 1440
College Director: V Refausse

Upper Bann College
of Further Education
Lurgan Road
Portadown
Co Armagh BT63 5BL
Tel: 028 3833 7111
Fax: 028 3839 7751
College Director: Dr Gordon Byrne

Library Service

The five Education and Library Boards provide library services in Northern Ireland, under the auspices of the Department of Education. As well as fixed libraries in main population centres, library provision includes mobile library services to homes, hospitals and schools. A list of the main public libraries is set out below.

Public Libraries

Andersonstown Library
Slievegallion Drive
Belfast BT11 8JP
Tel: 028 9050 9200

Antrim Library
41 Church Street
Antrim BT41 4BE
Tel: 028 9446 1942

Ardoyne Library
446-450 Crumlin Road
Belfast BT14 7GH
Tel: 028 9050 9202

Armagh Library
Market Street
Armagh BT61 7BU
Tel: 028 3752 4072

Armagh Public Library
43 Abbey Street
Armagh BT61 7DY
Tel: 028 3752 3142

Ballee Library
2 Neighbourhood Centre
Ballee Drive
Ballymena BT42 2SX
Tel: 028 2564 5761

Ballycastle Library
5 Leyland Road
Ballycastle BT54 6DP
Tel: 028 2076 2566

Ballyclare Library
School Street
Ballyclare BT39 9BE
Tel: 028 9335 2269

Ballyhackamore Library
1 Eastleigh Drive
Ballyhackamore BT4 3DX
Tel: 028 9050 9204

Ballymacarrett Library
19 Templemore Avenue
Belfast BT5 4PF
Tel: 028 9050 9207

Ballymena Library
25-31 Demesne Avenue
Ballymena BT43 7BG
Tel: 028 2566 4100

Ballymoney Library
Rodden Foot
Queen Street
Ballymoney BT53 6JB
Tel: 028 2766 3589

Ballynahinch Library
Main Street
Ballynahinch BT24 8DN
Tel: 028 9756 6442

Banbridge Library
Scarva Street
Banbridge BT32 3AD
Tel: 028 4062 3973

Bangor Branch Library
80 Hamilton Road
Bangor BT20 4LH
Tel: 028 9127 0591

Bellaghy Library
20 Castle Street
Bellaghy
Tel: 028 7938 6627

Belvoir Park Library
Drumart Square
Belfast BT8 7EY
Tel: 028 9064 4331

Bessbrook Library
12 Church Road
Bessbrook BT35 7AQ
Tel: 028 3083 0424

Braniel Library
Glen Road
Castlereagh BT5 7JH
Tel: 028 9079 7420

Broughshane Library
Main Street
Broughshane
Tel: 028 2586 1613

Brownlow Library
Brownlow Road
Brownlow
Craigavon BT65 5DP
Tel: 028 3834 1946

Bushmills Library
44 Main Street
Bushmills BT57 8QA
Tel: 028 2073 1424

Carnlough Library
Town Hall
Harbour Road
Carnlough BT44 0EQ
Tel: 028 2888 5552

Carrickfergus Library
2 Joymount Court
Carrickfergus BT38 7DN
Tel: 028 9336 2261

Carryduff Library
Church Road
Carryduff BT8 8DT
Tel: 028 9081 3568

Castlederg Library
Main Street
Castlederg BT81 7AY
Tel: 028 8167 1419

Castlerock Library
57 Main Street
Castlerock
Tel: 028 7084 8463

Castlewellan Library
Main Street
Castlewellan BT31 9DA
Tel: 028 4377 8433

Central Library
Royal Avenue
Belfast BT1 1EA
Tel: 028 9050 9150

Chichester Library
Salisbury Avenue
Belfast BT15 5EB
Tel: 028 9050 9210

Cloughfern Library
2a Kings Crescent
Newtownabbey BT37 0DH
Tel: 028 9085 4789

Coalisland Library
Ground Floor
Lineside
Coalisland BT71 4LT
Tel: 028 8774 0569

Coleraine Library
Queen Street
Coleraine BT52 1BE
Tel: 028 7034 2561

Comber Library
5 Newtownards Road
Comber BT23 5AV
Tel: 028 9187 2610

Cookstown Library
Burn Road
Cookstown BT80 8DJ
Tel: 028 8676 3702

Central Library, Belfast

Craigavon Divisional Library
24 Church Street
Portadown BT62 3DB
Tel: 028 3833 6122

Cregagh Library
409-413 Cregagh Road
Belfast BT6 0LF
Tel: 028 9040 1365

Creggan Library
Central Drive
Londonderry BT48 9QH
Tel: 028 7126 6168

Crossmaglen Library
The Square
Crossmaglen BT35 9AA
Tel: 028 3086 1951

Crumlin Library
Orchard Road
Crumlin BT29 4SD
Tel: 028 9442 3066

Cullybackey Branch Library
153 Tobar Park
Cullybackey BT42 1NW
Tel: 028 2588 1878

Cushendall Library
Mill Street
Cushendall BT44 0RR
Tel: 028 2177 1297

Dairy Farm Library
Dairy Farm Centre
Stewartstown Road
Dunmurry
Belfast BT17 0AW
Tel: 028 9043 1266

Derry Central Library
35 Foyle Street
Londonderry BT48 9AL
Tel: 028 7127 2300

Donaghadee Library
Killaughey Road
Donaghadee BT21 0BE
Tel: 028 9188 2507

Downpatrick Library
79 Market Street
Downpatrick BT30 6LZ
Tel: 028 4461 2895

Draperstown Library
The Square
High Street
Draperstown BT45 7AE
Tel: 028 7962 8249

Dromore Library
Town Hall
Market Square
Dromore BT25 1AW
Tel: 028 9269 2280

Dundonald Library
16 Church Road
Dundonald BT16 2LN
Tel: 028 9048 3994

Dungannon Library
Market Square
Dungannon BT70 1JD
Tel: 028 8772 2952

Dungiven Library
74 Main Street
Dungiven BT70 1JD
Tel: 028 7774 1475

Dunmurry Library
Upper Dunmurry Lane
Dunmurry
Tel: 028 9062 3007

Enniskillen Library
Halls Lane
Enniskillen BT74 7DR
Tel: 028 6632 2886

Falls Road Library
49 Falls Road
Belfast BT12 4PD
Tel: 028 9050 9212

Finaghy Library
13 Finaghy Road South
Belfast BT10 0BW
Tel: 028 9050 9214

Fintona Library
112 Main Street
Fintona BT78 2AH
Tel: 028 8284 1774

Fivemiletown Library
Main Street
Fivemiletown BT75 0PG
Tel: 028 8952 1409

Garvagh Library
Bridge Street
Garvagh BT51 5AF
Tel: 028 2955 8500

Gilford Library
37 Mill Street
Gilford BT63 6HQ
Tel: 028 3833 1770

Gilnahirk Library
Gilnahirk Rise
Belfast BT5 7DT
Tel: 028 9079 6573

Glengormley Library
40 Carnmoney Road
Glengormley BT36 7HP
Tel: 028 9083 3797

Greenisland Library
17 Glassillan Grove
Greenisland BT38 8PE
Tel: 028 9086 5419

Greystone Library
Greystone Road
Antrim
BT40 1JW
Tel: 028 9446 3891

Heritage Library
12-14 Bishop Street
Londonderry BT48 6PW
Tel: 028 7126 9792

Holywood Arches Library
4 Holywood Road
Belfast BT4 1NT
Tel: 028 9047 1309

Holywood Library
86-88 High Street
Holywood BT18 9AE
Tel: 028 9042 4232

Irvinestown Library
Main Street
Irvinestown BT95 1GL
Tel: 028 6862 1383

Keady Library
1 Bridge Street
Keady BT60 3RP
Tel: 028 3753 1365

Kilkeel Library
49 Greencastle Street
Kilkeel BT34 4BH
Tel: 028 4176 2278

Killyleagh Library
High Street
Killyleagh BT30 9QF
Tel: 028 4482 8407

Kilrea Library
27 The Diamond
Kilrea BT51 5QN
Tel: 028 2954 0630

Larne Library
36 Pound Street
Larne BT40 1SQ
Tel: 028 2827 7047

Laurelhill Community Library
22 Laurelhill Road
Lisburn BT28 2VM
Tel: 028 9266 4596

Ligoniel Library
53-55 Ligoniel Road
Belfast BT14 8BW
Tel: 028 9050 9221

Limavady Library
5 Connell Street
Limavady BT49 0EA
Tel: 028 7776 2540

Linenhall Library
17 Donegall Square North
Belfast BT1 5GB
Tel: 028 9032 1707

Lisburn Library
29 Railway Street
Lisburn BT28 1XP
Tel: 028 9260 1749

Lisburn Road Library
440 Lisburn Road
Belfast BT9 6GR
Tel: 028 9050 9223

Lisnaskea Library
Drumhaw
Lisnaskea BT92 0GT
Tel: 028 6772 1222

Lurgan Library
Carnegie Street
Lurgan BT66 6AS
Tel: 028 3832 3912

Maghera Library
1 Main Street
Maghera BT66 6AS
Tel: 028 7964 2578

Linenhall Library, Belfast

Magherafelt Library
The Bridewell
6 Church Street
Magherafelt BT45 6AN
Tel: 028 7963 2278

Moira Library
Backwood Road
Moira BT67 0LJ
Tel: 028 9261 9330

Moneymore Library
8 Main Street
Moneymore BT45 7PD
Tel: 028 8674 8380

Monkstown Library
Bridge Road
Monkstown
Tel: 028 9058 3138

Moy Library
The Square
Moy BT71 7SG
Tel: 028 8778 4661

Newcastle Library
141/143 Main Street
Newcastle BT33 0AE
Tel: 028 4372 2710

Newry Public Library
79 Hill Street
Newry BT34 1DG
Tel: 028 3026 4683

Newtownards Library
Regent Street
Newtownards BT23 4AB
Tel: 028 9181 4732

Newtownbreda Library
Saintfield Road
Belfast BT8 4HL
Tel: 028 9070 1620

Newtownstewart Library
2 Main Street
Newtownstewart BT78 9AA
Tel: 028 8166 1245

O'Fiaich Memorial & Archive
15 Moy Road
Armagh BT61 7LY
Tel: 028 3752 2981

Oldpark Library
46 Oldpark Road
Belfast BT14 6FF
Tel: 028 9050 9226

Omagh Library
1 Spillars Place
Omagh BT78 1HL
Tel: 028 8224 4821

Ormeau Library
Ormeau Embankment
Belfast BT7 3GG
Tel: 028 9050 9228

Poleglass Library
14 Good Shepherd Road
Belfast BT17 0PP
Tel: 028 9062 9740

Portadown Library
24-26 Church Street
Portadown BT62 3LQ
Tel: 028 3833 6122

Portaferry Library
47 High Street
Portaferry BT22 1QT
Tel: 028 4272 8194

Portglenone Library
19 Townhill Road
Portglenone BT44 8AD
Tel: 028 2582 2228

Portstewart Library
Town Hall, The Crescent
Portstewart BT55 7AB
Tel: 028 7083 2712

Randalstown Library
34 New Street
Randalstown BT41 3AF
Tel: 028 9447 2725

Rathcoole Library
2 Rosslea Way
Rathcoole
Newtownabbey BT37 9BJ
Tel: 028 9085 1157

Rathfriland Library
John Street
Rathfriland BT34 5QH
Tel: 028 4063 0661

Richhill Branch Library
1 Maynooth Road
Richhill BT61 9PE
Tel: 028 3887 0639

Saintfield Library
17 Fairview
Saintfield BT24 7AD
Tel: 028 9751 0550

Sandy Row Branch Library
127a Sandy Row
Belfast BT12 5ET
Tel: 028 9050 9230

Shankill Road Library
298 Shankill Road
Belfast BT13 2BN
Tel: 028 9050 9232

Shantallow Library
92 Racecourse Road
Shantallow
Londonderry BT48 8DA
Tel: 028 7135 4185

Sion Mills Library
Church Square
Sion Mills BT82 9HD
Tel: 028 8165 8513

Strabane Library
25 Butcher Street
Strabane BT82 8AJ
Tel: 028 7188 3686

Strathfoyle Library
22 Temple Road
Strathfoyle
Co Londonderry BT47 6TJ
Tel: 028 7186 0385

Suffolk Library
57 Stewartstown Road
Belfast BT11 9JP
Tel: 028 9050 9234

Tandragee Library
Market Street
Tandragee BT62 2BP
Tel: 028 3884 0694

Templepatrick Library
23 The Village
Templepatrick
BT39 0AA
Tel: 028 9443 2953

Tullycarnet Library
Kinross Avenue
Belfast BT5 7GF
Tel: 028 9048 5079

Waringstown Library
Main Street
Waringstown BT66 7QH
Tel: 028 3888 1077

Warrenpoint Library
Summer Hill
Warrenpoint BT34 3JB
Tel: 028 4175 3375

Waterside Library
The Workhouse
23 Glendermott Road
Waterside
Londonderry BT47 6BG
Tel: 028 7134 2963

Whitehead Library
17b Edward Road
Whitehead BT38 9RU
Tel: 028 9335 3249

Whiterock Library
195 Whiterock Road
Belfast BT12 7FW
Tel: 028 9050 9236

Whitewell Library
Ballygolan Primary School
Serpentine Road
Belfast
Tel: 028 9050 9242

Woodstock Road Library
358 Woodstock Road
Belfast BT6 9DG
Tel: 028 9050 9239

Key Issues Facing
Northern Ireland Education

This section of the Yearbook addresses four of the key issues facing the education sector in Northern Ireland:

- Integrated education and religion;
- Selection procedure - Post Primary Review Team;
- Pupil Teacher Ratios;
- Investment in Education.

Integrated Education and Religion

Many commentators agree that Northern Ireland's most fundamental problem is that of sectarian division between Protestants and Catholics. Despite the fact that the divisions date back for centuries, prejudices are passed from generation to generation and preserved by the fact that the two communities are segregated in many areas of everyday life, including education. There is a growing belief that integrated education could be a major contributor to breaking the cycle of prejudice.

The establishment of a set of schools designed specifically to facilitate the education of pupils from Roman Catholic and Protestant backgrounds side by side has been one of the major developments in Northern Ireland education over the last twenty years. There has been steady growth in integrated education during this period.

The first planned integrated school, Lagan College, opened in 1981, the second in 1985, and by 1995, this new sector had grown to have a total enrolment of 5,816 pupils. In the last five years this number has risen to 15,770 pupils, 4.6 per cent of the total primary/post-primary enrolment in Northern Ireland. Table 7.11 lists all of the major existing schools and shows how numbers have grown steadily.

Integrated education is popular, but as it is not yet available everywhere due to financial and logistical difficulties, particularly in getting new schools established, it may be some time before it realises its full potential. In 2000/01 some 1,140 applications for places in integrated education had to be turned away due to lack of places.

NI COUNCIL FOR INTERGRATED EDUCATION

Northern Ireland Council for Integrated Education (NICIE)
44 University Street
Belfast
BT7 1HB
Tel: (028) 9023 6200
Fax: (028) 9023 6237
Email: info@nicie.org.uk

Michael Wardlow, Chief Executive Officer

The Northern Ireland Council for Integrated Education (NICIE) was established in 1987 and is a voluntary body that acts as a central forum and umbrella organisation for integrated schools, groups or individuals that are interested in Integrated Education.
It works with parent groups to start new schools, supports existing integrated
schools and helps schools seeking to become integrated through the transformation process.

Integrated Education schools bring together pupils, staff and governors, in roughly equal numbers, from both Protestant and Catholic traditions, as well as those of other faiths or with no religious tradition.

There are currently 47 integrated schools, educating 15,770 pupils in 29 Primaries, 18 Colleges, located throughout Northern Ireland. In addition there are 17 integrated nurseries.

Selection Procedure: Post Primary Review Team

Brownlow College, Craigavon

The process of selection (the 11-plus examination) is at the heart of the Northern Ireland education system. Essentially it is the case that all children are placed in either Grammar or Secondary schools based on a test taken during their seventh year at school, when they are eleven years of age. It is widely accepted that this placement, coupled with the educational provision available thereafter, fundamentally affects each child's future prospects and the nature of society as a whole. In September 2000, following a major, wide ranging study, the report titled 'The Effects of the Selective System of Secondary Education in Northern Ireland' was published. It looked at the current system and considered possible alternatives.

Table 7.11: Integrated Schools in Northern Ireland

Opened	Location	Enrolment	School/College	Opened	Location	Enrolment	School/College
1981	Belfast	980	Lagan College	1995	Dungannon	432	Integrated College Dungannon
1985	Belfast	217	Forge CIPS	1995	Crossgar	156	Cedar IPS
1985	Belfast	799	Hazelwood College	1995	Omagh	540	Drumragh IC
1985	Belfast	402	Hazelwood IPS	1995	Loughbrickland	435	New-Bridge IC
1986	Newcastle	214	All Children's CIPS	1995	Portaferry	67	Portaferry CIPS
1987	Banbridge	394	Bridge IPS	1996	Lambeg	79	Hilden CIPS
1987	Portrush	217	Mill Strand IPS	1996	Coleraine	430	North Coast IC
1988	Dungannon	185	Windmill IPS	1996	Derriaghy	116	Oakwood IPS
1989	Ballymena	255	Braidside IPS	1996	Antrim	107	Rathenraw CIPS
1989	Enniskillen	105	Enniskillen IPS	1996	Ballymena	501	Slemish IC
1990	Omagh	180	Omagh IPS	1997	Castlewellan	47	Annsborough CIPS
1990	Portadown	197	Portadown IPS	1997	Whitehead	322	Ulidia IC
1991	Craigavon	355	Brownlow CIC	1997	Carrowdore	323	Strangford
1991	Garvagh	48	Carhill CIPS	1997	Derriaghy	520	Malone IC
1991	Larne	140	Corran IPS	1998	Bangor	502	Bangor Central CIPS
1991	Derry	397	Oakgrove IPS	1998	Kircubbin	100	Kircubbin CIPS
1992	Carrickfergus	203	Acorn IPS	1998	Rostrevor	70	Kilbroney CIPS
1992	Derry	779	Oakgrove IC	1998	Holywood	430	Priory CIC
1993	Belfast	193	Cranmore IPS	1998	Downpatrick	300	Down Academy CIC
1993	Belfast	240	Lough View IPS	1998	Lisburn	850	Forthill CIC
1993	Armagh	192	Saints and Scholars IPS	1999	Magherafelt	90	Spires IPS
1994	Enniskillen	391	Erne IC	2000	Carryduff	10	Millennium IPS (Independent)
1994	Newcastle	470	Shimna IC				

Source: Northern Ireland Council for Integrated Education

Five main models came to the fore:

- A system of delayed selection, perhaps at age 14;
- A system of all-through comprehensive schools, like that currently in operation in Scotland;
- A system using common primary and lower secondary schools, followed by differentiated upper secondary schools, as currently operated in France, Italy and other European countries;
- A system of differentiated post-primary schools with distinctive academic and vocational/technical routes;
- The status quo: selection at 11 years and a system of grammar and secondary schools.

The Current System

Significant strengths in the current selective system in Northern Ireland were identified including:

- The high academic standards achieved in grammar schools;
- The supportive environment provided in secondary schools for pupils who may not succeed in grammar schools;
- Secondary schools tend to draw their enrolment from more localised areas, possibly providing opportunities to strengthen the links between local communities and these schools.

Significant weaknesses in the current selective system in Northern Ireland were identified including:

- The perception that testing is unfair and places undue pressure on young children; this concern is shared by teachers, employers and society more generally;
- Primary teachers in some cases feel obliged to focus curricular attention narrowly on the requirements of the selection test, partly to assist each child in achieving their highest score and also because they feel they are judged in the public mind on the basis of their school's overall transfer test performance;
- Rather than simply identifying all the children suited to grammar schooling the testing procedure enables the grammar schools to admit only the pupils with high scores, possibly leaving many children, who have the academic

ability behind. Secondary schools, who then cater for the 'failures' are in turn accorded a lesser status than grammar schools in the eyes of most people. Teachers in secondary schools argue that they have to rebuild the self-confidence and esteem of many pupils who arrive in their schools with a sense of failure;

- In spite of the grading system which is designed so as not to label children as having passed or failed, this is still how results are generally interpreted;
- Increasingly parents feel obliged to pay for out-of-school coaching, and not all parents can afford to do so.

Success and Failure

With regard to the current system, the report concluded that the most important factor for a pupil achieving a high GCSE score is achieving a place in a grammar school.

The original purpose of the transfer test procedure was to identify pupils, from any background, not just those most financially advantaged, deemed able to cope with the academic curriculum provided in grammar schools.

However, the current performance patterns may imply that a higher proportion of pupils should have the opportunity to experience a grammar school education or equivalent. Interviews with pupils in both grammar and secondary schools indicated a strong difference in aspirations. The vast majority of those in grammar were planning to enter higher education whereas only a minority of those in secondary schools aspired to do so.

It would appear to be the case that success breeds success and "failure" breeds failure, but in the Northern Ireland selective system the success and the failure seem to be strongly dependent upon one another.

Table 7.11 shows how Northern Ireland compares with Scotland and England/Wales in terms of the spread of exam performance. Proportionately Northern Ireland has more high and low achieving schools, whereas the distribution in England/Wales and, even more so, Scotland shows a more even spread.

Table 7.12: Examination Performance Comparison Across the UK			
5+ GCSE grades (A*-C or equivalent)	Northern Ireland	England/Wales	Scotland
0 to 20% of pupils	17%	11%	3%
21 to 40% of pupils	37%	43%	12%
41 to 60% of pupils	13%	31%	38%
61 to 80% of pupils	3%	13%	34%
81 to 100% of pupils	31%	3%	14%
Total	100%	100%	100%

On the government's behalf the Independent Review Body on Post-Primary Education produced a major report called 'Education for the 21st Century'. The Review Body, chaired by Gerry Burns, made four key recommendations, which, if implemented, could mean fundamental reorganisation of Northern Ireland's educational system. They were:

- Abolition of the transfer test (the 11 plus);
- The ending of selection on academic grounds;
- The development of a 'Pupil Profile' assessment system;
- The creation of a 'collegiate system' of schools across Northern Ireland.

The Burns report called the 11 plus 'divisive' and argued that the exam leads to inequality of opportunity.

Response to the Post Primary Review Group Recommendations

The Review Group report (commonly referred to as the Burns report) published in October 2001 has stirred a major debate including all of the interested players from political parties through all kinds of educational organisations, churches, business groups and trade unions. At a political level, the Minister for Education, Martin McGuinness welcomed the report and indicated his personal support for the abolition of the transfer test. He then embarked on a major consultative exercise, which was completed in September 2002.

The consultative exercise was unprecedented in scale (proposals communicated to every household in Northern Ireland) and yielded over 1300 written responses, including over 500 from schools and 200,000 completed household response forms.

Disappointingly the Northern Ireland Assembly and the Education Committee divided along traditional lines on the issue with the Nationalist parties broadly in support of the Burns proposals and Unionist parties generally opposed.

Overall there was overwhelming support for the objectives of the Burns Report and general acceptance that the 11+ transfer test should be abolished. However, some of the support for abolition was conditional on a suitable alternative means of academic selection being found.

The many educational interests were divided on the broader principle of academic selection. Although there was support from all five Education and Library Boards, two-thirds of schools, CCMS and NICIE, there was opposition from the Governing Bodies Association, voluntary grammar schools and two-thirds of household respondents.

It is difficult to see in what way the government can move on academic selection given the strength of opinion on both sides of the argument. Some kind of academic selection at age 14 as opposed to age 11 may form some part of a compromise. There was broad support for the concept of pupil profiles but uncertainty about the extent to which it would be used for admission purposes. There was widespread opposition to the system of collegiates as proposed in the Burns Report although there was support for greater collaboration and networking between schools.

Such is the discussion over the proposals of the Post Primary Review Group that it is probable executive action on foot of the proposals will be tentative and slow. It is probable that the 11+ test will disappear but that some kind of academic selection may be retained. With the return to Direct Rule it is unlikely that much change will occur in the short term.

Pupil/Teacher Ratios

Pupil/teacher ratio is an issue close to the hearts of parents and teachers. Parents value lower class sizes. Governments are always keen to show how they have succeeded in reducing the pupil/teacher ratio.

Unfortunately, the ratio figures can be quite misleading. The following table indicates that the ratio in primary schools is about twenty pupils to each teacher. However to reach this figure all teachers will have been included, many of whom have no class duties. 'Floating teachers' such as many principals, vice-principals, supply teachers, reading recovery and special needs teachers give the impression of lower ratios.

311

Table 7.13 Pupil/Teacher Ratios		
Education Type	Pupil/Teacher Ratio 1988/89	Pupil/Teacher Ratio 2000/01
Nursery	24.6	24.4
Primary	23.2	20.2
Secondary	14.2	13.9
Grammar	15.9	15.4
Special	7.0	5.9
All Schools	**18.3**	**16.7**

The reality in the classroom is usually higher and in some cases significantly higher than indicated in the table. Nonetheless parents who look around may be surprised to find relatively low pupil/teacher ratios in certain schools or subjects as there can be considerable class-to-class variation against average ratios.

However overall, Northern Ireland enjoys pupil/teacher ratios which are significantly below the UK average in both primary and secondary education.

Investment in Education

There is a general consensus that for many years education in Northern Ireland (and perhaps in the UK as a whole) had been an area of under-investment. The Northern Ireland Executive prioritised this area, and planned capital expenditure in 2001/2002 is £99.7 million, rising to £108.9 million in 2002/2003. However, it is accepted that even these substantial sums will not bring Northern Ireland's ageing educational infrastructure up to modern standards. The problem is particularly acute in terms of outdated school buildings, many in a poor state of repair. A high percentage of Northern Ireland's classrooms are temporary or mobile buildings.

Until its suspension the Northern Ireland Executive had set itself some ambitious targets in this area in 2002 including:

- Reducing the maintenance backlog by 18 per cent;
- Replacing 260 temporary classrooms with permanent accommodation;
- Commencing 18 major works in the school building programme.

As in other sectors, one possible solution to the infrastructural deficit is PFI, or as it is now known, PPP (Public-Private Partnerships), whereby private sector capital can create the infrastructure and effectively lease it to the Department or Education and Library Board as the client. This approach has both supporters and opponents.

Those in favour of PPP argue that it is the only way of ensuring that necessary investment actually happens and all the construction and operational risks pass to the private sector developer or facilities manager.

Opponents contend that the process is complex and unwieldy, and that in order to give the private sector a good return on their investment, it *must* cost the taxpayer more in the long term.

The Treasury has developed public sector comparators which allow the public sector client to judge to some extent how the PPP proposition looks in terms of overall value against the alternative approach.

Nonetheless, while the debate continues, Northern Ireland's educational authorities have been steadily adopting the PPP approach to a number of key projects including:

- Rebuilding of main campus for Belfast Institute Further and Higher Education (Capital approx. £40 million);
- Secondary schools: Balmoral High School, Wellington College, Drumglass, St Genevieve's.

However, even with this PPP activity Northern Ireland's educational estate will require sustained investment in buildings and equipment in coming years. It is possible that much of the "catching up" that is essential can be achieved under the Reinvestment and Reform Initiative (RRI) which allows the Northern Ireland government to borrow considerable low cost funds for infrastructural development.

Delivery of Northern Ireland Education Service

Department of Education

The education system in Northern Ireland is administered by the Department of Education (NI), one of the ten departments devolved under the new arrangements for the government of Northern Ireland. The Department's stated aim and objective is:

"To ensure that the education service addresses the needs of the Northern Ireland community and to lead and support it in doing so".

Supporting objectives:

- Targeting under-achievement and increasing employability;
- Supporting teaching and learning;
- Targeting the needs of individuals;
- Promoting equity and a culture of inclusion;
- Improving the school estate;
- Supporting education partners;
- Promoting improvement and assuring quality in teaching and learning;
- Supporting the changing needs of today's youth;
- Promoting accountability.

Contact:
Rathgael House
Balloo Road
Bangor
BT19 7PR
Tel: 028 9127 9279
Fax: 028 9127 9100
E-mail: deni@nics.gov.uk
Web: www.deni.gov.uk

Statistics and Research Branch
Contact: Nicola Wilson
Tel: 028 9127 9311
Fax: 028 9127 9594
E-mail: nicola.wilson@deni.gov.uk

Further detailed information about the Department is set out in Chapter 4.

Overview of Education and Library Boards

The Education and Library (NI) Order 1972 took control of the provision of education and library services from local authorities, and placed it under the direction of new Education and Library Boards. Five new Boards were established in 1973 to cover Northern Ireland: Belfast, Northern, Western, Southern and South Eastern.

The Constitution of each Board is laid down primarily in the following legislation:

- Education and Libraries (NI) Order 1986;
- Education Reform (NI) Order 1989;
- Education and Libraries (NI) Order 1993;
- Education and Libraries (NI) Order 1997;
- Education and Libraries (NI) Order 1998.

Functions, Duties, Powers and Services

Within the public education system, Education and Library Boards have statutory responsibility for primary and secondary education within their respective areas. The system of education is divided into three stages:

- Primary Education: for pupils aged 5-11 in Key Stages 1 and 2;
- Secondary Education: for pupils aged 11-18 in Key Stages 3 and 4 and post-16 studies;
- Further Education: for people over compulsory school age.

Each Board must also have regard for the need for pre-school education. Boards are responsible for the provision of a youth service and library services to schools and the public.

The principal duties of each Board are:

- To contribute to the spiritual, moral, cultural, intellectual and physical development of the community;
- To ensure that there are sufficient schools for providing primary and secondary education;
- To secure special education provision for those children who have been identified as having special educational needs;
- To provide a comprehensive and efficient library service for people who live, work or undertake courses of study within its area;
- To secure the provision for their respective areas of adequate facilities for recreational, social, physical, cultural and youth service activities and for services ancillary to education.

In support of these main provisions the Board undertakes a range of duties and provides a variety of services including:

- Admission arrangements to schools;
- School transport, meals and milk;
- Music Service;
- Providing a range of services for children with special needs;
- Education welfare services, schools' psychological services and services relating to child protection;
- Provision of boarding and clothing grants;
- Monitoring the employment of school children for compliance with legislative requirements;
- Management and implementation of the transfer procedure;
- Facilitating the provision of student loans and grants;
- Maintenance of controlled and maintained schools, including payment of salaries, provision of a purchasing service and human resources;
- Appointment of boards of governors;
- Employment of teachers in controlled schools and other staff in controlled and maintained schools;
- Legal and insurance services.

Each Education and Library Board has 32-35 members, appointed by the Minister responsible for the Department of Education in Northern Ireland and representative of the following:

- Each Local Government District in the Board's area;
- Transferors' interests;
- Trustees of maintained schools;
- Those with an interest in the services provided by the Board.

Belfast Education and Library Board

40 Academy Street
Belfast
BT1 2NQ
Tel: 028 9056 4000
Fax: 028 9033 1714

Chairperson: Anne Odling-Smee
Chief Executive: David Cargo

Belfast Education and Library Board is the local education and library authority for the area served by Belfast City Council, covering, according to the 2001 census figures a population of 277,391. Approximately 65,000 children are enrolled in 178 schools in the Belfast Area. The Board provides 21 libraries, library services to hospitals and homes, a schools' library service, a teachers' reference library and the Northern Ireland Schools' Video Library.

The Board provides music tuition through the School of Music. It also provides a comprehensive youth service through the operation of 53 controlled youth organisations, and support for over 350 voluntary youth organisations. It also maintains two outdoor centres at Delamont and Drumalla, which are used extensively by people from a wide range of schools and youth organisations. Specialist resource and teachers' centres are located in Mountcollyer and Ulidia.

Expenditure

During the financial year 2000-2001, Belfast Education and Library Board spent a total of £174.8 million, the main portion of this going to schools (£154.5 million). A further £12 million went to other education services, bringing the total spent on education to £166.5 million. The remaining £8.4 million was split between Culture, Arts and Leisure, and Further and Higher Education.

Helpful Contact Numbers: BELB

Registry Fax	028 9033 1714
Central Library	028 9024 3233
Complaints	028 9056 4289
Education Welfare Service	028 9056 4098
Equal Opportunities	028 9056 4124
Health & Safety	028 9056 4162
Human Resources	028 9056 4010
LMS (Local Management of Schools)	028 9056 4205
School of Music	028 9032 2435
Student Awards	028 9056 4235
Transfer	028 9056 4082
Transport	028 9056 4270
Mountcollyer Technology Centre	028 9035 2435
Ulidia Centre for Resources & Training	028 9049 1058
Delamont	028 4482 1010
Drumalla	028 2888 5247

Board Membership

The total Board is comprised of 35 persons.

Chair: Mrs Anne Odling-Smee

Vice Chair: Cllr Jim Rodgers

Representative of Transferors of Schools:
Rev David Cooper, Rev Canon Walter Lewis,
Rev John Dickinson, Rev Dr Donald Patton

Representative of the Trustees of Maintained Schools:
Gerry Hamill, Finbarr McCallion, Rev John McManus,
James Toner

Ministerial Nominations:
Edwin Paynter, Carmel McKinney, Nigel Butterwick, Dr
Michael Harriott, Jim Cooper, Margaret Cruickshank, Mary
Campbell, Jim Collins, Dr Pamela Montgomery, Trevor
Blayney, Patricia Diamond, John MacVicar

Nominated by Belfast City Council: Cllr Catherine Molloy,
Cllr Nelson McCausland, Cllr Rev Eric Smyth, Cllr David
Browne, Cllr Jim Clarke, Cllr Jim Rodgers, William
Hutchinson, Cllr Nigel Dodds, Cllr Danny Dow, Cllr Chris
McGimpsey, Cllr Stephen McBride, Cllr Fred Proctor, Cllr
Harry Smith, Cllr Margaret Walsh

North Eastern Education and Library Board

County Hall
182 Galgorm Road
Ballymena
Co Antrim
BT42 1HN
Tel: 028 2565 3333
Fax: 028 2564 6071
Web: www.neelb.org.uk
Chairperson: James Currie
Chief Executive: Gordon Topping

The North Eastern Education and Library Board is the
local education and library authority for most of County
Antrim and the eastern part of County Londonderry,
comprising the Local Government Districts of Antrim,
Ballymena, Ballymoney, Carrickfergus, Coleraine, Larne,
Magherafelt, Moyle and Newtownabbey.

The population of the Board's area in the 2001 census
was 394,384. (The 2001 mid-year population estimate
was 395,514). School enrolment figures from
1999/2000 indicate that 74,657 children are enrolled in
schools within the Board's area. This includes 1984
children in 17 nursery schools; 37,461 in 214 primary

schools; 18,805 in 35 secondary schools; 947 in 11
special schools and 4,572 in 6 grammar schools. There
are also 9,306 pupils attending 11 voluntary grammar
schools and 866 pupils in 5 grant maintained integrated
schools, and 716 pupils in 2 grant maintained integrated
post-primary schools.

There are 36 branch libraries, 9 public service mobile
libraries and 4 schools' mobile libraries in the area. A
1994/1995 Youth Service Survey indicates that 38,839
young people aged 5-25 are members of youth
organisations within the Board's area. There are 37
controlled youth clubs and 482 voluntary youth
organisations.

The Board is the employing authority of approximately
10,745 people in full-time and part-time capacities.

Board Membership

Chairperson: J Currie

Vice-Chair: J Christie

Members: D D Barbour, J R Beggs MP, R F Cavan,
O M Church, J Convery, J M Crilly, M W Crockett,
M P Devine, U M Duncan, L Frazer, J A Gaston,
P A Gillespie, Rev D S Graham, L A Hicklin,
Rev J T Jamieson, M J Johnston, M Laverty,
J A McBride, K M McCann, A P McConaghy, S A McCrea,
Rev F J McDowell, P G McShane, N S Macartney,
N C Murray, C M Poots, J C Reid, Rev R B Savage,
A J Templeton, R Thompson, A D C Watson,
C Wegwermer, W T Wright

South Eastern Education and Library Board

Grahamsbridge Road
Dundonald
Belfast
BT16 2HS
Tel: 028 9056 6200
Fax: 028 9056 6266
Web: www.seelb.org.u

Chairperson: Rev Dr D J Watts
Chief Executive: Jackie Fitzsimons

Library Headquarters
Windmill Hill
Ballynahinch
BT24 8DH
Tel: 028 9756 6400
Fax: 028 9756 5072

The South Eastern Education and Library Board covers much of County Down, including the Local Government Districts of Ards, Castlereagh, Lisburn and North Down. The population of the Board's area in 2001 was 388,577. School enrolment figures indicate that at October 2001 there were 66,700 children attending schools in the area. The Board is responsible for 18 nursery schools, 11 nursery/pre-school units, 163 primary schools, 29 secondary schools, 10 grammar schools and 28 special units. The Board also provides or supports 31 public library service points, 3 outdoor education centres, 550 youth organisations, 2 resource centres and a music centre.

Expenditure

During the financial year ending 31 March 2001, the South Eastern Board spent a total of £228.4 million. The majority went on schools, with smaller amounts spent on library and other services.

Structure of the Board

The work of the Board is carried out through a committee structure; the committees being as follows:

- Audit Committee
- Chairmen's Committee
- Committee for the Management of Schools
- Education Committee
- Expulsions Committee
- Finance and Property Services Committee
- General Purposes Committee
- Library and Information Committee
- Teaching Appointments Committee
- Youth Committee

The principal departmental units are set out below.

Administration Unit:	Human Resources
	Property Services
	Transport
	Legal and Insurance
	Corporate and Business Planning
	Open Enrolment and
	Transfer Service

Chief Executive's Unit:	Internal Audit Unit
	Legal Service
Curriculum Unit:	Curriculum Advisory and Support Service
	Educational Psychology Service
	Educational Welfare Service
	Pre-school Education
	Special Education Service
	Youth Service
Finance Unit:	Accounting Support Unit
	Financial Support Unit
	Purchasing Unit
	Awards and Benefits Unit
	Direct Service Organisations Unit
Library and Information Service:	Library and Information Service
	Corporate Information Services
	IT Services

Contacts

Chief Executive:	Jackie Fitzsimons
Chief Finance Officer:	Ken Brown
Senior Education Officer:	Stanton Sloan
Chief Librarian:	Beth Porter
Senior Education Officer (admin):	Martin Graham

Board Membership

Chairperson: Rev D J Watts

Vice Chair: Cllr R Gibson

Members: Rev Dr J P O'Barry, Rev C W Bell, Cllr P A Butler, D Cahill, Cllr C Calvert, J Campbell, K Cleland, J L Colgan, S I Davidson, Cllr G N Douglas, Cllr R M Dunlop, Ald G Ennis, M P Flanagan, F A Gault, Cllr R Gibson, Cllr G H Gregory, Rev G N Haire, Ald C Hall, R Jones, R J McFerran, M M McGoran, M M McHenry, A McReynolds, D G Mullan, Cllr J Norris, Cllr C O'Boyle, E M Robinson, Rev Dr R A Russell, Cllr M Smith, G Tigchelaar, J D Uprichard, Cllr W M Ward, Cllr W G Watson, Rev Dr D J Watts, J Williams, Cllr A Wilson

Southern Education and Library Board

3 Charlemont Place
The Mall
Armagh
BT61 9AX
Tel: 028 3751 2200
Fax: 028 3751 2490
Web: www.selb.org

Chairperson: M Alexander
Chief Executive: Helen McClenaghan

Head of Corporate Services:	T Heron
Head of Educational Services:	W Burke
Chief Architect:	A McGee
Inter-Board Services Manager:	J Curran
Human Resources Manager:	Pat Keating

The Southern Education and Library Board is the local authority for education and library services in the Armagh, Banbridge, Cookstown, Craigavon, Dungannon and Newry and Mourne Local Government Districts.

The population of the area, as of April 2001 was 343,700 including 88,600 pupils. To serve this population the Board provides or maintains 18 nursery, 238 primary, 36 secondary, 3 grammar and 6 special schools. It also provides 23 public libraries, 12 youth centres and 3 outdoor education centres. Services are also offered to a further 12 voluntary grammar schools and 8 grant maintained integrated schools in the area, along with 448 voluntary youth clubs.

The Board is the employer of 7844 staff. It is required by law to have 2 statutory committees: the Library Committee and the Teaching Appointments Committee. It also has a number of other committees through which much of its detailed work is carried out:

- Education Committee;
- Services Committee;
- Direct Service Committee;
- Committee for Peripatetic Teachers;
- Teachers' Staffing Committee;
- Audit Committee;
- Special Education Committee;
- Consultants Selection Panel;
- Membership Committee;
- Special Business Committee;
- Policy Committee;
- Best Value Committee;
- Remuneration Committee.

Expenditure

During the financial year 2000/2001, the revenue budget for the Board was £225 million. The majority of this was delegated to schools, with smaller amounts going to various other areas.

Board Membership

Chairperson: Mrs M Alexander
Vice Chair: Very Rev L M McVeigh

P H Aiken, M Alexander, Cllr J F Bell, Cllr P Brannigan, S R Brownlee, Rev J Byrne, M P Campbell, Cllr E Corry, Ald F E Crowe, Dr P Cunningham, M E Donnell, Cllr J Feehan, S M B Fitzpatrick, E Gill, Cllr I E B Hanna, Cllr J Hanna, Ald G A Hatch, Cllr A B Lewis, C Mackin, Cllr W J Martin, W Mayne, P C McAleavey, Cllr P P McAleer, D A McBride, C M McCaul, Rev C D McClure, Cllr P McGinn, Cllr W J McIlwrath, Cllr B Monteith, Very Rev S Rice, J W Saunders, A G Sleator, Rev Canon F D Swann, Rev Canon W R Twaddell

Western Education and Library Board

1 Hospital Road
Omagh
Co Tyrone
BT79 0AW
Tel: 028 8241 1411
Fax: 028 8241 1400
Web: www.welbni.org
Chairperson: H Faulkner
Chief Executive: Joseph Martin

The Western Education and Library Board is the local authority for the provision of education, library and youth services in the District Council areas of Derry, Fermanagh, Limavady, Omagh and Strabane.

The area has a population of 281,215. There are over 63,000 pupils attending schools and over 137,000 registered library users. The Board provides or maintains 10 nursery, 191 primary, 10 special, 35 secondary/ high, 4 grammar schools and 16 public libraries. In addition, services are provided to 9 voluntary grammar and 5 grant-maintained integrated schools. The Board also makes extensive provision for youth facilities and over 400 registered youth groups are supported.

The Board has 32 members. The activities of the Board are managed through the Education, Library, Services, Finance and Youth Committees. The Board also has a Teaching Appointments Committee and an Audit Committee. Minutes of the Board and its committees are available for consultation at Headquarters Office, District Offices and Public Libraries.

The Western Board also has a responsibility, on behalf of the five Education and Library Boards, for the Classroom 2000 Project, which has as its purpose the design, development and operation of an ICT infrastructure to support the curricular, management and information needs of the major bodies within the education service in Northern Ireland.

Executive Organisation

Chief Executive: Joseph Martin

Curriculum: Sheila McCaul

Finance: Ciaran Doran

Library: Helen Osborn

Services: Arthur Rainey

The Board is managed by a Chief Executive through leadership of a team of four Departmental Heads, representing Curriculum, Finance, Library and Services. The Audit Section reports directly to the Chief Executive.

The purpose of the Curriculum Department is to provide a range of advice and support services to schools, youth groups and parents in order to improve the standard of pupils' and young persons' achievements and the quality of their learning experiences.

The purpose of the Finance Department is to secure maximum funding for the services, which the Board provides, and thereafter to allocate resources in accordance with the Board's corporate objectives, and to ensure that proper systems are available to enable financial monitoring and evaluation to take place.

The purpose of the Library Service is to provide access to a comprehensive range of books, information and library facilities in support of the educational, economic and cultural needs of people in the area.

The purpose of the Services Department is to provide the Board with a wide range of services including responsibility for school planning and capital provision, estate management, school administration and recurrent funding, human resources and support services.

Expenditure

During the financial year ending 31 March 2001, the Western Board's total expenditure was £229.6m. This was largely made up by a departmental grant, as well as funding from other sources. The majority of expenditure was on schools, with smaller amounts spent on library and other services.

Board Members

Chairperson: H Faulkner
Vice Chair: H Mullan

Members: M Bradley, A Brolly, E F Brunt, Dr J Cornyn, M Cunningham, P Donnelly, P Duffy, F G Durkan, P Fleming, M Garfield, Rev R Herron, D Hussey, R Irvine, J Kerr, N W Lambert, S MacCionnaith, J P Martin, E S McCaffrey, B T McCusker, B McElduff, D N McElholm, C McGill, M McLaughlin, D McNamee, S Morrow, H Mullan, J O'Kane, T O'Reilly, Archdeacon C T Pringle, D Rainey, S Shields, E Stevenson, E Waterson

Other Agencies and Organisations in Education

Staff Commision for Education and Library Boards

Forestview
Purdy's Lane
Belfast
BT8 7AR
Tel:028 9049 1461
Fax: 028 9049 1744
E-mail: info@staffcom.org.uk
Chairman: Maurice Moroney

The Staff Commission for Education and Library Boards is an Executive Non Departmental Public Body whose aim is to oversee recruitment, promotion, training and terms and conditions of employment for people working in Education and Library Boards in Northern Ireland.

CCEA

Rewarding Learning

CCEA
29 Clarendon Road,
Clarendon Dock,
Belfast BT1 3BG

Tel: 028 9026 1200
Fax: 028 9026 1234
E-mail: info@ccea.org.uk
Web: www.ccea.org.uk

CCEA is a unique educational body in the UK bringing together the three areas of curriculum, examinations and assessment.

The CCEA was set up by Government to provide advice on and support for what is taught in schools and colleges in Northern Ireland, and how it is assessed. The CCEA is responsible for assessment of pupils at Key Stages 1, 2 and 3, and accreditation of Records of Achievement. The Council conducts public examinations such as GCSE, CES, Certificate of Educational Achievement and Graded Objectives in Modern Languages for students aged 16 to 19 and beyond, and administers the transfer test (known as the 11 plus) on behalf of the Department of Education. The Council is also responsible for the regulation of GNVQs in Northern Ireland. In recent years there have been incidents of public concern over test content leaks and declarations of incorrect grades.

Chief Executive: Gavin Boyd
Head of Corporate Services: G Crossan
Head of Education Services: Dr A Walker

Membership of CCEA Council

CCEA's Council consists of a Chairman and 17 other members appointed by the Department of Education and includes representatives from education, industry and commerce as well as having two assessors from the Department.

Chairman: Dr Alan Lennon

Council for Catholic Maintained Schools (CCMS)

160 High Street
Holywood
Co Down
BT18 9HT
Tel: 028 9042 6972
Fax: 028 9042 4255
Chairman: Most Rev J McAreavey DD, Bishop of Dromore
Chief Executive: Donal Flanagan

The Council for Catholic Maintained Schools (CCMS), although entirely independent, has a role in relation to the management of Catholic Schools not unlike the role of an Education and Library Board in relation to controlled schools. It manages, on behalf of the voluntary maintained (Catholic) sector, matters such as staff recruitment and appointments, maintenance and finance. CCMS also has a strong input into the curriculum, where there is an emphasis on maintaining the appropriate ethos in the school environment.

Northern Ireland Higher Education Council

Adelaide House
39-49 Adelaide Street
Belfast
BT2 8FD
Tel: 028 9025 7777
Fax: 028 9025 7778
Chairman: Tony Hopkins CBE

The Northern Ireland Higher Education Council (NIHEC) is a non-executive advisory body established in April 1993. It provides advice to the Department for Employment and Learning on the planning and funding of higher education in Northern Ireland. It is particularly concerned with educational standards, facilities and research.

Training in Northern Ireland

Overview of Training

Overall training policy in Northern Ireland rests with the Department for Employment and Learning (DEL). DEL runs numerous focused training programmes using subcontractors for most of the delivery. These programmes range from basic work skills for school leavers, through to Executive Programmes for senior management and business executives.

There is also a tier of officially recognised training organisations (Registered Training Organisations, or RTOs) who deliver training programmes on the ground and who perform a valuable function in recruiting the right participants for each programme. The RTOs generally focus on training young people starting out on their working careers. (A list of RTOs is set out below).

A major trend in training is the increasing emphasis on IT skills, now considered as important as literacy and numeracy in a trainee's profile. However, traditional skills in the trades sector are still very important in Northern Ireland's training mix. Most of the training for joiners, plumbers, bricklayers, electricians, etc, is delivered at government training centres dispersed around Northern Ireland's main population centres. There are also specialist training centres for skills leading to qualified technician status, for example instrumentation, cable jointing, etc.

Department for Employment and Learning

Local Minister Carmel Hanna headed the Department for Employment and Learning, until the restoration of direct rule on 15 October 2002 when Minister of State Jane Kennedy of the Northern Ireland Office assumed responsibility for the department. The department has overall responsibility for training and raising skill levels generally across Northern Ireland.

Training and Employment Support Programmes

Until recently, the Department for Employment and Learning managed the Training and Employment Agency (T&EA), responsible for all government sponsored training and employment support programmes. Following the restructuring of the department, the Training and Employment Agency, previously a "next-step" agency has been integrated fully into DEL.

One board, the Learning and Skills Advisory Board, replaced the board of the Training and Employment Agency and the Further Education Consultative Committee.

Details of the many employment support programmes operated by the Department are set out below.

Skills and Employment

Jobskills

The Jobskills programme is the primary vocational training route for young people, which leads to Traineeships at NVQ Level 2 and to Modern Apprenticeships at NVQ Level 3.

DEL has made changes designed to re-focus Jobskills on the delivery of key skills, to address skill shortages and to encourage greater employment involvement in training, particularly at craft level.

New Deal

The New Deal is the central element in the Government's Welfare to Work strategy and has two main objectives:

- To help young and long-term unemployed people into jobs and to improve their prospects of progressing into and staying in employment; and
- To increase the employability of long-term unemployed people, thereby making a positive contribution contributing to sustainable levels of employment and a reduction in social exclusion.

New Deal For 25+

This New Deal is also aimed at people aged 25 and over who have been claiming Jobseeker's Allowance for 18 months or more. After a Gateway period (of up to 3 months), people who are still unemployed can progress to one of the following:

- Employment: a subsidised job with an employer;
- Education and Training: a vocationally relevant course lasting up to one year;
- Intensive Activity Period: up to 13 weeks of intensive training aimed at improving participants' workskills, work experience, motivation and providing help towards self-employment.

Community Employment Programmes

Worktrack

Worktrack is designed to complement New Deal. It is a waged programme providing the long-term unemployed with temporary employment with training for up to 26 weeks duration, focusing on the needs of the individual, with the aim of progressing participants into suitable employment at the earliest opportunity.

Enterprise Ulster

This statutory organisation aims to provide employment, training and work related experience for the unemployed through a range of activities mostly of an environmental or amenity nature.

Lifelong Learning

"Lifelong Learning: a New Culture for All" is DEL's plan for lifelong learning. The plan aims to increase the overall levels of and broaden participation in adult learning; to address clear deficiencies in basic literacy and numeric skills; to improve information about and access to learning opportunities by individuals and businesses.

Modern Apprenticeships

DEL has continued to encourage direct employer involvement in the delivery of Modern Apprenticeships. There are 10 individual training programmes, involving over 5,000 apprentices, in a range of sectors including electrical insulation telecommunications, printing, catering and hospitality. These programmes run alongside those being delivered by Jobskills.

Guidance Service

DEL's career officers provide a guidance service to all young people entering the labour market and to unemployed adults. In addition to this work with young people, Careers Officers also helped many thousands of adults with guidance and help with career changes.

Bridge to Employment

The main aim of this programme is to provide customised training courses to equip the unemployed and in particular long-term unemployed people with the skills necessary to compete for jobs on an equal basis with others. The programme, funded by the European Union Special Support Programme for Peace and Reconciliation, is specifically aimed at job opportunities created by inward investment and local expanding companies.

NI Skills Task Force

Following the Chancellor's Economic Initiative, a Skills Task Force for Northern Ireland has been established. The task force advises on Labour Market Research and Monitoring Activities, broad policy issues linked to the determination of skill needs in Northern Ireland and on measures, which might be taken to address future skills needs. Membership of the Task Force includes employers and trade union representatives, as well as senior officials from Government Departments and agencies.

Première 2

Première 2 is an intensive graduate management development programme, which aims to develop participants' employability in management whilst also seeking to improve business performance across growth companies in Northern Ireland.

Business Education Initiative (BEI)

BEI is an innovative programme aimed at offering undergraduate students from Northern Ireland and the border counties the opportunity to study business and management in the USA.

Management Development Pilot Programmes

Over recent years the following programmes were developed and implemented:

Management Standards

To promote management standards throughout Northern Ireland, DEL joined with the Management Charter Initiative (MCI) to commission a series of case studies using the standards in local companies. DEL has also been encouraging interest in Management NVQs, based on the management standards as part of their management developmental programmes.

Management Council

The Council consists of leading figures drawn from the private sector and industry influencers. Their overarching goal is the implementation of a management development strategy to strengthen the global competitiveness of Northern Ireland economy.

(Further detailed information on support for business in Northern Ireland is set out in Chapter 9.)

Training Organisations

What follows is an extensive (but not exhaustive) list of registered training organisations across Northern Ireland.

Abbey Training Services
314 Antrim Road
Glengormley
Newtownabbey BT36 8EH
Tel: 028 9084 0527

Advance Training & Development
South Eastern Education & Library Board
Youth Section Block 3
Grahamsbridge Road
Belfast BT16 2HS
Contact: Jimmy Peel
Tel: 028 9056 6938

Ballymena Training Centre
73 Fenaghy Road
Galgorm
Ballymena BT42 1HW
Contact: Mrs J McKay
Tel: 028 2565 6561

BCW Training Ltd
Unit 18
Leyland Road
Ballycastle
Co Antrim BT54 6EZ
Contact: Mr C Craig
Tel: 028 2076 2902

Beechvalley Training Co Ltd
Craigavon Crescent
Dungannon
Co Tyrone BT71 7BN
Tel: 028 8772 4440

Belfast Central Training Limited
Donegall House
98-102 Donegall Street
Belfast BT1 2GW
Contact: John Savage
Tel: 028 9032 4973

Belfast Centre of Learning
1 Rossmore Avenue
Ormeau Road
Belfast BT7 3HB
Contact: Marie Irvine
Tel: 028 9064 0446

Belfast College Of Training & Education Ltd
Franklin House
12 Brunswick Street
Belfast BT2 7GE
Contact: Colette Steele
Tel: 028 9023 2186

Belfast Institute Training & Employment Services
Jobskills Central Admin
Room F4, 5th Floor
Millfield Building
Belfast BT1 1HS
Contact: Anne-Marie Barr
Tel: 028 9026 5433

Blackwater House
Blackwater Road
Mallusk
Co Antrim BT36 4TZ
Contact: Pamela Morgan
Tel: 028 9034 2400

Brookfield Business School
333 Crumlin Road
Belfast BT14 7EA
Contact: Margaret Higgins
Tel: 028 9075 1293

Castlereagh College of Further Education
Montgomery Road
Belfast BT6 9JD
Contact: Una Carlin
Tel: 028 9079 7144

Causeway Institute of Further and Higher Education
2 Coleraine Road
Ballymoney
Co Antrim BT53 6BP
Contact: Mr I Williams
Tel: 028 2766 0404

Clanrye Employment & Training Services
The Abbey
Abbey Yard
Newry BT34 2EG
Contact: Liam Devine
Tel: 028 3026 7121

Coalisland Training Services Ltd
51 Dungannon Road
Coalisland
Co Tyrone BT71 4HP
Contact: Richard Thornton
Tel: 028 8774 8502

College Training & Employment Centre
72-76 Main Street
Limavady
Co Londonderry BT49 0ET
Contact: Alwin Stewart
Tel: 028 7776 2745

Construction Industry Training Board
17 Dundrod Road
Crumlin
Co Antrim BT29 4SR
Contact: Allan McMullen
Tel: 028 9082 5466

Cookstown Training
45a James Street
Cookstown
Co Tyrone BT80 8AA
Contact: Jennifer Hamilton
Tel: 028 8676 1145

CTRS Computer Training
The New Hope Centre
Erne Road
Enniskillen
Co Fermanagh BT74 6NN
Contact: Vera Samuel
Tel: 028 6632 8073

Customized Training Services Limited
Units 11 & 12
3-5 Main Street
Strabane BT82 8AR
Contact: Carmel Boyce
Tel: 028 7138 2260

Dairy Farm Jobskills
Unit 18
Dairy Farm Centre
Stewartstown Road
Belfast BT17 0EA
Contact: Ronan Heenan
Tel: 028 9061 8452

DDA Training Services Ltd
21 William Street
Dungannon
Co Tyrone BT70 1DX
Contact: Donal Laverty
Tel: 028 8772 6342

East Antrim Institute
400 Shore Road
Newtownabbey
Co Antrim BT37 9RS
Contact: John Blaney
Tel: 028 9085 5000

East Down Institute TES
Market Street
Downpatrick
Co Down BT30 6ND
Tel: 028 4461 5815

East Tyrone College
of Further Education
Circular Road
Dungannon
Co Tyrone BT71 6BQ
Contact: Tony Dardis
Tel: 028 8772 2323

Electrical Training Trust Ltd
Unit 57-59
Ballymena Business
Development Centre
62 Fenaghy Road
Ballymena BT42 1FL
Contact: Ronnie Geary
Tel: 028 2565 0750

Engineering Training Council
Interpoint
20-24 York Street
Belfast BT15 1AQ
Contact: David Hatton
Tel: 028 9032 9878

Enniskillen College of Agriculture
Levaghy
Enniskillen BT74 4GF
Contact: Seamus McAliney
Tel: 028 6634 4802

Enniskillen Training Centre
Killyhevlin Industrial Estate
Enniskillen
Co Fermanagh BT74 4EJ
Contact: Dermott Hevlin
Tel: 028 6632 2072

Federation of The Retail
Licensed Trade NI
91 University Street
Belfast BT7 1HP
Contact: Nichola Jamison
Tel: 028 9032 7578

Felden Training Centre
Mill Road
Newtownabbey
Co Antrim BT36 7BJ
Contact: Irvine Abraham
Tel: 028 9085 6421

Fermanagh College
1 Dublin Road
Enniskillen
Co Fermanagh BT74 6AE
Contact: Brian Rouse
Tel: 028 6632 2431

Fermanagh Training Ltd
Skills Centre
Killyhevlin Industrial Estate
Enniskillen
Co Fermanagh BT74 4EJ
Contact: Martin Maguire
Tel: 028 6632 4860

Greenmount College
22 Greenmount Road
Antrim BT41 4PU
Contact: John Fey
Tel: 028 9442 6674

Hugh J O'Boyle Training Limited
114 Irish Street
Downpatrick
Co Down BT30 6BT
Contact: John Carson
Tel: 028 4461 6438

Impact Training (NI) Ltd
16 Lanark Way
Belfast BT13 3BH
Contact: Florence Irvine
Tel: 028 9033 9910

Jennymount Training Services/
Hair Academy
Jennymount Court
Lanyon Buildings
North Derby Street
Belfast BT15 3HN
Contact: William McIlvoy
Tel: 028 9075 6658

Joblink - Limavady
42 Catherine Street
Limavady
BT49 9DB
Contact: Mairead Farren
Tel: 028 7772 2174

Joblink - North East
62-64 New Row
Coleraine BT52 1EJ
Contact: Colm McCaughan
Tel: 028 7032 8555

Joblink - Strabane
Abercorn House
Railway Street
Strabane BT82 8EF
Contact: Monica Langon
Tel: 028 7138 2811

Joblink - Waterloo House
48 Waterloo Street
Londonderry BT48 6HF
Contact: James Logue
Tel: 028 7137 0300

Joblink Braid Ltd
48-50 Linenhall Street
Ballymena BT43 5AL
Contact: Colin McCaughan
Tel: 028 2563 1800

JTM Youth &
Adult Employment Agency
9-11 Linenhall Street
Ballymena
Co Antrim BT43 5AJ
Contact: Trevor Magee
Tel: 028 2565 6567

JTM Youth &
Adult Employment Agency
29 Church Street
Ballymena
Co Antrim BT43 6DD
Contact: Patricia Cathcart
Tel: 028 2563 0033

JTM Youth &
Adult Employment Agency
24 The Diamond
Coleraine BT52 1DP
Contact: Stephen Gaston
Tel: 028 7035 6677

Larne Skills Development Limited
Units 10 & 11 Larne Business Centre
Bank Road
Larne BT40 3AW
Contact: Owen Vice
Tel: 028 2827 3337

LETS Training & Employment Ltd
100 Hill Street
Lurgan
Co Armagh BT66 6BQ
Contact: Miles Haughey
Tel: 028 3832 7307

Lisburn Institute
39 Castle Street
Lisburn
Co Antrim BT27 4SU
Contact: Mr McReynolds
Tel: 028 9267 7225

Lisburn Training Centre
4 Knockmore Road
Lisburn
Co Antrim BT28 2EB
Contact: Mr McReynolds
Tel: 028 9267 3437

Loughview Training College
1 Ballyclare Road
Glengormley
Newtownabbey BT36 5EX
Contact: Anne Irwin
Tel: 028 9080 1010

Maydown Training Centre
5 Carrakeel Drive
Maydown
Londonderry BT47 6UQ
Contact: Susanne Currie
Tel: 028 7186 0293

Maydown Youth Training Project
Ebrington Centre
Glendermot Road
Waterside
Londonderry BT47 6BG
Contact: Glen Barr
Tel: 028 7131 1005

Melbourne Training &
Employment Services Ltd
Brown Square
Peters Hill
Belfast
BT13 2GP
Contact: Jim Rogers
Tel: 028 9032 9931

Network Personnel Ltd
The Business Centre
80-82 Rainey Street
Magherafelt BT45 5AJ
Contact: Anne McBride
Tel: 028 7963 1032

Newry & Kilkeel Institute
Patrick Street
Newry
Co Down BT35 8DN
Contact: Mr Mullen
Tel: 028 30261071

Newry Training Centre
Ballinacraig Way
Newry
Co Down BT34 2QX
Contact: Mr Mullen
Tel: 028 3026 4721

North City Training Ltd
275 Antrim Road
Belfast BT15 2GZ
Contact: Liam McNeil
Tel: 028 9074 5408

North Down & Ards Institute (ITEC)
Victoria Avenue
Newtownards
Co Down BT23 7EH
Tel: 028 9181 8053

North Down Training Ltd
4-6 Conway Square
Newtownards
Co Down BT23 4DD
Contact: Nigel Finch
Tel: 028 9182 2880

North East Institute of Further And
Higher Education
Ballymena Campus
25 Castle Street
Ballymena BT43 7BT
Tel: 028 2565 2871

Nothern Ireland Hotel & Catering
College
Ballywillan Road
Portrush
Co Antrim BT56 8JL
Contact: Lucia Campbell
Tel: 028 7082 3768

Omagh College
2 Mountjoy Road
Omagh
Co Tyrone BT79 7AH
Contact: Victor Refauffe
Tel: 028 8224 5433

Omagh Training Centre
Woodside Avenue
Omagh
Co Tyrone BT79 7BT
Contact: Malachy McAleer
Tel: 028 8225 4955

Orchard Training Services Ltd
63 Park Road
Portadown
Co Armagh BT62 1DS
Contact: Ben Ferron
Tel: 028 3833 1573

Oriel Training Services
35 Main Street
Randalstown
Co Antrim BT41 3AB
Contact: Bill Clinton
Tel: 028 9447 8860

Peter Mark School Of Hairdressing
42 Great Victoria Street
Belfast BT2 7BA
Contact: Anita McArdle
Tel: 028 9031 1968

Sea Fish Industry Training Association
(NI) Ltd
The John Warnock Centre
The Harbour (Off Princess Anne Road)
Portavogie BT22 1EA
Tel: 028 4277 1556

Seven Towers Training Ltd
2-4 Railway Street
Ballymena
Co Antrim BT42 2AB
Contact: Kim Alexander
Tel: 028 2564 4003

Shantallow Training Services Ltd
Marion Hall
Steelstown Road
Londonderry BT48 8EU
Tel: 028 7135 1190

Southern Group Enterprises
Unit 22 Greenbank Industrial Estate
Newry BT34 2QU
Contact: Robert Barton
Tel: 028 3026 6924

Southern ITEC Limited
52 Armagh Road
Newry BT35 6DP
Contact: Briege Burns
Tel: 028 3026 8131

Spring Skills (Belfast)
Third Floor
Scottish Legal House
65-67 Chichester Street
Belfast BT1 4JD
Contact: Janice McBrinn
Tel: 028 9033 0331

Spring Skills (Derry)
1st Floor
50-54a Waterloo Street
Londonderry BT48 6HE
Contact: Janice McBrinn
Tel: 028 7137 3002

Spring Skills (Newry)
2 Marcus Street
Newry
Co Down BT34 1AZ
Contact: Janice McBrinn
Tel: 028 3026 4440

Springvale Training Ltd
200 Springfield Road
Belfast BT12 7DB
Contact: Marie Lyons
Tel: 028 9024 2362

Strabane Training Services Ltd
Ballycolman Industrial Estate
Strabane
Co Tyrone BT82 9PH
Contact: Eugene McCormick
Tel: 028 7138 2438

Springtown Training Centre
Springtown Industrial Estate
Londonderry
BT48 0LY
Contact: Suzanne Corrie
Tel: 028 7126 1026

The Link Works
11 Sugar Island
Newry
Co Down
BT35 6HT
Contact: Johnny Power
Tel: 028 3026 2777

Tourism Training Trust (NI) Ltd
Caernarvon House
19 Donegall Pass
Belfast BT7 1DQ
Contact: Billy Nelson
Tel: 028 9032 0625

Training Direct
NWIFHE
Strand House
20 Strand Road
Londonderry BT48 7AB
Contact: Suzanne Currie
Tel: 028 7137 2575

Transport Training Services Ltd
15 Dundrod Road
Nutts Corner
Crumlin BT29 4ST
Contact: Michael Finch
Tel: 028 9082 5653

Tyrone Training Services
38 Gortin Road
Omagh BT79 7HX
Contact: Sonya McAnulla
Tel: 028 8224 9999

Ulidia Community Vocational College
165-169 Albert Bridge Road
Belfast BT5 4PS
Contact: Raymond McDole
Tel: 028 9073 1030

Upper Bann Institute Of Further &
Higher Education
36 Lurgan Road
Portadown BT63 5BL
Tel: 028 3833 7111

Wade Training Armagh
59-65 Scotch Street
Armagh BT61 7DF
Tel: 028 3752 7955
Fax: 028 3752 7955

Wade Training Lurgan
45 Church Place
Lurgan BT66 6HD
Contact: Annesley Renshaw
Tel: 028 3832 9158

Wade Training Portadown
33 Castle Street
Portadown BT62 1BB
Contact: Emma Burden
Tel: 028 3833 7000

Workforce Training Services Ltd
90-120 Springfield Road
Belfast BT12 7AJ
Contact: Mr McGrath
Tel: 028 9024 7016

Worknet Jobskills
The Glenand Centre
Blackstaff Road
Kennedy Way Industrial Estate
Belfast BT11 9DT
Tel: 028 9020 8020

Workscene Training Organisation
Curran House
Twin Spires Centre
155 Northumberland Street
Belfast BT13 2JF
Contact: Seamus Twomey
Tel: 028 9031 1787

WRTC
10 Hydepark Road
Mallusk
Newtownabbey BT36 4PY
Contact: Gwen Patterson
Tel: 028 9084 5830

Young Help Trust
23-31 Waring Street
Belfast BT1 2DX
Tel: 028 9056 0120

CHAPTER 8

The Northern Ireland Economy

Overview of The Northern Ireland Economy

The Northern Ireland economy is a relatively small regional economy within the United Kingdom and in a European context is a highly peripheral and less favoured economic area.

Although Northern Ireland was traditionally the most industrialised part of Ireland it has gradually been overtaken economically by the adjacent Republic of Ireland economy, which has enjoyed a sustained boom in recent years.

The Northern Ireland economy has some unique characteristics that present structural challenges for the future. These include:

*   An over dependence on the public sector for employment and wealth;
*   A relatively small industrial and manufacturing base;
*   Traditional industries - shipbuilding, engineering, textiles and agriculture, all in crisis or long term decline;
*   Difficulty attracting quality international investment and tourism revenue because of political problems.

However, because these structural difficulties are fully recognised and considerable efforts deployed to counter them, Northern Ireland has an impressively resilient economic long-term performance. It does not collapse into slump in times of international cyclical downturn nor does it enjoy spectacular growth even when all western economies are experiencing a boom.

Although performance has certainly improved over recent years, Northern Ireland is not a major exporter and continues to depend heavily on the rest of the United Kingdom for its key export markets.

GDP and Economic Growth

Northern Ireland accounts for around 2.2 per cent of UK gross domestic product (GDP) and the proportion does not vary greatly around this figure. In recent years Northern Ireland GDP has grown, at rates that have been slightly above the UK average, from £9,329 million in 1989 to £17,003 million in 1999, or £10,050 per capita.

Table 8.1 below indicates that Northern Ireland not only accounts for a small share of UK GDP but also that per capita GDP in Northern Ireland lags behind the UK average by a considerable margin. Historically Northern Ireland GDP per capita has hovered around 75 per cent of the UK average although this improved noticeably in the later 1990s (possibly but not indisputably coinciding with the "peace process") reaching a peak of 81.5 per cent in 1995.

Although GDP per capita is 77.5 per cent of the UK average, it is no longer the lowest of the UK, with the North East of England now slightly lower.

Table 8.1: GDP and GDP per head in Northern Ireland 1989-1999[1]						
	GDP in NI			GDP per head in NI		
	£m	Growth	% of UK	£	Growth	% of UK Average
1989	9,329	–	2.1	5,893	–	74.7
1990	10,013	7.3	2.0	6,300	6.9	73.8
1991	10,890	8.8	2.1	6,787	7.7	76.4
1992	11,611	6.6	2.2	7,163	5.5	77.6
1993	12,437	7.1	2.2	7,610	6.2	78.7
1994	13,344	7.3	2.2	8,114	6.6	79.8
1995	14,297	7.1	2.3	8,654	6.7	81.5
1996	14,936	4.5	2.3	8,964	3.6	80.1
1997	15,952	6.8	2.3	9,507	6.1	80.1
1998	16,501	3.4	2.2	9,754	2.6	77.7
1999	17,003	3.0	2.2	10,050	3.0	77.5

Source: ONS

[1] GDP at factor cost, current prices UK excludes Extra-Regions

The services sector dominates Northern Ireland GDP, accounting for 69.1 per cent in 1998. The growth in the services sector has seen its share rise to this level from 64.5 per cent in 1989. In contrast manufacturing's share has declined from 20.1 per cent to 18.5 per cent in 1998. Although manufacturing's share has declined the sector in Northern Ireland has fared better than in other parts of the UK. Agriculture is an important employer but it now accounts for only 3.9 per cent of GDP.

Table 8.2: Northern Ireland's GDP by industrial sector, 1989 and 1998

	1989 %	1998 %
Agriculture, forestry and fishing	5.5	3.9
Mining and quarrying	0.5	0.5
Manufacturing	20.1	18.5
Electricity, gas and water	2.9	2.1
Construction	6.5	5.9
Services	64.5	69.1
Total	100.0	100.0

Source: ONS

Analysis of Northern Ireland's GDP by sector shows that the economy relies heavily on the public sector. In 1997 health and education accounted for more than the manufacturing sector with both public services accounting for a total of 21 per cent of GDP. Public administration and defence accounted for a further 10.4 per cent.

Comparisons with Republic of Ireland

Although Northern Ireland GDP performance compares favourably with other regions of the UK the comparison with the neighbouring economy of the Irish Republic is quite startling.

Table 8.3: Gross Domestic Product By Industry

Gross domestic product (GDP)

By industry (£ millions)	1990	1991	1992	1993	1994	1995	1996	1997	1998
Agriculture, hunting, forestry and fishing	488	512	641	576	634	794	809	741	653
Mining and quarrying of energy producing materials	10	10	9	9	11	12	9	9	10
Other mining and quarrying	30	29	34	50	74	91	65	72	77
Manufacturing	2,130	2,184	2,293	2,430	2,628	2,777	3,014	3,109	3,135
Electricity, gas and water supply	298	374	372	397	398	400	435	428	354
Construction	652	626	643	675	753	833	868	915	1,001
Wholesale and retail trade (including motor trade)	1,058	1,197	1,266	1,346	1,462	1,597	1,693	1,983	2,085
Hotels and Restaurants	246	259	281	314	330	378	407	459	505
Transport, storage and communication	540	606	639	649	738	793	812	900	938
Financial intermediation	312	326	432	515	618	592	558	583	591
Real estate, renting and business activities	924	1,015	1,064	1,230	1,347	1,477	1,615	1,869	2,175
Public administration and defence	1,445	1,789	1,883	1,967	1,933	1,941	1,960	1,969	1,966
Education	679	819	913	953	953	1,052	1,096	1,252	1,367
Health & social work	864	1,005	1,055	1,143	1,295	1,355	1,376	1,373	1,380
Other services	336	349	378	462	538	554	572	650	672
FISIM	-243	-210	-293	-278	-367	-348	-355	-362	-406
Gross Domestic Product (£m)	11,611	11,611	12,437	13,344	14,297	14,936	15,952	16,501	17,003

*FISIM = financial intermediation services indirectly measured

Source: NISRA

Only 10 years ago Northern Ireland was regarded as more prosperous as a region than its southern neighbour although both were acknowledged to be Objective 1 regions of the European Union (regions eligible for financial support from Europe where GDP per capita was below 75 per cent of the EU average). At that time Northern Ireland with just under half of the population of the Republic had about half the Republic's gross domestic product in absolute terms.

With the sustained boom in the Republic and the slower growth in Northern Ireland, the Province's GDP as a proportion of Republic of Ireland GDP has fallen from approximately 50 per cent in 1992 to under 30 per cent today and this general trend is predicted to continue, although much less dramatically. It is expected therefore that Northern Ireland's share of total all island GDP could fall to under 20 per cent.

It is expected that the rapid growth in the Republic will start to slow because of the global downturn but also now that the Republic is one of the EU's wealthier member states, the substantial assistance from Europe's structural funds will be phased out.

Remarkably although Northern Ireland has lost its Objective 1 status the Republic has retained Objective 1 for its border, midlands and western (bmw) region.

Employment and Unemployment in Northern Ireland

In UK terms Northern Ireland has, traditionally, been something of an unemployment black spot. However in recent years unemployment has been continually low by historic standards. Northern Ireland continues to suffer from higher levels of long-term unemployment, with nearly one third of unemployed claimants being classed as long term unemployed (i.e. being out of work more than 12 months).

The dominance of the public sector is reflected in Table 8.4 above which sets out the composition of Northern Ireland's employee base. The numbers employed in health, education and public administration combined are over twice the number employed in manufacturing. As with many developed economies the services sector's share of employment is dominant.

Table 8.4: Northern Ireland Employees in Employment by Sector June 2002

	June 2002
Agriculture	14,640
Mining & Quarrying	1,920
Manufacturing	97,210
Electricity, Gas & Water Supply	3,050
Construction	35,460
Wholesale & Retail Trade; Repairs	111,060
Hotels & Restaurants	39,340
Transport, Storage & Communication	27,010
Financial Intermediation	16,670
Real Estate, Renting & Business Activities	53,220
Public Administration & Defence	60,410
Education	66,970
Health & Social Work	98,460
Other Service Activities	30,360
Total Services	503,500
TOTAL	655,770

Source: DETI

In contrast the number employed in manufacturing has decreased from 101,660 in June 2001 to 97,210 in June 2002. This decrease in manufacturing employment has not been as dramatic as for the UK as a whole and shows that despite a downturn in many of Northern Ireland's traditional industries the overall manufacturing base although small is proving quite resilient.

The public sector dominance has come about through a number of factors: the abnormal political situation; large numbers employed in the security sector; and the complex institutions that have evolved since the creation of Northern Ireland in 1921. Although there has been a stabilising effect from a large public sector it is now recognised as a barrier to accelerating economic growth.

Table 8.5: Public Sector Employment 2002

	Male	Female	Total
NI Central Government	28,135	18,259	46,394
Bodies under the aegis of NI Central Government	19,386	51,557	70,943
UK Central Government	3,392	3,254	6,646
Local Government (District Councils)	6,085	4,303	10,388
Public Corporations	18,887	51,694	70,581
Total Public Sector Jobs	75,885	129,076	204,952
% of Employee Jobs	23.5%	38.7%	31.3%

Exports From Northern Ireland

Just under £11bn in value in goods and services (£10,866 million) were sold by Northern Ireland manufacturing companies in 2000/01 and of this 73 per cent were sold outside Northern Ireland. This compares with 68 per cent being exported in 1995/96.

Sales by Northern Ireland manufacturers grew by 8.5 per cent over the year. This continued the strong growth experienced over the past four years of £2,117 million, which equates to a 24 per cent increase over the period. The increases were due to strong performances by Northern Ireland manufacturers across all sectors despite the unfavourable sterling/euro exchange rate.

Table 8.6: Total Sales and Exports from Northern Ireland

	£m
1995/96	£8,618
1996/97	£8,749
1997/98	£9,082
1998/99	£9,340
1999/00	£10,017
2000/01	£10,866

Source: NIERC/DETI

Table 8.7 below shows that sales from Northern Ireland to the rest of the European Union expanded in the last reported year by 16.5 per cent. Cross-border exports also increased significantly over the year. Sales to the Republic of Ireland increased from £903m to £967m, a

rate of growth of 7.1 per cent, a disappointing figure given the efforts that are being made by government agencies to promote cross border trade. There was also an increase in sales within Northern Ireland with 2000/01 sales increasing by 5.5 per cent on the previous year.

Table 8.8 shows the make-up of sales and exports by economic sector. Although there was growth across a number of sectors, most of the growth in external and export markets has been driven by a small number of large firms in key sectors including transport equipment, food, drink and tobacco, and electrical and optical equipment. The majority of industrial sectors in Northern Ireland are heavily reliant on external markets for their sales. In seven of the twelve broad industrial sectors, external sales account for more than half of total sales. The transport equipment sector is the most export-oriented sector, selling three-quarters of all sales into markets outside the UK.

There are ongoing difficulties in other key sectors, notably the textiles and clothing sector and the meat processing and dairy sector, which have been hit by a number of crises in recent years. The importance of the performance of a few large firms is reflected by the fact that the three largest exporters accounted for one-quarter of all exports and the ten largest companies accounted for just under half of all exports.

Table 8.7 External Sales and Export Sales (current prices)

	1999/00 (revised) £m	2000/01 (provisional) £m	Share of Sales 2000/01
Total Sales	10,017	10,866	100
Northern Ireland	2,743	2,895	27
External Sales	7,274	7,971	73
Great Britain	3,300	3,813	35
Export Sales	3,974	4,158	38
Republic of Ireland	903	967	9
Rest of European Union	1,150	1,340	12
Rest of World	1,921	1,851	17

Source: NIERC/DETI

Table 8.8: Overview of Sales and Exports by Sector 2000/01

	Sales £m	Exports £m
Food, Drink & Tobacco	3,216	648
Electrical & Optical Equipment	2,116	1,173
Transport Equipment	913	603
Textiles, Clothing & Leather	821	208
Other Machinery & Equipment	626	339
Rubber & Plastics	560	266
Chemicals & Man-Made Fibres	475	309
Basic Metals & Fabricated Metal Products	531	199
Paper & Printing	448	106
Other Non-Metallic Mineral Products	459	98
Other Manufacturing	341	113
Wood & Wood Products	360	96
Total	**10,866**	**4,158**

Competitiveness

In a major UK and regional competitiveness study carried out in 2000 Northern Ireland ranked at 93.7 per cent of the UK average, above the rankings for Yorkshire and the Humber, Wales and the North East. Looking at sub-regions within Northern Ireland, the east of Northern Ireland ranked 66th of 149 and the north of Northern Ireland ranks 109th of 149. The south and west of Northern Ireland both rank near the bottom of the 149 regions at 132nd and 138th respectively (see table 8.9 below).

Putting these rankings into an international perspective, Northern Ireland, at 93.7 per cent of the UK average, ranks well below the Republic of Ireland (102.9 per cent). As can be seen from the table, the north of Northern Ireland ranks just below Chile; the south of Northern Ireland just below Hungary; and the west of Northern Ireland below Malaysia. Interestingly, the east of Northern Ireland ranks above both Wales and Scotland and at an index of 96.3 is on a par with the East Midlands.

Overall the picture is clear: despite having relatively low labour costs, Northern Ireland continues to lag behind other developed regions in terms of competitiveness.

Table 8.9: Index of Regional Competitiveness of Northern Ireland in a Global Context (UK=100)

Region	Index
United States	134.8
Finland	111.8
Denmark	104.5
RoI	102.9
UK (Average)	100.0
East of Northern Ireland	96.3
Northern Ireland	93.7
Spain	93.5
Chile	90.1
North of Northern Ireland	88.9
Hungary	85.5
South of Northern Ireland	85.2
Malaysia	84.3
West of Northern Ireland	84.0
Portugal	83.9
China	82.2
Italy	80.8

Source: Huggins, R "An Index of Competitiveness in the UK" Cardiff University, April 2000.

CENTRE FOR COMPETITIVENESS

Centre for Competitiveness
www.cforc.org

1st Floor Interpoint,
20-24 York Street
Belfast BT15 1AQ
Web: www.cforc.org
Email: compete@cforc.org
Tel: (028) 9046 8362
Fax: (028) 9046 8361

Director & Chief Executive
Bob Barbour

The Centre for Competitiveness (formerly the Northern Ireland Quality Centre) is a private sector, not for profit, membership organisation actively supporting the development of an internationally competitive economy in Northern Ireland through Innovation, Productivity Improvement and European Quality Excellence (EFQM).

The primary role of CforC is to assist local organisations - particularly SMEs - achieve sustainable competitive advantage through the provision of specialised support using up-to-date management methods, tools and techniques. CforC supports its members and clients and works in partnership with Invest Northern Ireland and other Public Sector bodies. CforC has a significant international network of best practice partnerships. See website for details.

Research & Devlopment in Northern Ireland

DETI has carried out a benchmarking survey of R&D in Northern Ireland over three year periods in the years 1999, 1996 and 1993. Comparing the levels of R&D spending between the three surveys, it can be seen that between 1996 and 1999 total civil expenditure on R&D increased by 6 per cent in real terms. In addition, over this period government funding towards business R&D has decreased by 40 per cent whilst business's own R&D expenditure has increased by 18 per cent. Earlier " 'pump-priming' support together with increased efforts to bring higher knowledge content jobs, such as those in R&D, to Northern Ireland has led to this shift towards private sector R&D investment.

As might be expected, R&D expenditure is concentrated in a small number of large companies. The ten biggest R&D spenders in 1999 accounted for 59 per cent of civil expenditure and five companies have appeared in the top ten in each of the three surveys. There is however, increased R&D activity in a growing number of companies. In 1999, nineteen companies spent more than £1 million on civil R&D compared with fifteen companies in 1996 and only eight in 1993.

Inward Investment

Northern Ireland continues to attract significant inward investment.

Table 8.10 shows the number of foreign owned companies operating in Northern Ireland and their home country location. The number of foreign-owned companies operating in Northern Ireland increased by over 40 per cent between 1996 and 2000, to nearly 500. The majority of the companies are from the Republic of Ireland and the US.

Table 8.10: Number of Foreign Owned Companies Operating in Northern Ireland by Country of Ownership, 1996 to 1999

Country	1996	1998	2000
Rep of Ireland	100	123	165
United States	71	111	146
France	23	23	36
Netherlands	17	30	26
Germany	17	22	26
Denmark	13	12	12
Japan	11	15	14
Switzerland	10	5	7
Canada	8	9	10
Australia	7	6	5
South Korea	6	8	7
Sweden	4	2	3
Finland	3	3	5
Belgium	3	5	3
South Africa	2	2	3
Portugal	1	1	4
Norway	1	1	9
Channel Islands	0	5	5
Isle of Man	0	4	3
Other Countries	7	2	4
All foreign owned companies	**304**	**389**	**497**

Source: NISRA

Table 8.11: Public Expenditure Plans: Draft Budget 2002-2003 October

2002 (£ million)	2001-02	2002-03	% Change
Agriculture and Rural Development	195.4	203.8	4.3
Culture, Arts and Leisure	72.6	77.4	6.6
Education	1,339.8	1,404.2	4.8
Employment and Learning	550.4	584.0	6.1
Enterprise, Trade and Investment	259.9	255.8	-1.6
Finance and Personnel	112.8	116.2	3.0
Health, Social Services and Public Safety	2,300.8	2,486.6	8.1
Environment	100.8	108.9	8.1
Regional Development	468.7	538.3	14.8
Social Development	414.9	450.5	8.6
Other Departments	5.4	5.6	4.1
OFMDFM	31.1	31.9	2.7
Northern Ireland Assembly	38.8	39.9	2.9
Total Departmental	**5,891.2**	**6,303.3**	**7.0**
Unallocated Executive Programme Funds	8.2	51.9	
Regional Rates and Other Items	-140.2	-264.1	
Total Other Adjustments	-132.0	-212.2	
Total Overall	**5,759.2**	**6,091.2**	**5.8**

Source: DFP 2002

Economic Forecast

There are few professional forecasts available in the UK (at a regional level) relating to the future of the Northern Ireland economy. The best available is produced between the Northern Ireland Economic Research Centre and Oxford Economic Forecasting (Dr Graham Gudgin) provide an expert forecast for all regions in the United Kingdom.

In recent years the forecast has pointed out that despite its well-publicised difficulties, the Northern Ireland economy taken as a region has been one of the star performers in the United Kingdom. Despite its outlying location, Northern Ireland's economic growth has been rapid and much closer to that of the South-East of England. It has easily outpaced growth in all the northern regions of the UK. Given Northern Ireland's structural disadvantages this is explained by competitive advantages such as low wages and a high level of government subsidies.

The Oxford forecast sees little medium term change in these fundamentals and therefore concludes that steady growth is set to continue.

By UK standards the overall performance projected, while continuing to lag the forecast for the Republic of Ireland, is creditable in the context of the United Kingdom. Some recent commentators have however taken a somewhat more pessimistic view arguing that further decline in the manufacturing sector and a shortfall in inward investment is now pushing up the unemployment rate above previous expectations.

Northern Ireland Ecomonic Conference 2003

Wednesday 8th October 2003

Now in its eighth consecutive year the Northern Ireland Ecomonic Conference has become the highlight of the Northern Ireland business calendar drawing top speakers and delegates from inside and outside Northern Ireland.

For details telephone bmf conferences on 028 9261 9933

Table 8.12: Economic and Demographic Indicators for Northern Ireland

	2001	2002	2003	2004	2005	2011
Population (000s)	1685	1691	1696	1701	1707	1713
(% pa)	0.3	0.3	0.3	0.3	0.3	0.4
GDP Growth Per Cent Per Annum	1.3	2.0	2.7	2.9	2.6	2.7
Personal Disposable Income (%pa)	7.0	2.1	2.1	2.7	2.6	2.6
Per Capita (UK=100)	85.4	85.6	85.6	85.6	85.5	85.5
Consumers Expend (%pa)	3.9	3.9	3.2	2.2	2.2	2.6
Per Capita (UK=100)	80.9	81.2	81.3	81.3	81.3	81.2
Unemployment Rate	5.0	4.9	4.9	5.0	5.4	5.7
Migration[1]	0.7	2.6	1.1	1.3	1.4	1.5
Self Employed (000s)	90	88	88	89	89	89
(% pa)	5.9	-2.9	0.8	0.8	0.2	0.1
Employment [2]						
Total Employment (000s)	746	752	756	761	766	770
(% pa)	0.6	0.9	0.5	0.7	0.6	0.6
Manufacturing (000s)	106	102	100	98	96	94
Private Serv. (000s)	272	273	275	279	283	288
Government Serv. (000s)	229	233	236	237	238	240

Source: NIERC/OEF

Notes: [1]Per 1000 of the population of working age.

[2]Employees plus the self-employed.

Table 8.13: Sectoral GDP Forecast (% Change)

	2002	2003	2004	2005
Agriculture	5.4	4.9	2.2	0.8
Extraction	7.2	3.4	0.2	-0.7
Manufacturing	-3.8	2.8	3.3	2.5
Food, Drink and Tobacco	-1.5	0.1	-0.2	-0.4
Textiles	5.6	-1.2	-2.0	-3.7
Wood Product Industries	-1.7	-1.7	-2.5	-3.0
Pulp, Paper and Printing	0.3	1.5	1.2	0.8
Coke Oil Refining and Nuclear Fuel	24.8	2.7	2.6	1.3
Chemical Industries	-5.5	2.5	4.5	4.2
Rubber and Plastic Industries	-4.4	3.6	3.9	2.8
Other Non Metal Mineral Products	1.5	4.1	4.2	3.6
Metals	-14.0	5.8	5.2	2.1
Machinery and Equipment	-10.1	2.8	2.0	0.8
Electrical and Optical Equipment	-2.3	6.7	8.2	7.2
Transport Equipment	-9.8	5.7	8.0	6.6
Other Manufacturing	0.5	1.2	0.9	0.4
Electricity, Water and Gas Systems	4.3	2.1	2.8	2.6
Construction	7.2	3.1	4.2	4.0
Distribution	3.1	2.2	2.2	2.0
Transport and Communication	3.6	3.6	5.3	5.2
Financial Services	3.4	4.2	5.1	4.6
Public Administration and Defence	1.1	-0.2	0.1	0.3
Education and Health and Social Work	3.2	2.7	2.6	2.3
Other Personal Services	1.1	5.7	1.4	2.4
Ownership of Dwellings	1.9	2.8	3.1	2.7
Financial Adjustment	4.0	4.5	5.6	4.9
All Industries	**2.0**	**2.7**	**2.9**	**2.6**

Source: NIERC/OEF

Northern Ireland Economic Research Centre (NIERC)

The Northern Ireland Economic Research Centre is an interdisciplinary research unit that conducts primary research on the Northern Ireland economy. The strategic aim of the Centre is to conduct policy related research that can contribute to accelerating economic growth in Northern Ireland. The Centre has gained a considerable reputation for its impact on government policy-making in Northern Ireland. Further information is available from:

NIERC, 22-24 Mount Charles, Belfast, BT7 1NZ
Tel: 028 9026 1800
Fax: 028 9033 0054
Web: www.qub.ac.uk/nierc

Table 8.14: Sectoral Employment[1] Forecast in Northern Ireland

	2001	2002	2003	2004	2005	2011
Agriculture	15	15	15	15	14	12
Extraction	2	2	2	2	2	1
Manufacturing	100	96	93	91	89	79
Food, Drink and Tobacco	19	18	18	17	17	15
Textiles	13	13	12	11	10	5
Wood Product Industries	3	3	3	3	3	3
Pulp, Paper and Printing	6	6	6	6	6	6
Coke Oil Refining and Nuclear Fuel	0	0	0	0	0	0
Chemical Industries	3	3	3	3	3	2
Rubber and Plastic Industries	7	7	6	6	6	6
Other Non Metal Mineral Products	6	6	6	6	6	6
Metals	7	6	6	6	6	5
Machinery and Equipment	7	6	6	6	6	5
Electrical and Optical Equipment	11	11	11	11	11	10
Transport Equipment	13	12	12	12	12	11
Other Manufacturing	4	4	4	4	4	4
Electricity, Water and Gas Systems	3	3	3	3	3	3
Construction	34	37	38	39	40	43
Distribution	109	111	110	111	112	115
Hotels and Restaurants	39	38	39	40	41	45
Transport and Communication	27	27	27	28	28	31
Financial Intermediation	16	16	16	16	16	16
Real Estate Renting and Insurance	52	54	55	58	60	78
Public Administration and Defence	59	61	60	60	59	60
Education, Health and Social Work	160	164	166	168	170	180
Other Personal Services	29	30	30	30	31	32
Total Employment[1]	**646**	**654**	**657**	**661**	**665**	**696**
% Change Per Annum	0.3	1.2	0.5	0.7	0.6	0.8

Source: NIERC/OEF

[1] Excluding Self Employment

Employment Forecast

Although further job losses are anticipated in manufacturing and in other sectors these are predicted to be more than off set by expansion in public and private services. Manufacturing in terms of employment will become a relatively small part of the economy. Employment projections by economic sector are shown in Table 8.14 above. The main sectors targeted for employment growth are the tradeable services sectors and in particular the ICT industries.

Sectoral Analysis of The Northern Ireland Economy

Agriculture and Food Sector

Agriculture, forestry and fishing are important elements of the local economy. The sector accounts for around 4.5 per cent of regional Gross Domestic Product (GDP) and 4 per cent of total employment. Proportionately, agriculture's contribution to employment in Northern Ireland is the highest of all UK regions and only in East Anglia does it provide a greater share of regional GDP.

There are around 22,000 active, mostly family-run, farm businesses in Northern Ireland with an average farm size of around 36 hectares. Although this is more than twice the average size of European farms it is half the size of farms in the United Kingdom. In common with other regions in developed countries there has been a long-term downward trend in the number of farms and the average farm size has increased gradually. Three-fifths of farm businesses own the land which they farm and the remainder are a mixture of owned land and land which is leased on short-term lettings basis.

There are approximately 400 food processors in Northern Ireland, employing around 19,000 people and generating approximately 20 per cent of the manufacturing sector's total external sales.

Table 8.15: Key Facts about Agriculture in Northern Ireland

	NI	UK	ROI
Gross Value Added (GVA)			
Agriculture as % of total GVA	2.6	0.8	3.9
Employment			
Agricultural employment ('000)	34	434	136
As % of total civil employment	5.0	1.6	8.5
Land Use			
As % of total area	78.2	70.0	62.9
Farms			
Number ('000)	29.9	240	144
Average agricultural area (ha)	35.5	66.6	29.3

Source: DARD 2000

Fisheries in Northern Ireland

Northern Ireland has three main fisheries harbours, Kilkeel (the biggest), Portavogie and Ardglass all in County Down. The total Northern Ireland fish catch has been in steady decline, mainly as a result of EU quota restrictions and depleting fish stocks. The total tonnage of fish landed is currently around 23,000 tonnes per annum with a value of £18 million. However, Northern Ireland has a value adding fish and food processing industry, which has external sales of fish produce of around £70 million per annum. It is generally recognised that the future for the Northern Ireland fishing industry is not bright with EU quota restrictions set to tighten further in the medium term.

Forestry in Northern Ireland

Northern Ireland has around 83,000 hectares of land under forestation of which approximately 61,000 is state owned, the remaining 22,000 in private ownership. The land area forested has grown slowly over the last 10 years although the level of planting of new forest has been falling in the same period. Although timber production has increased significantly from a volume of $188,000m^3$ in 1992 to $300,000m^3$ in 2000 its average price has fallen in the period resulting in an overall modest increase in value added.

Northern Ireland Agriculture and Food

In recent years the agri-food industry in Northern Ireland has been hit by a succession of crises. In 1996 BSE with the subsequent beef export ban hit the sector hard. It was then hit by the outbreak of foot and mouth disease in early 2001. These crises were against a backdrop of lower market and support prices. In addition the strength of sterling in relation to the Euro and the changing structure of the local food retailing market added to the challenges facing the sector. The food-retailing sector in Northern Ireland has seen a restructuring with the arrival of the large UK multiples. Local producers and processors have responded to this restructuring and significant value of food sourced in Northern Ireland is supplied annually to the top four multiples. In October 2002 Safeway announced plans for a £100 million investment programme in Northern Ireland. The other multiples are in an expansionary phase also.

338

Agriculture and Food Agencies

Livestock & Meat Commission for Northern Ireland

31 Ballinderry Road
Lisburn
BT28 2SL
Tel: 028 9263 3000
Fax: 028 9263 3001
Chief Executive: David Rutledge

The role of the Commission is to promote Northern Ireland beef and sheep meat in domestic and export markets.

DARD Veterinary Service

Dundonald House
Upper Newtownards Road
Stormont Estate
Belfast
BT4 3SB
Tel: 028 9052 0100
Fax: 028 9052 5012

Food Standards Agency

10c Clarendon Road
Belfast
BT1 3BG
Tel: 028 9041 7711
Fax: 028 9041 7726
Director: Morris McAllistair

The Food Standards Agency Northern Ireland is part of a UK-wide independent body accountable to both Parliament and the Northern Ireland Assembly. The agency's functions are to:

Provide advice to the public and to the Government on food safety, nutrition and diet;
Protect consumers through effective enforcement and monitoring;
Support consumer choice through accurate and meaningful labelling.

Under the terms of the legislation setting up the agency, an Advisory Committee for Northern Ireland was established to provide advice and information to the agency on matters relating to its functions in Northern Ireland. The agency is required to take the advice of the Advisory Committee into account when carrying out its functions or advising the Northern Ireland Assembly.

Agricultural and Horticultural Colleges and Research Institutes

Agriculture Research Institute For Northern Ireland (ARINI)

Large Park
Hillsborough
Co Down
BT26 6DR
Tel: 028 9268 2484
Fax: 028 9268 9594
Web: www.arini.ac.uk
Director: Dr C S Mayne

The institute was established in 1927 to research into crop and animal production. It provides farm demonstration opportunities for undergraduates within the Faculty of Agriculture and Food Science at The Queen's University of Belfast. Aspects of the research programme are integrated with postgraduate studies leading to post-primary degrees. It also provides specialist advice and support for agriculture advisory work carried out by government.

There are three colleges operated by the Department of Agriculture and Rural Development (DARD) forming an integral part of the DARD Agri-Food Development Service.

Enniskillen College of Agriculture

Levaghy
Enniskillen
Co Fermanagh
BT74 4GF
Tel: 028 6634 4800
Fax: 028 6634 4888

Enniskillen College of Agriculture is situated within a 136-hectare rural estate.

Greenmount College of Agriculture and Horticulture

22 Greenmount Road
Antrim
BT41 4PU
Tel: 028 9442 6666
Fax: 028 9442 6606

The primary function of Greenmount College is to develop people through education and training; and business and technology programmes for the agricultural and horticulture industries. The college offers a wide range of Diplomas and NVQ awards in both agriculture and horticulture.

The College Estate is comprised of several farms and units, which are combined to form three Agricultural Development Centres and a Horticultural Development Centre.

Principal: Mr J Fay

Loughry College: The Food Centre

Dungannon Road
Cookstown
BT80 9AA
Tel: 028 867 8100
Fax: 028 867 1043

Loughry College is a 'Centre of Excellence' for food and a major provider of education, training and technology services to the Northern

Ireland industry. The focus of the college is the food supply chain with particular emphasis on food processing. The college has the largest and best equipped Food Technology Centre in the UK.

Industry Associations

Dairy Council for Northern Ireland
456 Antrim Road
Belfast
BT15 5GB
Tel: 028 907 7 0113
Fax: 028 9078 1224
Chief Executive: Michael Johnston

The Dairy Council acts on behalf of both the production and processing sectors for the dairy industry.

Royal Ulster Agricultural Society
Show Grounds
Balmoral
Belfast
BT9 6GW
Tel: 028 9066 5225
Fax: 028 9066 1264
Chief Executive: Mr W H Yarr

Ulster Farmers Union
475 Antrim Road
Belfast
BT15 3DA
Tel: 028 9037 0222
Fax: 028 9037 1231
Web: www.ufuni.org
Director General (Acting):
Clarke Black

The Ulster Farmers Union is a voluntary organisation and is the largest representative group in Nothern Ireland agriculture.

Northern Ireland Food and Drink Association
Quay Gate House
15 Scrabo Street

Belfast
BT5 4BD
Tel: 028 9045 2424
Fax: 028 9045 3373
Director: Michael Bell

Major Agricultural and Food Companies

Agriculture Dairy Products

Armaghdown Creameries Ltd
30 Rathfriland Road
Banbridge
BT32 4LN
Tel: 028 4066 2742
Fax: 028 4066 2443
Principal Activity: dairy products
Chief Executive: David Graham

Avondale Foods (Craigavon) Ltd
Corcreeny
Lurgan
Craigavon
BT66 8TB
Tel: 028 3834 1619
Fax: 028 3834 3779
Principal Activity: Dairy products
Chief Executive: Derek Geddis

Ballyrashane Co-op Society Ltd
18 Creamery Road
Coleraine
BT52 2NE
Tel: 028 7034 3265
Fax: 028 7035 1653
Principal Activity: milk and dairy products
Chief Executive: Francis Kerr

Dale Farm
Shaftesbury Road
Bangor
BT20 3NL
Tel: 028 9146 7131
Fax: 028 9145 4574
Principal Activity: dairy products
Manager: Rowland Patterson

Dairy Produce Packers Ltd
Millburn Road
Coleraine
BT52 1QZ
Tel: 028 7035 6231
Fax: 028 7035 6412
Principal Activity: dairy products
Chief Executive: Alan McMinn

Dale Farm Dairies Ltd
Pennybridge Industrial Estate
Larne Road
Ballymena
BT42 3HB
Tel: 028 2564 5161
Fax: 028 2565 1108
Principal Activity: dairy products
Chief Executive: Neville Crukshanks

Dromona Quality Foods Ltd
456 Antrim Road
Belfast
BT15 5GD
Tel: 028 9037 2200
Fax: 028 9037 2211
Principal Activity: dairy products
Chief Executive: David Dobbin

Fane Valley Co-op Society Ltd
Alexander Road
Armagh
BT61 7JJ
Tel: 028 3752 2344
Fax: 028 3751 0511
Principal Activity: agricultural co-operative
Chief Executive: David Graham

Fayrefield Foods Ireland Ltd
123 York Street
Belfast
BT15 1AB
Tel: 028 9024 7448
Fax: 028 9032 6375
Principal Activity: dairy products
Managing Director: Richard Laird

Glanbia Cheese Ltd
35 Steps Road
Magheralin
Craigavon
BT67 0QY
Tel: 028 9261 1274
Fax: 028 9261 2464
Principal Activity: dairy products
Chief Executive: Conor Donovan

Golden Cow Dairies Ltd
25-29 Artabrackagh Road
Portadown
Craigavon
BT62 4HB
Tel: 028 3833 8411
Fax: 028 3835 0292
Principal Activity: dairy products
Chief Executive: Eamon Rice

Lakeland Dairies (Omagh) Ltd
46 Beltany Road
Omagh
BT78 5NF
Tel: 028 8224 6411
Fax: 028 8225 6496
Principal Activity: milk processing
Chief Executive: Michael Hanley

United Dairy Farmers
456 Antrim Road
Belfast
BT15 5GD
Tel: 028 9037 2237
Fax: 028 9037 2222
Principal Activity: milk collection and
sale
Chief Executive: David Dobbin

Meat and Poultry Processing

ABP Newry
Greenbank Industrial Estate
Warrenpoint Road
Newry
BT34 2PD
Tel: 028 3026 3211
Fax: 028 3026 1321

Principal Activity: meat processing
Chief Executive: Colin Duffy

Crossgar Poultry Ltd
11 Kilmore Road
Crossgar
Downpatrick
BT30 9HJ
Tel: 028 4483 0301
Fax: 028 4483 0724
Principal Activity: poultry processing
Chief Executive: Gerald Bell

Dungannon Meats Ltd
Granville Industrial Estate
Dungannon
BT70 1NJ
Tel: 028 8775 3338
Fax: 028 8775 3790
Principal Activity: meat processing
Chief Executive: Jim Dobson

Fleming Poultry
Ballymena Road
Ballymoney
BT53 7EX
Tel: 028 2766 5050
Fax: 028 2766 5045
Principal Activity: poultry processing
Chief Executive: Jennifer Patten

Foyle Meats Ltd
Lisahally
Campsie
Londonderry
BT47 6TJ
Tel: 028 7186 0691
Fax: 028 7186 0700
Principal Activity: meat processing
Chief Executive: Robert Watson

Grampian Country Pork
70 Molesworth Road
Cookstown
BT80 8PJ
Tel: 028 8676 3321
Fax: 028 8676 8524
Principal Activity: pork processing
Chief Executive: Bob Copsey

Henry Denny & Sons Ltd
6 Corcrain Road
Portadown
Craigavon
BT62 3UF
Tel: 028 3833 2411
Fax: 028 3833 4913
Principal Activity: pork processing
Chief Executive: Gareth Fitzgerald

Hiltonmaids Cookstown Ltd
Derryloran Industrial Estate
Sandholes Road
Cookstown
BT80 9LU
Tel: 028 8676 2106
Fax: 028 8676 2327
Principal Activity: meat processing
Managing Director: Tracey Acheson

Linden Foods
Granville Industrial Estate
Dungannon
BT70 1NJ
Tel: 028 8772 4777
Fax: 028 8772 4714
Principal Activity: meat processing
Joint Managing Directors:
Richard Moore, Gerry Maguire

Moy Park Ltd
The Food Park
39 Seagoe Industrial Estate
Craigavon
BT63 5QE
Tel: 028 3835 2233
Fax: 028 3836 8011
Principal Activity: poultry processing
Chief Executive: Trevor Campbell

O'Kane Poultry Ltd
170 Larne Road
Ballymena
BT42 3HA
Tel: 028 2564 1111
Fax: 028 2566 0680
Principal Activity: poultry processing
Chief Executive: Billy O'Kane

Omagh Meats Ltd
52 Doogary Road
Omagh
BT79 0BQ
Tel: 028 8224 3201
Fax: 028 8224 3013
Principal Activity: meat processing
Chief Executive: Richard Watson

WD Meats Ltd
Lower Newmills Road
Coleraine
BT52 2JR
Tel: 028 7035 6111
Fax: 028 7035 4903
Principal Activity: meat processing
Chief Executive: Francis Dillon

Drinks Companies

Bass Ireland Ltd
Ulster Brewery
Glen Road
Belfast
BT11 8BY
Tel: 028 9030 1301
Fax: 028 9062 4884
Principal Activity: brewing
Managing Director: Robert Magee

Bushmills Distillery Ltd
2 Distillery Road
Bushmills
BT57 8XH
Tel: 028 2073 1521
Fax: 028 2073 1339
Principal Activity: whiskey
manufacture
Chief Executive: Gill Jefferson

Cantrell & Cochrane Ltd
468-472 Castlereagh Road
Belfast
BT5 6RG
Tel: 028 9079 9335
Fax: 028 9070 7206
Principal Activity:
soft drinks manufacturer
Chief Executive: Colin Gordon

Coca-Cola HBC Ltd
The Green
Lambeg
Lisburn
BT27 5SS
Tel: 028 9267 4231
Fax: 028 9267 1049
Principal Activity: drinks bottling and
distribution
Executive Director: John Barrett

Guinness Northern Ireland Ltd
Apollo Road
Adelaide Industrial Estate
Belfast
BT12 6PJ
Tel: 028 9066 1611
Fax: 028 9066 9889
Principal Activity: drinks distribution
Chief Executive: Jude Lynch

Other Food Processing

Allied Bakeries (NI) Ltd
2/12 Orby Link
Belfast
BT5 5HW
Tel: 028 9070 4545
Fax: 028 90793411
Principal Activity: bakery products
Managing Director: Alan Hempton

Andrews Holdings Ltd
71-75 Percy Street
Belfast
BT13 2HW
Tel: 028 9032 2451
Fax: 028 9023 3591
Principal Activity: animal feed and
flour milling
Chief Executive: Michael Moreland

Cuisine de France
Unit 5
Blaris Industrial Estate
Altona Road
Lisburn
BT27 5QB

Tel: 028 9260 3222
Fax: 028 9260 3072
Principal Activity: bakery products
Managing Director: Hugo Kane

Gallaher Ltd
201 Galgorm Road
Ballymena
BT42 1HS
Tel: 028 2564 6666
Fax: 028 2566 5210
Principal Activity: tobacco products
Chief Executive: Nigel Dunlop

Mothers Pride Bakeries
Apollo Road
Belfast
BT12 6LP
Tel: 028 9038 1131
Fax: 028 9038 1131
Principal Activity: bakery products
Managing Director: Alan Stephens

Ormeau Bakery
307 Ormeau Road
Belfast
BT7 3GN
Tel: 028 9049 1001
Fax: 028 9049 1247
Principal Activity: bakery products
Chief Executive: Paul Rothwell

Pritchitt Foods Ltd
46 Belfast Road
Newtownards
BT23 4TU
Tel: 029 9182 4800
Fax: 028 9181 3538
Principal Activity: food products
Chief Executive: Diane Hunter

Rockall Seafoods Ltd
The Harbour
Kilkeel
Newry
BT34 4AX
Tel: 028 4176 2809
Fax: 028 4176 2022

Principal Activity: fish sales
Chief Executive: Wesley Newell

Tayto
Tandragee Castle
Tandragee
Craigavon
BT62 2AB
Tel: 028 3884 1466
Fax: 028 3884 0085
Principal Activity: snack food
manufacturer
Chief Executive: Arthur Anderson

Irwins Bakery Ltd
5 Diviny Drive
Portadown
Craigavon
BT63 5WE
Tel: 028 3833 2421
Fax: 028 3833 3918
Principal Activity: bakery products
Managing Director: Brian Irwin

Food Wholesaling and Retailing

Dunnes Stores Ltd
28 Hill Street
Newry
BT34 1AR
Tel: 028 3026 7111
Fax: 028 3026 8119
Principal Activity: food retailing
Managing Director: Frank Dunne

John Henderson Ltd
Hightown Avenue
Mallusk
Newtownabbey
BT36 4RT
Tel: 028 9034 2733
Fax: 028 9034 2484
Principal Activity: food distribution
Managing Director: Martin Agnew

J&J Haslett Ltd
20 The Cutts
Derriaghy
Belfast
BT17 9HN
Tel: 028 9030 1188
Fax: 028 9060 0197

Principal Activity: food wholesaling
and retailing
Managing Director: Peter Kealy

J Sainsbury
Darnley Store
10 Darnley Mains Road
Glasgow
G53 7RH
Tel: 0141 6386 495
Fax: 0141 6212 897

Principal Activity: food retailing
District Manager, Scotland & NI:
David Millburn

Musgrave Cash & Carry
1/15 Dargan Crescent
Duncrue Road
Belfast
BT3 9HJ
Tel: 029 9078 4800
Fax: 028 9037 0607

Pennyburn Industrial Estate
Londonderry
BT48 0LU
Tel: 028 7130 5700
Fax: 028 7130 5729

Principal Activity: wholesalers
General Managers: Russell Miller and
David McLaughlin

Musgrave SuperValu-Centra Ltd
1-19 Dargan Drive
Belfast harbour Estate
Belfast
BT3 9JG
Tel: 028 9077 5959
Fax: 028 9078 7101

Principal Activity: retail franchising
Divisional Managing Director: Nigel
Briggs

NI Co-op Society Ltd
75 Belfast Road
Carrickfergus
Co Antrim
BT38 8PH
Tel: 028 9335 7500
Fax: 028 9335 7505

Principal Activity: food retailing
Chief Officer: Paul Slocombe

Safeway
1009 Upper Newtownards Road
Dundonald
Belfast
BT16 0RN
Tel: 028 9048 9222
Fax: 028 9048 8700

Principal Activity: food retailing
Area Manager: Peter Darroch

SHS Group Ltd
63 Church Road
Newtownabbey
BT36 7LQ
Tel: 028 9086 8031
Fax: 028 9086 4425

Principal Activity: food broking and
distribution
Group Managing Director: Michael
Howard

Tesco NI
17 Clarendon Road
Clarendon Dock
Belfast
BT1 3BG
Tel: 028 9033 4800
Fax: 028 9033 4860

Principal Activity: food retailing
Store Director: Richard Baker

Energy Sector

Energy Policy In Northern Ireland

Northern Ireland, historically, has faced a number of major energy challenges. A lack of indigenous resources has meant over-dependence on others for fuel and comparatively high energy prices for final customers.

Recent policy priorities have included physical interconnection in order to give Northern Ireland access not only to a more secure infrastructure but to more competitive energy prices in Great Britain. Interconnection also creates diversity, reducing single fuel over-dependence and creating choice for customers. There has also been an emphasis on reducing the harmful impact of energy infrastructure on the environment.

Work on these policy priorities has progressed steadily in recent years: Northern Ireland was interconnected to Great Britain's gas system in 1992 bringing natural gas to the province for the first time. The arrival of gas reduced considerably the over-dependence on Heavy Fuel Oil in the power sector and at the same time introduced a much cleaner fuel source with obvious benefits for the environment.

Electrical interconnection with Great Britain has now been accomplished with the construction of Northern Ireland's 500MW interconnector with Scotland. This opens up many interesting possibilities for electricity trading between Britain and Ireland. Interconnection is also beneficial for the environment locally. In recent years electrical interconnection between the two systems in Ireland has also been re-established and strengthened. In 2001, the Department of Enterprise, Trade and Investment together with the Department of Public Enterprise in the Irish Republic undertook a joint study on the 'all-island energy sector'. However, a cogent all island energy strategy has not yet emerged.

After a number of years of debating Northern Ireland's future energy needs a number of major projects have been announced recently in the energy sector that will shape the future of the industry locally. The devolved government announced that it planned to part fund the building of a natural gas pipeline to the northwest and also a cross border pipeline that will bring natural gas to Newry and Craigavon in the south east of Northern Ireland. This work is now underway. In addition, a new power station project for the north west was announced to replace the existing Coolkeeragh power station and work also began on the replacement of Northern Ireland's largest power station at Ballylumford with a new gas fired combined cycle power station.

The development of North/South and East/West interconnection along with the independent power projects will introduce an unprecedented degree of competition into the Northern Ireland energy market and should impose downward pressure on prices. The gradual change to a fully competitive market will also require restructuring and cost-effective trading and settlement system to be put in place. This will be a formidable task for the authorities.

A further policy priority continues to be the promotion of energy efficiency and greater use of renewable sources of energy. Northern Ireland boasts a number of successful wind farm projects and hydro and biomass power generation schemes.

The year 2002 has seen volatility in international oil prices and policy focus has returned to the issue of energy prices, in particular electricity prices, and what can be done to reduce the costs differential between Northern Ireland on the one hand and the rest of the UK and the Irish Republic where average prices can be significantly lower.

A high percentage of low-income households in Northern Ireland are described as "fuel poor" in that the cost of energy required to adequately service their homes is disproportionately high. The issue has now become a high priority for the energy regulatory authority OFREG and a number of consumer groups.

It is expected that Northern Ireland's energy policy will change little following the supension of the devolved adminstration although there is a fear that implementation of decisions already taken will be slower than under a local administration.

Major Energy Companies

AES Kilroot Power Station
Larne Road
Carrickfergus
BT38 7LX
Tel: 028 9335 1644
Fax: 028 9335 1086
Principal Activity: power generation
Managing Director: Shane Lynch

Airtricity (Northern Ireland)
20 Adelaide Street
Belfast
BT2 8GB
Tel: 028 9051 7153
Fax: 028 9051 7001
Principal Activity: electricity supply
Chief Executive: Mark Ennis

Energia

Energia House
62 Newforge Lane
Belfast
BT9 5NF
Tel: 028 9068 5900
Fax: 028 9068 5902

Website: www.energia.ie
Email: sales@energia.ie
Principal Activity: energy supply
Managing Director:
Dr Allister McQuoid (pictured)

Energia is an all island electricity supplier with customers on both sides of the border. It is a subsidiary of the Viridian Group.

Northern Ireland Electricity
120 Malone Road
Belfast
BT9 5HT
Tel: 028 9066 1100
Fax: 028 9068 9117
Principal Activity: electricity transmission and distribution

COOLKEERAGH ESB

Coolkeeragh ESB Ltd, is the joint venture between Coolkeeragh power and ESB International to build the new 400MW natural gas combined cycle power plant at Coolkeeragh in the Northwest. The new plant will offer substantial benefits in terms of providing competitive low cost electricity, which will contribute in the drive to reduce costs for the consumer, and will act as the anchor customer for the new gas pipeline to the Northwest.

Coolkeeragh ESB Ltd
2 Electra Road
Maydown
Londonderry BT47 6UL

Tel: (028) 7186 1177
Website: www.coolkeeragh.com
Email: ccgt@coolkeeragh.co.uk

ESB INDEPENDENT ENERGY

ESB Independant Energy is a subsidiary company of the ESB Group and one of the largest suppliers in the liberalised electricty market in Northern Ireland. Offering customers a unique combination of competitive price and premium service our offering is based on understanding the business, energy usage patterns and the needs of our customers.

ESB Independant Energy
59 Petrie Way
O'Donovan Road
Derry
BT48 8PW

LoCall: 0845 309 8138
Website: www.esbie.ie
Email: info@esbie.ie

Managing Director: Harry McCracken

OFREG
Brookmount Buildings
42 Fountain Street
Belfast
BT1 5EE
Tel: 028 9031 1575
Fax: 028 9031 1740
Principal Activity: gas and electricity regulation

Director General:
Douglas McIldoon

Phoenix Natural Gas Limited
197 Airport Road West
Belfast
BT3 9ED
Tel: 028 9055 5555
Fax: 028 9055 5500
Principal Activity: natural gas distribution and supply
Chief Executive: Peter Dixon

Premier Power Limited
Islandmagee
Larne
Co Antrim
BT40 3RS
Tel: 028 9338 1100
Fax: 028 9338 1240
Principal Activity: power generation
Chief Executive: Bill Cargo

Energy Efficiency Advice Centres

Belfast Energy Centre

1-11 May Street
Belfast
BT1 4NA
Tel: 028 9024 0664
Fax: 028 9024 6133
Programme Co-ordinator: Orla Ward

Foyle Regional Energy Agency (FREA)

1st Floor Offices
3-5 London Street
Londonderry
BT48 6RQ
Tel: 028 7137 3430
Fax: 028 7130 8389
Email: info@foyleenergy.org
Acting Manager: Lawrence Arbackle

ENERGY IRELAND YEARBOOK

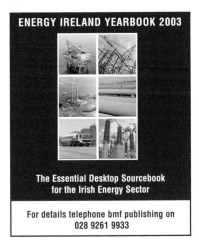

ENERGY IRELAND YEARBOOK 2003

**The Essential Desktop Sourcebook
for the Irish Energy Sector**

For details telephone bmf publishing on
028 9261 9933

Western Regional Energy Agency and Network (WREAN)

1 Nugents Entry
Townhall Street
Enniskillen
Co Fermanagh
BT74 7DF
Tel: 028 6632 8269
Fax: 028 6632 9771
Email: all@wrean.co.uk
Manager: Nigel Brady

Neighbourhood Energy Action (NEA)

64-66 Upper Church Lane
Belfast
BT1 4QL
Tel: 028 9023 9909
Fax: 028 9043 9191
Web: www.northern -
ireland.nea.ork.uk
Principal Activity: energy campaigning charity
Director: Majella McCloskey

SUSTAINABLE ENERGY IRELAND

Sustainable Energy Ireland
Glasnevin, Dublin 9
Tel: (00 353 1) 8369080
Fax: (00 353 1) 8372848
Email: info@sei.ie
Website: www.sei.ie

Chief Executive Officer:
David Taylor

Industry and Public Sector:
Peter Brabazon
Corporate Services:
Majella Kelleher
Consumer Awareness: Tom Halpin
Strategy and Development:
Kevin O'Rourke

Sustainable Energy Ireland, formerly the Irish Energy Centre, is Ireland's national energy authority. The Authority promotes and assists environmentally and economically sustainable production, supply and use of energy, in support of Government policy, across all sectors of the economy.

Sustainable Energy Ireland is organised into five divisions with offices in Dublin, Cork and Sligo. The Authority's Renewable Energy Information Office is located in Bandon, Co. Cork.

Coolkeeragh Power Station

Manufacturing Sector

Manufacturing in Northern Ireland

Following a decade of relative stability in the manufacturing sector in Northern Ireland in 2001 manufacturing employment fell by 3.8 per cent placing Northern Ireland fifth in the UK regional growth league.

2001 saw a fall of 5,640 manufacturing jobs making it the third worst performing sector in Northern Ireland after agriculture and the utilities sectors. Of the six manufacturing sectors, food, drink and tobacco; chemicals and "other manufacturing" all increased their output whilst fabricated metals, textiles and clothing and engineering slumped significantly. Engineering was the weakest performing sector in 2001 with a fall of 25 per cent overall.

In terms of employment, textiles and clothing and electrical and optical were worst affected shedding 3,040 and 2,560 jobs respectively. Output in the textiles and clothing sector fell by 17.6 per cent and there was virtually no new job creation, although the sector is still a substantial employer with 12,510 employees. The electrical and optical equipment sector slipped from being the third to the fourth largest employer in Northern Ireland.

The continuing strength of the pound has had a huge impact on exports to the eurozone and many manufacturing companies have faced unprecedented pressure on margins.

Over the period 1995-2000, NI manufacturing output increased by 29 per cent. The biggest sectoral increase over this period was in engineering and allied industries (an increase of 78 per cent). The largest decrease (approximately 16 per cent) occurred in the leather, textile and textile products industries.

There is now growing concern about the continued shrinkage of Northern Ireland's already comparatively small manufacturing base. Closure of any of Northern Ireland's major manufacturers could reduce the overall employment figure significantly.

Manufacturing Companies: General

Acheson & Glover Ltd
127 Crievehill Road
Fivemiletown
BT75 0SY
Tel: 028 8952 1275
Fax: 028 8952 1886
Principal Activity: bricks
Managing Director:
Raymond Acheson

John Finlay Ltd
Tullyvannon
Ballygawley
Dungannon
BT70 2HW
Tel: 028 8556 8666
Fax: 028 8556 8447
Principal Activity: concrete products
Managing Director: Stephen Finlay

Quinn Group Ltd
Head Office
Derrylin
Enniskillen
BT92 9AU
Tel: 028 6774 8866
Fax: 028 6774 8800
Principal Activity: concrete products
Managing Director: Sean Quinn

RJ Hall & Sons Ltd
Homebright House
Hillview Industrial Estate
Belfast
BT14 7BT
Tel: 028 9035 1707
Fax: 028 9075 3833
Principal Activity: brushes
Managing Director:
Desmond McClelland

Readymix Northern Ireland
RMC House
Upper Dunmurry Lane
Belfast
BT17 0AJ

Tel: 028 9061 6611
Fax: 028 9061 9969
Principal Activity: concrete
Managing Director: Joe Doyle

Robert Wright & Son Coachworks Ltd
Galgorm Industrial Estate
Fenaghy Road
Ballymena
BT42 1PY
Tel: 028 2564 1212
Fax: 028 2564 9703
Principal Activity: coaches
Managing Director: Jeff Wright

Rusch Manufacturing (UK) Ltd
Portadown Road
Lurgan
Craigavon
BT66 8RD
Tel: 028 3832 5771
Fax: 028 3832 4306
Principal Activity: medical devices
Managing Director: Gerry McCaffery

Tyco Healthcare
20 Garryduff Road
Ballymoney
BT53 7AP
Tel: 028 2766 3234
Fax: 028 2766 4799
Principal Activity: syringes
Plant Manager: Robin Eakin

Tyrone Crystal Ltd
Killybrackey
Dungannon
BT71 6TT
Tel: 028 8772 5335
Fax: 028 8772 6260
Principal Activity: crystal
manufacturing
Managing Director: Hugo Wilson
Chief Executive: Vacant

Walter Alexander & Company
Hydepark Industrial Estate
Mallusk
Newtownabbey

BT36 8RP
Tel: 028 9034 2006
Fax: 028 9034 2678
Principal Activity: coach builders
Works Manager: Steven McClough

THALES AIR DEFENCE

THALES
THALES AIR DEFENCE

Thales Air Defence Limited
Alanbrooke Road
Belfast
BT6 9HB
Tel: +44 (0) 2890 465200
Fax: +44 (0) 2890 465201
www.thales-ad.co.uk

Thales Air Defence, formerly known as Shorts Missile Systems, is a world-class defence company based in Belfast, Northern Ireland.

We have a rich heritage of high technology, state of the art products including Seacat, Blowpipe, Javelin and Starburst. Starstreak, our latest product, is the nucleus of our current business and forms the basis of our future growth and expansion into other defence fields.

Thales Air Defence is part of the Thales Group - a key player in the European defence and aerospace electronics markets. Within the Group Thales Air Defence is recognised as the centre of excellence for missile design and manufacture.

Engineering

Traditionally engineering has been a vital sector of the economy employing over 30,000 people and accounting for a quarter of all manufacturing jobs. There has been strong growth over the last five years with the 25,949 employed in 1996, rising to around 31,000 in March 2001. Large companies dominate, although there are many active small businesses also. Despite a worldwide shift from manufacturing into services the sector continues to perform strongly in Northern Ireland.

Aerospace

The aerospace sector was hit hard by the aftermath of the events in New York on 11 September 2001. Bombardier Aerospace, the biggest player in the Northern Ireland aerospace sector has announced 681 job losses due to take effect by early 2003. A cluster of aerospace-related manufacturing companies has grown around Bombardier Aerospace. Local companies now manufacture aircraft seats, while RFD in Dunmurry are world leaders in the design and production of life rafts and other life-saving equipment for aircrafts. RFD have continually expanded in recent years with acquisitions in the US, Italy and Australia. The position overall in the aerospace sector in Northern Ireland appears to have stabilised.

Automotive Sector

In the automotive sector the Visteon plant in Belfast, previously the automotive components division of Ford Motor Company employs 600 people in automotive systems manufacture. The Montupet plant at Dunmurry on the outskirts of Belfast employs a similar number in the production of aluminium and alloy engine blocks and wheels for the major European motor manufacturers. In Craigavon Nacco Materials Handling have over 800 employees producing forklift trucks for worldwide markets.

Shipbuilding

Extreme difficulties continue for Belfast shipyard Harland and Wolff owned by Norwegian shipping company Fred Olsen Energy. The yard continues to fight for its survival. It recently announced further swingeing job cuts reducing employment at the yard to an all time low of around 150. Many commentators believe it has now gone beyond the point where it can recover its overall ship building capacity.

Outlook

Outside the three main sectors Northern Ireland has a significant light engineering base, coach building, shelving systems etc. This sub-sector is performing well. Anxiety in the overall engineering sector relates mainly to the prospects of some of the larger companies and the implications for employment should any more of these face market difficulties.

Manufacturing Companies: Engineering

Arntz Belting Co Ltd
Pennyburn Pass
Londonderry
BT48 0AE
Tel: 028 7126 1221
Fax: 028 7126 3386
Principal Activity: fan belts
Chief Accountant: Tommy Smith

Bemac EMS Ltd
19a Ballinderry Road
Lisburn
BT28 2SA
Tel: 028 9267 7634
Fax: 028 9266 0258
Principal Activity: sheet metal parts
Managing Director: David Munroe

Bombardier Aerospace
Airport Road
Belfast
BT3 9DZ
Tel: 028 9045 8444
Fax: 028 9073 3396
Principal Activity: aircraft equipment
Vice President: Michael Ryan

BE Aerospace
2 Moor Road
Kilkeel
Newry
BT34 4NG
Tel: 028 4176 2471
Fax: 028 4176 4297
Principal Activity: aircraft seats
Vice President: John Sharkey

Copeland Ltd
Ballyray Industrial Estate
Sandholes Road
Cookstown
BT80 9DG
Tel: 028 8676 0100
Fax: 028 8676 0110
Principal Activity: compressors
Manager: Declan Billington

Camco Products & Services
Cloughfern Avenue
Doagh Road
Monkstown
Newtownabbey
BT37 0UH
Tel: 028 9036 4444
Fax: 028 9085 2766
Principal Activity: manufacture oil well equipment
Managing Director: Damien Canavan

Crane Stockham Valve Ltd
Alexander Road
Belfast
BT6 9HJ
Tel: 028 9070 4222
Fax: 028 9040 1582
Principal Activity: valves
Commercial Director: Paul Clarke

Denroy Plastics & Denman International
Balloo Industrial Estate
Balloo Drive
Bangor
BT19 2QY
Tel: 028 9127 0936
Fax: 028 9127 7553
Principal Activity: injection moulding
Managing Director: John Rainey

FG Wilson Engineering Ltd
Old Glenarm Road
Larne
BT40 1EJ
Tel: 028 2826 1000
Fax: 028 2826 1111
Principal Activity: generators
Chief Executive Officer: Don Perry

Fisher Engineering Ltd
Main Street
Ballinamallard
Enniskillen BT94 2FY
Tel: 028 6638 8521
Fax: 028 6638 8706
Principal Activity: steelwork
Managing Director: Ernie Fisher

John Ashe
66-69 Queen Street
Ballymena
BT42 2BF
Tel: 028 2565 3569
Fax: 028 2564 1002
Principal Activity: mechanical seals & couplings
General Manager: Hubert Dunlop

Glen Electric Ltd
Greenbank Industrial Estate
Rampart Road
Newry
BT34 2QU
Tel: 028 3026 4621
Fax: 028 3026 6122
Principal Activity: electrical products
Managing Director: Brian McLoran

Harland & Wolff SHI Ltd
Queens Island
Belfast
BT3 9DE
Tel: 028 9045 7040
Fax: 028 9045 8515
Principal Activity: shipbuilding
Chief Executive Officer:
Brynjulv Mugaas

Heyn Engineering
1 Corry Place
Belfast Harbour Estate
Belfast
BT3 9AH
Tel: 028 9035 0022
Fax: 028 9035 0012
Principal Activity: engineering
Managing Director: Alec Toland

Howden Power
Sirocco Works
Channel Commercial Park
Queens Road
Belfast
BT3 9DT
Tel: 028 9045 7251
Fax: 028 9073 2980

Principal Activity: industrial fans & gas reheaters
Production Director: David McMinn

Langford Lodge Engineering Co
97 Largy Road
Crumlin
BT29 4RT
Tel: 028 9445 2451
Fax: 028 9445 2161
Principal Activity: precision engineering
Managing Director: Denis Burrell

Mivan Ltd
Newpark
Greystone Road
Antrim
BT41 2QN
Tel: 028 9448 1000
Fax: 028 9448 1015
Principal Activity: ship outfitting/shop fitting
Chief Executive: Ivan McCabrey

Montupet UK Ltd
The Cutts
Dunmurry
Belfast
BT17 9HN
Tel: 028 9030 1049
Fax: 028 9030 3030
Principal Activity: aluminium components
Managing Director: Daniel Cofflard

Morphy Richards (NI) Ltd
Balloo Industrial Estate
16 Balloo Avenue
Bangor
BT19 7QT
Tel: 028 9146 8811
Fax: 028 9146 4009
Principal Activity: household appliances
Managing Director: Ken Ferguson

Munster Simms
Old Belfast Road
Bangor
Tel: 028 9127 0531
Fax: 028 9146 6421
Managing Director: Brian Batchelor

NACCO Materials Handling Ltd
Carn Industrial Estate
Portadown
Craigavon
BT63 5RH
Tel: 028 3835 4499
Fax: 028 3833 9977
Principal Activity: forklift trucks
Managing Director: Alan Little

RFD Ltd
Kingsway
Dunmurry
Belfast
BT17 9AF
Tel: 028 9030 1531
Fax: 028 9062 1765
Principal Activity: life rafts
Managing Director: Uel McChesney

Rotary Group Ltd
5 Trench Road
Mallusk
Newtownabbey
BT36 4XA
Tel: 028 9083 1200
Fax: 028 9083 1201
Principal Activity: electrical mechanical & ventilation engineers
Managing Director: Thomas Jennings

Ryobi Aluminium Casting (UK) Ltd
5 Meadowbank Road
Trooperslane Industrial Estate
Carrickfergus
BT38 8YF
Tel: 028 9335 1043
Fax: 028 9335 5644
Principal Activity: aluminium castings manufacture
Managing Director: John Hughes

SDC Trailers Ltd
116 Deerpark Road
Toomebridge
Co Antrim BT41 3SS
Tel: 028 7965 0765
Fax: 028 7965 0042
Principal Activity: commercial trailers
Managing Director: Darren Donnelly

Seagoe Technology
Church Road
Seagoe
Portadown
Craigavon BT63 5HU
Tel: 028 3833 3131
Fax: 028 3833 3042
Principal Activity: storage heaters
Managing Director: Neil Stewart

Sperrin Metal Products Ltd
Cahore Road
Draperstown
Magherafelt
BT45 7AP
Tel: 028 7962 8362
Fax: 028 7962 8972
Principal Activity: shelving systems
Director: Patrick Gormley

TK-ECC Ltd
770 Upper Newtownards Road
Dundonald
Belfast
BT16 1UL
Tel: 028 9055 7200
Fax: 028 9055 7300
Principal Activity: car components
Managing Director: Leslie Boyd

Visteon (Ford Motor Company)
Belfast Plant
Finaghy Road North
Belfast
BT11 9EF
Tel: 028 9060 8300
Fax: 028 9060 8490
Principal Activity: car parts
Plant Manager: John McLoughlin

Electronics

The Electrical and Electronics sector employs around 10,000 people in Northern Ireland, equivalent to over 10 per cent of all manufacturing employment. UK and Northern Ireland electronics companies have among the lowest operating costs in Europe, particularly labour related costs, which account on average for approximately 57 per cent of core costs for this sector. Therefore, the Belfast area is particularly attractive to international electronics companies seeking a base within the European Union. The information and communications technologies (ICT) sub sector's share of overall output from the sector is expected to grow by almost 50 per cent over the next ten years.

Northern Ireland is the base for several leading electronics companies including AVX, Seagate Technologies and Nortel Networks.

There are also a growing number of local companies operating in specialist niches within the electronics sector. Many of these companies have been spun out of Northern Ireland's two universities, which have internationally renowned electronics research centres. The focus of the centres has been on the information and communication technologies. The ICT sub-sector is expected to dominate the electronics sector within the next five years, in contrast to the consumer electronics sector, which is not expected to grow at anything like the same pace.

Northern Ireland is a world leader in Digital Signal Processing (DSP) with Queen's University renowned for developing this important technology, which powers nearly every sector of the electronics industry. Queen's is one of a few universities in the UK that has its own silicon fabrication facilities, which are based in the university's Northern Ireland Semiconductor Research Centre. DSP chips are being used in an ever-increasing range of electronic products from mobile phones to consumer appliances.

Northern Irleand has also been at the forefront of innovative microchip technology for compressing digital still video. This leading edge technology is used in a range of applications from satellite imaging to digital cameras.

The University of Ulster also has a research centre, which specialises in medical electronics technology. Like the centre at Queen's there have been a number of commercial spin offs from this centre.

Major Electronics Companies

AVX Ceramics Ltd
Hillmans Way
Ballycastle Road
Coleraine
BT52 2ED
Tel: 028 7034 4188
Fax: 028 7035 5527
Principal Activity: electrical
components
Vice President: Martin McGuigan

Analogue NI Ltd
5 Hannahstown Hill
Belfast
BT17 0LT
Tel: 028 9061 5599
Fax: 028 9061 6788
Principal Activity: electronic
equipment
Company Secretary: Celesta Forte

BIA Systems
Antrim Road
Ballynahinch
BT24 8AN
Tel: 028 9756 6200
Fax: 028 9756 6256
Principal Activities:
Telecommunications
Operations Director: Stephen
Donnelly

Contex Ltd
63 Greystone Road
Antrim
BT41 2QN
Tel: 028 9446 3035
Fax: 028 9442 8094
Principal Activity: manufacture
electronic components
Managing Director: Mark Macusaka

Elite Electronic Systems Ltd
Lackaboy Industrial Estate
Killyvilly
Enniskillen
BT74 4RL
Tel: 028 6632 7172
Fax: 028 6632 5668
Principal Activity: PCB's electronics
manufacturer
Managing Director: Ron Balfour

Fujitsu Telecommunications (Ireland)
10 Antrim Technology Park
Belfast Road
Muckamore
Antrim
BT4 11Q
Tel: 028 9442 8394
Fax: 028 9442 8395
Principal Activity:
telecommunications equipment
manufacture
General Manager: Paddy Turnbull

Getty Connections Ltd
Belfast Road
Carrickfergus
BT38 8BG
Tel: 028 9336 4741
Fax: 028 9336 5894
Principal Activity: telephone
equipment
Managing Director: Brian Getty

Irlandus Circuits
Annesborough Industrial Estate
Craigavon
BT67 9JJ
Tel: 028 3832 6211
Fax: 028 3832 4037
Principal Activity: printed circuit
boards
Joint Managing Directors: Roy Adair,
Sean Ritchie

Nortel Networks
Doagh Road
Newtownabbey
BT36 6XA
Tel: 028 9036 5111
Fax: 028 9036 5285
Principal Activity:
telecommunications equipment
Managing Director: Chris Conway

Partsnic UK Company Ltd
1 Sloefield Drive
Carrickfergus
BT38 8GD
Tel: 028 9336 0338
Fax: 028 9336 2223
Principal Activity: electronics
components
Managing Director: S E Kim

Seagate Technology
1 Disc Drive
Springtown Industrial Estate
Londonderry
BT48 0BF
Tel: 028 7127 4000
Fax: 028 7127 4202
Principal Activity: electronic &
computer equipment
Managing Director: John Spangler

Sintec Europe
72 Silverwood Road
Lurgan
Craigavon
BT66 6NB
Tel: 028 3831 4336
Fax: 028 3832 3297
Principal Activity: sub contract
manufacturer for electronics
Managing Director: Kieran Leonard

Textiles and Clothing

The Northern Ireland Textiles & Apparel Association is the representative body of the textiles and clothing industry in Northern Ireland. The sector employs in the region of 17,000 people and contributes over £900m to the economy - this in itself represents around 15 per cent of all manufacturing turnover in Northern Ireland.

The textiles and clothing sector comprises businesses in yarns, fibres, threads, fabric (woven, non-woven and knitted) garments, carpets, household furnishings and industrial textiles. The Northern Ireland textiles and apparel industries comprise of a small number of large publicly owned companies (mostly UK based), together with a significant number of small, often family run, businesses. The top eight companies account for almost half of total employment in the sector. Textiles manufacturing has a 200-year history in Northern Ireland, originating in the world famous Irish linen industry. Many textile manufacturers however, are now focused on adding value to traditional products towards technical textiles and finishes. High tech textiles such as carpets, synthetic and yarns are now as well known as Northern Ireland's linen sector in terms of quality worldwide. Ulster Carpet Mills in Portadown supplies carpet to over 20 countries.

The clothing sector became a major employer in the 1950s and 1960s evolving originally from the linen sector. Today several thousand people are employed in the manufacture of shirts, lingerie, sports and leisurewear in Northern Ireland. Much of this employment is based in the northwest with companies such as Desmonds, Adria, Glenaden and Graham Hunter Shirts manufacturing for UK retailers and global brands. The northwest is also the location for manmade fibre giant DuPont.

In recent times the sector has come under extreme pressure. The strength of sterling and pressure from cheaper imports has led to a number of factory closures. Also individual plants were completely dependent on major high street retailers for business. When the retailers found difficulties in the global marketplace their Northern Ireland based suppliers suffered directly.

The Northern Ireland Textiles and Apparel Association (NITA), the industry body in Northern Ireland, has been to the forefront of the drive toward higher added-value. The 'Brand to Win' programme focuses on consumer marketing and seeks to develop the potential for Northern Ireland firms to reach end consumers directly. In addition to focusing on the higher added value segments of the industry much of the labour intensive elements of the industry are increasingly outsourced. The present employment level is expected to fall to 13,500 over the next five years as more production is moved offshore. The textile and clothing industry is focusing on items of higher quality fabric, high design content and higher quality finish. In addition, companies are also focusing on quick response times, an area where they can develop an advantage over overseas competitors.

Industry Association

Northern Ireland Textile & Apparel Association
5c The Square
Hillsborough
Co Down
BT26 6AG
Tel: 028 9268 9999
Fax: 028 9268 9968
Director: Linda MacHugh

Major Textiles and Clothing Companies

3M Industrial Tapes
5-7 Balloo Drive
Bangor
BT19 2PB
Tel: 028 9127 8200
Fax: 028 9145 1072
Principal Activity: industrial tape manufacture
Plant Manager: Phil Ward

Adria Ltd
Beechmount Avenue
Strabane
BT82 9BG
Tel: 028 7138 2568
Fax: 028 7138 2910
Principal Activity: ladies hosiery/socks
Managing Director: David Taylor

Barbour Campbell Threads Ltd
Hilden Mill
Hilden
Lisburn
BT27 4RR
Tel: 028 9267 2231
Fax: 028 9267 8048
Principal Activity: thread manufacturer
Managing Director: Massimo Petronio

Ben Sherman
Portadown Road
Lurgan
Craigavon
BT66 8RE
Tel: 028 3832 4121
Fax: 028 3832 4436
Principal Activity: uniforms, shirts
Managing Director: Myles Gray

British Textile Manufacturing Company
25 Ballymena Road
Ballymoney
BT53 7EX
Tel: 028 2766 3368
Fax: 028 2766 5479
Principal Activity: knitwear
Managing Director: Robert Francey

Carpets International
7 Saintfield Road
Killinchy
Newtownards
BT23 6RJ
Tel: 028 9754 1441
Fax: 028 9754 1594
Principal Activity: carpet yarns
General Manager: Lewis Rodgers

Desmond & Sons Ltd
Drumahoe
Londonderry
BT47 3SA
Tel: 028 7134 4901
Fax: 028 7131 1447
Principal Activity: clothing manufacturer
Managing Director: Denis Desmond

Dinsmore
25 Greenfield Road
Kells
Ballymena
BT42 3JL
Tel: 028 2589 1203
Fax: 028 2589 2295
Principal Activity: dyeing and finishing textiles
Director: Stephen Dinsmore

Ferguson Irish Linen
54 Scarva Road
Banbridge
BT32 3AU
Tel: 028 4062 3491
Fax: 028 4062 2453
Principal Activity: textiles
Managing Director: David Neilly

Herdmans Ltd
11 Mill Avenue
Sion Mills
Strabane
BT82 9HE
Tel: 028 8165 8421
Fax: 028 8165 8909
Principal Activity: flax spinning
Managing Director: Neville Orr

Interface Europe
Silverwood Industrial Estate
Lurgan
Craigavon
BT66 6LN
Tel: 028 3831 2600
Fax: 028 3831 2666
Principal Activity: carpet tiles
General manager: Richard Nicholson

Magee Clothing Ltd
Paradise Avenue
Ballymena
BT42 3AE
Tel: 028 2564 6211
Fax: 028 2564 5111
Principal Activity: men's clothing
Chief Executive: Ian McEvoy

Octopus Sportswear Ltd
Unit 1
Dublin Road Industrial Estate
Strabane
BT82 9EA
Tel: 028 7188 2320
Fax: 028 7188 2902
Principal Activity: sports
manufacture
Managing Director: Kieran
Kennedy

Regency Spinning Ltd
Comber Road Industrial Estate
Comber
Newtownards
BT23 4RX
Tel: 028 9181 8836
Fax: 028 9182 0569
Principal Activity: textiles
manufacture
Manager: J Johnson

Saintfield Yarns Ltd
Saintfield Industrial Estate
Saintfield
Ballynahinch
BT24 7AL

Tel: 028 9751 1096
Fax: 028 9751 1459
Principal Activity: yarns
Managing Director: Graham Smith

Saville Row Shirt Co Ltd
Curran Road
Castledawson
Magherafelt
Co Derry
BT45 8AF
Tel: 028 7946 5000
Fax: 028 7946 8074
Principal Activity: shirts, nightwear,
ties, uniforms
Managing Director: Jeffrey Doltis

Ulster Weavers Home Fashions
Maldon Street
Donegall Road
Belfast
BT12 6NZ
Tel: 028 9032 9494
Fax: 028 9032 6612
Principal Activity: textile
manufacturers
Managing Director: Ian McMorris

Huhtamaki Lurgan Ltd
Inn Road
Lurgan
Craigavon
BT66 7JW
Tel: 028 3832 7711
Fax: 028 3832 1782
Principal Activity: moulded fibre
products
Managing Director: Steve
Chapman

William Clark & Sons Ltd
Upperlands
Maghera
BT46 5RZ
Tel: 028 7964 2214
Fax: 028 7954 7257
Principal Activity: textile
manufacture
Financial Director: Richard Semple
Marketing and Sales Director:
Robert Clarke

Irish Linen

Pharmaceutical, Polymer and Chemical Manufacture

Northern Ireland has been a base for the manufacture of chemicals since the mid 1950s. During the 1960s and 1970s Northern Ireland had a significant chemicals sector, which was dominated by the manufacture of man made fibres. ICI, Courtaulds, Monsanto, DuPont and British Enkalon had world scale plants in Northern Ireland. There were also a number of smaller plants supplying process chemicals and services to these plants including a large BOC plant at Maydown. The recession in the man-made fibres sector in the early 1980s saw the closure of all these plants except DuPont which still operates on the Maydown site, although now with only two plants. However, Maydown will be the world's largest elastane production centre.

Although the manufacturing of bulk commodity chemicals has declined there have been two notable successes in the higher added value pharmaceuticals manufacturing sector; pharmaceutical manufacturing company Galen in Portadown and Norbrook Laboratories in Newry.

However, Richardson Fertilisers who manufactured nitric acid for the production of agricultural fertilisers suffered from overcapacity for several years and announced the closure of the plant in October 2002 with the loss of 250 jobs.

There are now no upstream polymer companies in Northern Ireland and any plastic and polymers manufacturing is in the lower value added extrusion segment of the industry. Northern Ireland continues to have a major tyre manufacturing centre at the Michelin plant in Ballymena, Co Antrim.

Galen Pharmaceuticals, Craigavon

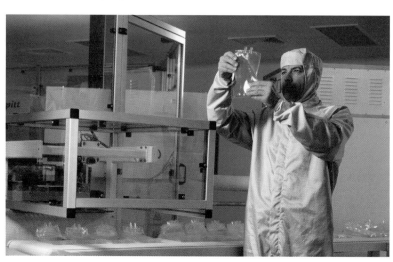

Major Companies: Chemicals and Pharmaceuticals

BOC Gases Ltd
Prince Regent Road
Castlereagh
Belfast
BT5 6RW
Tel: 028 9040 1441
Fax: 028 9040 1379
Principal Activity: medical & industrial gases
Operations Manager: Bob Loade

DuPont UK Ltd
PO Box 15
Maydown Works
Londonderry
BT47 6TH
Tel: 028 7186 0860
Fax: 028 7186 4222
Principal Activity: manmade fibres
Site Manager: Pat Carroll

Galen Holdings plc
22 Seagoe Industrial Estate
Craigavon
BT63 5UA
Tel: 028 3833 4974
Fax: 028 3835 0206
Principal Activity: pharmaceuticals
Chief Executive: John King

Norbook Laboratories Ltd
Station Works
Camlough Road
Newry
BT35 6JP
Tel: 028 3026 4435
Fax: 028 3026 1721
Principal Activity: veterinary pharmaceutical manufacturer
Managing Director:
Dr Edward Haughey

Perfectseal Ltd
Springtown Industrial Estate
Londonderry
BT48 0LY
Tel: 028 7128 7000
Fax: 028 7128 7401
Principal Activity: medical packaging
General Manager: Keith McCracken

Randox Laboratories Ltd
55 Diamond Road
Crumlin BT29 4QY
Tel: 028 9442 2413
Fax: 028 9445 2912
Principal Activity: clinical diagnostic reagents
Managing Director:
Dr Peter Fitzgerald

Plastics and Polymers

Creative Composites Ltd
Blaris Industrial Estate
Altona Road
Lisburn
BT27 5QB
Tel: 028 9267 3312
Fax: 028 9260 7381
Principal Activity: reinforced plastic
Chairman: R J Kelly

Brett Martin Ltd
24 Roughfort Road
Mallusk
Newtownabbey
BT36 4RB
Tel: 028 9084 9999
Fax: 028 9083 6666
Principal Activity: PVC plastic sheeting
Managing Director: Lawrence Martin

Dessian Products Ltd
9 Apollo Road
Adelaide Industrial Estate
Belfast BT12 6HP
Tel: 028 9038 1118
Fax: 028 9066 0741
Principal Activity: uPVC windows
Managing Director: Des Longmore

Huhtamaki
180 Gilford Road
Craigavon
BT63 5LE
Tel: 028 3833 3161
Fax: 028 3836 7280
Principal Activity: plastic containers
Site Manager: Alan Matchett

Kent Plastics UK Ltd
Derrychara Road
Enniskillen
BT74 6JG
Tel: 028 6632 3131
Fax: 028 6632 7410
Principal Activity: decorative plastics
Managing Director:
Dennis McKinney

Leaf Technologies
64 Mallusk Road
Newtownabbey
BT36 4QE
Tel: 028 9034 2090
Fax: 028 9034 2147
Principal Activity: injection moulding
Managing Directors: Nigel Brabbins and Brian Dickie

Michelin Tyre plc
Ballymena Factory
190 Raceview Road
Ballymena
BT42 4HZ
Tel: 028 2566 3600
Fax: 028 2566 3628
Principal Activity: heavy weight tyres
Factory Manager: John Lancaster

Polypipe (Ulster) Ltd
Dromore Road
Lurgan, Craigavon
BT66 7HL
Tel: 028 3888 1270
Fax: 028 3888 2344
Principal Activity: plastic pipe fittings
Managing Director: Henry White

Information and Communications Technology (ICT) Sector

2002 saw a downturn in the telecommunications and IT sector and the loss of employment largely as a result of the global downturn. Figures from the June 2002 annual survey by Momentum, the Northern Ireland ICT Federation show that employment had fallen by approximately 1,000 and turnover was also down. The survey found that the decrease in turnover was a reflection of the more difficult trading conditions faced by the sector.

Northern Ireland has now a sizeable telecommunications and IT sector, with several large multi-nationals and a cluster of substantial local IT and software companies.

The information and communications technology sector (ICT) employs 17,000 people, which accounts for approximately 3.0 per cent of the total workforce in Northern Ireland.

The importance of the sector has been fully recognised by policy makers: In the government's Strategy 2010 blueprint for Northern Ireland's economic future, specific targets are established for growth in turnover in the various high-tech sub-sectors while an overall target to make high-tech industry account for up to 6 per cent of total employment by 2010 has been established.

2002 saw a boost to the ICT sector with the launch of the Northern Ireland Science Park (NISP). The NISP aims to be a centre of excellence for research and development operations in Northern Ireland.

Telecommunications Sector

The telecoms sector is an important employer in the province with employment estimated at around 7,500. Northern Ireland has several major companies, both equipment manufacturers and service providers and several small niche telecommunications companies.

With the bursting of the 'dotcom bubble' the excessive valuations seen in this sector retreated to much more realistic levels. The telecommunications sector has been hit particularly hard, with major providers taking on significant levels of debt to pay for third generation network licences.

Nortel Networks is possibly the largest external investor in the Northern Ireland telecoms sector and a major international player in its own right. Its Belfast site is its largest European manufacturing base for transmission equipment and components. The Monkstown plant employed 1,250 staff of which around 25 per cent are active in research and development Activity. Nortel has been hit by the downturn in the sector and following the 2, 000 job losses world wide and 125 jobs lost at the local Monkstown plant in 2001, the company announced further significant job cuts in 2002.

Another major international player is the Japanese telecoms giant Fujitsu which has made several significant investments in the province in recent years. This year Fujitsu Telecommunications announced a new software engineering centre in Belfast to serve the North American market. The centre once fully established is expected to employ 400 product engineers and will have full design and testing capability for the next generation of internet products.

Among the telecommunications and related service providers, the leading telecoms company in Northern Ireland is BT Northern Ireland. BT has now several competitors in Northern Ireland, including NTL who are completing a major programme of providing Northern Ireland with a new fibre-optic cable network to carry a range of telecoms, IT and entertainment services to Northern Ireland customers. NTL employs around 350 people in Northern Ireland and has around 80,000 customers including 9,000 for its broadband services. The arrival of real competition has extended customer choice and imposed downward pressure on prices.

Other companies present in the market are Cable and Wireless and the Republic of Ireland's leading telecoms company Eircom, as well as Nevadatele.com a subsidiary of GB telecoms transmission company Energis.

In mobile telecommunications all the major UK players have operations in Northern Ireland with Vodafone the largest player.

Telecommunications Companies

BT

www.bt.com

2002 proved to be a successful year for BT Northern Ireland as it largely weathered the downward trend in the market place experienced by many leading telecommunications and IT companies.

Mr Bill Murphy
Managing Director
of BT Regions

The company remains Northern Ireland's number one Internet Service Provider and is a major supplier of communications technology to corporates and government.

Over the last decade BT Northern Ireland has spent more than £1bn in Northern Ireland's communications infrastructure and £1mn a week on wired and wireless projects in the last year alone.

With more than 600,000 customers BT Northern Ireland serves a population of 1.7 million with a network of over 700,000 exchange lines.

Its commitment to Northern Ireland, its people and the economy is evident and is well placed to grow and compete in 2003.

Eircom NI
2 Clarendon Road
Belfast
BT1 3BG
Tel: 028 9089 0000
Fax: 028 9043 4566
Principal Activity: telecommunications
Chief Executive: Chris Kingham

CABLE & WIRELESS

CABLE & WIRELESS

Post Quarry Corner
Upper Newtownards Road
Belfast
BT16 1UD
email: michelle.mcguire@cw.com
Tel: +44 (028) 9055 5247
Fax: +44 (028) 9055 5111

Michelle McGuire
Business
Manager

Cable & Wireless are a well known Telecoms Company in the Northern Ireland market. Its success has been built on a business to business basis concentrating on customer service as well as a competitive pricing policy.

Michelle McGuire currently heads up the Northern Ireland Sales Team promoting the depth and breath of Cable & Wireless capabilities both within the Public and Private sector providing Local and Worldwide Reach to their customers.

Cable & Wireless are the only providers of the Government Secure Internets (GSI) and Criminal Justice Extranet (CJX) to governing bodies throughout the United Kingdom.

Cable & Wireless is debt free, backed by $4.0 Billion in net cash with strong cash-flows from operations ensuring its continued existence and growth in the Northern Ireland market.

Nevada tele.com
1 Cromac Avenue
Belfast BT7 2JA
Tel: 0808 1401400 (freephone)
Tel: 028 9072 0400
Fax: 028 9095 9401
Web: www.nevadatele.com
Principal Activity: telecommunications
Chief Executive: Leslie Harris

NTL

ntl:business

209 Airport Road West
Belfast
BT3 9EZ

ntl business is a leading national and local provider of integrated business communications, specialising in the provision of Voice, Data and Broadband, products and services. It is one of the largest business-to-business communications providers in the UK, with revenues totalling £600 million.

ntl business offers innovative, cost-competitive bundles and bespoke solutions to large blue chip corporations, public sector organisations, small and medium sized businesses and carriers.

Through the delivery of innovative and cost-competitive products and services, led by a strong management team, ntl business is committed to providing excellent customer service to new and existing customers alike.

Contact : 0800 052 9000

ORANGE

Orange PCS Ltd
Quay Gate House
15 Scrabo Street
Belfast
BT5 4BD
Tel: 028 9073 6600
Fax: 028 9073 6601

Eric Carson
General
Manager,
Orange
in Northern
Ireland

Orange is Northern Ireland's fastest growing mobile, or wirefree™, network. Launched in 1998 as part of a £200 million investment, Orange currently provides coverage to more than 99% of the population through a network of over 300 radio transmitter sites.

Orange has more than 350,000 customers in Northern Ireland. It employs 80 people locally, mainly through 8 Orange Shops.

Orange is in the middle of a two year, £15m network investment programme to build on the spread and depth of its existing coverage and prepare the network for the launch of third generation (3G) advanced services due this year.

PATTERSON ELECTRONICS

12 Falcon Road
Belfast BT12 6RD
Tel: 028 9038 1387
Fax: 028 9038 1741
Email: info@patterson-electronics.com
Website: www.patterson-electronics.com

Patterson Electronics Ltd, a locally owned company in the mobile communications business for over 30 years, are Motorola's sole authorised two-way radio and paging dealer in Northern Ireland and sole Northern Ireland dealer for Kenwood Two-way radio.

Patterson Electronics Ltd were the first mobile Communications Company in Northern Ireland to attain comprehensive ISO9000 and DTI RQAS (Radio Quality Assurance Scheme) certification.

The business has grown over the years to become a "one-stop" communications supplier with an ever growing range including:

Motorola Two-Way Radio
Kenwood Two-Way Radio
Licence Exempt Radio
Walkie-Talkie and Event Radio Hire
Wide-area Radio Systems
Trunked Radio Systems
Shopwatch and Radiolink Systems
Motorola Paging Systems
Alcatel Phone Systems
Fleet/Vehicle Tracking
Mobile Data

VODAFONE

16 Wellington Park
Belfast
BT9 6DJ
Website: www.vodafone.co.uk
Call our business team today on
0800 052 5200.

Byrom Bramwell
Managing
Director

Mobile technology is advancing fast - with Vodafone leading the way. Mobilising your business brings more effective results, enabling you to reach new markets with a competitive edge. Working in partnership with your company, Vodafone delivers the most appropriate solution for your business and budget. Fleet management, voicemail, internet and multimedia services, Mobile EPOS for instant customer payments and professional friendly advice from start to finish. Whatever your company requires, no one works harder than Vodafone.

Call our business team today on
0800 052 5200.

Vodafone. The world's leading innovator in mobile communications.

IT and Software Sector

Although 2002 has been a difficult year for the technology sector across the globe, the software sector in Northern Ireland remains a key sector for economic growth. The Northern Ireland software and IT sector now consists of over 200 organisations employing over 5,000 IT professionals actively developing software. Northern Ireland's universities and technical colleges produce around 1,000 IT graduates each year to meet the growing demands of the sector. It is considered that Northern Ireland has now developed some critical mass in this sector.

The software and IT sector is the fastest growing sector in the local economy and there has been significant inward investment by large international software companies including Nortel Networks, Fujitsu, Liberty Information Technology, Abbey National, Northbrook Technology and Segue Software.

Northbrook Technology is a subsidiary of the Illinois-based $25 billion capitalised Allstate Corporation, which is the largest personal insurance company in the US. The company has over 100 software professionals in a £4 million centre in Belfast's Cathedral Quarter supporting the company's operations across the US.

In addition to Northbrook there has also been inward investment by other leading financial services companies including Boston-based Liberty Information Technologies and the UK bank Abbey National. Liberty Information Technologies has over 100 people writing software for US insurance giant Liberty Mutual and Abbey National has over 150 people developing software for management information systems for use in-house.

Unibol is part of the UniComp Group, which is based in Marietta, Georgia and employs around 80 people in Belfast developing software to enable older IBM mainframes to run the latest computer applications. Data analysis Risk Technology (DART) which has a software development centre at the Antrim Technology Park provides specialist software to many of the leading financial services companies.

Although it has announced job cuts in 2002, Nortel Networks remains one of the larger high-tech investors in Northern Ireland. The major Canadian-owned telecommunications equipment company has an R&D division, the Northern Ireland Telecommunications Engineering Centre (NITEC) at its plant in Newtownabbey. Established in 1988, the centre employs over 300 hardware and software engineers in the development of synchronous digital hierarchy fibre optic multiplexers for transport, access and broadband products for the Internet.

Although there is now an impressive list of inward investors in this sector, the majority of software and IT companies in Northern Ireland are locally owned. The Northern Ireland Software Industry Federation, now known as Momentum, has over 100 member companies.

Leading local software and IT companies include Apion, Kainos software, CEM Systems, Unibol, Absec and Lagan technologies. This local 'cluster' of software and IT companies are growing fast and are exporting a wide range of products and services to markets worldwide.

The level of activity of Northern Ireland-based IT and software companies is across a wide range of activities including systems development, Internet products and services, new financial services applications, telecommunications related products and services, management information systems and manufacturing systems development.

Belfast-based Apion is a market leader in software development for advanced wireless and Internet telecommunications internationally. Kainos now employs over 250 software engineers and is a world leader in document management products.

IT and Software Companies

Aepona
Interpoint Building
20-24 York Street
Belfast
B15 1AQ
Tel: 028 9026 9100
Fax: 028 9026 9111
Principal Activity: computer software
Managing Director: Liam McQuillan

Audio Processing Technology (APT)
Unit 6
Edgewater Road
Belfast
BT3 9JQ
Tel: 028 9037 1110
Fax: 028 9037 1137
Web: www.aptx.com
Principal Activity: computer software
Managing Director: Noel McKenna

BIC Systems
Sydenham Business Park
201 Airport Road West
Belfast
BT3 9ED
Tel: 028 9053 2200
Fax: 028 9056 0056
Web: www.bicsystems.com
Principal Activity: computer systems
Managing Director: Ed Vernon

Black Box Network Services
12 Enterprise Park
Greystone Road
Antrim
BT41 1JZ
Telephone: 028 9442 8325
Web: www.blackbox.co.uk

CEM Systems
Unit 4
Ravenhill Business Park
Ravenhill Road
Belfast
BT6 8AW
Tel: 028 9045 6767
Fax: 028 9045 4535
Web: www.cemsys.com
Principal Activity: computer systems
Managing Director: Richard Fulton

Claritas Software
7 Springrowth House
Ballinske Road
Springtown
Londonderry
BT48 0MA
Tel: 028 7129 1111
Fax: 028 7129 1110
Web: www.claritassoftware.com
Principal Activity: computer software
design
Managing Director: Plunkett Devlin

Consilium Technologies
Consilium House
Technology Park
Belfast Road
Antrim
BT41 1QS
Tel: 028 9448 0000
Fax: 028 9448 0001
Web www.task.co.uk
Principal Activity: computer software
Director: Colin Reid

First Derivatives
Kilmorey Business Park
Kilmorey Street
Newry
BT34 2DH
Tel: 028 3025 2242
Fax: 028 3025 2060
Web: www.firstderivatives.com
Principal Activity: financial software
Managing Director: Brian Conlan

Fujitsu Telecommunications Software Ireland (FTSI)
Springvale Business Park
Belfast
BT12 7DY
Tel: 028 9031 6300
Fax: 028 9031 0174
Principal Activity: telecoms software
Executive Vice-President: M. Fujisaki

Kainos Software
Kainos House
4-6 Upper Crescent Street
Belfast
BT7 1NZ
Tel: 028 9023 6868
Fax: 028 9057 1101
Principal Activity: computer software
Managing Director: Brendan Mooney

FUJISTU

Fujitsu Siemens Computers
9 Lanyon Place
Belfast
BT1 3FJ
web: www.fujitsu-siemens.com
Tel: (028) 9072 5140
Fax: (028) 9066 7268

Fujitsu Siemens Computers is one of Europe's leading computer companies and offers one of the world's most complete product and solution portfolios.World-leading IT products answer the needs of personal computing and enterprise computing with:

Notebooks
PC
Workstations
Intel- and Unix-based servers
Mainframes
Enterprise storage solutions

Lagan Technologies
Lagan Court
20 Wildflower Way
Belfast
BT12 6TA
Tel: 028 9050 9300
Fax: 028 9050 9339
Web: www.lagan.com
Principal Activity: computer software
Managing Director: Des Speed

Liberty Information Technologies
9-21 Clarendon House
Adelaide Street
Belfast
BT2 8DJ
Tel: 028 9044 5500
Fax: 028 9044 5511
Web: www.liberty-it.co.uk
Principal Activity: financial software
Managing Director: Gordon Bell

Meridio Ltd
Harvester House
4 Adelaide Street
Belfast
BT2 8GA
Tel: 028 9072 5600
Fax: 028 9072 5601
Web: www.meridio.com
Principal Activity: computer software
Managing Director: Frank Graham

Northbrook Technology of Northern Ireland
39 Corporation Street
Belfast
BT1 3JL
Tel: 028 9034 6500
Web: www.northbrooktechnology.com
Principal Activity: software development
Chief Executive: Bro McFearan

Northland Computer Services
5 Northland Road
Londonderry
BT48 7HX

Tel: 028 7136 3168
Fax: 028 7136 0002
Managing Director: Jim O'Donnell

Parity Solutions Ltd
Unit 1
Technology Park
Belfast Road
Antrim
BT41 1QS
Tel: 028 9446 4901
Fax: 028 9446 0702
Principal Activity: software
Chairman: Paul McWilliams

Singularity
100 Patrick Street
Londonderry
BT48 7EL
Tel: 028 7126 7767
Fax: 028 7126 8085
Principal Activity: computer software
Managing Director: Padraig Canavan

SX3 (Service & Systems Solutions) Ltd
Hillview House
61 Church Road
Newtownabbey
BT36 7SS
Tel: 028 9068 8000
Fax: 028 9066 3579
Principal Activity: computer services
Managing Director: Robert Bailes

Stream International
Ulster Science & Technology Park
Buncrana Road
Londonderry
BT48 0NB
Tel: 028 7130 3030
Fax: 028 7130 3040
Principal Activity: technical support
Director: Kevin Houston

Unibol
UniComp House
Victoria Business Park
Westbank Road
Belfast

BT3 9UB
Tel: 028 9056 1000
Fax: 028 9056 1001
Principal Activity: computer software
Managing Director: Dr L Graham

Western Connect
25D Bishop Street
Londonderry
BT48 6PR
Tel: 028 7137 0726
Fax: 028 7137 4726
Principal Activity: computer software
Managing Director: Ann Marie Slavin

ti SOLUTIONS

t.i.solutions Ltd.
Thomas Andrews House
Queens Road, Queens Island
Belfast BT3 9DU
Tel: (028) 9053 4570
Fax: (028) 9053 4577
Website: www.tisolutions.biz
Email: info@tisolutions.biz

t.i.solutions is dedicated to the delivery of fully managed IT Solutions for SME's and public organisations. The Solutions the company provides are uniquely tailored and delivered seamlessly and professionally.

t.i.solutions supports clients in achieving their strategic goals via our Compass Service Suite. Compass services can fit any budget and range from helpdesk services to complete turnkey IT support.

As a trusted ICT Partner t.i.solutions offers advice on how to get the best out of your technology investment. t.i.solutions' mission is to help its clients achieve their business goals by giving them IT direction.

Transport and Distribution Sector

The public road network in Northern Ireland is nearly 25,000 km in length with nearly one tenth of that figure class one roads and motorways. Unclassified roads account for the largest portion of all roads at 60 per cent of total road length.

The number of vehicles licensed for use in Northern Ireland's roads now stands at over 730,730. In the year 2000 there were 84,977 new registrations of private cars in Northern Ireland. One fifth of these new registrations were for imported cars from the Republic of Ireland due to the favourable exchange rate and differences in taxation on new cars. Over the ten-year period from 1991 to 2000, the Northern Ireland licensed vehicle stock increased by 31 per cent compared with 19 per cent in Scotland, 16 per cent in England and 14 per cent in Wales. Despite having good quality roads and for the most part less crowded roads, Northern Ireland has a serious road accident problem and persistently records higher levels of road traffic injuries than the rest of the UK.

Translink is the major provider of public transport services in Northern Ireland, through its three operating companies Citybus, Ulsterbus and Northern Ireland Railways (NIR). European funding, and a cash injection of £105 million from the Northern Ireland Executive to be awarded over the coming three years have enabled the commencement of a major programme of upgrades at Translink sites across Northern Ireland. New integrated bus and rail centres have been completed at Bangor and Coleraine, a new bus depot opened in Magherafelt and major refurbishment and restoration work at Carrickfergus. 20 new double decker and 38 single decker buses entered service in 2002 and a number of new luxury coaches were added to the Ulsterbus Tours fleet.

Prior to this injection of funding financial support for Northern Ireland's bus and rail networks was much lower than in Great Britain. However, it is hoped that these previous funding deficits will be a thing of the past as under the new Regional Transport Strategy (RTS) £3 billion has been promised for the development of public transport infrastructure and roads over the next ten years.

Translink has also completed relaying the railway track between Belfast and Bangor and a series of additional safety related systems are now being installed. Rolling stock is at least 19 years old on average and currently consists of 36 locomotives and 105 carriages and trailers. Spanish manufacturer CAF was awarded an £80 million contract in Spring 2002 for new rolling stock.

Northern Ireland has a small but fully integrated rail network covering 211 miles of track services to Derry and Portrush in the north-west; Larne, Belfast and Bangor along the eastern seaboard; Newry in the south and onwards to Dublin, in the Republic of Ireland. Rail passenger journeys decreased by 8 per cent over the last five years. 6 million journeys made in 2000/01 generating passenger receipts of £14 million.

Airports

Belfast International is the largest of the region's three main airports. It was ranked ninth in a list of 20 busiest UK airports ordered by number of terminal passengers. In 1999, it accounted for 1.8 per cent of all passengers (just over 3 million) throughout the United Kingdom. Since it opened in 1983 Belfast City Airport has increased its passenger numbers to 1.28 million and was placed fourteenth in the league table of UK airports. In October 2001 British Airways announced that it was ending its Belfast to London shuttle service and bmiBritish Midland initially moved its services on the same route from Belfast International to Belfast City Airport, but now operates from both airports. Between 1995 and 2000 there was a 33 per cent increase in the number of terminal passengers using Belfast International Airport and a 1 per cent increase at Belfast City Airport.

Seaports

Northern Ireland has four main seaports, which in order of importance are: Belfast, Larne, Warrenpoint and Derry. The Port of Belfast benefits from a safe, accessible, deepwater harbour, which is ideally placed to service middle corridor routes across the Irish Sea Ports in the North-West of England such as Heysham and Liverpool. The designation of Liverpool as channel tunnel rail freight hub with a quayside rail link facilitates access to the European rail network and rapid onward transit of goods to the continent. Heysham and Liverpool also offer links to Great Britain's extensive motorway network and its main centres of population and manufacturing.

Public Road and Rail Transport

Translink Ltd
Central Station
East Bridge Street
Belfast
BT1 3PB
Tel: 028 9089 9400
Fax: 028 9089 9401
Principal Activity: public transport
Managing Director: Ted Hesketh

Sea Transport Companies

Belfast Freight Ferries Ltd
Victoria Terminal 1
Dargan Road
Belfast
BT3 9LJ
Tel: 028 9077 0112
Fax: 028 9078 1217
Principal Activity: shipping/RORO
Secretary: Claire Jenkins

Belfast Harbour Commissioners
Harbour Office
Corporation Square
Belfast
BT1 3PB
Tel: 028 9055 4422
Fax: 028 9055 4411
E-mail: info@belfast-harbour.co.uk
Web: www.belfast-harbour.co.uk
Principal Activity: Harbour Authority
Chief Executive: Gordon Irwin

Coastal Container Line Ltd
Victoria Terminal 3
West Bank Road
Belfast
BT3 9JL
Tel: 028 9037 3200
Fax: 028 9037 1333
Principal Activity: ship operators
Chief Executive: Ken Wharton

G Heyn & Sons Ltd
1 Corry Place
Belfast Harbour Estate
Belfast
BT3 9AH
Tel: 028 9035 0000
Fax: 028 9035 0011
Principal Activity: shipping agents
Managing Director:
Michael Maclaren

PORT OF LARNE

9 Olderfleet Road, Larne
Northern Ireland, BT40 1AS
Tel: (028) 2887 2100
Fax: (028) 2887 2209
Website: www.portoflarne.co.uk
Email: info@portoflarne.co.uk

The Port of Larne combines a unique geographical advantage with ongoing investments to ensure that it is the best-equipped and most efficient RoRo port on the Irish Sea.

Nine ferries operate up to 40 arrivals and departures each day to and from four ports in Great Britain - Larne to Cairnryan and Troon in Scotland, and Fleetwood and Liverpool in England - making it the first choice for both commercial and tourist customers.

The Port of Larne provides an excellent Distribution Centre which includes frozen, chilled and ambient areas. The Centre offers a complete range of services including next day delivery, break bulk and order picking from stock.

Londonderry Port & Harbour
Harbour Office
Port Road
Lisahally
Londonderry
BT47 6FL
Tel: 028 7186 055
Fax: 028 7186 1168
Principal Activity:
pilotage, storage, cranes
Chief Executive: Stan McIlvenny

Norse Merchant Ferries
Victoria Terminal 2
Westbank Road
Belfast
BT3 9JN
Tel: 028 9077 9090
Fax: 028 9077 5520
Web: www. norse-irish-ferries.co.uk
Principal Activity: sea transport
General Manager: Philip Shepherd

P&O European Ferries
Larne Harbour
Larne
BT40 1AQ
Tel: 028 2887 2200
Fax: 028 2887 2129
Principal Activity: sea transport
General Manager: Denis Galway

Sea-Truck Ferries
Ferry Terminal
The Docks
Warrenpoint
Newry
BT34 3JR
Tel: 028 4175 4400
Fax: 028 4177 3737
Principal Activity: ferry service
Director: Karen Donaldson

The Right Connection...

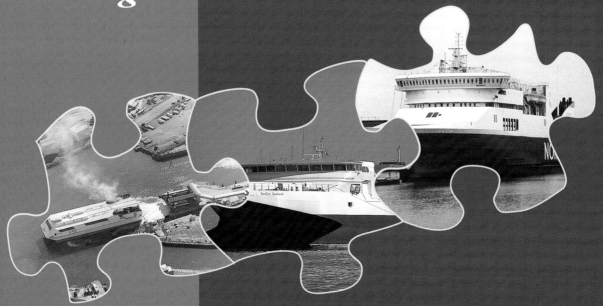

...For Trade & For Travel

Stena Line
Passenger Terminal
Corry Road
Dock Street
Belfast
BT3 9SS
Tel: 028 9088 4089
Fax: 028 2827 5278
Principal Activity:
transport ferry service
Port Service Manger: Billy Wicks

Warrenpoint Harbour Authority
The Docks
Warrenpoint
Newry
BT34 3JR
Tel: 028 4177 3381
Fax: 028 4175 2875
Principal Activity: harbour authority
Chief Executive: Quentin Goldie

Air Transport Companies

Belfast City Airport
Sydenham By-Pass
Belfast
BT3 9JH
Tel: 028 9093 9093
Fax: 028 9093 5007
Principal Activity: airport operator
Airport Director: John Doran

Belfast International Airport
Belfast
BT29 4AB
Tel: 028 9442 2888
Fax: 028 9445 2096
Principal Activity: airport operator
Managing Director: Albert Harrison

British European Airways
City Airport
Belfast
BT3 9JH
Tel: 08705 676 676
Principal Activity: air transport
Manager: Andrea Hayes

bmi - British Midland
Suite 2
Fountain Centre
College Street
Belfast BT1 6ET
Tel: 028 9024 1188
Fax: 028 9024 1183
Principal Activity: airline
Regional Manager: Valerie Ward

City of Derry Airport
Airport Road
Londonderry
BT47 3PY
Tel: 028 7181 0784
Fax: 028 7181 1426
Principal Activity: airport
Airport Manager: John Devine

National Air Traffic Service
Belfast International Airport
Belfast
BT29 4AA
Tel: 028 9442 2955
Fax: 028 9442 2643
Principal Activity: air traffic services
General Manager: William Henry

Servisair Ltd
Belfast International Airport
Crumlin
BT29 4AA
Tel: 028 9448 4600
Fax: 028 9442 2010
Principal Activity:
general air transport support
Manager: Ronnie McClune

Distribution Companies

Royal Mail Northern Ireland Ltd
20 Donegall Quay
Belfast
BT1 1AA
Tel: 0845 774 0740
Fax: 0870 241 5967
Principal Activity: postal delivery
Managing Director:
Michael Kennedy

Parcel Force Worldwide
Unit 24
2 Westbank Way
The Harbour Industrial Estate
Belfast
BT3 9PF
Tel: 028 9077 7270
Fax: 028 9077 7226
Principal Activity: postal services
General Manager: Kieran Carribine

Dukes Transport (Craigavon) Ltd
11 Vicarage Road
Craigavon
BT62 4HF
Tel: 028 3833 4477
Fax: 028 3835 0777
Principal Activity: road transport
operators
Managing Director: Winston Duke

Montgomery Transport Ltd
607 Antrim Road
Newtownabbey
BT36 4RF
Tel: 028 9084 9321
Fax: 028 9083 2746
Principal Activity:
transport haulage company
Managing Director: Harold
Montgomery

Woodside Haulage Ltd
61 Carrickfergus Road
Ballynure
Ballyclare
BT39 9QJ
Tel: 028 9335 2255
Fax: 028 9334 0427
Web: www.woodside-haulage.co.uk
Principal Activity: road haulage
Managing Director: David McComb

Tradeable Services Sector

Financial Services in Northern Ireland

Tradeable services derive from financial and business services and range from consultancy, accountancy, architecture, estate agency through to the newer services such as call centres, employment agencies and multimedia. Belfast is currently ranked within the top ten most popular centres globally for call centre operators.

Employment in the financial services sector in Northern Ireland has grown steadily over the past decade. Most of this growth has been in the non-traditional area of financial services including real estate renting and business activities sub-sector. The traditional side of the financial services sector, financial intermediation which includes mainstream retail banking has seen a decline in employment numbers over the same period largely as a result of productivity and automation initiatives taken by the banks.

Some economic commentators suggest that most national economies can only support one physical centre for international financial activity. This is clearly the case for the UK with London being the main centre for international services and the other regional centres, including Belfast, focusing on providing financial services for their own region.

Competition in the financial services sector has increased over the last five years with the introduction of legislation facilitating the deregulation of the sector and many building societies becoming banks. In recent years several of the Republic of Ireland banks and building societies have entered the Northern Ireland market.

Bank mergers in the 1970s in Northern Ireland and Republic of Ireland had led to the creation of two Northern-based clearing banks and two clearing banks headquartered in Dublin. In Northern Ireland there are the Ulster Bank (now owned by Royal Bank of Scotland) and the Northern Bank (wholly owned by the National Australian Bank) and in the Republic of Ireland there are Bank of Ireland and Allied Irish Bank (AIB). All four main banks have operations north and south, with AIB calling its Northern Ireland subsidiary First Trust Bank.

The remainder of the deposit taking institutions are branches of the UK building societies and financial services providers and locally based credit unions. With the Northern Ireland financial services sector being largely companies headquartered outside Northern Ireland with regional offices, local demand will determine the demand for their services rather than broad international developments. As Northern Ireland is the only part of the UK that shares a land border with a Euro participant, the banking and financial services sector in Northern Ireland is already dealing in Euros.

The growth of financial services in Northern Ireland has occurred in recent years, at a time when the rest of the UK is experiencing some concentration in the sector. The major driver of local growth has been call-centres and while there are issues over the long-term value of some call-centre operations, investment from blue-chip companies like Halifax, Abbey National and Prudential has served to position Northern Ireland as a leading call centre location.

Northern Ireland also has a competitive insurance industry although most of the main players are regional offices of large UK or European insurance houses. Increasingly also at the brokerage level there has been a concentration within the industry, with the larger brokerages buying out the independents. During the past year NIE sold its sizeable financial services subsidiary Open+Direct to a £100million management buyout.

Set out below are listings of Northern Ireland's leading tradeable services organisations including banks, insurance companies, building societies and stockbrokers. Extensive listings of other business services providers including accountants, legal advisors, PR consultants, etc. are set out in Chapter 9 "A Guide to Doing Business in Northern Ireland".

Major Banks

FIRST TRUST BANK

Registered Office: 4 Queen's Square
Belfast
BT1 3DJ
Registered Number NI 18800
Web: www.firsttrustbank.co.uk
Tel: (028) 9032 5599

Managing
Director:
Dennis Licence

First Trust Bank operates in
Northern Ireland as a trading name
of AIB Group (UK) plc.

One of Northern Ireland's main
clearing Banks, First Trust Bank
offers a wide range of personal and
business services through its
extensive network of 65 Branches
Province-wide. It is committed to
investing in new emerging
technologies, demonstrated through
the provision of Internet Banking
(Online), Telephone Banking
(Phoneline), Electronic Business
Banking solutions and the Bank's
ATM network.

In addition, First Trust Bank's
Business Banking Division, Credit
Card Services and Finance &
Leasing teams offer specialised
services for customers.

ULSTER BANK

Registered Office
Ulster Bank Group
Head Office, 11-16
Donegall Square East,
Belfast BT1 5UB

Tel: (028) 9027 6000
Fax: (028) 9027 5507
Email:
webmaster@ulsterbank.com
Website:
www.ulsterbank.com

Martin J Wilson
Group Chief
Executive

Ulster Bank Group operates in both
Northern Ireland and the Republic of
Ireland and is a member of The
Royal Bank of Scotland Group, the
second largest banking group in
Europe. Ulster Bank acts as a full
service institution to its customers,
providing a comprehensive range of
retail banking, business banking,
investment banking and capital
markets services to corporate,
personal and institutional clients.

Ulster Bank is fully committed to its
Branch network, which extends to
213 outlets, complemented by over
400 ATM's and Internet and
Telephone banking.

Directors and Executives

Directors
Dr Alan Gillespie - Chairman
Fred Goodwin

Martin J Wilson - Group Chief
Executive
Niamh Brennan
William Burgess
Richard Houghton
Tony McArdle
Peter McKie
Brenda McLaughlin
Miller McLean
Peter Malone
John McNally
Declan O'Neill
Martin Rafferty
Tom Reid

Divisional Heads
John McNally - Corporate Banking
and Financial Markets
Tony McArdle - Retail Banking
Graham Lee - Human Resources
Richard Houghton - Group Finance
John West - Manufacturing
Tom Reid - Change Management
Ronnie Hanna - Group Communications
John McDonnell - Group Risk

Company Secretary
Anne Gribbon

Bank of Ireland
4-8 High Street
Belfast
BT1 2BA
Tel: 028 9024 4901
Fax: 028 9023 4388
Principal Activity: banking services
General Manager: David Magowan

Northern Bank Ltd
PO Box 183
14 Donegall Square West
Belfast
BT1 6JS
Tel: 028 9024 5277
Fax: 028 9089 3245
Principal Activity: banking services
Chief Executive: Don Price

Insurance and Life Assurance Companies

ALLIANZ

Allianz Northern Ireland
Allianz House, 21 Linenhall Street,
Belfast BT2 8AB
Tel: (028) 9089 5600
Fax: (028) 9043 4222
Web: www.allianz-ni.co.uk

Head of Allianz Northern Ireland: Adrian Toner

Allianz Northern Ireland is a leading local insurer and part of the Allianz global network. As part of this network, Allianz Northern Ireland enjoys unrivalled access to risk and product knowledge. Working with a network of over one hundred brokers and intermediaries, the company has established itself as a market leader in all lines of personal and commercial insurance, providing an efficient and comprehensive service to the local business community. Expanding on the principles of local expertise combined with global presence, Allianz is also recognised as an authority in the niche areas of marine credit and guarantee, which are particularly relevant to the commercial and industrial requirements of Northern Ireland.

Abbey Insurance Brokers
10 Governor Place
Carrickfergus
BT38 7BN
Tel: 028 9335 1525
Fax: 028 9336 2509
Principal Activity: insurance
Senior Partner: Frazer Evans

Aon McMillen
31 Bedford Street
Belfast
BT 2 7FP
Tel: 028 9024 2771
Fax: 028 9031 3644
Principal Activity: insurance brokers
Managing Director: Patrick McMillen

AXA Insurance
Windsor House
9-15 Bedford Street
Belfast
BT2 7FT
Tel: 028 9033 3222
Fax: 028 9024 2864
Principal Activity: insurance
Director: Tim Scott

Co-operative Insurance Society Ltd
Lombard House
10-20 Lombard Street
Belfast
BT1 1RD
Tel: 028 9043 8233
Principal Activity: financial advisors
Managing Director: Dennis Garden

Norwich Union
5 Donegall Square South
Belfast
BT1 5AN
Tel: 028 9032 2232
Fax: 028 9024 8511
Principal Activity: insurance companies
Branch Manager: John Boyd

Open+Direct
Arnott House
12-16 Bridge Street
Belfast
BT1 1LU
Tel: 028 9026 0900
Fax: 028 926 0978
Managing Director: Paul Elliott

Pearl Assurance plc
2 Donegall Square East
Belfast
BT1 5HH
Tel: 028 9032 1938
Fax: 028 9023 7833
Principal Activity: insurance
Branch Manager: Paul McMullan

Prudential Assurance Co Ltd
Beacon House
27 Clarendon Road
Belfast
BT1 3PD
Tel: 0845 720 000
Fax: 028 9089 6000
Principal Activity: insurance
Regional Manager: Adrian Clement

Royal Sun Alliance Insurance Plc
Sun Alliance House
42 Queen Street
Belfast
BT1 6HL
Tel: 028 9024 4433
Fax: 028 9026 2357
Principal Activity: insurance
General Manager: Peter Gallagher

Willis Insurance
78-86 Dublin Road
Belfast
BT2 7BY
Tel: 028 9024 2131
Fax: 028 9032 1087
Principal Activity: insurance
Managing Director: Jim Halliday

Zurich Assurance
Zurich House
31 Clarendon Road
Belfast
BT1 3DP
Tel: 028 9024 4488
Fax: 028 9023 2823
Principal Activity: insurance brokers
General Manager: George Higginson

Zurich Insurance
7 Upper Queen Street
Belfast
BT1 6QD
Tel: 028 9024 5222
Fax: 028 9023 2435
Principal Activity: insurance
Area Manager (NI): James Shields

Building Societies

Abbey National plc
Imperial House
6 Donegall Square East
Belfast
BT1 5HL
Tel: 0845 765 4321
Fax: 028 9023 5379
Branch Manager: Andrea Buchanan

Alliance & Leicester plc
63 Royal Avenue
Belfast
BT1 1FT
Tel: 028 9024 1957
Fax: 028 9031 4366
Principal Activity: building society
Regional Manager: Gary Mills

Bradford & Bingley plc
2 Chichester Street
Belfast
BT1 4LA
Tel: 028 9032 2665
Fax: 028 9032 9338
Principal Activity: building society
Area Director: Ian McDonnell

Britannia Building Society
47 Arthur Street
Belfast
BT1 4BG
Tel: 028 9024 1639
Fax: 028 9031 0876
Principal Activity: building society
Branch Manger: Christine Wilson

Irish Nationwide Building Society
18 Donegall Square East
Belfast
BT1 5HE
Tel: 028 9055 0093
Fax: 028 9055 0094
Principal Activity: building society
General Manager: Gary McCollum

Irish Permanent plc
Suite 1
Clarence Chamber
19-20 Donegall Square East
Belfast
BT1 5HB
Tel: 028 9023 5100
Fax: 028 9023 4647
Principal Activity: building society
Regional Manager: Gordon Boal

Derry Provident Building Society
31A Carlisle Road
Londonderry
BT48 6JJ
Tel: 028 7137 0037
Fax: 028 7137 1508
Principal Activity: building society
Managing Director: Colin Jeffrey

Progressive Building Society
Progressive House
33-37 Wellington Place
Belfast
BT1 6HH
Tel: 028 9024 4926
Fax: 028 9033 0431
Principal Activity: building society
Managing Director: William Webb

Halifax Building Society
Donegall Square North
Belfast
BT1 5GL
Tel: 0845 720 3040
Fax: 028 9027 8233
Principal Activity: financial services
Branch Manager: Jim Porter

Woolwich plc
17 Castle Place
Belfast
BT1 1EL
Tel: 028 9024 6506
Fax: 028 9043 9651
Principal Activity: building society
Area Manager: Elaine Dixon

Other Financial Services Companies

Anglo Irish Bank
14-18 Great Victoria Street
Belfast
BT2 7BA
Tel: 028 9033 3100
Fax: 028 9026 9090
Web: www.angloirishbank.ie
Principal Activity: financial services
Branch Manager: Neil Adair

Bank of Scotland (Ireland) Ltd
4th Floor
Bedford House
16-22 Bedford Street
Belfast
Tel: 028 9033 0033
Fax: 028 9033 0030
Principal Activity: financial services
Regional Manager: Eugene McGale

Halifax

Stokes House
17-25 College Square East
Belfast
BT1 6DE
Tel: 028 9026 6400
Fax: 028 9023 9843
Principal Activity:
pensions and investment
Area Manager: John Sell

HFC Bank plc

44-46 High Street
Belfast
BT1 2BF
Tel: 028 9032 4400
Fax: 028 9032 4300
Principal Activity: financial services
Manager: Julie-Anne Burns

HSBC

4th Floor
5 Donegall Square South
Belfast
BT1 5JP
Tel: 028 9043 4565
Fax: 028 9088 4853
Principal Activity: financial services
Regional Manager: Steve Clayton

Lombard & Ulster Group Ltd

11-16 Donegall Square East
Belfast
BT1 5UD
Tel: 028 9027 6276
Fax: 028 9027 6279
Principal Activity: financial services
Area Director: James Conn

Provident Personal Credit Ltd

2nd Floor
10 Royal Avenue
Belfast
BT1 1DB
Tel: 028 9032 3735
Fax: 028 9033 1339
Principal Activity: financial services
Area Manager: Mark Horner

Stockbrokers

BWD Rensburg Ltd

St Georges House
99-101 High Street
Belfast
BT1 2AH
Tel: 028 9032 1002
Fax: 028 9024 4852
Principal Activity: stockbrokers
Senior Investment Director:
Kenneth McCaw

Cunningham Coates Ltd

19 Donegall Street
Belfast
BT1 2HA
Tel: 028 9032 3456
Fax: 028 9023 1479
Principal Activity: stockbrokers
Managing Director: Randell Herron

Edward Jones Investments

Cavehill House
32 Waterloo Gardens
Belfast
BT15 4EY
Tel: 028 9068 7715
Fax: 028 9068 2580
Principal Activity: stockbrokers
Managing Director: Patrick Mahony

Construction and Property

Up to 45,000 people are employed in the construction industry in Northern Ireland which, although employment levels tend to fluctuate, contributes 8 per cent of GDP. The representative body for the construction industry in Northern Ireland is the Construction Employers Federation. One of the main players is the Construction Industry Training Board (CITB), which ensures that the industry is properly staffed and trained. There has been something of a boom in private house building in recent years (although a slow down in public sector house building) and a number of major development projects including Laganside are underway in Belfast.

Ardmac Performance Contracting Ltd
Unit 15
Annesborough Industrial Estate
Craigavon
BT67 9JD
Tel: 028 3834 7093
Fax: 028 3834 1604
Principal Activity: interior
Managing Director: Kevin McAnallen

B Mullan & Sons (Contractors)
Bovally House
11-13 Anderson Avenue
Limavady
BT49 0TF
Tel: 028 7772 2337
Fax: 028 7776 4780
Principal Activity: stone, asphalt
Managing Director: Sean Mullan

Farrans (Construction) Ltd
99 Kingsway
Dunmurry
Belfast
BT17 9NU
Tel: 028 9061 1122
Fax: 028 9062 9753
Principal Activity: construction
Managing Director: John Gillivray

Felix O'Hare & Co Ltd
88 Chancellors Road
Newry
BT35 8LS
Tel: 028 3026 1134
Fax: 028 3026 1397
Principal Activity: builders
Managing Director: John Parr

Gilbert Ash (NI) Ltd
47 Boucher Road
Belfast
BT12 6HR
Tel: 028 9066 4334
Fax: 028 9066 3634
Principal Activity: building contractors
Managing Director: Tony Reynolds

Graham Construction
Lagan Mills
Dromore
BT25 1AS
Tel: 028 9269 2291
Fax: 028 9269 3412
Principal Activity: building contractors
Managing Director: Michael Graham

J Kennedy & Co (Contractors) Ltd
1 Letterloan Road
Macosquin
Coleraine
BT51 4PP
Tel: 028 7035 2211
Fax: 028 7035 6308
Principal Activity: builders
Manager: Danny Kennedy

Karl Construction Ltd
92 Old Ballyrobin Road
Muckamore
Antrim BT41 4TJ
Tel: 028 9442 5600
Fax: 028 9442 8178
Principal Activity: builders
Managing Director: A Blackbourne

Lagan Holdings Ltd
19 Clarendon Road
Clarendon Dock
Belfast
BT1 3BG
Tel: 028 9026 1000
Fax: 028 9026 1010
Principal Activity: quarrying civil engineering & construction group
Managing Director: Michael Lagan

Mivan Construction Ltd
Newpark
Greystone Road
Antrim
BT41 2QN
Tel: 028 9448 1000
Fax: 028 9448 1015
Principal Activity: construction
Managing Director: Ivan McCabrey

PJ Conway (Contractors) Ltd
58 Moneymore Road
Magherafelt
BT45 6HG
Tel: 028 7963 2001
Fax: 028 7963 3038
Principal Activity: building contractors
Proprietor: Patrick Conway

Redland Tile & Brick Ltd
61 Largy Road
Crumlin
BT29 4RR
Tel: 028 9442 2791
Fax: 0870 564 2742
Principal Activity: roofing services
Sales Manager: Billy Wright

RJ Maxwell & Son Ltd
209 Bushmills Road
Coleraine
BT52 2BX
Tel: 028 7034 3281
Fax: 028 7035 3346
Principal Activity: civil engineering
Managing Director: Willy McNabb

Tourism Sector

2001 saw a total increase in visitors to Northern Ireland with numbers growing by 31 per cent from 1.41 million in 1997 to 1.85 million in 2001. During 2001 over 1.8 million staying visitors came to Northern Ireland to visit friends and relatives, for business, on holiday or other purposes. This figure includes visitors from Great Britain, the Republic of Ireland, North America, Europe and elsewhere. It is estimated that tourism contributed 2.3 per cent to GDP in 2001. During 2000 the Northern Ireland tourism industry earned £329 million, against £322 million in 1999, of which £265 million came from staying visitors in Northern Ireland, and £64 million from domestic holiday spending.

Visitor tourism to Northern Ireland increased by 1 per cent in 2000 over 1999. This was in spite of decreases in the two main markets, Great Britain by 5 per cent and the Republic of Ireland by 1 per cent. These decreases were balanced by an increase of 37 per cent in the European market and in the other long haul markets: North America (+20%), Australia and New Zealand (+20%) and elsewhere (+32%). As in 1999 over 18 per cent (306,000) of all visitors were pure holidaymakers.

A significant number of Northern Ireland residents also holiday in the region, and the home holiday sector experienced a slight improvement in 2000. In 1999 home holidays accounted for 510,000 trips, and a holiday spend of £57 million whilst in 2000 home holidays accounted for 588,000 trips and a home holiday spend of £64 million.

The reduction in visitors from the Irish Republic was largely attributed to the continued strength of sterling, civil unrest in Northern Ireland during the summer months and disruption of the cross border rail service.

Visitors from the United States have increased by 120 per cent since 1993. Total visitors for 2000 were 110, 000, of which almost 50 per cent were pure holiday visitors. Revenue has also doubled in the last 6 years, totalling £29 million in 2000.

The main body responsible for the development of tourism in Northern Ireland is the Northern Ireland Tourist Board, which operates under the aegis of the Department of Enterprise, Trade and Investment. Investment in product development continued with £20 million gross capital investment spent during the year. This included assistance towards development of a wide variety of accommodation and visitor facilities across Northern Ireland.

The Tourism Development Scheme (TDS) financed through NITB and DETI, made available £1.6 million, primarily for the development of tourism related accommodation. During 2000 offers of support to the value of £4.43 million were issued, including £2.25 million for the development of a 145 bedroom 4 star hotel in Derry. The scheme also supported a number of tourism amenities and attractions, including the replacement of the rope footbridge at Carrick-a-Rede by The National Trust and visitor facilities at the Giant's Causeway. Spend under TDS at £3.4 million during 2000 was lower than forecast due to delays in a number of major hotel projects. However, a 120 bedroom four star hotel at Shaws Bridge was completed.

The EU, through the Tourism Sub-Programme 1994-99, Interreg 2, and the Special Support Programme for Peace and Reconciliation has also contributed substantially towards supporting the marketing of Northern Ireland as an attractive tourism destination, and in helping to develop tourist infrastructure, amenities and attractions. Projects receiving EU capital support included the St Patrick's Visitor Centre in Downpatrick which opened in March 2001 and the establishment of the former Shane's Castle narrow gauge railway along part of the Portrush coast to the Giant's Causeway tramway.

Throughout the year the Northern Ireland Tourist Board continued to administer the Challenge Fund, aimed to improve the competitiveness of the tourism industry. Offers amounting to £2.76 million were made to a diverse range of projects including a new 70-bed hostel in Enniskillen, and a visitor management project in the Mournes.

The level of employment in Northern Ireland supported by tourism revenue is estimated at 17,000 - a significant proportion of the total workforce.

CHAPTER 9

A Guide to Doing Business in Northern Ireland

The Northern Ireland Business Environment

This section of the Northern Ireland Yearbook 2003 is aimed primarily at individuals or group considering going into business for the first time and people and organisations based outside Northern Ireland who are thinking of developing business opportunities within Northern Ireland. It sets out a detailed description of the environment for business in Northern Ireland as well as the main practical considerations such as company registration, regulations, compliance, employment and taxation.

The Northern Ireland Economic Environment

Northern Ireland is an increasingly attractive location for those seeking to establish a new branch of an existing business or those seeking to build a completely new enterprise.

It is characterised by a youthful and well-educated population, a low cost base and one of the most technologically advanced network infrastructures in Europe as the following tables show. Further analysis of the Northern Ireland economy and its key sectors is set out in Chapter 8.

Table 9.1: European Union Population Comparison

Country	% Aged 0-40
Sweden	52.1
Germany	53.1
Italy	53.5
United Kingdom	54.9
France	56.8
Netherlands	57.5
Northern Ireland	**59.7**

Source: European Union Business Incentives Report 2001

Throughout the 1990s, Northern Ireland enjoyed the fastest economic growth of any region of the United Kingdom. In 1999 Gross Domestic Product was £17,003 million ($24,707 million). Between 1989 - 1999, real GDP per head increased by 22.6 per cent (2.1 per cent per year) in Northern Ireland compared to 18.2 per cent (1.7 per cent per year) increase for the UK as a whole.

It can also be seen that the Northern Ireland economy in line with western European economies is increasingly dependant on the services sector. This now accounts for almost 70 per cent of total GDP.

Table 9.2: Origins of GDP by Industrial Sector

Sector	% of total GDP
Services	68.5
Manufacturing	19.0
Construction	6.0
Agriculture	4.0
Electricity, Gas, Water	2.0
Mining and Quarrying	0.5
Total	**100**

Source: Northern Ireland Annual Abstract of Statistics 2001

Over the past five years the performance of Northern Ireland's manufacturing sector has significantly exceeded the UK average.

Table 9.3: Manufacturing Output 1996-2002

Country	% Change
United Kingdom	1.4
Northern Ireland	19.2

Source: DETI 'Quarterly Strategic Information Report'

Output growth has been accompanied by a significant rise in investment by the region's productive industries. Between 1995 and 2000, it increased by 91 per cent compared to a UK rise of 18.5 per cent. The UK is the second largest recipient of Foreign Direct Investment (FDI) globally and holds 20 per cent of all FDI stock in the EU and 8 per cent worldwide. Northern Ireland has captured a proportional share of this investment.

Table 9.4: Northern Ireland Exports

Exports 2000	Value £ million	% of total exports
Transport Equipment	603	14.5
Electrical & Optical Equipment	1173	28.5
Chemicals & Man Made Fibres	673	16.0
Food, Drink and Tobacco	648	15.5
Non Metallic Manufacturing Products	315	7.5
Other Machinery & Equipment	339	8.0
Textiles	208	5.0
Basic Metals/ Fabricated Metal Products	199	5.0
Total	**4158**	**100.0**

Source: NIERC, DETI 'Sales and Exports 00/01' June 2002

Traditionally a very inward looking economy, Northern Ireland has developed an increasing export focus, with exports now accounting for 38 per cent of total sales by Northern Ireland companies up from 28 per cent in 1991/92. The June 2002 export survey shows that sales to markets outside Europe grew by 25 per cent over the last five years to £1.85 billion. These markets now account for almost half of Northern Ireland's total exports.

Northern Ireland Labour Force

Table 9.5: Employment in Northern Ireland 2001

Total at Work	625, 740	% Workforce
Agriculture	15, 640	2.0
Industry	140, 900	21.0
Services	488, 650	75.0

Source: Northern Ireland Annual Abstract of Statistics 2001

Unemployment, which is currently at its lowest level since records began, has fallen steadily from a peak of 17.2 per cent in 1986 to 5.7 per cent in April 2002, compared with the current EU average of 8.4 per cent.

The Northern Ireland labour force is well trained and educated and although unemployment is low there are no significant skills shortages.

On average, labour costs are 32 per cent lower in Northern Ireland than in the US. Northern Ireland is unquestionably labour cost competitive with other developed economies.

Table 9.6: Index of Costs for Manufacturing Workers 2001

Country	Index
Germany	116
Japan	111
USA	100
Europe average	93
France	83
Canada	81
United Kingdom	80
Northern Ireland	**68**

Source: US Bureau of Labour Stats September 2001 Industrial Relations

In addition to relatively low cost labour by western standards, Northern Ireland is also a stable environment in terms of its industrial relations, with a lower incidence of industrial disputes than its European neighbours.

Table 9.7: International Comparisons of Labour Disputes 1995-1999

Country	Index
Denmark	300
Spain	150
Finland	125
France	100
Ireland	100
Italy	75
Sweden	45
Netherlands	25
UK average	23
Northern Ireland	**23**
Europe average	50

Source: UK National Statistics 'Regional Trends' 2001

Levels of staff absenteeism due to sickness in Northern Ireland are the lowest in the United Kingdom.

Productivity

Northern Ireland's manufacturing efficiency in terms of productivity has been increasing at almost twice the rate of the United Kingdom average.

Table 9.8: Manufacturing Productivity 1996-2001

Country	% change
Northern Ireland	27.7
UK average	14.5

Source: DETI, 'Quarterly Strategic Information Report' June 2002

Education of Labour Force

There are a total of 348,600 pupils in Northern Ireland schools (00/01), with approximately 21,000 schoolteachers and a ratio of 17.3 pupils per teacher.

In the most recent PISA (Programme for International Student Assessment - OECD), which covers the reading, mathematical and scientific abilities of 15 year olds in 32 countries, Northern Ireland significantly exceeds the OECD average in all three areas.

Table 9.9: Public Expenditure on Education as % of total Public Expenditure

Country	%
Northern Ireland	**22.0**
USA	14.4
ROI	13.5
Spain	12.8
UK	12.6
Portugal	12.6
France	11.1
Germany	9.5
Japan	9.8
Netherlands	9.8

OECD, N.I Assembly Public Expenditure Plans 2001-02

On average students in Northern Ireland obtain higher grades on standardised exams than they do elsewhere in the UK - almost 38 per cent of those who sat the highest exam at High School achieved the top pass mark ratings compared to the UK national average of only 29.5 per cent.

Northern Ireland's two universities have had major successes in a United Kingdom comparison of research work. The results of the Research Assessment Exercise 2001, demonstrate that 53 per cent of the departments assessed at the University of Ulster and 82 per cent of those at the Queen's University of Belfast are carrying out work of national and international excellence.

Infrastructure and Utilities

Electricity

The electrical power system is 3-phase AC operating at 50Hz with transmission systems of 275kV and 110kV serving a wide distribution network of 33kV and 11kV. Low voltage supplies are 230/400 volts although many large factories take supply at 11kV or 33kV. A range of tariffs is available although most large companies are charged on the basis of an Electricity Purchase Agreement. Rates vary considerably depending on the pattern of usage and voltage of supply. However, as a guide, most large companies pay an average price between 3.5p and 6p per kWh.

The Northern Ireland electrical grid has been strengthened considerably in recent years with physical interconnection with both the Republic of Ireland grid and Great Britain.

Telecoms

Northern Ireland has an advanced resilient, digital telecommunications network that provides high-speed voice and data connections. It was the first region in the UK to develop a fully fibre-optic infrastructure, and is part of a UK network that supplies greater bandwidth than the rest of Europe combined.

The cost of a typical 3 minute call from Northern Ireland to mainland Europe is on average 45 per cent cheaper than other EU tariffs, whilst contacting the US is up to 30 per cent less expensive.

Gas

Until relatively recently when a gas pipeline was built across the Irish sea, Northern Ireland had no natural gas network. Phoenix Natural Gas commenced supplying its first major customers in Belfast in January 1997. To date there are over 3,000 industrial and commercial customers using natural gas, saving an estimated £6 million between them on energy costs against their previous fuels. Natural gas is, however, currently only available in the Greater Belfast area although there are plans to extend the network significantly both northwest and south over the next few years.

Contract customers, using above 25,000 therms (732,000 kWh) per annum, can expect to pay between 1.1p and 1.4p per kWh depending upon the size of load, load factor, contract duration etc. For large customers with equipment capable of firing on alternative fuels, "interruptible supply" contracts are available at prices below the 1.1p per kWh level.

VODAFONE

16 Wellington Park
Belfast
BT9 6DJ
Website: www.vodafone.co.uk
Call our business team today on
0800 052 5200.

Byrom Bramwell
Managing Director

Mobile technology is advancing fast - with Vodafone leading the way. Mobilising your business brings more effective results, enabling you to reach new markets with a competitive edge. Working in partnership with your company, Vodafone delivers the most appropriate solution for your business and budget. Fleet management, voicemail, internet and multimedia services, Mobile EPOS for instant customer payments and professional friendly advice from start to finish. Whatever your company requires, no one works harder than Vodafone.

Call our business team today on
0800 052 5200.

Vodafone. The world's leading innovator in mobile communications.

Table 9.10: Rate for a Three-Minute Trunk Call at Peak Hours - U.S.$

From	Northern Ireland	Republic of Ireland	France	Germany	Netherlands	Belgium	USA
Northern Ireland	0.11	0.17	0.21	0.21	0.21	0.21	0.21
Republic of Ireland	0.34	N/A	0.83	0.83	0.83	0.83	0.40
France	0.25	0.32	N/A	0.25	0.25	0.25	0.27
Germany	0.27	0.27	0.27	N/A	0.27	0.27	0.27
Netherlands	0.15	0.28	0.18	0.17	N/A	0.18	0.15
Belgium	0.43	0.59	0.43	0.43	0.43	N/A	0.43
USA	0.24	0.45	0.45	0.45	0.45	0.57	N/A

Source - Tarrifica PBI Media. July 2001

Water

For industry, metered water costs are made up of two separate charges. The first is a volumetric charge for each cubic metre of water registered on the meter, the second is a yearly standing charge which depends on the internal diameter of the metre supply pipe, (e.g. 41-50mm equates to £289 per annum).

Domestic customers are not charged directly for water although there had been growing pressure on Northern Ireland's devolved administration to introduce some kind of charging structure for water in line with the rest of the UK.

Property and Accommodation

New, purpose built and fitted out office space is available throughout Northern Ireland from $13/£9/€14 per square foot in the greater Belfast area. Belfast currently offers the lowest net-rent of any large city in the UK.

Table 9.11: Cost of Office Space per Sq Foot by Location

Region	City	Cost per sq foot ($)
UK and Ireland	Belfast	20.90
	Birmingham	51.80
	Dublin	52.74
	Glasgow	30.36
	London (City)	112.23
	London (West End)	146.33
	Manchester	52.16
USA	Chicago	35.72
	New York (Mid Town)	63.22
	San Francisco	46.74
	Washington	47.94
EU	Amsterdam	34.58
	Madrid	51.53
	Paris	76.39
Asia Pacific	Hong Kong	70.37
	Tokyo (Inner Central)	122.34

Source: 'World Office Rents', CB Richard Ellis
July 2001, DTZ Research 2001

Specialist incubator units at the Northern Ireland Science Park and the University of Ulster Science and Research Park provide state-of-the-art accommodation and support during the start-up phase for knowledge-based industries.

New business parks such as Invest NI's Global Point International Business Park have flexible leasing at costs that are among the lowest in Europe. Invest Northern Ireland's Speculative Build Initiative will involve the private sector in the provision of property of up to 30,000 sqft (sub divisible into units of 5000 sqft) at a number of locations throughout Northern Ireland. These units are primarily suitable for companies operating in the Information, Communication and Telecoms sectors.

Transport Connections

At the end of 2000-01 there were 24,728 kilometres of public roads in Northern Ireland. Traffic congestion is minimal, compared to main routes in Britain, although larger towns and cities do experience problems during the conventional morning and evening rush hours. The well developed road infrastructure links all major commercial and industrial areas with seaports and airports.

Seaports

Over 80 international shipping lines operate out of Northern Ireland's 5 commercial seaports. 90 per cent of Northern Ireland's total trade, and almost 50 per cent of the Republic of Ireland's freight traffic, leaves through these ports. There are 150 sailings a week to destinations in the United Kingdom, including regular sailings to the USA, Continental Europe and the rest of the world. 8,800 ships carrying 15.5 million tonnes of cargo leave Belfast port each year. Over 60 per cent of Northern Ireland's sea borne trade is shipped through the Port of Belfast.

Airports

Serving over 3 million passengers a year Belfast International Airport is the principal gateway to the north of Ireland. It is the most technically advanced airport in Ireland and the fifth largest regional air cargo centre in the UK. Airfreight services are currently provided by regular scheduled passenger aircraft and an increasing number of dedicated freighter aircraft. Leading companies operating services from the 24-hour centre at Belfast International Airport are DHL and TNT, while Royal Mail also has a large presence there.

Belfast City Airport has opened a new £21 million terminal as a result of rapidly growing passenger traffic. More than 1.3 million passengers now pass through the terminal each year.

(Further details of Northern Ireland's sea crossings and connections and airline services are set out in Chapter 13, A Visitor's Guide to Northern Ireland.)

Formation and Registration of Companies in Northern Ireland

Forming a company in Northern Ireland is an uncomplicated process, although all companies registered in Northern Ireland are required to register with Companies House, submit accounts and annual returns and follow general procedures relating to registration.

Business entities may be incorporated or unincorporated. Incorporated bodies have a legal status separate from that of their owners and may sue and be sued in their own name. Incorporated bodies include private limited companies, public limited companies and unlimited companies. An unincorporated body may be a sole proprietorship or a partnership.

Registering a Company

There are four main types of company:
- Private company limited by shares - members' liability is limited to the amount unpaid on shares they hold;
- Private company limited by guarantee - members' liability is limited to the amount they have agreed to contribute to the company's assets if it is wound up;
- Private unlimited company - there is no limit to the members' liability;
- Public limited company (PLC) - the company's shares may be offered for sale to the general public and members' liability is limited to the amount unpaid on shares held by them.

A limited company has the fundamental advantage of being a legal entity separate from its members. An unlimited company lacks the advantage that most people seek from incorporation that of the limited liability of its members.

Limited liability companies have the advantage that the member's liability to contribute to the debts of the company have a fixed limit, which is always clear. The limit is set by issuing shares, (a company limited by shares) or by taking guarantees (a company limited by guarantee) from the members that they will contribute up to a fixed amount to the debts of the company when it is wound up or when it needs money in particular circumstances.

The Companies Act generally allows one or more persons to form a company for any lawful purpose by subscribing to its memorandum of association. However, a public company or an unlimited company must have at least two subscribers.

Company Formation

Those seeking to register a new company must submit the following:
- Form 10 summary of a companies officers, registered company address etc;
- Form 12 declaration of compliance;
- Memorandum of Association;
- Articles of Association;
- Fee of either £20 or £80.

Form 10 gives details of the first director(s), secretary and the address of the intended registered office. The company's directors must give their date of birth, occupation and details of other directorships they have held within the last five years. Each director appointed and each subscriber (or their agent) must sign and date the form. Form 10 is available from the Companies Office in Belfast or from any of the company registration agents for which details are given below.

The same person can be both a director and company secretary, provided there is another director. A sole director cannot also be the company secretary.

Form 12 is a statutory declaration of compliance with all the legal requirements relating to the incorporation of a company. It must be signed by a solicitor who is forming the company, or by one of the people named as director or company secretary on Form 10. It must be signed in the presence of a commissioner for oaths, a notary public, a JP or a solicitor.

Form 12 must be signed and dated after all other documents are signed and dated, as Form 12 confirms that all other documentation is complete. Form 12 is available from the Companies Office in Chichester Street, Belfast, or online. (Full contact details are given below).

Provided standard forms of memorandum and Articles of Association are being used documentation may be processed in one working day.

Completed and signed documentation should be forwarded to Companies House who will issue a Certificate of Incorporation. Processing of registration in a standard period of time has a £20 fee; the standard period is three to ten working days. Same day registration has a fee of £80, and is possible provided that Companies House receives all necessary documentation before 3pm.

The Memorandum of Association and Registration

It is essential that a company has a memorandum of association to specify its constitution and objects.

The memorandum of every company must state:

- The name of the company;
- Where the registered office of the company is to be situated;
- The objects of the company; (The object of a company may simply be to carry on business as a general commercial company.);
- That the liability of the members is limited;
- The maximum amount of capital the company may raise and its division into shares of a fixed amount.

The memorandum of a company limited by shares or by guarantee must also state that the liability of its members is limited. The memorandum of a company limited by guarantee must also state that each member undertakes to contribute to the assets of the company if it should be wound up whilst he is a member, or within one year after he ceases to be a member. These assets may then be used for payment of the debts and liabilities of the company contracted before he ceases to be a member, and of the costs, charges and expenses of winding up, and for the adjustment of the rights of the contributories amongst themselves, such amounts as may be required.

Articles of Association

The Articles of Association is a document setting out the rules for the running of the company's internal affairs and contains clauses addressing matters such as the issue and transfer of shares, the appointment and removal of directors, the conduct of shareholders and directors meetings and payment of dividends.

In the case of an unlimited company or a company limited by shares, articles of association signed by the subscribers to the memorandum and prescribing regulations for the company are registered. In the case of an unlimited company having a share capital, the articles must state the amount of share capital with which the company proposes to be registered.

Company Names

The choice of name for a company is of considerable importance and is subject to a number of restrictions.

The name of a public company must end with the words "public limited company". In the case of a company limited by shares or guarantee the company must have "limited" as its last word unless exempted under s.30 of the Companies Act 1986.

It is prohibited to register a company name which is the same as a name appearing in the registrar's index of company names or a name which would in the opinion of the Secretary of State for Northern Ireland constitute a criminal offence or is offensive.

A company may not be registered by any name, unless with the approval of the Secretary of State, which would give the impression that the company is connected in any way with government or the local authority.

If a company goes into insolvent liquidation a person who was acting as a director of the insolvent company is not permitted to act as a director of a new company with the same or a similar name. This restriction lasts for five years and aims to prevent the misuse of limited liability companies by putting one into liquidation, leaving the debts behind and starting another.

Registration and its Consequences

A company's memorandum and articles must be delivered to the Registrar of Companies. Accompanying the memorandum must be a statement in the prescribed form containing the names and details of the director or directors of the company and the person who is or is to be the first secretary or joint secretary of the company.

The statement should be signed by all those named as a director or secretary. The statement should specify the intended situation of the company's registered office on incorporation.

The registrar of companies will not register a company's memorandum unless satisfied that all requirements in respect of registration have been complied with. Subject to such compliance the registrar will retain and register the memorandum and articles.

Effect of Registration

Following registration of a company's memorandum, the registrar of companies will give a certificate that the company is incorporated and in the case of a limited company that it is limited. The certificate may be signed by the registrar or authenticated by his official seal. From the date of incorporation contained in the certificate the subscribers of its memorandum shall be a body corporate by the name contained in the memorandum.

Location of Registered Office

A company registered in Northern Ireland is required to have a registered office located in Northern Ireland. Upon formation the proposed registered office of a company and other details should be notified to the Registrar of Companies on Form G21. Any change to the registered address should be notified to Companies House on Form G295. Smaller companies frequently use their accountant's office as their registered address.

Publication of the Company Name

The name and address of a company must be present on company letterheads and other documentation. The name of the company must be displayed outside every place of business including the registered office. Under the terms of the Companies Act 1986 there is a requirement to state the company's name, place of registration, registered number and the address of its registered office on all business letters, notices and official publications, bills of exchange, promissory notes, endorsements, cheques, orders for money or goods, invoices, receipts and letters of credit. Failure to do so may leave the company and officers liable to a fine and may lead to personal liability for a director or agent.

In the case where a company, which is incorporated outside Northern Ireland, wishes to establish a presence within Northern Ireland certain disclosure and registration requirements must be met.

There are two registration regimes applicable in Northern Ireland, where a company has established a place of business in Northern Ireland, or established a branch in Northern Ireland. Once the applicable regime has been determined registration must occur within one month of the date of establishment.

To qualify as a branch the business entity must be part of a company and conduct business in Northern Ireland on behalf of the company. Local decision-making management would also be indicative of branch status. If the activities carried on by the entity are mainly ancillary or incidental to the core business of the organisation then those activities may be insufficient to constitute a branch although they may be sufficient to amount to the establishment of a place of business. To register as a branch the company must deliver prescribed documents to the Register of Companies. These include:

- A completed form BR1 Return Delivered for Registration of a Branch of a Part XXIII company which gives details of its date and country of incorporation, company number, officers and their authority to bind the company and location of branches;
- A certified copy of its charter statutes or Memorandum and Articles;
- Copies of the latest accounting documents;
- A registration fee of £35.00;
- Any amendments to registered details must be delivered within 21 days and special rules apply to the registration of charges or mortgages over assets.

Whilst there is no statutory definition for "establishing" a place of business the establishment of a place of business at a specific location and with a degree of permanency or recognisability as being a location of the business will suffice.

To register as having "established" a place of business in Northern Ireland companies must deliver the following documents to the Register of Companies:

- Using the prescribed form 641 a list of the directors and secretary with their details and the names and addresses of those resident in Northern Ireland authorised to accept notices on behalf of the company;
- A certified copy of its charter, statutes or Memorandum and Articles;
- A statutory declaration made by an authorised person stating the date upon which the company's place of business in Northern Ireland was established;

- The registration fee;
- Any alterations in registered details must be delivered within 21 days;
- A company, which has established a place of business in Northern Ireland, does not need to file any accounting documentation at its initial registration. However, for each subsequent financial year it must file accounts and the Director's report as if the company were incorporated under the 1986 Order.

Partnerships

A partnership has many fewer formalities to be complied with than a limited company, however, the members of a partnership are liable for all the debts incurred by the business they run. If large losses are made they must contribute their own money to clear the debts of the business. In practice with small businesses there may be little distinction between partnership and limited status, as banks will not lend money without first securing guarantees from those running the business so that if the company cannot pay its debts, the personal assets of those in charge will meet such debts.

Limited Partnerships

A limited partnership consists of:

- One or more persons called general partners, who are liable for all the debts and obligations of the firm; and
- One or more persons called limited partners, who contribute a sum or sums of money as capital, or property valued at a stated amount. Limited partners are not liable for the debts and obligations of the firm beyond the amount contributed.

A limited partnership must be registered under the Limited Partnership Act. To register as a limited partnership a statement (Form LP5) signed by all the Partners must be delivered to Companies House.

Limited Liability Partnerships

The Limited Liability Partnerships Act, which came into force on 6 April 2001, introduced a new form of association partnerships with limited liability.

A limited liability partnership is an alternative corporate vehicle providing the benefits of limited liability but allowing members the flexibility of organising their internal structure as a traditional partnership.

Any new or existing firm of two or more persons will be able to incorporate as a limited liability partnership. Incorporation of a limited liability partnership will be by registration at Companies House through a similar process to registration of a company.

Limited liability partnerships have similar disclosure requirements to a company including the filing of accounts. Limited liability partnerships will also be required to:

- File an annual return;
- Notify any changes to the limited liability partnership's membership;
- Notify any changes to the members names and residential addresses;
- Notify any change to their registered office address.

Joint Ventures

An overseas company may form a base in Northern Ireland by joining with an established company. Such joint ventures are usually as a limited company or as a partnership.

Accounts and Audit

Every company has a duty to keep accounting records sufficient to show and explain the company's transactions and should disclose with reasonable accuracy at any time the financial position of the company. Directors must ensure that the balance sheet and profit and loss account is compliant with their obligations under the terms of the Companies Act. Accounting records should contain day to day entries of all sums of money received and expended by the company and the matters in respect of which the receipt and expenditure takes place, and a record of the assets and liabilities of the company.

If a company's business involves dealing in goods, the accounting records should contain statements of stock held by the company at the end of each financial year of the company, all statements of stocktakings from which any statement of stock has been or is to be prepared and except in the case of goods sold by way of ordinary retail trade, statements of all goods sold and purchased, showing the goods and the buyers and sellers in sufficient detail to enable all these to be identified.

If a company fails to comply with these provisions every officer of the company who is in default becomes guilty of an offence unless he shows that he acted honestly and that in the circumstances in which the business operated the default was excusable.

A company's accounting records may be held at its registered office or such other place as the directors may think fit, and should be open to inspection by the company's officers at all times. A private company should keep its accounting records for three years from the date upon which they were made.

Annual Accounts

The directors of every company have a duty to prepare a set of accounts for each financial year. These accounts must include a profit and loss account, a balance sheet signed by a director, an auditors report signed by the auditor, notes to the accounts, and if relevant, group accounts.

Small and medium sized enterprises (SMEs) may abbreviate the accounts they submit to Companies House. All limited and public limited companies must submit their accounts to the Registrar. Unlimited companies need only deliver accounts to the Registrar if during the period covered by the accounts, the company was:

- A subsidiary or a parent of a limited undertaking;
- A banking or insurance company;
- A qualifying company within the meaning of the Partnerships and Unlimited Companies (Accounts) Regulations 1993;
- Operating a trading stamp scheme.

A company's first accounts stem from the date of incorporation not the first day of trading. Subsequent accounts start on the day after the previous accounts ended. If a company's first accounts cover a period of more than twelve months they must be delivered to the Registrar within 22 months of the date of incorporation for private companies.

Directors of private limited companies usually have a maximum of ten months from the accounting reference date to deliver accounts to the Registrar. The accounting reference date is the date to which accounts must be prepared. Public limited companies usually have seven months to deliver their accounts from the accounting reference date.

Whilst accountants may prepare the company accounts it is the responsibility of the director to ensure that accounts are filed on time. Late filing penalties are enforced against those companies whose accounts are late. These penalties are shown top right:

Table 9.12 Penalties for Late Filing of Company Accounts

Length of Delay	Private Company	Public Company
3 months or less	£100	£500
3 months 1 day to 6 months	£250	£1000
6 months 1 day to 12 months	£500	£2000
More than 12 months	£1000	£50000

Qualification of a Company as Small or Medium Sized

Companies qualifying as small or medium may prepare and deliver abbreviated accounts to the Registrar. Certain small companies with a turnover of less than £1 million, (£250,000 for companies with charitable status) and assets of less that £1.4 million can claim exemption from audit.

Public companies and certain companies in the regulated sectors cannot qualify as small or medium sized. For other companies, the size of the company (and in the case of a parent company the size of the group headed by it) in terms of its turnover, balance sheet total (meaning the total of the fixed and current assets) and average number of employees determines whether it is classed as small or medium.

To be classified as a small company at least two of the following conditions must be met:

- Annual turnover must be £2,800,000 or less;
- The balance sheet total must be £1,400,000 or less;
- The average number of employees must be 50 or fewer.

To be a medium sized company at least two of the following conditions must be met:

- Annual turnover must be £11,200,000 or less;
- The balance sheet total must be £5,600,000 or less:
- The average number of employees must be 250 or fewer.

If the company is a parent company it cannot qualify as a small or medium sized enterprise unless the group headed by it is also small or medium sized.

The abbreviated accounts of a small company must include:

- The abbreviated balance sheet and notes;
- A special auditor's report unless the company is also claiming audit exemption.

The abbreviated accounts of a medium company must include:

- The abbreviated profit and loss account;
- The full balance sheet;
- A special auditor's report;
- The directors' report;
- Notes to the accounts.

The special auditor's report should state that in the auditor's opinion the company is entitled to deliver abbreviated accounts and that they have been properly prepared in accordance with requirements of the Companies Act.

Company Governance

Company Officers

Every company must have formally appointed company officers at all times.

A private company must have at least:

- One director;
- One secretary - formal qualifications are not required. A company's sole director cannot also be the company secretary.

A public company must have at least:

- Two directors;
- One secretary - formally qualified.

All company officers have wide responsibilities in law.

After incorporation Companies House must be notified about:

- The appointment of a new officer - use Form 288a;
- An officer's resignation from the company - use Form 288b;
- Changes in an officer's name or address or any of the other details originally registered on Form 10 - use Form 288c.

Company Directors

Anyone of good standing may act as a company director subject to a few exceptions. Every company director has personal responsibility to ensure that statutory documents are delivered to the Registrar of Companies particularly:

- Accounts (only for limited companies);
- Annual returns (Form 363);
- Notice of change of directors or secretaries or their details (Forms 288 a/b/c);
- Notice of change of registered office (Form 287).

Company Secretaries

The company secretary of a public limited company must be qualified. However the company secretary of a private limited company requires no formal qualifications.

Northern Ireland Registrar of Companies
64 Chichester Street
Belfast
BT1 4JX
Tel: 028 9023 4488
Fax: 028 9054 4888

Off- the- Shelf Companies

Ready-made companies may be acquired from enterprises, which register a number of companies and hold them dormant until they are purchased. This may save time where a company is needed quickly for a particular enterprise. These ready-made companies are formed with the objects of a general commercial company having the power to carry on any trade or business.

Company Registration Agents

Cleaver Fulton Rankin

50 Bedford Street
Belfast BT2 7FW
Tel: 028 9024 3141
Fax: 028 9024 9096

Company Registration Agents

138 University Street
Belfast BT7 1HJ
Tel: 028 9032 9984
Fax: 028 9023 2221

The Company Shop

79 Chichester Street
Belfast BT1 4JE
Tel: 028 9055 9955
Fax: 028 9055 0078

Comperia Ltd

26 Donard Avenue
Newtownards BT23 4NF
Tel: 028 9181 0284
Fax: 028 9181 9470

Legal Support Services Ltd

352 Antrim Road
Belfast BT15 5AE
Tel: 028 9037 0001
Fax: 028 9077 6986

Taxation of Businesses in Northern Ireland

Company Taxation

The levels of corporate and personal taxation in Northern Ireland are among the lowest in Europe.

\multicolumn{2}{c}{Table 9.13: EU Main CorporateTax Rates 2001 (%)}	
Country	**% Rate**
Belgium	42
Italy	36
France	35
Netherlands	34
Spain	34
Austria	34
Portugal	32
Luxembourg	31
United Kingdom	**30**
Germany	22
\multicolumn{2}{c}{Source: Invest NI 2002}	

The UK has among the lowest corporate tax rates in Europe, making it one of the most competitive and attractive business locations. Since April 2000, a lower "small companies" rate of 10 per cent applies to the income of resident companies in the UK, with marginal relief available to companies with profits from £10,000 to £50,000.

Corporation Tax

Corporation tax is based on the total profits, income and capital gains, arising in an accounting period. The Corporation tax year runs from 1 April to 31 March. Where an organisation has an accounting period not coinciding with the corporation tax year, and the rate of tax varies from one year to the next, the company's profits are distributed pro rata over the two years.

The Corporation Tax Self Assessment (CTSA) regime applies in respect of all accounting periods ending after 30 June 1999. Under CTSA, companies compute their own tax and larger organisations are required to make payments on account.

A company is required to complete a detailed tax return in respect of each accounting period. The return contains a section requiring a computation of corporation tax and a self-assessment of liability. The return must usually be filed within twelve months of the end of the accounting period. Penalties of up to £1000 may be imposed for failure to submit a return and should the failure continue beyond six months, liability may increase to a tax related penalty of up to 20 per cent.

Under the terms of the Corporation Tax Self Assessment scheme a company's self-assessment stands unless amended by the company concerned or by the Inland Revenue. Where a company fails to make a return, the Inland Revenue will determine the tax due.

Payment of Corporation Tax

Corporation tax must be paid no later than nine months and one day from the end of the company's accounting period. This due and payable date predates the date for filing a return. Under self-assessment large companies must operate a quarterly account.

A large company is defined for this purpose as one with taxable profits and UK dividend income exceeding £1.5 million in a particular accounting period. Where a company is a member of a group or has associated companies this limit is divided by the number of associated companies plus one.

Where quarterly payments on account are to be made, they fall due as follows: six months and 14 days from the start of the accounting period; nine months and 14 days from the start of the accounting period; twelve months and 14 days from the start of the accounting period; and three months and 14 days from the end of the accounting period.

Interest on tax paid late runs from the due and payable date with respect to the final liability. The rate of interest on underpaid tax is currently 5 per cent and the interest on overpaid tax 3.75 per cent. During the period leading up to the due date different rates apply. Under CTSA interest on overdue tax is deductible when computing accessible profits and interest on overpaid tax is taxable.

Tax Audits

Under the terms of CTSA, the Inland Revenue has one year from the due filing date to commence an enquiry into a company's return. Where errors are discovered during the period of the enquiry the return may be corrected. However, once the period of the enquiry has expired, the return stands, unless deficiencies emerge of which the Inland Revenue could not reasonably have been made aware on the basis of the information available at the time.

Appeal Procedures

Where disputes arise over a self-assessment, assessment or determination and resolution cannot be achieved with the local tax office, an appeal is heard before the General or Special Commissioners.

Rates of Corporation Tax

The current rate of corporation tax is 30 per cent applicable to all of a company's taxable profits including capital gains, whether retained or distributed.

A reduced rate of 20 per cent applies where taxable profits do not exceed £300,000. The overall rate increases on a sliding scale from 20-30 per cent for profits between £300,00 and £1,500,000. Where taxable profits do not exceed £10,000 a starting rate of 10 per cent applies and a marginal rate applies to taxable profits between £10,000 and £50,000.

Table 9.14: UK Corporation Tax Rates

Band £000	%
0-10	10.0
10-50	22.5
50-300	20.0
300-1.5m	32.5
Over 1.5m	30.0

Capital Gains

Capital gains are computed according to separate rules and once computed are chargeable to corporation tax. Capital gains are computed by deducting from the base cost of the asset and an adjustment for inflation (indexation). The base cost is normally the acquisition price (plus enhancement expenditure), but where the asset was held at 31 March 1982, its market value at that date may normally be substituted for the base cost if greater. The inflation adjustment is restricted where necessary to the amount required to reduce the un-indexed gain to zero. Where a loss is sustained indexation is not available.

Dividends received by UK resident companies from other UK resident companies are exempt from corporation tax. Dividends from abroad are subject to corporation tax, both under domestic legislation and the UK's tax treaties.

Business expenses are deductible but must be incurred wholly and exclusively for the purposes of the taxable activity.

Depreciation and Capital Allowances

Depreciation of capital assets is not an allowable deduction. Deductions in lieu of depreciation are granted in respect of capital expenditure on certain classes of assets. These deductions known as capital allowances apply to the following:

Table 9.15 Assets Eligible for Deductions in lieu of Depreciation

Asset	Deduction
Industrial Buildings (factories and workshops but not commercial or retail premises)	4 per cent per annum straight line
Hotels	4 per cent per annum straight line
Plant and Machinery (including furniture and office equipment)	25 per cent per annum on a reducing balance
Agricultural Buildings and Works	4 per cent per annum straight line
Mineral Extraction	25 per cent or 10 per cent on a reducing balance
Scientific Research	100 per cent in the year of expenditure
Patent Rights	25 per cent per annum on a reducing balance

For expenditure on plant and machinery incurred between 12 May 1998 and 11 May 2002 a "first year allowance" of 100 per cent is available to most small and medium sized enterprises (SMEs) resident in Northern Ireland. The plant and machinery must be used in Northern Ireland by the SME claiming the allowance.

Draft legislation to enable companies to benefit from tax relief on the cost of intellectual property, goodwill and other intangible assets is currently under consideration. No relief is currently available with amortisation of intangible assets included in the statutory accounts being added back in the corporation tax computations as disallowable expenditure.

Research and Development Tax Credits

Research and development tax credits were introduced for small companies with effect from 1 April 2000. Qualifying companies may claim 150 per cent of qualifying revenue research and development expenditure against taxable profits or potentially claim 16 per cent of the 150 per cent as a repayment. The government proposes to extend this type of relief.

Interest and Other Charges on Income

Rules concerning the treatment of corporate debt have been significantly amended since 1996. Under the new rules, the tax treatment is intended to mirror the accounting treatment, provided that the company follows one of the two authorised accounting methods, namely the accruals basis or the mark to market basis.

Under the accruals basis, loan relationships are shown at cost, and payments and receipts are allocated to the accounting period to which they relate, on the assumption that every payable amount is paid when it becomes due. Under the mark to market basis, appropriate mostly for investment dealing, each loan relationship is accounted for in each accounting period at its fair value, and payments and receipts are allocated to the period in which they become due and payable.

Other charges on income, such as patent royalties and donations to charity are deductible from total profits (including capital gains). A deduction is available for a charge on income only when paid. Income tax at a basic rate, 22 per cent must be deducted from charges on income, and the tax must be accounted for on a quarterly basis to the Inland Revenue.

Expenses, which are non-deductible in computing taxable profits, include:

- Depreciation of capital assets;
- Non specific bad debt provisions;
- Entertaining expenses (excluding staff entertainment);
- Corporation tax;
- Capital expenditure;
- Expenditure incurred more than seven years before trading begins;
- Dividends and other distributions.

Personal Taxation

Table 9.16: EU Personal Tax (Higher) Rates 2000

Country	% Rate
Netherlands	60
Belgium	55
France	54
Germany	51
Austria	50
Italy	46
Greece	45
Ireland	44
Spain	40
Portugal	40
United Kingdom	40

Source: Invest UK 'Key Facts' 2002

The UK has the lowest "top rate" of personal taxation in the EU, and a starting rate of just 10% for most sources of income. In the UK, income becomes liable for taxation if it falls within one of the four schedules listed top right:

Table 9.17 Income Tax Schedules

Schedule	Description
Schedule A	Rental income from land and property in the UK
Schedule D	
Case I	Income from trade
Case II	Income from a profession or vocation
Case III	Interest, annuities or other annual payments
Case IV	Income from foreign securities
Case V	Income from foreign possessions
Case VI	Miscellaneous income
Schedule E	Income from employment and pensions
Schedule F	Dividends and distributions from other UK companies

Each schedule and case has its own rules for computing income and deductions. The computed income is then aggregated to produce an individual's total income, which is taxable. The tax year commences on the 6 April and ends on the following 5 April. The income assessable in any tax year is the income of that year.

A self-assessment system was introduced on 6 April 1996 for taxpayers whose liability is not satisfied solely by deductions under PAYE. The Inland Revenue sends tax returns to these taxpayers shortly after the end of the tax year. Taxpayers may choose between self-assessments in which case they must complete the return and calculate their own tax payable and file by 31 January and leaving it up to the Inland Revenue to compute tax payable, in which case completed returns must be filed by 30 September. Interest and penalty charges will be incurred if the return is not filed on time.

The Inland Revenue has been trying to move the tax return process on-line but the response from taxpayers has not been as enthusiastic as had been hoped.

PAYE System

Employers on a cumulative basis deduct tax and National Insurance contributions under the PAYE (Pay As You Earn) system. Deductions are made according to a code number for each employee issued by the Inland Revenue.

The code number takes into account the employees' allowances, benefits and credits, so that the correct amount of tax should have been deducted by the end of the tax year.

PAYE income tax and primary employee's National Insurance Contributions (NIC) deductions must be applied to virtually all payments of income assessable to Schedule E tax and /or NIC. Deductions cannot be made from payments in kind but a suitable adjustment is made to the employee's PAYE code number to allow for the tax due.

Every employer with a sufficient tax presence in the United Kingdom is obliged to operate PAYE. Special rules apply if the employee is not resident or ordinarily resident in the UK.

Persons operating PAYE are required to account monthly to the Inland Revenue for sums deducted in the previous tax month (from the 6th of one calendar month to the 5th of the next). Employers with small payrolls may apply for quarterly accounting.

At the end of the tax year the employer must provide a certificate of pay and tax deducted to each employee and a return of deductions in respect of all employees to the Inland Revenue, together with the payment of any balance of deductions outstanding. These returns and payments must be submitted to the Inland Revenue by 19 May of the following tax year. Interest is charged on late payment of end of year balances and penalties are imposed for late filing of returns.

Income tax

For the income tax year 2001-2002 the income tax bands after allowances are as follows:

Table 9.18 Income Tax Bands (after allowances)	
First £1,880	Lower Rate 10%
Next £27,520	Basic Rate 22%
Balance over £29,400	Higher Rate 40%

Income tax is computed by aggregating income under the various schedule and cases and subjecting the result (total income) to tax at three progressive rates, after deducting personal and other allowance and deductions.

INLAND REVENUE

www.inlandrevenue.gov.uk

Inland Revenue Northern Ireland (IRNI) is one of seven regional offices of the Inland Revenue.

Naomi Ferguson
Director
Inland Revenue
Northern Ireland

IRNI is committed to delivering a quality service to our customers. We will work to deliver the department's aim, which is to administer the tax system fairly and efficiently and make it as easy as possible for individuals and businesses to understand and comply with their obligations and receive their tax credits and other entitlements.

Our aim is to be an organisation that values and develops its people recognising that diversity and equality of opportunity are essential to the success and effectiveness of IRNI.

The names of the various income tax rates used in the United Kingdom are listed below:

Table 9.19 UK Income Tax Rates	
Lower Rate	10%
Savings Rate	20%
Basic Rate	22%
Higher Rate on Dividends	32.5%
Discretionary Trusts	34%
Higher Rate	40%

Inland Revenue Offices

Belfast 1

Beaufort House
31 Wellington Place
Belfast
BT1 6BH
Tel: 028 9053 2300
Fax: 028 9053 2310
Textphone: 028 9023 4081

Belfast 2

Olivetree House
23 Fountain Street
Belfast
BT1 5EP
Tel: 028 9053 2300
Fax: 028 9053 2682
Textphone: 028 9053 2786

Belfast 7

Dorchester House
52-58 Great Victoria Street
Belfast
BT2 7QH
Tel: 028 9050 5000
Fax: 028 9050 5107
Textphone: 028 9050 5634

Ballymena

Kilpatrick House
38-54 High Street
Ballymena
BT43 6DR
Tel: 028 2563 3022
(self-assessment)
Tel: 028 2563 3000 (other enquiries)
Fax: 028 2563 3001
Textphone: 028 2563 3053

Coleraine

Fern House
1A Adelaide Avenue
Coleraine
BT52 1ES
Tel: 028 7032 2069
(self-assessment)
Tel: 028 7032 2000 (other enquiries)
Fax: 028 7032 2001
Textphone: 028 7032 2038

Craigavon

Marlborough House
Central Way
Craigavon
BT64 1AH
Tel: 028 3831 2103
(self-assessment)
Tel: 028 3834 1131 (other enquiries)
Fax: 028 3831 2040
Textphone: 028 3831 2087

Enniskillen

Abbey House
Head Street
Enniskillen
BT74 7JL
Tel: 028 6634 4500
Fax: 028 6634 4566
Textphone: 028 6634 4523

Lisburn

Moira House
121 Hillsborough Road
Lisburn
BT28 1LA
Tel: 028 9266 5230
Fax: 028 9260 3385
Textphone: 028 9260 6071

Londonderry

Foyle House
Duncreggan Road
Londonderry
BT48 0AA
Tel: 028 7130 5239
(self-assessment)
Tel: 028 7130 5100 (other enquiries)
Fax: 028 7130 5101
Textphone: 028 713 5254

Newry

Downshire House
22-23 Merchants Quay
Newry
BT35 6HS
Tel: 028 3025 5570
(self-assessment)
Tel: 028 3025 5555 (other enquiries)
Fax: 028 3025 5600
Textphone: 028 3025 5522

Other Tax Offices

Belfast Provincial Collector of Taxes

Dorchester House
52-58 Great Victoria Street
Belfast BT2 7QE
Tel: 028 9050 5784
Fax: 028 9050 5774

Business Support Team

Level 8, Beaufort House
31 Wellington Place
Belfast BT1 6BH
Tel: 028 9053 2755
Fax: 028 9053 2524

Capital Taxes Office

Dorchester House
52-58 Great Victoria Street
Belfast BT2 7QE
Tel: 028 9050 5353
Fax: 028 9050 5305

Directors Office

Level 9, Dorchester House
52-58 Great Victoria Street
Belfast BT2 7QE
Tel: 028 9050 5000
Fax: 028 9050 5055
Textphone: 028 9050 5059

Regional Customer Service Manager

Level 8, Beaufort House
31 Wellington Place
Belfast BT1 6BH
Tel: 028 9053 2437
Fax: 028 9053 2524
Textphone: 028 9023 4081

Stamp Office

Dorchester House
52-58 Great Victoria Street
Belfast BT2 7QE
Tel: 028 9050 5127
Fax: 028 9050 5130

Tax Credit Helpline

Dorchester House
52-58 Great Victoria Street
Belfast BT2 7WF
Tel: 0845 609 7000
Textphone: 0845 607 6078

National Insurance

National Insurance is the major labour oncost in the United Kingdom and can add up to 10 per cent to salary costs. Social Security Taxes in the form of "National Insurance contributions" are payable by individuals and employers. There are six classes of contributions. The greatest share of revenue is raised by Class one contributions, paid by employers and employees. For employees, NICs are payable at a single rate of 10 per cent on the excess of gross earnings (excluding most benefits in kind) over £87 per week (equivalent to £4,535 per year). However, once gross earnings exceed £29,000 per year, the upper earnings limit, no further NICs are payable on the excess. No NICs are payable if earnings do not exceed the lower earnings limit (LEL). For 2001-2002 the LEL is £87 per week or £4535 per year.

Helpline Numbers

National Insurance
Tel: 0845 915 4655

Construction Industry Scheme
Subcontractors queries
Tel: 0845 3000 581

Contractors queries
Tel: 0845 733 5588

Existing Employers
Tel: 0845 7143 143

National Minimum Wage
Tel: 0845 6000 678

New Employers
Tel: 0845 6070 143

Self-Assessment
Tel: 0845 9000 444

National Insurance Contributions Offices

Headquarters
24-42 Corporation Street
Belfast BT1 3DR
Tel: 028 9025 1411
Fax: 028 9054 3354
Textphone: 028 9054 3340

Belfast
3rd Floor, Lancashire House
5 Linenhall Street
Belfast BT2 8AA
Tel: 028 9054 2920
Fax: 028 9054 2955
Textphone: 028 9054 2942

Banbridge
Bridgewater House
25 Castlewellan Road
Banbridge
BT32 4AX
Tel: 028 4062 1600
Fax: 028 4062 1616
Textphone: 028 4062 1648

Antrim
Castle Street
Antrim
BT41 4JE
Tel: 028 9442 6500
Fax: 028 9442 6555
Textphone: 028 9442 6460

Londonderry
Foyle House
Duncreggan Road
Londonderry
BT48 0AA
Tel: 028 7130 5260
Fax: 028 7130 5222
Textphone: 028 7130 5254

Value Added Tax (VAT)

VAT is a tax which VAT registered businesses charge when they supply their goods and services in the UK or the Isle of Man, but there are some exceptions. It is also a tax on goods, and some services, that are imported or acquired from outside the UK.

VAT does not apply to certain services. These include loans of money, some property transactions, insurance and certain types of education and training. Supplies, which are exempt from VAT, do not form part of taxable turnover.

There are three rates of VAT in the UK:

- 17.5 per cent (standard rate);
- 5 per cent (reduced rate);
- 0 per cent (zero rate).

Businesses will probably have to register for and charge VAT if:

- Taxable turnover reaches or is likely to reach a set limit, known as the VAT registration threshold;
- A business has been taken over as a going concern; or
- Goods are acquired from other European Community countries.

The VAT registration threshold was raised to £52,000 in the 2000 Budget. But businesses may opt to register for VAT if taxable turnover is less than this. Turnover is the amount of money going through the business, not just the profit.

The VAT which registered businesses charge and collect from customers is payable to Customs & Excise and is know as 'output tax'. The VAT which businesses are charged by their suppliers is called 'input tax' and can normally be reclaimed from Customs, although there are some exceptions.

Most businesses collect more VAT than they pay to their suppliers, and therefore pay the surplus VAT to Customs. However, if a business's input tax is more than its output tax, the difference will be refunded.

Most businesses must fill in a VAT return and pay the surplus VAT to Customs every quarter. Small businesses may opt to make just one return a year, although they may be asked to make interim payments. Businesses, which regularly pay out more, VAT than they collect, may fill in a return every month and obtain a refund.

Customs and Excise: Importing and Exporting

HM Customs and Excise
Custom House
Custom House Square
Belfast BT1 3ET
Tel: 028 9056 2600
Web: www.hmce.gov.uk

Registration & Deregistration
Tel: 0845 711 2114
Fax: 028 3026 4165

Debt Management
Tel: 028 9056 2600
Fax: 028 9056 2975

Complaints and Suggestions
Tel: 028 9056 2617
Fax: 028 9056 2970

National Advice Service
Tel: 0845 010 9000
Text-phone for the deaf or hard of hearing:
0845 000 0200

Customs & Excise is the UK Government department responsible for the collection and administration of VAT and excise duties as well as looking after Import & Export formalities. The department provides a range of support services for businesses that may need advice or assistance in operating any of these regimes.

- The National Enquiry Service deals with all general telephone enquiries via a single telephone number - 0845 010 9000. This service is available Monday to Friday from 8am to 8pm;

- If the enquiry is more complex, or a written response is required, the Written Enquiry Service may be contacted at the above address or by e-mail to enquiries.ni@hmce.gsi.gov.uk;

- The local Business Support Team offers support for businesses in Northern Ireland. This support can take the form of a one to one consultation for a single business or a seminar for a group of businesses with a common interest, such as cross border trade. The Business Support Team may be contacted at the above address or by telephone on 028 9056 2600;

- The Customs & Excise Website www.hmce.gov.uk contains further information and visitors to the site may download a wide range of information notices and leaflets.

All Customs & Excise support services are provided free of charge.

Importing and Exporting

If a business involves importing or exporting goods, there are certain requirements, which must be complied with, such as declaration of imports and exports to Customs & Excise and payment of any duties or VAT due.

Some imported goods are also liable to duties; further information on those goods affected is available from Customs and Excise.

With the establishment of the internal market across the European Union import/export procedures have been greatly simplified. However, there are numerous compliance requirements relating to trade with non-EU member states.

Employment of Staff in Northern Ireland

Introduction

The employment of staff for business in Northern Ireland entails much more than the payment of salary and overhead costs. Employers will need to be aware of a plethora of legal employment requirements and regulations across a range of headings. Some of the regulation derives from the Social Chapter of the European Union and is governed by European Directives (see below).

The remainder comes from the particular requirements deemed necessary for Northern Ireland in terms of ensuring fairness and equality in the employment sphere.

The table to the right sets out the main sources of legislation in relation to employment law in Northern Ireland and provides an overview of the obligations and entitlements of both the employer and the employee.

Unfair Dismissal

Unfair dismissal in Northern Ireland is determined by the Rome Convention on the Law Applicable to Contractual Obligations transposed into UK and Northern Ireland law by the Contracts (Applicable Law) Act, 1990.

Discrimination in Northern Ireland

Equality legislation in Northern Ireland comprises the Fair Employment and Treatment (NI) Order 1998, the Disability Discrimination Act 1995, the Race Relations (NI) Order 1997, the Equal Pay Act (NI) 1970 and the Sex Discrimination (NI) Order 1976.

Public Holidays

Public holidays include bank holidays, holidays by Royal Proclamation and "common law holidays". Banks are not allowed to operate on bank holidays.

There is no statutory entitlement to bank or other public holidays, these are days where an employee may receive paid or unpaid leave depending on the terms of their contract. Where employees work on a public holiday to which they are entitled under the terms of their contracts, compensation for doing so is a matter for resolution under the terms of their contract.

Bank holidays in Northern Ireland include the traditional "12th" holiday of the 12th and 13th July, the August Bank Holiday, 25th and 26th December, 1st January, and May Day.

Table 9.20 Overview of Employment Entitlements and Obligations

Working Time:
Working Time (NI) Regulations 1998.
Employees may choose to work in excess of 48 hours per week

Notice:
Employment Rights (NI) Order 1996

Length of Service	Notice
One month	1 week
2-3 year	2 week
3-4 years	3 weeks
12 years or more	up to 12 weeks

Annual Leave and Public Holidays:
Employment Rights (NI) Order 1996

Minimum Wage:
The Minimum Wage (NI) Act 1998
The minimum hourly rate is currently £4.20 per hour (aged 22+) or £3.60 per hour (aged 18-21)

Equality:
The Sex Discrimination (NI) Order 1976, The Equal Pay Act (NI) 1970, the Race Relations (NI) Order 1997, the Disability Discrimination Act 1995, The Fair Employment and Treatment (NI) Order 1998.
Anti-discrimination provisions include:
- 5 discriminatory grounds - sex, race, (includes membership of the travelling community), religious belief, political opinion and disability
- Discriminatory grounds of family status, marital status, age and sexual orientation are not included
- The Part-time Workers (Prevention of Less Favourable Treatment) Regulations (NI) 2000

Unfair Dismissal:
Employment Rights (NI) Order 1996
- Time limit - 3 months from the date of the dismissal or within such further period as the Tribunal considers reasonable
- Compensation: a basic award which would usually equate to the amount an employeewould have received had they been made redundant;

Whistleblowers:
The Public Interest Disclosure (NI) Order 1998
Provides protection for workers who are dismissed or victimised as a result of making certain disclosures

Redundancy:
Employment Rights (NI) Order 1996
Service below the age of 18 may not be included in calculating statutory redundancy. Statutory redundancy pay is subject to a ceiling of £240 per week. A collective redundancy arises where 20 or more employees are dismissed as redundant at one establishment within a period of 90 days or less. Where a collective redundancy arises, consultation with employee representatives must begin in good time.

Human Rights:
The Human Rights Act 1998
Article 8 confers the right to respect for family and private life.

Annual Leave

Annual leave is usually accrued over "leave years" from the date of employment or the date of the commencement of the organisation's leave year. If an employee joins an organisation during the course of the leave year their annual leave entitlement is calculated pro rata to the full leave year. Under the terms of the Working Time Regulations (Northern Ireland) 1998 entitlement to statutory leave for part years is proportionate to the amount of leave year that the employee works.

Holidays and Holiday Pay

Entitlement to holidays and holiday pay for most workers is determined by their contract of employment subject to the minimum conditions of the Working Time Regulations (Northern Ireland) 1998. Most employees have the statutory right to receive from their employers a written statement of employment details; although not a contract in itself this statement provides evidence of many of the terms of the contract. These must include provisions relating to holidays, including public holidays and holiday pay.

Restrictions on Taking Holidays

Restrictions on the taking of annual leave may be stated in the contract of employment, implied from custom and practice or incorporated into individual contracts from a collective agreement between the employer and trade unions.

Maternity Leave

Maternity rights are set out in the Employment Relations (Northern Ireland) Order 1996 and the Maternity and Parental Leave Regulations (Northern Ireland) 1999.

- Pregnant employees are entitled to 18 weeks of ordinary maternity leave regardless of length of service:
- Women who have completed one year's service with their employer are entitled to take additional maternity leave commencing at the end of ordinary maternity leave and finishing 29 weeks after the birth.

Parental Leave

Parental leave is a new entitlement to take time off to look after a child or to make arrangements for a child's welfare. Parents may use this entitlement to spend more time with their children and strike a balance between work and family commitments. Employees qualify for this entitlement following one year's service with the employer.

Time Off for Dependants

All employees have the right to take a reasonable period of time off work to deal with an emergency involving a dependant and not be victimised or dismissed for doing so.

Disability Issues

Issues relating to disability are legislated for under the Disability Discrimination Act 1995 which makes it unlawful to discriminate against disabled persons in connection with employment, the provision of goods, facilities and services or the disposal or management of premises.

For businesses and organisations it is unlawful to treat disabled people less favourably than other people for a reason related to their disability (December 1996). Organisations are required to make reasonable adjustments for disabled people, such as providing extra help or making changes to the way they provide their services (October 1999) and may have to make reasonable adjustments to the physical features of their premises to overcome physical barriers to access (2004).

European Directives Impacting on Employment in Northern Ireland

Directive Implementing the Principle of Equal Treatment Between Persons Irrespective of Racial or Ethnic Origin (The Race Directive)

The Race Directive was formally adopted on 29 July 2000 and must be implemented by member states by 19 July 2003. The Directive prohibits both direct and indirect discrimination on grounds of race or ethnic origin.

Framework Directive on Equal Treatment in Employment and Occupation

The purpose of this Directive is to implement in member states the principle of equal treatment in respect of access to employment of all persons, regardless of their age, sexual orientation, religion, belief or disability.

Draft EU Directive on Information and Consultation at the National Level (the National Works Council Directive)

The purpose of this directive is to set out minimum requirements for the right to information and consultation of employees.

Directive on Fixed Term Work

This directive was introduced with the aim of preventing fixed term employees being treated less favourably than employees on permanent or "continuing" contracts.

Other Regulation of Business in Northern Ireland

Introduction

In addition to the regulation of fundamental business concerns such as employment, taxation and governance, businesses are subject to extensive regulation in many other areas.

Depending on the nature of the business being started it may be affected by legislation and regulations regarding:

- Planning and Building Control;
- Health and safety;
- Fire precautions;
- Environmental protection;
- Intellectual property;
- Fair trading;
- Data protection;
- Licensing;
- Insurance.

Planning Permission, Buildings/Premises

All development activity on a site or premises is subject to planning regulations overseen by the Planning Service. This can include as small a matter as installation of external signage right through to refurbishment and new build. The Planning Service has a network of regional offices (these are listed in Chapter 4).

In addition to planning authorisations all developments require building control approvals. Building control is a function of the Department of the Environment with local offices organised through local offices.

Further information is available from the Building Control department of the relevant local authority.

Health and Safety

Company directors are responsible for the effect their business may have on the health and safety of employees and members of the public and may need to register with the Health & Safety Executive (HSE) or Local Authority. Further information is available from the Health and Safety Executive. Depending on the activities a company is engaged in and the extent of the danger it may present to staff and the public there are exacting procedures, which are legally binding. Larger businesses are required to produce a Health and Safety Policy statement and to publicise same.

Health & Safety Executive for Northern Ireland (HSENI)
83 Ladas Drive
Belfast BT6 9FR
Tel: 028 9024 3249
Fax: 028 9023 5383

Fire Precautions

All business premises are required to have adequate levels of protection against fire hazard. This includes the installation (and regular checking) of equipment such as fire extinguishers and blankets. Staff should be trained in necessary action to combat fire - a clear fire drill should be established and in larger premises a fire alarm system must be installed. Certain businesses may require a fire certificate, particularly if the business is a guesthouse, hotel or residential nursing home.

Environmental Protection

There are environmental regulations that may apply to a business if it:

- Uses refrigeration or air-conditioning equipment, fire equipment or solvents for cleaning;
- Produces, imports, exports, stores, transports, treats, disposes of or recovers waste;
- Produces, imports or exports packaging;
- Produces packaging waste.

The Environment Agency provides advice for business and industries. For more information contact:

Tel: 028 9054 0540
Web: www.environment-agency.gov.uk/epns/

Department of Environment contacts are set out below:

Environmental Protection
Headquarters
Calvert House
23 Castle Place
Belfast BT1 1FY
Tel: 028 9025 4754

Information and Education
Commonwealth House
35 Castle Street
Belfast BT1 1GU
Tel: 028 9054 6533

Industrial Pollution & Radiochemical
Inspectorate
Calvert House
23 Castle Place
Belfast BT1 1FY
Tel: 028 9025 4754

Intellectual Property

'Intellectual property' describes things such as business names, patents and inventions. Businesses should protect their own company name and logo, along with any inventions, product designs or copyrights and must also respect other people's intellectual property rights. The Patent Office can provide useful information and advice.

Tel: 08459 500 505.
Web: www.patent.gov.uk
Web: www.intellectualproperty.gov.uk

Fair Trading

The Office of Fair Trading (OFT) is responsible for protecting consumers by promoting effective competition, removing trading malpractice and publishing appropriate guidance. The OFT also issues consumer credit licences. More information is available by contacting The Office of Fair Trading:

Web: www.oft.gov.uk or
Tel: 08457 224499.
For information about consumer credit licences:
Tel: 0207 211 8608.

Data Protection

Where a business involves keeping detailed information about people, it must be careful about the sort of information it keeps and how it is used or shared in relation to the Data Protection Act. There is a requirement to register if such detailed or private information is held on computer. Further information is available from:

Data Protection Office
Tel: 01625 545745
Web: www.dataprotection

Licensing

Most business sectors are specifically regulated and participants are often individually licensed to engage in particular activities. A licence is required for many businesses, not just casinos or public houses. For example, a licence is required to run a hotel, a guesthouse, or a mobile shop. Companies should always check whether the business requires a licence to trade.

Insurance

Company directors are required to take out Employers' Liability Insurance to cover the consequences of possible accidents in the workplace. Depending on the nature of the business directors or staff may also wish to investigate personal indemnity insurance.

A list of Northern Ireland's leading insurance companies is included in the business services listings, which follow later in this chapter.

Sources of Support for Business

BELFAST FIRST STOP SHOP LTD

Belfast First Stop Business Shop Ltd
14 Wellington Place
Belfast
BT1 6GE
Tel: (028) 9027 8399
Fax: (028) 9027 8398
Email: info@firststopshop.co.uk
Website: www.firststopshop.co.uk

Belfast First Stop Business Shop provides an information, advisory and signposting service for potential and existing businesses. Assistance is principally for those based in the Belfast City Council area, but anyone with a new business idea is encouraged to visit the shop to avail of its services.

The First Stop Shop is an independent organisation with established links to both public and private sector agencies involved in enterprise development in Belfast. The First Stop Shop has an extensive information library and a highly experienced, qualified team of people who can provide advice and counselling as well as signposting to other business development agencies.

Invest Northern Ireland

A new agency, Invest Northern Ireland has been established to co-ordinate industrial development efforts. Professor Fabian Monds has been appointed as Chairman and Leslie Morrison as the new Chief Executive.

The agency falls under the auspices of the Department of Enterprise, Trade and Investment, which is the principal department responsible for providing business support for the private sector in Northern Ireland.

Invest Northern Ireland

64 Chichester Street
Belfast BT1 4JX
Tel: 028 9023 9090
Fax: 028 9054 0490
E-Mail: info@investni.com
Web: www.investni.com

Invest Northern Ireland

Upper Galwally
Belfast BT8 6TB
Tel: 028 9023 9090
Fax: 028 9049 0490

Invest Northern Ireland

17 Antrim Road
Lisburn BT28 3AL
Tel: 028 9023 9090
Fax: 028 9049 0490

Invest Northern Ireland has drawn together the activities previously carried out by the Industrial Development Board (IDB), Local Enterprise Development Unit (LEDU), Industrial Research and Technology Unit (IRTU), and certain functions of the Northern Ireland Tourist Board (NITB) and the Business Support Division of the Training and Employment Agency (T&EA).

Invest Northern Ireland's mission is "to accelerate the development in Northern Ireland, applying expertise and resources to encourage innovation and achieve business success, increasing opportunity for all within a renewed culture of enterprise".

There are also five Invest Northern Ireland Regional Offices:

Belfast:	028 9024 2582
Ballymena:	028 2564 9215
Londonderry:	028 7126 7257
Newry:	028 3026 2955
Omagh:	028 8224 5763

There are plans to open further regional offices in Enniskillen, Coleraine and Craigavon.

Invest Northern Ireland Local Offices

North Western Local Office
13 Shipquay Street
Londonderry BT48 6DJ
Tel: 028 7126 7257
Fax: 028 7126 6054
E-mail: nwlo@investni.com
Manager: Gerard Finnegan

North Eastern Local Office
Clarence House
86 Mill Street
Ballymena BT43 5AF
Tel: 028 2564 9215
Fax: 028 2564 8427
E-mail: nelo@investni.com
Acting Manager: Claire Herron

Eastern Local Office
25-27 Franklin Street
Belfast BT2 87DT
Tel: 028 9024 2582
Fax: 028 9024 9730
E-mail: elo@investni.com
Manager: Tim Losty

Southern Local Office
6-7 The Mall
Newry BT34 1BX
Tel: 028 3026 2955
Fax: 028 3026 5358
E-mail: slo@investni.com
Acting Manager: Mark Bleakney

Western Local Office
Kevlin Buildings
47 Kevlin Avenue
Omagh BT78 1ER
Tel: 028 8224 5763
Fax: 028 8224 4291
E-mail: wlo@investni.com
Acting Manager: Ethna McNamee

Invest NI CEO, Leslie Morrison (second right) visits AVX, Coleraine

Organisation Structure of Invest Northern Ireland

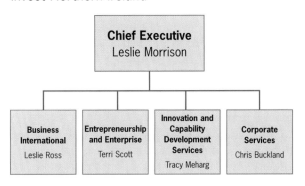

Business International

Managing Director: Leslie Ross
Tel: 028 9064 5304

Director of International
Sales and Marketing: Colin Lewis
Tel: 028 9054 5330

Director of International
Health Technologies and
Consumer Products: Ian Murphy
Tel: 028 9054 5322

Director of International Electronics
and Industrial Products: Derek Lynn
Tel: 028 90545324

Director of International ICT: Jeremy Fitch
Tel: 028 9054 5123

The Business International Directorate is responsible for inward investment and global indigenous companies. Through its network of offices throughout Europe, including Great Britain, North America and Asia Pacific, Invest Northern Ireland works with overseas companies to help identify investment opportunities, source data and set up reconnaissance visits.

Entrepreneurship and Enterprise

Managing Director: Prof Terri Scott
Tel: 028 9082 8092

Director of Local Economic
Development Including Property: Graham Davis
Tel: 028 9049 0552

Director of Enterprise Support: Kevin McCann
Tel: 028 9049 0576

Director of Entrepreneurship
and Start Up Sector: Vacant

The Entrepreneurship and Enterprise Directorate is responsible for pre-existing LEDU companies, indigenous IDB client companies and NITB client companies.

Innovation and Capability Development Services

Managing Director: Tracy Meharg
Tel: 028 9054 5101

Director of Innovation,
Research and Technology: Diarmuid McClean
Tel: 028 9262 3151

Director of Trade Development Services: Alan Hingston
Tel: 028 9055 9203

Director of Business
Improvement Services: Victor Jordan
Tel: 028 9054 4859

Director of Knowledge Management: Jim Sayers
Tel: 028 9062 3056

The Innovation and Capability Development Services Directorate is responsible for research and development, business development programmes, the former business support division of the T&EA and e commerce initiatives including the Information Age initiative.

Corporate Services

Managing Director: Chris Buckland
Tel: 028 9064 4873

Director of HR and
Internal Communications: Liam Hagan
Tel: 028 9054 4889

Director of Finance: Alan Neville
Tel: 028 9082 8038

Director of Investment Appraisal: Charles Harding
Tel: 028 9054 5369

Director of Strategic Management and Planning:
Carol Keery, Bernie O'Hare, Maurice Patterson
Tel: 028 9054 5299

Head of ICT and e-business: Vacant

Corporate Communications: Rosie Clarke
Tel: 028 9054 5194

The Corporate Services Directorate is responsible for corporate affairs and administration.

Invest Northern Ireland: Business Start Up Assistance, Grants and Funding Opportunities

Support for Start Up Business

As well as providing advice and assistance on every aspect of setting up a business in Northern Ireland, Invest Northern Ireland also maintains a portfolio of land pre-approved for development and a range of property available for immediate leasing.

Also available is a package of financial incentives, recruitment and training support customized to each company's needs. This can include:

- Tax free capital grant of up to 50% on buildings and equipment;
- Employment grant as each new worker is recruited;
- R&D grants up to 50 per cent for innovative market led products and processes;
- Rent grants;
- Access to share capital and loans on commercial terms;
- A total recruitment and selection service at no extra cost;
- Training grants of up to 50% of eligible training costs;
- Free pre-employment training.

A list of business support programmes operated by or through Invest Northern Ireland is available for all Invest NI offices.

Cross border Business Support Initiatives

As well as support for business development in Northern Ireland there is considerable assistance available to companies wishing to operate on a cross-border basis.

International Fund for Ireland Initiatives

Contact: Rodney Baird Tel: 028 9076 8832.

Business Enterprise and Technology Programme

The programme aims to promote the development of new products, identify new market opportunities, and encourage partnerships, alliances and joint ventures.

Initiatives include:

- The North American Partnership, which develops linkages between Irish Southern border firms and US companies;

- The American Business Internship Programme (AMBIT);
- The Ron Brown programme of intensive management training in the US;
- The Research and Development between Ireland and North America or Europe (RADIANE).

Peace II

The European Union has allocated substantial funding for the purposes of helping sustain the "peace" in Northern Ireland including a number of economic measures. The funding known as "Peace II" covers a range of initiatives and is administered overall by the Special EU Programmes Body and a number of other intermediary bodies including Co-operation Ireland.

Details on the funding available under the Peace II initiative are to be found in Chapter 10, the European Union and Economic Support Initiatives in Northern Ireland.

InterTradeIreland

InterTradeIreland also provides a range of funding opportunities and business support initiatives; details of where to contact InterTradeIreland are to be found in Chapter 2, The Government of Northern Ireland.

Local Government: Support for Economic Development

Local councils play a role in the development of enterprise through their Economic Development Units. There is no generic approach to enterprise promotion at local government level, rather each local council area will operate a disparate range of programmes and initiatives depending on the level of funding available.

Enterprise Northern Ireland

Enterprise Northern Ireland is the association of enterprise Agencies in Northern Ireland. Local Enterprise Agencies provide a range of services, including:

- A single point of contact for government-backed small business initiatives;
- Advice on business start-up;
- Access to low cost loans, grant aid and other finance sources;
- Practical support in the use of IT for small businesses;
- Various programmes to support business growth;
- Provision of industrial and office accommodation.

Local Enterprise Agencies

There are 31 active Enterprise Agencies in Northern Ireland, employing around 200 staff, operating from 40 locations.

Belfast

Argyle Business Centre Ltd
39 North Howard Street
Belfast BT13 2AP
Tel: 028 90 233777
Fax: 028 90 313446
E-mail: admin@abc-ni.co.uk
Web: www.abc-ni.co.uk
Manager: Frank Hamill

Brookfield Business Centre
333 Crumlin Road
Belfast BT14 7EA
Tel: 028 9074 5241
Fax: 028 9074 8025
E-mail: bob.mcneill@brookfieldcampus.com
Web: www.flaxtrust.com
Manager: Bob McNeill

Castlereagh Enterprises Ltd
Dundonald Enterprise Park
Enterprise Drive
Carrowreagh Road
Dundonald
Belfast BT16 0QT
Tel: 028 9055 7557
Fax: 028 9055 7558
E-mail: enterprise@Castlereagh.com
Web: www.castlereagh.com
Manager: Bob McNeill

East Belfast Enterprise Park Ltd
308 Albertbridge Road
Belfast BT5 4GX
Tel: 028 9045 5450
Fax: 028 9073 2600
E-mail: info@eastbelfast.org
Web: www.eastbelfast.org
Manger: Roisin Boyle

Farset Enterprise Park Ltd
638 Springfield Road
Belfast BT12 7DY
Tel: 028 9024 2373
Fax: 028 9043 8967
E-mail: admin@farset.com
Web: www.farset.com
Manager: William Bradley

Glenwood Enterprise Ltd
Glenwood Business Centre
Springbank Industrial Estate
Poleglass
Belfast BT17 0QL
Tel: 028 9061 0311
Fax: 028 9060 0929
E-mail: office@glenwoodbc.com
Web: www.glenwoodbc.com
Manager: Eamon Foster

Investment Belfast
40 Linenhall Street
Belfast BT2 8BA
Tel: 028 90 331136
Fax: 028 90 331137
E-mail: info@investment-belfast.co.uk
Web: www.investment-belfast.co.uk
Chief Executive: Brendan Mullan

Laganside Corporation
Clarendon Building
15 Clarendon Road
Belfast BT1 3BG
Tel: 028 90 328507
Fax: 028 90 332141
E-mail: info@laganside.com
Web: www.laganside.com
Chief Executive: Mike Smith

North City Business Centre Ltd
2 Duncairn Gardens
Belfast BT15 2GG
Tel: 028 9074 7470
Fax: 028 9074 6565
E-mail: michael@north-city.co.uk
Web: www.north-city.co.uk
Centre Manager: Michael McCorry

Ormeau Business Park
8 Cromac Avenue
Belfast BT7 2JA
Tel: 028 9033 9906
Fax: 028 9033 9937
E-mail: info@ormeaubusinesspark.com
Web: www.ormeaubusinesspark.com
Development Officer: Patricia McNeill

ORTUS:
The West Belfast Enterprise Board
Twin Spires Centre
155 Northumberland Street
Belfast BT13 2JF
Tel: 028 9031 1002
Fax: 028 9031 1005
E-mail: hq@ortus.org
Web: www.ortus.org
Manager: Sean Toal

Townsend Enterprise Park Ltd
28 Townsend Street
Belfast BT13 2ES
Tel: 028 9089 4500
Fax: 028 9089 4502
E-mail: admin@townsend.co.uk
Web: www.townsend.co.uk
Manager: George Briggs

West Belfast Development Trust
Work West
301 Glen Road
Belfast BT11 8BU
Tel: 028 9061 0826
Fax: 028 9062 2001
E-mail: c.ferris@workwest.co.uk
Web: www.workwest.co.uk
Manager: Claire Ferris

Westlink Enterprise Limited
T/A Westlink Enterprise Centre
30-50 Distillery Street
Belfast BT12 5BJ
Tel: 028 90 331549
Fax: 028 90 330803
E-mail: hq@ortus.org
Web: www.ortus.org
Manager: Sean Toal

Co Antrim

Acorn the Business Centre
2 Riada Avenue
Garryduff Road
Ballymoney BT53 7LH
Tel: 028 2766 6133
Fax: 028 2766 5019
E-mail: enquiries@acornbusiness.co.uk
Manager: Bobby Farren

Antrim Enterprise Agency
58 Greystone Road
Antrim BT41 1JZ
Tel: 028 9446 7774
Fax: 028 9446 7292
E-mail: admin@antrimenterprise.com
Web: www.antrimenterprise.com
Manager: Jennifer McWilliams

Ballymena Business Development Centre Ltd
Galgorm Industrial Estate
62 Fenaghy Road
Galgorm
Ballymena BT42 1FL
Tel: 028 2565 8616
Fax: 028 630 830
E-mail: bb.dc@virgin.net
Web: www.bbdc.co.uk
Manager: Melanie Christie

Carrickfergus Enterprise
Agency Ltd (CEAL)
8 Meadowbank Road
Troopers Lane Industrial Estate
Carrickfergus BT38 8YF
Tel: 028 9336 9528
Fax: 028 9336 9979
E-mail: carrickenterprise@dnet.co.uk
Web: www.ceal.co.uk
Business Development Officer:
Kelli Bagchus

Larne Enterprise
Development Co (LEDCOM)
Ledcom Industrial Estate
Bank Road
Larne BT40 3AW
Tel: 028 2827 0742
Fax: 028 2827 5653
E-mail: info@larne.com
Web: www.ledcom.org
Chief Executive: Ken Nelson

Lisburn Enterprise Organisation
Enterprise Crescent
Ballinderry Road
Lisburn BT28 2BP
Tel: 028 9266 1160
Fax: 028 9260 3084
E-mail: project@lisburn-enterprise.co.uk
Web: www.lisburn-enterprise.co.uk
Chief Executive: Aisling Owens

Mallusk Enterprise Park
2 Mallusk Drive
Newtownabbey BT36 3GN
Tel: 028 9083 8860
Fax: 028 9084 1525
Chief Executive: Melanie Humphrey

Moyle Enterprise Co Ltd
61 Leyland Rd
Ballycastle BT54 6EZ
Tel: 028 2076 3737
Fax: 028 2076 9690
E-mail: moyle.enterprise@dnet.co.uk
Web: www.moyle-enterprise.com
Manager: Colette McMullan

Co Armagh

Armagh Business Centre
2 Loughgall Road
Armagh BT61 7NJ
Tel: 028 3752 5050
Fax: 028 3752 6717
Manager: Tracy Gale

Craigavon Industrial Development
Organisation Ltd (CIDO)
Carn Industrial Estate
Craigavon BT63 5RH
Tel: 028 3833 3393
Fax: 028 3835 0390
Chief Executive: Jim Smith

CIDO Business Complex
Charles St
Lurgan BT66 6HG
Tel: 028 3834 7020
Fax: 028 3834 7052
Chief Executive: Jim Smith

Co Londonderry

Coleraine Enterprise Agency Ltd
Unit 7, Loughanhill Industrial Estate
Coleraine BT52 2NR
Tel: 028 7035 6318
Fax: 028 7035 5464
E-mail: info@coleraine enterprise.co.uk
Web: www.coleraine-enterprise.co.uk
Manager: Ray Young

Creggan Enterprises Ltd
Rath More Centre
Blighs Lane
Londonderry BT48 0LZ
Tel: 028 7137 3170
Fax: 028 7137 3440
Chairperson: Conal McFeeley

Dunamanagh & District Community
Association Ltd
2a Lisnarragh Road
Dunamanagh BT82 0QL
Tel: 028 7139 7097
Business Manager: Albert Allen

Eurocentre West Ltd
Unit 25b
Pennyburn Industrial Estate
Buncrana Road
Londonderry BT48 0LU
Tel: 028 7136 4015
Fax: 028 7726 6032
E-mail: fdecw@aol.com
Contact: Denis Feeney

Glenshane Business Park
50 Legavallon Rd
Dungiven BT47 4QL
Tel: 028 7774 2494
Fax: 028 7774 2393
Manager: M Kelly

Glenshane Enterprise Centre
414a Ballyquinn Rd
Dungiven BT47 4NQ
Tel: 028 7774 2511
Contact: Tony McCall

Limavady Small Business Centre
Aghanloo Industrial Estate
Aghanloo Road
Limavady BT49 0HE
Tel: 028 7776 5655
Fax: 028 7776 5707
E-mail: martin.devlin@roevalleyenterprise.com
Web: www.lysba.com
Manager: Martin Devlin

Maghera Development Association
10b Coleraine Rd
Maghera BT46 5BN
Tel: 028 7964 5425
Fax: 028 7964 5425

Noribic Ltd
North West Institute for Further &
Higher Education
Strand Road
Londonderry BT48 7BY
E-mail: noribic@nwifhe.ac.uk
Web: www.noribic.com
Chief Executive: Barney Toal

Roe Valley Enterprises Ltd
Aghanloo Industrial Estate
Aghanloo Road
Limavady BT49 0HE
Tel: 028 7776 2323
Fax: 028 7776 5707
Manager: Martin Devlin

Workspace (Draperstown) Ltd
The Business Centre
7 Tobermore Road
Draperstown BT45 7AG
Tel: 028 7962 8113
Fax: 028 7962 8975
E-mail: info@workspace.org
Web: www.workspace.org.uk
Chief Executive: Brian Murray

Co Down

Ards Business Centre Ltd
Jubilee Rd
Newtownards BT23 4YH
Tel: 028 9181 9787
Fax: 028 91 820625
E-mail: postbox@ardsbusiness.com
Web: www.ardsbusiness.com
Chief Executive: Margaret Patterson

Banbridge District Enterprises Ltd
Scarva Road Industrial Estate
Banbridge BT32 3QD
Tel: 028 4066 2260
Fax: 028 4066 2325
E-mail: info@bdelonline.com
Web: www.bdelonline.com
Manager: Ciaran Cunningham

Down Business Centre
45 Saul Road
Downpatrick BT30 6PA
Tel: 028 44 616416
Fax: 028 44 616419
E-mail: business@downbc.co.uk
Web: www.downbc.co.uk
Chief Executive: Joe McCoubrey

Newry and Mourne Enterprise Agency
Enterprise House
Win Business Park
Canal Quay
Newry BT35 6PH
Tel: 028 3026 7011
Fax: 028 3026 1316
E-mail: nmcoop@dial.pipex.com
Web: www.nmea.net
Manager: Conor Patterson

North Down Development
Organisation Ltd
Enterprise House
Balloo Avenue
Balloo Industrial Estate
Bangor BT19 7QT
Tel: 028 9127 1525
Fax: 028 9127 0080
E-mail: mail@nddo.u-net.com
Web: www.nndo.u-net.com
Chief Executive: Lynne Vance

Stranney Enterprises
35 Ballylucas Road
Downpatrick BT30 8AZ
Tel: 028 44 851521
Fax: 028 44 851827
Web: www.winviz21.com
Manager: Stephen Stranney

Co Fermanagh

Belcoo Enterprise Ltd
Railway Road
Belcoo BT93 5FJ
Tel: 028 66 386536
Fax: 028 66 386377
Chairman: Harold Johnston

Fermanagh Enterprise Ltd
Enniskillen Business Centre
Lackaghboy Industrial Estate
Tempo Rd
Enniskillen BT74 4RL
Tel: 028 6632 3117
Fax: 028 6632 7878
Web: www.fermanaghenterprise.com
Manager: John Tracey

Irvinestown Trustee Enterprise Co
Irvinestown Business Park
Market Yard
Mill St
Irvinestown BT94 1GR
Tel: 028 6862 1977
Fax: 028 6862 8414
Manager: Jenny Irvine

Kesh Development Association
Charitable Trust
Mantlin Road
Kesh BT93 1TU
Tel: 028 6863 2158
Fax: 028 6863 2158
E-mail: dev@kesh.org.uk
Manager: Glenn Moore

Lisnaskea Community Enterprise
Drumbrughas North
Lisnaskea BT92 0PE
Tel: 028 6772 1081
Fax: 028 6772 1088
Manager: Kieran Kelly

Rosslea Enterprises Ltd
Rosslea Enterprise Centre
Liskilly
Rosslea BT92 7FH
Tel: 028 6775 1851
Contact: Jane Collins

South West Fermanagh Development
Organisation Ltd
Teemore Business Complex
Teemore BT92 9BL
Tel: 028 6774 8893
Fax: 028 6774 8493
E-mail: teemorecomplex@hotmail.com
Web: www.shannon-erne.co.uk
Contact: James Barron

Co Tyrone

Acumen Cross-Border Support Agency
Unit B10, Omagh Business Complex
Great Northern Road
Omagh BT78 5LU
Tel: 028 8225 0404
Fax: 028 8225 0416
Web: www.acumenprogramme.com
Director: Willie Maxwell

Castlederg and District Enterprises
Drumquin Rd
Castlederg BT81 7PX
Tel: 028 8167 0414
Fax: 028 8167 0731
Director: Gerald Sproule

Coalisland and District Development
Association Ltd
51 Dungannon Rd
Coalisland BT71 4HP
Tel: 028 8774 7215
Fax: 028 8774 8695
Chief Executive: Pat McGirr

Cookstown Enterprise Centre Ltd
Derryloran Industrial Estate
Sandholes Road
Cookstown BT80 9LU
Tel: 028 8676 3660
Fax: 028 8676 3160
Web: www.cookstownenterprise.com
Chief Executive: Jim Eastwood

Dungannon Enterprise Centre Ltd
2 Coalisland Road
Dungannon BT71 6JT
Tel: 028 8772 3489
Fax: 028 8775 2200
Web: www.dungannonenterprise.com
Centre Manager: Brian McAuley

Omagh Enterprise Co Ltd
Gortrush Industrial Estate
Great Northern Road
Omagh BT78 5LB
Tel: 028 8224 9494
Fax: 028 8224 9451
E-mail: oecl@compuserve.com
Manager: Nicholas O'shiel

Strabane Industrial Properties Ltd
Strabane Enterprise Agency
Orchard Road
Strabane BT82 9FR
Tel: 028 7138 2518
Fax: 28 7188 45311
E-mail: seagency@aol.com
Chief Executive: Christina Mullen

Business Services Listings

Legal Services

Association of Personal Injury Lawyers
Tel: 0115 958 0585
Web: www.apil.com

Cleaver Fulton Rankin
50 Bedford Street
Belfast BT2 7FW
Tel: 028 9024 3141
Fax: 028 9024 9096
E-mail: cfr@cfrlaw.co.uk
Web: www.cfrlawonline.com

Crawford Scally and Co
45 Bowling Green
Strabane BT82 8BW
Tel: 028 7188 3591
Fax: 028 7138 2298

D&E Fisher
8 Trevor Hill
Newry BT34 1DN
Tel: 028 3026 1616
Fax: 028 3026 7712

Edward Dougan & Co
14 The Diamond
Rathcoole
Newtownabbey BT37 9BJ
Tel: 028 9086 2800
Fax: 028 9085 3000

Elliott Duffy Garrett
Royston House
34 Upper Queen Street
Belfast BT1 6FD
Tel: 028 9024 5034
Fax: 028 9024 1337
E-mail: egd@egdsolicitors.co.uk

Ferguson & Co
Scottish Amicable House
11 Donegall Square South
Belfast BT1 5JE
Tel: 028 9032 2998
Fax: 028 9032 6241

Francis Hanna and Co
75/77 May Street
Belfast BT1 3JL
Tel: 028 9024 3901
Fax: 028 9024 4215

Kelly & Co Ltd
Clarendon House
4 Clarendon Street
Londonderry BT48 7NB
Tel: 028 7136 6612
Fax: 028 71367 1845

Jack McCann & Son
20 Ballymoney Road
Ballymena BT43 5BY
Tel: 028 2564 2388
Fax: 028 2565 1292

McClelland & Company
40 Main Street
Crumlin BT29 4UR
Tel: 028 9445 4994
Fax: 028 9445 4995

McCullough & Company
St John's Court
734 Upper Newtownards Road
Dundonald BT16 1RJ
Tel: 028 9048 2800
Fax: 028 9048 2428

Madden & Finucane
88 Castle Street
Belfast BT1 1HE
Tel: 028 9023 8007
Fax: 028 9043 9276

39-41 Shipquay Street
Londonderry BT48 6DL
Tel: 028 7126 1726
Fax: 028 7126 1826

69 Church Street
Downpatrick BT30 6EH
Tel: 028 4461 9200
Fax: 028 4461 7322

40a Irish Street
Armagh BT61 7EP
Tel:028 3753 2107
Fax: 028 3751 0733

Tughan & Co
Marlborough House
30 Victoria Street
Belfast BT1 3GS
Tel: 028 9055 3300
Fax: 028 9055 0096

33 High Street
Lurgan BT66 8AH
Tel: 028 3834 2621
Fax: 028 3834 1278

Wilson Nesbitt
33 Hamilton Road
Bangor BT20 4LF
Tel: 028 9127 1035

77 High Street
Holywood BT18 9AQ
Tel: 028 9042 8600

City Link Business Park
Durham Street
Belfast BT12 4HB
Tel: 028 9032 3864

Management Consultants and Accountants

Capita Business Services Ltd
425 Holywood Road
Belfast BT4 2PL
Tel: 028 9076 3910
Fax: 028 9076 1698
Web: www.capitaconsulting.co.uk

Grant Thornton
Water's Edge
Clarendon Dock
Belfast BT1 3BH
Tel: 028 9031 5500
Fax: 028 9031 4036

Paul Hagerty and Co
11 The Square
Rostrevor BT34 3AX
Tel: 028 4173 9340
Fax: 028 4173 9342
E-mail: info@paulhagerty.co.uk
Web: www.paulhagerty.co.uk

KPMG
Stokes House
College Square East
Belfast BT1 6DH
Tel: 028 9024 3377
Fax:028 9089 3893

McClure Watters
Thomas House
14-16 James St South
Belfast BT2 7GA
Tel: 028 9023 4343
Fax: 028 9043 9077

McKeague Morgan & Co
40 University Street
Belfast BT7 1F2
Tel: 028 9024 2612

Co. REGISTRATION AGENTS

Holdfast Limited

Established in 1963,
The Company provides:

- Company Formations &
  Shelf Companies

- Provision Of Registered
  Office Address

- Company Secretarial
  Services

138 University Street
Belfast BT7 1HJ
Tel: (028) 9032 9984
Fax: (028) 9023 2221
Website: www.cra-ni.com
Email: holdfast@cra-ni.com

DELOITTE & TOUCHE

Deloitte & Touche

19 Bedford Street
Belfast
BT2 7EJ
Tel: 028 9032 2861
Fax: 028 9023 4786
Web: www.deloitte.co.uk

Paul Clarke,
Senior Partner

Deloitte & Touche is the UK's fastest growing major professional services firm with over 10,000 staff nationwide, and a fee income of £713.6 million in 2001/2002, representing a 15.7% growth rate on the previous year.

For the second consecutive year, the firm was ranked in The Sunday Times "100 Companies To Work For 2002" accentuating our position as the employer of choice for top talent, attracting and retaining the most able people.

Employing more than 140 people locally, Deloitte & Touche Belfast provides fully integrated services that include accounting, business advisory, audit, tax, management consulting, orporate finance and reorganisation services offering our clients the best possible opportunities and services with access to our global capabilities and extensive network.
Our clients include local plcs, subsidiaries of global organisations and locally owned businesses.

Moore Stephens
7 Donegall Square West
Belfast BT1 6JH
Tel: 028 9032 9481
Fax: 028 9043 9185

PricewaterhouseCoopers
Waterfront Plaza
8 Laganbank Road
Belfast BT1 3LR
Tel:028 9024 5454
Fax:028 9041 5600

Insurance Advisers

Aon McMillen
31 Bedford Street
Belfast BT2 7FP
Tel: 028 9024 2771
Fax: 028 9031 3644

Bartholomew and James
26 Linenhall Street
Belfast BT2 8NU
Tel: 028 9024 1651
Fax: 028 9024 0441

CJ Higgins
22 Mallusk Road
Glengormley BT36 8PP
Tel: 028 9083 0830

Dawson Whyte
43 Malone Road
Belfast BT9 6RX
Tel: 028 9066 4414
Fax: 028 9066 4414

Hughes & Company
4 Jubilee Road
Newtownards BT23 4WN
Tel: 028 9181 7375
Fax: 028 9181 6236

Laing & Company Limited
142 High Street
Holywood BT18 9HS
Tel: 028 9042 5125
Fax: 028 9042 5126

Trevor Lunn Insurances
36 Bachelors Walk
Lisburn BT28 1XN
Tel: 028 9267 3164
Fax: 028 9267 4835

Office Accommodation Services

The Communications Centre
27 Shore Road
Holywood BT18 9HX
Tel: 028 9042 5412
Fax: 028 9042 7094

Elmwood House Business Centre
44-46 Elmwood Avenue
Belfast BT9 6AZ
Tel: 028 9066 4941
Fax: 028 9068 2007

McDowall House Business Centre
83 University Street
Belfast BT7 1HP
Tel: 028 9022 0442
Fax: 028 9022 0441

Montrim House
105 University Street
Belfast BT7 1HP
Tel: 028 9058 6606
Fax: 028 9058 6607

Regus
33 Clarendon Dock
Laganside
Belfast BT1 3BG
Tel: 028 9051 1200
Fax: 028 9051 1201

Premier Business Centres
20 Adelaide Street
Belfast BT2 8GB
Tel: 028 9051 7000
Fax: 028 9051 7001
Web: www.premgroup.com

Commercial Property Agents

Ardmore Commercial
397 Lisburn Road
Belfast BT9 7EW
Tel: 028 9066 2299
Fax:028 9066 5454

Brown McConnell Clark
11 Rosemary Street
Belfast BT1 1QF
Tel: 028 9032 0634
Fax: 028 9024 8810

Hamilton Osborne King
Lindsay House
10 Callendar Street
Belfast BT1 5EN
Tel: 028 9027 0000
Fax: 028 9027 0011
E-mail: property@hk.co.uk
Web: www.hok.co.uk

Insignia Richard Ellis Gunne
Scottish Provident Building
Donegall Square West
Belfast BT1 6JL
Tel: 028 9043 8555
Fax: 0298 9043 9444
Web: www.insignia-re.com

Lambert Smith Hampton
4-10 May Street
Belfast BT1 4NJ
Tel: 028 9032 7954
Fax: 028 9024 4057
E-mail: belfast@lsh.co.uk

McKibbin Commercial
Property Consultants
1st Floor
Callender House
58-60 Upper Arthur Street
Belfast BT1 4GP
Tel: 028 9050 0100
Fax: 028 9050 0101
E-mail: property@mckibbin.co.uk

McQuitty Lisk Associates
483 Lisburn Road
Belfast BT9 7EZ
Tel: 028 9066 0085
Fax: 028 9066 1161

O'Connor Kennedy Turtle
Scottish Provident Buildings
7 Donegall Square West
Belfast BT1 6JH
Tel: 028 9024 8181
Fax: 028 9024 8188
E-mail: Belfast@okt.co.uk

The Whelan Partnership
44 Upper Arthur Street
Belfast BT1 4GJ
Tel: 028 9044 1000
Fax: 028 9033 2266

IT Support

IP OPTIONS

Solutions Based On Experience

IP Options House
15 Dunraven Park
Belfast BT5 5LF
Tel: (028) 9029 0019
Fax: (028) 9080 1658

IP Options Ltd
Coolmine Enterprise Centre
Coolmine
Dublin 15
Tel: (+353) 1 8243772
Fax: (+353) 1 8243773
www.ipoptions.com

Managing Director: Gerard Lundy

IP Options are a TCP/IP Service and Consultancy Company specialising in Security, Systems & Network Integration and Messaging across multiple platforms.

Our consultants have excellent technical knowledge in security, telecommunications, integration and messaging. We have planned, designed and implemented major IT infrastructures for many of the largest blue chip companies both in Ireland and abroad.

IP Options can design and implement tailored solutions, based on our extensive knowledge of the best-of-breed security, networking and messaging products available in the marketplace. We can provide full implementation services, including project management, consultancy, comprehensive documentation, end user training and full post-implementation support.

GRAFTON RECRUITMENT

Grafton Recruitment
35-37 Queen Square
Belfast BT1 3FG
Tel: (028) 9024 2824
Fax: (028) 9024 2897

Website: www.grafton-group.com
email: hq@grafton-group.com

Barbara O'Hare
Chief Executive

Founded in 1982 Grafton Recruitment has established itself as a world-class provider of recruitment solutions to various industry sectors.

With a presence in 9 countries worldwide and a network of 26 branch operations in Ireland they employ over 300 specialist recruiters who operate in their respective niche markets, including Accountancy & Finance, Languages, Commercial, Healthcare, IT, Engineering, Industrial, Public Sector & Executive selection.

Ranked 18 in the top 100 companies in a recent business survey they are the single largest supplier of permanent, temporary and contract staffing solutions in Ireland today.

This success has culminated in Grafton recently being awarded one of the highest accolades in British Industry - the Queen's Award for Enterprise, which recognises excellence, innovation, professionalism and sustained growth within their industry.

Recruitment Agencies

Apple Recruitment Services
8 Bedford Street
Belfast BT2 7FB
Tel: 028 9024 9747
Fax: 028 9024 2203

Blythe Grace
405 Lisburn Road
Belfast BT9 7EW
Tel: 028 9066 3377
Fax: 028 9066 4466

Diamond Recruitment
16 Donegall Square South
Belfast BT1 5JF
Tel: 028 9055 8080
Fax: 028 9055 8100

First Choice Selection Services Limited
Sinclair House
Royal Avenue
Belfast BT1 1EX
Tel: 028 9031 3693
Fax: 028 9031 3693
Web: www.first-choice-rec.com

Kennedy Recruitment
31-35 May Street
Belfast BT1 4NG
Tel: 028 9033 0555
Fax: 028 9033 2878
Web: www.kennedyrecruitment.co.uk

Lynn Recruitment
48-50 Bedford Street
Belfast BT2 7FG
Tel: 028 9023 4324
Fax: 028 9023 4383
Web: www.lynn-recruitment.co.uk

Manpower
50-56 Wellington Place
Belfast BT1 6GF
Tel: 028 9023 6860
Fax:028 9023 9379

Merc Partners
12b Clarendon Road
Belfast BT1 3BG
Tel: 028 9072 5750
Fax: 028 9072 5751
Web: www.mercpartners.co.uk

Printers, Graphic Designers and Signage

Printers

Dargan Press Ltd
5 Round Tower Centre
Dargan Crescent,
Belfast BT3 9JP
Tel: 028 9077 4478
Fax: 028 9077 4771

Dorman & Sons Ltd
Unit 2, 2a Apollo Road
Boucher Road
Belfast BT12 6BF
Tel: 028 9066 6700
Fax: 028 9066 1881

Graham & Sons Ltd
51 Gortin Road
Omagh BT79 7HZ
Tel: 028 8224 9222
Fax: 028 8224 9886

Johnston Printing Ltd
Mill Road
Kilrea BT51 5RJ
Tel: 028 2954 0312
Fax: 028 2954 1070
Web: www.johnston-printing.co.uk

LM Press Ltd
47 High Street
Lurgan BT66 8AH
Tel: 028 3832 2412
Fax: 028 3832 1820

Limavady Printing Co Ltd
26c Catherine Street
Limavady BT49 9DB
Tel: 028 7776 2051
Fax: 028 7776 2132
Web: www.limprint.com

Northern Whig
107 Limestone Road
Belfast BT15 3AH
Tel: 028 9035 2233
Fax: 028 9035 2181

Print-N-Press
Hamilton House
Foyle Road
Londonderry BT48 6SR
Tel: 028 7126 3868
Fax: 028 7137 1817

Priory Press
31a Hibernia Street
Holywood BT18 9JE
Tel: 028 9042 2918
Fax: 028 9042 7030

Graphic Designers

Ardmore Design
Ardmore House, Pavilions
Holywood BT18 9JQ
Tel: 028 9042 5344
Fax: 028 9042 4823
Web: www.ardmore.co.uk

Catalyst
95 University Street
Belfast BT7 1HP
Tel: 028 9043 8925
Fax: 028 9032 8839
E-mail: info@catalystdesign.co.uk
Web: www.catalystdesign.co.uk

Darragh Neely Associates
Ama Communication Centre
Newtownards Road
Bangor BT19 7TA
Tel: 028 9151 6034
Fax: 028 9147 2797
Web: www.daraghneelyassociates.com

GCAS Design
Russell Court, 38–52 Lisburn Road
Belfast BT9 6AA
Tel: 028 9055 7700
Fax: 028 9024 5741
E-mail: design@gcasgroup.com
Web: www.gcasgroup.com

IPR Communications Group
27 Shore Road
Holywood BT18 9HX
Tel: 028 9042 5412
Fax: 028 9042 7094
E-mail: ipr@d-n-a.net

KR Graphics
121 University Street
Belfast BT7 1HP
Tel: 028 9033 3792
Fax: 028 9033 0549

Leslie Stannage Design
93 Botanic Avenue
Belfast BT7 1JN
Tel: 028 9023 7377
Fax: 028 9033 0549

Rocket
3 Pavilions Office Park
Kinnegar Drive
Holywood BT18 9JQ
Tel: 028 9022 7700
Web: www.rocket-design.com

Slater Design
The Old Sorting Office
Strand Avenue
Holywood BT18 9AA
Tel: 028 9042 1133
Fax: 028 9042 1122

TDP Advertising
75 University Street
Belfast BT7 1HE
Tel: 028 9032 2882
Fax: 028 9033 2727
E-mail: mail@tdpadvertising.co.uk
Web: www.tdpadvertising.co.uk

Signage

Signs Express (Belfast C.W.)
Unit 14
Abbey Enterprise Park
Mill Road
Newtownabbey BT36 7BA
Tel: 028 9086 5647
Fax: 028 9086 9224
Web: www.signsexpressirl.com
E-mail: belfast@signsexpress.co.uk

Full listings for providers of
IT support, Graphic Designers,
ISPs, Advertising and PR
Consultants are more fully listed in
Chapter 11, Communications and
the Media in Northern Ireland.

Chapter 10

The European Union

The European Union

Introduction

The European Union was established following World War Two, with the process of European integration launched on 9 May 1950 when France officially proposed to create "the first concrete foundation of a European federation". Six countries Belgium, Germany, France, Italy, Luxembourg and the Netherlands joined. Since then there have been four waves of accessions:

- 1973: Denmark, Ireland and the United Kingdom;
- 1981: Greece;
- 1986: Spain and Portugal;
- 1995: Austria, Finland and Sweden.

The EU currently has 15 member states and is preparing for the accession of 13 eastern and southern European countries.

The European Union is built on a unique institutional system and is based on the rule of law and democracy; its member states delegate sovereignty to common institutions representing the interests of the Union as a whole. All decisions and procedures are derived from the basic treaties ratified by the member states. Whilst the role of the Commission is traditionally perceived to be to uphold the interests of the Union as a whole, each national government is represented by the Council and individual citizens in the European parliament, which is a directly elected legislature.

Two other institutions, the Court of Justice and the Court of Auditors support the "institutional triangle" of Commission, Council and parliament and are supported by a further five bodies:

- European Central Bank;
- Economic and Social Committee;
- Committee of the Regions;
- European Investment Bank;
- European Ombudsman.

The principal objectives of the Union are to:

- Establish European Citizenship (Fundamental Rights; Freedom of Movement; Civil and Political Rights);
- Ensure freedom, security and justice (Cooperation in the field of Justice and Home Affairs);
- Promote economic and social progress (single market; Euro, the common currency; job creation; regional development; environmental protection);
- Assert Europe's role in the world (common foreign and security policy; the European Union in the world).

Enlargement Candidate Countries:	
Bulgaria	Malta
Czech Republic	Poland
Estonia	Romania
Cyprus	Slovenia
Latvia	Slovakia
Lithuania	Turkey
Hungary	

Source: www.europa.eu.int

The Institutions of the European Union

The European Council of Ministers

The Council Of Ministers
Rue de la Loi 175
B–1048 Brussels
Tel: +32 2 285 61 11
Fax: +32 2 285 7397
Web: www.ue.eu.int
E-mail: public.info@consilium.eu.int

The Council of the European Union consists of relevant ministers from all of the member states, and is the European Union's main decision-making body. Its representatives come together regularly at ministerial level. According to the matters on the agenda, the Council meets in different compositions: foreign affairs, finance, education, telecommunications, etc. It co-ordinates the broad economic, foreign and security policies of member states and shares legislative and budgetary authority with the European parliament. The Council generally co-ordinates the activities of member states and adopts measures in the fields of policing and judicial co-operation in criminal matters.

The Council of Ministers is supported by the Committee of the Permanent Representatives (COREPER), which prepares the positions for the ministers prior to their Council meetings. Each country has its own permanent representation team.

European Parliament, Strasbourg

The European Commission

200 rue de la Loi
B–1049
Brussels
Tel: +32 2 299 11 11
Web: www.europa.eu.int
E-mail: sg-info@cec.eu.int
President: Romano Prodi

Windsor House
9–15 Bedford Street
Belfast
BT2 7EG
Tel: 028 9024 0708
Fax: 028 9024 8241
Head of Representation: Eddie McVeigh

President:	Romano Prodi
Vice-Presidents:	
Administrative Reform	Neil Kinnock
Relations with the European	
Parliament, Transport and Energy	Loyola de Palacio
Members of the Commission:	
Competition	Mario Monti
Agriculture, Rural Development and Fisheries	Franz Fischler
Enterprise and the Information Society	Erkki Liikanen
Internal Market	Frederik Bolkestein
Research	Philippe Busquin
Economic and Monetary Affairs	Pedro Solbes Mira
Development and Humanitarian Aid	Poul Nielson
Enlargement	Günter Verheugen
External Relations	Christopher Patten
Trade	Pascal Lamy
Health and Consumer Protection	David Byrne
Regional Policy and, ad personam, Inter-Governmental Conference	Michel Barnier
Education and Culture	Viviane Reding
Budget	Michaele Schreyer
Environment	Margot Wallström
Justice and Home Affairs	António Vitorino
Employment and Social Affairs	Anna Diamantopoulou
Secretariat General of the Commission:	
Secretary-General:	David O'Sullivan
Deputy Secretary-General:	Bernhard Zepter
Assistant:	François Genisson

The European Commission's members are nominated by the member states. It initiates draft legislation, presents legislative proposals to parliament and the Council and is the executive body of the European Union, implementing legislation, budget and programmes adopted by the European parliament and the Council of the European Union. In addition, the Commission represents the EU internationally, negotiates international agreements (chiefly trade and co-operation) and acts as guardian of the Treaties with the Court of Justice, ensuring that Community law is properly applied.

The Commission consists of 20 Commissioners. A President, assisted by two Vice-Presidents, heads the Commission. Each member state has at least one of its nationals serving on the Commission at any one time, and the larger member states – France, Germany, Italy, Spain and the United Kingdom – have, at present, two. The members of the Commission are appointed 'by common accord' of the governments of the member states for a renewable term of five years. The seat of the European Commission is in Brussels.

The Commission enjoys wide legislative powers delegated from the Council and certain autonomous legislative powers under the Treaties: but its principal role is setting the general policy agenda for the European Union. Although the Council adopts European legislation, in most cases these institutions may only act on legislative proposals from the Commission itself. In the past, the right of legislative initiative has enabled the Commission to act as the engine of European integration. The Commission also has important investigative, enforcement and quasi-judicial functions, including the

power to act against member states believed to be in breach of Community law: It also has powers in relation to the supervision and enforcement of the Community's rules on competition and state aids. The latter can extend to the imposition of extremely heavy fines (subject to rights of appeal) on individuals, undertakings or groups of undertakings found to be breach of the law.

The European Commission is not simply an executive body; in particular, it has a key role to play in the management of the European Union's annual budget of over 80 billion Euro. Most of this sum represents farm spending allocated by the European Agricultural Guidance and Guarantee Fund and by the Structural Funds: in general terms, running the Community's Common Agricultural Policy is perhaps the single biggest task of the Commission.

Details of the Commission, which took office in 1999 for a five-year period, are set out opposite and a list of the top commission officals is set out below.

Directorates-General

Each Directorate-General is headed by a Director-General reporting to the Commissioner who takes overall political and operational responsibility for the work of the Directorate-General. An individual Commissioner's portfolio may well cover the work of more than one Directorate-General. The allocation of portfolios to

Directorate-General	Director
Legal Service	Michel Petit
Press and Communication Service	Jonathan Faull
Economic and Financial Affairs	Klaus Regling
Enterprise	Fabio Colasanti
Competition	Alexander Schaub
Employment and Social Affairs	Odile Qunitin
Agriculture	José Manuel Silva Rodríguez
Transport and Energy	François Lamoureux
Environment	James Currie
Research	Achille as Mitsos
Joint Research Centre	Finbarr McSweeney
Information Society	Robert Verrue
Fisheries	Steffen Smidt
Internal Market	John Mogg
Regional Policy	Guy Crauser
Taxation and Custom Unit	Michel Vanden Abeele
Education and Culture	Nikolaus Van Der Pas
Health and Consumer Protection	Robert Coleman
Justice and Home Affairs	Adrian Fortescue
External Relations	Guy Legras
Trade	Peter Carl Mogens
Development	Jacobus Richelle
Enlargement	Eneko Landaburu
Europe Aid Cooperation Office	Giorgio Bonacci
Humanitarian Aid Office – ECHO	Costanza Adinolfi
Eurostat	Yves Franchet
Personnel and Administration	Horst Reichenbach
Internal Audit Service	Jules Muis
Budget	Jean-Paul Mingasson
Financial Control	Edith Kitzmantel
European Anti-Fraud Office	Franz-Hermann Bruener
Joint Interpreting and Conference Service	Marco Benedetti
Translation Service	Brian McCluskey
Office for Official Publications of the European Communities	Thomas L. Cranfield

individual Commissioners is decided collectively, although the President makes initial proposals. The Commissioners meet collectively as the College of Commissioners once a week, act by majority and operate under the political guidance of the President.

The European Parliament

The European Parliament
Allée du Printemps
B.P. 1024/F
F–67070 Strasbourg Cedev
Tel: +33 03 08 17 40 01
Fax:+33 03 88 25 65 01
E-mail: civis@europarl.eu.int
Web: www.europarl.eu.int/

Elected every five years by individual citizens in each of the member states, the European parliament represents the democratic voice of the 374 million citizens of the European Union.

The European parliament is composed of members from each of the fifteen member states in broad proportion to their population. The parliament shares legislative and budgetary authority with the European Council and exercises democratic and political supervision over the other institutions.

The European parliament has three essential functions:

- Shares with the Council the power to legislate, i.e. to adopt European laws (directives, regulations, decisions), assisting in maintaining the democratic legitimacy of the texts adopted;
- Shares budgetary authority with the Council and can therefore influence spending. At the end of the procedure it adopts the budget in its entirety;
- The parliament exercises democratic supervision over the Commission approving the nomination of Commissioners. It has the right to censure the Commission, and also exercises political supervision over all the institutions.

The UK has an entitlement of 87 European parliament seats. Of this, Northern Ireland returns 3 MEPs by an election held every 5 years. In this case Northern Ireland is a single constituency, and the three European MPs are elected by proportional representation, the Single Transferable Vote (STV).

The current MEPs, returned in June 1999, are:

Ian Paisley MP MLA

Party	DUP
European Political Group	Non-attached
Constituency Contact	Rhonda Paisley
	256 Ravenhill Road
	Belfast BT6 8GJ
	Tel: 028 9045 4255
	Fax: 028 9045 7783
Brussels Contact	European Parliament
	Rue Wiertz
	B–1047 Brussels, Belgium
	Tel:+ 32 2 284 5410
	Fax: + 32 2 284 9410

Jim Nicholson

Party	UUP
European Political Group	European People's Party and European Democrats
Constituency Contact	Cunningham House
	429 Holywood Road
	Belfast BT4 2LN
	Tel: 028 9076 5500
	Fax: 028 9024 6738
Brussels Contact	European Parliament
	Rue Wiertz
	B–1047 Brussels, Belgium
	Tel: + 32 2 284 5933
	Fax: + 32 2 284 9933

John Hume MP

Party	SDLP
European Political Group	Party of European Socialists
Constituency Contact	Ronan McCay
	5 Bayview Terrace
	Derry BT48 7EE
Brussels Contact	Tom Lyne
	European Parliament
	Rue Wiertz
	B–1047 Brussels, Belgium
	Tel: + 32 2 284 5190
	Fax: + 32 2 284 9190

The European Court of Justice

The Court of Justice ensures that Community law is uniformly interpreted and effectively applied. It has jurisdiction in disputes involving member states, EU institutions, businesses and individuals.

The Court of Justice currently consists of 15 Judges and eight Advocates General who are appointed for a renewable term of six years. The task of the Judges and Advocates General is to make reasoned submissions on the cases brought before the European Court of Justice in advance of the Court handing down its final decision.

The European Court of Justice is the highest and sole judicial authority in matters of Community law. Its responsibilities encompass three main areas:

- Monitoring the application of Community law;
- Interpretation of Community law;
- Further shaping of Community law.

The Court of Justice acts as a constitutional court when disputes between Community institutions are before it or legislative instruments are up for review for legality; as an administrative court when reviewing the administrative acts of the Commission or of national authorities applying Community legislation; as a labour court or industrial tribunal when dealing with freedom of movement, social security and equal opportunities; as a fiscal court when dealing with matters concerning the validity and interpretation of directives in the fields of taxation and customs law; as a criminal court when reviewing Commission decisions imposing fines; and as a civil court when hearing claims for damages or interpreting the Brussels convention on the enforcement of judgements in civil and commercial matters.

The European Court of Auditors

The Court of Auditors checks that all the Union's revenue has been received and all its expenditure incurred in a lawful and regular manner and that financial management of the EU budget has been sound. The Court of Auditors consists of 15 members, corresponding to the present number of member states.

The duties of the Court of Auditors include:

- Examining the accounts of all revenue and expenditure of the Community;
- Examining the accounts of all revenue and expenditure of all bodies set up by the Community;
- Ascertaining whether all revenue has been received and all expenditure incurred in a 'lawful and regular manner' and whether financial management has been sound;
- Assisting the European parliament and the Council in exercising their powers of control over the implementation of the budget;
- Submitting annual reports at the close of each financial year;
- Submitting observations, opinions or special reports on specific questions.

European Central Bank

The European Central Bank frames and implements European monetary policy; it conducts foreign exchange operations and ensures the smooth operation of payment systems. Its chief tasks are to:

- Maintain the stability of the European currency, the Euro;
- Control the amount of currency in circulation.

In order to carry out its tasks the European Central Bank's independence is guaranteed by numerous legal provisions. The European Central Bank consists of a Governing Council and an Executive Board. The Governing Council comprises the governors of the national central banks and the members of the Executive Board of the European Central Bank. The Executive Board, which is made up of the President, Vice President and four other members, is effectively in charge of running the European Central Bank.

The European Single Currency

Following agreement by EU leaders in 1998 on European and Monetary Union, 1st January 1999 saw the adoption of the single currency by France, Spain, Portugal, Germany, The Netherlands, Austria, Belgium, Finland, Italy, Luxembourg and Ireland. From 1st January 2002 note and coins became available and the European Single Currency became a reality.

The Euro zone is comparable in size with the United States economy, already including 320 million consumers and accounting for one fifth of the world's GDP. Northern Ireland is the only region of the UK to have a land border with a country operating in the Euro zone and the impact has been substantial.

European Investment Bank

The European Investment Bank exists to assist the Community in its role as financing agency for a 'balanced and steady development' of the common market. It provides loans and guarantees in all economic sectors, especially to promote the development of less-developed regions, to modernise or convert undertakings or create new jobs and to assist projects of common interest to several member states. The 15 member states are all members of the Bank.

European Economic and Social Committee

Rue Ravenstein 2
1000 Brussels
Belgium
Tel:+32 2 546 9011
Fax:+32 2 513 4893
E-mail: info@esc.eu.int

The Economic and Social Committee is a consultative body made up of representatives of Europe's main interest groups: employer's organisations, trade unions, farmers, consumer groups, professional associations, etc. From the 15 member states 222 members of the committee are selected. It is non-political, and exists to advise the European parliament, European Commission and the European Council. It supports the role of civil society organisations in non-EC countries to foster better relations with similar bodies, termed 'institution building'. The Committee is divided into three groups: employers, workers and various interests. They draw up opinions on draft EU legislation and issues affecting European society.

Northern Ireland has two representatives attached to the European Economic and Social Committee:

Northern Ireland European Economic and Social Committee Members (under review)

Bill Tosh

Contact Details:
Foy Cottage, Whitestown, Greenol, Co Louth
Tel/Fax: +353 429373090
E-mail: billtosh@btinternet.com
Group Group I: Employers (Proposed by CBI)
Committee Membership: Economic and Monetary Union and Social Cohesion; Transport; Energy; Infrastructure and Information Society

John Simpson (Vice President)

Contact Details: 3 Glenmachan Drive, Belfast BT4 2RE
Tel / Fax: 028 9076 9399
E-mail: johnvsimpson@compuserve.com
Group Group III: Various Interests
Committee Membership: Economic and Monetary Union and Social Cohesion; Single Market; Production and Consumption

The European Committee of the Regions

Rue Montoyer, 92–102
B–1000 Brussels
Belgium
Tel: +32 2 282 2211
Fax: +32 2 282 2325

The European Committee of the Regions was established under the Maastricht Treaty, to represent local and regional authorities in the European Union. Its aim is to strengthen social and economic cohesion of member states, towards European integration. The Committee meets in plenary session 5 times a year to measure opinions on relevant issues. Like the Economic and Social Committee, the Committee of the Regions consists of 222 representatives of regional and local authorities in the member states.

There are a number of areas in which the Council or the Commission are required to seek the views of the Committee, namely:

- Education
- Culture;
- Public Health;
- Trans-European networks;
- Transport
- Telecommunications and energy infrastructure;
- Economic and Social Cohesion;
- Employment policy;
- Social legislation.

The Council also consults the Committee regularly, but without any legal obligation.

Northern Ireland Members of the Committee of the Regions

Dermot Nesbitt MLA

Political Party: UUP
Contact: Cunningham House, 429 Holywood Road
Belfast BT4 2LN
Tel: 028 9076 5500
Fax: 028 9024 6738
Type of Membership: Full Member

Alban Magennis MLA

Political Party: SDLP
Contact: 121 Ormeau Road
Belfast BT7 1SH
Tel: 028 9024 7700
Fax: 028 9023 6699
Type of Membership: Full Member

George Savage MLA

Political Party: UUP
Contact: 'Watties Hill'
147 Dromore Road, Donacloney
Craigavon BT66 7NR
Tel: 028 3882 0401
Fax:028 3882 0401
Type of Membership: Alternate Member

Margaret Ritchie

Political Party: SDLP
Contact: 24 Strangford Road, Downpatrick, Co Down
Type of Membership: Alternate Member

Northern Ireland in Europe

Northern Ireland has a recognised presence in Europe and is no longer seen as a region on the periphery but a keen participant within the structures and institutions of the European Union.

Improvements in infrastructure, the peace dividend to which the Special Support Programme for Peace and Reconciliation has contributed over £370 million and further resources from the EU Structural Funds aimed at promoting economic development have heightened popular awareness of the role of the EU within the region.

Northern Ireland has faced great social and economic disadvantage and in the recent past the region has focused upon gaining economic parity with other member states of the European Union. Current indicators demonstrate that rising prosperity, falling unemployment and reduced emigration are now trends. However, the categorisation of Northern Ireland as "lagging behind" in the early 1990s saw the region being eligible for Objective 1 status under the EU's Structural Funds. Nonetheless, even with the economic progress that has been made Northern Ireland as a region has a GDP per capita that is still only 80% of the EU average.

The European Commission has worked to develop relationships within the new Northern Ireland Assembly and the recent establishment of the Northern Ireland Executive Brussels office operated by the Office of the First Minister and Deputy First Minister reinforces a growing profile for the interests of Northern Ireland government within the Community. This, coupled with the work of the Commission's representation in Belfast ensures that Brussels is au fait with Northern Ireland developments and vice versa.

Local authorities are an important level of government in European terms and many now have a dedicated European Liaison Officer to keep them informed of developments and co-ordinate their applications for European funding. Currently there are 26 local liaison officers, one for each of the local authorities in Northern Ireland.

The Northern Ireland Government and Legislative Process in a European Context

Northern Ireland has three MEPs with a range of knowledge and experience of working for Northern Ireland; two Northern Ireland representatives on the Committee of the Regions and the Northern Ireland representation on the Economic and Social Committee.

At the UK level, EU policy is a non-transferred matter and the majority of decisions on EU policy are taken at national level. Since devolution, as the decisions taken are mostly implemented at regional level, the UK government has recognised that the devolved administrations have a significant role to play in EU issues.

This role is formalised in the Memorandum of Understanding and the Concordats on Co-ordination of European Union Policy and the Joint Ministerial Council (JMC). Policy is still made through London; the difference now is the ability for the Northern Ireland departments to influence policy on those specific issues which have a clear regional perspective.

The Concordats, which govern the relationships on EU matters between the UK government, and Northern Ireland, make specific reference to the involvement of the North South Ministerial Council. However, the details on how this is to happen have yet to be determined.

The main Institutions in the UK Government include the Whitehall departments who still liaise with their Northern Ireland counterparts; the Cabinet Office European Sub Committee and Secretariat who are responsible for policy co-ordination, the Foreign Office who hold responsibility for policy at the EU institutional level

EU policies and legislation impact on a wide range of matters in Northern Ireland; 80 per cent of policies in the Programme for Government and up to 60 per cent of all legislation. The degree to which Northern Ireland can influence EU policy depends primarily on its links with London.

Since EU policy decisions are taken at national level it is argued that Northern Ireland should focus on defining areas where there are distinctions in the Northern Ireland position and where returns can be maximised. Due to resource constraints only a limited number of areas may be chosen as priority areas. The experience of other regional parliaments suggests that if there is insufficient planning or co-ordination, the outcome will be volumes of effort with little realisable benefit for Northern Ireland.

There is some disquiet that Assembly Committees have little opportunity to exert influence on the development and implementation of policy; their first view of European Directive and Commission decisions often occurs when the department brings subordinate legislation forward. To address this concern there are currently plans within OFMDFM to take a more proactive approach to build capacity within all departments to become engaged with European issues, particularly beyond the remit of implementing legislation. This will be supported by plans to form a Standing Committee on EU Affairs within the next Assembly.

Other possibilities under consideration include: the establishment of an Assembly Information Desk in Brussels, possibly in the Office of the Northern Ireland Executive in Brussels, or operating as a shared resource with other regions; appointment of a Junior Minister with responsibility for European Affairs, to manage relationships with the European Parliament and Commission and to support and co-ordinate European matters within the Assembly.

The European Policy Unit OFMDFM

In July 2000 a new unit, the European Policy Co-ordination Unit (EPCU) was set up by the Office of the First Minister and the Deputy First Minister. The European Policy Coordination Unit provides a central policy and coordination role for the departments in developing their relationship with the EU. The EPCU provides liaison with the Cabinet Office European Secretariat and can send a representative to Cabinet and Foreign and Commonwealth Office (FCO) official meetings. It provides support for the Northern Ireland ministers at the Joint Ministerial Committee (JMC) and UK Ministerial Committees on European Co-ordination.

It approaches its work under six headings:
- Establishing agreed areas for Northern Ireland in Europe;

- Ensuring that Northern Ireland interests are taken into account in the formulation of the UK's EU policy;
- Improving understanding of the EU among Northern Ireland Departments and wider society;
- Increasing Northern Ireland influence in EU institutions;
- Raising a Northern Ireland positive profile in Europe;
- Administration of the EU programme for Peace and Reconciliation in Northern Ireland and the Border Regions.

Office of the Northern Ireland Executive in Brussels

The Office of the Northern Ireland Executive in Brussels was opened in May 2001 to liaise with the EU Institutions on issues affecting Northern Ireland. The Director and Deputy Director work under the umbrella of UKRep.

The role of the office is to monitor the development of policies by the EU institutions relevant to Northern Ireland; provide up to date information to ministers and departments; ensure Northern Ireland interests are fully represented in policy developments by EU institutions; raise a positive profile of Northern Ireland amongst European policy makers and to foster mutually beneficial links between Northern Ireland and other regions of Europe.

However, the key point of influence remains the policy making process in London. As EU policy is a reserved power, the primary means of contributing Northern Ireland input to policy development in EU institutions lies with Northern Ireland departments influencing the common UK policy in Council and through the work of the Northern Ireland MEPs in the parliament.

European Funding and Northern Ireland

European funding falls broadly into the following categories:
- Structural Funds Packages, which are drawn up between the European Commission and regional authorities, to identify the needs and priorities of the particular region. Packages are managed at regional level and projects are based in the region in question.
- Community initiatives which are special forms of assistance, which aim to address problems,

identified by the European Commission as being common throughout the EU. They are financed by the Structural Funds and managed at regional level.

- EU funding programmes which have a theme and correspond with EU policy areas. They are managed by the Directorates-General and all projects must be transactional in nature.
- Ad hoc calls for proposals issued by various Directorates-Generals of the European Commission.
- Aid to applicant countries and to other non-member states of the EU in order to support economic restructuring and democratic reforms.

Structural Funds

Four main inter related funds known as the Structural Funds are used to finance EU activities for social and economic development throughout the regions. These are:

The European Regional Development Fund (ERDF)

Provides financial support to regional development programmes in order to reduce socio-economic imbalances.

The European Social Fund (ESF)

The main instrument of community social policy and provides financial assistance for vocational training, retraining and job creation schemes.

The European Agricultural Guidance and Guarantee Fund (EAGGF)

Financial instrument for agriculture and rural development policy and finances development in rural areas throughout the European Union.

The Financial Instrument for Fisheries Guide (FIFG)

Enhances the competitiveness of the fisheries sector and strives to maintain the balance between fishing capacity and resources.

Within the 2000–2006 period the total budget for the Structural Funds Europe-wide amounts to 195 billion Euro, including 10.44 billion Euro for the Community initiatives representing over one third of the European Union's total budget.

Reform of the Structural Funds

Agenda 2000 was the action programme concluded in 1999 at the Berlin European Council to strengthen Community policies and to give the European Union a new financial framework in consideration of the potential full membership of the EU of 12 countries from Central and Eastern Europe by 2010.

The European Commission has accordingly refined its priority objectives for the classification of the regions. The Structural Funds are then used in different combinations in order to address the three priority objectives.

Objective One

Aims to promote development and structural adjustment of regions whose development are lagging behind. Regions with a GDP per capita of less than 75% of the Community average are eligible for Objective 1 funding.

Objective Two

Aims to support the economic and social conversion of areas experiencing structural problems. For the 2000–2006 period, areas with structural difficulties have been divided into four distinctive categories: industrial, rural, urban and fisheries dependent zones.

Objective Three

Aims to support the adaptation and modernisation of education, training and employment policies and systems. It replaces the former Objectives 3 and 4 and reflects the new Title on Employment in the Treaty of Amsterdam.

Transitional Support

Under the terms of the Agenda 2000 reforms those regions which were eligible for Objective 1 funding during the 1994–1999 period but who have lost this entitlement for 2000–2006 will be given transitional assistance. This system of phasing out support is designed to avoid a sudden cessation of European funding and to consolidate the achievements of structural assistance in the previous period.

Northern Ireland has been classified as an Objective 1 in transition region for the funding period 2000–2006 as the level of GDP per capita had attained around

80 per cent of the EU average; around five per cent above the threshold for Objective 1 status.

The Cohesion Fund

A Cohesion Fund was set up in 1993 to run alongside the Structural Funds. The role of the fund is to finance transport and environment infrastructure in those member states where GDP is less than 90 per cent of the EU average (Greece, Ireland, Spain, Portugal). Eighteen billion Euro has been allocated to the Cohesion fund for 2000–2006.

The Community Support Framework in Northern Ireland (CSF)

The details of the Structural Funds assistance to Northern Ireland are laid down in the Northern Ireland Community Support Framework (CSF) 2000–2006. The CSF for the region was agreed following the submission of the Northern Ireland Structural Funds Plan and the subsequent negotiations between the European Commission and the Northern Ireland authorities.

A total of 1.3 billion Euro has been allocated to the Northern Ireland Community Support Framework for the period 2000–2006 (The breakdown is 57% ERDF, 33% ESF, 8% EAGGF and 2% FIFG).

The Northern Ireland Community Support Framework 2000–2006 aims to achieve a transition to a more peaceful, stable, prosperous, fair and outward looking society, sustained by a better physical environment. This aim is carried over into five priorities and nine Horizontal Principles, while the CSF itself is divided into two operational programmes.

- Northern Ireland Programme for Building Sustainable Prosperity 2000–2006; 890 million Euro (£590 m);
- EU Programme for Peace and Reconciliation in Northern Ireland and the Border Region of Ireland 2000–2004; 425 million Euro (£280 m).

Northern Ireland Programme for Building Sustainable Prosperity 2000–2006 (Transitional Objective 1 Programme)

This Transitional Objective 1 operational programme is the largest component of the Community Support Framework, accounting for 68 per cent of the Structural Funds allocated. This programme will therefore be the main instrument for the realisation of the economic and social development identified in the Community Support Framework. The designated priorities under the programme are set out in the table below along with the relevant points of contact in government.

Priority 1	**Economic Growth and Competitiveness**
Priority 1a	Business Competitiveness
1.1	Business Support
1.2	Research and Technology Development and Technology Transfer
1.3	Tourism
1.4	Local Economic Development
1.5	Information Society

Contact:
Howard Keery, DETI, Room 31, Netherleigh,
Massey Avenue, Belfast BT4 2JP

Tel: 028 9052 9328
Fax: 028 9052 9485
E-mail: Howard.Keery@detini.gov.uk

1.6 Roads and Transport

Contact: Stephen Creagh
Department of Regional Development, Clarence Court,
10–18 Adelaide Street, Belfast, BT2 8GB
Tel: 028 9054 0827
Fax: 028 9054 0081
E-mail: Stephen.Creagh@drdni.gov.uk

1.7 Telecommunications

Contact: Trevor Forsythe
Invest NI, 17 Antrim Road, Lisburn, BT28 3AL
Tel: 028 9262 3138
Fax: 028 9267 6054
E-mail: Trevor.Forsythe@irtu.detini.gov.uk

1.8 Energy

Contact: David Stanley
DETI, Netherleigh,
Massey Avenue, Belfast, BT4 2JP
Tel: 028 9052 9240
Fax: 028 9052 5449
E-mail: David.Stanley@detni.gov.uk

Priority 2   Employment

2.1	Education and Skills Development
2.2	Tackling the Flows into Long Term Unemployment
2.3	Promoting a Labour Market Open to All
2.4	Improving Opportunities for Lifelong Learning
2.5	Education and Training ICT and Infrastructure Support
2.6	Developing Entrepreneurship
2.7	Human Resource Development in Companies
2.8	The Advancement of Women

Contact: John Neill
European Unit, DEL, Adelaide House,
39–49 Adelaide Street, Belfast BT2 8FD
Tel: 028 9025 7646
Fax: 028 9025 7646
E-mail: John.Neill@delni.gov.uk

Priority 3   Urban and Social Revitalisation

3.1	Urban Revitalisation
3.2	Advice and Information Services
3.3	Community Sustainability
3.4	Investing in Early Learning

Contact: Don Harley
DSD, 5th Floor Churchill House,
Victoria Square, Belfast BT2 4BA
Tel: 028 9056 9307
Fax: 028 9056 9303
E-mail: Don.Harley@dsdni.gov.uk

Priority 4   Agriculture, Rural Development, Forestry and Fisheries

4.1	Training
4.2	Improving Processing and Marketing of Agricultural Products
4.3	Forestry
4.4	Setting up of Farm Relief and Farm Management Services
4.5	Marketing of Quality Agricultural Products
4.6	Basic Services for the Rural Economy and Population
4.7	Renovation and Development of Villages and Protection and Conservation of the Rural Heritage
4.8	Diversification of Agricultural Activities and Activities Close to Agriculture to Provide Multiple Activities or Alternative Incomes
4.9	Development and Improvement of Infrastructure Connected with the Development of Agriculture
4.10	Encouragement for Tourist and Craft Activities

4.11	Protection of the Environment in Connection with Agriculture, Forestry and Landscape Conservation and the Improvement of animal Welfare
4.12	Financial Engineering
4.13	Fisheries
4.14	Axis I Adjustment of Fishing Effort
4.15	Axis II Renewal and Modernisation of the Fleet
4.16	Axis III Ports, Aquaculture, Processing and Marketing
4.17	Axis IV Other Measures

Contact: Noel Cornick
DARD, Room 355B, Dundonald House
Upper Newtownards Road, Belfast BT4 3SB
Tel: 028 9052 4557
Fax: 028 9052 4148
E-mail: Noel.Cornick@dardni.gov.uk

Priority 5   The Environment

5.1	Sustainable Management of the Environment and Promotion of the Natural and Built Heritage

Contact: Stephen Creagh
DRD, Clarence Court,
10–18 Adelaide Street, Belfast, BT2 8GB
Tel:028 9054 0827
Fax:028 9054 0081
E-mail: Stephen.Creagh@drdni.gov.uk

European Documentation Centres

There are 2 European Documentation Centres based in Northern Ireland. Their role is to provide a resource to students and academics.
The centres have extensive collections of EU information sources and access to EU databases.

European Documentation Centre

The Main Library, Queen's University, Belfast BT7 1NN
Tel: 028 9024 5133 ext 3605
Fax: 028 9033 5040
Web: www.qub.ac.uk/lib/wherelib/
Contact: Marie Griffiths

European Documentation Centre

The Library, University of Ulster, Cromore Road
Coleraine BT52 1SA
Tel: 028 7032 4029
Fax: 028 7032 4928
E-mail: je.peden@ulst.ac.uk
Web: www.ulst.ac.uk/library

EU Programme for Peace and Reconciliation in Northern Ireland and the Border Region of Ireland 2000–2004 (PEACE II)

Peace II accounts for 38 per cent of the Structural Funds allocated and complements the Programme for Building Sustainable Prosperity. It also aims to build upon the creative cross-community approaches to funding adopted under the Special Support Programme for Peace and Reconciliation 1994 –1999 (Peace I).

The Peace II Programme is designed to address the legacy of "The Troubles" and aims to reinforce progress towards a peaceful and stable society and to promote reconciliation. It also aims to take the opportunities arising from the peace process and contribute to reconciliation by promoting appropriate cross community contacts.

Two specific objectives can be identified in relation to the overall aim of the Programme:

- Objective 1   Addressing the legacy of conflict
- Objective 2   Taking opportunities arising
from Peace

The Priorities for the PEACE II Programme along with funding allocations are set out in the tables to the right.

The five priorities have been sub divided into an extensive list of measures aimed at achieving the key objectives of the programme. Details of the measures, the bodies appointed to implement them, and contact information are set out in the tables below.

The intermediary funding bodies associated with the various measures and relevant abbreviations are set out according to the key (right).

Priority 1	**Economic Renewal**
	This has an allocation of 153.67 million Euro in Northern Ireland

Priority 2	**Social Integration, Inclusion and Reconciliation**
	This has an allocation of 107.04 million Euro in Northern Ireland

Priority 3	**Locally Based Regeneration and Development Strategies**
	This has an allocation of 86.05 million Euro in Northern Ireland

Priority 4	**Outward and Forward Looking Region**
	This has an allocation of 86.05 million Euro in Northern Ireland.

Priority 5	**Cross Border Co-operation**
	This has an allocation of 39.72 million Euro in Northern Ireland.

Table Explaining Abbreviations	
DETI	Department of Enterprise, Trade and Investment
DRD	Department for Regional Development
EGSA	Educational Guidance Service for Adults
ADM/CPA	Area Development Management/Combat Poverty Agency
TWN	Training for Women Network
DARD	Department of Agriculture and Rural Development
RDC	Regional Development Council
IRTU	Industrial Research and Technology Unit
CRC	Community Relations Council
SELB	Southern Education and Library Board
NIVT	Northern Ireland Voluntary Trust
NIPPA	Northern Ireland Pre Schools Playgroup Association
DE	Department of Education
DSD	Department for Social Development
OFMDFM	Office of the First Minister and Deputy First Minister
LSP	Local Strategy Partnership
SEUPB	Special EU Programmes Body
NITB	Northern Ireland Tourist Board

Priority	Measure		Implementing Body	Contact	Telephone
1. Economic Renewal	1.1	**Business Competitiveness and Development**			
	1.1a	Economic Revitalisation	Invest NI	Sharon Polson	028 9023 9090
	1.1b	Trade Development	Invest NI	Carol Keery	028 9023 9090
	1.1c	Financial Engineering	DETI NI	Michael Pollock	028 9025 7330
	1.1d	Business Competitiveness	DRD	Michael Pollock	028 9025 7330
	1.1e	Business Competitiveness in the Border Region	ADM/CPA	Aillish Quinn	00 353 47 71340
	1.2	**Sustainable Tourism Development**	DCAL NI DARD	Barry Davison Angela Kelly	028 9025 8870 028 9052 5435
	1.2a	Water Based Tourism			
	1.2b	Natural Resource Rural Tourism	PROTEUS EGSA ADM/CPA	Pat Donnelly Kevin Donaghy Aillish Quinn	028 9037 1023 028 9024 4274 00353 47 71340
	1.3	**New Skills and New Opportunities**	Invest NI ADM/CPA	Sharon Polson Aillish Quinn	028 9023 9090 00 353 47 71340
	1.4	**Promoting Entrepreneurship**	TWN Playboard ADM/CPA	Norma Shearer Hunter Blair Aillish Quinn	028 9077 7199 028 9080 3380 00 353 47 71340
	1.5	**Positive Action for Women**	DARD	Lesley Fay	028 9054 5893
	1.6	**Training for Farmers**	DARD	Robert Erne	028 9054 5869
	1.7	**Diversification of Agricultural Activities**	RDC	Director of Programmes	028 8676 6980
	1.7a	Obtaining Alternative Employment			
	1.7b	Part-Time Employment	IRTU	Boyd McDowell	028 9262 3143
	1.8	**Technology Support for the Knowledge Based Economy**	DETI	Information Age Initiative	028 9052 6577
	1.8a	Innovation Technology and Networking	DARD	Seamus Hughes	028 9054 7116
	1.8b	Information Age			
	1.9	**Investment in Agricultural Holdings**	RDC RDC	Director of Programmes	028 8676 6980
	1.10	**Basic Services for the Rural Economy and Population**			
	1.10a	Retail Services			
	1.10b	Basic Services for Rural Economy			
2. Social Integration, Inclusion and Reconciliation	2.1	Reconciliation for Sustainable Peace	CRC ADM/CPA	Duncan Morrow Aillish Quinn	028 9022 7500 00 353 47 71340
	2.2	Developing Children	SELB	Gregory Butler	028 3741 5381
	2.3	Skilling and Building			
	2.4	**Reconciliation of Victims**			
	2.4a	Pathways to Inclusion	NIVT	Roisin Owens	028 9024 5927
	2.4b	Integration and Reconciliation			
	2.4c	Inclusion of Target Groups in Border Region	ADM/CPA	Aillish Quinn	00 353 47 71340
	2.5	Investing in Childcare	NIPPA	Siobhan Fitzpatrick	028 9066 5220
	2.6	Promoting Active Citizenship	NIVT ADM/CPA	Felicity McCartney Aillish Quinn	028 9024 5927 00 353 47 71340
	2.7	Developing Weak Community Infrastructure	NIVT ADM/CPA	Roisin Owens Aillish Quinn	028 9024 5927 00 353 47 71340

Priority		Measure	Implementing Body	Contact	Telephone
	2.8	Accompanying Infrastructure	DE	Richard Hodgett	028 9127 9567
			DSD	Don Harley	028 9056 9307
			NIPPA	Siobhan Fitzpatrick	028 9066 5220
			OFMDFM	Karen Jardine	028 9052 0198
			ADM/CPA	Aillish Quinn	00 353 47 71340
	2.9	**Renovation and Development of Villages and Protection and Conservation of Rural Heritage**			
	2.9a	Conservation of the Rural Heritage	RCN	Michael Hughes	028 8676 6670
	2.9b	Renovation	RDC	Director of Programmes	028 8676 6980
	2.10	Encouragement for Tourist and Craft Activities	RDC	Director of Programmes	028 8676 6980
	2.11	Area Based Regeneration	DSD	Don Harley	028 9056 9307
3. Locally Based Regeneration and Development Strategies	3.1	Local Economic Initiatives for Developing the Social Economy	Contact Local LSP		
	3.2	Locally based Human Resource, Training and Development Strategies	Contact Local LSP		
	3.3	Building Better Communities	Contact Local Task Force		
	3.4	Improving Our Rural Communities	Contact Local Task Force		
4. Outward and Forward Looking Region	4.1	Networking	OFMDFM SEUPB	Kenny Knox	028 9052 2563
	4.2a	Marketing the Region as a Tourism Destination	NITB Taskforces	Caroline Bell	028 9023 1221
	4.2b	Enhancing the Region as a Tourism Destination	NITB Taskforces	Caroline Bell	028 9023 1221
5. Cross Border Co-operation	5.1	Increasing Cross-Border Development Opportunities	Co-operation Ireland	Gina McIntyre	028 9032 2445
	5.2	Public Sector Co-operation	SEUPB		028 8225 5750
	5.3	Developing Cross Border Reconciliation and Understanding	ADM/CAPA	Aillish Quinn	00 353 47 71340
	5.4	Promoting Joint Approaches to Social, Education, Training and Human Resource Development	ADM/CPA	Aillish Quinn	00 353 47 71340
	5.5	Education, Cross Border School and Youth Co-operation	DE DES	Richard Hodgett Mary O'Driscoll	028 9127 9567 00 353 1889 2179
	5.6	**Agriculture and Rural Development Cooperation**			
	5.6a	Cross Border Community Development	DARD DAFRD	Stephen Hogg Siobhan Stack	028 9052 4597 00 353 1607 2949
	5.6b	Cross Border Diversification	DARD DAFRD	Seamus Hughes Fergus Phelan	028 9054 7119 00 353 1607 2949
	5.7	Fishing and Aquaculture	NI Seafood Bord Iascaigh Mhara	Niall Heaney Gerry Honer	028 9052 2373 00 353 1619 9688

Special EU Programmes Body

EU House
6 Cromac Place
Belfast BT7 2JB
Tel: 028 90 2666 660
E-mail: info@seupb.org
Chief Executive: John McKinney

The full text of the PEACE II Operational Programme can be found at: www.europe-dfpni.gov.uk
Application details can be found at: www.eugrants.org/
Information on Peace I can be found at: www.eu-peace.org/

The Special EU Programmes Body is the key player in managing the overall allocation process relating to Peace II and is the best source of information on the initiative.

Other European Union Initiatives

Community Initiatives are special forms of assistance proposed by the Commission to Member states. Implemented throughout the European Union they are financed by Structural Funds aimed at solving specific problems and are additional in financial terms to a region's Community Support Framework.

The Community Initiatives have three defining features:

- Encouraging transactional, cross border and interregional co-operation;
- Increased involvement of people on the ground "bottom up approach";
- Support through a real partnership of those involved in Community initiatives.

Reform of Community Initiatives

The number of Community Initiatives has been reduced with the reform of the Structural Funds under Agenda 2000. There are now 4 Community Initiatives for the period 2000–06 each financed by a Structural Fund; 118 million Euro has been allocated to Northern Ireland for this purpose. These are:

- Interreg III
- Leader +
- EQUAL
- Urban II

Details of these initiatives are set out below.

INTERREG III

The main objective is to strengthen economic and social cohesion in the Community through the promotion of cross border, transnational and international co-operation and balanced development of the community territory. This is to be achieved through the promotion of integrated regional development within neighbouring regions.

INTERREG III has 3 strands:

- Strand A: cross-border co-operation
- Strand B: transnational co-operation
- Strand C: interregional co-operation

81 million Euro has been allocated to Northern Ireland for INTERREG.

Contact:
The Special EU Programmes Body
European Union House
Monaghan, Co Monaghan.
Tel:00353 47 71251
Fax: 00353 47 71258
E-mail: INTERREG@seupb.ie
Web: www.eugrants.org

Leader +

Leader + encourages the design and implementation of innovative development strategies for rural areas. Leader + achieves this by establishing partnerships at a local level.

Leader + comprises three strands:

- Strand 1: support for integrated and innovative development strategies for rural areas
- Strand 2: support for interregional and transnational co-operation
- Strand 3: networking for all EU rural areas

15 million Euro has been allocated to Northern Ireland.

Contact:
Angela Kelly, Rural Development Division, DARD, Dundonald House, Belfast BT4 3SB
Tel: 028 9052 4201
Fax: 028 9052 4776
E-mail: Angela.Kelly@dardni.gov.uk
Web: www.dardni.gov.uk

EQUAL

Equal aims to promote new means to tackle all forms of exclusion, discrimination and inequality in relation to the labour market and leads on from two earlier initiatives: ADAPT and EMPLOYMENT.

EQUAL comprises three strands:
- Strand A: Tackling discrimination and inequalities linked to the labour market
- Strand B: Networking projects at national level to enable information exchanges and the dissemination of best practice
- Strand C: Joint work by the Commission and member states to learn the lessons of good practice

The Northern Ireland EQUAL Programme will target two priorities:
- Employability
- Equal opportunities for men and women

12 million Euro has been allocated to Northern Ireland for this project.

Contact:
John Neill, Head of European Unit, Adelaide House, 39–49 Adelaide Street, Belfast, BT2 8FD
Tel: 028 90 257874
Fax: 028 90 257646
E-mail: john.neill@delni.gov.uk
Web: www.equal.ecotec.co.uk

Pat Donnelly, Chief Executive
PROTEUS, 8 Edgewater Road, Belfast, BT3 9JQ
Tel: 028 90 37 0123
Fax: 028 90 37 0124
E-mail: pat.donnelly@proteus-ni.org
Web: www.proteus-ni.org

Urban II

The initiative aims to promote the design and implementation of innovative development models for the economic and social regeneration of urban areas in crisis and aims to strengthen exchanges of information and experience on sustainable urban development in the EU.

Approximately 50 towns with a population of 10,000+ may be eligible for the Urban initiative. The urban areas included may be inside or outside Objective 1 and 2 areas and must fulfil at least three of the following conditions:

- High long term unemployment;
- Low rate of economic activity;
- High level of poverty and exclusion;
- The need for structuring adjustment due to economic and social difficulties;
- High proportion of immigrants, ethnic minorities or refugees;
- Low level of education, major gaps in terms of qualifications and a high rate of pupil failure;
- Unstable demographic environment;
- Particularly poor environmental conditions.

10 million Euro has been allocated to Northern Ireland.

Each Urban programme must include measures for strengthening information exchanges and sharing experience on the regeneration of urban areas in crisis.

Contact:
Mike Thompson, Belfast Regeneration Office,
Brookmount Buildings, 42 Fountain Street
Belfast BT1 5EE
Tel: 028 9025 1973
Fax: 028 90 25 1939
E-mail: mike.thompson@dsdni.gov.uk

Business: European Information Centre

Aimed at providing the business community (with emphasis on the SME sector) with information on European developments. The centre has access to EU databases including Tenders Electronic Daily (TED) carrying daily listings for requests for tenders for EU public contracts.

Euro Info Centre

Invest NI, Upper Galwally, Belfast BT8 6TB
Tel: 028 9023 9090
Fax: 028 9049 0490

Northern Ireland Innovation Relay Centre (IRC)

The IRC funded by the EU aims to promote the transfer of innovative technology to and from Northern Ireland.

Innovation Relay Centre

Invest NI, 17 Antrim Road, Lisburn BT28 3AL
Tel: 028 9023 9090
Fax: 028 9049 0490

Other Centrally Managed Programmes

SME Development Initiatives

Entrepreneurs or Businesses seeking European business and commercial information and assistance with Community funding should contact:

Euro Info Centre
Invest NI
64 Chichester Street
Belfast BT1 4JX
Tel: 028 9023 9090
Fax: 028 9054 5000

Joint European Venture Programme

The programme aims to stimulate the establishment of joint ventures between European SMEs. JEV has an indicative budget of 85 million Euro.

JEV Information Unit
6 Rue Jean Monnet
L–2180 Luxembourg

Contact:
Greater London Enterprise Ltd
28 Park Street
London SE1 9EQ
Tel: 0207 403 0300
Fax: 0207 403 1742

Business Angels Networks

Under the Business Angels programme the Commission finances up to 50% of the costs of feasibility studies for the creation of such networks, as well as a maximum of 50% of the costs of pilot actions aimed at establishing a regional or national network.

European Business Angels Network
Avenue des Arts 12, Bte 7
B–1210 Brussels
Belgium
Tel: 00 32 22 18 43 13
Fax: 00 32 22 18 45 83
E-mail: info@eban.org
Web: www.eban.org

Mutual Guarantee Scheme

Mutual Guarantee Schemes involve private groupings of companies, often linked to sector specific interest groups, to provide loan insurance to banks.

Enterprise Directorate General
Access to Finance
Rue de la Loi 200 (SC-27 04/04)
B–1049 Brussels
Tel: 00 322 295 91 86
Fax: 00 322 295 21 54

ETF Start Up (European Technology Facility) – Venture Capital

The programme aims to support equity investments in SMEs which have a higher risk profile.

Enterprise Directorate General
Access to Finance
Rue de la Loi (SC-27 04/04)
B–1049 Brussels
Tel: 00 322 295 91 86
Fax: 00 322 295 21 54

I-Tec

I-Tec is part of the Innovation Programme of the European Commission and aims to encourage early stage investments in technologically innovative SMEs.

Enterprise Directorate General
Innovation Policy
Office EUFO 2/2197
L–2920 Luxembourg
Tel: 00 352 4301 39194
Fax: 00 352 4301 34544

Social, Health and Human Rights Initiatives

DAPHNE

DAPHNE is a four-year programme 2000–2003 supporting preventative measures to fight violence against children, young people and women. The programme has a total budget of 20 million Euro.

European Commission
Directorate General for Justice and Home Affairs
(Unit A.1) LX 46 5/08
Rue de la Loi 200
B–1049 Brussels
Fax: 00 322 299 67 11

Education, Training and Youth

Socrates

Socrates is the EU Action Programme for education. It aims to promote the European dimension and improve the quality of education by encouraging co-operation between participating countries. 31 countries can participate in the programme, which will run from 2002–2006, and 185 million Euro has been allocated to the programme.

Bernie McAllister/Liz McBain
European Schools West, 2nd Floor
Norwich Union House, 7 Fountain Street
Belfast BT1 5EG
Tel: 028 9024 8220
Fax: 028 9023 7592
E-mail: Bernie.McAllister@britishcouncil.org
Web: www.socrates-uk.net

Jean Monnet Project

The Jean Monnet Project "European Integration in University Studies" aims to facilitate the introduction of European integration studies in Universities. The project awards funds on a co-financing basis for a start up period of three years, in exchange for a commitment by the University to maintain the teaching activities for a further four years.

Jean Monnet Project
DG for Education and Culture
European Commission
200 Rue de la Loi
B–1049 Brussels
Belgium
Tel: 00 322 296 03 12
Fax: 00 322 296 31 06

Leonardo da Vinci

Leonardo da Vinci is the action programme for implementing the European Union's vocational training policy, thereby supporting and supplementing action taken by the member states. It aims to use transnational co-operation to enhance quality, promote innovation and support for the European dimension of vocational training systems and practices.
The British Council
10 Spring Gardens
London SW1A 2BN
Tel: 0207 389 4389
Fax: 0207 389 4426
E-mail: Leonardo@britishcouncil.org
Web: www.leonardo.org.uk

Youth

Youth is focussed on the promotion of co-operation in youth related matters. 520 million Euro has been allocated to the project.

Youth Council for Northern Ireland
European Bureau
Forestview, Purdy's Lane
Belfast BT8 7AR
E-mail: info@youthcouncil-ni.org.uk
Web: www.youthcouncil-ni.org.uk

Culture 2000

Culture 2000 is the first Community Framework programme in the area of culture. The Programme seeks to develop a common cultural area by promoting transnational co-operation between creative artists, cultural players and institutions throughout the EU. 167 million Euro has been allocated to Culture 2000, which will be administered by the European Commission.

Geoffrey Brown
EUCLID
46–48 Mount Pleasant
Liverpool L3 5SD
Tel: 0151 709 2564
Fax: 0151 709 8647
E-mail: info@euclid.info
Web: www.euclid.info

Media Plus

Media Plus aims to create an environment, which promotes the European cinematographic, audiovisual and multi media industry.

Northern Ireland Film & Television Commission
21 Alfred Street
Belfast BT2 8ED
Tel: 028 9023 2444
Fax: 028 9023 9918
E-mail: info@niftc.co.uk
Web: www.niftc.co.uk

Financial Assistance for Town Planning

European Commission
Directorate General for Education and Culture
Unit "Communication with the public-partnerships with civil society – Town Twinning"
200 Rue de la Loi VM-2 4/35

B–1049 Brussels
Belgium
E-mail: towntwinning@cec.eu.int
Web: www.europa.eu.int/comm/dg10

Employment and Training

DEL is the government department responsible for European funding for training and employment in Northern Ireland.

Department for Employment and Learning
European Unit
Adelaide House
39–49 Adelaide Street
Belfast BT2 8FD
Tel: 028 9025 7644
Fax: 028 9025 7646
E-mail: European.unit@nics.gov.uk

PROTEUS

Proteus is the contact point for the EQUAL initiative and some measures under PEACE II, as well as its role administering training and employment programmes on behalf of the Department for Employment and Learning.

8 Edgewater Office Park
Edgewater Road
Belfast BT3 9JQ
Tel: 028 9037 1023
Fax: 028 9077 3543
E-mail: administrator@proteus-ni.org

The European Employment Service (EURES)

Eures links to a network of over 400 centres throughout Europe providing information on vacancies, recruitment and living and working conditions throughout Europe.

EURES Section
Gloucester House
Chichester Street
Belfast BT1 4RA
Tel: 028 9025 2270
Fax: 028 9025 2288
E-mail: Nicola.mchugh@delni/gov.uk
Web: europa.eu.int/comm./employmentsocial

Rural Carrefours

Carrefours are part of a regional network providing information to all sectors of the agricultural and rural community. They provide regional information and will assist in the search for European partners and help place students seeking work placements in other EU member states.

Carrefour Ulster
Clogher Valley Rural Centre
47 Main Street
Clogher BT76 0AA
Tel: 028 8554 8872
Fax: 028 8554 8203
E-mail: carrefours_Ulster@dnet.co.uk
Web: www.clogher.com/carrefour

Education

The European Resource Centre for Schools and Colleges

Norwich Union House
7 Fountain Street
Belfast BT1 5EG
Tel: 028 9024 8220
Fax: 028 9023 7592
E-mail: Jonathan.Stewart@britishcouncil.org

The British Council

Education and Training Group
Norwich Union House
7 Fountain Street
Belfast BT1 5EG
Tel: 028 9024 8220
Fax: 028 9023 7592
E-mail: liz.mcbain@britishcouncil.org

European Bureau

Youth Council for Northern Ireland
Forestview
Purdy's Lane
Belfast BT8 7AR
Tel: 028 9064 3882
Fax: 028 9064 3874
E-mail: dguilfoyle@youthcouncil-ni.org.uk
Web: www.youthcouncil-ni.org.uk

Local Strategy Partnerships in Northern Ireland

The Local Strategy Partnership Boards established to oversee the implementation of Priority 3 Locally Based Regeneration and Development Initiatives will have responsibility for measures relating to the social economy and human resource and development initiatives under Peace II.

Priority 3 accounts for approximately 20 per cent of the EU's Structural Funds allocation to the EU Programme for Peace and Reconciliation in Northern Ireland. The EU allocations will be supplemented by national public and private funds to produce a total of 114.73 million Euros.

The Peace II Programme details a vision for the Local Strategy Partnerships building upon the previous structures of District Partnerships, which were established under the EU Programme for Peace and Reconciliation (Peace I). It is intended that the LSPs will be more integrated and sustainable and have greater autonomy in their decision making than the District Partnership Boards. There are two key changes in the new LSPs from the old District Partnership model:

- District Councils are to be involved in the work of local partnerships at a corporate level, not only through the participation of individual district councillors or council officers and
- Statutory agencies at local level are to be actively involved in partnership work, to ensure that the broad strategic direction of Departments and their Agencies take full account of the views and priorities of local communities operating at the local level.

It is envisaged that the role of LSPs will develop into a long-term strategy and that they will establish a remit extending beyond the distribution of EU Structural funds. In furtherance of these aims the central decision making role of the Northern Ireland Partnership Board has not been repeated for Peace II. Responsibility for decision making will rest at local level and the Special EU Programmes Body and the Monitoring Committee will focus upon:

- Ensuring compliance with the Structural Funds Regulations, the Peace II Programme document and the Programme Complement and
- Playing a supportive role for LSPs in association with the new Regional Partnership Board.

The overall strategic aim of Peace II is to "reinforce progress toward a peaceful and stable society and to promote reconciliation". Applications under the programme must contain at least one of two of the specific objectives i.e. they must address the legacy of conflict and/or take the opportunities arising from peace. Peace II Partnerships focus on specific needs in the partnership areas and involve a more structured contribution from the statutory sector which it is hoped will ensure greater sustainability and avoid the criticisms levelled of a lack of sustainability following Peace I.

Local Strategy Partnerships (LSPs) consist of two strands:

- Government (local government and statutory sector) and

The "four pillars" of the:

- Voluntary sector;
- Business;
- Agriculture;
- Trade Unions.

The aim is to achieve a balance of local interests and the development of a structured involvement of the statutory sector in the Partnerships. Partnerships are required to be inclusive and provide equity of standing between the various strands and seek to be open and accountable to their local communities, demonstrate fairness in the allocation of funding in their control and produce structures and mechanisms to enable auditing of all aspects of their work.

Whilst there is no definitive membership quota set for membership of the LSPs it is recommended that a maximum of twenty-eight should not be exceeded. Nominations for members of the LSP occur at a local level and the procedure for processing nominations is determinable at individual local level. However, the process utilised must be documented and submitted to the SEUPB for approval as part of the Global Grant Allocation Agreement.

A listing of Local Strategy Partnerships is set out below (A–Z). The listing includes contact details and membership for each LSP.

A–Z Listing of Local Strategy Partnerships

Antrim LSP

The Steeple, Antrim BT41 1BJ
Tel: 028 9446 3113
Fax: 028 9446 4469
Contact: Geraldine Girvan

Members	Nominating Sector
Jacqueline Barnes	Community/Voluntary
Gilbert Bell	NEELB
Andy Brown	ICTU
John Clarke	UFU
Thomas Burns	Antrim Borough Council
Sam Dunlop	Antrim Borough Council
Alison Flynn	Invest NI
Oliver Frawley	Community/Voluntary
Linda Houston	Community/Voluntary
Andrew Little	Chamber of Commerce
Damien Lynch	Chamber of Commerce
Sam Magee	Antrim Borough Council
Brian Mawhinney	Community/Voluntary
John McKee	DARD
Martin McManus	Antrim Borough Council
Stephen Murray	NHSSB
Stephen Nicholl	Antrim Borough Council
Freda Waite	Antrim Enterprise Agency
Adrian Watson	Antrim Borough Council
Robert Chesney	UFU
Kieron Murphy	NIHE
Christine Harper	DEL

Ards

Council Offices, Crepe Weavers Industrial Estate, 20 Comber Road Newtownards BT23 4RX
Tel: 028 9182 6913
Fax: 028 9182 8040
Partnership Manager: Tom Rowley

Members	Nominating Sector
Cllr Angus Carson	Ards Borough Council
Cllr Linda Clelland	Ards Borough Council
Cllr Margaret Craig, (Mayor)	Ards Borough Council
Cllr Robert Gibson	Ards Borough Council
Cllr Hamilton Lawther	Ards Borough Council
Cllr Alan McDowell	Ards Borough Council
Mrs Bertie Duncan	Institute of Directors
Ms Jackie Brown	Chamber of Commerce
Tony McMullan	NIPSA
Margaret Adair	NIPSA
Harry Liddy	NIPSA

Trevor Kerr	Invest NI
Lester Black	SEELB
Gordon Orr	PSNI
Derek McClure	Action Mental Health
John Smyth	Rural Community Network
Artie Spence	Ards Development Bureau
Hilary Forrester	Women's Aid
Carol McNamara	NIPPA
Caroline Mahon	Upper Ards Community Assoc.
David Stewart	UFU
Professor Sydney Salmon	UCHT

Armagh LSP

Council Offices, Place Demesne, Armagh BT60 4EL
Tel: 028 3752 9600
Fax: 028 3752 9601
Contact: Denise O'Hare/Sharon O'Gorman

Members	Nominating Sector
Cllr P Brannigan	Armagh City and District Council
Cllr B Hutchinson	Armagh City and District Council
Cllr C Rafferty	Armagh City and District Council
Cllr J A Speers	Armagh City and District Council
Cllr R W Turner	Armagh City and District Council
Mr V Brownlees	Armagh City and District Council
D McCammick	Armagh City and District Council
A Hamilton	Invest NI
J Dobbin	NIHE
E Hamilton	Armagh and Dungannon HSS
V McKevitt	DARD
C Donaghy	SHSSB
H McClenaghan	SELB
R Jay	Queen's University Armagh
I Mathews	Ballymore Open Centre
A Gibson	Armagh Chamber of Commerce
I Grimes	ICTU
E Kelly	Crosscurrents
A Rutledge	Recruitment and Training
J Fogarty	ICTU
G Mallon	Keady and District Community
J Doherty	Rutledge Recruitment and Training
T W Johnston	Markethill District Enterprises
K McAnallen	Armagh City Hotel

Ballymena LSP

Ardeevin, 4 Wellington Court, Ballymena BT43 6EQ
Tel: 028 2563 3930
Fax: 028 2563 9785
Contact: Majella McAllister

Members	Nominating Sector
Arthur Crewe	Northern Ireland Housing Executive
G Irwin	NEELB
John Fenton	NHSSB
Claire O'Neill	North East Institute
Cllr R Stirling	Ballymena Borough Council
Cllr Hubert Nicholl	Ballymena Borough Council
Cllr Neill Armstrong	Ballymena Borough Council
Cllr L Scott	Ballymena Borough Council
Cllr Declan O'Loan	Ballymena Borough Council
Cllr Maurice Mills	Ballymena Borough Council
Claire Herron	Invest NI
Vacant	Portglenone Enterprise Group Ltd
Ms Sylvia Gordon	Ballymena Women's Aid
Michael Scullion	Glenravel Environmental Assoc.
Deirdre McAuley	Ballymena Citizens Advice Bureau
Jane Gribbin	Ballymena Community Forum
Colum Best	Dunclug and District Community
James Edmondson	Ulster Farmers Union
Gerry Lawn	Ballymena Chamber of Commerce
Gerry Bonar	Ballymena Chamber of Commerce
Maureen McAuley	ICTU
Gerald Bradley	ICTU

Ballymoney LSP

Borough Offices, Riada House, 14 Charles Street
Ballymoney BT53 6DZ
Tel: 028 2766 2280
Fax: 028 2766 5150
Contact: Nigel Freeburn

Members	Nominating Sector
Cllr Bill Kennedy	Ballymoney Borough Council
Cllr Mervyn Storey	Ballymoney Borough Council
Cllr Cecil Cousley	Ballymoney Borough Council
Cllr James Simpson	Ballymoney Borough Council
Cllr Malachy McCamphill	Ballymoney Borough Council
John Dempsey	Ballymoney Borough Council
Sam Vallelly	Causeway Trust
Anne Connolly	Education
Geoff Spence	Invest NI
John McKee	DARD
Joe Patton	Rural Development
Vince Boyle	NIAPA
Jonathan Payne	Retail
Heather Hargy	Retail

Michael Fleming	Industrialist
Mac Pollock	Trade Union
Rae Kirk	Community/Voluntary
Pat Crossley	Community/Voluntary
Veronica McKinley	Community/Voluntary
Denis Connelly	Community/Voluntary

Banbridge LSP

Civic Building, Downshire Road, Banbridge BT32 3JY
Tel: 028 4066 0600
Contact: Joanne Morgan

Members	Nominating Sector
Cllr Ian Burns	Banbridge District Council
Cllr William J Martin	Banbridge District Council
Cllr Frank McQuaid	Banbridge District Council
Cllr Cassie McDemott	Banbridge District Council
Cllr Wilfred McFadden	Banbridge District Council
Robert Gilmore	Banbridge District Council
Nigel Jess	Private Tourism Provider
John Dawson	Banbridge Rotary Club
Patrick Kelly	ROMAL Community Network
Tony Gates	Mourne Heritage Trust
Pamela Johnston	Banbridge & District Gateway Club
Nigel Smith	Banbridge & District Sports
Anne Cromie	Banbridge Community Network
Brian Hewitt	ICTU
Sharon Currans	NIPSA
William Cromie	UFU
Esther Ervin	UFU
Aidan McCullough	TADA Rural Network
Kathleen Donnely	Training and Employment Agency
Helen McClenaghan	SELB
Eamon McKeown	NIHE
Vince McKevitt	DARD
Denis Preston	Craigavon and Banbridge HSS
Eamon Mulvenna	Invest NI

Belfast LSP

5th Floor, Premier Business Centre, 20 Adelaide Street
Belfast BT2 8GB
Tel: 028 9032 8532
Fax: 028 9032 7306
Contact: Deirdre McBride

Members	Nominating Sector
Cllr David Alderdice	Belfast City Council
Cllr David Browne	Belfast City Council
Cllr Patrick Convery	Belfast City Council
Cllr Ian Crozier	Belfast City Council
Cllr Danny Lavery	Belfast City Council
Cllr Marie Moore	Belfast City Council

Cllr Hugh Smyth	Belfast City Council
Tim Losty	Invest NI
Dr Paula Kilbane	EHSSB
Billy Gamble	Dept. for Regional Development
Alison McQueen	Department for Social Development
Kieran Brazier	Dept. of Employment and Learning
Maurice Johnston	NIHE
George Campbell	BELB
Dr Eddie Jackson	Belfast City Council
Sam Burns	Community/Voluntary Sector
Marie Cavanagh	Community/Voluntary Sector
Sammy Douglas	Community/Voluntary Sector
Eileen Howell	Community/Voluntary Sector
Liam Maskey	Community/Voluntary Sector
Bill Patterson	Community/Voluntary Sector
Judith Willoughby	Community/Voluntary Sector
John Lilly	Business/Private Sector
Maria McAllister	Business/Private Sector
Jackie McCoy	Business/Private Sector
Brendan Mackin	Trade Union
Manus Maguire	Trade Union
Anne McVicker	Trade Union
Brian Megahey	Agriculture

Carrickfergus LSP

The Wilson Endowed Building, 15 Lancasterian Street, Carrickfergus BT38 7AB
Tel: 028 9335 1438
Contact: Deirdre Convery

Members	Nominating Sector
Brenda Leslie	Carrickfergus Women's Forum
Sandara Kelso	NIMBA
Karen Montgomery	Community/Voluntary
Muriel Todd	Trade Union
Beverley Heaney	Trade Union
Sam Crowe	Business
David Mitchell	Business
James Macauley	Business
Edward Adamson	UFU
Ald Roy Beggs	Carrickfergus Borough Council
Cllr Robin Cavan	Carrickfergus Borough Council
Cllr Terry Clements	Carrickfergus Borough Council
Cllr May Beattie	Carrickfergus Borough Council
Cllr Janet Crampsie	Carrickfergus Borough Council
Alan Cardwell	Carrickfergus Borough Council
Dermot Curran	NIHE
Geoffrey McGeagh	NEELB
Stephen Murray	NHSSB
Noel Brown	Invest NI

Castlereagh LSP

Civic and Administrative Offices, Bradford Court
Upper Galwally, Belfast BT8 6RB
Tel: 028 9048 7997
Partnership Coordinator: Mike Wilson

Members	Nominating Sector
Cllr Jack Beattie	Castlereagh Borough Council
Cllr Claire Ennis	Castlereagh Borough Council
Cllr Vivienne Stevenson	Castlereagh Borough Council
Cllr Frank Gallagher	Castlereagh Borough Council
Cllr David Drysdale	Castlereagh Borough Council
Cllr Joanne Bunting	Castlereagh Borough Council
Cllr Jim White	Castlereagh Borough Council
Cllr Geraldine Rice	Castlereagh Borough Council
Cllr Cecil Hall	Castlereagh Borough Council
Cllr Brian Hanvey	Castlereagh Borough Council
Fred McKenna	Community/Voluntary
Janice Cherry	Community/Voluntary
Rosemary Reynolds	Community/Voluntary
Richard Mills	Community/Voluntary
Elizabeth Walker	Community/Voluntary
Gilmore Andrews	Community/Voluntary
Timothy Morrow	Agricultural and Rural
Michael Watson	Agricultural and Rural
Stephen McAuley	Business
Helen Mathews	Business
Jack McComiskey	Business
Ray Hamilton	Business
Brenda Smith	Trade Union
Jim Barbour	Trade Union
Karen Bradbury	Statutory
Paul Carland	Statutory
Alan Gregg	Statutory
Campbell Dixon	Statutory

Coleraine LSP

Cloonavin, 66 Portstewart Road, Coleraine BT52 IEU
Tel: 028 7034 7034
Contact: Patricia McCallion

Members	Nominating Sector
Nevin Oliver	Causeway HSS Trust
Joan Baird	NIHE
Gerard Finnegan	Invest NI
Nigel Kyle	PSNI
Prof Peter Roebuck	University of Ulster
Wavell Moore	Coleraine Borough Council
Cllr David Barbour	Coleraine Borough Council
Cllr Eamon Mullan	Coleraine Borough Council
Cllr Maurice Bradley	Coleraine Borough Council
Lorna Carson	ICTU
Dr Arthur Williamson	AUT
Liz Baird	Coleraine Rural and Urban Network

Angela Welch	Advice Services in Coleraine
Diana McClelland	Leader and UFU
Alison Harbison	Agivey Network and NIAPA
Eddie Clements	Coleraine Enterprise Agency
Ian Donaghy	Coleraine Town Partnership
David Alexander	Causeway Chamber of Commerce

Cookstown LSP

Gortalowry House, 94 Church Street, Cookstown BT80 8HX
Tel: 028 8676 4714
Manager: Maggie Bryson

Members	Nominating Sector
Cllr Trevor Wilson	Cookstown District Council
James McGarvey	Cookstown District Council
Ian McCrea	Cookstown District Council
Oliver Molloy	Cookstown District Council
John McNamee	Cookstown District Council
Adrian McCreesh	Statutory
Michael McGuckin	Statutory
Michael May	Statutory
David Bradshaw	Statutory
Helen McClenaghan	Statutory
Ursula Marshall	Community/Voluntary
William Wilkinson	Community/Voluntary
May Devlin	Community/Voluntary
Hilary Mallon	Trade Union
Vera McElhone	Trade Union
Raymond McGarvey	Business
Jim Eastwood	Business
Wilbert Mayne	Social Partner

Craigavon LSP

Civic Centre, Lakeview Road, Craigavon BT64 1AL
Tel: 028 3831 2571
Project Officer: Jillian McAreavey

Members	Nominating Sector
Cllr Jonathan Bell	Craigavon Borough Council
Mark Bleakney	Statutory Representative
Ald Frederick Crowe	Craigavon Borough Council
Gerard Devlin	Trade Union Representative
Kathleen Donnellly	Statutory Sector Representative
Jill England	Statutory Sector Representative
Clifford Forbes	Community/Voluntary Sector
Ignatius Fox	Agricultural/Rural Representative
Philomena Horner	Community and Voluntary Sector
Cllr Dolores Kelly	Craigavon Borough Council
Teddy Martin	Trade Union Representative
Jim McCammick	Business Sector Representative

Helen McClenaghan	Statutory Sector Representative
Isabel Murray	Business Sector Representative
Cllr John O'Dowd	Craigavon Borough Council
David Riley	Agricultural/Rural Representative

Derry LSP

98 Strand Road, Londonderry BT48 6DQ
Tel: 028 7137 6505
Contact: Oonagh McGillion

Members	Nominating Sector
Clionagh Boyle	Community/Voluntary
Cllr Mary Bradley	Community/Voluntary
Noel Cochrane	Agriculture/Rural
Catherine Cooke	Community/Voluntary
Keith Cradden	Statutory
Eamonn Deane	Community/Voluntary
Edyth Dunlop	Community/Voluntary
Des Farrell	Private
Gerard Finnegan	Statutory
Cllr Lynn Fleming	Derry City Council
Martin Gallagher	Community/Voluntary
Cllr Joe Millar	Derry City Council
Hugh Hegarty	Private
Margaret Kelly	Statutory
Cathal Logue	Statutory
Conal McFeely	Community/Voluntary
Cllr Jim McKeever	Derry City Council
Jennifer McLernon	Statutory
Anne Molloy	Trade Union
Eamonn Molloy	Observer
Donald Montgomery	Agriculture/Rural
Ruth Moore	Community/Voluntary
Declan O'Hare	Statutory
Cllr Gerry O'hEara	Derry City Council
Joe O'Kane	Statutory
Cllr William O'Connell	Derry City Council
Helen Osborn	Statutory
Des Rainey	Trade Union
Cllr Pat Ramsey	Derry City Council

Down LSP

8-10 Irish Street, Downpatrick BT30 6BP
Tel: 028 4461 7667
Contact: David Patterson

Members	Nominating Sector
Helen Honeyman	Harmony Community Trust
Sean O'Rourke	Newcastle 2000
Sean Garland	St Dymphna's Association
Francis Casement	Racecourse Road Community

Marion Flanagan	Ballynahinch Regeneration
Jacquie Richardson	NIPPA, Drumaroad Playgroup
Eamonn King	Down District CAB
Adrian Smyth	Business in the Community
Crosby Clelland	Rural Business
Ian Irwin	Craft Sector/Tourism
Peter Bunting	ICTU
Marion Ritchie	ICTU
Elizabeth Fleming	UFU
Graham Furey	UFU
Lawrence Clarke	Down Lisburn Trust
Vincent McKevitt	DARD
Ian McCrickard	NIHE
Anne Beggs	Invest NI
James Peel	SEELB
David Smyth	East Down Institute
Peter Craig	Down District Council
Carmel O'Boyle	Down District Council
Dermot Curran	Down District Council
John Doris	Down District Council
Eamon McConvey	Down District Council
Robert Burgess	Down District Council
Eddie Rea	Down District Council

Dungannon and South Tyrone LSP

Circular Road, Dungannon BT71 6DT
Tel: 028 8772 0315
Programme Manager: Ursula Quinn

Members	Nominating Sector
Cllr J Canning	Statutory
Cllr J I Cavanagh	Statutory
Cllr S McGuigan	Statutory
Cllr W J McIlwrath	Statutory
Cllr K Magennis	Statutory
David Bradshaw	Invest NI
Iain Frazer	Dungannon Borough Council
Helen McClenaghan	SELB
Kieran Lavelle	DARD
Mary Patterson	Armagh and Dungannon HSST
Daragh Shields	DEL
John Quigley	NIHE
Wilfred Mitchell	Community
Monika Donnelly	Community
Jennifer Hamilton	Community
Annette McGahan-McMurray	Community
Mary O'Neil	Community
John Downey	Community
Sean Donnelly	NIAPA
Jean Elliott	UFU
Martin Devlin	ICTU
Roy Wilkins	John Stevenson & Co
Norman Adams	ASM Howarth Accountants

Fermanagh LSP

Enniskillen Business Centre, Tempo Road, Enniskillen BT74 7BA
Tel: 028 6632 9225
Contact: Helen Maguire

Members	Nominating Sector
John Treacy	Fermanagh Enterprise Ltd
Eamonn Cox	Fermanagh Business Initiative
Tanya Cathcart	Fermanagh Lakeland Tourism
Margaret Gallagher	FLAG
John Sheridan	UFU
Vacant	NIAPA
Anne Beattie	NATFHE
Brendan Hueston	TG&WU
Leanne Lyttle	Fermanagh Young Farmers
Jenny Irvine	ITEC
Gerry Maguire	Fermanagh Access Group
Lauri McCusker	Cornagrade Community Assoc.
Brenda Whitley	Fermanagh Women's Aid
Jennifer Long	DARD
Henry Robinson	DRD Road Service
Vincent Ryan	Sperrin Lakeland H&SC Trust
Thelma Fitzgerald	Invest Northern Ireland
Seamus Gunn	T&EA
Iris Barker	WELB
Glynis Henry	WH&SSB
Cllr Robin Martin	Fermanagh District Council
Cllr Bertie Kerr	Fermanagh District Council
Cllr Harold Andrews	Fermanagh District Council
Cllr Gerry Gallagher	Fermanagh District Council
Cllr Paddy Gilgunn	Fermanagh District Council
Cllr Tom O'Reilly	Fermanagh District Council

Larne Development Partnership

Smiley Buildings
Victoria Road
Larne BT40 1RU
Tel: 028 2827 0742

Contact: Patricia Brennan

Members	Nominating Sector
Fred Dodds	Trade Union
William Breen	Trade Union
Jonathan Moore	UFU
Ivan McMullan	UFU
Dermot Murphy	FG Wilson
Norma Shannon	Larne Traders Forum
William Adamson	NIE
Geoffrey Kerr	Larne Community Development
Anne Marie McCartan	Barnardos
Karen Moore	Carnlough Community Group
Janetta Scott	Ballycarry Community Assoc.

Jacqueline Moore	Larne Millenium Initiative
Catherine Lynas	Inter Church Tuesday Group
Cllr Martin Wilson	Larne Borough Council
Cllr Brian Dunn	Larne Borough Council
Cllr Winston Fulton	Larne Borough Council
Geraldine Mulvenna	Larne Borough Council
Trevor Clarke	Larne Borough Council
Morris Crum	Larne Borough Council
Olive Hill	DETI
Pat Davison	NHSSB
Gilvert Bell	NEELB
Phyllis Craig	NIHE
John McKee	DARD
Inspector Noel Rogan	PSNI

Limavady LSP

7 Connell Street, Limavady BT49 0HA
Tel: 028 7776 0306
Contact: Martin Quinn

Members	*Nominating Sector*
Edwin Stevenson	Limavady Borough Council
Leslie Cubitt	Limavady Borough Council
Michael Coyle	Limavady Borough Council
Dessie Lowry	Limavady Borough Council
Marian Donaghy	Limavady Borough Council
Boyd Douglas	Limavady Borough Council
John Stevenson	Town Clerk and Chief Executive
Michael Gormley	WHSSB
Noel Hegarty	Invest NI
Brendan Doherty	NIHE
Bridie Mullin	WELB
Kevin Murphy	DARD
Wayne McCabe	PSNI
Joe O'Kane	T&EA
Damien Corr	Community/Voluntary
Brenda Macqueen	Community/Voluntary
Raymond Wright	Community/Voluntary
Raymond Craig	Community/Voluntary
Dolores O'Kane	Community/Voluntary
Gerard Lynch	Community/Voluntary
Martin Devlin	Business
Alistair Smyth	Business
Vacancy	Business
Alan Hunter	Agriculture
Nigel McLaughlin	Agriculture
Ian Buchanan	Rural Development
Ian Heaslett	Trade Union
Tony Squires	Trade Union

Lisburn Partnership

Lagan Valley Island, 1 The Island, Lisburn BT27 4RL
Tel: 028 9260 5406
Contact: Alice O'Kane

Members	*Nominating Sector*
Cllr Jim Dillon	Lisburn City Council
Ald Ivan Davis	Lisburn City Council
Cllr James Baird	Lisburn City Council
Cllr Betty Campbell	Lisburn City Council
Cllr Peter O'Hagan	Lisburn City Council
Cllr Paul Butler	Lisburn City Council
Cllr Gary McMichael	Lisburn City Council
Cllr James Tinsley	Lisburn City Council
Sarah Browne	Down Lisburn Trust
Monica Meehan	SEELB
Richard Christie	Invest NI
TBC	DEL
John Bourke	Probation Board for NI
Danny Cochrane	NIHE
Annie Armstrong	Twinbrook & Poleglass Forum
Fiona McCaulsand	Old Warren Partnership
Gillian Gibson	Footprints Women's Centre
John Lyttle	Voluntary Service Lisburn
Claire Hanna	Lisburn YMCA
Roy Hanna	TADA Rural Network
Joe Vallely	Surestart
Jean McQuitty	Chamber of Commerce
Eamon Foster	Glenwood Business Centre
Aisling Owens	Lisburn Enterprise Organisation
Bumper Graham	NIC ICTU
Jim Quinn	NIC ICTU
Gregg Shannon	UFU
Robert Poots	UFU

Magherafelt LSP

Council Offices, 50 Ballyronan Road, Magherafelt BT45 6EN
Tel: 028 7939 7979
Contact: Chris McCarney

Members	*Nominating Sector*
Cllr Thomas Catherwood	Magherafelt District Council
Cllr John Kelly	Magherafelt District Council
Cllr Kathleen Lagan	Magherafelt District Council
Cllr R A Montgomery	Magherafelt District Council
John McLaughlin	Magherafelt District Council
Cheryl Chambers	Invest NI
Michael McSorley	DOE Planning Service
Muriel Crockett	
Faith Wood	
Heather McAleese	UFU
Seamus Davey	

Chris McAleer	Citizens Advice Bureau
William McKeown	Yardmaster International
Gerry Kelly	NEELB
Brian Murray	Workspace Draperstown
Austin Kelly	
Gerard McGuckin	NWIFHE
Brendan Clarke	
Kevin Murphy	DARD
Elaine Doherty	NHSSB

Moyle LSP

Sheskburn House, 7 Mary Street, Ballycastle BT54 6QH
Tel: 028 2076 2225
Contact: Caitriona McNeill

Members	Nominating Sector
Donnell Black	Agricultural/Rural
Cllr Madeleine Black	Moyle District Council
Anna Burleigh	Trade Union
Marian Cavanagh	Voluntary/Community
Ann Creith	Voluntary/Community
Nigel Flynn	Statutory
Paul Gallagher	
Cllr Helen Harding	Moyle District Council
Cllr George Hartin	Moyle District Council
Sharon Kirk	Voluntary/Community
Richard Lewis	Moyle District Council
Andrew McAllister	Voluntary/Community
Eileen McAuley	Voluntary/Community
Gerry McCloskey	Statutory
Tommy McDonald	Private
Seamus McErlean	Agricultural/Rural
John McKee	Statutory
Cllr Oliver McMullan	Moyle District Council
Catrina McNiell	Agricultural/Rural
Anne Morrison	Moyle District Council
Esther Mulholland	
Mary O'Kane	Statutory
Trevor Robinson	Statutory
Ruth Wilson	Statutory

Newry and Mourne LSP

Town Hall, Newry BT35 6NR
Tel: 028 3026 6933
Contact: Una Magill

Members	Nominating Sector
Cllr Martin Cunningham	Newry and Mourne City Council
Cllr Michael Carr	Newry and Mourne City Council
Cllr Danny Kennedy	Newry and Mourne City Council
Cllr Isaac Hanna	Newry and Mourne City Council
Cllr Josephine O'Hare	Newry and Mourne City Council
Cllr Pat McElroy	Newry and Mourne City Council
Cllr Jim McCreesh	Newry and Mourne City Council
Cllr Brendan Curran	Newry and Mourne City Council
Jim Bagnall	NIHE
Mary Young	Invest NI
Eric Bowyer	Newry and Mourne HSS Trust
Billy Gamble	DRD
Helen McClenaghan	SELD
Vincent McKevitt	DARD
Mairead White	Atticall CA
Betty Moffett	Bessbrook Development
Damian McKevitt	Drumalane/Fathom Park
Maynard Hanna	Ulster British Forum
Tom McKay	ROSA Ltd
Marian Patterson	ICTU
Gordon Coulter	Toughglass
Jerome Mullen	Newry Chamber of Commerce
Michael Hughes	Vitafresh
Hugh O'Neill	LEADER
Sharon Porter	UFU
Paddy Tiernan	NIAPA
Tom Moore	ICTU
Evelyn Patterson	ICTU

Newtownabbey LSP

Mossley Hill, Newtownabbey BT36 5QA
Tel: 028 9034 0194
Fax: 028 9034 0196
Contact: David Hunter

Members	Nominating Sector
Ald W P Girvan	Council/Statutory
Cllr N P Hamilton	Council/Statutory
Ald R N Hutchinson	Council/Statutory
Cllr M F Langhammer	Council/Statutory
Cllr N P McClelland	Council/Statutory
Cllr K W Robinson	Council/Statutory
Cllr E Turkington	Council/Statutory
Cllr D E Walker	Council/Statutory
Veronica Gillen	Council/Statutory
Stella Hewitt	Council/Statutory
Keery Irvine	Council/Statutory
Maureen Wright	Council/Statutory
Anne Craven	Community Development Agency
Sheila McAvoy	Bridge Youth Centre
Sharon Parkes	Ballyclare Community Concerns
Victor Robinson	Community Development Agency
John Scott	Ballyduff Community Group
Brian Hunter	Business Representative
Roy Kennedy	UFU
Brian McAvoy	NIC/ICTU
Pat McCudden	Business Representative

441

John Ross	Business Representative
Mr Sandy Sherrard	UFU
Ms Marjorie Trimble	NIC/ICTU

North Down LSP

Town Hall, The Castle. Bangor BT20 4BT
Tel: 028 9127 8028
Contact: Jan Nixey

Members	Nominating Sector
David Jackson	Ulster Farmers Union
Janette McNulty	ICTU
John Graham	ICTU
Margaret Ferguson	Holywood Chamber of Trade
Ian Pennick	SIGNAL
Michael Dunlop	Bangor Chamber of Commerce Ltd
Patrick Gregg	North Down Community Network
Pat Bowen	NITAP
Stephen Dunlop	North Down Community Network
Christine Sloan	Bangor YMCA
James Henderson	Shopmobility Bangor
Ronnie Boyle	Age Concern
Aidan Ferguson	Invest NI
Sybil Skelton	SEELB
W Woodside	PSNI
Robert Mahaffy	NIHE
Cecil Worthington	UCHT
Cllr Alan Chambers	NDBC
Ald Leslie Cree	NDBC
Cllr Stephen Farry	NDBC
Ald Valerie Kingham	NDBC
Ald Ellie McKay	NDBC
Cllr Alan Graham	NDBC

Omagh LSP

Tourist Info Centre, 1 Market Street, Omagh BT78 1EE
Tel: 028 8225 0202
Contact: Harry Parkinson

Members	Nominating Sector
Sean Begley	Omagh District Council
Sean Clarke	Omagh District Council
Liam McQuaid	Omagh District Council
Gerry O'Doherty	Omagh District Council
Oliver Gibson	Omagh District Council
Reuben McKelvey	Omagh District Council
Johnny McLaughlin	Omagh District Council
Danny McSorley	Omagh District Council
Conor McGale	FOCUS/Urban Community
Monica Coyle	FORUM/Rural Community
Brigid McAleer	OWAN

Kieran Downey	CAP and Disabled Access Group
Marion Blayney	Early Years/Youth Sector
Paschal McCrumlish	Omagh Traders Association
Joe Doherty	DETI
Nicholas O'Shiel	Omagh Chamber of Commerce
Vincent Ryan	Sperrin Lakeland Trust
Rosemary Watterson	WELB
Sean Nugent	DARD
Alistair McKane	DOE/DSD
Eileen McFarline	NIPSA
Geraldine Keys	Unison
Gary Hawkes	UFU
Jim Maguire	Leader

Strabane LSP

47 Derry Road, Strabane BT82 8DY
Tel: 028 7138 1309
Fax: 028 7138 1346
E-mail: slsp@strabanedc.com
Web: www.strabanelsp.com
Project Officer: Patrick O'Doherty

Members	Nominating Sector
Cllr Ivan Barr	Strabane District Council
Mrs Anne Bradley	Strabane and District Community
Seamus Kelly	NIHE
Isaac Crilly	Tyrone Quality Livestock
Seamus Devine	Community/Voluntary Sector
Cllr John Donnell	Strabane District Council
Brian Forbes	Strabane Trade Union Council
Paul Gallagher	Community/Voluntary Sector
Mary Gormley	Invest NI
Cllr Derek Hussey	Strabane District Council
Conor Loughrey	c/o DRD Road Service
Paddy Mackey	WELB
Cllr Thomas McBride	Strabane District Council
Georgina McClintock	Sion Mills Community Association
Felix McCrossan	Strabane Trade Union Council
Cllr Claire McGill	Strabane District Council
Cllr Charlie McHugh	Strabane District Council
Cllr Eugene McMenamin	Strabane District Council
Eamonn McTernan	Strabane District Council
Christina Mullen	Strabane Enterprise Agency
Sean Nugent	DARD
Ken Strong	DSD
Howard Pollock	North Tyrone Ulster Farmers Union
Derek Reaney	Derry and Raphoe Action
Ken Sayers	Business in the Community
William Sayers	Ballylaw Regenereration Group
Gordon Spear	Castlederg Chamber of Commerce
Desmond Stewart	St Vincent de Paul

CHAPTER 11

Communications and the Media in Northern Ireland

EST?
1870
BELFAST TELEGRAPH

Belfast Telegraph Offices

The Media in Northern Ireland

Northern Ireland is a veritable hotbed of media and communications activity. Over the period of the last 30 years of political instability the province has attracted highly disproportionate international media attention, which has created a degree of media and communications sophistication normally associated with much larger places.

Northern Ireland has a comparatively high level of newspaper readership despite having a relatively small market. Surveys have shown that almost three quarters of the adult population read at least one paid-for newspaper daily – nearly 900,000 readers a day. There are only four home-produced daily papers in Northern Ireland – one evening, two morning and one Sunday. Of these regional titles only the nationalist Irish News is genuinely local in ownership, being controlled by a local business family. It's unionist counterpart the News Letter has been owned by the Mirror Group Newspapers since 1996. The main evening newspaper, the Belfast Telegraph, which was formerly owned by the Canadian-based Thomson Regional Newspapers, was sold to the English-based Trinity Holdings in 1995 before being recently acquired by Tony O'Reilly's Independent Newspaper Group. The Belfast Telegraph has a monopoly on the popular evening paper market and this is reflected in that it is one of Northern Ireland's most profitable businesses.

In addition to the four local newspapers there are Northern Ireland and Irish editions of many of the British papers. British newspapers, broadsheet and tabloid, are widely read in Northern Ireland. There is also some readership of the leading Southern Irish papers who have been making efforts to increase circulation in Northern Ireland in recent years.

Table 11.1 Circulation and Readership Figures for Northern Ireland Newspapers 2002		
Newspaper	**Circulation**	**Readership**
Belfast Telegraph	111,407	338,000
Sunday Life	96,093	313,000
Irish News	50,031	193,000
The News Letter	32,784	98,000
Source: Newspapers		

Just under 23m people in the UK hold a television licence. It's a dynamic industry, which continues to develop at a rapid rate. In addition to the five terrestrial channels, BBC1, BBC2, ITV, Channel 4 (S4C in Wales) and Channel 5, there are now hundreds more available on satellite, cable and digital – and a thriving independent production sector. The BBC is the UK's main public service broadcaster, run by a board of governors and funded by the licence fee. In addition to its two terrestrial channels, the corporation runs several digital services including BBC Knowledge and BBC Choice and a news channel, BBC News 24.

ITV is made up of 15 regionally based television companies and GMTV, the national breakfast-time service, licensed by the ITC and funded through advertising. The ITV Network Centre commissions and schedules programmes and, as with the BBC, 25 per cent of programmes must come from independent producers. There are over 1,500 independent production companies in the UK which generate over £1bn of programming.

Channel 4 and S4C (the fourth channel in Wales) were set up to provide programmes with a distinctive character and which appeal to interests not catered for by ITV and are also funded through advertising. S4C also has to provide a certain amount of Welsh language programming. Channel 4 has two digital services, FilmFour and E4, a youth entertainment channel.

Channel 5 began broadcasting in 1997 and now reaches about 80% of the population. It is advertising-funded and its remit is to show programmes of quality and diversity.

Satellite and cable services are funded mainly through subscriptions. The UK's largest supplier is BSkyB, with over 5m subscribers.

Digital television is expanding rapidly. It has been taken up by about a third of the population and offers the potential to access over 200 channels and other services including interactive TV and the Internet. The government expects all television transmissions to be digital between 2006 and 2010.

There are also several teletext services available through both the BBC and commercial TV which carry news, sport, travel, weather and other information and also offer subtitling.

BBC has a regional organisation In Northern Ireland, BBC NI, and in addition to showing network programmes has an autonomous news and current affairs department. The regional independent television company UTV, formerly known as Ulster Television, is the most popular of the two television stations and attracts around 43 per cent of the Northern Ireland television audience against 30 per cent for BBC.

BBC has also a local radio station with bases in both Belfast and the north west (BBC Radio Foyle). Independent radio has also a strong foothold in the local radio market.

An increasing proportion of Northern Ireland households now receive the Southern Irish national broadcaster RTE and there is an estimated subscriber base of 80,000 cable multi-channel services subscribers and a fast rising subscriber base for satellite services.

Northern Ireland is well served by a growing community of communications professionals beyond those in the media. Some of the world's largest communications organisations have Belfast offices in the fields of advertising, public relations and other communications services. With the establishment of Northern Ireland's own devolved government and administration this sector has continued to grow and to offer new specialisms.

Belfast-based advertising agencies have won international recognition for their work and some of Northern Ireland's leading communications businesses have established strong customer bases in markets outside Northern Ireland.

James Kerr, BBC Business Editor

Northern Ireland Newspapers
Local Daily/Sunday Newspapers

Belfast Telegraph
124–144 Royal Avenue
Belfast BT1 1EB
Tel: 028 9026 4000
Fax: 028 9055 4506
Web: www.belfasttelegraph.co.uk
E-mail: editor@belfasttelegraph.co.uk

Managing Director: Derek Carvell
Tel: 028 9026 4160

Editor: Ed Curran

Deputy Editor: Jim Flanagan

News Editor: Paul Connolly
Tel: 028 9026 4420
Fax: 028 9055 4540

Deputy News Editor: Ronan Henry

Features Editor: John Caruth

Political Correspondents: Noel McAdam, Chris Thornton

Business Editor: Nigel Tilson

Business Correspondents: Robin Morton, Maurice Neill

Agriculture Editor: Michael Drake

Education Correspondent: Kathryn Torney

Sports Editor: John Laverty

Assistant Editors (Sports): Graham Hamilton, John Taylor

Pictures Editor: Gerry FitzGerald

Commercial Director: John Leslie
Tel: 028 9026 4162
Fax: 028 9033 1332

Advertising Services: Simon Mann
Tel: 028 9026 4462
Fax: 028 9033 1332

Marketing Director: Ramsay Fawell
Tel: 028 9026 4138
Fax: 028 9055 4523

Circulation & Resources: Roy Lyttle
Tel: 028 9026 4022

Sales & Promotions Director: Richard McClean
Tel: 028 9026 4395
Fax: 028 9055 4577

Irish News
113–117 Donegall Street
Belfast BT1 2GE
Tel: 028 9032 2226
Fax: 028 9033 7505 (News)
Fax: 028 9033 7508 (Advertising)
E-mail: newsdesk@irishnews.com
Web: www.irishnews.com

Chairman: James Fitzpatrick
Managing Director:
Dominic Fitzpatrick

Editor: Noel Doran

Assistant Editor: Stephen O'Reilly

News Editor: Steven McCaffery
Tel: 028 9033 7544

Features: Joanna Braniff

Head of Content: Fiona McGarry

Business Editor: Gary McDonald

Pictures Editor: Brendan Murphy

Political Correspondent:
William Graham

Travel Editor: James Stinson

Sports Editor: Thomas Hawkins

Derry Correspondent:
Seamus McKinney
Tel: 028 7137 4455

Marketing Manager: Vacant
Tel: 028 9032 2226

Advertising Manager:
Paddy Meehan
Tel: 028 9033 7516
Fax: 028 9033 7508

Deputy Advertising Manager:
Sean Higgins
Tel: 028 9033 7509
Fax: 028 9033 7508

News Letter
46–56 Boucher Crescent
Belfast BT12 6QY
Tel: 028 9068 0000
Fax: 028 9066 4412
Web: www.newsletter.co.uk

Managing Director: Martin Gower

Editor: Vacant

Deputy Editor: Helen Greenaway

Night Editor: Vacant

News Editors: Ric Clarke,
Steven Moore
Tel: 028 9068 0005

Political Correspondent:
Stephen Dempster

Business Correspondent:
Adrienne McGill

Farming Life: David McCoy

Travel & Tourism: Geoff Hill

Women's Editor: Sandra Chapman

Sports Editor: Brian Millar

Pictures Editor: John Rush

Advertising Manager: Shona Rafferty
Tel: 028 9068 0000

Sales & Marketing Manager:
William Berkeley
Tel: 028 9068 0000

Promotions Manager: Catherine Byrne
Tel: 028 9068 0000

Classified Advertising:
Tel: 028 9031 3566
Fax: 028 9066 4420

Sunday Life
124–144 Royal Avenue
Belfast BT1 1EB
Tel: 028 9026 4300
E-mail: betty.arnold@belfasttelegraph.co.uk
Web: www.sundaylife.co.uk

Editor: Martin Lindsay
Tel: 028 9026 4309

Deputy Editor: Martin Hill
Tel: 028 9026 4305

News Editor: Martin Hill
Tel: 028 9026 4311

Women's Editor: Andrea McVeigh
Tel: 028 9026 4315

Pictures Editor: Darren Kidd
Tel: 028 9026 4317

Sports Editor: Jim Gracey
Tel: 028 9026 4308

Local Weekly Newspapers

Andersonstown News
2 Hannahstown Hill
Belfast BT17 0LY
Tel: 028 9061 9000
Fax: 028 9062 0602
Web: www.irelandclick.com

Editor: Robin Livingstone

Antrim Guardian
5 Railway Street
Antrim BT41 4AE
Tel: 028 9446 2624
Fax: 028 9446 5551

Editor: Liam Heffron

Antrim Times
22–24 Ballymoney Street
Ballymena BT43 6AL
Tel: 028 2565 3300
Fax: 028 2564 1517
Web: www.mortonnewspapers.com

Editor: Dessie Blackadder

Armagh Observer/
Armagh – Down Observer
Ann Street
Dungannon BT70 1ET
Tel: 028 8772 2557
Fax: 028 8772 7334

Editor: Desmond Mallon

Ballyclare Gazette
36 The Square
Ballyclare BT39 9BB
Tel: 028 9335 2967
Fax: 028 9335 2449
Web: www.ulsternet-ni.co.uk

Editor: Stephen Kernohan

Ballymena Chronicle
& Antrim Observer
Ann Street
Dungannon BT70 1ET
Tel: 028 8772 2557
Fax: 028 8772 7334

Editor: Desmond Mallon

Ballymena Guardian
83–85 Wellington Street
Ballymena BT43 6AD
Tel: 028 2564 1221
Fax: 028 2565 3920

Editor: Morris O'Neill

Ballymena Times
22–24 Ballymoney Street
Ballymena BT43 6AL
Tel: 028 2565 3300
Fax: 028 2564 1517
Web: www.mortonnewspapers.com

Editor: Dessie Blackadder

Ballymoney Times
6 Church Street
Ballymoney BT53 6HS
Tel: 028 2766 6216
Fax: 028 2766 7066
Web: www.mortonnewspapers.com

Editor: Lyle McMullen

Banbridge Chronicle
14 Bridge Street
Banbridge BT32 3JS
Tel: 028 4066 2322
Fax: 028 4062 4397

Editor: Bryan Hooks

The Banbridge Leader
25 Bridge Street
Banbridge BT32 3JL
Tel: 028 4066 2745
Fax: 028 4062 6378
Web: www.mortonnewspapers.com

Editor: Damien Wilson

Bangor Spectator Group
Spectator Buildings, 109 Main Street
Bangor BT20 4AF
Tel: 028 9127 0270
Fax: 028 9127 1544

Editor: Paul Flowers

Belfast News
46–56 Boucher Crescent
Belfast BT12 6QY
Tel: 028 9068 0000
Fax: 028 9066 4412

Editor: Julie McClay

Carrick Times
19 North Street
Carrickfergus BT38 7AQ
Tel: 028 9335 1992
Fax: 028 9336 9825

Editor: Terence Ferry

Carrickfergus Advertiser
31a High Street
Carrickfergus BT38 7AN
Tel: 028 9336 3651
Fax: 028 9336 3092

Editor: Stephen Kernohan

Coleraine Chronicle
20 Railway Road
Coleraine BT52 1PD
Tel: 028 7034 3344
Fax: 028 7034 3606

Editor: Anthony Toner

Coleraine Times
71 New Row, Market Court
Coleraine BT52 1EJ
Tel: 028 7035 5260
Fax: 028 7035 6186
Web: www.mortonnewspapers.com

Editor: David Rankin

Community Telegraph
124–144 Royal Avenue
Belfast BT1 1EB
Tel: 028 9026 4396
Fax: 028 9055 4585

Editor: Robin Young

The County Down Outlook
Castle Street, Rathfriland
Newry BT34 5QR
Tel: 028 4063 0202
Fax: 028 4063 1022

Editor: Stephen Patton

County Down Spectator
109 Main Street
Bangor BT20 4AF
Tel: 028 9127 0270
Fax: 028 9027 1544

Editor: Paul Flowers

Craigavon Echo
14 Church Street
Portadown BT62 3LQ
Tel: 028 3835 0041
Fax: 028 3835 0203

Editor: David Armstrong

The Cross Examiner
Rathkeeland House, 1 Blaney Road
Crossmaglen BT35 9JJ
Tel: 028 3086 8500
Fax: 028 3086 8580
E-mail: theexaminer@btconnect.com

Editor: Gerry Murray

The Democrat
Ann Street
Dungannon BT70 1ET
Tel: 028 8772 2557
Fax: 028 8772 7334

Editor: Desmond Mallon

Derry Journal
22 Buncrana Road
Londonderry BT48 8AA
Tel: 028 7127 2200
Fax: 028 7127 2260
Web: www.derryjournal.com

Editor-in-Chief: Patrick McArt

Derry News
26 Balliniska Road
Springtown Industrial Estate
Londonderry BT48 0LY
Tel: 028 7129 6600
Fax: 028 7129 6611

Editor: Garbhan Downey

Down Democrat
74 Margaret Street
Downpatrick BT30 6LZ
Tel: 028 4461 6600
Fax: 028 4461 6221
Web: www.downdemocrat.com

Editor: Terry McLaughlin

Down Recorder
2–4 Church Street
Downpatrick BT30 6EJ
Tel: 028 4461 3711
Fax: 028 4461 4624
Web: www.thedownrecorder.com

Editor: Paul Symington

The Dromore Leader
30a Market Square
Dromore BT25 1AW
Tel: 028 9269 2217
Fax: 028 9269 9260

Editor: Damien Wilson

Dungannon News and Tyrone Courier
58 Scotch Street
Dungannon BT70 1BD
Tel: 028 8772 2271
Fax: 028 8772 6171
Web: www.ulsternet-ni.co.uk

Editor: Ian Greer

Dungannon Observer
Ann Street
Dungannon BT70 1ET
Tel: 028 8772 2557
Fax: 028 8772 7334

Editor: Desmond Mallon

East Antrim Advertiser
8 Dunluce Street
Larne BT40 1JG
Tel: 028 2827 2303
Fax: 028 2826 0255

Editor: Hugh Vance

East Antrim Gazette
20 Main Street
Larne BT40 1SS
Tel: 028 2827 7450
Fax: 028 2826 7333

Editor: Stephen Kernohan

East Antrim Guardian
5 Railway Street
Antrim BT41 4AE
Tel: 028 9446 2624
Fax: 028 9446 5551

Editor: Liam Heffron

Fermanagh Herald
30 Belmore Street
Enniskillen BT74 6AA
Tel: 028 6632 2066
Fax: 028 6632 5521
Web: www.fermanaghherald.com

Editor: Pauline Leary

Fermanagh News
Ann Street
Dungannon BT70 1ET
Tel: 028 8772 2557
Fax: 028 8772 7334

Editor: Desmond Mallon

Impartial Reporter
8–10 East Bridge Street
Enniskillen BT74 7BU
Tel: 028 6632 4422
Fax: 028 6632 5047
Web: www.impartialreporter.com

Editor: Denzil McDaniel

Journal Extra
22 Buncrana Road
Londonderry BT28 8AA
Tel: 028 7127 2200
Fax: 028 7127 2270

Editor: Patrick McArt

The Lakeland Extra
8–10 East Bridge Street
Enniskillen BT74 7BT
Tel: 028 6632 4422
Fax: 028 6632 5047
Web: www.impartialreporter.com

Editor: Denzil McDaniel

Larne Gazette
20 Main Street
Larne BT40 1SS
Tel: 028 2827 7450
Fax: 028 2826 0733

Editor: Stephen Kernohan

Larne Times
8 Dunluce Street
Larne BT40 1JG
Tel: 028 2827 2303
Fax: 028 2826 0255
Web: www.mortonnewspapers.com

Editor: Hugh Vance

The Leader
20 Railway Road
Coleraine BT52 1PD
Tel: 028 7034 3344
Fax: 028 7034 3606

Editor: Jarvis Grant

Lisburn Echo
12a Bow Street
Lisburn BT28 1BN
Tel: 028 9260 1114
Fax: 028 9260 2904
Web: www.mortonnewspapers.com

Editor: David Fletcher

Londonderry Sentinel
Suite 3, Spencer House
Spencer Road,
Londonderry BT47 1AA
Tel: 028 7134 8889
Fax: 028 7134 1175
Web: www.mortonnewspapers.com

Editor: William Allen

Lurgan & Portadown Examiner
Ann Street
Dungannon BT70 1ET
Tel: 028 8772 2557
Fax: 028 8772 7334

Editor: Desmond Mallon

Lurgan Mail
4a High Street
Lurgan BT66 8AW
Tel: 028 3832 777
Fax: 028 3832 5271
Web: www.mortonnewspapers.com

Editor: Richard Elliott

Mid-Ulster Echo
52 Oldtown Street
Cookstown BT80 8EF
Tel: 028 8676 1364
Fax: 028 8676 4295
Web: www.mortonnewspapers.com

Editor: John Fillis

Mid-Ulster Mail
52 Oldtown Street
Cookstown BT80 8EF
Tel: 028 8676 2288
Fax: 028 8676 4295
Web: www.mortonnewspapers.com

Editor: John Fillis

Mid-Ulster Observer
Ann Street
Dungannon BT70 1ET
Tel: 028 8772 2557
Fax: 028 8772 7334

Editor: Desmond Mallon

Morton Newspapers Limited
2 Esky Drive
Carn Industrial Estate Area
Portadown BT63 5YY
Tel: 028 3839 3939
Fax: 028 3839 3940
Web: www.mortonnewspaper.com

Antrim/Ballymena Times,
Ballymoney/Coleraine Times,
Carrickfergus/Larne/Newtownabbey
Times, Roe Valley/Londonderry
Sentinel, Lurgan Mail, Portadown
Times, Castlereagh/Dromore/
Ulster Star, Banbridge Leader,
Tyrone Times, Magherafelt/
Cookstown Mid-Ulster Mail & Echo,
Craigavon Echo, Lisburn Echo,
North-West-free

Group Editor: David Armstrong

**Mourne Observer &
County Down News**
Castlewellan Road
Newcastle BT33 0JX
Tel: 028 4372 2666
Fax: 028 4372 4566

Editor: Terence Bowman

Newry Democrat
45 Hill Street
Newry BT34 1UF
Tel: 028 3025 1250
Fax: 028 3025 1017
Web: www.newrydemocrat.com

Editor: Caroline McEvoy

The Newry Reporter
4 Margaret Street
Newry BT34 1DF
Tel: 028 3026 7633
Fax: 028 3026 3157

Editor: Austin Smyth

Newtownabbey Times
14 Portland Avenue
Glengormley BT36 8EY
Tel: 028 9084 3621
Fax: 028 9083 7715

Editor: Judith Watson

**Newtownards Chronicle
& Co Down Observer**
25 Frances Street
Newtownards BT23 3DT
Tel: 028 9181 3333
Fax: 028 9182 0087

Editor: John Savage

Newtownards Spectator
109 Main Street
Bangor BT20 4AF
Tel: 028 9127 0270
Fax: 028 9127 1544

Editor: Paul Flowers

North Belfast News
253 Antrim Road
Belfast BT15 2GZ
Tel: 028 9058 4444
Fax: 028 9058 4450
Web: www.irelandclick.com

Editor: Sean Mag Uidhir

North West Echo
Suite 3, Spencer House
Spencer Road BT47 1AA
Tel: 028 7134 2226
Fax: 028 7134 1175
Web: www.mortonnewspapers.com

Editor: William Allen

Northern Constitution
20 Railway Road
Coleraine BT52 1PD
Tel: 028 7034 3344
Fax: 028 7034 3606

Editor: Maurice McAleese

Northern Newspaper Group
20 Railway Street
Coleraine BT52 1PD
Tel: 028 7034 3344
Fax: 028 7034 3606

Group Editor: Maurice O'Neil

Coleraine Chronicle, Ballymena
Guardian, Antrim Guardian,
Newtownabbey Guardian, The Leader,
Northern Constitution

Observer Group
Ann Street
Dungannon BT70 1ET
Tel: 028 8772 2557
Fax: 028 8772 7334

Group Editor: Desmond Mallon

Armagh/Down Observer, Dungannon
Observer, Fermanagh News, Lurgan
and Portadown Examiner,
Mid-Ulster Examiner

Portadown Times
14a Church Street
Portadown BT62 3LQ
Tel: 028 3833 6111
Fax: 028 3835 0203

Editor: David Armstrong

Roe Valley Sentinel
32A Market Square
Limavady BT49 0AA
Tel: 028 7772 2234
Fax: 028 7776 4090
Web: www.mortonnewspapers.com

Editor: William Allen

Strabane Chronicle
15 Upper Main Street
Strabane BT82 8AS
Tel: 028 7188 2100
Fax: 028 7188 3199

Editor: Michelle Canning

Strabane Weekly News
25–27 High Street
Omagh BT78 1BD
Tel: 028 8224 2721
Fax: 028 8224 3549

Editor: Wesley Atchison

Tyrone Constitution
25–27 High Street
Omagh BT78 1BD
Tel: 028 8224 2721
Fax: 028 8224 3549

Editor: Wesley Atchison

Tyrone Times
Unit B, Butter Market Centre
Thomas Street
Dungannon BT70 1HN
Tel: 028 8775 2801
Fax: 028 8775 2819

Editor: Paul McCreary

Ulster Farmer
Ann Street
Dungannon BT70 1ET
Tel: 028 8772 3153
Fax: 028 8772 7334

Editor: Desmond Mallon

Ulster Gazette and Armagh Standard
56 Scotch Street
Armagh BT61 7DQ
Tel: 028 3752 2639
Fax: 028 3752 7029

Editor: Richard Stewart

Ulster Herald
10 John Street
Omagh BT78 1DT
Tel: 028 8224 3444
Fax: 028 8224 2206
Web: www.ulsterherald.com

Editor: Daragh McDonald

Ulster Star
12a Bow Street
Lisburn BT28 1BN
Tel: 028 9267 9111
Fax: 028 9260 2904

Editor: David Fletcher

National Newspapers (Belfast Offices)

The Mirror
415 Holywood Road
Belfast BT42 2GU
Tel: 028 9056 8000
Fax: 028 9056 8005

Editor: Craig McKenzie

News Editor: Joe Gorrod

The Times
Queen's Building
Royal Avenue
Belfast BT1 5AU
Tel: 029 9023 3711
Fax: 028 9023 3588

Chief Ireland Correspondent:
Chris Walker

The Sunday Mirror
415 Holywood Road
Belfast BT4 2GU
Tel: 028 9056 8000
Fax: 028 9056 8005

Editor: John Cassidy

Sunday People
415 Holywood Road
Belfast BT4 2GU
Tel: 028 9056 8000
Fax: 028 9056 8005

Editor: Greg Harkin

The Sunday Times
72 High Street
Belfast BT1 2BE
Tel: 028 9043 8208
Fax: 028 9043 8209

Northern Ireland Editor: Liam Clarke

Republic of Ireland Newspapers (Belfast Offices)

Irish Independent
(Sunday Independent and Evening Herald)
7 North Street
Belfast BT1 1PA
Tel: 028 9032 9436
Fax: 028 9024 5726

Belfast Correspondent: John Devine

Irish Times
Fanum House
110 Great Victoria Street
Belfast BT2 7BE
Tel: 028 9032 3324
Fax: 028 9023 1469

Northern Editor: Gerry Moriarty

Sunday World
3–5 Commercial Court
Lower Donegall Street
Belfast BT1 2NB
Tel: 028 9023 8118
Fax: 028 9023 8120

Editor: Jim McDowell

News Agencies

Press Association
Queen's Building, Royal Avenue
Belfast BT1 1DB
Tel: 028 9024 5008
Fax: 028 9043 9246

Ireland Editor: Derick Henderson

Political Editor: Dan McGinn

Reuters
2nd Floor, Fanum House
Great Victoria Street
Belfast BT2 7BE
Tel: 028 9031 5253
Fax: 028 9031 0160

Correspondent: Alex Richardson

Magazines and Periodicals

Angling Ireland (Monthly)
124 Low Road, Islandmagee
Larne BT40 3RF
Tel: 028 9338 2610
Fax: 028 9338 2610
Web: www.anglingireland.com

Editor: Frank Quigley

An Phoblacht (Weekly)
535e Falls Road
Belfast BT11 9AA
Tel: 028 9060 0279
Fax: 028 9060 0207
Web: www.irlnet.com/aprn

Editor: Martin Spain

Auto Trader (Weekly)
James House, Dargan Crescent
Belfast BT3 9JU
Tel: 028 9037 0444
Fax: 028 9037 2828

Managing Director: Craig Stevens

BBM Magazine (Monthly)
2 Gregg Street
Lisburn BT27 5AN
Tel: 028 9266 7000
Fax: 028 9266 8005
Web: www.bbmag.com

Editor: Judith Farrell

Belfast Magazine (Monthly)
5 Churchill Street
Belfast BT15 2BP
Tel: 028 9020 2100
Fax: 028 9020 2177
Web: www.glenravel.com
Editor: Joe Baker

BNIL - Bulletin of Northern Ireland Law (Monthly)
SLS Legal Publications Ltd
School of Law, Queen's University
Belfast BT7 1NN
Tel: 028 9027 3597
Fax: 028 9032 6308

Editor: Deborah McBride

The Big List (Fortnightly)
Flagship Media Group Ltd
48–50 York Street
Belfast BT15 1AS
Tel: 028 9031 9008
Fax: 028 9072 7800
Web: www.thebiglist.co.uk
Editor: Brendan McKeown

Business Eye (Monthly)
Buckley Publications
The Mount, 2 Woodstock Link
Belfast BT6 8DD
Tel: 028 9073 5859
Fax: 028 9073 5858
Web: www.businesseye.co.uk
Editor: Richard Buckley

Carsport Magazine (Monthly)
Greer Publications
5B Edgewater Business Park
Belfast Harbour Estate
Belfast BT3 9JQ
Tel: 028 9078 3200
Fax: 028 9078 3210
Editor: Patrick Burns

Catering & Licensing Review (Monthly)
Greer Publications
5B Edgewater Business Park
Belfast Harbour Estate
Belfast BT3 9JQ
Tel: 028 9078 3200
Fax: 028 9078 3210
Editor: Kathy Jensen

Chartered Institute of Transport
(Annual Review)
Mainstream Publications Ltd
139–140 Thomas Street
Portadown BT62 3BE
Tel: 028 3833 4272
Fax: 028 3835 1046
Web: www.mainstreampublishing.co.uk
Managing Editor: Helen Beggs

Cheltenham Racecourse
(Annual Review)
Mainstream Publications Ltd
139–140 Thomas Street
Portadown BT62 3BE
Tel: 028 3833 4272
Fax: 028 3835 1046
Web: www.mainstreampublishing.co.uk
Managing Editor: Helen Beggs

Church of Ireland Gazette (Weekly)
C of I Publishing Co
3 Wallace Avenue
Lisburn BT27 4AA
Tel: 028 9267 5743
Fax: 028 9266 7580
Web: www.gazette.ireland.anglican.org
Editor: Rev Canon Ian Ellis

Club Review
B101 Portview Trade Centre
Newtownards Road
Belfast BT4 1RX
Tel: 028 9045 9864
Fax: 028 9045 9034
E-mail: info@media-marketing.net
Editor: Harry Beckinsale

Constabulary Gazette (Monthly)
Ulster Journals Ltd
39 Boucher Road
Belfast BT12 6UT
Tel: 028 9068 1371
Fax: 028 9038 1915
Web: www.media-marketing.net
Editor: Bob Catterson

County Down Outlook
Castle Street
Rathfriland BT34 5QR
Tel: 028 4063 0202
Fax: 028 4063 1022
Editor: Stephen Patton

Elegant Style (Monthly)
CM&A
8 Dufferin Court
Dufferin Avenue
Bangor BT20 3BX
Tel: 028 9145 7554
Fax: 028 9145 7430
Editor: Margaret Henderson

Energy - Phoenix Gas (Annual)
Mainstream Magazines Ltd
139–140 Thomas Street
Portadown BT62 3BE
Tel: 028 3839 2000
Fax: 028 3835 1071
Web: mainstreampublishing.co.uk
Managing Editor: Karen McAvoy

Enterprise - Belfast–Dublin Train
(Quarterly)
Mainstream Magazines Ltd
139–140 Thomas Street
Portadown BT62 3BE
Tel: 028 3839 2000
Fax: 028 3835 1071
Web: mainstreampublishing.co.uk
Managing Editor: Karen McAvoy

Equestrian (Bi-monthly)
Mainstream Publications Ltd
139–140 Thomas Street
Portadown BT62 3BE
Tel: 028 3833 4272
Fax: 028 3835 1046
Web: mainstreampublishing.co.uk
Managing Editor: Phillip Hardy

Epsom Derby (Annual)
Mainstream Publications Ltd
139–140 Thomas Street
Portadown BT62 3BE
Tel: 028 3833 4272
Fax: 028 3835 1046
Web: mainstreampublishing.co.uk
Managing Editor: Helen Beggs

Export & Freight (8 issues pa)
Mainstream Publications Ltd
139–140 Thomas Street
Portadown BT62 3BE
Tel: 028 3833 4272
Fax: 028 3835 1046
Web: mainstreampublishing.co.uk
Managing Editor: Helen Beggs

Extraction Industry Ireland
(Annual Review)
Mainstream Publications Ltd
139–140 Thomas Street
Portadown BT62 3BE
Tel: 028 3833 4272
Fax: 028 3835 1046
Web: mainstreampublishing.co.uk
Managing Editor: Helen Beggs

Farmers' Journal - Impartial Reporter
(Weekly)
8–10 East Bridge Street
Enniskillen BT74 7BT
Tel: 028 6632 4422/425
Fax: 028 6632 5047
Web: www.impartialreporter.com
Editor: Denzil McDaniel

Farming Life - News Letter (Weekly)
46–56 Boucher Crescent
Belfast BT12 6QY
Tel: 028 9068 0033
Fax: 028 9066 4432

News Editor: David McCoy

Farm Week (Weekly)
Morton Newspapers Ltd
14 Church Street
Portadown BT62 3QU
Tel: 028 3833 9421
Fax: 028 3835 0203
Web: www.mortonnewspapers.co.uk

Editor: Hal Crowe

Food Technology & Packaging
(Quarterly)
Greer Publications
5B Edgewater Business Park
Belfast Harbour Estate
Belfast BT3 9JQ
Tel: 028 9078 3200
Fax: 028 9078 3210

Editorial Contact: Jackie Scott

Fortnight (Monthly)
11 University Road
Belfast BT7 1NH
Tel: 028 9023 2353
Fax: 028 9023 2650
Web: www.fortnight.org

Editor: Malachi O'Docherty

Funeral Times (Quarterly)
1 Annagh Drive
Portadown BT63 5WF
Tel: 028 3835 5060
Fax: 028 3833 6959

Editor: Ian Millen

Garage Trader (Quarterly)
Mainstream Publications Ltd
139–140 Thomas Street
Portadown BT62 3BE
Tel: 028 3833 4272
Fax: 028 3835 1046
Web: www.mainstreampublishing.co.uk

Managing Editor: Janice Uprichard

Getting Married in Northern Ireland
Mainstream Publications Ltd
139–140 Thomas Street
Portadown BT62 3BE
Tel: 028 3833 4272
Fax: 028 3835 1046

Web: www.mainstreampublishing.co.uk
Editor: Karen McAvoy

The Gown (Monthly during term)
c/o Students Union
Queen's University
University Road
Belfast BT7 1NF
Tel: 028 9032 4803
Fax: 028 9023 6900

Editor: Vicky McMahon

Guide to Industrial Estates (Quarterly)
Mainstream Publications Ltd
139–140 Thomas Street
Portadown, BT62 3BE
Tel: 028 3833 4272
Fax: 028 3835 1046

Web: www.mainstreampublishing.co.uk

Managing Editor: Helen Beggs

Home Life Magazine (Monthly)
42a High Street
Lurgan BT66 8AU
Tel: 028 3832 4006
Fax: 028 3832 5213

Editor: Margaret Kinsella

Horizon Magazine (Monthly)
Unit 11, Broomfield Industrial Estate
333 Crumlin Road
Belfast BT14 7EA
Tel: 028 9074 5573
Fax: 028 9074 5573

Editor: Eddie McAteer

Industrial & Manufacturing
Engineer (Quarterly)
Mainstream Publications Ltd
139–140 Thomas Street
Portadown BT62 3BE
Tel: 028 3833 4272
Fax: 028 3835 1046

Web: www.mainstreampublishing.co.uk

Managing Editor: Paul Beattie

Institute of Export (Annual Review)
Mainstream Publications Ltd
139–140 Thomas Street
Portadown BT62 3BE
Tel: 028 3833 4272
Fax: 028 3835 1046

Web: www.mainstreampublishing.co.uk

Managing Editor: Helen Beggs

Interview - Belfast International Airport
Magazine (Quarterly)
Mainstream Magazines Ltd
139–140 Thomas Street
Portadown BT62 3BE
Tel: 028 3839 2000
Fax: 028 3835 1071
Web: mainstreampublishing.co.uk

Managing Editor: Karen McAvoy

Ireland's Equestrian (Bi-monthly)
Mainstream Publications
139–140 Thomas Street
Portadown BT62 3BE
Tel: 028 3833 4272
Fax: 028 3835 1046
Web: mainstreampublishing.co.uk

Editor: Phillip Hardy

Ireland's Homes,
Interiors & Living (Monthly)
Unit 65, Dunlop Commercial Park
4 Balloo Drive
Bangor BT19 7QY
Tel: 028 9147 3979
Fax: 028 9145 7226

Senior Editor: Samantha Blair

Publisher: Mike Keenan

Ireland's Horse Trader (Bi-monthly)
Mainstream Publications Ltd
139-140 Thomas Street
Portadown BT62 3BE
Tel: 028 3833 4272
Fax: 028 3835 1046
Web: www.mainstreampublishing.co.uk

Editor: Phillip Hardy

Ireland's Pets (Bi-monthly)
Mainstream Publications Ltd
139-140 Thomas Street
Portadown, Co Armagh BT62 3BE
Tel: 028 3833 4272
Fax: 028 3835 1046
Web: www.mainstreampublishing.co.uk

Editor: Phillip Hardy

Irish Farmers Journal
Northern Ireland Editorial Office
69 Ballyrainey Road
Newtownards BT23 5AF
Tel: 028 9181 2054
Fax: 028 9182 0946

Editor: James Campbell

Irish Country Sports and Country Life
(Quarterly)
PO Box 62
Portadown BT62 1XP
Tel: 028 3885 1326/028 9048 3873
Fax:028 3885 2237/028 9048 0195

Editor: Emma Cowan

Keystone - Construction Industry
(Bi-monthly)
Flagship Media Group Ltd
48–50 York Street
Belfast BT15 1AS
Tel: 028 9031 9008
Fax: 028 9072 7800

Editor: Cathy Lang

LÁ (Irish Language Newspaper)
(Weekly)
Teach Basil, 2 Cnoc Bhaile hAnnaidh
Béal Feirste BT17 0LY
Tel: 028 9060 5050
Fax: 028 9060 5544
Web: www.nuacht.com

Eaghatoir: Ciarán Ó Pronntaigh

Licensed Catering News (LCN) (Monthly)
Ulster Magazines Ltd
8 Lowes Industrial Estate
31 Ballynahinch Road
Carryduff BT8 8EH
Tel: 028 9081 5656
Fax: 028 9081 7481

Editor: Linda Brooks

Materials Handling (Annual Review)
Mainstream Publications Ltd
139–140 Thomas Street
Portadown BT62 3BE
Tel: 028 3833 4272
Fax: 028 3835 1046

Web: www.mainstreampublishing.co.uk

Managing Editor: Helen Beggs

Neighbourhood Retailer & Forecourt
Technology (10 issues pa)
Penton Publications Ltd
Penton House, 38 Heron Road
Sydenham Business Park
Belfast BT3 9LE
Tel: 028 9045 7457
Fax: 028 9045 6611

Managing Editor: Bill Penton

New Houses In Northern Ireland
(Quarterly)
Mainstream Magazines Ltd
139–140 Thomas Street
Portadown BT62 3BE
Tel: 028 3839 2000
Fax: 028 3835 1071
Web: mainstreampublishing.co.uk

Managing Editor: Karen McAvoy

The Northern Builder Magazine
(Quarterly)
Unit 22, Lisburn Enterprise Centre
Ballinderry Road Industrial Estate
Lisburn BT28 2BP
Tel: 028 9266 3390
Fax: 028 9266 6242
Web: www.northernbuilder.co.uk

Editor: Alan Bailie

Northern Business Mail
(Bi-monthly)
Flagship Media Group Ltd
48–50 York Street
Belfast BT15 1AS
Tel: 028 9031 9008
Fax: 028 9072 7800

Editor: Michael Bashford

Northern Farmer (The Irish News)
(Weekly)
113–117 Donegall Street
Belfast BT1 2GE
Tel: 028 9032 2226
Fax: 028 9033 7451

Editor: John Manley

Northern Ireland Legal Quarterly
(Quarterly)
SLS Legal Publications Ltd
School of Law, Queen's University
Belfast BT7 1NN
Tel: 028 9027 3597
Fax: 028 9032 6308

Editor: Prof Brigid Hadfield

Northern Ireland Medicine Today
(Monthly)
Penton Publications Ltd
Penton House, 38 Heron Road
Sydenham Business Park
Belfast BT3 9LE
Tel: 028 9045 7457
Fax: 028 9045 6611

Managing Editor: Bill Penton

Northern Ireland Travel & Leisure
News (Monthly)
Unit 1, Windsor Business Park
16–18 Lower Windsor Avenue
Belfast BT9 7DW
Tel: 028 9066 6151
Fax: 028 9068 3819
Web: www.nitravelnews.com

Editor: Brian Ogle

Northern Ireland
Veterinary Today (Quarterly)
Penton Publications Ltd
Penton House, 38 Heron Road
Sydenham Business Park
Belfast BT3 9LE
Tel: 028 9045 7457
Fax: 028 9045 6611

Managing Editor: Brian McCalden

Northern Ireland
Visitors' Journal (Annual)
Penton Publications Ltd
Penton House, 38 Heron Road
Sydenham Business Park
Belfast BT3 9LE
Tel: 028 9045 7457
Fax: 028 9045 6611

Managing Editor: Bill Penton

Northern Woman (Monthly)
Greer Publications
5B Edgewater Business Park
Belfast Harbour Estate
Belfast BT3 9JQ
Tel: 028 9078 3200
Fax: 028 9078 3210

Editor: Stephanie Berkeley

Perspective - Royal Society of Ulster
Architects Journal (Bi-monthly)
Marlborough House
348 Lisburn Road
Belfast BT9 6GH
Tel: 028 9066 1666
Fax: 028 9068 1888

Editor: Wendy McCague

Plant & Civil Engineer (6 issues pa)
69 Glen Road
Comber BT23 5QS
Tel: 028 9187 2656

Editor: Michael McRitchie

Plumbing & Heating (Quarterly)
Mainstream Magazines Ltd
139–140 Thomas Street
Portadown BT62 3BE
Tel: 028 3839 2000
Fax: 028 3835 1071
Web: www.mainstreampublishing.co.uk

Managing Editor: Karen McAvoy

The Presbyterian Herald (10 issues pa)
Church House
Fisherwick Place
Belfast BT1 6DW
Tel: 028 9032 2284
Fax: 028 9024 8377
Web: www.presbyterianireland.org

Editor: Rev Arthur Clarke

Property News (Monthly)
1 Annagh Drive
Carn Industrial Estate
Portadown BT63 5RH
Tel: 028 3835 5060
Fax: 028 3833 6959

Editor: Graham Brown

Recruitment (Weekly)
48–50 York Street
Belfast BT15 1AS
Tel: 028 9031 9008
Fax: 028 9072 7800
Web: www.jobsnation.net

Editor: Steven Preston

Regional Film & Video (Monthly)
Flagship Media Group Ltd
48–50 York Street
Belfast BT15 1AS
Tel: 028 9031 9008
Fax: 028 9072 7800
Web: www.4rfv.co.uk

Editor: Gavin Bell

Retail Forecourt &
Convenience Store (Bi-monthly)
Ulster Magazines Ltd
Lowes Industrial Estate
31 Ballynahinch Road
Carryduff BT8 8EH
Tel: 028 9081 5656
Fax: 028 9081 7481

Editor: Linda Brooks

Retail Grocer (Monthly)
Ulster Magazines Ltd
Lowes Industrial Estate
31 Ballynahinch Road
Carryduff BT8 8EH
Tel: 028 9081 5656
Fax: 028 9081 7481

Editor: Linda Brooks

Specify (Construction Industry)
(Bi-monthly)
Greer Publications
5B Edgewater Business Park
Belfast Harbour Estate
Belfast BT3 9JQ
Tel: 028 9078 3200
Fax: 028 9078 3210

Editor: Billy McAllister

Team Talk (Gaelic Football) (Monthly)
8 Sperrin View, Lough Macrory
Omagh BT79 9NB
Tel: 028 8076 0769
Fax: 028 8076 0804

Editor: Kenneth Curran

Ulster Architect Magazine (Monthly)
Addemo Press Ltd
182 Ravenhill Road
Belfast BT6 8EE
Tel: 028 9073 1636
Fax: 028 9073 8927

Editor: Ann Davey Orr

Ulster Bride (Bi-Annual)
Ulster Journals Ltd
39 Boucher Road
Belfast BT12 6UT
Tel: 028 9068 1371
Fax: 028 9038 1915

Editor: Pauline Roy

Ulster Farmer (Weekly)
Observer Newspapers
Ann Street
Dungannon BT70 1ET
Tel: 028 8772 2557
Fax: 028 8772 7334

Editor: Desmond Mallon

ULSTER BUSINESS

Greer Publications
5B Edgewater Business Park
Belfast Harbour Estate
Belfast BT3 9JQ
Tel: 028 9078 3200
Fax: 028 9078 3210
Web: www.ulsterbusiness.com

Editor:
Russell Campbell

Published monthly, Ulster Business is
Northern Ireland's best known
business magazine. Highlighting the
issues that are dominating the world
of business in Northern Ireland, the
magazine is very widely read by senior
business people and policymakers all
over Northern Ireland.

Ulster Grocer (Monthly)
Greer Publications
5B Edgewater Business Park
Belfast Harbour Estate
Belfast BT3 9JQ
Tel: 028 9078 3200
Fax: 028 9078 3210

Editor: Kathy Jenson

Ulster Homes (Quarterly)
Ulster Journals Ltd
39 Boucher Road
Belfast BT12 6UT
Tel: 028 9068 1371
Fax: 028 9038 1915

Editor: Billy McAllister

Ulster Tatler Series (Monthly)
Ulster Journals Ltd
39 Boucher Road
Belfast BT12 6UT
Tel: 028 9068 1371
Fax: 028 9038 1915

Editor: Richard Sherry

Ulster Tatler Wine &
Dine Guide (Annual)
Ulster Journals Ltd
39 Boucher Road
Belfast BT12 6UT
Tel: 028 9068 1371
Fax: 028 9038 1915

Editor: Walter Love

United News - Farming (Monthly)
Greer Publications
5B Edgewater Business Park
Belfast Harbour Estate
Belfast BT3 9JQ
Tel: 028 9078 3200
Fax: 028 9078 3210

Editor: Kathy Jenson

Wedding Journal (Quarterly)
Penton Publications Ltd
Penton House, 38 Heron Road
Sydenham Business Park
Belfast BT3 9LE
Tel: 028 9045 7457
Fax: 028 9045 6611
Web: www.weddingjournalonline.com

Managing Editor: Bill Penton

Women's News (Monthly)
109–113 Royal Avenue
Belfast BT1 1FF
Tel: 028 9032 2823
Fax: 028 9043 8788

Publishers

Ambassador
Providence House
Ardenlee Street
Belfast BT6 8QJ
Tel: 028 9045 0010
Fax: 028 9073 9659
Web: www.ambassador-productions.com

Director: Samuel Lowry

Appletree Press Ltd
14 Howard Street South
Belfast BT7 1AP
Tel: 028 9024 3074
Fax: 028 9024 6756
Web: www.appletree.ie

Beyond the Pale Publications
2nd Floor, 2–6 Conway Street
Belfast BT13 2DE
Tel: 028 9043 8630
Fax: 028 9043 9707
Web: www.btpale.com

Blackstaff Press
Wildflower Way
Apollo Road
Belfast BT12 6TA
Tel: 028 9066 8074
Fax: 028 9066 8207
E-mail: info@blackstaffpress.com
Web: www.blackstaffpress.com

bmf Publishing
Deramore House
76 Main Street
Moira BT67 0LQ
Tel: 028 9261 9933
Fax: 028 9261 9951
E-mail: bmf@dnet.co.uk

bmf Publishing is a dynamic new publishing house specialising in factual information-packed books aimed at business and government both inside Northern Ireland and further afield.

Recent titles include:

- The Northern Ireland Yearbook 2003
- Energy Ireland Yearbook 2003
- The Governance of Northern Ireland
- A Guide to Doing Business in Northern Ireland.

bmf Publishing also offers a contract research and publishing facility to its growing client base.

All bmf publications will be available online in 2003.

BMG Publishing
5 Emerson House
14B Ballynahinch Road
Carryduff BT8 8DN
Tel: 028 9081 7333
Fax: 028 9081 7444

Campbell Visuals
14 West Bank Road
Belfast BT3 9JL
Tel: 028 9077 7700
Fax: 028 9077 7700
www.campbellvisuals.com

Colourpoint Books
Unit D5, Ards Business Centre
Jubilee Road
Newtownards BT23 4YH
Tel: 028 9182 0505
Fax: 028 9182 1900

Cottage Publications
Laurel Cottage
15 Ballyhay Road
Donaghadee BT21 0NG
Tel: 028 9188 8033
Fax: 028 9188 8063
E-mail: info@cottage-publications.com

Creagh Media Publications
644 Antrim Road
Belfast BT15 4EL
Tel: 028 9077 0776
Fax: 028 9077 2577
E-mail: creaghmedia7@netscapeonline.co.uk

Editoral Solutions
537 Antrim Road
Belfast BT15 3BU
Tel: 028 9077 2300
Fax: 028 9078 1356
E-mail: michael@editorialsolutions.com
Web: www.editorialsolutions.com

GCAS Publications
Russell Court
Lisburn Road
Belfast BT9 6AA
Tel: 028 9055 7700
Fax: 028 9024 5741
Web: www.gcasgroup.com
Managing Director:
Robin Hetherington

Greer Publications
5b Edgewater Business Park
Belfast Harbour Estate
Belfast BT3 9JQ
Tel: 028 9078 3200
Fax: 028 9078 3210

Guildhall Press
Unit 4, Community Service Units
Bligh's Lane
Londonderry BT48 0LZ
Tel: 028 7136 4413
Fax: 028 7137 2949
Web: www.ghpress.com

Linenhall Library
17 Donegall Square North
Belfast BT1 5GD
Tel: 028 9032 1707
Fax: 028 9043 8586
E-mail: info@linenhall.com

Locksley Press Ltd
10a Bridge Street
Lisburn BT28 1XY
Tel/Fax: 028 9260 3195
Freephone: 0800 9178104
Web: www.locksleybrief.co.uk

Mainstream Publications Ltd
139–140 Thomas Street
Portadown BT62 3BE
Tel: 028 3833 4272
Fax: 028 3835 1046
Web: www.mainstreampublishing.co.uk

Mathematics Publishing Co
45 Blackstaff Road
Clough
Downpatrick BT30 8SR
Tel: 028 4485 1211
Fax: 028 4485 1566

Medical Communications Ltd
Ulster Bank Building
142–148 Albertbridge Road
Belfast BT5 4GS
Tel: 028 9080 9090
Fax: 028 9080 9097

N.I. Media Ltd
41 Royal Avenue
Belfast BT1 5AB
Tel: 028 9058 5000
Fax: 028 9058 5001

Outlook Press
Castle Street
Rathfriland BT34 5QR
Tel: 028 4176 9995
Fax: 028 4063 1022

Penton Publications Ltd
Penton House, 38 Heron Road
Sydenham Business Park
Belfast BT3 9LE
Tel: 028 9045 7457
Fax: 028 9045 6611
E-mail: info@pentonpublications.co.uk

Tendering Services Ireland
Coolmaghery
156 Pomeroy Road, Donaghmore
Dungannon BT70 2TY
Tel: 028 8776 7313
Fax: 028 8776 7030
E-mail: enquiries@irishtendersdirect.com
Web: www.irishtendersdirect.com

tSO Ireland
(the Stationery Office)
16 Arthur Street
Belfast BT1 4GD
Tel: 028 9023 8451
Fax: 028 9023 5401
Web: www.ukstate.com

Ulster Historical Foundation
Balmoral Buildings
12 College Square East
Belfast BT1 6DD
Tel: 028 9033 2288
Fax: 028 9023 9885
E-mail: enquiry@uhf.org.uk
Web: www.ancestryireland.com

Ulster Magazines Ltd
Lowes Industrial Estate
31 Ballynahinch Road
Carryduff BT8 8EH
Belfast BT7 1PT
Tel: 028 9081 5656
Fax: 028 9081 7481

White Row Press
135 Cumberland Road
Dundonald
Belfast BT16 2BB
Tel: 028 9048 2586
Fax: 028 9079 5464
E-mail: whiterow@whiterow.freeserve.co.uk

WG Baird
Newpark Industrial Estate
Antrim BT41 2RS
Tel: 028 9446 3911
Fax: 028 9446 6250
E-mail: wgbaird@wgbaird.com
Web: www.wgbaird.com

Belfast Telegraph Printing Press

457

Television and Radio

Associated Press Television

Vision House
56 Donegall Pass
Belfast BT7 1BU
Tel: 028 9022 1555
Fax: 028 9023 5547

BBC

B B C Northern Ireland

British Broadcasting Corporation
Broadcasting House
Ormeau Avenue
Belfast BT2 8HQ
Tel: (028) 9033 8000
Fax: (028) 9033 3800

The Northern Ireland region of the
BBC broadcasts regional radio and
television programmes and
contributes to the BBC's United
Kingdom and World Services output.
BBC Radio Ulster broadcasts
6,119 hours of indigenous
programmes and the region transmits
736 hours of regional television per
year. BBC Foyle, based in Derry,
broadcasts 1,315 hours of
programmes per year.

National Governor BBC NI:
Professor Fabian Monds, CBE

Controller: Anna Carragher

Secretary, BBC NI: Mark Adair

Head of News and Current Affairs:
Andrew Colman

Head of Marketing and Development:
Peter Johnston

Head of Drama: Robert Cooper

Editor Foyle: Ana Leddy

Head of Finance and Business Affairs:
Crawford MacLean

Head of Personnel: Liz Torrans

Head of Programme Operations:
Stephen Beckett

Head of Entertainment: Mike Edgar

Head of Factual and Learning:
Bruce Batten

Head of Broadcasting: Tim Cooke

Let's Talk Studio, BBC

Press Office
Tel: 028 9033 8226/906
Fax: 028 9033 8279
Web: www.bbc.co.uk

Editors BBC NI:

Editor Sport: Edward Smith

Editor Music: Declan McGovern

Editor Specialist Factual:
Deirdre Devlin

Editor Entertainment: Alex Johnston

Editor Broadcasting: Fergus Keeling

Editor Learning Unit:
Kieran Hegarty

Editor New Media: David Sims

Editor Newsgathering:
Michael Cairns

Editor Popular Factual Unit:
Clare McGinn

News Correspondents:

Political Editor: Mark Davenport

Business Editor: James Kerr

Health Correspondent: Dot Kirby

Chief Security Correspondent:
Brian Rowan

Education & Arts Correspondent:
Maggie Taggart

Ireland Correspondents:
Denis Murray, Tom Coulter

Ireland Producer: Kevin Kelly

Sport Producer: Padraig Coyle

BBC Radio Foyle (MW 792, FM 93.1)

8 Northland Road
Londonderry BT48 7JD
Tel: 028 7137 8600
Fax: 028 7137 8666
Web: www.bbc.co.uk/northernireland
Managing Director: Ana Leddy
Head of News: Eimer O'Callaghan

BBC Radio Ulster (92.4/95FM)

Broadcasting House
Ormeau Avenue
Belfast BT2 8HQ
Tel: 028 9033 8000
Fax: 028 9033 8804 (General)
Fax: 028 9033 8806 (News)
Web: www.bbc.co.uk
Head of News and Current Affairs:
Andrew Colman

Belfast City Beat (FM 96.7)

50 Stranmillis Embankment
Belfast BT9 5DF
Tel: 028 9020 5967
Fax: 028 9020 0023
Web: www.citybeat.co.uk
Managing Director: John Rosborough

Channel 9 TV

Springrowth House
Ballinska Road
Springtown
Londonderry BT48 0LY
Tel: 028 7128 9900
Fax: 028 7128 9901
Fax: 028 7129 9911 (News)
Web: www.c9tv.tv

Station Manager: Gary Porter
News Editor: Jimmy Cadden

City Beat DJ, Kenny Tosh

Cool FM (FM 97.4)
Kiltonga Industrial Estate
Belfast Road
Newtownards BT23 4ES
Tel: 028 9181 7181
Fax: 028 9181 4974
Web: www.coolfm.co.uk

Managing Director: David Sloan

Downtown Radio
Kiltonga Industrial Estate
Belfast Road
Newtownards BT23 4ES
Tel: 028 9181 5555
Fax: 028 9181 8913 (General)
Fax: 028 9181 7878 (News)
Web: www.downtown.co.uk

Chairman: James Donnelly

Managing Director: David Sloan

News/Sports Editor: Harry Castles

Political Correspondent:
Eamonn Mallie

All Northern Ireland AM 102.6,
Derry FM 102.4,
Enniskillen & Omagh FM 96.6

GMTV Belfast ITN
Ascot House
24–31 Shaftesbury Square
Belfast BT2 7DB
Tel: 028 9023 0923
Fax: 028 9043 9395

Ireland Correspondent: Carl Dinnen
Tel: 028 9043 9138

Broadcast Journalists:
Siobhan McGarry, Peter Gregory

ITN
(Independent Television News)
Ascot House
24–31 Shaftesbury Square
Belfast BT2 7DB
Tel: 028 9023 0786
Fax: 028 9043 9395
Web: www.itn.co.uk

Ireland Correspondent: Mark Webster
Tel: 028 9023 0786

Video Journalist: Victoria Hawthorne
Tel: 028 9023 0786

Q97.2FM Causeway Coast Radio
24 Cloyfin Road
Coleraine BT52 2NU
Tel: 028 7035 9100
Fax: 028 7032 6666
Web: www.q97.2fm

Managing Director: Frank McLaughlin

Station Manager: David Devenney

News Editors: Bob McCracken,
Caroline Fleck

Q102.9 FM
The Riverside Suite
Old Waterside Railway Station
Duke Street
Londonderry BT47 6DH
Tel: 028 7134 6666
Fax: 028 7131 177

Managing Director: Frank McLaughlin

Station Manager: David Austin

News Editor: Roger Donnelly

Ulster Television plc
Havelock House
Ormeau Road, Belfast BT7 1EB
Tel: 028 9032 8122
Fax: 028 9024 605
Web: www.u.tv

Newsroom:
Tel: 028 9026 2000
Fax: 028 9023 8381

Press Office:
Tel: 028 9026 2187
Fax: 028 9026 2219

Chairman: John B McGuckian

Managing Director: John McCann

Head of News & Current Affairs:
Rob Morrison

Controller of Programming:
Alan Bremner

News Producer: Chris Hagan

Political Correspondent: Ken Reid

Sports Editor: Adrian Logan

Producer of 'Kelly': Patricia Moore

Editor of 'Insight': Trevor Birney

Head of Engineering: Bob McCourt

Head of Press & Public Relations:
Orla McKibbin

Lynda Bryans, UTV

Communications and Service Providers

Advertising Agencies

AndersonSpratt Group
Anderson House
409 Holywood Road
Belfast BT4 2GU
Tel: 028 9080 2000
Fax: 028 9080 2001
Web: www.asgh.com

Ardmore Advertising & Marketing Ltd
Ardmore House
Pavillions Office Park
Holywood BT18 9JQ
Tel: 028 9042 5344
Fax: 028 9042 4823
Web: www.ardmore.co.uk

A V Browne Advertising Ltd
46 Bedford Street
Belfast BT2 7GH
Tel: 028 9032 0663
Fax: 028 9024 4279
Web: www.avb.co.uk

Coey Advertising & Design
Victoria Lodge
158 Upper Newtownards Road
Belfast BT4 3EQ
Tel: 028 9047 1221
Fax: 028 9047 1509

Concept Advertising & Marketing
8 Glenshesk Park, Dunmurry
Belfast BT17 9BA
Tel: 028 9061 0508
Fax: 028 9030 0648

Design & Place Recruitment
Advertising
409 Holywood Road
Belfast BT4 2GU
Tel: 028 9080 2010
Fax: 028 9080 2011
Web: www.andersonspratt.com

McCANN ERICKSON

McCANN-ERICKSON BELFAST

McCann-Erickson
31 Bruce Street
Belfast
BT2 7JD
Tel: (028) 9033 1044
Fax: (028) 9033 1266
Website: www.mccann-belfast.com
E-mail: info@europe.mccann.com

Chief Executive
David Lyle

Executive Creative
Director
Julie Anne Bailie

World-Class Excellence is the
consistent product at
McCann-Erickson Belfast. As the
professional market-leader McCann is
far ahead in winning Effectiveness and
Creative Awards internationally.
Uniquely with in-house psychologists
to research, test and measure
effectiveness, McCann's creative
output dominates in both awareness
and the power to influence target
audiences.

McCann's full service expertise spans
in-house media (Universal McCann)
event management, sponsorship and
integrated marketing - but Chief
Executive David Lyle adds "creativity
is key" while Julie Anne Bailie,
Executive Creative Director stresses
that "engaging ideas are essential to
make integrated communications
come alive".

Fire imc
10 Dargan Crescent
Belfast BT3 9JP
Tel: 028 9077 4388
Fax: 028 9077 6906
Web: www.fireimc.co.uk

Fox Advertising
1 Union Buildings
Union Place
Dungannon BT70 1DL
Tel: 028 8772 2962
Fax: 028 8772 9719

GCAS Advertising Limited
Russell Court
38–52 Lisburn Road
Belfast BT9 6AA
Tel: 028 9055 7700
Fax: 028 9024 5741
Web: www.gcasgroup.com

Genesis Advertising Ltd
4 Mount Charles
Belfast BT7 1NZ
Tel: 028 9032 8737
Fax: 028 9031 2245
Web: www.genesis-advertising.co.uk

Higher Profile Advertising
74 Ballycrochan Road
Bangor BT19 6NF
Tel: 028 9127 1016
Fax: 028 9127 1016

KR Graphics
121 University Street
Belfast BT7 1HP
Tel: 028 9033 3792
Fax: 028 9033 0549
Web: www.krgraphics.co.uk

The Levy McCallum
Advertising Agency
10 Arthur Street
Belfast BT1 4GD
Tel: 028 9031 9220
Fax: 028 9031 9221
Web: www.levymccallum.co.uk

Millennium Advertising
& Marketing Ltd
Emerson House
14b Ballynahinch Road
Carryduff
Belfast BT8 8DN
Tel: 028 9081 5522
Fax: 028 9081 5351
Web: www.millennium-advertising.co.uk

WALKER COMMUNICATIONS

walker**communications**
design / advertising / web

The Old Post Office
43 High Street
Holywood, BT18 9AB

Tel: 028 9042 5555
Fax: 028 9042 1222
www.walkercommunications.co.uk

We don't do advertising...
We don't do design...
We don't do web...

We connect you with your customer
using powerful, distinctive
expressions, thrusting your business
into new realms of opportunity.

MRB Creative
24 College Gardens
Belfast BT9 6BS
Tel: 028 9066 3663
Fax: 028 9066 3600
Web: www.mrbcreative.com

Navigator Blue
The Baths
18 Ormeau Avenue
Belfast BT2 8HS
Tel: 028 9024 6722
Fax: 028 9023 1607
Web: www.navigatorblue.com

RLA Northern Ireland Limited
86 Lisburn Road
Belfast BT9 6AF
Tel: 028 9066 4444
Fax: 028 9068 3497
Web: www.rla.co.uk

TDP Advertising
76 University Street
Belfast BT7 1HE
Tel: 028 9032 2882
Fax: 028 9033 2727
Web: www.tdpadvertising.co.uk

Shandwick Design
425 Holywood Road
Belfast BT4 2GU
Tel: 028 9076 1007
Fax: 028 9076 1941
E-mail: 028 9076 3490
Web: www.belfastdesign.shandwick.com

Broadcasting and Studio Services

Associated Press Television
Vision House
56 Donegall Pass
Belfast BT7 1BU
Tel: 028 9022 1555
Fax: 028 9023 5547

Audio Processing Technology Ltd
Unit 6, Edgewater Road
Belfast BT3 9JQ
Tel: 028 9037 1110
Fax: 028 9037 1137

BBC Northern Ireland
Broadcasting House
25 Ormeau Avenue
Belfast BT2 8HD
Tel: 028 9033 8000
Fax: 028 9033 8800
Web: www.bbc.co.uk

BBC Radio Foyle
8 Northland Road
Londonderry BT48 7JD
Tel: 028 7137 8600
Fax: 028 7137 8666
Web: www.bbc.co.uk

Belfast City Beat
50 Stranmillis Embankment
Belfast BT9 5FL
Tel: 028 9020 5967
Fax: 028 9020 0023
Web: www.citybeat.co.uk

CASP Enterprises
4 Ballycrummy Road
Armagh BT60 4LB
Tel: 028 3752 3914
Fax: 028 3752 7100

CB Productions
31 Hillsborough Road
Carryduff BT8 8HS
Tel: 028 9081 4477
Fax: 028 9081 5976

Cool FM
Kiltonga Industrial Estate
Belfast Road
Newtownards BT23 4ES
Tel: 028 9181 7181
Fax: 028 9181 4974
Web: www.coolfm.co.uk

Downtown Radio Ltd
Kiltonga Industrial Estate
Belfast Road
Newtownards BT23 4ES
Tel: 028 9181 5555
Fax: 028 9181 8913
Web: www.downtown.co.uk

Duplitape
100 Duncairn Gardens
Belfast BT15 2GL
Tel: 028 9074 7411
Fax: 028 9029 9001

Elmstree Studio
12 Turmore Road
Newry BT34 1PJ
Tel: 028 3026 5913
Fax: 028 3026 5913

EMS The Studio
12 Balloo Avenue
Bangor BT19 7QT
Tel: 028 9127 4411
Fax: 028 9127 4412

Jingle Jangle
The Strand
156 Holywood Road
Belfast BT4 1NY
Tel: 028 9065 6769
Fax: 028 9067 3771

Laganside Studios Ltd
Units 2–3 Ravenhill Business Park
Ravenhill Road, Belfast BT6 8AW
Tel: 028 9045 0231
Fax: 028 9045 9499

Mach Two
412 Beersbridge Road
Belfast BT5 5EB
Tel: 08707 300030
Fax: 028 9047 1625

Q97.2FM
24 Cloyfin Road
Coleraine BT52 2NU
Tel: 028 7035 9100
Fax: 028 7032 6666
Web: www.q97.2fm

Q102.9FM
The Riverside Suite
The Old Waterside Railway Station
Duke Street
Londonderry BT47 6DH
Tel: 028 7134 4449
Fax: 028 7131 1177
Web: www.q102.fm

Radio Telefis Eireann
Fanum House
Great Victoria Street
Belfast BT2 7BE
Tel: 028 9032 6441
Fax: 028 9033 2222

TV3 Television Network
46 Bradbury Place
Belfast BT7 1RU
Tel: 028 9043 5465

UTV plc
Havelock House
Ormeau Road
Belfast BT7 1EB
Tel: 028 9032 8122
Fax: 028 9024 6695
Web: www.u.tv

Graphics, Multimedia and Communications

MORPHEUS MULTIMEDIA LTD

Regus House
33 Clarendon Dock
Laganside
Belfast BT1 3BG
Tel: 028 9051 1256
Fax: 028 9051 1201
Web: www.morpheus.ie
E-mail: morpheus@morpheus.ie

Morpheus Media specializes in CD-R Duplication, DVD, CD-Rom, Business Cards CDs and VHS 2 DVD.

We supply a fast, efficient, quality service from 1 unit upwards, 48 hour turnaround on up to 5,000 units.

All our services can be tailored to your needs.

Television, Film and Video Production

About Face Media
Townsend Enterprise Park
Townsend Street
Belfast BT13 2ES
Tel: 028 9089 4555
Fax: 028 9089 4502

Acron Film & Video Ltd
13 Fitzwilliam Street
Belfast BT9 6AW
Tel: 028 9024 0977
Fax: 028 9022 2309

Another World Productions
2nd Floor, 11 Lismore House
23 Church Street
Portadown BT62 3LN
Tel: 028 3833 2933
Fax: 028 3839 6941

Arcom Interactive
157 High Street
Holywood BT18 9HU
Tel: 028 9042 6334
Fax: 028 9039 7715

Brian Waddell Productions Ltd
Strand Studios, 5–7 Shore Road
Holywood BT18 9HX
Tel: 028 9042 7646
Fax: 028 9042 7922

Christian Communications Networks (Europe) Ltd
646 Shore Road
Whiteabbey BT37 0PR
Tel: 028 9085 3997
Fax: 028 9036 5536

Extreme Film & TV Productions Ltd
Crofton House
128 Warren Road
Donaghadee BT21 0DD
Tel: 028 9188 8900
Fax: 028 9188 8901

Macmillan Media
729 Lisburn Road
Belfast BT9 7GU
Tel: 028 9050 2150
Fax: 028 9050 2151

MGTV
Victoria House
1A Victoria Road
Holywood BT18 9BA
Tel: 028 9020 0060
Fax: 028 9059 2000

Miracles Production
154 Upper Newtownards Road
Belfast BT4 3EQ
Tel: 028 9047 3838
Fax: 028 9047 3839

Northland Broadcast
30 Chamberlain Street
Londonderry BT48 6LR
Tel: 028 7137 2432
Fax: 028 7137 7132

Nosedive Animation Studio
Units 2–3, Laganside Studio
Ravenhill Business Park
Belfast BT6 8AW
Tel: 028 9022 2410
Fax: 028 9022 2410

The Picturehouse
The Strand
156 Holywood Road
Belfast BT4 1NY
Tel: 028 9065 1111
Fax: 028 9067 3771

Stirling Productions Ltd
137 University Street
Belfast BT7 1HP
Tel: 028 9033 3848
Fax: 028 9024 9583

Straight Forward Film & Television Productions Ltd
Ground Floor, Crescent House
14 High Street
Holywood BT18 9AZ
Tel: 028 9042 6298
Fax: 028 9042 3384

Tyndall PR Productions
58 Edentrillick Road
Hillsborough BT26 6HS
Tel: 028 9268 9444
Fax: 028 9268 9224

Visionworks Television Ltd
Vision House, 56 Dongall Pass
Belfast BT7 1BU
Tel: 028 9024 1241
Fax: 028 9024 1777

Westway Film Production Ltd
32 Shipquay Street
Londonderry BT79 4SW
Tel: 028 7130 8383
Fax: 028 7130 9393

Public Relations/Public Affairs Consultancies

Aiken PR
Marlborough House
348 Lisburn Road
Belfast BT9 6GH
Tel: 028 9066 3000
Fax: 028 9068 3030

Anderson Spratt Group Public Relations
Hollywood House, Innis Court
High Street
Holywood BT18 9HT
Tel: 028 9042 3332
Fax: 028 9042 7730

Cactus PR & Communications Ltd
38 Heron Road
Belfast BT3 9LE
Tel: 028 9045 7700
Fax: 028 9045 6622

Carmah Communications
39a Main Street
Bangor BT20 5AF
Tel: 028 9127 5965
Fax: 028 9127 5284

Cherton Enterprise Limited
Korona
164 Upper Newtownards Road
Belfast BT4 3EQ
Tel: (028) 9065 4007
Fax: (028) 9065 4008
Website: www.cherton.co.uk

Citigate Northern Ireland Ltd
157–159 High Street
Holywood BT18 9HU
Tel: 028 9039 5500
Fax: 028 9039 5600

Compton Communications
17 Station Road
Holywood BT18 0BP
Tel: 028 9042 7949
Fax: 028 9042 8459
E-mail: john@comptoncom.co.uk

Cooper Keaney Communication Ltd
Unit 4, Riversedge
14 Ravenhill Road
Belfast BT6 8DN
Tel: 028 9020 3992
Fax: 028 9020 0430

Davidson Cockcroft Partnership
Bamford House
91–93 Saintfield Road
Belfast BT8 7HR
Tel: 028 9040 2296
Fax: 028 9040 2291

Doris Leeman Public Relations
27 Berwick View
Moira BT67 0SX
Tel: 028 9261 1044
Fax: 028 9261 1979

Franklin Creative Communications
Wellington House
39 Wellington Park
Belfast BT9 6DN
Tel: 028 9068 1041
Fax: 028 9068 7747

GCAS Public Relations Ltd
Russell Court
38–52 Lisburn Road
Belfast BT9 6AA
Tel: 028 9055 7777
Fax: 028 9023 0142

GCC Stormont Strategy Ltd
The Red Barn
Whiterock Road
Killinchy BT23 6PT
Tel: 028 9754 1899
Fax: 028 8754 1890

Icon Public Relations & Design
39 Wellington Park
Belfast BT9 6DN
Tel: 028 9068 1041
Fax: 028 9068 7747

Inform Communications

13 University Street
Belfast BT7 1FY
Tel: 028 9023 3550
Fax: 028 9033 1017

John Laird Public Relations Ltd
104 Holywood Road
Belfast BT4 1NU
Tel: 028 9047 1282
Fax: 028 9065 6022

WEBER SHANDWICK

425 Holywood Rd.
Belfast BT4 2GU
Tel: 028 9076 1007
Fax: 028 9076 1012

Managing Director:
Brenda Boal

The Belfast office of Weber
Shandwick was established in
1992. It is Northern Ireland's
largest public relations,
interactive marketing and
visual communications company.

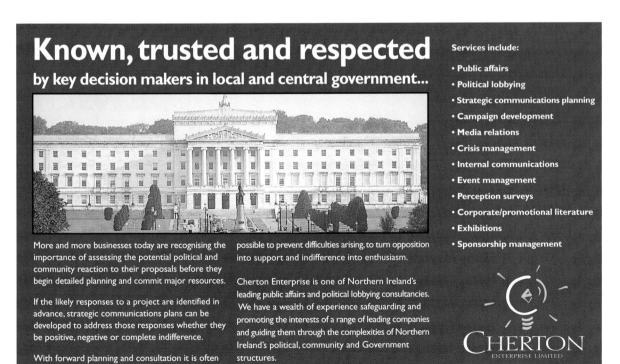

CROCKARD COMMUNICATIONS

CROCKARD
COMMUNICATIONS

Crockard Communications
36 Martinez Avenue
Belfast
BT5 5LY
Tel / Fax: (028) 9087 7290
Email: info@crockard.co.uk

Joanne
Crockard
Managing
Director

Crockard Communications delivers effective, creative PR/communications for private and public sector clients.

The business is led by Joanne Crockard, MIPR, Dip.Man (OUBS), a journalist and PR consultant who specialises in dealing with challenging PR and communication briefs.

Joanne Crockard has worked with the news and business media locally and nationally for 20 years and is equally adept at handling major hard news developments, customer crises, or 'softer' news events such as product launches and events.

Media relations, crisis management, corporate communications, event and issues management, are the main services which this consultancy offers. Viridian, Phoenix Gas, Premier Power, Hilton Belfast are some of the blue chip companies she has advised and the anchor client of Crockard Communications is the cross-border government agency, The Ulster-Scots Agency.

Lagan Consulting (Public Affairs)

Deramore House
76 Main Street
Moira BT67 0LQ
Tel: 028 9261 3216
Fax: 028 9261 9951
E-mail: owen.mcquade@laganconsulting.com

Life Communications

46 Bedford Street
Belfast BT2 7FF
Tel: 028 9024 8805
Fax: 028 9024 8806

Morrow Communications Ltd

Hanwood House
Pavillions Office Park
Kinnegar Drive
Holywood BT18 9JQ
Tel: 028 9039 3837
Fax: 028 9039 3830

The PR Agency

721A Lisburn Road
Belfast BT9 7GU
Tel: 028 9022 2422
Fax: 028 9022 2423

Event Management Organisations

bmf Business Services

Deramore House
76 Main Street
Moira BT67 0LQ
Tel: 028 9261 9933
Fax: 028 9261 9951
E-mail: bmf@dnet.com

Class Acts Promotions

39 Wellington Park
Belfast BT9 6DN
Tel: 028 9068 1041
Fax: 028 9068 7747

Creative Events

1 Dublin Road
Belfast BT2 7HB
Tel: 028 9023 5001
Fax: 028 9023 5003

Happening Creative Communications

65 Eglantine Avenue
Belfast BT9 6EW
Tel: 028 9066 4020
Fax: 028 9038 1257

THE DISPLAY TEAM

International Exhibition, Conference and Creative Shopfitting Designers & Contractors

6 Greenway Industrial Estate
Conlig
Newtownards
BT23 7SU
Tel: 028 9127 5616
Fax: 028 9127 5612
E-mail: sales@thedisplayteam.co.uk
Web: www.thedisplayteam.co.uk

In the pursuit of excellence The Display Team combine first-class production and installation resources with craft and creative skills.
We have achieved a reputation second to none in the highly competitive display markets for Exhibition Stands, Conference Backdrops, Product Launches, Awards Ceremonies, Themed Interiors, Graphics etc.

We provide a total service from conception to completion, with each stage carefully controlled to ensure that each project is on time, within budget and to agreed specification. We work locally, nationally and internationally for a wide range of clients including many 'blue-chip' organisations.

Mitchell Kane Associates
The Technology Centre
Townsend Street
Belfast BT13 2ES
Tel: 028 9089 4504
Fax: 028 9089 4514

Morrow Communications Ltd
Hanwood House
Pavillions Office Park
Kinnegar Drive
Holywood BT18 9JQ
Tel: 028 9039 3837
Fax: 028 9039 3830

Project Planning International
Montalto Estate
Spa Road
Ballynahinch BT24 8PT
Tel: 028 9756 1993
Fax: 028 9756 5073

SR Events and PR
43 Coastguard Lane
Orlock
Bangor BT19 6LR
Tel/Fax: (028) 9188 8291
Email: SREventsandPR@aol.com

Conference Venues

The conference market in Northern Ireland is worth an estimated £5–6 million per annum equating to an approximate spend of £160 per delegate. Whilst the total UK conference market generates income of £6–7 billion, purpose built conference developments such as the Odyssey complex and the Waterfront Hall enable Northern Ireland to compete with other UK conference destinations, heightening the profile of Belfast and Northern Ireland as an attractive conference centre for international events, and generating greater economic revenue for the city.

A brief summary of some of Northern Ireland's premier conference venues follows below:

Note: all delegate figures are for theatre style conferences (rows of chairs without tables).

Belfast

Belfast Castle
Antrim Road
Belfast BT15 5GR
Tel: 028 9077 6925
Fax: 028 9037 0228

Contact: Brenda Toland, Manager

Facilities: Full range of audio-visual equipment

Max No of Delegates: 490

Belfast Waterfront Hall,
Conference & Concert Centre
2 Lanyon Place
Belfast BT1 3WH
Tel: 028 9033 4400
Fax: 028 9024 9862

Contact: Andrew Kyle,
Sales & Marketing Manager

Facilities: Full audio-visual range, simultaneous translation, sound & lighting, recording, broadcast facilities, ISDN.

Max No of Delegates: 2,000

Dukes
65–67 University Street
Belfast BT7 1HL
Tel: 028 9023 6666
Fax: 028 9023 7177

Contact: Yvonne McNally,
General Manager

Facilities: Audio-visual Equipment, OHP & screen, roving microphone, air conditioning.

Max No of Delegates: 150

Europa Hotel
Great Victoria Street
Belfast BT2 7AP
Tel: 028 9032 7000
Fax: 028 9032 7800

Contacts: Jo-Anne Crossley, Events Manager, Debbie Stevens, Events Co-ordinator

Facilities: ISDN facilities, Internet access, full range of audio-visual equipment, air conditioning, sound proofing.

Max No of Delegates: 1,480

JURYS INN BELFAST

Fisherwick Place
Great Victoria Street
Belfast
BT2 7AP
Tel: (+44 28) 9053 3500
Fax: (+44 28) 9053 3511
Website: www.jurysdoyle.com
Email: jurysinnbelfast@jurysdoyle.com

Located in the centre of Belfast, adjacent to the Opera House, the City Hall and the city's main commercial district, Jurys Inn Belfast is an ideal venue for board meetings, seminars, training, recruitment and press conferences. Three of the Inn's conference rooms are state-of-the-art, client-designed and client-driven Dedicated Meeting Rooms - now recognised as being the ultimate solution for small and medium-sized meetings.

Quotation and queries: Contact Jurys Inn Belfast directly or call the Jurys Doyle Central Conference Desk at 0845 3000165 or mail to conference@jurysdoyle.com

Fitzwilliam International Hotel
Belfast International Airport
Belfast BT29 4ZY
Tel: 028 9442 2033
Fax: 028 9442 3500

Contact: Laura Maxwell, Conference & Banqueting Co-ordinator

Facilities: Full range of audio-visual equipment

Max No of Delegates: 590

PARK AVENUE HOTEL

PARK
AVENUE
HOTEL

Park Avenue Hotel
158 Holywood Road
Belfast
BT4 1PB
Tel: (028) 9065 6520
Fax: (028) 9047 1417
Website: www.parkavenuehotel.co.uk
Email: frontdesk@parkavenuehotel.co.uk

The Park Avenue Hotel offers 56 ensuite bedrooms which are equipped with satellite televisions, direct dial telephones, modem connections, trouser press, iron, ironing board, tea and coffee making facilities, disabled facilities, free car parking and a fitness room.

The Griffin Restaurant offers an extensive menu to suit all tastebuds. Alternatively our Bistro menu is served daily in Gelston's Corner Bar.

Our brand new conference centre can accommodate just about any combination of meetings, seminars, lectures, exhibitions and launches. We have a variety of suites that can be adapted for your needs.

The Park Avenue Hotel is the closest hotel to Belfast City Airport and lies only 10 minutes from the heart of the city. The hotel is also in close proximity to the Odyssey Arena and the Waterfront Hall and has excellent links to the outer ring roads and all transport stations and ferry terminals

Hilton Belfast
2 Lanyon Place
Belfast BT1 3LP
Tel: 028 9025 7828
Fax: 028 9025 7830

Facilities: Fully equipped business & communications centre

Max No of Delegates: 400

Holiday Inn Express
Inex Conference Centre
106 University Street
Belfast BT7 1HP
Tel: 028 9031 1909
Fax: 028 9031 1910

Contact: Philip Rees, Commercial Director

Facilities: ISDN communication technology, photocopying, fax, and secretarial and catering services.

Max No of Delegates: 300

Queen's University of Belfast
University Road
Belfast BT7 1NN
Tel: 028 9024 5133
Fax: 028 9024 789

Contact: Julie McCrory, Conference Manager

Facilities: Range of audio-visual equipment, teleconferencing, PA system, catering.

Max No of Delegates: 900

Stormont Hotel
Upper Newtownards Road
Belfast BT4 3LP
Tel: 028 9065 1066
Fax: 028 9048 0240

Contact: Roslin Wilson, Sales Manager

Facilities: Full audio-visual range, blackout, natural light and air-conditioning.

Max No of Delegates: 400

The Wellington Park Hotel
21 Malone Road,
Belfast BT9 6RU
Tel: 028 9038 1111
Fax: 028 9066 5410

Contact: Tracy Cecil, Anne Johnston

Facilities: Full audio-visual range including latest state of the art equipment: Visualisor in the McWilliam suite, ISDN line, air conditioning, secretarial services, computer link ups.

Max No of Delegates: 350

Co Antrim

Ballygally Castle Hotel
Coast Road
Ballygally BT40 2QZ
Tel: 028 2858 3212
Fax: 028 2858 3681

Contact: Sheila Carr

Facilities: Full range of Audio-visual equipment

Max No of Delegates: 200

The Dunadry Hotel & Country Club
2 Islandreagh Drive
Dunadry BT41 2HA
Tel: 028 9443 4343
Fax: 028 9443 3389

Contact: John Mooney
Business Development Co-ordinator

Facilities: Full audio-visual range.

Max No of Delegates: 350

Ross Park Hotel
Business & Conference Centre
20 Doagh Road
Kells BT42 3LZ
Tel: 028 2589 1385
Fax: 028 2589 8178

Contact: Lesley Ramsey, Conference Manager.

Facilities: Audio-visual equipment, ISDN, air-conditioning, secretarial service, fax, photocopying, complete facilities for disabled delegates.

Max No of Delegates: 420

Templepatrick Hilton
Castle Upton Estate
Templepatrick, Co Antrim BT39 0DD
Tel: 028 9443 5500
Fax: 028 9443 5511

Contact: Wilma Lindsay, Conference & Banqueting Sales Manager

Facilities: Full line audio-visual range, ISDN line, modern line, business centre and PA system.

Max No of Delegates: 500

Templeton Hotel
882 Antrim Road
Templepatrick BT39 0AH
Tel: 028 9443 2984
Fax: 028 9443 3406

Contact: Claire Kerr
Conference and Banqueting Manager

Max No of Delegates: 250

Co Armagh

Armagh City Hotel
2 Friary Road
Armagh BT60 4FR
Tel: 028 3751 8888
Fax: 028 3751 2777

Contact: Gary Hynes
Conference and Banqueting
Sales Manager

Max No of Delegates: 1200

Carngrove Hotel
2 Charlestown Road
Portadown BT63 5PW
Tel: 028 3833 9222
Fax: 028 3833 2899

Contact: Mrs B Currie,
General Manager

Facilities: Range of
audio-visual equipment.

Max No of Delegates: 300

Seagoe Hotel
22 Upper Church Lane
Portadown BT63 5JE
Tel: 028 3833 3076
Fax: 028 3835 0210

Contact: Cathy McDowell

Facilities: Range of
audio-visual equipment.

Max No of Delegates: 300

Co Down

Burrendale Hotel & Country Club
51 Castlewellan Road
Newcastle BT33 0JY
Tel: 028 4372 2599
Fax: 028 4372 2328

Contact: Fiona O'Hare
Conference and Banqueting Manager

Max No of Delegates: 200

The Culloden Hotel
142 Bangor Road
Holywood BT18 0EX
Tel: 028 9042 5223
Fax: 028 9042 6777

Contact: Allyson Hastings,
Event Co-ordinator

Facilities: Full audio-visual range, complimentary parking, natural light, blackout, air conditioning.

Max No of Delegates: 300

Marine Court Hotel
The Marina
Bangor BT20 5ED
Tel: 028 9145 1100
Fax: 028 9145 1200

Facilities: Fax, photocopying, Internet access, and secretarial service.

Max No of Delegates: 450

Slieve Donard Hotel
Newcastle BT33 0AH
Tel: 028 4372 1066
Fax: 028 4372 4830

Contact: Nora Hannah,
Business Manager

Facilities: Full audio-visual range, air-conditioning, natural light and blackout.

Max No of Delegates: 1,515

Co Fermanagh

Killyhevlin Hotel
Dublin Road
Enniskillen BT74 76RW
Tel: 028 6632 3481
Fax: 028 6632 4726
Web: www.killyhevlin.com

Contact: David Morrison

Facilities: Fax, photocopying, OHP and screens.

Max No of Delegates: 300

Manor House Country Hotel
Killadeas
Irvinestown BT94 1NY
Tel: 028 6862 2200
Fax: 028 6862 1545

Contact: Bronagh Donnelly,
Functions Manager

Facilities: Fax, photocopying, OHP and screens.

Max No of Delegates: 400

Co Londonderry

City Hotel
Queen's Quay
Londonderry BT48 7AS
Tel: 028 7136 5800
Fax: 028 7136 5801

Contact: Colette Brennan,
Conference and Banqueting Manager

Max No of Delegates: 350

Everglades Hotel
Prehen Road
Londonderry BT47 2PA
Tel: 028 7134 6722
Fax: 028 7134 9200

Contact: Rodney Stewart,
Conference & Banqueting Manager

Facilities: Full audio-visual range, natural light, blackout and air-conditioning.

Max No of Delegates: 640

Inn at the Cross
171 Glenshane Road
Londonderry BT47 3EN
Tel: 028 7130 1480
Fax: 028 7130 1394

Contacts: Muriel or Ivan Millar,
Hotel Proprietors.

Conference and Banqueting
Co-Manager: Matt Doherty

Facilities: Selection of audio-visual equipment, microphones, photocopying, and fax.

Max No of Delegates: 300

TOWER HOTEL DERRY

Tower Hotel Derry
★★★★ (4 Star RAC)
Butcher Street
Londonderry
BT48 6HL
Tel: (028) 7137 1000
Fax: (028) 7137 1234
Website: www.towerhotelgroup.com
Email: reservations@thd.ie

General Manager
Ian Hyland

Tower Hotel Derry provides exceptional conference facilities, including a fully equipped business centre with four meeting rooms, including a prestigious boardroom, and a conference and banqueting suite catering for up to 300 guests.

Radisson Roe Park
Roe Park
Limavady BT49 9LB
Tel: 028 7772 2222
Fax: 028 7772 2313

Contact: Kerrie McCauley,
Event Co-ordinator

Facilities: Extensive range of audio-visual equipment, stage, and microphone.

Max No of Delegates: 1,090

Co Tyrone

Fir Trees Hotel
Dublin Road
Strabane BT82 9EA
Tel: 028 7138 2382
Fax: 028 7138 3116

Contact: Tracy Smullen,
General Manager

Max No of Delegates: 300

Glenavon House Hotel
52 Drum Road
Cookstown BT80 8JQ
Tel: 028 8676 4949
Fax: 028 8676 4396

Contact: Paula Wilson, Manager

Facilities: Fax, photocopying, audio-visual equipment, and secretarial services.

Max No of Delegates: 400

Silver Birch Hotel
5 Gortin Road
Omagh BT79 7DH
Tel: 028 8224 2520
Fax: 028 8224 9061

Contact: Harriet Robinson,
Receptionist/Function Co-ordinator.

Facilities: OHP, range of audio-visual equipment.

Max No of Delegates: 420

Printers

Dargan Press Ltd
5 Round Tower Centre
Dargan Crescent
Belfast BT3 9JP
Tel: 028 9077 4478
Fax: 028 9077 4771

Dorman & Sons Ltd
Unit 2, 2a Apollo Road
Boucher Road
Belfast BT12 6BF
Tel: 028 9066 6700
Fax: 028 9066 1881

Graham & Sons Ltd
51 Gortin Road
Omagh BT79 7HZ
Tel: 028 8224 9222
Fax: 028 8224 9886

Johnston Printing Ltd
Mill Road
Kilrea BT51 5RJ
Tel: 028 2954 0312
Fax: 028 2954 1070
Web: www.johnston-printing.co.uk

LM Press Ltd
47 High Street
Lurgan BT66 8AH
Tel: 028 3832 2412
Fax: 028 3832 1820

Limavady Printing Co Ltd
26c Catherine Street
Limavady BT49 9DB
Tel: 028 7776 2051
Fax: 028 7776 2132
Web: www.limprint.com

Northern Whig
107 Limestone Road
Belfast BT15 3AH
Tel: 028 9035 2233
Fax: 028 9035 2181

Print-N-Press
Hamilton House
Foyle Road
Londonderry BT48 6SR
Tel: 028 7126 3868
Fax: 028 7137 1817

Priory Press
31a Hibernia Street
Holywood BT18 9JE
Tel: 028 9042 2918
Fax: 028 9042 7030

Graphic Designers

Ardmore Design
Ardmore House
Pavillions
Holywood BT18 9JQ
Tel: 028 9042 5344
Fax: 028 9042 4823
Web: www.ardmore.co.uk

Catalyst
95 University Street
Belfast BT7 1HP
Tel: 028 9043 8925
Fax: 028 9032 8839
E-mail: info@catalystdesign.co.uk
Web: www.catalystdesign.co.uk

Coppernoise
Unit 5-6 Ormeau Business Park
8 Cromac Avenue
The Gasworks
Belfast BT7 2JA
Tel: 028 9031 1933
Fax: 028 9031 1541
E-mail: info@coppernoise.com
Web: www.coppernoise.com

Darragh Neely Associates
Ama Communication Centre
Newtownards Road
Bangor BT19 7TA
Tel: 028 9151 6034
Fax: 028 9147 2797
Web: www.darraghneelyassociates.com

GCAS Design
Russell Court
38–52 Lisburn Road
Belfast BT9 6AA
Tel: 028 9055 7700
Fax: 028 9024 5741
E-mail: design@gcasgroup.com
Web: www.gcasgroup.com

IPR Communications Group
27 Shore Road
Holywood BT18 9HX
Tel: 028 9042 5412
Fax: 028 9042 7094
E-mail: ipr@d-n-a.net

KR Graphics
121 University Street
Belfast BT7 1HP
Tel: 028 9033 3792
Fax: 028 9033 0549

Leslie Stannage Design
93 Botanic Avenue
Belfast BT7 1JN
Tel: 028 9023 7377
Fax: 028 9033 0549

Rocket
3 Pavilions Office Park
Kinnegar Drive
Holywood BT18 9JQ
Tel: 028 9022 7700
Web: www.rocket-design.com

Slater Design
The Old Sorting Office
Strand Avenue
Holywood BT18 9AA
Tel: 028 9042 1122
Fax: 028 9042 1133

TDP Advertising
75 University Street
Belfast BT7 1HE
Tel: 028 9032 2882
Fax: 028 9033 2727
E-mail: mail@tdpadvertising.co.uk
Web: www.tdpadvertising.co.uk

Signage

SIGNS EXPRESS

creating signs that create business

Signs Express (Belfast C.W.)
Unit 14
Abbey Enterprise Park
Mill Road
Newtownabbey
BT36 7BA
Tel: (028) 9086 5647
Fax: (028) 9086 9224
Email: belfast@signsexpress.co.uk
Website: www.signsexpressirl.com

Brendan O'Donnell
Managing Director

- Interior Signs
- Exterior Signs
- Vehicle Livery
- Exhibition Displays
- Window Graphics
- Banners
- Health & Safety
- Full Colour Images

Signs Express (Belfast) opened in August 1999 and has already established its reputation as a professional sign company supplying clients including British Telecom, The Odyessy Arena, Harry Corry, Mercedes and Subway.

New Media

Internet Access Service Providers (ASPs)

Note: The listing below is for Northern Ireland based Internet access providers who provide access to the Internet. Internet service providers (ISPs) offer access through leased lines and provide hosting and design services.

BTNI
Riverside Tower
5 Lanyon Place
Belfast BT1 3BT
Tel: 0800 800 800
(Business Enquiries)
Tel: 028 9032 7327
(General Switchboard)
Web: www.bt.com

Firenet Internet
Knockmore Industrial Estate
Moira Road
Lisburn BT28 2EJ
Tel: 028 9267 0600
Fax: 028 9267 0916
Web: www.firenet.co.uk

Nevada tele.com
1 Cromac Avenue
Belfast BT7 2JA
Tel: 0808 140 1400
Fax: 028 9095 9401
Web: www.nevadatele.com

The Internet Business
Holywood House
1 Innis Court
Holywood BT18 9HF
Tel: 028 9042 4190
Fax: 028 9042 4709
Web: www.tibus.net

Unite Solutions
Edgewater Road
Belfast BT3 9JQ
Tel: 028 9077 7338
Fax: 028 9077 7313
Web: www.unite.net

UTV Internet
31 Bruce Street
Belfast BT2 7JD
Tel: 0845 2470000
Fax: 028 9020 1203
Web: www.u.tv

Website Hosting and Design

Note: the above ISPs all offer web site development and design services as do most advertising agencies and some PR agencies. The listings below are companies whose main business is website design.

Aurion
Laganside Studios
Ravenhill Business Park
Belfast BT6 8AW
Tel: 028 9045 5244
Fax: 028 9045 3157
Web: www.aurion.co.uk

Biznet Solutions
133–137 Lisburn Road
Belfast BT9 7AG
Tel: 028 9022 3224
Fax: 028 9022 3223
Web: www.biznet-solutions.com

Create Focus
Unite 36
Ledcom Industrial Estate
Bank Road
Larne BT40 3AW
Tel: 028 2827 5018
Fax: 028 2827 5188
Web: www.creatfocus.com

Memsis
2A Derryvolgie Avenue
Belfast BT9 6FL
Tel: 028 9080 6999
Fax: 028 9080 6060
Web: www.memsis.com

Net Works
Russell Court
38–52 Lisburn Road
Belfast BT9 6AA
Tel: 028 9055 7700
Fax: 028 9024 5741
Web: www.networksforyou.co.uk

Parc Computing Limited
Enkalon Business Centre
25 Randalstown Road
Antrim BT41 4LJ
Tel: 028 9442 9242
Fax: 028 9442 9253
Web: www.parc-computing.co.uk

Revelations Internet.com
27 Shaftesbury Square
Belfast BT2 7DB
Tel: 028 9032 0337
Fax: 028 9032 0432
Web: www.revelationsinternet.com

Sugarcube
1B Castle Street
Carrickfergus BT38 7BE
Tel: 028 9332 9662
Fax: 028 9335 5507
Web: www.sugarcube.co.uk

Other Media Organisations

Independent Television Commission
Albany House
75 Great Victoria Street
Belfast BT2 7AF
Tel: 028 9024 8733
Fax: 028 9032 2828

Institute of Public Relations (IPR)
c/o Happening Creative
Communications
65 Eglantine Avenue
Belfast BT9 6EW
Tel: 028 9066 4020
Fax: 028 9038 1257
Web: www.happen.co.uk

Northern Ireland Film Commission
21 Ormeau Avenue
Belfast BT2 8HD
Tel: 028 9023 2444
Fax: 028 90239918
Web: www.nifc.co.uk

Northern Ireland Government Affairs Group
c/o Conor McGrath
Lecturer in Political Communication
University of Ulster, Jordanstown
Newtownabbey BT37 0QB
Tel: 028 9036 6178
Fax: 028 9036 6872

Media and Communications Training

Lagan Consulting (Public Affairs Training)
Deramore House
76 Main Street
Moira BT67 0LQ
Tel: 028 9261 9933
Fax: 028 9261 9951
E-mail: info@laganconsulting.com

Northern Visions
4 Lower Donegall Place
Belfast BT1 2FN
Tel: 028 9024 5495
Fax: 028 9032 6608
Web: www.northernvisions.org

University of Ulster
School of Design and Communication
York Street
Belfast BT15 1ED
Tel: 028 9032 8515
Fax: 028 9032 1048

University of Ulster
School of Media and Performing Arts
Cromore Road
Coleraine BT37 0QB
Tel: 028 7032 4196
Fax: 028 7032 4964

AndersonSpratt Group Public Relations
Hollywood House
Innis Court
High Street
Holywood BT18 9HT
Tel: 028 9042 3332
Fax: 028 9042 7730

Macmillan Media
729 Lisburn Road
Belfast BT9 7GU
Tel: 028 9050 2150
Fax: 028 9050 2151

Photographic Libraries

Chris Hill Photographic
17 Clarence Street
Belfast BT2 8DY
Tel: 028 9024 5038
Fax: 028 9023 1942
Web: www.scenic-ireland.com

Pacemaker Press
787 Lisburn Road
Belfast BT9 7GX
Tel: 028 9066 3191
Fax: 028 9068 2111
Web: www.pacemakerpressintl.com

Esler Crawford Photography
37A Lisburn Road
Belfast BT9 7AA
Tel: 028 9032 6999
Fax: 028 9033 1542

Roger Kinkead Photo Library
20 Lynden Gate
Portadown BT63 5YH
Tel: 028 3839 4553

CHAPTER 12

Representative Groups and Associations

Introduction

Northern Ireland has a vast number of representative groups and associations, large and small, commercial and not-for-profit, covering a wide spectrum of the economic and social life of its people. The main groups are listed A–Z below under appropriate categories.

These listings have been extensively researched but they are by no means exhaustive.

Some organisations may fall into more than one categorisation due to the breadth of their activities.

Business, Trade Associations and Representative Bodies

Anglo North Irish Fish Producers Organisation Limited
The Harbour, Kilkeel BT34 4AX
Tel: 028 4176 2855
Fax: 028 4176 4904
Chief Executive: Alan McCulla

Arts and Business
53 Malone Road, Belfast BT9 6RY
Tel: 028 9066 4736
Fax: 028 9066 4500
Director: Alice O'Rawe

Association of Landscape Contractors of Ireland
4 Gorse Hill, Moneyrea,
Co Down BT23 6XA
Tel: 028 9044 9024
Fax:028 9044 9024
Web: www.alci.org.uk
Chairman: Laurence McMinn

Association of Municipal Engineers
C/o McAdam Design, 18 Victoria Avenue, Newtownards BT23 7EB
Tel: 028 9181 2831
Fax: 028 9181 1847
Secretary: Mark Oliver

Association of Northern Ireland Colleges
Unit 3, The Sidings Business Park Antrim Road, Lisburn BT28 3AJ
Tel: 028 9262 7512
Fax: 028 9262 7594
Web: www.anic.ac.uk
Chief Executive: John Patterson

Association for Residential Care
47 Henderson Avenue,
Cavehill Road
Belfast BT15 5FL
Tel: 028 9022 9020
Fax: 028 9020 9300
Manager: Siobhan Bogues

Belfast Naturalists Field Club
78 Kings Road, Belfast BT5 6JN
Tel: 028 90 797 155
Honorary Secretary:
Professor Richard S J Clarke

British Association of Social Workers BASW (NI)
216 Belmont Road, Belfast
BT4 2AT
Tel: 028 9067 2247
Fax: 028 9065 6273
Web: www.basw.co.uk
Professional Officer:
Eileen Ashenhurst

British Cattle Society
22 Ballynahonemore Road,
Armagh BT60 1JD

British Council
2nd Floor, Norwich Union House
7 Fountain Street, Belfast BT1 5EG
Tel: 028 9024 8220
Fax: 028 9023 7592
Web: www.britishcouncil.co.uk
Director: Ann Malamah-Thomas

Chambers of Commerce

Chambers of Commerce represent the business community in Northern Ireland at a local level and are active in dealing with local issues which have implications for the commercial life of a locality. The Northern Ireland Chamber of Commerce and Industry and the regional Chamber of Commerce network currently represents more than 4000 businesses in Northern Ireland.

Members are drawn from every sector of the business community including senior management from major industrial sites, smaller scale retailers and service providers. As well as being an authentic voice for local business and undertaking the representational work which that entails, local Chambers of Commerce are very active in charitable work in their respective areas

The Northern Ireland Chamber of Commerce and Industry
Chamber of Commerce House
22 Great Victoria Street
Belfast BT2 7BJ
Tel: 028 9024 4113
Fax: 028 9024 7024
Web: www.northernirelandchamber.com
President: Victor Haslett

Antrim Borough Chamber of Commerce
C/o Antrim Enterprise Agency Ltd
58 Greystone Road, Antrim
BT41 1JZ
Tel: 028 9446 7774
Fax: 028 9446 7292
Contact: Ms Siobhan Donnelly

Armagh Chamber of Commerce
18 Russell Street, Armagh
BT61 9BB
Tel: 028 3752 3163
Fax: 028 3741 5111
Contact: Mr Godfrey Abbott

Ballycastle Chamber of Commerce
A D McAuley Newsagent, 31 Castle
Street, Ballycastle BT54 6AS
Tel: 028 2076 2648
Contact: Mr Fintan McAuley

Ballymena Chamber of Commerce
C/o Bank of Ireland, 153
Church Street
Ballymena BT43 6DG
Tel: 028 2565 2443
Fax: 028 2564 8138
Contact: Mr Gerry Lawn

Ballymoney Chamber of Commerce
C/o Thomas Taggart & Sons
Solicitors
27 Church Street
Ballymoney BT53 6HF
Tel: 028 2766 0940
Fax: 028 2766 4708
Contact: Mr Lewis Richards

Bangor Chamber of Commerce
C/o 65b Main Street
Bangor BT20 5AF
Tel: 028 9146 0035
Fax: 028 9146 0035
Contact: Mr Evan Ward

Belleek Chamber of Commerce
Main Street, Belleek BT93 3FX
Tel: 028 6865 8942
Contact: Ms Bridie Gormley

Carrickfergus Chamber of Commerce
C/o Wadsworth Estate
Tower House, 33–35 High Street,
Carrickfergus BT38 7AN
Tel: 028 9336 0707
Fax: 028 9336 7368
Contact: Mr Peter Wadsworth

Castlederg Chamber of Commerce
11–12 The Diamond
Castlederg BT81 7AR
Tel: 028 8167 1974
Fax: 028 8167 1974
Contact: Mr Gordon Speer

Coleraine Chamber of Commerce
2 Abbey Street, Coleraine
BT52 1DS
Tel: 028 7034 4067
Fax: 028 7032 1416
Contact: Prof. C. Barnett

Cookstown Chamber of Commerce
PO Box 27, Cookstown
Tel: 028 8676 6023
Contact: Mr Raymond McGarvey

Downpatrick Chamber of Commerce
C/o J Laverty & Co,
18 English Street
Downpatrick BT30 6AB
Tel: 028 4461 6413
Contact: Mrs Eileen Laverty

Dromore Chamber of Commerce
C/o 21 Bridge Street, Dromore
BT25 1AN
Tel: 028 9269 9478
Contact: Mrs Erica Pepper

Enniskillen Chamber of Commerce
C/o Old Gate Lodge, Drumawill,
Enniskillen BT74 5NQ
Tel: 028 6632 4595
Contact: Mrs Jennifer McCrea

Fivemiletown Chamber of Commerce
Four Ways Hotel, 41 Main Street,
Fivemiletown BT75 0PG
Tel: 028 8952 1260
Fax: 028 8952 2061
Contact: Mr Brunt

Holywood Chamber of Trade and Commerce
C/o David Ferguson & Associates
45 Church View, Holywood
BT18 9DP
Tel: 028 9042 7135
Fax: 028 9042 7943
Contact: Ms Margaret Ferguson

Irvinestown Chamber of Commerce
C/o Irvinestown Rectory, Enniskillen
Road, Irvinestown BT94 1GL
Tel: 028 6862 1225
Contact: Rev Raymond Thompson

Kilkeel Chamber of Commerce
C/o Dunnes Stores, 18 Greencastle
Street, Kilkeel BT34 4BH
Tel: 028 4176 2265
Contact: Mr Tom O'Hanlon

Limavady Chamber of Commerce, Industry & Trade
C/o Main Street, Limavady
BT49 0EY
Tel: 07713 273123
Contact: Mr Douglas Miller

Lisburn Chamber of Commerce
3a Bridge Street, Lisburn
BT28 1XZ
Tel: 028 9266 6297
Contact: Mr Sam Johnston

Lisnaskea Chamber of Commerce
C/o Market Yard, Lisnaskea
BT92 0PL
Tel: 028 6772 1081
Fax: 028 6772 1088
Contact: Mr John McIlwaine

Londonderry Chamber of Commerce
1 St Columbs Court, Bishop Street,
Derry BT48 6PT
Tel: 028 7126 2379
Fax: 028 7128 6789
Contact: Mr Niall Birthistle

Magherafelt Chamber of Commerce
37 Rainey Street
Magherafelt BT45 5AB
Tel: 028 7963 2392
Contact: Mr Michael McLarnon

Newcastle Chamber of Commerce

C/o 51 Main Street
Newcastle BT33 0AD
Tel: 028 4372 4903
Fax: 028 4372 4263
Contact: Mr Peter Law

Newry Chamber of Commerce

C/o Town Hall, Bank Parade
Newry BT35 6HR
Tel: 028 3025 0303
Contact: Mr Gerard O'Hare

Omagh Chamber of Commerce

2nd Floor, 33 Market Street
Omagh BT78 1EE
Tel: 028 8225 9595
Fax: 028 8225 9596
Contact: Mr Nicholas O'Shiel

Portadown Chamber of Commerce

C/o Alexander Gill & Sons Ltd
42 Meadow Lane
Portadown BT62 3NJ
Tel: 028 3833 2875
Contact: Mr Robin Gill

Portrush Chamber of Commerce

C/o 110 Dunluce Road
Portrush BT56 8NB
Tel: 028 7082 2783
Fax: 028 7082 4524
Contact: Mr David Alexander

Portstewart Chamber of Commerce

C/o 17 Ballyleese Park
Portstewart BT55 7QA
Tel: 028 7083 2960
Contact: Mr Peter Bayliss

Strabane Chamber of Commerce

C/o Safeway (Ireland) Ltd
2 Branch Road, Strabane BT82
Tel: 028 7138 2365
Contact: Mr Hugh Kelly

Carrickfergus Gasworks Preservation Society

6 Twinburn Crescent, Monkstown
Newtownabbey BT37 0ER
Tel: 028 90 862 974

Coal Advisory Service (NI)

Unit 18a Lowes Industrial Estate
31 Ballynahinch Road
Carryduff, Belfast BT8 8EH
Tel: 028 9081 2182
Fax: 028 9081 2145
Director: Ken Thompson

CBI (Confederation of British Industry)

Scottish Amicable Building
11 Donegall Square South
Belfast BT1 5JE
Tel: 028 9032 6658
Fax: 028 9024 5915
Web: www.cbi.org.uk
Chairman: Dr Ian McMorris
Vice Chairman: Mark Ennis
Director: Nigel Smyth

CBI is a leading umbrella organisation and representative group for industry and business in Northern Ireland. It coordinates policy positions on behalf of industry for presentation to government on a range of major issues.

CBI / IBEC Joint Business Council

Also based at the address above and at the offices of the CBI counterpart in the Republic of Ireland, IBEC.
Contact: William Poole, Business Development Director

Centre for Competitiveness

Interpoint, 20–24 York Street
Belfast BT15 1AQ
Tel: 028 9046 8362
Fax: 028 9046 8361
Web: www.cforc.org
Chief Executive: Bob Barbour

The Centre for Competitiveness is a private sector, not for profit, membership organisation actively supporting the development of an internationally competitive economy in Northern Ireland.

Construction Employers Federation

143 Malone Road, Belfast BT9 6SU
Tel: 028 9087 7143
Fax: 028 9087 7155
Web: www.cefni.co.uk
Managing Director: Mr W A Doran

CONSTRUCTION INDUSTRY TRAINING BOARD

Nutts Corner Training Centre
17 Dundrod Road, Crumlin
BT29 4SR
info@citbni.org.uk
www.citbni.org.uk
Tel: (028) 9082 5466
Fax: (028) 9082 5693

Chief Executive:
Allan McMullen

As one of the largest employers in the Province, employing around 47,000 people and with a turnover in excess of £1.6bn per annum, the construction industry makes a major contribution to the economy of the Province.

The importance of training cannot be ignored in such a large and diverse industry. The construction industry in Northern Ireland is unique in having a structure of contractors and sub-contractors, many of whom are self employed or working in a small group. Therefore it is essential to have an effective umbrella organisation to be responsible for high quality training, which might not otherwise take place. The Construction Industry Training Board fulfils this role.

East Belfast Traders Association
Unit 1a, 321 Beersbridge Road
Belfast BT5 5DS
Fax Only: 028 9022 6464

Electrical Contractors Association
45 Sunningdale Park, Bangor
Tel: 028 9147 9527

Engineering Employers Federation
2 Greenwood Avenue, Belfast
BT4 3JL
Tel: 028 9059 5050
Fax: 028 9059 5059
Web: www.eef.org.uk
Director: Peter Bloch

Federation of Master Builders
42a–44a New Row
Coleraine BT52 1AS
Tel: 028 7034 0999
Fax: 028 7034 0998
Web: www.fmb.org.uk
Administrator: Jim Morrison

Federation of Small Businesses
20 Adelaide Street, Belfast
BT2 8GB
Tel: 028 9051 7024
Fax: 028 9051 7120
Web:www.nireland.policy@fsb.org.uk
NI Press Officer: Glyn Roberts

Federation of the Retail Licensed
Trade
91 University Street, Belfast
BT7 1HP
Tel: 028 9032 7578
Fax: 028 9032 7578
Web: www.ulsterpubs.com/
Chief Executive: Nicola Jamison

The Federation represents around
1,100 pubs, hotels and restaurants
in Northern Ireland.

Freight Transport Association Ltd
2–10 Duncrue Road, Belfast
BT3 9BP
Tel: 028 9074 5975
Fax: 028 9074 5979
Web: www.fta.co.uk
Manager: Chris Campbell

Institute of Directors
4 Royal Avenue, Belfast BT1 1DA
Tel: 028 9023 2880
Fax: 028 9023 2881
Web: www.iod.com
Chairman: Denis Rooney
Divisional Director: Linda Brown

Institute of Export (NI Branch)
Tel: 028 9146 2141
E-mail: j.stewart@denmanbrush.com
Chairperson: Mr Jim Stewart

Irish Guild of Master Craftsmen
123–125 Main Street
Bangor BT20 4AE

Irish Linen Guild
5c The Square
Hillsborough BT26 6AG
Tel: 028 9268 9999
Fax: 028 9268 9968
Web: www.irishlinen.co.uk
Director: Linda MacHugh

Founded in 1928, the Irish Linen
Guild is a promotionqal organisation
drawing its membership from all
sections of the Irish linen industry.

Irish Trade Board
53 Castle St, Belfast BT1 1GH

Knitwear, Footwear & Apparel Trades
(KFAT)
The Knitting Centre, 6 London
Road, Kilmarnock KA3 7AD
Tel: 01563 535 888

Livestock & Meat Commission for
Northern Ireland
Lissue House, 31 Ballinderry Road
Lisburn BT28 2FL
Tel: 028 9263 3000
Fax: 028 9263 3001
Web: www.lmcni.com
Chief Executive: David Rutledge

Mastic Asphalt Federation (NI)
C/o Mr H Crothers
Durastic Roofing & Cladding
12–16 Sanda Road, Whitehouse
Newtownabbey BT37 9UB
Tel: 028 9085 4515
Fax: 028 9085 4348

Momentum
(Formerly Northern Ireland Software
Federation)
123–137 York Street
Belfast BT15 1AB
Tel: 028 9033 3939
Fax: 028 9033 3454

National Association of Shopkeepers
and Self-Employed Business People
338a Beersbridge Road
Belfast BT5 5DT
Tel: 028 9045 9036

National Association for the Self
Employed
Tel: 028 9042 7797

National Farmers' Union
72 High Street, Newtownards
BT23 7HZ
Tel: 028 9181 4218
Fax: 028 9181 1574
Group Secretary: Ms HJ Murphy

National Federation of Retail
Newsagents
Yeoman House, 11 Sekforde Street,
London EC1
Tel: 020 7253 4225
Fax: 020 7250 0927

National House Building Council
59 Malone Road, Belfast BT9 6SA
Tel: 028 9068 3131
Fax: 028 9068 3258
Web: www.nhbc.co.uk
Regional Director: Tom Kirk

North Belfast Traders Association
Unit 3, North City Business Centre
Duncairn Gardens, Belfast
BT15 2GF

Northern Ireland Aerospace Consortium

Northern Ireland Technology Centre
Cloreen Park, Malone Road
Belfast BT9 5HN
Tel: 028 9027 4505
Fax: 028 9066 3715
E-mail: Sharon.devlin@niac.org.uk
Chairperson: Dr Paul Madden

Northern Ireland Agricultural Producers' Association

15 Molesworth St
Cookstown BT80 8NX
Tel: 028 8676 5700
Fax: 028 8675 8598
Chairman: Sean Clarke

Northern Ireland Amusement Caterers Trade Association

Hydepark Industrial Estate
58 Mallusk Road
Newtownabbey BT36 4PX
Tel: 028 9084 8731
Fax: 028 9083 3104
Secretary: Mr JH Sander

Northern Ireland Bankers' Association

Stokes House
17–25 College Square East
Belfast BT1 6DE
Tel: 028 9032 7551
Fax: 028 9033 1449
Contact: Bill McAlister

Northern Ireland Brickmakers' Association

61 Largy Road, Crumlin BT29 4RR

Northern Ireland Chamber of Trade

PO Box 444, Belfast BT1 1DY
Tel: 028 9023 0444
Fax: 028 9023 0444
Director: Joan Roberts

Northern Ireland Childminding Association

16–18 Mill St
Newtownards BT23 4LU
Tel: 028 9181 1015
Fax: 028 9182 0921
Web: www.nicma.org
Director: Bridget Nodder

Northern Ireland Consumer Committee for Electricity

Brookmount Buildings
42 Fountain Street, Belfast
BT1 5EE
Tel: 028 9031 1575
Fax: 028 9031 1741
Web: www.ofreg.nics.gov.uk
Chairperson: Felicity Huston

Northern Ireland Council for Ethnic Minorities

Ascot House
24–31 Shaftesbury Square
Belfast BT2 7DB
Tel: 028 9023 8645
Fax: 028 9031 9485
Executive Director: Patrick Yu

Northern Ireland Dairy Association

Quay Gate House, 15 Scrabo Street
Belfast BT5 4BD
Tel: 028 9045 2292
Fax: 028 9045 3373
Director: Paul Archer

Northern Ireland Dyslexia Association

17a Upper Newtownards Road
Belfast BT4 3HT
Tel: 028 9066 0111

Northern Ireland Fish Producers' Organisation

1 Coastguard Cottages, Harbour
Road, Portavogie
Newtownards BT22 1EA
Tel: 028 4277 1946
Fax: 028 4277 1696
E-mail: nifpo@aol.com
Chief Executive: Mr Richard James

Northern Ireland Food & Drink Association

Quay Gate House, 15 Scrabo Street
Belfast BT5 4BD
Tel: 028 9045 2424
Fax: 028 9045 3373
Web: www.nifda.co.uk
Director: Michael Bell

Northern Ireland Furniture Manufacturers Group

C/o Mr T Doak, Balmoral Furniture,
Moffett & Sons Ltd, Seymour Hill Mews
Dunmurry, Belfast BT17 9PW
Tel: 028 9030 1411
Fax: 028 9061 0785

Northern Ireland Grain Trade Association (NIGTA)

Cuinne na Chaireil, 27 Berwick
View, Moira BT67 0SX
Tel: 028 9261 1044
Fax: 028 9261 1979
E-mail: doris@leemanpr.demon.co.uk
Contact: Doris Leeman

Northern Ireland Heritage Gardens Committee

PO Box 252, Belfast BT9 6GY
Tel: 028 90 668 817
Contact: David Gilliland

Northern Ireland Hotels Federation

The Midland Building, Whitla Street
Belfast BT15 1JP
Tel: 028 9035 1110
Fax: 028 9035 1509
Web: www.nihf.co.uk
Director General: Janice Gault

NI Local Government Association

123 York Street, Belfast BT15 1AB
Tel: 028 9024 9286
Fax: 028 9023 3328
Email: hm@nilga.org.uk
Chief Executive: Heather Moorhead

Northern Ireland Interactive Multi Media Association (NIMA)

Regus Hse, 33 Clarendon Dock,
Belfast BT1 3BG
Tel: 028 9051 1226
Web: www.niima.ni.org
Contact: Dr Robert Bunn
NIMA has been established to
support the emerging multi media
industry in Northern Ireland.

Northern Ireland Master Butchers'
Association
38 Oldstone Hill
Muckamore BT41 4SB
Tel: 028 9446 5180
Fax: 028 9446 5180
Secretary: Mr H Marquess

Northern Ireland Master Plumbers'
Association
C/o Mr W Crawford
Crawford Sedgwick & Co
38 Hill Street
Belfast BT1 2LB
Tel: 028 9032 1731
Fax: 028 9024 7521
Secretary: Mr W Crawford

Northern Ireland Meat Exporters
Association
24 Ballydown Road
Banbridge BT32 3RP
Tel: 028 4062 6338
Fax: 028 4062 6083
Web: www.nimea.co.uk
Chief Executive: Cecil Mathers

Northern Ireland Museums Council
66 Donegall Pass, Belfast
BT7 1BU
Tel: 028 9055 0215
Fax: 028 9055 0216
Web: www.nimc.co.uk
Director: Chris Bailey

Northern Ireland Optometric Society
PO Box 20202, Banbridge
Co.Down BT32 4SD
Tel: 028 40 629 978
Fax: 028 90 629 978
General Secretary: Leanora Keating

Northern Ireland Quarry Owners'
Association
C/o Mr B Frair, Jackson Andrews,
Andras House, 60 Great Victoria St
Belfast BT2 7ET
Tel: 028 9023 3152
Fax: 028 9033 2757
E-mail: belfast@jackson-andrews.co.uk
Secretary: B Frair

Northern Ireland Seafood
Quay Gate House, 15 Scrabo St
Belfast BT5 4BD
Tel: 028 9045 2829
Fax: 028 9045 3373
Web: www.niseafood.co.uk
Chief Executive: Dennis Law

Northern Ireland Software Federation
(See under Momentum)

Northern Ireland Textile & Apparel
Association
5c The Square
Hillsborough BT26 6AG
Tel: 028 9268 9999
Fax: 028 9268 9968
Web: www.nita.co.uk
Director: Linda MacHugh.

Northern Ireland Timber Trade
Association
13 Churchill Drive
Carrickfergus BT38 7LH
Tel: 028 9336 2784
Secretary: Mr T G Rankin

Pharmaceutical Society
73 University Street, Belfast
BT7 1HL
Tel: 028 9032 6927
Fax: 028 9043 9919
Chief Executive: Sheila Maltby

Professional Craftsmen Association
14 Northland Row
Dungannon BT71 6AP
Tel: 028 8772 5377
Chairman: Paul Devlin

Retail Motor Industry Federation
107a Shore Road, Belfast
BT 15 3BB
Tel: 028 9037 0137
Fax: 028 9037 0706
Regional Manager: Noel Smyth

Royal Life Saving Society
4 Albert Drive, Belfast BT6 9JH
Tel: 028 9070 5644
Web: www.rlssdirect.co.uk
Contact: Jim McCurry

Social Economy Agency
45–47 Donegall Street
Belfast BT1 2FG
Tel: 028 9096 1115
Fax: 028 9096 1116
Regional Manager: Eamonn Donnelly

Ulster Archaeological Society
C/o Dept of Archaeology
Queen's University, Belfast BT7 1QF
Tel: 028 90 273 186

Ulster Chemists' Association
73 University Street, Belfast
BT7 1HL
Tel: 028 9032 0787
Fax: 028 9031 3737
President: Siobhan O'Reilly

Ulster Farmers' Union
475 Antrim Road, Belfast
BT15 3BJ
Tel: 028 9037 0222
Fax: 028 9037 1231
Chief Executive: Clarke Black
President: John Gilliland

Ulster Federation of Credit Unions
56 Sandy Row, Belfast BT12 5EW
Tel: 028 9023 6301
Co-ordinator: Gladys Copeland

Ulster Launderers' Association
C/o Patrick Bryson, Standard
Laundry
213 Donegall Avenue
Belfast BT12 6LU
Tel: 028 9032 7295
Fax: 028 9031 4026
Contact: Patrick Bryson

Ulster GAA Writers Association
20 Stewartstown Park
Belfast BT11 9GL
Tel: 028 9060 0833
Web: www.ulstergaawriters.com

Wildlife Trust
30 Claggan Lane
Cookstown BT80 8PX
Tel: 028 8676 3576
Web: www.wildlifetrusts.org

YMCA National Council
27–41 High St, Belfast BT1 2AB
Tel: 028 9032 7757
Fax: 028 9043 8809
Chief Executive: Stephen Turner

Professional Institutes and Associations

Architects Registration Board
8 Weymouth Street, London W1W 5BU
Tel: 020 7580 5861
Web: www.arb.org.uk
Chief Executive: Robin Vaughan

Association of Belfast Doctors on Call
The Old Casualty, Crumlin Road
Belfast BT14 6AB
Tel: 028 9074 4447
Fax: 028 9074 9999
Manager: Kerry Cavanan

Association of Chartered Certified
Accountants (ACCA)
29 Lincoln's Inn Fields
London WC2A 3EE
Tel: 020 7396 7000
Fax: 020 7396 7070
Email: info@accaglobal.com

Association of Consulting Engineers
(NI Branch)
C/o Taylor and Fagan, Riversedge
11 Ravenhill Road, Belfast
BT6 8DN
Tel: 028 9045 4401
Fax: 028 9045 8400
Secretary: Bill Taylor

Association of Southern Area Doctors
on Call
The Square, Moy
Dungannon BT71 7SG
Tel: 028 8778 9713

British Dental Association
The Mount, 2a Woodstock Link
Belfast BT6 8DD
Tel: 028 9073 5856
Fax: 028 9073 5857

NI Administrative Secretary:
Alison McMaster

British Medical Association
16 Cromac Place, Cromac Wood,
Ormeau Road, Belfast BT7 2JB
Tel: 028 9026 9666
Fax: 028 9026 9665
E-mail: info.belfast@bma.org.uk
Regional Service Co-ordinator:
Avril Campbell

Chartered Institute of Building
PO Box 1268, Bangor, BT20
5DYTel: 028 9147 9883
Fax: 028 9147 9884

Chartered Institution of Building
Surveyors
c/o The Caldwell Partnership
8 Lorne Street, Belfast BT9 7DU
Tel: 028 9066 9456
Fax: 028 9066 2219
Honorary Secretary: Mark Taylor

Chartered Institute of Housing
Carnmoney House
Edgewater Office Park
Belfast BT3 9JQ
Tel: 028 9077 8222
Fax: 028 9077 8333
E-mail: ni@cih.org
Chief Executive: David Butler

Chartered Institute of Management
Accountants (CIMA)
26 Chapter Street
London SW1P 4NP
Tel: 020 7663 5441
Web: www.cimaglobal.com
NI Secretary: Geoffrey Troughton
Tel: 028 9268 3727
Email: gtroughton@lineone.net

Chartered Institute of Marketing
22 Great Victoria St, Belfast
BT2 7BJ
Tel: 028 9024 4113
Fax: 028 9024 7024
Regional Director: Mike Maguire

Chartered Institute of Public Finance
and Accountancy
30–31 College Gardens
Belfast BT9 6BT
Tel: 028 90 26 6770
Fax: 028 9068 3185
Contact: David Nicholl
    The Accountancy Institute which
represents in the main professional
accountants operating in the public
sector.

Chartered Institute of Purchasing and
Supply
Easton House, Easton on the Hill,
Stamford, Lincolnshire PE9 3NZ
Tel: 01780 756 777
Fax: 01780 751 610
Contact: Sarah Lewithwaite

Chartered Society of Physiotherapy (CSP)
Merrion Business Centre
58 Howard Street, Belfast BT1 6PJ

Chief Executives' Forum
Lancashire House, 5 Linenhall St
Belfast BT2 8AA
Tel: 028 9054 2966
Fax: 028 9054 2970
Web: www.ceforum.org
Secretary: A McKinley

The Chief Executives' Forum is the
association of chief executive
officers of public bodies in Northern
Ireland. The Forum aims to support
the democratic process by
promoting excellence in public
service and encourage innovation
and development of leadership.

The General Council of the Bar in
Northern Ireland
Royal Courts of Justice
Belfast BT1 3JP
Tel: 028 9024 1523
Fax: 028 9023 1850
Chairman: Mr Reg Weir QC
The Bar Council is responsible for
the maintenance of the standards,

honour and independence of the bar, and through its Professional Conduct Committee, also receives and investigates any complaints against members of the Bar in their professional capacity.

The Law Society

Law Society House, 98 Victoria Street
Belfast BT1 3JZ
Tel: 028 9023 1614
Fax: 028 9023 2606
E-mail: info@lawsoc-ni.org
President: Mr Allan Hewitt

The Law Society is set up by Royal Charter and its powers and duties are to regulate the solicitor's profession in Northern Ireland. It operates through a Council of thirty members, all practicing solicitors who serve on a voluntary basis.

The Institute of Chartered Accountants in Ireland

11 Donegall Square South
Belfast BT1 5JE
Tel: 028 9032 1600
Fax: 028 9023 0071
Director: Heather Briars

Institution of Chemical Engineers

(Irish Branch: Northern Section)
Department of Chemical Engineering
Queens University Belfast
Tel: 028 9027 4255
Fax: 028 9028 1753
Contact: Dr Ronnie Magee

Institution of Civil Engineers

C/o Construction Employers Federation, 143 Malone Road
Belfast BT9 6SU
Tel: 028 9087 7157
Regional Secretary: Wendy Blundell

Institution of Electrical Engineers (NI Branch)

1 Glenbrae, Church Road, Holywood, Co Down BT18 9SD
Tel: 028 9042 8281
Web: www.ieeni.com
E-mail: glenbrae@lineone.net
Secretary: Mr WA Biggerstaff

The Institution of Electrical Engineers is a professional organisation, registered as a charity in the UK.

Institute of Financial Accountants

Burford House, 44 London Road, Sevenoaks, Kent TN13 1AS
Tel: 01732 458 080
Fax: 01732 455 848
E-mail: mail@ifa.org.uk
Web: www.accountingweb.co.ukifa

Institute of Management

PO Box 34, Newtownards
BT23 6ST
Tel: 028 9754 2451
Tel: 0207 497 0580 (London)
Web: www.inst-mgt.org.uk

Institute of Management Services

Stowe House, Netherstowe, Lichfield
Staffordshire WS13 6TJ
Tel: 01543 251 346
Fax: 01543 266 811
E-mail: admin@ims-stowe.fsnet.co.uk

The Institute operates through a network of regions throughout the UK and abroad, which work in conjunction with other professional institutes in their region.

Institution of Mechanical Engineers

105 West George Street
Glasgow G2 1QL
Tel: 0141 2217156
Regional Manager: Sandra Mulligan

Institute of Ophthalmology

11–43 Bath Street, London
EC1V 9EL
Tel: 0207 608 6800
Fax: 0207 608 6851

Institute of Personnel and Development

Weavers Court Business Park
Linfield Road, Belfast BT12 5LA
Tel: 028 9022 4005
Web: www.cipd.co.uk
Vice Chairperson: Lynne Stephenson

Institute of Psychiatry

De Crespigny Park
London SE5 8AF
Tel: 0207 848 0140
Fax: 0207 701 9044
Web: www.iop.kcl.ac.uk

Institute of Public Relations

The Old Trading House, 15 Northburgh Street
London EC1V OPR
Tel: 0207 253 5151
Fax: 0207 553 3771
E-mail: info@ipr.org.uk

Royal College of General Practitioners (NI)

44 Elmwood Avenue, Belfast
BT9 6AZ
Tel: 028 9066 7389
Fax: 028 9066 7389
Web: www.rcgp.org
Regional Manager: Valerie Fiddis

Royal College of Midwives

Friends Provident Building
58 Howard St, Belfast BT1 6PJ
Tel: 028 9024 1531
Fax: 028 9024 5889
Web: www.rcm.org.uk
NI Board Secretary:
Brendan Hughes

Royal College of Nursing

17 Windsor Avenue, Belfast
BT9 6EE
Tel: 028 9066 8236
Fax: 028 9038 2188
Acting Board Secretary:
Hilary Herron

Royal Institute of British Architects
66 Portland Place,
London W1B 1AD
Tel: 020 7307 3700
Web: www.architecture.com/

Royal Institute of Chartered Surveyors
(NI Branch)
9/11 Corporation Square
Belfast BT1 3AJ
Tel: 028 9032 2877
Fax: 028 9023 3465
Director: Ian Murray

Royal Society of Ulster Architects
2 Mount Charles, Belfast BT7 1NZ
Tel: 028 9032 3760
Fax: 028 9023 7313
Web: www.rsua.org.uk
Director: Frank McCloskey

Royal Town Planning Institute
(NI Branch)
2 Mount Charles, Belfast BT7 1NZ
Tel: 028 9032 3760
Fax: 028 9023 7313
Chairman: John Turner

Society of Radiographers (SOR)
297 Providence Square
Mill St, London SE1 2EW
Tel: 0207 740 7200

Trades Unions

Northern Ireland has a variety of trades union organisations covering a wide spectrum of economic life. For the most part the unions are regional parts of UK-based national unions, or in quite a number of cases, all-island unions, or unions active throughout the British Isles. There are a few union organisations unique to Northern Ireland.

Generally, Northern Ireland has a reasonably good industrial relations record and relations between management and trades unions across the economic sectors are positive and professional. There has

been a long-term decline in individual membership of trades unions but formal union-centred industrial relations procedures still operate in many workplaces.

Irish Congress of Trade Unions (ICTU)
3 Crescent Gardens, Belfast
BT7 1NS
Tel: 028 9024 7940
Fax: 028 9024 6898
Assistant General Secretary:
Peter Bunting

The Irish Congress of Trade Unions is the umbrella organisation of, and provides leadership for, the entire trades union movements in Ireland, North and South. It is organised on a regional basis, which includes a Northern Ireland section.
ICTU negotiates with government directly on national labour issues and carries out research on behalf of the union movement.

Amalgamated Engineering & Electrical Union (AEEU)
Unit 1, City Link Business Park
8 Albert Street
Belfast BT12 4HB
Tel: 028 9024 5785
Fax: 028 9024 5939
Web: www.aeeu.org.uk

4 Foyle Road, Derry BT48 7FR
Tel: 028 7126 1622
Fax: 028 7136 6025
Regional Secretary:
Peter Williamson

Amalgamated Transport & General Workers Union (ATGWU)
102 High Street, Transport House
Belfast BT1 2DL
Tel: 028 9023 2381
Fax: 028 9032 9904
56–58 Carlisle Road, Derry
BT48 6JW
Tel: 028 7126 4851

Acting Regional Secretary:
James Elsby

Association of First Division Civil Servants (AFDCS)
Room 3 Craigantlet Buildings
Stoney Road, Belfast BT4 3SX

Association of Teachers and Lecturers (ATL)
397a Holywood Road, Belfast
BT4 2LS
Tel: 028 9047 1412
Fax: 028 9047 1535
Office Administrator: Evelyn Rogers

Association of University Teachers (AUT)
C/o Dr S Lowry, Faculty of Science, University of Ulster
Coleraine BT52 1SA
Tel: 028 7034 4141

Bakers, Food & Allied Workers Union (BFAWU)
80 High Street, Belfast BT1 2BG
Tel: 028 9032 2767
Regional Officer: John Halliday

British Actors' Equity Association (EQUITY)
114 Union St, Glasgow G1 3QQ
Tel: 0141 248 2472
Fax: 0141 248 2472
Web: www.equity.org.uk
Secretary: Drew McFarland

Broadcasting, Entertainment, Cinematograph & Theatre Union (BECTU)
373–377 Clapham Road
London SW9 9BT
Tel: 0207 346 0900
Fax: 0207 346 0901
General Secretary: Roger Bolton

Communication Managers' Association (CMA)
Royal Mail House, 20 Donegall Quay
Belfast BT1 1AA
Tel: 028 9089 2288
Secretary: Bobby Smith

Communication Workers' Union (CWU)
8–10 Exchange Place
Belfast BT1 2NA
Tel: 028 9032 1771
Fax: 028 9043 9390
Chairman: John McLoughlin

Connect
C/o Mr A Gibb
BT plc Riverside Tower
5 Lanyon Place, Belfast BT1 3BT

Counteract
2nd Floor Philip House
123–137 York Street
Belfast BT15 1AB
Tel: 028 9023 7023
Fax: 028 9031 3585
Web: www.counteract.org
Director: William Robinson

National Farmers' Union
72 High Street
Newtownards BT23 7HZ
Tel: 028 9181 4218
Fax: 028 9181 1574
Group Secretary: Ms HJ Murphy

Prospect
75–79 York Road, London SE1 7AQ
Tel: 020 7902 6600
Fax: 020 7902 6667
E-mail: enquiries@prospect.org.uk
General Secretary: Paul Noon

Fire Brigades' Union (FBU)
7 Kerrymount Avenue
Belfast BT8 6NL

GMB
3–4 Donegal Quay, Belfast
BT1 3EA
Tel: 028 9031 2111
Fax: 028 9031 2333
Senior Organiser: Pat Dyer

Graphical Paper & Media Union
(GMPU)
Unit A First Floor
Loughside Industrial Park
Dargan Crescent, Belfast BT3 9SP
Tel: 028 9077 8550
Fax: 028 9077 8552
Branch Secretary: Davy Edmont

Irish Bank Officials Association (IBOA)
93 St Stephen's Green, Dublin 2
Tel: 01 475 5908
Fax: 01 478 0567
Secretary: Larry Broderick

Irish National Teachers Association
(INTO)
23 College Gardens, Belfast
BT9 6BS
Tel: 028 9038 1455
Fax: 028 9066 2803
E-mail: info@ni.into.ie
Northern Secretary:
Mr Frank Bunting

Manufacturing Science & Finance
(MSF)
7 Donegall Place, Belfast BT1 2FN
Tel: 028 9032 6688
Fax: 028 9032 6699
Web: www.msf.org.uk
Regional Officer: Jack Nicholl

National Association of Head Teachers
31 Church Road, Holywood
BT18 9BU
Tel: 028 9077 6633
Fax: 028 9077 4777
E-mail: fernt@naht.org.uk
Regional Officer: Fern Turner

National Association for Probation
Officers (NAPO)
C/o Ms E Richardson, PBNI
80/90 Great Patrick St
Belfast BT1 1LD
Tel: 028 9032 6688

National Association of Schoolmasters
/ Union of Women Teachers (NASUWT)
Ben Madigan House, Edgewater
Road
Belfast BT3 9JQ
Tel: 028 9078 4480
Fax: 028 9078 4489
Web: www.teachersunion.org.uk
Regional Officer: Tom McKee

National Association of Teachers in
Further & Higher Education (NATFHE)
475 Lisburn Road, Belfast
BT9 7EZ
Tel: 028 9066 5501
Fax: 028 9066 9225
Web: www.natfhe.org.uk
Regional Officer: Jim McKeown

National Farmers' Union
72 High Street
Newtownards BT23 7HZ
Tel: 028 9181 4218
Fax: 028 9181 1574
Group Secretary: Ms H J Murphy

National Union of Journalists (NUJ)
Headland House
308–312 Gray's Inn Road
London WC1X 8DT
Tel: 0207 278 7916
Fax: 0207 837 8143

National Union of Rail, Maritime &
Transport Workers (RMT)
180 Hope St, Glasgow G2 2UE
Tel: 0141 332 1117
Fax: 0141 333 9583
Regional Organiser: Steve Todd

Northern Ireland Musicians
Association (NIMA)
3rd Floor, Unit 4, Fortwilliam
Business Park, Dargan Road,
Belfast BT3 9JZ
Tel: 028 9037 0037
Fax: 028 9037 0037
NIWA Organiser: Mr Hamilton

NI Public Service Alliance (NIPSA)
Harkin House, 54 Wellington Park
Belfast BT9 6DP
Tel: 028 9066 1831
Fax: 028 9066 5847
Web: www.nipsa.org.uk
General Secretary: Jim McCusker

The National Union of Students (NUS-USI)
NUS-USI, 29 Bedford Street
Belfast BT2 7EJ
Tel: 028 9024 4641

Fax: 028 9043 9659
E-mail: info@nistudents.com
Web: www.nistudents.com
Manager: Peter O'Neill
Convenor 2002–2003:
Ben Archibald
Deputy Convenor: Andy Ward

Belfast Institute of Further and Higher
Education Students Union
Room A24, College Square East
Belfast BT1 6DJ
Union Tel: 028 9024 9040
Union Fax: 028 9026 5101
College Tel: 028 9026 5000

Queen's University of Belfast Students
Union
University Road
Belfast BT7 1PE
Union Tel: 028 9032 4803
Union Fax: 028 9023 6900
E-mail: info@qubsu.org
College Tel: 028 9024 5133
Web: www.qubsu.org

University of Ulster Students Union
Cromore Road, Coleraine
BT52 1SA
Union Tel: 028 7032 4319
Union Fax: 028 7032 4915
College Tel: 08700 400 700
E-mail: su.president@uusu.org
Web: www.uusu.org

Jordanstown Site
Shore Road, Co Antrim BT37 0QB
Union Tel: 028 9036 6050
Union Fax: 028 9036 6817
E-mail: su.edwel@uusu.org
E-mail: vp.jordanstown@uusu.org
College Tel: 08700 400 700

Derry Site
Magee College, Northlands Road,
Derry BT48 7JL
Union Tel: 028 7137 5226
Union Fax: 028 7137 5415
College Tel: 08700 400 700
E-mail: vp.magee@uusu.org

Belfast Site
York Street, Belfast BT15 1ED
Union Tel: 028 9026 7302
Union Fax: 028 9026 7351
College Tel: 08700 400 700
E-mail: vp.belfast@uusu.org
E-mail: su.enquiries@uusu.org

Public Commerce Services Union
(PCS)
10 Mounthill Court, Cloughmills
Co Antrim BT44 9QU
Tel: 028 2563 3096
Contact: Alastair Donaghy

Royal College of Nursing
17 Windsor Avenue, Belfast
BT9 6EE
Tel: 028 9066 8236
Fax: 028 9038 2188
Board Secretary: Hilary Herron

Services Industrial Professional
Technical Union (SIPTU)
3 Antrim Road, Belfast BT15 2BE
Tel: 028 9031 4000
Fax: 028 9031 4044
Regional Secretary: George Hunter

Ulster Farmers' Union
475 Antrim Road, Belfast
BT15 3BJ
Tel: 028 9037 0222
Fax: 028 9037 1231
Web: info@ufunq.com/
Chief Executive: Clarke Black

Ulster Teachers' Union (UTU)
94 Malone Road, Belfast BT9 5HP
Tel: 028 9066 2216
Fax: 028 9066 3055
Web: www.utu.edu/home.html/
Secretary: Ray Calvin

Union of Construction, Allied Trades &
Technicians (UCATT)
Rooms 108 / 110, Midland
Building, Whitla Street, Belfast
BT15 1JP
Tel: 028 9075 1866
Fax: 028 9075 1867
E-mail: admin@ucatt.org.uk
Regional Secretary: Terry Lally

Union of Shop, Distributive & Allied
Workers (USDAW)
40 Wellington Park, Belfast
BT9 6DN
Tel: 028 9066 3773
Fax: 028 9066 2133
Area Organiser: Bob Gourley

UNISON
Unit 4, Fortwilliam Business Park,
Dargan Road, Belfast BT3 9JZ
Tel: 028 9037 0971
Fax: 028 9077 9772
Secretary: Inez McCormack

Affiliated Councils of Trade Unions
Belfast & District
C/o Transport House
102 High Street, Belfast BT1
Contact: Pearse McKenna

Craigavon & District
47 Cranny Road
Portadown BT63 5SP
Contact: Dr A Evans

Derry
23/25 Shipquay St, Derry
BT48 6DL
Contact: Mr J McCracken

Fermanagh
C/o 5/7 Queen St
Enniskillen BT74 7JR
Contact: Mr D Kettyles

Newry
24 Cherrywood Grove
Newry BT34 1JJ
Contact: Mr J Murphy

North Down
88 Balfour St
Newtownards BT23 4EF
Contact: Mr W Holland

Charitable, Support and Voluntary Organisations

Northern Ireland has an extensive and very active voluntary sector, which includes a wide range of charitable and support organisations. Many of these organisations are affiliated to an umbrella body, the Northern Ireland Council for Voluntary Action (NICVA), an organisation that has been appointed on occasions by the European Commission as an intermediary body to distribute substantial EU funding in Northern Ireland.

It is worth noting that as a region of the UK, Northern Ireland records very high comparative levels of deprivation and it is not surprising therefore that so much voluntary endeavour is required. For example, Northern Ireland has considerably higher levels of homelessness and disability than UK averages and the charities and support groups operating in these areas are necessarily significant players.

Action Cancer

Action Cancer House
1 Marlborough Park, Belfast
BT9 6XS
Tel: 028 9080 3344
Fax: 028 9080 3356
Web: www.actioncancer.org
Chief Executive: Peter Quigley

Action for Dysphasic Adults NI

Graham House, Knockbracken
Healthcare Park
Saintfield Road, Belfast BT8 8BH
Tel: 028 9040 1389
Fax: 028 9079 1965
Web: www.speechmatters.org
Chief Executive: Caroline Little

Action Multiple Sclerosis

Knockbracken Healthcare Park
Saintfield Road, Belfast BT8 8BH
Tel: 028 9079 0707
Fax: 028 9040 2010
E-mail: info@actionms.co.uk
Web: www.actionms.co.uk
Director: Anne Walker

ADAPT Fund for Ireland

109 Royal Ave
Belfast BT1 1FF
Tel: 028 9023 1211
Fax: 028 9024 0878
E-mail: info@adaptni.org
Development Manager:
Caroline Shiels

ACTION MENTAL HEALTH

Action Mental Health
Mourne House
19 Knockbracken Healthcare Park
Saintfield Road
BELFAST
BT8 8BH

Tel: (028) 9040 3726
Fax: (028) 9040 3727
Email:
mail@actionmentalhealth.org.uk

Chief Executive: Ian Walters

Action Mental Health celebrates its 40th Anniversary in 2003. The company provides a range of training and employment services to people recovering from mental illness. It operates in 15 locations across Northern Ireland.

Age Concern NI

3 Lower Crescent, Belfast
BT7 1NR
Tel: 028 9024 5729
Fax: 028 9023 5497
Chief Executive: Chris Common

Aids Helpline NI

7 James Street South
Belfast BT2 8DN
Tel: 028 9024 9268
Free Helpline: 0800 137437
Fax: 028 9032 9845
Web: www.aidshelpline.org.uk
Director: Geraldine Campbell

Alcoholics Anonymous

7 Donegall Street Place
Central Service Office
Belfast BT1 2FN
Tel: 028 9043 4848
Fax: 028 9043 4848
Web: www.alcoholicsanonymous.ie

Alzheimers Disease Society

86 Eglantine Avenue, Belfast
BT9 6EU
Tel: 028 9066 4100
Fax: 028 9066 4440
Regional Manager: Marjorie Magee

Amnesty International NI Region

80a Stranmillis Road, Belfast
BT9 5AD
Tel: 028 9066 6216
Fax: 028 9066 6164
Web: www.amnesty.org
Development Officer: Patrick Corrigan

Anti-Poverty Network

61 Duncairn Gardens
Belfast BT15 2GB
Tel: 028 9087 7777
Fax: 028 9087 7799
Information Officer: Frances Dowds

Ards Society for Mentally Handicapped Children
203 South Street
Newtownards BT23 4JY
Tel: 028 9181 5363

Armagh Confederation of Voluntary Groups
1 College Street, Armagh
BT61 9BT
Tel: 028 3752 2282
Fax: 028 3752 2286
Web: www.acvg.com
Co-ordinator: vacant

Arthritis Care NI
Ballymena Business Centre
62 Fenaghy Road, Ballymena
BT42 1FL
Tel: 028 9448 1380
Fax: 028 2563 2477
Web: www.arthritiscare.org.uk
Director: Sharon Sinclair

Arthritis Care West
76 Clanabogan Road
Omagh BT78 1SJ
Tel: 028 8225 0380
Fax: 028 8225 0380
E-mail: annettemoore.acni@virgin.net
Contact: Annette Moore

Arthritis Research Campaign
15 Summerhill Parade
Belfast BT5 7HF
Tel: 028 9048 4783
Fax: 028 9048 4783
Appeals Manager: Charlotte Trinder

Arts and Disability Forum
Unit 45, Westlink Enterprise Centre
30–50 Distillery Street
Belfast BT12 5BJ
Tel: 028 9023 9450
Fax: 028 9024 7770
Web: www.ads.dnet.co.uk
Development Officer: Avril Crawford

ASH
C/o Ulster Cancer Foundation
40–42 Eglantine Avenue
Belfast BT9 6DJ

Tel: 028 9066 3281
Fax: 028 9066 0081
Web: www.ulstercancer.org
Head of Education and Training:
Gerry McElwee

Association of Independent Advice Centres (AIAC)
303 Ormeau Road, Belfast
BT7 3GG
Tel: 028 9064 5919
Fax: 028 9049 2313
Web: www.aiac.net/
Director: Bob Strong

Association of Mental Health
80 University Street, Belfast
BT7 1HE
Tel: 028 9032 8474
Fax: 028 9023 4940
Chief Executive: Alan Ferguson

Association for Spina Bifida & Hydrocephalus
Graham House
Knockbracken Healthcare Park
Saintfield Road, Belfast BT8 8BH
Tel: 028 9079 8878
Fax: 028 9079 7071
Regional Manager: Margaret Young

Barnardos
NI Regional Office
542–544 Upper Newtownards Road
Belfast BT4 3HE
Tel: 028 9067 2366
Fax: 028 9067 2399
Web: www.barnardos.org.uk
Senior Director: Linda Wilson

BBC Children in Need
Broadcasting House, Ormeau Ave
Belfast BT2 8HQ
Tel: 028 9033 8221
Fax: 028 9033 8922
National Co-ordinator:
Sheila Jane Malley

Belfast Central Mission
5 Glengall Street, Belfast
BT12 5AD
Tel: 028 9024 1917
Fax: 028 9024 0577
Superintendent: David Kerr

The Quayside Project
16 South Street
Newtownards BT23 1JT
Tel: 028 9182 7783
Fax: 028 9182 7784
Team Leader: John Turtle

Belfast and Co Down Railway Trust
9 Abbey Gardens, Millisle,
Newtownards
Tel: 0800 980 1242
Contact: Bob Pue

Belfast Common Purpose
Beacon House, 27 Clarendon Road
Belfast BT1 3BG
Tel: 028 9089 2273

Blind Centre for Northern Ireland
70 North Road, Belfast BT5 5NJ
Tel: 028 9065 4366
Fax: 028 9060 0051
Web: www.bcni.co.uk
Chief Executive: Dean Huston

Board for Social Responsibility
Church of Ireland House
61–67 Donegall Street
Belfast BT1 2QH

12 Talbot Street, Belfast BT1 2LD
Tel: 028 9023 3885
Fax: 028 9032 1756
Web: www.cofiadopt.org.uk
Chief Executive: Ian Slane

Brainwaves NI
68 Cable Road, Whitehead
Co Antrim BT38 9PZ
Tel: 028 9337 2505
Fax: 028 9335 3995
Honorary Secretary: Kate Ferguson

British Deaf Association
Wilton House
5–6 College Street North

Belfast BT1 6AR
Tel: 028 9072 7400
Tel: 028 9072 7407
Web: www.britishdeafassocation.org.uk
Community Development Manager:
Majella McAteer

Diabetics UK
8 Bridgewood House
Newforge Business Park
Newforge Lane
Belfast BT9 5NW
Tel: 028 9066 6646
Fax: 028 9066 6333
E-mail: n.ireland@diabetes.org.uk
Web: www.diabetes.org.uk
National Manager: Kate Fleck

British Red Cross
87 University Street, Belfast
BT7 1HP
Tel: 028 9024 6400
Fax: 028 9032 6102
Regional Director: Norman McKinley

British Red Cross Therapeutic Care
Service
20 Hamilton Road, Bangor
BT20 4LE
Tel: 028 9146 6915
Fax: 028 9147 3976
Regional Service Co-ordinator:
Norma Groves

Bryson House
28 Bedford Street, Belfast BT2 7EE
Tel: 028 9032 5835
Fax: 028 9043 9156
Director: Jo Marley

Bryson House is a Northern Ireland Charity committed to identifying and developing sustainable responses to existing and emerging social needs. The charity provides a range of services including environmental, family and caring, training and voluntary services.

Bryson House Charity
7a Main St, Ballynahinch
BT24 8DN
Tel: 028 9756 4366

Web: www.brysonhouse.org
Project Manager: Margaret Coffey

C A C D P
5 College Square North, Belfast
Tel: 028 9043 8161
Fax: 028 9043 8161
Minicom: 028 9043 8161
National Development Officer
Northern Ireland: Cilla Mullan

Carers Northern Ireland
58 Howard Street, Belfast
BT1 6PJ
Tel: 028 9043 9843
Fax: 028 9032 9299
E-mail: info@carersni.demon.co.uk
Director: Helen Ferguson

Cancer Research Campaign Northern Ireland
Unit 3, Leslie Office Park, 393
Holywood Road
Belfast BT4 2LS
Tel: 028 9065 6575
Fax: 028 9065 6585
E-mail: northernireland@crc.org.uk
Web: www.crc.org.uk
Shops Manager: William McKinley

Cats Protection
NI Shelter, 270 Belfast Road,
Dundonald BT16 1UE
Tel: 028 9048 0202
Fax: 028 9048 6614
Manager: Janice Watts

Child Accident Prevention Trust
23A/B Mullacreevie Park,
Killylea Road
Armagh BT60 4BA
Tel: 028 3752 6521
Fax: 028 3752 6521
E-mail: safetycentra@aol.com
Web: www.capt.org.uk
NI Manager: Rosie Mercer

Challenge Work Skills
2 Old Lurgan Road
Portadown BT63 5SG
Tel: 028 3839 2170
Carer Facilitator: Maria Boyle

Charles Sheils Charity
Circular Road, Dungannon
BT71 6BJ
Tel: 028 8772 2138
Superintendent: Averill Griffith

Chernobyl Children Appeal
52c Monaghan Street
Newry BT35 6AA
Tel: 028 3026 0142

Chest Heart Stroke Association
21 Dublin Road, Belfast BT2 7HB
Tel: 028 9032 0184
Fax: 028 9033 3487
Web: www.nicha.com
Chief Executive: Andrew Dougal

Child Care (NI)
216 Belmont Road, Belfast
BT4 2AT
Tel: 028 9065 2713
Fax: 028 9065 0285
Web: www.childcareni.org.uk
Director: Mary Cunningham

Childline
3rd Floor Offices
The War Memorial Building
9–13 Waring Street, Belfast
BT1 2EU
Tel: 028 9032 7773
Fax: 028 90181 8131
Web: www.childline.org.uk
Acting Director: Liz Osborne

Children in Crossfire
2 St Joseph's Avenue, Derry
BT48 6TH
Tel: 028 7126 9898
Fax: 028 7126 6630
E-mail:
ciara.donnelly@childreincrossfire.org
Director: Richard Moore

Children's Law Centre
3rd Floor, Phillip House
123–137 York Street
Belfast BT15 1AB
Tel: 028 9024 5704
Fax: 028 9024 5679
E-mail: info@childrenslawcentre.org
Director: Paddy Kelly

Cleft Lip & Palate Association
43 Ashley Avenue, Belfast
BT9 7BT
Tel: 028 9066 5115
Web: www.clapa.com

Community Arts Forum
15 Church St, Belfast BT1 1PG
Tel: 028 9024 2910
Fax: 028 9031 2264
Web: www.community-arts-forum.org
Director: Heather Floyd

Community Evaluation NI
295 Ormeau Road, Belfast
BT7 3GG
Tel: 028 9064 6355
Fax: 028 9064 1118
Web: www.ceni.org
E-mail: info@ceni.org
Director: Mr Brendan McDonnell

Community Relations Information Centre
21 College Square East
Belfast BT1 6DE
Tel: 028 9022 7555
Fax: 028 9022 7550
E-mail: info@community-relations.org.uk
Manager: Patricia O'Neill

Community Work Education and Training Network
Phillip House, 123–127 York St
Belfast BT15 1AB
Tel: 028 9023 2618
Fax: 028 9027 8196
E-mail: cwetn@compuserve.com
Co-ordinator: Peggy Flanagan

Conservation Volunteers NI
159 Ravenhill Road, Belfast
BT6 0BP
Tel: 028 9064 5169
Fax: 028 9064 4409
Web: www.cvni.org.uk
E-mail: info@cvni.org.uk
Senior Manager: Ian Humphreys

Community Technical Aid NI Ltd
445 Ormeau Road, Belfast
Tel: 028 9064 2227
Fax: 028 9064 2467
E-mail: info@community
    technicalaid.org
Director: Colm Bradley

Community Transport Association
Graham House
Knockbracken Health Care Park
Saintfield Road, Belfast BT8 8BH
Tel: 028 9040 3535

Concern Worldwide NI
47 Frederick Street, Belfast
BT1 LW
Tel: 028 9033 1100
Fax: 028 9033 1111
E-mail: infobelfast@concern.org.uk
Head of NI Operations: David Gough

Co-operation Ireland
7 Botanic Avenue, Belfast BT7 1JG
Tel: 028 9032 1462
Fax: 028 9024 7522
Web: www.cooperationireland.org
E-mail: info@cooperationireland.org
Chief Executive: Tony Kennedy
Operations Director:
Anne Anderson Porter

Co-operation Ireland is a leading charitable organisation unique to Northern Ireland. Its central mission is to develop practical cooperation between people North and South of the border with the Irish Republic. It is increasingly expanding its role in reconciling different traditions North and South, to include reconciliation of the different traditions within the North. Co-operation Ireland operates numerous social, economic, youth and community programmes and is an EU-appointed intermediary body for distribution of EU funds for certain programmes in Northern Ireland.

COMMUNITY RELATIONS COUNCIL

Community Relations Council

Community Relations Council
6 Murray Street
Belfast BT1 6DN
Tel: (028) 9022 7500
Fax: (028) 9022 7551
Website: www.community-relations.org.uk
E-mail: info@community-relations.org.uk

Chief Executive:
Dr Duncan Morrow

The Community Relations Council (CRC) was established in 1990 as a registered charity. It aims to help organisations and individuals to create a society free from sectarianism.

CRC is a development agency for peace in Northern Ireland and provides advice and support to community relations initiatives and projects in the voluntary and community sector. Almost 500 grants are awarded each year. CRC also offers advice and guidance to public sector organisations in meeting the section 75 (2) statutory duty under the NI Act (1998) to promote 'Good Relations'.

Corrymeela Community Belfast
8 Upper Crescent, Belfast
BT7 1NT
Tel: 028 9050 8080
Fax: 028 9050 8070
E-mail: enquiries@corrymeela.org.uk
Leader of the Community:
Rev Trevor Williams

Council for the Homeless NI

153 University Street
Belfast BT7 1HR
Tel: 028 9024 6440
Fax: 028 9024 1266
E-mail: info@chni.org.uk
Director: Ms Ricky Rowledge

Crossroads Caring for Carers

Head Office, 7 Regent Street,
Newtownards BT23 4AB
Tel: 028 9181 4455
Fax: 028 9181 2112
E-mail: mail@crossroadscare.co.uk
Chief Executive: Christine Best

CRUSE Bereavement Care NI

Knockbracken Heathcare Park,
Saintfield Road, Belfast BT7 8BH
Tel: 028 9079 2419
Fax: 028 9079 2474

Cruse is the leading bereavement charity in the UK. The organisation currently has 178 branches and over 6,300 volunteers throughout the UK.

Cystic Fibrosis Association

1 Circular Road East
Holywood BT18 0HA
Tel: 028 9127 2781
Web: www.acfa.org.uk

Cystic Fibrosis Trust

178 Moyola Terrace, Obin Street,
Portadown
Tel: 028 3833 4491

Disability Action

Portside Business Park
189 Airport Road West
Belfast BT3 9ED
Tel: 028 9029 7880
Fax: 028 9029 7881
Textphone: 028 9029 7882
E-mail: hq@disabilityaction.org
Chief Executive: Monica Wilson

CO-OPERATION IRELAND
"Making Peace Work"

The Leading Peace-Building Charity

Did you know?

- There are more 'peace walls' in Belfast today than before the peace process started
- The attitudes held by people living in Northern Ireland today are as polarised or even more polarised than they were before the peace process started
- Many children reach adulthood with little or no appreciation for 'the other tradition'

Co-operation Ireland is working to change this. Through our programmes with schools and community groups our work crosses all communities promoting practical co-operation at ground level. In addition we distribute funds for the European Union Programme for Peace and Reconciliation for cross-border businesses and other projects.

We need your help to allow groups the opportunity to build peace by assisting us directly, sponsoring an activity or supporting an event.

Each year we organise a range of fundraising events to raise money for our work. These include:

- Golfing Events
- Gala Dinners
- BorderTrek - Co-operation Ireland's flagship cycling event
- Sporting Events
- Music Events

Together we can build peace

For information on our programmes and how you can assist us, please contact us at:

www.cooperationireland.org
Tel: 028 9032 1462
Fax: 028 9024 7522

Downs Syndrome Association NI

Graham House
Knockbracken Healthcare Park
Saintfield Road, Belfast BT7 8BH
Tel: 028 9070 4606
Fax: 028 9070 4075
Web: www.downs-syndrome.org.uk
E-mail: downs.sysdrome@cinni.org
Regional Director: Alan Hanna

Downtown Women's Centre

109–113 Royal Avenue
Belfast BT1 1FF
Tel: 028 9024 3363
Fax: 028 9023 7884
Director: Elizabeth Hendron

Dungannon & District Women's Centre

11 Feeny's Lane
Dungannon BT70 1TX
Tel: 028 8772 6615
Fax: 028 8722 6615
Acting Co-ordinator: Eilish McCabe

East Antrim Therapy Centre

Unit 24, Ledcom Industrial Estate
Bank Road, Larne
Tel: 028 2827 4670
Fax: 028 2827 4670
E-mail:
info@oxygentherapycentre.co.uk
Centre co-ordinator: Lorna Liddle

East Belfast Independent Advice Centre

85 Castlereagh Street,
Belfast BT5 4NS
Tel: 028 9096 3003
Fax: 028 9096 3004
Manager: Karen McNamee

Family Planning Association NI
113 University Street
Belfast BT7 1HP
Tel: 028 9032 5488
Fax: 028 9031 2212
Co-ordinator: Dr Audrey Simpson

Federation of Women's Institutes
209–211 Upper Lisburn Road,
Belfast BT10 0LL
Tel: 028 9030 1506
Fax: 028 9043 1127
E-mail: wini:btconnect.com
General Secretary: Irene Sproule

Fibromyalgia Support Group
18 Woodcot Avenue, Bloomfield
Belfast BT5 5JA
Fax: 028 9065 4243
E-mail: msni@fsmsnifreeserve.co.uk
Chairperson: Mrs Romayne Wright

Friedrich's Ataxia Group (NI)
4 Kingsway Close, Cherryvalley
Belfast BT5 7HA
Tel: 028 9048 4046
Web: www.ataxia.org.uk
Contact Member: Ida Walker

Friends in the West
Rathmourne House
143 Central Promenade
Newcastle BT33 0EU
Tel: 028 4372 3300
Fax: 028 4372 6210
Contact: Julian Armstrong

Friends of the Earth
7 Donegall Place, Belfast BT1 2FN
Tel: 028 9023 3488
Fax: 028 9024 7556
Head of Campaigns and
Development: John Woods

Gamblers Anonymous
18 Donegall Street, Belfast
BT1 2GP
Tel: 028 9024 9185
Web: www.gambersanonymous.org

Gay Lesbian Youth Northern Ireland
E-mail: admin@glyni.org.uk
Web: www.glyni.org.uk

Gingerbread
169 University Street
Belfast BT7 1HR
Tel: 028 9023 4568/9023 1417
Fax: 028 9024 0740
E-mail: enquiries:gingerbreadni.org
Director: Marie Cavanagh

Guide Dogs for the Blind
NI Training Centre
15 Sandown Park South
Belfast BT5 6HE
Tel: 028 9047 1453
Fax: 028 9065 5097
E-mail: Belfast:gdba.org.uk
District Team Manager: Peter Swan

Habitat for Humanity NI
Unit 29, 638 Springfield Road
Belfast BT12 7DY
Tel: 028 9024 3686
Fax: 028 9033 1878
E-mail: belfast@habitat.co.uk
Executive Director:
Peter Farquharson

Hearing Dogs for the Deaf
12 Main St, Crawfordsburn
BT19 1JE
Tel: 028 9185 3669
Contact: Mrs A Jameson

Help the Aged
Ascott House, Shaftesbury Square
Belfast BT2 7DB
Tel: 028 9023 0666
Fax: 028 9024 8183
Advice: 0800 808 7575
Web: www.helptheaged.org.uk
E-mail: helptheagedni@hta.org.uk
NI Executive: Anne O'Reilly

Home Start
533 Antrim Road, Belfast
BT15 3BS
Tel: 028 9077 8999
Fax: 028 9078 1656
Web: www.home-start.org.uk
Scheme Organiser: Patricia Friel

Imperial Cancer Research Fund
593 Lisburn Road, Belfast

BT9 7GS
Tel: 028 9038 2113
Manager: Gwen Kennedy

International Fund for Ireland
PO Box 2000, Belfast BT4 2QY
Tel: 028 9076 8832
Fax: 028 9076 3313
Joint Director General:
Mr Sandy Smith

International Voluntary Service
122 Great Victoria Street
Belfast BT2 7BG
Tel: 028 9023 8147
Fax: 028 9024 4356
E-mail: georget@ivsni.co.uk
Co-ordinator: Colin McKinty

Lifestart Family Centre
13 Dunluce Court, Derry BT48 0PA
Tel: 028 7126 9833
Fax: 028 7126 0233
Contact: Margaret McCann

Macmillan Cancer Relief
82 Eglantine Avenue, Belfast
BT9 6EU
Tel: 028 9066 1166
Fax: 028 9066 3661
Fundraising Manager: Paul Sweeney

Make a Wish Foundation UK
4 Fairway Drive, Upper Malone
Road Belfast BT9 5ND
Tel: 028 9080 5580

Marie Curie Cancer Care
Kensington Road, Belfast
Tel: 028 9067 4200
      (Hospice/Nursing Service)
Tel: 028 9067 1210 (Fundraising)
Services Manager: Maeve Hully

Meningitis Research Foundation
71 Botanic Avenue, Belfast
BT7 1JL
Tel: 028 9032 1283
Fax: 028 9032 1284
Freephone: 0800 800 3344
E-mail: info@meningitis-ni.org
NI Manager: Diane McConnell

Mencap
416 Ormeau Road
Belfast BT7 3HY
Tel: 028 9049 2666
Fax: 028 9049 3373
Web: www.mencap.org
Regional Director: Maureen Piggott

Mencap offers a range of services, information and support for children and adults with learning difficulties.

Multiple Sclerosis Society – Northern Ireland
The Resource Centre
34 Annadale Avenue, Belfast
BT7 3JJ
Tel: 028 9080 2802
Web: www.mssocietyni.co.uk
E-mail: providingthestrength@
    mssociety.ni.co.uk
Director: Kieran Harris

National Autistic Society
University Road, Belfast BT7 1N
Tel: 028 9027 4547
Fax: 028 9027 4547

National Deaf Children's Society
Wilton House
5–6 College Square North
Belfast BT1 6AR
Tel: 028 9031 3170
Fax: 028 9027 8205
E-mail: nioffice@ndcsni.co.uk
Development Manager:
Pauline Walker

National Schizophrenia Fellowship
Windhurst
Knockbracken Healthcare Park
Saintfield Road, Belfast BT8 8BH
Tel: 028 9040 2323
Fax: 028 9040 1616
E-mail: info.nireland@rethink.org
Director: Liz Cuddy

National Trust
Rowallane, Saintfield BT24 7LH
Tel: 028 9751 0721
Fax: 028 9751 1242
Web: www.nationaltrust.org.uk
Director: Ruth Laird

The National Trust is a registered charity, which owns and manages a range of historic properties and estates on behalf of the public and for their future preservation. The Trust now cares for over 248,000 hectares of countryside, almost 600 miles of coastline and more than 200 buildings and gardens.

Nexus Institute Belfast
119 University Street
Belfast BT7 1HP
Tel: 028 9032 6803
Fax: 028 9023 7392
E-mail: dominica@nexusinstitute.org
Director: Dominica McGowan

Nexus Institute Derry
38 Clarendon Street, Derry BT48 7ET
Tel: 028 7126 0566
Fax: 028 7130 8399
Web: www.nexusinstitute.org
Project Manager: Helena Bracken

Northern Ireland Children's Holiday Scheme
547 Antrim Road, Belfast
BT15 3BU
Tel: 028 9037 0373
Fax: 028 9078 1161
E-mail: niches@utvinternet.com
Director: Jackie Chalk

Northern Ireland Foster Care Association
216 Belmont Road, Belfast
BT4 2AT
Tel: 028 9067 3441
Fax: 028 9067 3241
E-mail: info.nifca@dnet.co.uk
Director: Kate Lewis

Northern Ireland Gay Rights Association
PO Box 44, Belfast

Northern Ireland Home Accident Prevention
Nella House
Dargan Crescent, Belfast BT3 9JP
Tel: 028 9050 1160
Fax: 028 9050 1164
Secretary: Janice Bisp

Northern Ireland Leukaemia Research Fund
University Floor, Tower Block,
Belfast City Hospital, Lisburn Road
Belfast BT9 7AB
Tel: 028 9032 2603
Director: Ms A Henry

NIPPA Childhood Fund
6e Wildflower Way
Apollo Road, Belfast BT12 6TA
Tel: 028 9066 2825
Fax: 028 9038 1270

1a Pottinger Street, Cullybackey, Ballymena
Tel: 028 2588 2345
Fax: 028 2588 2338
Chief Executive: Siobhan Fitzpatrick

Northern Ireland Agoraphobia & Anxiety Society
27–31 Lisburn Road, Belfast BT9 7AA
Tel: 028 9023 5170
Fax: 028 9024 5535
Contact: Fiona McFarland

Northern Ireland Association of Citizens Advice Bureaux
11 Upper Crescent, Belfast
BT7 1NT
Tel: 028 9023 1120
Fax: 028 9023 6522
E-mail: enquires@niacab.org
Chief Executive: Derek Alcorne

The Citizens Advice Bureau originated as an emergency service and now addresses debt and consumer issues, benefits, housing, legal matters, employment and immigration.

Each bureau is affiliated to the National Association of Citizens Advice Bureau (NACAB).

Northern Ireland Cancer Fund For Children
2nd Floor
46 Botanic Avenue, Belfast
BT7 1JR
Tel: 028 9080 5599
Fax: 028 9080 3858
General Manager: Gillian Creevy

Northern Ireland Council For Voluntary Action (NICVA)
61 Duncairn Gardens,
Belfast BT15 2GB
Tel: 028 9087 7777
Fax: 028 9087 7799
E-mail: nicva@nicva.org
Director: Seamus McAleavey

The Northern Ireland Council for Voluntary Action is an umbrella group for Northern Ireland charities, community and voluntary groups.

Northern Ireland Hospice
74 Somerton Road, Belfast
BT15 3LH
Tel: 028 9078 1836
Fax: 028 9037 0585
Web: www.nihospice.com/
E-mail: information@nihospice.com
Administration Director: Tom Hill

Northern Ireland Hospice Children's Service
18 O'Neill Road
Newtownabbey BT36 6WB
Tel: 028 9077 7635
Fax: 028 9077 7521
Web: www.nihospice.com
E-mail: children@nihospice.com
Head of Home: Patricia O'Callaghan

Northern Ireland ME Association
Bryson House
28 Bedford Street, Belfast
Tel: 028 9043 9831
Fax: 028 9043 9831

Northern Ireland Mixed Marriage Association
28 Bedford Street, Belfast
Tel: 028 9023 5444
Fax: 028 9043 4544
Web: www.nimma.org.uk
E-mail: nimma@nireland.com
Contact: Nigel Speirs

Northern Ireland Preschool Playgroup Association
1A Pottinger Street, Cullybackey,
Ballymena BT42 1BP
Tel: 028 2588 2345
Fax: 028 2588 2338
Training Co-ordinator:
Jennifer Montgomery

Northern Ireland Transplant Association
51 Circular Road, Belfast BT4 2GA
Tel: 028 9076 1394
Web: www.nita.org.uk
E-mail: nitransplant@email.com
Chairman: David Robinson

Northern Ireland Women's Aid Federation
129 University Street
Belfast BT7 1HP
Tel: 028 9024 9041
Fax: 028 9023 9296
Web: www.niwaf.org
E-mail: niwaf@dnet.co.uk
Director: Angela Courtney

NSPCC NI
Jennymount Court
North Derby Street, Belfast
BT15 3HN
Tel: 028 9035 1135
Fax: 028 9035 1100
Web: www.nspcss.org.uk
Divisional Director NI: Ian Elliott

Organisation of the Unemployed NI
14 May Street, Belfast BT1 4NL
Tel: 028 9031 0862
Fax: 028 9031 4975

Oxfam Northern Ireland
52–54 Dublin Road, Belfast
BT2 7HN
Tel: 028 9023 0220
Fax: 028 9023 7771
Web: www.oxfamireland.org
E-mail: oxfam@oxfamni.org.uk
Corporate Services Manager:
Julie McSorley

P A N D A
21 University Street, Belfast BT7 1FY
Tel: 028 9020 7307
Fax: 028 9020 8700
Co-ordinator: Arthur Magill

PAPA (Parents and Professionals and Autism) NI
Knockbracken Park, Saintfield Road
Belfast BT8 8BH
Tel: 028 9040 1729
Fax: 028 9040 3467
Web: www.autismni.org
Director: Arlene Cassidy

Parents Advice Centre
Franklin House, 12 Brunswick Street, Belfast BT2 7GE
Tel: 028 9040 1729
Fax: 028 9031 2475
Web: www.pachelp.org
E-mail: belfast@pachelp.org
Chief Executive: Pip Jaffa

PHAB
Knockbracken Health Park
Saintfield Road, Belfast BT8 8BH
Tel: 028 9050 4800
Fax: 028 9079 6070
Web: www.phabni.org
E-mail: info@phabni.org
Chief Executive: Trevor Boyle

Praxis Care Group

29–31 Lisburn Road, Belfast
BT9 7AA
Tel: 028 9023 4555
Fax: 028 9024 5535
Chief Executive: Nevin Ringland
Praxis Care is a new charity formed
out of the amalgamation of four
established charities in the mental
health area – Praxis Mental
Healthcare, Respond, Northern
Ireland Agoraphobia and Challenge.

The Princes Trust
5 Jenny Mount Court,
North Derby Street
Belfast BT15 3HN
Tel: 028 9074 5454
Fax: 028 9074 8416
Web: www.princes-trust.org.uk
E-mail: ptnire@princes-trust.org.uk
Director: Tommy Fagan

Prisoners Enterprise Project (South
Belfast)
127–145 Sandy Row
Belfast BT12 5ET
Tel: 028 9024 4449
Fax: 028 9024 4471
Co-ordinator: Bill Newman

The Rainbow Project
2-6 Union Street
Belfast BT1 2JF
Tel: 028 9031 9030
Fax: 028 9031 9031
Web: www.rainbow-project.com
E-mail: info@rainbow-project.com
Chairman: Frank Toner

Rape Crisis and Sexual Abuse Centre
29 Donegall Street, Belfast
BT1 2FG
Tel: 028 9024 9696

Reach Across
21 The Diamond, Derry BT48 6HP
Tel: 028 7128 0048
Fax: 028 7128 0058
Web: www.reach-across.co.uk
E-mail: reach-across@hotmail.com
Youth co-ordinator:
Barney McGuigan

Relate NI
74–76 Dublin Road, Belfast
BT2 7HP
Tel: 028 9032 3454
Fax: 028 9031 5298
Web: www.relateni.org
Chief Executive: Gerald Clark

Respond
25–31 Lisburn Road, Belfast
BT9 7AA
Tel: 028 9031 0883
Fax: 028 9024 5535
Director: Irene Sloan

Royal National Institute for the Blind
40 Linenhall Street, Belfast
BT2 8BA
Tel: 028 9032 9373
Fax: 028 9027 8119
Web: www.info@rnib.org.uk
Director: Susan Reid

Royal National Institute for the Deaf
(RNID)
Wilson House, 5 College Square
North, Belfast BT1 6AR
Tel: 028 9023 9619
Fax: 028 9031 2032
Director: Brian Symmington

Royal National Lifeboat Institution
Unit 1, Lifeboat House
Lesley Office Park
393 Holywood Road
Belfast BT4 2LS
Tel: 028 9047 3665
Fax: 028 9047 3668
Regional Manager: Patricia Mathison

PARKINSON'S DISEASE SOCIETY

Parkinson's Disease Society
Dunsilly Lodge
Dunsilly
Antrim
Northern Ireland
BT41 2JH
Tel / Fax: (028) 9442 8928

Bill Canning
Regional Manager

The Aims of the PDS

To help people with Parkinson's and
their relatives with the problems
arising from Parkinson's

To collect and disseminate
information on Parkinson's

To encourage and provide funds for
research into Parkinson's

There are branches throughout
Northern Ireland which meet
regularly.

National Helpline: 0808 800 0303

Royal Society for the Prevention of
Accidents
Nella House, Dargan Crescent
Belfast BT3 9JP
Tel: 028 9050 1160
Fax: 028 9050 1164
Manager: Janice Bisp

Royal Society for the Protection of Birds
Belvoir Park Forest, Belvoir Drive
Belfast BT8 7QT
Tel: 028 9049 1547
Fax: 028 9049 1669
Web: www.rspb.org.uk
Director: Dr Robert Brown

Save the Children Fund
15 Richmond Park, Belfast
BT10 0HB
Tel: 028 9062 0000
Fax: 028 9043 1314
Web: www.scfuk.org.uk
Marketing Area Manager:
Nichola James

Shelter (Northern Ireland)
1–5 Coyles Place, Belfast BT9 1EL
Tel: 028 9024 7752
Fax: 028 9024 5771
E-mail: shelter@fsnet.co.uk
Campaign Officer: Laurence Moffat

Simon Community Northern Ireland
57 Fitzroy Avenue, Belfast
BT9 1HT
Tel: 028 9023 2882
Fax: 028 9032 6839
Chief Executive: Carol O'Bryan

The Simon Community is one of Northern Ireland's largest charities, with over 200 staff with an annual budget in excess of £4m. Simon Community provides a wide range of services to homeless people including the provision of over 1,000 short-stay accommodation places all across Northern Ireland. In addition to lobbying for more appropriate accommodation for homeless people and better access to public services Simon Community is also focusing on the causes of homelessness and policy changes that could lead to greater prevention of this growing social problem.

Spina Bifida and Hydrocephalus Association (NI) (ASBAH)
Graham House
Knockbracken Healthcare Park
Saintfield Road, Belfast BT8 8BH
Tel: 028 9079 8878
Fax: 028 9079 7071
Web: www.asbah.org
E-mail: margarety@asbah.org
Regional Manager: Margaret Young

St John's Ambulance
Knockbracken Healthcare Park
Belfast BT8 8RA
Tel: 028 9079 9393
Fax: 028 9079 3303
Chief Executive: Dr Sheila McRandall

Tara Counselling & Personal Development Centre
11 Holmview Terrace, Omagh
Co Tyrone BT79 0AH
Tel: 028 8225 0024
Fax: 028 8225 0023
Administration Officer: Anne Devlin

Trocaire
50 King Street, Belfast BT1 6AD
Tel: 028 9080 8030
Fax: 028 9080 8031
Web: www.trocaire.org
Regional Manager: Roisin Thanki

Twins & Multiple Birth Association
Tel: 028 9065 4609
Fax: 028 9065 4609

Ulster Society for the Prevention of Cruelty to Animals
28 Benvarden Road
Ballymoney BT53 8AF
Tel: 028 2074 2788
Fax: 028 2074 1556
Web: www.planetpets-uspca.co.uk
Manager: Paddy Duffy

Ulster Cancer Foundation
40–42 Eglantine Avenue
Belfast BT9 6DX
Tel: 028 9066 3281
Fax: 028 9066 0081

Web: www.ulstercancer.org
E-mail: info@ulstercancer.org
Chief Executive: Arlene Spiers

North West Regional Office
14–16 The Diamond, Derry
BT47 0HN
Tel: 028 7128 8878
Fax: 028 7128 8879

Ulster Wildlife Trust
Ulster Wildlife Centre
3 New Line, Crossgar
Downpatrick BT30 9EP
Tel: 028 4483 0282
Fax: 028 4483 0888
E-mail: ulsterwt@clx.co.uk
Chief Executive: Dr David Erwin

Victim Support NI
Annsgate House, 70–74 Ann Street
Belfast BT1 4AH
Tel: 028 9024 4039
Fax: 028 9031 3838
E-mail: info@victimsupportni.org.uk
Chief Executive: Oliver Wilkinson

Voluntary Organisations Forum
47 Henderson Avenue
Cavehill Road
Belfast BT15 5FL
Tel: 028 9071 9119
Fax: 028 9020 9300
Director: Siobhan Bogues

Voluntary Service Belfast
70–72 Lisburn Road, Belfast
BT9 6AF
Tel: 028 9020 0850
Fax: 028 9020 0860
E-mail: info@vsb.org.uk
Director: Bill Osborne

War on Want
1 Rugby Avenue, Belfast BT7 1RD
Tel: 028 9023 2064
Fax: 028 9032 8019
Director: Ian McClelland

The Woodland Trust
1 Dufferin Court, Dufferin Avenue,
Bangor BT20 3BX
Tel: 028 9127 5787

Fax: 028 9127 5942
E-mail: wtni@woodland-trust.org.uk
Operations Director: Patrick Gregg

Women's Aid Belfast
Womens Aid, 49 Malone Road
Belfast BT9 6RY
Tel: 028 9066 6049
Fax: 028 9068 2874
Web: www.womensaid.org.uk
E-mail: admin@
     belfastwomensaid.co.uk
Management co-ordinator:
Margot Hesketh

Women's Aid Coleraine
23 Abbey Street, Coleraine
BT52 1DX
Tel: 028 7032 1263
Fax: 028 7032 0270
Administrator: Evelyn Morrow

Women's Aid Craigavon
198 Union Street, Lurgan
Craigavon BT66 8EQ
Tel: 028 3834 3256

Fax: 028 3834 8755
E-mail: info@craigavon
     banbridgewomensaid.org.uk

Women's Aid Fermanagh
24 Church Street
Enniskillen BT74 7EJ
Tel: 028 6632 8898
Fax: 028 6632 8859
Co-ordinator: Hazel Hayes

Women's Aid Newry
7 Downshire Place
Newry, Co Down BT34 1DZ
Tel: 028 3025 0765
Fax: 028 3026 9606
Co-ordinator: Gail McFerran

Women's Forum NI
PO Box 135, Belfast BT5 5WA
Tel: 028 9446 0251
Fax: 028 9446 0251
E-mail: anneking@lineone.net
Chairman: Ruth Graham

Youth and Community Organisations

An Crann / The Tree
10 Arthur St, Belfast BT1 4GD
Tel: 028 9024 0209
Fax: 028 9024 0219
E-mail: ancrann1@compuserve.com
Honorary Secretary: Dennis Greig

Ardglass Development Association
19 High Street, Ardglass
Tel: 028 4484 2404
Chairperson: Mary McCargoe

Ballymena Community Forum
37 Glendun Drive
Ballymena BT43 6SR
Tel: 028 2565 1032
Fax: 028 2565 1035
Web: www.ballymenacommunity
     forum.org
Contact: Corinna Peterson

Ballynafeigh Community Development Association
283 Ormeau Road, Belfast BT7 3GG
Tel: 028 9049 1161
Fax: 028 9049 2393
Web: www.bcda.net
Contact: Katie Hallon

Ballysillan Community Forum
925–927 Crumlin Road
Belfast BT14 8AB
Tel: 028 9039 1272
Fax: 028 9039 1259
Contact: Jane Field

Belfast Community Theatre Workshop
Crescent Arts Centre
2–4 University Road
Belfast BT7 1AH
Tel: 028 9031 0900
Fax: 028 9024 6748
E-mail: bct.comm.arts@ntlworld.com
Contact: Fintan Brady

Belfast Interface Project
Glendinning House, 6 Murray St
Belfast BT1 6DN
Tel: 028 9024 2828
Fax: 028 9024 2828
E-mail: bip@cinni.org

Belfast Travellers Education & Development Group
13a Glen Road, Belfast BT11 8BA
Tel: 028 9020 3337
Fax: 028 9080 9191
E-mail: info@ b-t-e-d-g@niireland.com/
Director: Paul Noonan

Belfast Traveller Support Group
Unit 12 Blackstaff Complex
77 Springfield Road
Belfast BT12 7AE
Tel: 028 9020 5330
Fax: 028 9020 5331
E-mail: btsp@cinni.org

Belfast Unemployed Resource Centre
45–47 Donegall Street
Belfast BT1 2FG
Tel: 028 9096 1111
Fax: 028 9096 1110
Manager: Joyce Green

Belfast Youth and Community Group
1–5 Donegall Lane, Belfast BT1 2LZ
Tel: 028 9024 4640
Fax: 028 9031 5629
E-mail: bycg@dial.pipex.com

Belfast Economic Resource Centre
1–5 Coyles Place, Belfast BT7 1EL
Tel: 028 9024 1924
Fax: 028 9024 6985
E-mail: office@boysandgirlsclub-ni.org.uk
Director of Programmes: Terry Watson

Business in the Community
770 Upper Newtownards Road, Dundonald, Belfast BT16 1UL
Tel: 028 9041 0410
Fax: 0289041 9030
E-mail: gillian.mckee@bitcni.org.uk
PR Director: Gillian McKee

Boys Brigade Northern Ireland Headquarters
National Training Centre
Rathmore House
126 Glenarm Road, Larne BT40 1DZ
Tel: 028 2827 2794
Fax: 028 2827 5150
Director: Alec Hunter

Catholic Guides of Ireland, Northern Region
285 Antrim Road, Belfast BT15 2G2
Tel: 028 9074 0835
Fax: 028 9074 1311
E-mail: guides@ northern.freeserve.co.uk
Chairperson: Eilish Smyth

Central Community Relations Unit
Block A, Level 5, Room A5.18
Castle Buildings, Stormont
Belfast BT4 3SG
Tel: 028 9052 8258
Fax: 028 9052 8426
Principal Officer: Denis Ritchie

Challenge for Youth
40–46 Edward Street
Belfast BT1 2LP
Tel: 028 9023 6893
Fax: 028 9024 0718
Manager: David Gardiner

Children's Law Centre
Phillip House, York St
Belfast BT15 1AB
Tel: 028 9024 5704
Fax: 028 9024 5679
E-mail: info@childrenslawcentre.org
Director: Ms Paddy Kelly

Children's Project NI
290 Antrim Road, Belfast BT15 5AN
Tel: 028 9074 1536
Fax: 028 9080 5578
E-mail: cpnibfast@yahoo.co.uk
Director: Gary Rocks

Chinese Welfare Association (NI)
133–135 University Street
Belfast BT7 1HP
Tel: 028 9028 8277
Fax: 028 9028 8278
E-mail: cwa.anna@cinni.org
Chief Executive: Anna Lo

Clogher Valley Rural Centre
Creebought House, 47 Main Street, Clogher, Co Tyrone BT76 0AA
Tel: 028 8554 8872
Fax: 028 8554 8203
E-mail: seank@cu.dnet.co.uk
Manager: Sean Kelly

The Clonard / Fitzroy Fellowship
5 Sunbury Avenue, Belfast BT5 5NU
Tel: 028 9065 4353
Contact: Mrs M Rintoul

Colin Glen Trust
163 Stewartstown Road
Belfast BT17 0HW
Tel: 028 9061 4115
Fax: 028 9060 1694
E-mail: info@colinglentrust.org
Chief Executive: Tim Duffy

Community Arts Forum
15 Church Street, Belfast BT1 1PG
Tel: 028 9024 2910
Fax: 028 9031 2264
Web: www.cast.ie/
E-mail: admin@cast.ie
Director: Heather Floyd

Community Bridges Programme
16 Donegall Square South
Belfast BT1 5JF
Tel: 028 9031 3220
Fax: 028 9031 3180
E-mail: community.bridge@dnet.co.uk
Programme Coordinator: Joe Hinds

Community Change
Philip House, 123 York Street
Belfast BT15 1AB
Tel: 028 9023 2587
Fax: 028 9031 2216
E-mail: info@communitychange-ni.org
Head of Agency: Alison Wightman

Community Development Centre North Belfast
22 Cliftonville Road, Belfast
BT14 6JX
Tel: 028 9028 4400
Fax: 028 9028 4401
E-mail: info.nbcdc@ntlworld.com
Senior Administrator:
Heather Stewart

Community Development & Health Network
Ballybot House, 28 Corn Market
Newry BT35 8BG
Tel: 028 3026 4606
Fax: 028 3026 4626
E-mail: cdhn@btconnect.com
Director: Ruth Sutherland

Community Dialogue
373 Springfield Road
Belfast BT12 7DG
Tel: 028 9032 9995
Fax: 028 9033 0482
E-mail: admin@commdial.org
Directors: Brian Lennon and
David Halloway

Community Empowerment Larne
Stylux Business Park
Glenarm Road, Larne
Tel: 028 2826 7552
205a Linn Road, Larne
Tel: 028 2827 3953

Community Evaluation Services (NI)
295 Ormeau Road, Belfast BT7 3GU
Tel: 028 9064 6355
Fax: 028 9064 1118
E-mail: info@ceni.org
Director: Brendan McDonnell

Community Information Technology Unit
45–47 Donegall Street
Belfast BT1 2FG
Tel: 028 9096 1104
Fax: 028 9096 1110
E-mail: citu@burc.org
Director: Brendan Mackin

Community Network Portadown
4 Market Lane, Portadown
BT62 3JY
Tel: 028 3835 1710
Fax: 028 3836 2494
E-mail: comnet@globalnet.co.uk
Director: Patricia Cooke

Community Organisations of South Tyrone & Areas
56a Main Street, Augher BT77 0BG
Tel: 028 8554 9819
Fax: 028 8554 9821
E-mail: costa.augher@virgin.co.uk
Network Development Officer:
Lorraine Griffin

Community Relations Training and Learning Consortium
2 Coalisland Road
Dungannon BT71 6JT

Tel: 0771 466 0506
Fax: 028 8772 9611
E-mail: info@crtlc.org
Co-ordinator: Elaine Rowan

Community Restorative Justice
195 Whiterock Road
Belfast BT12 7FW
Tel: 028 9027 8359
E-mail: uscrji@ukonline.co.uk
Administrator: Chrissie MacSiacais

Community Technical Aid NI
445–449 Ormeau Road
Belfast BT7 3GQ
Tel: 028 9064 2227
Fax: 028 9064 2467
E-mail:
info@communitytechnicalaid.org
Director: Colm Bradley

Community Transport Association UK
Graham House, Saintfield Road
Belfast BT7 8BH
Tel: 028 9040 3535
E-mail:
bryan@communitytransport.com
Regional Development Officer:
Bryan Miles

Community Work Education and Training Network
Philip House, York Street
Belfast BT15 1AB
Tel: 028 9023 2618
Fax: 028 9031 2216
Co-ordinator: Peggy Flanagan

Cornerstone Community
443–445 Springfield Road
Belfast BT12 7DL
Tel: 028 9032 1649
Fax: 028 9032 7323
E-mail: cornerstone@cornerstone.co.uk
Administrator: Geraldine Connolly

Counteract
Philip House, 123–137 York Street
Belfast BT15 1AB
Tel: 028 9023 7023
Fax: 028 9031 3585
E-mail: counteract@btconnect.com
Director: William Robinson

Devenish Partnership Forum
26 Yoan Road, Kilmacormick,
Enniskillen BT74 6EI
Tel: 028 6632 7808
Fax: 028 6632 7808
Web: www.devenish.partnership@
    cinni.org
Manager: John Guthrie

Duke of Edinburgh Award NI
28 Wellington Park, Belfast
BT9 6DL
Tel: 028 9050 9550
Fax: 028 9050 9555
E-mail: nireland@theaward.org
Secretary: Eric Rainey

Dunlewey Substance Advice Centre NI Ltd
226 Stewartstown Road
Belfast BT17 0LB
Tel: 028 9061 1162
Fax: 028 9060 3751
E-mail: dsac@btclick.com
Director: Annette Goodall

East Belfast Community Development Agency
269 Albertbridge Road
Belfast BT5 4PY
Tel: 028 9045 1512
Fax: 028 9073 8039
E-mail: inf@ebcda.com
Director: Mrs Maggie Andrews

Enkalon Foundation
25 Randalstown Road
Antrim BT41 4LJ
Tel: 028 9446 3535
Fax: 028 9446 5733
E-mail: enkfoundation@lineone.net
Secretary: John Wallace

Falls Community Council
275–277 Falls Road
Belfast BT12 6FD
Tel: 028 9020 2030
Fax:028 9020 2031
E-mail: fallscommunitycouncil.org
Director: Eileen Howell

Fermanagh Access and Mobility Group
36 Eastbridge Street
Enniskillen BT74 7BT
Tel: 028 6634 0275
E-mail: fermanaghaccess@swiftsoft.net
Chairperson: Gerry Maguire

Fermanagh Rural Community Initiative
8b Queen Elizabeth Road
Enniskillen BT74 7DG
Tel: 028 6632 6478
Fax: 028 6632 5984
E-mail: frci@totalserve.co.uk
Manager: Ciaran Rooney

Fermanagh Volunteer Bureau
12 Belmore Street
Enniskillen BT74 7DG
Tel: 028 6632 8438
Fax: 028 6632 2061
E-mail: info@fermanaghrb.org
Chairperson: Martin Lawson

Girls Brigade Northern Ireland
16 May Street, Belfast BT1 4NL
Tel: 028 9023 1157
Fax: 028 9032 3633
E-mail: info@girlsbrigadeni.com
National Secretary: Doreen Tennis

Greater Shankill Community Council
17 Shankill Road, Belfast
BT13 1FT
Tel: 028 9032 5536
Fax: 028 9024 4469
Manager: Mr Bill Patterson

Greater Shankill Early Years Project
Alessie Centre, 60 Shankill Road
Belfast BT13 2BB
Tel: 028 9087 4000
Fax: 028 9087 4009
E-mail: irene@earlyyears.org.uk
Administration Manager:
Irene Cooke

Greater Twinbrook and Poleglass Community Forum
Unit W2, Dairyfarm Centre,
Stewartstown Road, Belfast BT17
0AW

Tel: 028 9060 4004
Fax: 028 9060 4104
Director: Sean Gibson

Greater West Belfast Community Association
76–78 Hamill Street
Belfast BT12 4AA
Tel: 028 9032 8295
Fax: 028 9032 8295
E-mail: gwbca@aol.com
Manager: Mary O'Rawe

Groundwork NI
Midland Building, Whitla Street
Belfast BT15 1NH
Tel: 028 9074 9494
Fax: 028 9075 2373
E-mail: info@groundworkni.co.uk
Executive Director: Mary McKee

Guide Association
Lorne House, Station Road,
Craigavad, Holywood BT18 0BP
Tel: 028 9042 5212
Fax: 028 9042 6025
E-mail: ulsterhq@guides.org.uk
Ulster administrator: Claire Bradley

Holywell Trust
10–12 Bishop Street, Derry BT48 6PW
Tel: 028 7126 1941
Fax: 028 7126 9332
E-mail: holywell.trust@business.ntl.com
Director: Eamonn Deane

Housing Rights Service
72 North Street, Belfast BT1 1LD
Tel: 028 9024 5640
Fax: 028 9031 2200
E-mail: hrs@housing-rights.org.uk
Director: Janet Hunter

Horizon Project
234 Upper Lisburn Road
Belfast BT10 0TA
Tel: 028 9060 5424
Fax: 028 9060 5423
E-mail: horizonbel@
    admins.freeserve.co.uk
Co-ordinator: George Simms

Initiative on Conflict Resolution and
Ethnicity (INCORE)
Aberfoyle House, Northland Road
Derry BT48 7JA
Tel: 028 7137 5500
Fax: 028 7137 5510
E-mail: incore@incore.ulst.ac.uk
Director: Professor Marie Fitzduff

Larne Community Development Project
Unit 25, Ledcom Industrial Estate
Larne BT40 3AW
Tel: 028 2826 7976
E-mail: info@larnecdp.org.uk
Chairperson: Geoffrey Kerr

Law Centre NI Belfast
124 Donegall Street, Belfast
BT1 2GY
Tel: 028 9024 4401
Fax: 028 9023 9938
E-mail: admin.belfast@lawcenteni.org
Director: Les Allamby

Leonard Cheshire NI Regional Office
5 Boucher Plaza, 4–6
Boucher Road
Belfast BT12 6HR
Tel: 028 9024 6247
Fax: 028 9024 6395
E-mail: info@ni.leonard-cheshire.org.uk
Regional Director: Roisin Foster

Lifeline
C/o 113 Strandburn Drive,
Sydenham, Belfast BT4 1NB
Tel: 028 9065 8328
Chairperson: Mrs Lindsey

Lifestart Foundation NI
11 Bishops Street, Derry BT48 6PL
Tel: 028 7136 5363
Fax: 028 7136 5334
E-mail: lifestart@foni.freeserve.co.uk
Director: Dolores McGuinness

Ligoniel Improvement Association
148 Ligoniel Road, Belfast
BT14 8DT
Tel: 028 9039 1225
Fax: 028 9039 1723
E-mail: wolfehill@greeuk.com
Director: Tony Morgan

LINC
218 York Street, Belfast BT15 1GY
Tel: 028 9027 8163
Fax: 028 907 45983
E-mail: billy.linc@cinni.lorg
Programme Manager: Billy Mitchell
Chairperson: Rev Philip Bell

Link Community Association
7 Avoca Park, Belfast BT11 9BH
Tel: 028 9020 0774
Fax: 028 9020 0774
Chairperson: Barbara Lynn

Lisburn Inter Church Project
22 Batchelors Walk, Lisburn
BT28 1XJ
Tel: 07092336691
Fax: 028 9260 1299
E-mail: info@licp.org
Co-ordinator: Kerry Nicholson

Lower North Belfast Community
Council
The Castleton Centre
30–42 York Road, Belfast
BT15 3HE
Tel: 028 9020 8100
Fax: 028 9020 1103
Programmes Manager:
Stephen Nicholl

Lurgan Council for Voluntary Action
Mount Zion House, Edward Street
Lurgan BT66 6DB
Tel: 028 3832 2066
Fax: 028 3834 8612
E-mail: info@lcva.co.uk
Director: Edwin Graham

Magnet Young Adult Centre
81a Hill Street, Newry BT34 1DG
Tel: 028 3026 9070
Fax: 028 3026 8132
E-mail: magnet-centre@fsnet.co.uk
Senior Youth Worker:
Eugene Donnelly

Mediation Network for Northern
Ireland
10 Upper Crescent, Belfast
BT7 1NT

Tel: 028 9043 8614
Fax: 028 9031 4430
Web: www.mediation-network.org.uk
E-mail: info@mediationnorthernireland.org
Director: Brendan McAllister

Mornington Community Project NI
117 Ormeau Road, Belfast
BT7 1SH
Tel: 028 9033 0911
Fax: 028 9023 4730
E-mail: ken.mornington@ciini.org
Director: Ken Humphrey

Multicultural Resource Centre
9 Lower Crescent, Belfast
BT7 1NR
Tel: 028 9024 4639
Fax: 028 9032 9581
Web: www.mcrc.co.uk
Chief Officer: Nadette Foley

Neighbourhood Energy Action
64–66 Upper Church Street
Belfast BT1 4QL
Tel: 028 9023 9909
Fax: 028 9043 9191
E-mail: northern.ireland@nea.org.uk
Director: Majella McCloskey

Newtownabbey Community
Development Agency
Ferbro Buildings, 333 Antrim Road,
Newtownabbey BT36 5DZ
Tel: 028 9083 8088
Fax: 028 9083 0108
Director: Victor Robinson

NIACRO Belfast
169 Ormeau Road, Belfast
BT7 1SQ
Tel: 028 9032 0157
Fax: 028 9023 4084
E-mail: info.niacro@cinni.org
Chief Executive: Alwyn Lyner

NIACRO Community Relations Project
16 Russell Street, Armagh BT61 9AA
Tel: 028 3751 5910
Fax: 028 3751 5919
E-mail: jennys.niacro@cinni.org
Manager: Margaret Montgomery

North Belfast Community
Development Centre
22 Cliftonville Road, Belfast
BT14 6JX
Tel: 028 9028 4400
Fax: 028 9028 4401
E-mail: info.nbcdc@ntlworld.com
Chairperson: Brendan Bradley

Northern Ireland Association of Youth
Clubs
'Hampton', Glenmachan Road
Belfast BT4 2NL
Tel: 028 9076 0067
Fax: 028 9076 8799
E-mail: info@youthaction.org
Director: June Trimble

Northern Ireland Council for Ethnic
Minorities
3rd Floor, Ascot House
24–31 Shaftesbury Square
Belfast BT2 7DB
Tel: 028 9023 8645
Fax: 028 9031 9485
E-mail: nicem@nireland.freeserve.co.uk
Executive Director: Patrick Yu

Peace People
Fredheim, 224 Lisburn Road
Belfast BT9 6GE
Tel: 028 9066 3465
Fax: 028 9068 3947
E-mail: peacepeople@gn.apc.org
Chairperson: Gerry Graham

The Phoenix Centre
Unit 14 Bluestone Business Centre,
Moyraverty Road West
Craigavon BT65 5HD
Tel: 028 3832 7614
Fax: 028 3832 7614
Manager: Pearl Snowdon

Poleglass Residents Association
Sallygarden Lane, Belle Steel Road,
Poleglass, Belfast BT17 0PB
Tel: 028 9062 7250
Fax: 028 9062 7250
E-mail: poleglass@hotmail.com
Chairperson: George Rogan

Quaker House Belfast
Joint Project
7 University Avenue, Belfast
BT7 1GY
Tel: 028 9024 9293
E-mail: quaker.house@ntlworld.com
Representative: Mark Chapman

Rural Community Network
38a Oldtown Street
Cookstown BT80 8EF
Tel: 028 8676 6670
Fax: 028 8676 6006
E-mail:
info@ruralcommunitynetwork.org
Chairperson: Roy Hanna

Sandy Row Community Forum
C/o Sandy Row Community Centre
63–75 Sandy Row, Belfast
BT12 5ER
Tel: 028 9023 8446
Fax: 028 9022 5335
Chairperson: Ernie Corbett

Scout Association
Old Milltown Road, Belfast
BT8 7SP
Tel: 028 9049 2829
Fax: 028 9049 2830
E-mail: info@scoutsni.com
Executive Commissioner:
Ken Gillespie

Scouting Foundation Northern Ireland (CSI)
Lisburn Enterprise Centre
Ballinderry Road, Lisburn
Tel: 028 9266 7696
Fax: 028 9266 7897

Shankill Lurgan Community Projects
53 Edward Street BT66 6DB
Tel: 028 3832 4680
Fax: 028 3832 6272
Manager: Mr Hugh Casey

Share Centre
Smiths Strand, Lisnaskea
BT92 0EQ
Tel: 028 6772 2122
Fax: 028 6772 1893
E-mail: info@sharevillage.org
Director: Oliver Wilkinson

Speedwell Project
Parkanaur Forest Park
Dungannon BT70 3AA
Tel: 028 8776 7392
Fax: 028 8776 1794
E-mail: speedwell.trust@btinternet.com
Director: Jean Kelly

Strabane Community Unemployment
Resource Centre
13a Newton Street
Strabane BT82 8DN
Tel: 028 7138 3927
Fax: 028 7138 3927
Manager: Betty Bradley

Training for Women Network Ltd
Unit 9, Edgewater Office Park
Belfast BT3 9JQ
Tel: 028 9077 7199
Fax: 028 9077 0887
E-mail: info@trainingforwomennetwork.org
Chairperson: Alice Higgins

Traveller Movement NI
30 University Street, Belfast
BT7 1FZ
Tel: 028 9020 2727
Fax: 028 9020 2005
E-mail: info@tmni.org
Director: Margaret Donaghy

Ulster Community Investment Trust
13–19 Linenhall Street
Belfast BT2 8AA
Tel: 028 9031 5003
Fax: 028 9031 5008
E-mail: info@ucitld.com
Chief Executive: Brian Howe

University for Industry Learndirect
400 Springfield Road, Belfast
Tel: 028 9090 0070
E-mail: info@ufi.com
Head of UFI in Northern Ireland:
Mark Langhammer

WAVE Trauma Centre
5 Chichester Street Park South
Belfast BT15 5DW
Tel: 028 9077 9922
Fax: 028 9078 1165
E-mail: wavetc@clara.co.uk
Chief Executive: Sandra Peake

West Belfast Economic Forum
148–158 Springfield Road
Belfast BT12 7DR
Tel: 028 9087 4545
Fax: 028 9087 5050
E-mail: info@wbef.org

West Belfast Parent Youth Group
141–143 Falls Road
Belfast BT12 6AF
Tel: 028 9023 6669
Fax: 028 9023 5564
E-mail: marieosbourne@btconnect.co.uk
Centre Manager: Marie Osborne

Women into Politics
109–113 Royal Avenue
Belfast BT1 1FF
Tel: 028 9024 3363
Fax: 028 9023 7884
Director: Elizabeth Hendron

Women's Resource & Development Agency
6 Mount Charles, Belfast BT7 1NZ
Tel: 028 9023 0212
Fax: 0289024 4363
E-mail: info@wrda.net
Chairperson: Louise O'Mara

Young Persons Project
2 Old Lurgan Road, Portadown
Tel: 028 3839 1155
Fax: 028 3839 3718
Manager: Peadar White

YMCA National Council
Memorial House, 9–13 Waring Street
Belfast BT1 2EU
Tel: 028 9032 7757
Fax: 028 9043 8809
E-mail: admin@ymca-ireland.org
National Secretary: Stephen Turner

Youth Initiatives
Central Office, 128b Lisburn Road
Belfast BT9 6HA
Tel: 028 9066 3710
Fax: 028 9066 8229
31 Colin Road, Dunmurry
Tel: 028 9030 1174

Youth Link NI
143a University St, Belfast
BT7 1HP
Tel: 028 9032 3217
Fax: 028 9032 3247
E-mail: info@youthlink.org.uk
Director: Rev Patrick White

YouthAction
Northern Ireland
Hampton, Glenmachan Park
Belfast BT4 2PJ
Tel: 028 9076 0067
Fax: 028 9076 8799
Director: June Trimble

YouthNet
7 James St South, Belfast
BT2 8DN
Tel: 028 9033 1880
Fax: 028 9033 1977
E-mail: youthnet-ni@dnet.co.uk
Director: Denis Palmer

Religious, Political and Cultural Organisations

Despite the fact that Northern Ireland has endured many years of conflict it is a deeply religious place by Western European standards.

Church attendances remain the highest of any region in the UK and there is a high ratio of churches to population. The Community is overwhelmingly Christian with the main four churches being Roman Catholic, Presbyterian, Church of Ireland and Methodist, with a strong evangelical tradition within Northern Ireland Protestantism. Most of the other major world religions are represented in Northern Ireland in relatively small numbers. The section below lists the various Churches found in Northern Ireland, with additional contact details for the larger institutions.

Irish Council of Churches
Inter-Church Centre
48 Elmwood Avenue, Belfast BT9 6AZ
Tel: 028 9066 3145
Fax: 028 9038 2780
E-mail: icpep@email.com
Web: www.irishchurches.org
General Secretary: Dr R D Stevens

Bahá'í Faith
64 Old Dundonald Road
Dundonald BT16 1XS
Tel: 028 9048 0500
Fax: 028 9041 0100

Baptist Union of Ireland
117 Lisburn Road, Belfast BT9 7AF
Tel: 028 9047 1908
Fax: 028 9047 1363

Belfast Islamic Centre
38 Wellington Park, Belfast BT9 6DN
Tel: 028 9066 4465
Fax: 028 9091 3148
Web: www.belfastislamiccentre.com
Contact: Kamar Abdul

Belfast Synagogue
49 Somerton Road, Belfast BT15
Tel: 028 9077 7974

Bethel Temple
95 Main St, Portglenone
Ballymena BT44 8HR
Tel: 028 2582 1167
Contact: David Lamont

Buddhist Centre
18 Eastleigh Crescent
Belfast BT5 6HT
Tel: 028 9028 4872
Web: www.potalacentre.org.uk

Roman Catholic Church
The Roman Catholic Church administers Ireland as a single unit, divided into 4 ecclesiastical Provinces. The Province of Armagh comprises of 6 dioceses, which together cover the whole of Northern Ireland and a proportion of the Republic of Ireland.

Catholic Bishops in the Province of Armagh

Most Rev Séan Brady,
Archbishop of Armagh
Ara Coeli, Cathedral Road
Armagh BT61 7QY
Tel: 028 3752 2045
Fax: 028 3752 6182

Most Rev Seamus Hegarty,
Bishop of Derry
Bishop's House,
St Eugene's Cathedral
Derry BT48 9AP
Tel: 028 7126 2302
Fax: 028 7137 1960

Most Rev Francis Lagan,
Auxiliary Bishop of Derry
9 Glen Road, Strabane
Co Tyrone BT82 8BX
Tel: 028 7188 4533
Fax: 028 7188 4551

Most Rev Patrick Walsh, Bishop of
Down and Connor
Lisbreen, 73 Somerton Road
Belfast BT15 4DE
Tel: 028 9077 6185
Fax: 028 9077 9377

Most Rev Anthony Farquhar,
Auxiliary Bishop of Down and
Connor
Lisbreen, 73 Somerton Road
Belfast BT15 4DE
Tel: 028 9077 6185
Fax: 028 9077 9377

Most Rev John McAreavey,
Bishop of Dromore
Bishop's House, 44 Armagh Road
Newry BT35 6PN
Tel: 028 3026 2444
Fax: 028 3026 0496

Christian Brothers
The Abbey Monastery, Courtney Hill,
Newry BT34 ED
Tel: 028 3026 4475

Church of Ireland
Church of Ireland House
61–67 Donegall Street
Belfast BT1 2QH
Tel: 028 9032 2268
Fax: 028 9032 1635

The Church of Ireland divides the island of Ireland into two Provinces, Armagh and Dublin. The majority of its members are in Northern Ireland; this congregation is administered under the province of Armagh.

The General Synod of the Church of Ireland, consisting of the archbishops and bishops, with 216 representatives of the clergy and 432 representatives of the laity, has chief legislative power in the Church.

Church of Ireland Bishops in the Province of Armagh

The Right Honourable the
Lord Eames of Armagh
The See House, Cathedral Close,
Armagh BT61 7EE
Tel: 028 3752 7144 (O)
Fax: 028 3752 7823

The Right Rev Michael Jackson
Lord Bishop of Clogher

The Right Rev Dr James Mehaffey,
Lord Bishop of Derry and Raphoe
The See House, 112 Culmore Road
Derry BT48 8JF
Tel: 028 7135 1206 (H)
Tel: 028 7126 2440 (O)
Fax: 028 7135 2554

The Right Rev H C Miller,
Lord Bishop of Down and Dromore
The See House
32 Knockdere Park South
Belfast BT5 7AB
Tel: 028 9047 1973
Fax: 028 9065 0584

The Right Rev J E Moore,
Lord Bishop of Connor
Bishop's House
113 Upper Road, Greenisland
Carrickfergus BT38 8RR
Tel: 028 9086 3165
Fax: 028 9036 4266

Church of Jesus Christ of the Latter
Day Saints
403 Holywood Road, Belfast
Tel: 028 9076 8250
President: Eric Noble

Conference of
Religious of Ireland
369 Springfield Road
Belfast BT12 7DJ
Tel: 028 9031 3944
Fax: 028 9031 3947
Contact: Sister Brighde Vallely

Elim Pentecostal Church
122a Alexandra Park Avenue
Belfast BT15 3GJ
Tel: 028 9074 4404
Fax: 028 9074 8422
Senior Minister: John Legg

Free Presbyterian Church
Martyrs Memorial
356 Ravenhill Road
Belfast
Moderator: Rev I Paisley

The Free Presbyterian Church has grown rapidly in Northern Ireland over the past 30 years. It was founded and is still headed by Rev, Ian Paisley, founder and leader of one of Northern Ireland's main political parties, the Democratic Unionist Party.

International Society for Krishna Consciousness
Inis Rath Island, Geaglum
Derrylin, Enniskillen, Co Fermanagh
Tel: 028 6772 1512
Web: www.iskon.org.uk

Jehovah's Witnesses
9 Belmont Park, Belfast BT4 3DU
Tel: 028 9028 2126

Methodist Church in Ireland
Mission House, 13 University Road
Belfast BT7 1NA
Tel: 028 9032 0078
Fax: 028 9043 8700

The Methodist Church divides Ireland into eight district synods, each containing a number of circuits. Each synod is headed by a District Superintendent. The Methodist Conference meets around the island every year, and elects a President as overall head of the Church.

President: Rev Harold Good
49 Old Forge Manor, Belfast BT10 0HY
Tel: 028 9060 4200

Secretary: Rev E T I Mawhinney
1 Fountainville Avenue
Belfast BT9 6AN
Tel: 028 9032 4554
Fax: 028 9023 9467

District Superintendents

Belfast District:
Rev Dr W B Fletcher
33a Ardenlee Avenue, Belfast BT6 0AA
Tel: 028 9045 5121

Down District: Rev Robin P Roddie
16 Brooklands Road, Newtownards,
Co Down BT23 4TL
Tel: 028 9181 5959

Enniskillen and Sligo District:
Rev Aian Ferguson
Aldersgate, 47 Chanterhill Road,
Enniskillen, Co Fermanagh BT74 6DE
Tel: 028 6632 2244

North East District:
Rev Paul Kingston
33 Highgrove Drive, Ballyclare
Co Antrim BT39 9XH
Tel: 028 9332 2272
Fax: 028 9332 2272

North West District:
Rev I D Henderson
Glebe Crest, Donegal
Tel: 00353 73 23588

Portadown District:
Rev W James Rea
35 Thomas Street, Portadown
BT62 3NU
Tel: 028 3833 3030

Methodist Administration

Trustees of the Methodist Church in Ireland
1 Fountainville Avenue
Belfast BT9 6AN
Tel: 028 9032 4554
Fax: 028 9023 9467
Secretary: Rev E T I Mawhinney
Treasurer: Rev K H Thompson

10 Margaretholme, Claremont Road,
Sandymount, Dublin 4
Tel: 00353 1 668 3353

Lay Treasurer: R B Lilburn
Non-Subscribing Presbyterian Church of Ireland
C/o 'Druncorran',
102 Carrickfergus Road
Larne BT49 3JX
Tel: 028 2827 2600

Presbyterian Church in Ireland
Church House, Fisherwick Place
Belfast BT1 6DQ
Tel: 028 9024 7453
Fax: 028 9024 8377
Web: www.presbyterianireland.org

General Assembly Moderator:
Rev Dr Alastair Dunlop
Tel: 028 9032 2284
Fax: 028 9024 8366

Clerk of the Assembly: Very Rev Dr Samuel Hutchinson

The Presbyterian Church in Ireland is divided into congregations or parishes, collectively containing over 280,000 members. The congregations are grouped into 21 district presbyteries. Eighteen of these are in the North, with the majority of Presbyterians in the South of Ireland in Dublin and the border counties. The Church is governed by an annual General Assembly, which is composed of representatives from every congregation. The General Assembly elects a Moderator each June, to act as the chief public representative of Presbyterians in Ireland.

Quakers Religious Society of Friends
Friends Meeting House
Frederick Street, Belfast BT1 2LW
Tel: 028 9082 6708

Salvation Army
12 Station Mews, Sydenham
Belfast BT4 1TL
Tel: 028 9067 5000
Fax: 028 9067 5011
Web: www.salvationarmy.org.uk
Public Relations: Mrs Pamela Neil

Seventh Day Adventist Church
9 Newry Road, Banbridge BT32 3HF
Tel: 028 4062 6361
Fax: 028 4062 6361

Sikh Cultural Centre
Simpsons Brae, Derry BT47 6DL
Tel: 028 7134 3523

Ulster Humanist Association
25 Riverside Drive, Lisburn BT27 4HE
Tel: 028 9267 7264

Cultural Organisations

Grand Orange Lodge
of Ireland
Schomberg House
368 Cregagh Road, Belfast BT6 9EY
Tel: 028 9070 1122
Fax: 028 9040 3700

Grand Master: Robert S Saulters
Deputy Grand Master: Alfred E Lee
Deputy Assistant Grand Masters:
Rev, Stephen Dickinson,
William Ross
Grand Secretary: Denis J Watson

The Orange Order is possibly Northern Ireland's best-known 'cultural' organisation, with an active membership of over 100,000 men and women. It is a Protestant organisation steeped in the heritage of Protestant struggle for religious freedoms in the seventeenth century. The Order has formal links all over the world with similar institutions and is best known for its colourful militaristic marches during the summer. The major date in the Orange calendar is the twelfth of July, known simply as 'The Twelfth Day', when King William fought the Battle of the Boyne, which is celebrated by Orangemen everywhere. However, Orange marches have become increasingly controversial, in certain parts of Northern Ireland, in recent years.

Latin American Community and
Cultural Association
C/o Multicultural Resources Centre
12 Upper Crescent, Belfast BT7 1NB
Tel: 028 9024 4639
E-mail: launida@mcrc.co.uk
Chairperson: Cony Ortiz

Ulster Scots Heritage Council
218 York Street, Belfast BT15 1GY
Tel: 028 9074 6939
Fax: 028 9074 6980
Director: Nelson McCausland

Ulster Scots Historical & Cultural
Society
Tel: 028 7133 8457

Political Organisations

Committee on the Administration of
Justice
45–47 Donegall St, Belfast BT1 2FG
Tel: 028 9096 1122
Fax: 028 9024 6706
Web: www.caj.org.uk
Director: Martin O'Brien

New Ireland Group
C/o 85 Charlotte St
Ballymoney BT53 6AZ
Tel: 028 2766 2235

Political Parties

Details of Northern Ireland's main political parties are set out in Chapter 3.

Sporting, Leisure and Arts Organisations

Badminton Union of Ireland
House of Sport, Upper Malone Road
Belfast BT9
Tel: 028 9038 3810
General Secretary: John Feeney

Belfast Giants Ice
Hockey Club
Unit 2, Ormeau Business Park
8 Cromac Avenue, Belfast BT7
Tel: 028 9059 1111
Contact: Richard Gowdy

British Association for Shooting and
Conservation
The Courtyard Cottage
Galgorm Castle, Ballymena
Tel: 028 2565 2349

British Horse Society
(NI Region)
60 Windmill Road
Hillsborough BT26 6LX
Tel: 028 9268 3801
Fax: 028 9268 3801
Web: www.bhsireland.co.uk
E-mail: bhsireland@aol.com
Contact: Susan Irwin

Council of University
Sports Administrators
Queens PEC, Botanic Gardens
Belfast BT9 5EX
Tel: 028 9068 1126
Fax: 028 9068 1129
Contact: Paul Mc Cann
Tel: 00353 8 7278 0278

Canoeing Association of Northern
Ireland (CANI)
C/o House of Sport
Upper Malone Road, Belfast BT9 5LA
Tel: 028 9146 9907
Contact: Dawn Coulter

Disability Sports NI
Development Avenue
Unit 10 Ormeau Business Park
8 Cromac Avenue, Belfast BT7 2JA
Tel: 028 9050 8255
Fax: 028 9050 8256
Web: www.dsni.co.uk
E-mail: email@dsni.co.uk
Contact: Mr Kevin O'Neill

Eventing Ireland
98 Shore Street, Killyleagh BT30 9QJ
Tel: 028 4482 8734
Fax: 028 4482 1166
Secretary: Margaret Spiers

Fitness Northern Ireland
147 Holywood Road
Belfast BT17 9NH
Tel: 028 9065 1103
Contact: Mrs D Reid

Gaelic Athletic Association: Ulster Council
House of Sport, Upper Malone Road
Belfast BT9 5LA
Tel: 028 9038 3815
Fax: 028 9068 2757
Development Officer: Seamus McGrattan

The Gaelic Athletic Association is Northern Ireland's leading participant sports organisation. It presides over Gaelic football, hurling, camogie and handball, as well as a range of other cultural activities.

Golfing Unions of Ireland, Ulster Branch
58a High Street, Holywood BT18 9AE
Tel: 028 9042 3708
Fax: 028 9042 6766
Branch Secretary: Mr B Edwards

International Sport Kickboxing Association UK
Dundela Social Club
Wilgar Street, Belfast
Tel: 028 9065 6414
Contact: Billy Murray

International Swimming Teachers Association
4 Firfields, Lough Road
Antrim BT41 4DJ
Tel: 028 9448 7050
E-mail: natiinfo@aol.com
Regional Organiser NI: Des Cossum

Irish Amateur Swimming Association
House of Sport
Upper Malone Road, Belfast
Tel: 028 9038 3807
DevelopmentOfficer:Ruth McQuillan

Irish Bowling Association
78 North Road, Belfast BT5 5NL
Tel: 028 9065 5076
Fax: 028 9065 5076
E-mail: iba@btinternet.com
Honorary Secretary: Mr J Humphreys

Irish Football Association
20 Windsor Avenue, Belfast BT9 6EE
Tel: 028 9066 9458
Fax: 028 9066 7620
General Secretary: Mr David Bowen
The IFA presides over soccer in Northern Ireland.

Ulster Branch, Irish Hockey Association
House of Sport, Upper Malone Road
Belfast BT9 5LA
Tel: 028 9038 3819
Fax: 028 9068 2757
E-mail: alan@ulsterhockey.com
Development Officer: Alan McMurray

Irish Indoor Bowling Association
204 Kings Road, Belfast BT5 7HX
Tel: 028 9048 3536
Secretary: Mr D Hunter

Irish Ladies Golf Union, Northern District
12 The Meadows, Strangford Road
Downpatrick BT30 6LN
Tel: 028 4461 2286
Contact: Mrs A Dickson

Irish Rugby Football Union (Ulster Branch)
85 Ravenhill Park, Belfast BT6 0DG
Tel: 028 9064 9141
Fax: 028 9049 1522
Web: www.ulsterrugby.com
E-mail: lyn@ulsterrugby.com
Honorary Secretary: Mr J Gardiner

Irish Table Tennis Association
House of Sport, Upper Malone Road
Belfast
Tel: 028 9038 3811

Irish Water Polo Association, Ulster Branch
78 Wateresk Road
Castlewellan BT31 9EZ
Contact: Ms J Lightbody

Irish Water Skiing Federation, Northern Ireland Sub-Committee
2 Shelling Hill, Lisburn BT27 5NZ
Contact: Mr P Gray

Irish Women's Bowling Association
30 Cromlyn Fold
Hillsborough BT26 6SD
Tel: 028 9268 8254
Fax: 028 9268 8808
Honorary Secretary: Ms J Fleming

Irish Women's Indoor Bowling Association
101 Skyline Drive, Lambeg
Lisburn BT27 4HW
Secretary: Mrs D Miskelly

Karate Association
Oliver Brunton Schools of Karate NI,
35 College Street
Belfast BT1 6BU
Tel: 028 9061 6453
Chairman: Oliver Brunton

Motor Cycle Racing Association
38 Carr Road, Lisburn BT27 6YG
Contact: Mr W McKibbin

Motor Cycle Union of Ireland, Ulster Centre
23 Kinnegar Rocks
Donaghadee BT21 0EZ
Contact: Mr T Reid

Mountaineering Council of Ireland
Mr R Connell, Concra
Castleblayney, Co Monaghan

Northern Ireland Amateur Fencing Union
58 St Anne's Crescent
Newtownabbey BT36 5JZ
Contact: Mr J Courtney

Northern Ireland Amateur Gymnastics Association
House of Sport, Upper Malone Road
Belfast BT9 5LA
Tel: 028 9038 3813
Contact: Mrs L Phillips

Northern Ireland Amateur Weightlifters' Association
130 Brooke Drive, Belfast BT11 9NR
Tel: 028 9080 3876
Secretary: Mr S Dougan

Northern Ireland Area of British Model Flying Association
'Strawberry Hill', 28 Carlston Avenue
Cultra, Holywood BT18 0NF
Tel: 028 9042 4113
E-mail: morrisdoyle@freenet.co.uk
Secretary: Mr M Doyle

Northern Ireland Athletic Association
Athletics House, Old Coach Road
Belfast BT9 5PR
Tel: 028 9060 2707
Fax: 028 9030 9939
Web: www.niathletics.org
E-mail: info@niathletics.org
Secretary: Mr J Allen

Northern Ireland Boys Football Association
15 Beechgrove Rise, Belfast BT6 0NH
Tel: 028 9079 4677
Contact: Mr J Weir

Northern Ireland Cricket Association
House of Sport, Upper Malone Road
Belfast BT9 5LA
Tel: 028 9038 3805
Fax: 028 9068 2757
E-mail: brian@nica.freeserve.co.uk
Cricket Development Officer:
Brian Walsh

Northern Ireland Federation of Sub
Aqua Clubs
56 Ballykeel Road
Moneyreagh BT23 6BW
Contact: Mr R Armstrong

Northern Ireland Ice Hockey
Association
25 Channing Street, Belfast BT5 5GP
Contact: Mrs B Carter

Northern Ireland Ice Skating
Association
15 Bromcote Street, Bloomfield Road
Belfast BT5 5JL
Tel: 028 9096 6876
Contact: Mr J Passmore

Northern Ireland Ju Jitsu Association
281 Coalisland Road
Dungannon BT71 6ET
Tel: 028 8774 6940
Secretary: Mr J Canning

Northern Ireland Olympic Wrestling
Association
312 Stranmillis Road, Belfast BT9 5EB
Contact: Mr P Mooney

Northern Ireland Orienteering
Association
62 Wheatfield Crescent,
Belfast BT14 7HT
Contact: Ms V Cordner

Netball Northern Ireland
House of Sport, Upper Malone Road
Belfast BT9 5LA
Tel: 028 9038 3806
Fax: 028 9068 2757
E-mail: netballnorthernireland@
          houseofsport.fsnet.co.uk
Netball Development Officer:
K Harrup

Northern Ireland Schools Football
Association
20 Moira Drive, Bangor BT20 4RN
Contact: Mr B Gilliland

Northern Ireland Ski Council
43 Ballymaconnell Road
Bangor BT20 5PS
Tel: 028 9145 0275
Web: www.niweb.com/niid/sport/skiing

Northern Ireland Sports Association
for People with Learning Disabilities
1 Clare Hill Road, Moira BT67 0PB
Contact: Mr N Logan

NISSU
29 Rossdowney Road, Derry BT47 1PB
Contact: Mr M Mace

Northern Ireland Ten Pin Bowling
Federation
13 Wanstead Road
Dundonald BT16 2EJ
Contact: Ms K Payne

Northern Ireland Trampoline
Association
Fir Tree Grove, 40 Monlough Road
Ballygowan BT23 6NH
Contact: Mr T Clifford

Northern Ireland Tug of War
Association
22 Annahugh Road
Loughall BT61 8RQ
Contact: Mr C McKeever

Northern Ireland Volleyball Association
21 Broughton Park, Belfast BT6 0BD
Contact: Mr D Orr

Northern Ireland Women's Football
Association
11 Ravenhill Gardens, Belfast BT6 8GP
Contact: Ms M Muldoon

Northern Cricket Union of Ireland
33 Dalboyne Park, Lisburn BT28 3BU
Contact: Mr W Carroll

Northern Ireland Alkido Association
57 Glenview Avenue, Belfast BT5 7LZ
Contact: Mr P Bradley

Northern Ireland American Football
Association
108 Victoria Rise
Carrickfergus BT38 7UR
Contact: Ms L Sleator

Northern Ireland Archery Society
10 Llewellyn Drive, Lisburn BT27 4AQ
Contact: Mr K Blair

Northern Ireland Billiards and
Snooker Association
2 Rockgrove Valley
Ballymena BT43 5HF

Northern Ireland Blind Sports
12 Sandford, Belfast BT5 5NW
Secretary: Ms L Royle

Northern Ireland Cricket Association
20 Pine Street, Waterside
Derry BT47 3QW
Contact: Mr B Dougherty

Northern Ireland Judo Federation
C/o Judo Office, House of Sport
Upper Malone Road, Belfast BT9 5LA
Tel: 028 9038 3814
Contact: Miss L Bradley

Northern Ireland Karate Board
58 Downview Park West
Belfast BT15 5HP
Tel: 028 9028 8609
Contact: Ms N Sleator

Northern Ireland Karting Association
6 Innisfree Park
Newtownards BT23 4AY
Tel: 028 9181 4987
Fax: 028 9182 2190
Contact: Mr K Wilkinson

Northern Ireland Martial Arts
Commission
C/o House of Sport
Upper Malone Road, Belfast BT9 5LA
Tel: 028 9038 1222
Web: www.sportsni.org

Northern Ireland Pool Association
8 Birch Drive, Bangor BT19 1RY
Contact: Mr J Humphrey

Northern Ireland Ski Council
43 Ballymaconnell Road
Bangor BT20 5PS
Contact: Mr P White

Northern Ireland Sports Council
House of Sport, Upper Malone Road
Belfast BT9 5LA
Tel: 028 9068 2757
Chief Executive: Eamonn McCartan

The Sports Council is the leading
government agency charged with the
development of all sport across
Northern Ireland. It works closely with
the Department of Culture, Arts and
Leisure, governing bodies and youth
organisations.

Northern Ireland Sports Forum
C/o House of Sport
Upper Malone Road, Belfast BT9 5LA
Tel: 028 9038 3825
Contact: Mr K McLean

Northern Women's Cricket Union of
Ireland
18 Belvedere Park, Belfast BT9 5GS
Contact: Miss S Owens

Royal Life Saving Society, Ulster
Branch
4 Albert Drive, Belfast BT6 9JH
Tel: 028 9070 5644
Web: www.rlssdirect.co.uk
Contact: Mrs K McCurry

Royal Scottish Country Dance Society
1 Rosevale Avenue
Drumbeg, Dunmurry BT17 9LG
Tel: 028 9061 4197
Contact: Mrs M Jordan

Royal Ulster Yacht Club
101 Clifton Road, Bangor BT20 5HY
Tel: 028 9146 5002

Royal Yachting Association
(Northern Ireland Council)
House of Sport, Upper Malone Road,
Belfast BT9 5LA
Tel: 028 9038 1222
Contact: Mr H Boyle

Taekwondo Association of Northern
Ireland
20 Lester Avenue, Lisburn BT28 3QD
Contact: Mr S Nicholson

Ulster Angling Federation
4 Mill Road, Annalong BT34 4RH
Tel: 028 4376 8531
Contact: Mr A Kilgore

Ulster Aviation Society
16 Ravelston Avenue
Newtownabbey BT36 6PF
Tel: 028 9084 4100

Ulster Basketball Association
2 Ravensdene Crescent
Belfast BT6 0DB
Tel: 028 9064 8000
Contact: Ms M Matthews

Ulster Branch, Badminton Union of
Ireland
C/o House of Sport
Upper Malone Road, Belfast BT9 5LA
Contact: Mr T Clarke

Ulster Branch, Irish Amateur Rowing
Union
47 Colenso Parade, Belfast BT9 5AN
Contact: Ms C Harrison

Ulster Branch, Irish Hockey
Association
Hockey Office, House of Sport
Upper Malone Road, Belfast BT9 5LA
Tel: 028 9038 3826
Contact: Mr W Clarke

Ulster Branch, Irish Table Tennis
Association
38 Ballynahinch Road
Carryduff, Belfast BT8 8DL
Tel: 028 9081 3378
Contact: Mr M Guy

Ulster Branch, Irish Triathlon
Association
13 Main Street, Limavady
Co Londonderry BT49 0EP
Tel: 028 7772 2617
President: Peter Jack

Ulster Branch, Tennis Ireland
17 Tennyson Avenue
Bangor BT20 3SS
Tel: 028 9146 5155
Contact: Mr G Stevenson

Ulster Camogie Council
10 Stang Road, Cabra
Hilltown BT34 5TG
Contact: Ms H McAleavey

Ulster Coarse Fishing Federation
29 Georgian Villas, Hospital Road,
Omagh BT79 0AT
Contact: Mr R Refausse

Ulster Council, Irish Federation of Sea
Anglers
17 Coolshinney Close
Magherafelt BT45 5DR
Tel: 028 7963 3198
Fax: 028 7963 3198
Secretary: Mr P Divito

Ulster Cycling Federation
C/o Mrs Rose Reilly, 18 Belturbet Road
Cornahoule BT92 9AZ
Contact: Mr P N Clarke

Ulster Deaf Sports Council
Wilton House, 5 College Square North
Belfast
Tel: 028 9031 2255

Ulster Federation of Rambling Clubs
40 Clontara Park, Lisburn BT27 4LB
Tel: 028 9260 1030
Honorary Secretary: Mr H Goodman

Ulster Flying Club
Newtownards Airport, Portaferry Road
Newtownards BT23 8SG
Tel: 028 9131 3327
Fax: 028 9131 4575
Chief Flying Instructor:
David Hodgkinson

Ulster Gliding Club
Ballyscullion, Seacoast Road
Bellarena
Tel: 028 7775 0301

Ulster Handball Council
13 Dunmurry Lodge
Belfast BT10 0GR
Contact: Mr R Maguire

Ulster Hang Gliding and Paragliding
Club
10 Woodhall, Moira
Co Down BT67 0NG
Tel: 028 9261 9828
Contact: Mr M Piggott

Ulster Provincial Council, Irish
Amateur Boxing Association
10 Tonagh Heights
Draperstown BT45 7DD
Tel: 028 7962 8450
Fax: 028 7962 8450
Secretary: Mr J Noonan

Ulster Region Swim Ireland

House of Sport, Upper Malone Road
Belfast BT9 5LA
Tel: 028 9038 3807
Fax: 028 9068 2757
Web: www.swim-ulster.com
E-mail: ann@swim-ulster.com
Development Officer: Ruth McQuillan

Ulster Squash

18 Dundela Avenue, Belfast BT4 3BQ
Contact: Mrs R Irvine

Ulster Society of Amateur Dancing

47 Upper Lisburn Road, Finaghy
Belfast BT10 0GX

Ulster Vintage Car Club

11 Ballynahinch Road, Saintfield
Ballynahinch BT24 7AE

Ulster Women's Hockey Union

168 Upper Newtownards Road
Belfast BT4 3ES
Contact: Mrs J Patterson

Yoga Fellowship of Northern Ireland

19 Elsmere Park, Belfast BT5 7QZ
Tel: 028 9079 1213
Contact: Mrs M Harper

Wild Geese Skydiving Club

116 Carrowreagh Road
Garvagh BT51 5LQ
Tel: 028 2955 8609
Fax: 028 2955 7050
Web: www.wildgeese.demon.co.uk
E-mail: parachute@wildgeese.demon.co.uk
Chief Instructor: Maggie Penny

World Ju-Jitsu Federation Northern Ireland

PO Box 1263
Belfast East Delivery, Belfast
Tel: 028 9079 7041

Arts

Belfast Festival at Queen's

25 College Gardens, Belfast BT9 6BS
Tel: 028 9066 7687
Web: www.belfastfestival.com

Cathedral Quarter Arts Festival

20 North Street Arcade
Belfast BT1 1 PB
Tel: 028 9023 2403
Fax: 028 9031 9884
E-mail: cqaf@hotmail.com
Web: www.cqaf.com

Cinemagic

2nd Floor, Fountain House
17–21 Donegall Place
Belfast BT1 5AB
Tel: 028 9031 1900
Fax: 028 9031 9709
E-mail: Ingrid@cinemagic.org.uk
Web: www.cinemagic.org.uk
Contact: Ingrid Arthurs

Classical Music Society

Foyle Arts Centre, Lawrence Hill
Derry BT48 7NJ
Tel: 028 7126 1449
Fax: 028 7130 9091
E-mail: info@classicalmusicsociety.com

Community Arts Forum

15 Church Street, Belfast BT1 1PG
Tel: 028 9024 2910
Fax: 028 9031 2264
Web: www.caf.ie
E-mail: admin@caf.ie
Acting Director: Heather Floyd

Community Theatre Association of Belfast

15 Church Street, Belfast BT1 1PG
Tel: 028 9024 2247
Web: www.newbelfaststarts.org

Crescent Arts Centre

2–4 University Road, Belfast BT7 1NH
Tel: 028 9024 2338
Fax: 028 9024 6748
E-mail: info@crescentarts.org
Acting Manager: Liz Donnan

Feile an Phobail

Tel: 028 90 313 440
E-mail: 028 90 313 440

Northern Ireland Film Commission

21 Ormeau Avenue, Belfast BT2 8HD
Tel: 028 9023 2444
Fax: 028 9023 9918
E-mail: info@nifc.co.uk
Contact: Richard Taylor

Northern Ireland Media Education Association (NIMEA)

C/o Belvoir Park Primary School,
Belvoir Drive, Belfast BT8 7DL
Tel: 028 9049 1810
Fax: 028 9049 2356
E-mail: dmccartney@belvoirps.belfast.ni.sch.uk
Contact: David McCartney

Ulster Orchestra

Elmwood Hall at Queen's
89 University Road
Belfast BT7 1NF
Tel: 028 9066 4535
Fax: 028 9066 2761
Box Office: 028 9066 8798
Web: www.ulster-orchestra.org.uk
Chief Executive: David Byers

CHAPTER 13

Lifestyle and Visitors' Guide to Northern Ireland

CARRICK-A-REDE
ROPE BRIDGE

Introduction

This chapter of the Northern Ireland Yearbook 2003 aims to provide a perspective on the social and lifestyle aspects of life in Northern Ireland, with listings of places to go, things to see and where to eat, drink and stay across Northern Ireland.

We hope that the practical information, timetables, reservations contacts and general information will be of interest and practical use to those visiting Northern Ireland and also those who already live here, in arranging trips for family, friends and colleagues.

Transport Services in Northern Ireland
By Air

Northern Ireland has three airports: Belfast International, Belfast City and City of Derry. Belfast International is also known as Aldergrove, and is the largest of the three. Situated near Templepatrick, 20 miles outside Belfast, it is one of the busiest airports in the United Kingdom, with chartered departures to European and Mediterranean destinations, as well as a number of direct-chartered flights to the USA.

Belfast City Airport is situated on the outskirts of East Belfast, with a similar range of flights to Belfast International. Belfast City Airport, which has been growing rapidly, has recently opened a new terminal, which coincides with the transferral of British Midland flights to the City Airport. City of Derry is much smaller, with domestic flights and connecting flights for onward travel from larger airports. There are a number of smaller airfields including Enniskillen and Newtownards.

The September 11 terrorist strikes in New York plummeted the global airline industry into crisis. The knock-on effect in Northern Ireland was a rationalisation of services between the two main airports.

Recent developments in the local air travel sector have seen the City Airport being put up for sale by its parent Bombardier Aerospace, owner of the company locally known as Shorts and the buyout of British Airway's budget airline operation GO by rival Easyjet

Belfast International Airport
Tel: 028 9442 2888
Website: www.belfastairport.com

bmi

Donington Hall
Castle Donnington
Derby
DE74 2SB
Sales centre (UK Only): 0870 60 70 555
Callers from outside the UK +44 1332 854 854
Group reservations: 01332 854 500
Text phone for the deaf: 01332 854 015

The best of both worlds when you fly bmi

Wherever you are flying to, bmi offers a greater choice in air travel between Belfast and the rest of Europe. bmi is the only carrier to fly between Belfast and London Heathrow with 8 daily flights from Belfast City Airport and 3 daily flights from Belfast International Airport. Passengers can also reach an extensive network of European destinations by connecting with other bmi flights at London Heathrow or over 729 destinations in 124 countries across the globe with bmi's STAR Alliance airline partners.

Even more reasons to book bmi

bmi has a low cost fares structure which is available on all routes, except transatlantic routes from Manchester and german routes. All fares are one-way so that you can mix and match to get the best value possible. Additionally, there are no more minimum overnight stay requirements and if you book on-line a £2.50 discount applies. There is the added flexibility of making changes to your original booking for a small administration fee.

All bmi flights offer a 2 cabin service with business class passengers enjoying a host of benefits including access to executive lounges, a range of check-in options and a full in-flight service.

For further information on bmi schedules and fares, visit us at flybmi.com

Direct Flights to and from Belfast International Airport

Destination	Airline	Days of Service
Luton	EJ	Daily
Edinburgh	EJ/GO	Daily
Amsterdam	EJ	Daily
Glasgow	EJ/GO	Daily
Liverpool	EJ	Daily
Stanstead	GO	Daily
Bristol	GO	Daily
Birmingham	BA	Daily
London-Heathrow	BM	Daily

Direct flights to and from Belfast City Airport

Destination	Airline	Days of Service
East Midlands	BM	Daily
Heathrow	BM	Daily
Isle of Man	P/M	Daily
Gatwick	BE	Daily
London City	BE	Daily
Bristol	BE	Daily
Leeds	BE	Daily
Bradford	BE	Daily
Newcastle	BE	Daily
Birmingham	BE	Daily
Glasgow	BE	Daily

AIRLINE KEY

EJ	Easyjet
BM	British Midland
GO	Go
BA	British Airways
P	Platinum
M	Manx
BE	British European
BRA	British Regional Airways

Reservation Telephone Numbers

bmi British Midland	0870 670 0555
Easyjet	0870 600 0000
Aer Lingus	0845 973 7747
British Airways	0845 773 3377
British European	0870 567 6676
British Regional Airlines	0845 773 377
Ryanair	028 7181 3302
Go	0845 605 4321

The best way to travel to Belfast city centre from International Airport is the Airbus, which runs regularly between the Europa Bus Centre and the Airport.

Airport Business Centre: Available for a full range of business facilities such as conferences and exhibitions.

Belfast City Airport

Tel: 028 9093 9093
Website: www.belfastcityairport.com

Ten minutes from Belfast City Centre, via Sydenham by-pass. The airport can be reached by rail from Central Station to Sydenham Halt, or City bus No 21 from City Hall.

Taxis are easily accessible from Belfast City Airport to the city centre.

City of Derry Airport

Airport Road, Derry
Tel: 028 7181 0784
British Airways
Ryanair
British Airways fly directly between Derry and Glasgow and Derry and Manchester. Taxis are available from the Airport to Derry city centre.

By Sea

Northern Ireland has four main ports, of which Belfast and Larne are the principal passenger ports. Ferry operators sail from Belfast and Larne to various Scottish ports including Stranraer, Troon and Cairnryan. Belfast also has passenger routes to Liverpool and Heysham.

Sea Carriers

Seacat

(Between Belfast and Stranraer)

Seacat Terminal, Donegall Quay, Belfast BT1 3AL
Seacat, a catamaran, travels between Belfast and Stranraer four times a day in each direction, and five times a day in August and September. The crossing takes about one hour 30 minutes.

Isle of Man Steam Packet Co

(summer sailings between Belfast and Douglas, Isle of Man)
Northern Road, Belfast BT3 9JN

Norse Irish Ferries

(between Belfast and Liverpool)
Victoria Terminal Two, West Bank Road, Belfast.
Ferry between Belfast and Liverpool takes about eight hours 30 minutes. There is one sailing every day.

Stena Line

(between Belfast and Stranraer)
Sea Terminal, Corry Road, Belfast BT3 9SS
Ferry between Belfast and Stranraer takes one hour 45 minutes. There are ten sailings per day.

P&O European Ferries

(between Larne and Cairnryan)
Larne Harbour, Larne BT40 1AQ
Ferry between Larne and Cairnryan takes 2 hours 15 minutes; Jetliner takes one hour. There are nine ferry sailings per day Monday–Friday, overnight ferry.

Destination	Carrier	Reservations
Stranraer	Stena Line	028 9074 7747
Troon	Superseacat	08705 523523
Heysham	Superseacat	08705 523523
Liverpool	Norse Irish Ferries	028 9077 9090
Douglas (Isle of Man)	Isle of Man Steam Packet Company	08705 523523

Destination	Carrier	Sailing Time	Reservations
Stranraer	Stena Line	1.75 hrs	08705 707070
Stranraer	Stena Line	3.25 hrs	08705 707070
Troon	SeaCat	2.5 hrs	08705 523523
Heysham	SeaCat	4 hrs	08705 523523
Douglas	Isle of Man	4.75 hrs	08705 523523
Liverpool	Norse Irish	8 hrs	028 9077 9090
Cairnryan	P&Q European	1 hrs	08702 424 7777
Cairnryan	P&Q European	1.75 hrs	08702 424 7777

Rail and Bus Services

Translink is the all-embracing title of Northern Ireland's three main public transport companies: Citybus, Northern Ireland Railways (NIR) and Ulsterbus, that merged in January 1995, as a result of a change in government transportation policy, which sought to encourage greater use of public transport. The parent company is the Northern Ireland Transport Holding Company, with a Chairman, a Board of Directors, a Managing Director of Group Operations and a Senior Management Team. Over 70 million passenger journeys are undertaken on Translink services each year.

Citybus Services

Citybus provides bus services within the Greater Belfast area, usually red single and double decker vehicles.

Citybus Route Numbering

Buses travelling out of the City Centre display their route number and destination. Buses travelling into the City Centre show the route number and the destination of their next journey out of the City Centre. All inward buses stop in the City Centre before travelling on to their new destination.

Citybus Sunday Services

Citybus services numbered 1–100 operate on Monday to Saturday only. On Sundays there are circular routes numbered 101–121. A special Citybus Sunday services timetable is available from the Citybus Kiosk, Donegall Square West.

City Stoppers

Ulsterbus services in the 500 series will stop to pick up and set down within the Citybus Zone along the Lisburn Road and the Falls Road. Citybus tickets are accepted by drivers on these services.

Citybus Fares and Tickets

Travel Cards: Offer 7 days' unlimited travel within a defined area of the City. They are available from Citybus Ticket Agents and the Citybus Kiosk at Donegall Square West and include:

- Gold cards: Unlimited travel throughout the entire City Zone.
- Silver cards: Unlimited travel in one of three sectors in the City Zone.

4 Journey Ticket for City Zone: Allows 4 single journeys within the City Zone to and from the City Centre.

4 Journey Ticket for Newtownabbey area: Allows 4 single journeys on Ulsterbus and Citybus services except City Express within the Newtownabbey area to and from Belfast City Centre.

Day Tickets: Offer unlimited travel within the City Zone or a combination of the City Zone and other Zones. Day tickets are available from the driver.

City Zone Fares: Any length of journey within the City Zone.

Off-Peak Saver Fares: Travel within the City Zone between 09.30 and 14.00 Monday to Friday only.

Ulsterbus Services

Ulsterbus services featuring blue single decker buses and coaches cover the whole of Northern Ireland. The Europa Bus Centre in Belfast concentrates on destinations in Armagh, Tyrone, Derry, Fermanagh, West Down, the Republic of Ireland and Cross-Channel services. Buses also run from here to connect with the ferry terminals and airports, as well as the Royal Group of Hospitals. The Laganside Bus Centre, which was built to replace the old Oxford Street Station, is the main hub for North Down and Antrim destinations.

Goldline Services:

Express services operate non-stop, serving all major towns in Northern Ireland. A special Goldline timetable is available from bus stations.

Special Services

Translink have introduced a number of new or improved services which include:

Centrelink

The Centrelink service links the main Belfast City Centre bus and rail stations with stops in the City Centre close to shops, bars and restaurants. The service is free to passengers with a valid bus or rail ticket. The services run approximately every 12 minutes Monday to Saturday.

Nightlink

Nightlink services are operated by Citybus and Ulsterbus providing a special weekend service from the City Centre on Friday and Saturday nights to main provincial towns. Nightlink serves Newtownabbey, Carrickfergus, Bangor, Newtownards, Comber/Ballygowan, Ballynahinch, Down-patrick (02.00 only), Lisburn, Antrim and Ballyclare/Doagh (02.00 only) and departs from Donegall Square West at 01.00 and 02.00. Tickets cost £3 and are available on-board the buses or from the Citybus Kiosk.

Rural Transport

In association with the Department for Regional Development, Translink operate services in rural areas. They are designed to provide access to the nearest market town and to make it easier to get out and about at evenings and weekends.

Go Services

Go Services operate on quality bus corridors, (dedicated busways) which reduce journey times on main routes to and from the City Centre. Both Ulsterbus (service no 18A) and Citybus (service nos 83 and 84) operate on this route and the buses are branded with the distinctive 'Go' logo. Passengers benefit from new and improved shelters, high frequency of service and detailed information at every stop along the route.

Ulsterbus Fares and Tickets

Return Tickets: Offer a saving over the cost of two single tickets.

10 Journey Tickets: Valid for 10 journeys in either direction between specified stages for one month from date of purchase. (Non-refundable).

40 Journey Commuter Tickets: Valid for 20 return journeys within one month from date of purchase. (Non-refundable). Can be purchased in advance.

Monthly Tickets: Valid for unlimited travel between designated points one month from date of purchase. (Non-refundable). Can be purchased in advance.

Group Travel: Discount is available for parties of 10 or more making travel arrangements at least 24 hours in advance. Contact your local station for details.

Excursion Fares: Available on certain bus services for shopping and off-peak journeys. Contact your local station for details.

Sunday Rambler Ticket: Unlimited travel on all scheduled Ulsterbus services within Northern Ireland on Sundays. Must be purchased in advance and the outward journey made before 15.00hrs.

Northern Ireland Railways (NIR)

Railway services operate on a fairly limited network which connects Belfast South to the border with the Irish Republic and onwards to Dublin and the CIE network. NIR extends East along the North Down Coast to Bangor and North–West to Ballymena, Coleraine and Derry. NIR'S network operates services from Belfast to Bangor, Lisburn, Derry, Portrush and Dublin. There are no separate 'tube' or underground or urban rail networks in Northern Ireland. The Cross-Harbour Rail-Link opened in November 1994, finally unifying the Northern Irish Rail system.

Great Victoria Street railway station opened in September 1995, adjoining the Europa Bus Centre in Belfast City Centre, making it the first integrated public transport facility in Northern Ireland, combining bus, rail and car-parking facilities.

NI Railway Fares and Tickets

Singles: Valid on day of issue only, between two stations.

Day Returns: Valid on day of issue only, with return journey on same day.

Monthly Return: Outward journey is valid on date of issue only, return journey is valid up to one month from the date shown on ticket.

7–Day Weekly Ticket: Seven days unlimited travel between any two designated stations (valid Monday to Sunday.)

Monthly Moneysavers: Unlimited travel between any two designated stations for a full calendar month. Unrestricted travel on the NIR Railways Network at weekends.

Contract Tickets: Books of 40 single tickets may be purchased for some journeys with Northern Ireland. For details telephone: 028 9033 3000.

Sunday Day Tracker: Unlimited travel on all scheduled train services within Northern Ireland on Sunday

Group Travel: Discount of up 15 per cent for parties of 10 or more passengers on all services. Further details are available from NIR Travel. Telephone: 028 9089 9434.

Belfast/Dublin Rail Services

First Plus and Enterprise Class Rail Travel

First Plus and Enterprise Class accommodation is provided on most trains between Belfast and Dublin. (Some services offer Enterprise Class only). Check railway timetable for details.

Seat Reservations

Individual seats may be reserved free of charge if you are travelling First Plus. Telephone: 028 9089 9409 for advance booking and seat reservation.

Enterprise Catering Service

A catering bar and trolley service is in operation on most scheduled Enterprise services.

Enterprise Fares and Tickets

Singles: Available for Enterprise Class and First Plus travel.

Day Returns: Available Monday to Thursday and Saturday for Enterprise Class only. (This is a promotional ticket and may be withdrawn at any time.)

Family Day Return Fares: Available for Enterprise Class travel only. Valid for two adults and up to four children, on any train, any day.

One Month Return Fares: Available for First Plus and Enterprise Class travel.

Family One Month Returns: Available for Enterprise Class travel only and valid for two adults and up to four children. Return journey valid for up to one month from date shown on ticket.

Cross Border Contract Tickets: Books of 20 single journey tickets are available between Belfast/Dublin and Portadown/Dublin. Contact NIR Travel for further information telephone: 028 9023 0671.

7–Day Weekly Ticket: 7 days' unlimited travel between Belfast, Portadown or Newry to selected cross border stations.

Monthly Tickets: Unlimited travel for one month between Belfast, Portadown or Newry to selected cross border stations.

Free travel on the DART: Passengers in possession of a valid Enterprise ticket can travel free of charge on the DART between Connolly Station and Tara Station/Pearse Station.

Integrated Bus and Rail Tickets

Freedom of Northern Ireland Tickets: 1 Day, 3 out of 8 Day and 7 Day Freedom of Northern Ireland tickets are available from main bus and rail stations, offering unlimited travel on all scheduled bus and rail services within Northern Ireland.

Pupil Tickets: Available for return travel from home to school by one mode or a combination of modes of travel. Application forms can be obtained from main bus and rail stations, or by writing to the Pupil Ticket Office, Translink, Milewater Road, Belfast, BT3 9BG or telephone: 028 9035 4074.

Translink Commuter Travelcards: Commuter Travelcards are valid for one year and offer at least 15 per cent discount compared with the purchase of monthly tickets. They provide unlimited travel between two chosen points (by one mode or a combination of modes of travel) and also Freedom of the Northern Ireland Network at weekends for the relevant operating company/ companies.

Railway Contact Numbers

NIR Timetable Enquiries	028 9089 9411
Enterprise First Plus reservations	028 9089 9409
Ulsterbus Travel Centre	028 9033 7004
NIR Travel Ltd	028 9023 0671
Parcelink	028 9089 9422
Call centre (Timetable enquiries)	028 9035 4007
Enterprise bookings	028 9035 4007
Compliments and Complaints	028 9089 9463

Lost Property Enquiries
(Mon-Fri office hours only)

Citybus Telephone:	028 9045 8345
NI Railways Telephone:	028 9074 1700
Ulsterbus Telephone:	028 9033 3000

Administration Offices
Office Hours: Mon-Thurs 0845-1730 Fri 0845-1400

Managing Director's Office, Human Resources, Marketing, Operations:
Central Station, Belfast BT1 3PB
Tel: 028 9089 9400

Fax: 028 9089 9401

Finance, Purchasing, Infrastructure, Property:
Milewater Road, Belfast BT3 9BG
Tel: 028 9035 1201
Fax: 028 9035 1474
Website: www.translink.co.uk
E-mail: feedback@translink.co.uk

Bangor Linkline Tickets: A pilot integrated ticketing scheme operates in the Bangor area. Tickets allow travel on either train or bus between any Central Zone Station in Belfast to Bangor and outer surrounding areas.

Concession Fares for Bus and Rail

Senior Citizens Pass: Senior Citizens who are 65 years of age and over and resident in Northern Ireland can travel on bus and rail services in Northern Ireland free of charge. War disabled passengers can avail of concession fares on presentation of a concession pass. Under the Department of Social Welfare free travel scheme senior citizens resident in Northern Ireland are entitled to free cross border bus or rail travel from any point in Northern Ireland to any point in the Republic of Ireland.

Blind persons: Registered Blind persons are entitled to free travel on all scheduled local and cross border bus and train services on presentation of a Blind Persons' Concession Pass.

Students: Concessions are available on certain tickets to students on presentation of an International Student Identity Card with a Travelsave Stamp.

Young People/Children: Young persons 5 years of age and under 16 years are entitled to a 50 per cent reduction on all local, cross border and cross channel fares. Between 16 and 21 years of age concession fares are available on rail season tickets only.

Jobseeker/Gateway: Reduced bus and rail fares are available to any person currently unemployed and actively seeking employment, or to any person on the Gateway period of the New Deal Initiative on production of an authenticated permit.

Tours and Private Hire

In addition to the scheduled bus and rail services, passengers can also avail of the following:

Ulsterbus Tours: Located in the Europa Bus Centre, Ulsterbus Tours offer coach holidays throughout Ireland, UK and Europe; short break holidays; themed weekends, special interest trips and private/corporate hire. For further information on coach tours telephone: 028 9033 7004 and private hire telephone: 028 9033 7006.

Citybus Tours: Provide a range of day tours from scenic drives to Mystery & Intrigue Tours. For further information on tours and private hire telephone: 028 9045 8484.

Car Hire and Taxi Services

Car hire is a popular way of exploring Northern Ireland, especially the more remote rural areas which are not served by public transport. Cars can be hired from various depots throughout the region. A typical family car will cost around £190 per week, or £90 for a weekend, exclusive of VAT and insurance.

Driving Information

General rules of the road are the same as in Great Britain, ie drive on the left; overtake on the right. Speed limits are 30 miles per hour in built up areas, 60mph on single carriageways and 70 mph on motorways and dual carriageways. Seatbelts are compulsory for drivers and all passengers; motorcyclists must wear crash helmets. Parking is available on-street or in car parks.

Avis: Tel: 0870 6060100
Belfast International Airport: 028 9442 2333
Belfast City Airport: 028 9045 2017
City of Derry Airport: 028 7181 1708

Budget: Tel: 0500 933700
Belfast City Centre: 028 9023 0700
Belfast City Airport: 028 9045 1111
Belfast International Airport: 028 9442 3332

Europcar: Tel: 0800 0680303
Belfast International Airport: 028 9442 3444
Belfast City Airport: 028 9043 0904
City of Derry Airport: 028 7181 2773

Hertz:
Belfast International Airport: 028 9442 2533
Belfast City Airport: 028 9073 2451
City of Derry Airport: 028 7181 1994

McCausland:
Belfast City Centre: 028 9033 3777, 028 9023 5171
Belfast International Airport: 028 9442 2022
Belfast City Airport: 028 9045 4141

Taxis

Taxis are relatively inexpensive in Northern Ireland. Public taxis, often black 'London' Hackney cabs, can pick up in the street or from taxi ranks. Alternatively, there are many private taxi firms, many of which have waiting rooms.

Northern Ireland Tourist Board

St Anne's Court
59 North Street
Belfast BT1 1NB
Tel: 028 9023 1221
Fax: 028 9024 0960

Regional Tourism Organisations

Derry Visitor & Convention Bureau

44 Foyle Street
Londonderry BT48 6AT
Tel: 028 7137 7577
Fax: 028 7137 7992
E-mail: info@derryvisitor.com
Website: www.derryvisitor.com
The Derry Visitor and Convention Bureau is the Regional Tourism Organisation for the area. The Bureau promotes the city and its hinterland as a major tourist and conference destination as well as providing a complete range of visitor services.

Kingdoms of Down

40 West Street
Newtownards, Co. Down
Tel: 028 9182 2881
Fax: 028 9182 2202
E-mail: info@kingdomsofdown.com

Fermanagh Lakeland Tourism

Wellington Road
Enniskillen BT74 7EF
Tel: 028 6634 6736
Fax: 028 6632 5511
Website: www.fermanaghlakelands.com

Causeway Coast & Glens

11 Lodge Road
Coleraine BT52 1LU
Tel: 028 7032 7720
Fax: 028 7032 7719
Website:www.causewaycoastandglens.com

Tourist Information Centres

Antrim

16 High Street, Antrim BT41 4AN
Tel: 028 9442 8331

Armagh

40 English Street, Armagh BT61 7BA
Tel: 028 3752 1800

Ballycastle

Sheskburn House
7 Mary Street, Ballycastle BT54 6QH
Tel: 028 2076 2024

Banbridge

Newry Road, Banbridge
Tel: 028 4060 3322

Bangor

34 Quay Street, Bangor BT20 5ED
Tel: 028 9127 0069

Belfast City Airport

Sydenham Bypass, Belfast BT3 9JH
Tel: 028 9073 2451

Carrickfergus

Antrim Street, Carrickfergus
Co Antrim BT38 7DJ
Tel: 028 9336 6455

Coleraine

Railway Road, Coleraine
Co Londonderry BT52 1PE
Tel: 028 7034 4723

Cookstown

Burn Road, Cookstown BT80 8DN
Co Tyrone
Tel: 028 8676 6727

Downpatrick

Market Street
Downpatrick BT30 6LZ, Co Down
Tel: 028 4461 2233

Dungannon (Killymaddy)

Ballygawley Road
Dungannon BT70 1TF, Co Tyrone
Tel: 028 8776 7259

Enniskillen

Wellington Road, Enniskillen
Co Fermanagh BT74 7EF
Tel: 028 6632 3110

Giant's Causeway

44 Causeway Rd., Bushmills
Co Antrim BT57 8SU
Tel: 028 2073 1855

Kilkeel

28 Bridge Street, Kilkeel
Co Down BT34 4AD
Tel: 028 4176 2525

Larne

Narrow Gauge Road, Larne
Co Antrim BT40 1XB
Tel: 028 2826 0088

Newcastle

Central Promenade
Newcastle, Co Down BT33 0AA
Tel: 028 4372 2222

Newtownards

Regent Street, Newtownards
Co Down BT23 4AD
Tel: 028 9182 6846

Omagh

Market Street, Omagh
Co Tyrone BT78 1EE
Tel: 028 8224 7831

Portrush

Sandhill Drive, Portrush
Tel: 028 7082 3333

Places to Visit in Northern Ireland

In and around Belfast

Belfast is a rapidly developing city undergoing massive investment; new apartment blocks, the Waterfront Hall, the five-star Hilton hotel and the new Odyssey Complex, built at a cost of over £100 million, symbolise a new Belfast.

Belfast Welcome Centre – Gateway to Northern Ireland

35–47 Donegall Place, Belfast
Tel: 028 9024 6609
This information centre has street plans of Belfast City, as well as information on attractions and contact details for the tours listed below.

Tours
Belfast Citybus Tour

Tel: 028 9045 8484
Bus tour with commentary. Duration 3½ hours. Leaves Castle Place at 1.30pm, Mon–Sat, in summer.

City Tour

From the City Hall to the Shipyard and the Zoo, this includes the main sights of Belfast City. Mon–Sat 1pm.

Living History Tour

Duration 2½ hours. Leaves main post office in Castle Place Tuesday, Thursday and Sunday at 1pm. Commentary complements a tour of the historic city, including recent historical events.

Lagan Boat Trips

1 Donegall Quay
Tel: 028 9033 0844
E-mail: info@laganboatcompany.com
Website: www.laganboatcompany.com

Trips along the river Lagan to see the highlights of Belfast's regenerated waterfront. Daily departures.

Leprechaun Tour Guiding Service

Tel: 028 3884 0054
Complete Blue Badge Guiding Service for Northern Ireland. Driver/coach, bi-lingual and city guides, itinerary planning, film location, familiarisation trips, courier duties, factory visits, port/airport reception.

Black Taxi Tours

Tel: 028 9064 2264
Many of the well-known sights of Belfast and Northern Ireland, with commentary. The alternative sights of Belfast include the political murals – a unique cultural experience.

Mini-Coach

Tel: 028 9032 4733
Tours of Belfast, Causeway Coast, Newcastle, Downpatrick, Mount Stewart House & Gardens, Lisburn, Hillsborough, Airport & Ferry transfers.

Murphy's Travel

Tel: 028 9069 3232
Range of tailor-made minibus tours to suit clients in and around Belfast for 1–14 persons. Blue Badge Guides. Specialities include: linen history, golf packages and bird-watching trips.

TourUlster Guided Tours

Tel: 07050 382856
Specialising in small, informal groups (up to 6 people) allowing maximum flexibility with each tour. Services include itineraries for larger groups, special interest tours plus scenic, cultural heritage, sports/activity trips and city tour.

Ulsterbus Tours

Tel: 028 9066 6630
A selection of tours of the main attractions of Northern Ireland and Southern Ireland depart daily in summer from the Europa BusCentre. Destinations include National Trust properties, seaside resorts, sporting and entertainment events.

View of City Hall from Donegall Square West

Places to See

City Hall

Donegall Square, Belfast
Tel: 028 9027 0456
A magnificent building in Portland stone, the centrally-located City Hall is seat of Belfast City Council. Tours June–Sept, Mon–Fri 10.30, 11.30 and 2.30pm. Every Sat at 2.30pm Oct–May, Mon–Sat 2.30pm. No tours on Bank or Public Holidays. Special group tours may be booked in advance. Tours last 1 hour. Admission Free.

Ulster Museum

Stranmillis Road
(in Botanic Gardens), Belfast
Tel: 028 9038 3000
Northern Ireland's largest museum houses major permanent and visiting collections, as well as a permanent exhibition of Irish art. Open Mon–Fri 10am–5pm, Sat 1–5pm, Sun 2–5pm.

Botanic Gardens

A beautiful city park hosting the Ulster Museum and the Victorian Palm House, full of exotic plants. The Palm House and Tropical Ravine are open April through Sept., Mon to Fri 10am to noon and 1pm to 5pm. Sat–Sun and Bank holidays 1pm to 5pm Oct–March 10am to noon and 1pm to 4pm Mon–Fri. Sat–Sun and Bank holidays 1pm to 4pm.

Harbour Commissioners Office

Belfast Harbour Commissioners, Harbour Office
Corporation Square, Belfast
Tel: 028 9055 4422
Paintings, sculptures, stained glass, Belfast's seafaring history. Public access to the Harbour Office is limited.

Harland & Wolff Shipyard

Queen's Island, Belfast BT3
Once one of the world's greatest shipyards, employing 30,000 men at its peak. Birthplace of the Titanic. The giant cranes, Samson and Goliath, are among Belfast's best-known landmarks. Public access to the shipyard is limited: write to Public Affairs Office.

International Rose Gardens

Sir Thomas and Lady Dixon Park, Upper Malone Road, Belfast
Over 25,000 shrub roses confirm why Northern Ireland has been a world centre of rose expertise for generations. The rose trials beds are where newly bred varieties from all over the world are tried out. International Rose Week takes place annually in July.

St Anne's Cathedral

Lower Donegall Street, Belfast
Begun in 1899, using stone from all 32 counties in Ireland, consecrated in 1904. Always open. Free guided tour Mon–Sat 10am–4pm. (Across St Anne's Square, opposite is the tourist information centre).

Belfast Zoo and Castle

Antrim Road, Belfast
Tel: 028 9077 6277
Picturesque Mountain Park on the slopes of Cave Hill overlooking the city. Open 7 days a week 10am to 5pm (closes 2.30pm in winter). Visit the heritage centre in Belfast Castle. Tel: 028 9077 6925.

Linen Hall Library

17 Donegall Square North, Belfast
Tel: 028 9032 1707
Established 1788 'to improve the mind and excite a spirit of general enquiry'. Thomas Russell, one of the past Librarians, was executed for his revolutionary activities in 1803. Today the Library is popular with Belfast's literary set. It is open weekdays until 5.30pm (4pm on Sat). Tour of library by arrangement. Reading room and café.

Royal Ulster Rifles Museum

5 Waring Street, Belfast
Tel: 028 9023 2086
Open Mon–Thur 10am–12.30pm, 2–4pm, 3pm closing Fri. Appointments may be necessary.

Fernhill House: The People's Museum

Glencairn Road, Belfast
Tel: 028 9071 5599
History of the Shankill district from the early 19th Century, Home Rule and World Wars I and II. Open Mon–Sat 10am–4pm, Sun 1–4pm.

The Giant's Ring

Off Ballylesson Road, South Belfast
A neolithic ceremonial earthwork. Near Shaw's Bridge.

Lagan Weir Lookout

Donegall Quay, Belfast
Tel: 028 9031 5444
The Weir stands on the site of the original ford across the river. Interactive exhibits on the river, construction of the Weir and the history of the Lagan. At night, the Weir and nearby road and rail bridges are spectacularly floodlit. Occasional special events. Open Mon–Fri 11am–5pm, Sat noon–5pm, Sun 2–5pm (closed on Monday in winter and shorter hours).

Odyssey

Queen's Quay, Belfast BT3 9QQ
General enquiries: 028 9045 1055
Main features are an indoor Arena, home of Belfast Giants Ice Hockey team; Sheridan IMAX and the

Warner Village 12-screen multiplex cinema; The Pavilion, a development of restaurants, bars and shops and the W5 Interactive Discovery Centre.

whowhatwherewhenwhy - W5

W5 at Odyssey, 2 Queen's Square
Belfast
BT3 9QQ
Tel: (028) 9046 7700
Web: www.w5online.co.uk

W5 is Ireland's first and only interactive discovery centre and is located at the Odyssey complex in the heart of Belfast. The centre has 140 amazing interactive exhibits which offer hours of fantastic fun for visitors of all ages. Attractions include a laser harp, giant racetrack and lie detector. Open: Mon–Sat 10am–6pm, Sun 12 noon–6pm. Last admission 5pm.

St George's Market

Corner of May Street and Oxford Street (opposite the Hilton Hotel) Belfast
Tel: 028 9027 0386
Elegant recently restored building, built in 1896; it is the oldest continually operated market in Northern Ireland. Market days are Tuesday and Friday mornings with the Farm and Speciality Market every Saturday morning. Special craft and design fairs, exhibitions, festive events and concerts are also held.

Central Library

Royal Avenue, Belfast
Tel: 028 9050 9150
Collection of early Belfast printed books. Also photographs, maps, and exhibitions. It is open Mon–Fri 9.30am–5.30pm (until 8pm Mon & Thur), Sat 9.30am–1pm.

Stormont

The Northern Ireland parliament building, 4 miles from Belfast city centre, is now where the new Northern Ireland Assembly meets. Features include an imposing entrance and avenue leading to palatial Parliament Buildings.

Near Belfast

Carrickfergus Castle

Tel: 028 9335 1273
Open April–Sept Mon–Sat 10am–6pm. Sun 2–6pm. June–Aug Sun noon–6pm. Oct–March Mon–Sat 10am–4pm, Sun 2–4pm. Last admission ½ hour before closing.

St Nicholas Parish Church

The Church dates from the 12th century. The father of the poet Louis MacNiece (1907–63) was rector here. The poet was born in Belfast 'between the mountain and the gantries'.

Ulster Folk and Transport Museum

The Ulster Folk and Transport Museum is one of Northern Ireland's leading visitor attractions depicting life in Northern Ireland in bygone days. (See MAGNI above right).

Knight Ride/Heritage Plaza

Tel: 028 9336 6455
Exhibition and monorail ride through the history of Carrickfergus from the 6th century. Open 1 April–30 Sept Mon to Sat 10am to 6pm, Sun noon to 6pm. 1 Oct to 31 Mar Mon–Sat 10am–5pm Sun noon to 5pm.

MUSEUMS & GALLERIES OF NI (MAGNI)

Ulster Folk & Transport Museum
Tel: (028) 9042 8428
Ulster Museum
Tel: (028) 9038 3000
Ulster American Folk Park
Tel: (028) 8224 3292
Armagh County Museum
Tel: (028) 3752 3070

The National Museums and Galleries of Northern Ireland (MAGNI) comprise the Ulster Museum, the Ulster Folk and Transport Museum, the Ulster American Folk Park and the Armagh County Museum. These museums were merged to form a single organisation under the Museums and Galleries (Northern Ireland) Order on 1 April 1998. MAGNI's collections promote access to and awareness of the arts, humanities and sciences, the culture, way of life, diversity, migration and settlement of peoples, and to the heritage of Northern Ireland. The interactive science centre W5 (whowhatwhenwherewhy), which opened in 2001 and which is situated at the Odyssey Arena in Belfast, is a wholly-owned subsidiary.

Carrickfergus Gasworks

Tel: 028 9335 1438

The only Victorian coal gasworks in Ireland (1855–1964). Guided tours can be arranged by appointment.

Andrew Jackson Centre

Tel: 028 9336 6455

Boneybefore. Plus US Rangers exhibition. June–Sept 10am–6pm Mon–Fri, Sat–Sun 2–6pm. April, May & Oct closes at 4pm & 1–2pm.

Hillsborough Tourist Information Centre

The Courthouse, Hillsborough

Tel: 028 9268 9717

Exhibition on the history of law and order. The fort is open 10am–7pm Tues–Sat, 2–7pm Sun. In winter it closes at 4pm. The parish church is always open (organ recitals at Easter).

Hillsborough Castle

Tel: 028 9268 1309

Residence of the Secretary of State. Tours must be booked.

John Ballance's Birthplace

Glenavy, Lisburn

Tel: 028 9264 8492

7 miles northwest of Lisburn, signposted off A30. John Ballance, New Zealand's prime minister 1891–93, was born in this house, open April to Sept 11am–5pm Tues–Fri 2–5pm, Sat–Sun, bank holidays 11am–5pm.

Irish Linen Centre/Lisburn Museum

Market Square, Lisburn

Tel: 028 9266 3377

The history of the linen industry in Ireland is recorded here. The Museum also hosts regular visiting exhibitions.

Open Mon–Sat 9.30am–5pm

In and Around Derry (Londonderry)

Tourist Information Centre

44 Foyle Street, Derry BT48 6AT

Tel: 028 7126 7284

Ask about guided tours of the city walls and tours by horse-drawn vehicles. The Foyle Civic bus tour leaves the Ulsterbus centre, Foyle Street, Tues 2pm during July and August.

The City Walls

These famous walls, which date back to the early part of the seventeenth century, have withstood several sieges, the most celebrated lasting 105 days. There are fine views from the top of the walls which encircle the old city, a circuit of one mile. Open to the public from dawn until dusk. Admission free.

The Tower Museum

Union Hall Place

Tel: 028 7137 2411

The 'Story of Derry' chronicles the history of the city from its geological formation through to the present day. In the O'Doherty Tower, above the museum, artefacts from Spanish Armada ships wrecked off the Irish coast in 1588 are on display. Open 10am–5pm Tues–Sat Sept–June and bank holiday Mondays. 10am–5pm Mon–Sat July–Aug. 2pm–5pm Sun. Adults £3.95 Child/Concession £1.50 Family £8.00 Adult Groups £3.45 per person.

The Guildhall

Guildhall Square

Tel: 028 7137 7335

This impressive neo-Gothic style building, with its distinctive tower and fine collection of stained glass windows, still functions as the seat of the City's council. Open 9.00am–5.00pm Mon–Fri.

DERRY VISITOR & CONVENTION BUREAU

Derry Visitor and Convention Bureau
44 Foyle Street
Derry
BT48 6AT
Tel: (028) 7137 7577
Fax: (028) 7137 7992
Web: www.derryvisitor.com

The Derry Visitor and Convention Bureau (DVCB) was the first Visitor and Convention Bureau to be set up in Ireland and is the Regional Tourism Organisation for the area. The Bureau promotes the city and its hinterland as a tourist and conference destination as well as providing a complete range of visitor services. It is also a membership organisation supported by the public and private sector and Derry City Council. The DVCB is the cornerstone of future tourist development in Derry and markets the city energetically at home and abroad.

St Columb's Cathedral

London Street

Tel: 028 7126 7313

St Columb's Church of Ireland Cathedral and Chapter House Museum – the most historic building in the city, built in 1633. Open Mon–Sat all year, 9.00am–5.00pm summer, 9am–1pm and 2–4pm in winter. Groups welcome, admission £1.00.

St Eugene's Cathedral

This Roman Catholic cathedral was completed in 1903 in a Gothic style. Open daily.

Long Tower Church

Bishop Street (just outside walls) Stained glass by Meyer of Munich, built in 1784 on site of the great medieval church of Templemore. The holy well of St Columb is nearby. Open daily.

Workhouse Museum

23 Glendermott Road, Waterside
Tel: 028 7131 8328
The Workhouse Museum houses a number of exhibitions on Victorian hardship, workhouses, the Famine, living in Victorian Derry and the city's role in the Battle of the Atlantic. Open Jan–June, Mon–Thur and Sat 10am–4.30pm July–Aug, Mon–Sat 10am–4.30pm Sept–Jan Mon–Thur & Sat 10am–4.30pm. Friday Closed. Admission Free.

The Calgach Centre – Fifth Province

4-22 Butcher Street
Tel: 028 7137 3177
Incorporates the Genealogy Centre and the Fifth Province. (Conference facilities available). Mon–Fri 10am– 4pm. Admission Free.

The Genealogy Centre

Tel: 028 7126 9792
Has a computerised genealogical database with records dating back to the early 1600s. Open weekdays 9am–1pm and 2–5pm.

The Fifth Province

By using a variety of dramatic effects and audio-visual techniques, brings to life the history and culture of the Celts. Mon–Fri 9.30am– 4.00pm.

HISTORIC WALLED CITY OF DERRY

Economic Development Programme
DERRY CITY COUNCIL

98 Strand Road
Derry BT48 7NN
Tel: 028 7136 5151
Fax: 028 7126 4858
Web: www.derrycity.gov.uk

Through its Economic Development Programme, Derry City Council has pulled together an inter-agency team to capitalise on the tourism potential of the 17th Century City Walls. The project aim is to create a sustainable visitor management strategy for Northern Ireland's largest historic monument. In line with the Department for Social Development's "Heart of the City" Report, the project will be implemented in ways that will strengthen the identity and character of the Walled City to reinforce its cultural tourism role.

The Walled City is unique in combining built heritage, cultural venues, creative industries, museums, galleries, shops and a vibrant evening economy within a compact City quarter. This unique tourism product adds vital critical mass to Northern Ireland as a tourism destination within an island of Ireland marketing strategy. Alongside the Causeway and Belfast, the Walled City has the potential to play a significant part in increasing visitor numbers to NI and boosting the tourism sector's contribution to GDP.

As a first step in the plan Derry City Council and the Foyle Civic Trust have secured £2million of Heritage Lottery funds to implement a Townscape Heritage Initiative within the Walled City. The focus of this initiative will be to enhance the built heritage of premises in ways, which bring back for new economic benefit, under-utilised premises.

The Foyle Valley Railway Centre

Foyle Road
Tel: 028 7126 5234
The Foyle Valley Railway Centre celebrates the outstanding railway history of the city. It has working diesel railcars that run on a picturesque three-mile track through the nearby Riverside Park. Open April-Sept, Tue-Sat 10am–4pm. Oct–Mar, Sat only 12noon–4pm.

Harbour Museum

Harbour Square
Tel: 028 7137 7331
Traditional Museum and Picture Gallery principally dealing with the maritime history of the city. Exhibits include a replica of the 30ft curragh in which St Columba sailed to Iona in 563. Temporary exhibitions are regularly displayed. Open Mon–Fri 10am–1pm and 2.00pm–4.30pm.

The Amelia Earhart Centre

Ballyarnett Country Park
Tel: 028 7135 4040 or
    028 7137 7331
3 miles north of Derry – take the A2. The centre was erected to commemorate the site where Amelia Earhart unexpectedly landed in

1932, the first woman to fly the Atlantic solo. Cottage exhibition open by appointment. Mon–Fri 10am–4pm. Please advise the centre of group visits in advance. Admission Free.

Gliding at Magilligan

86 Shore Road, Ballyhalbert, Newtownards BT22 1BJ
Tel: 028 4275 8777
or Bellarena clubhouse
Tel: 028 7775 0301
Contact Bod Rodwell
From the viewpoint on Bishop's Road, 853ft above the sea, you can see sailplanes and hang gliders over Magilligan Point. Sailplanes take off from the airfield at Bellarena.

Limavady

A plaque in Main Street marks home of Jane Ross, who preserved the Londonderry Air, more famously known as "Danny Boy". She is buried in the parish churchyard nearby. A mile south of the town, the Roe Valley Country Park is a treasure house of old mills and bleach greens – reminders of the local linen industry.

Mussenden Temple

Tel: 028 7084 8728
Starting from Limavady, the Coleraine bus travels to the old demesne of ruined Downhill Palace. Walk up through the grounds (always open) to the temple on the cliff edge open noon–6pm Sat–Sun and bank holidays April–Sept, Mon–Sun July–Aug.

In and Around Armagh

Tourist Information Centre

40 English Street, Armagh
Tel: 028 3752 1800
For such a small city, Armagh has a very large number of buildings listed as being of architectural and historical importance, with many clustered round the fine Anglican cathedral or close to the Mall, where cricket is played.

Armagh County Museum

Tel: 028 3752 3070
The Mall. The Ionic schoolhouse is one of Ireland's best small museums. Its library, art gallery and natural history room are especially interesting. Works by AE George Russell (1867–1935) born in Lurgan and James Sleator (1889–1950), the Armagh portrait painter. Open Mon to Fri 10am to 5pm, Sat 10am–1pm and 2–5pm.

Planetarium

Tel: 028 3752 3689
College Hill, in the grounds of Armagh Observatory, founded 1790 by Primate Robinson and designed by Francis Johnston. Open Mon–Fri 10am–4.45pm, Sat 1.15–4.45pm. Self-guided tours of the observatory grounds include sundials and barometer telescopes.

Armagh Public Library (Robinson Library)

Tel: 028 3752 3142
Near Anglican cathedral. Theology, science, archaeology and travel collections, original letters of Jonathan Swift and registers of archbishops from medieval times. Open 9.30am–1pm, 2–4pm Mon–Fri.

St Patrick's Trian

English Street, Armagh
Tel: 028 3752 1801
Incorporates three exhibitions: Armagh Story, Land of Lilliput, Least of all the Faithful – Saint Patrick's Testament. Open daily.

Palace Stables

Tel: 028 3752 9629
Heritage centre in the stables of the former Archbishop's Palace. Carriage rides, working stables, exhibitions, crafts and licensed restaurant. Icehouse, 18th-century chapel. Open daily.

Royal Irish Fusiliers Museum

Sovereign's House
The Mall, Armagh
Tel: 028 3752 2911
Call the curator for admission times.

Navan Fort

Tel: 028 3752 5550
Off the A28, 2 miles west of Armagh City. There are fine views from the top of this huge prehistoric mound which features prominently in the Ulster Cycle of epic myths. When the armies of Connaught invaded Ulster they were repelled single handedly by Cuchulain, the heroic warrior known as 'the Hound of Ulster'.

Apple Blossom Time

Tel: 028 3752 1800
A signposted apple blossom trail, starting and finished in Armagh city, winds through the 'orchard county' in May.

Ardress House

Annaghmore, Portadown
Tel: 028 3885 1236
7 miles west of Portadown on B28. 17th century manor house, plasterwork by Michael Stapleton, working farmyard. National Trust property. Open April–Sept.

The Argory

Tel: 028 8778 4753
Off the B27 west of Portadown. A neoclassical mansion lit by acetylene gas. National Trust property. Open April–Sept.

Gosford Forest Park

Tel: 028 3755 1277
Off A28 near Markethill. Associated with Dean Swift. Mock-Norman castle, walled garden, walks.

Moneypenny's Lock

Portadown

Tel: 028 3832 2205

Exhibition in lock keeper's house on the Newry Canal. Heyday of the lightermen, restored outhouses. Open Easter–Sept, weekends, afternoons, 2-mile walk along towpath from Bridge Street carpark.

Lough Neagh Discovery Centre

Oxford Island, Lough Neagh

Tel: 028 3832 2205

History of the lough, 'working water' computer and wildlife exhibition. Birdwatching, walks, boat trips and coffee bar. Open daily 10am–7pm (shorter hours during winter).

Keady Heritage Centre

Keady

Tel: 028 3753 9928

Local industrial archaeology exhibits in a former mill.

Tayto Factory

Tandragee

Tel: 028 3884 0249

Guided tours of the popular potato crisp factory, located in a castle. Mon–Thur 10.30am and 1.30pm. Not suitable for children under 5 years. Booking essential.

Around The Giant's Causeway

The Giant's Causeway, a peculiar formation of basalt rock, is Northern Ireland's most popular visitor attraction. The hexagonal columns are a symbol of the region throughout the world.

Giant's Causeway Centre

Tel: 028 2073 1855

Open July & August 10.00am – 7.00pm, June & Sept 6.00pm, 4.30p, in winter. Several craft and gift shops. Tourist information and bureau de change. National Trust

tea room. Causeway minibus service to Giant's Causeway.

To get there:

From Belfast – bus and train excursions throughout summer. Details from Translink on 028 9033 3000 or 028 9089 9411.

The Bushmills Bus – In summer (July–August) an open top bus travels the scenic route between Coleraine and Bushmills, stopping at Portstewart, Portrush, Portballintrae and the Causeway. The bus follows part of the route of the famous Giant's Causeway hydro-electric tramway. Regular departures from Coleraine bus station. More details from Ulsterbus Tel: 028 7034 3334.

From Portrush – Take bus no 172 from Dunluce Avenue (turn right opposite rail station). Journey distance – 9 miles. Details from Ulsterbus.

Causeway Coast & Glens

11 Lodge Road, Coleraine BT52 1LU

Tel: 028 7032 7720

Fax: 028 7032 7719

Website:

www.causewaycoastandglens.com

Boat Trips off the Causeway

Pleasure and sea angling boats from Portrush and Portstewart, April–Oct. Contact the nearest tourist information centre.

Whitepark Bay

National Trust leaflet available from shop at Giant's Causeway. Spectacular cliffs and beaches, although swimmers are advised to avoid east end of bay (fierce currents).

Youth hostel Tel: 028 2073 1745 at west end, near Portbraddan hamlet

and St Gobhan's church – smallest church in Ireland (12ft x 6ft).

Carrick-a-Rede Rope Bridge

Tel: 028 2073 1159

On A2, 5 miles west of Ballycastle. The bridge spans a chasm 80ft above the sea between the mainland and a small island. It is in position during the fishing season only April–Sept 10am–6pm, July–Aug until 8pm. Access along cliff path, 15-minute walk from National Trust's carpark at Larrybane information centre. Not for the faint hearted.

Dunluce Castle

Tel: 028 2073 19838

On A2, 3 miles east of Portrush. Open April & Sept Tues–Sat 10am–6pm and Sun 2pm–7pm, June–Aug Sun 2pm–6pm.

Bonamargy Friary

On A2, $\frac{1}{2}$ mile east of Ballycastle. Extensive ruins of Francisan friary, burial place of Sorley Boy MacDonnell.

Dunluce Centre

Portrush

Tel: 028 7082 4444

Simulated thrill ride, adventure play area, myths and legends, wildlife sights and sounds of the north coast.

Waterworld

Portrush

Tel: 028 7082 2001

Indoor water centre – giant water flumes, fun pools, water cannon, pirate ships and Jacuzzis.

Old Bushmills Distillery

Bushmills

Tel: 028 2073 1521

Guided tours of the world's oldest licensed distillery.

Leslie Hill Open Farm

Ballymoney
Tel: 028 2766 6803
Garden, blacksmith's forge, carriage displays.

Beaches

There are five impressive Blue Flag beaches on the Causeway Coast – Benone, Portstewart, two at Portrush, and Ballycastle in the east.

Glens of Antrim

Ossian's grave

Off the A2, 3 miles south of Cushendun. Megalithic tomb on slopes of Tievebulliagh mountain. The warrior-bard Ossian was the son of the legendary Finn McCool. A cairn nearby commemorates John Hewitt, the 20th Century Ulster poet.

Pony Trekking in the Glens

Watertop Farm, 188 Cushendall Rd.
Ballycastle, BT54 6RN
Tel: 028 2076 2576

Arthur Ancestral Home

Tel: 028 2588 0781
From Cushendall, the scenic A43 runs south-west through Glenariff to Ballymena, with Cullybackey beyond, a detour to the ancestral home of Chester Alan Arthur, US President 1881–1885. Open April–Sept Mon–Sat.

Sea Fishing

Red Bay Boats, Coast Road
Cushendall
Tel: 028 2177 1331
Boats for hire, tackle, rods, reels and live bait.

Oul' Lammas Fair (August)

Tel: 028 9033 7004
A major visitor attraction in the annual recreational calendar, including horse trading, stalls, dulse and 'Yellow Man'. Ulsterbus runs trips to the fair both days, from Belfast.

Rathlin Island

Tel: 028 2076 9299
Forty-five minutes by ferry from Ballycastle. Daily all year: 2 crossings in each direction weather permitting. 1 June – 30 Sept: 4 crossings each way. Overnight accommodation available.

Ards Peninsula and Co Down

For more information about the area contact:
Kingdoms of Down
40 West Street
Newtownards BT23 4EN
Tel: 028 9182 2881
Fax: 028 9182 2202
Website:
www.visitkingdomsofdown.com
Buses depart regularly from Belfast (Laganside Bus Centre) for Portaferry. For Mount Stewart ask to be dropped at Clay Gate. Tel: 028 9033 3000

Aquarium (Exploris)

Portaferry
Tel: 028 4272 8062
The marine life of Strangford Lough. The interactive centre includes large aquatic 'touch tanks' containing all kinds of creatures. Other tanks display anything from seahorses to sharks! Open Mon–Fri 10am–6pm, Sat 11am–6pm, Sun 1–6pm (shorter hours in winter).

Portaferry Visitor Centre

Tel: 028 4272 9882
Restored stable with exhibitions on Strangford Lough and Portaferry. Audio-visual display on the tower houses of County Down. Open Easter–Sept Mon–Fri 10am–5pm, Sun 2–6pm.

Portaferry–Strangford Ferry

Runs across the narrows, linking the Ards peninsula with the main body of county Down, every half hour, 7.45am–10.45pm, all year (carries 20 cars).

Sea Fishing

For trips from Portaferry to fish Strangford Lough, contact Des Rogers 028 4272 8297 and John Murray 028 4272 8414, offshore fishing from Donaghadee Quinton Nelson 028 9188 3403. Booking essential.

Summer Cruises

Departing from Bangor, Groomsport and Donaghadee. For more details contact 028 9127 0069 or 028 9182 6846.

North Down Heritage Centre

Tel: 028 9127 1200
Open 10.30am–4.30pm Tues–Sat and Sunday afternoon. Longer hours in July–Aug, Mon–Sat.

Ballycopeland Windmill

Tel: 028 9054 3037
One mile west of Millisle. One of only two working windmills left in Ireland. Open during June–Sept, from Tues to Sat, 10am–6pm and Sun 2–6pm.

Scrabo Country Park

Tel: 028 9181 1491
Tower on top dominates Strangford Lough, views over Newtownards and the whole of north Down. Tower open Easter Sat–Tue, May Bank Holidays, June–Sept Sat–Thur 10.30–6pm. Various walks through country park – open daily. From Newtownards take A21 towards Comber. Signposted after 2 miles to Scrabo carpark.

Greyabbey

Tel: 028 4278 8585
Visit the 'physic garden' where

medicinal plants are grown in trellised beds, in the grounds of this ruined 12th-century abbey. Open April–Sept Tues–Sat 10am–7pm, Sun 2–7pm.

Mount Stewart House

Tel: 028 4278 8387

Fine gardens created by the Seventh Marchioness of Derry. Refreshments available in house. Shop. Open April–Oct.

Castle Espie

Tel: 028 9187 4146

On Strangford Lough shore near Comber. Internationally renowned wildlife centre with a large collection of ducks, geese and swans. Viewing from hides or from coffee room. Open Mon–Sat 10.30am–5pm, Sun 11.30am–6pm (shorter hours in winter).

Delamont Country Park

Tel: 028 4482 8333

2 miles south of Killyleagh. Fine views of, and access to, Strangford Lough. Ten feet high Millennium Stone.

Castle Ward

Tel: 028 4488 1204

A mile west of Strangford village, the estate has a formal garden, parkland, sawmills, restored 1830s cornmill, unusual collection of wildfowl, Victorian laundry. Close by are two 15th-century castles, Old Castle Ward and Audley's Castle. House itself is open April–Oct. Known for its midsummer series of opera performances in its grounds.

St Patrick's Country and the Mournes

Slemish Mountain

St Patrick's first acquaintance with Ireland was, in fact, with County Antrim, particularly Slemish mountain (1,437 ft) where the boy slave is said to have herded swine for his master Miluic. For centuries this solitary extinct volcano has been a place of pilgrimage on St Patrick's Day (17th March). Follow the signposts from Broughshane village.

Coach Tours

Tel: 028 4461 2233

There is a special tour of St Patrick's Country during the Festival Week (March) led by a local historian. Contact Downpatrick Tourist Information Centre on the above number.

Down County Museum

Tel: 028 4461 4922

Fax: 028 4461 4456

The Mall, Downpatrick. This former jail, with an 18th-century cell block, has been superbly restored as a museum. Open all year.

Down Cathedral

Tel: 028 4461 4922

Fax: 028 4461 4456

The stone marking the place where St Patrick is believed to have been buried is in the churchyard. Cathedral closes at 5pm. For guided tours, contact Cathedral office. Open all year.

Saul Church

Built to mark the 1,500th anniversary of St Patrick's arrival in Ireland. Exhibition. Open daily until 6pm.

Slieve Patrick

On top of the hill is a huge granite statue of the saint. The base has interesting bronze panels, including a scene in which St Patrick defies the druids.

Downpatrick Railway Museum

Market Street

Tel: 028 4461 5779

Restored section of the Belfast–Newcastle main line runs to the grave of an ancient Viking King. Trips available on the steam locomotive Guinness July–Aug Sun afternoons.

Struell Wells

Healing wells and bath houses in rocky valley 2 miles east of Downpatrick have strong associations with St Patrick. One of the wells is said to cure eye ailments.

Quoile Pondage

Strangford Road, Downpatrick

Tel: 028 4461 5520

Quoile Pondage, where the Quoile river joins Strangford Lough, is a national nature reserve. Once a salt-water basin, it is now fresh water. Visit the Quoile interpretative centre nearby.

Brontë Interpretative Centre

Drumballyroney, Rathfriland

Tel: 028 4063 1152

Patrick Brontë, father of the novelist sisters, was parish schoolmaster here. Open March–Oct Tues–Fri 11am–5pm Sat & Sun 2–6pm.

Silent Valley

Tel: 028 9074 1166

A large reservoir in the heart of the Mourne mountains, Silent Valley is the main source of water to Belfast city. Open daily all year. Visitor centre, café.

Newry Museum

Bank Parade

Tel: 028 3026 6232

History of the 'Gap of the North,' robes of the Order of St Patrick, restored 18th-century room with period furniture. Mon–Fri 10.30am–4.30pm.

Fermanagh Lakelands

Tourist Information Centre
Wellington Road
Enniskillen BT74 7EF
Tel: 028 6632 3110
Fax: 028 6632 5511
Website: www.soeasygoing.com
Close to jetty and bus station,
accommodation-booking service,
crafts, souvenirs and books.

Cruising on the Waterways
Hire cruiser companies include:

Aghinver Boat Company
Tel: 028 6863 1400

Belleek Charter Cruising
Tel: 028 6865 8027

Carrick-Craft
Tel: 028 6774 8868

Carrybridge Boat Company
Tel: 028 6638 7034

Corraquill Cruising
Tel: 028 6774 8712

Erincurrach Cruising
Tel: 028 6864 1737

Erne Marine
Tel: 028 6634 8267

Lochside Cruisers Ltd
Tel: 028 6632 4368

Manor House Marine
Tel: 028 6862 8100

Lough Erne Cruises
Tel: 028 6632 2882
A 2–hour waterbus cruise of the
lower lough, calling at Devenish
Island, departs Enniskillen 'Round O'
pier three times a day in July and
August. On some days there is also
an evening trip. In May, June and
September, cruises are less
frequent. The waterbus has a
covered deck, a bar and
refreshments. Tel: 028 6862 1493

Shuttle Ferries to the Islands
Devenish and White Islands, both on
the lower lough, are accessible by
ferry in the main holiday season
every day 10am–7pm. For
Devenish: depart Trory off A32, 3
miles north of Enniskillen,
Easter–Sept. For White Island:
depart Castle Archdale marina, off
B82, south of Kesh, April–Sept. For
ferry times contact Fermanagh
Tourist Information Centre.

Enniskillen Castle
Tel: 028 6632 5000
This medieval castle houses
Fermanagh's county museum where
you can learn about the battling
Maguires, who had their
headquarters here. The castle also
houses the museum of the famous
Royal Inniskilling Fusiliers and there
is a heritage centre. The castle is
open 10am–5pm Tues–Fri, 2–5pm
Mon, 2–5pm Sat May–Sept, 2–5pm
Sat–Sun July–Aug.

Florence Court and Castle Coole
Tel: 028 6634 8249
These two fine houses, in National
Trust care, are open to the public.
Florence Court is set among
dramatic hills. Castle Coole is a
palatial neoclassical mansion. Call
028 6632 2690 for opening hours
or ask at Fermanagh Tourist
Information Centre in Enniskillen.

Crom Estate
Upper Lough Erne, Newtownbutler
Tel: 028 6773 8118
An important nature conservation
area, it has 1900 acres of woodland,
an exhibition centre and a tearoom.

Belleek
Tel: 028 6865 8631
This pretty village, famous for its fine
porcelain china (for tour of pottery
and interesting museum, Telephone
028 6865 8501) is also home to the

ExplorErne Centre which tells the
story of the Fermanagh Lakeland.

Marble Arch Caves
Tel: 028 6634 8855
Near Florence Court off A32 leaving
Enniskillen on the Sligo Road. The
tour begins with a short underground
boat trip past stalactites. Open mid
March–Sept every day, weather
permitting. Tours 10.30am–5pm.
Closing times vary.

Fermanagh From the Air
Tel: 028 6632 2771
Trial flights available in four-seater
aircraft from Enniskillen (St Angelo)
Airport, Tues–Sun.

Tyrone and the Sperrins

Tourist Information Centre
1 Market Street, Omagh
Tel: 028 8224 7831
The high Sperrins are splendid
walking country frequented by
golden plover, red grouse, and
thousands of sheep. Sawel is at
2240ft the highest mountain in the
range. It is very accessible and
offers wide panoramas. Sperrin
Hillwalking Festivals run annually
from June to October.

Sperrin Heritage Centre
Cranagh
Tel: 028 8164 8142
Craft shop.

Blessingbourne Museum
Fintona Road, Fivemiletown
Tel: 028 8952 1221
Small coach and carriage museum.
Open Easter–September by
arrangement.

An Creagán Centre
Tel: 028 8076 1112
Situated off A505 between Omagh
and Cookstown. Interpretative
exhibition of the archaeology,
environment and folklore of the area.

Craft shop, licensed restaurant, conference facilities, self-catering cottages. April–Sept Mon–Sun 11am–6.30pm, Oct–March Mon–Sat 11am–4.30pm.

Ulster Plantation Centre

Draperstown
Tel: 028 7962 7800
The story of the Plantation of Ulster brought alive in a stunning multimedia presentation. Interactive area, tearoom and shop. Open Easter–Sept Mon–Sat 10am–5pm, Sun 1pm–5pm Oct–Easter, 10am–5pm, closed Sat & Sun.

Kinturk Visitor Centre

Tel: 028 8673 6512
Close to Ardboe Cross, 10 miles east of Cookstown..

Ulster History Park

Tel: 028 8164 8188
Outdoor museum featuring reconstructions of homes and monuments from the Stone Age to the 17th century Plantation period. Visitor centre houses an exhibition gallery, a.v. presentations, cafeteria and gift shop. Open April–June, Sept daily 10am–5.30pm July–August daily 10am–6.30pm Oct–March Mon–Fri 10am–5pm.

Ulster American Folk Park

Omagh
Tel: 028 8224 3292
Museum of Emigration. Indoor Museum galleries and 23 original reconstructed buildings from both sides of the Atlantic. Ship and Dockside Gallery, craft shop and restaurant. Open 10.30am–6pm daily (summer) Mon–Fri (winter) 10.30–5pm.

Springhill House

Tel: 028 8674 8210
On B18, Moneymore–Coagh Road. Good example of fortified manor house. Open April–Sept.

Cornmill Heritage Centre

Coalisland
Tel: 028 8774 8532

Woodrow Wilson Ancestral Home

Strabane
Tel: 028 7188 3735
028 8224 3292
Telephone for details.

Gray's Printing Press

Main Street, Strabane
Tel: 028 7188 4094
John Dunlop, printer of the American Declaration of Independence, learned his trade here.

Grant Ancestral Home

Ballygawley
Tel: 028 8776 7259
South-east of Omagh (20 miles) is the home of the maternal ancestors of Ulysses Simpson Grant, US President 1869–77. It is open April–Sept Tues–Sat 12noon–5pm, Sun 2pm–6pm.

Wellbrook Beetling Mill

Tel: 028 8675 1735
Beetling is the final process in linen manufacture: the cloth is hammered (beetled) to give an even finish and sheen.

Benburb Valley
Heritage Centre

Milltown Road, Benburb
Tel: 028 3754 9752/3754 9885
Ten miles south of Dungannon. Guided tours of 19th-century linen mill on the banks of the old Ulster Canal.

Northern Ireland's Forests

Northern Ireland's forests are expanding and are open throughout the year, providing facilities and areas for recreational activities such as walking. Forests are listed by county.

Co Antrim

Ballycastle Forest, Glenarm Forest, Glenariff Forest Park, Tardree Forest, Ballyboley Forest, Ballypatrick Forest, Portglenone Forest, Randalstown Forest, Rea's Wood

Co Armagh

Gosford Forest Park, Slieve Gullion Forest Park

Co Down

Tollymore Forest Park, Castlewellan Forest Park, Donard Forest, Rostrevor Forest, Drumkeeragh Forest, Belvoir Park Forest, Cairn Wood

Co Fermanagh

Florence Court Forest Park, Ely Lodge Forest, Lough Navar Forest, Castle Caldwell Forest, Castle Archdale Forest, Marble Arch Wood, Spring Grove.

Co Londonderry

Coleraine Woods – Sommerset, Mountsandel, Castleroe, Springwell Forest, Binevenagh

Co Tyrone

Gortin Glen Forest Park, Drum Manor Forest Park, Parkanaur Forest Park, Pomeroy Forest, Seskinore Forest, Knockmany Forest, Fardross Forest

The National Trust

National Trust properties are located across Northern Ireland and offer a wealth of opportunities for the walking enthusiast. Many scenic coastal and countryside sites in Trust care include waymarked walking routes. The Trust also maintains scenic estates and gardens, including properties such as: Mount Stewart, Castle Ward and Rowallane in County Down, Castle Coole, Florence Court and the Crom Estate in County Fermanagh. For further information contact the Marketing and Communications Department on Tel: 028 9751 0721.

Where to Stay in Northern Ireland

Until relatively recently Northern Ireland has been undersupplied with quality hotel accommodation. In fact, on the occasions when there has been a major international event in the region, hotel accommodation has simply been insufficient to meet demand.

However, over the last few years hoteliers, supported by Government tourism policy and the Northern Ireland Tourist Board, have invested heavily in new and improved accommodation. Five years ago Northern Ireland did not have a single 5-star hotel; now it has two. Most of the leading hotels now have well-equipped leisure centres. A number of the big international hotel chains have recently established a presence, including Hilton, Radisson, Ramada and Holiday Inn.

Main Hotels Listing

The following hotel listing is arranged according to the Northern Ireland Tourist Board's 'star' ranking system. A description of each category in the system follows below.

NITB Star System

Five Star *****

Hotels of an international standard with luxurious and spacious guest accommodation including suites. High quality restaurants with table d'hôte and à la carte dinner menus.

Four Star ****

Large hotels with a high standard of comfort and service in well appointed premises. All bedrooms ensuite. Cuisine meets exacting standards. Comprehensive room service.

Three Star ***

Good facilities with a wide range of services. All bedrooms ensuite. Food available all day.

Two Star **

Good facilities with a reasonable standard of accommodation, food and services. Most bedrooms are ensuite.

One Star *

Hotels with acceptable standards of accommodation and food. Some bedrooms have ensuite facilities.

Belfast Hotels

Belfast Hilton International *****
4 Lanyon Place, Belfast BT1 3LP
Tel: 028 9027 7000
Fax: 028 9027 7277
Website: www.hilton.com
195 Rooms

Culloden Hotel *****
142 Bangor Road,
Holywood BT18 0EX
Tel: 028 9042 5223
Fax: 028 9042 6777
Website: www.hastingshotels.com
79 Rooms

Europa Hotel ****
Great Victoria Street
Belfast BT2 7AP
Tel: 028 9032 7000
Fax: 028 9032 7800
Website: hastingshotels.com
240 Rooms

Holiday Inn Belfast ****
Ormeau Avenue, Belfast BT2 8HR
Tel: 08704 009005
Fax: 028 9062 6546
170 Rooms

Malone Lodge Hotel ****
60 Eglantine Avenue
Belfast BT9 6DY
Tel: 028 9038 8000
Fax: 028 9038 8088
E-mail: info@malonelodgehotel.com
Website: ww.malonelodgehotel.com
51 Rooms

McCausland Hotel ****
34–38 Victoria Street
Belfast BT1 3GH
Tel: 028 9022 0200
Fax: 028 9022 0220
E-mail: info@mccauslandhotel.com
Website: www.mccauslandhotel.com
61 Rooms

Ramada Hotel ****
Shaws Bridge, Belfast BT8 7XP
Tel: 028 9092 3500
Fax: 028 9092 3600
E-mail: info@ramadabelfast.com
Website:
www.ramadabelfast.com
120 Rooms

Rayanne House
60 Demesne Road, Holywood
Co. Down BT18 9EX
Tel: 028 9042 5859

Stormont Hotel ****
587 Upper Newtownards Road
Belfast BT4 3LP
Tel: 028 9065 1111
Fax: 028 9048 0240
Website:
www.hastingshotels.com
105 Rooms

Nsq ****

Donegall Square South
elfast BT1 5JD
el: 028 9024 1001
ax: 028 9024 3210
ooms: 23

ellington Park Hotel ****
1 Malone Road, Belfast BT9 6RU
el: 028 9038 1111
ax: 028 9038 5055
ebsite: www.mooneyhotelgroup.com
5 Rooms

eechlawn House Hotel ***
Dunmurry Lane, Belfast BT17 9RR
el: 028 9060 2010
ax: 028 9060 2080
ebsite: www.beechlawnhotel.co.uk
2 Rooms

enedicts of Belfast ***
7–21 Bradbury Place
elfast BT7 1RQ
el: 028 9059 1999
ax: 028 9059 1990
2 Rooms

ukes Hotel ***
5–67 University Street
elfast BT7 1HL
Tel: 028 9023 6666
Fax: 028 9023 7177
Website: dukes-hotel.com
21 Rooms

Express Holiday Inn ***
106 University Street
Belfast BT7 1HP
Tel: 028 9031 1909
Fax: 028 9031 1910
Website: www.holidayinn-ireland.com
114 Rooms

Jurys Inn Belfast***
Fisherwick Place
Great Victoria Street
Belfast BT2 7AP
Tel: 028 9053 3500
Fax: 028 9053 3511
Email:jurysinnbelfast@jurysdoyle.com
Website: www.jurysdoyle.com
190 Rooms

Lansdowne Court Hotel***
657 Antrim Road, Belfast BT15 7EF
Tel: 028 9077 3317
Fax: 028 9037 0125
25 Rooms

Park Avenue Hotel ***

158 Holywood Road
Belfast BT4 1PB
Tel: 028 9065 6520
Fax: 028 9047 1417
56 Rooms
Email: marketing@parkavenuehotel.co.uk
Website: www.parkavenuehotel.co.uk

Belfast City Travelodge**
15 Brunswick Street,
Belfast BT2 7GE
Tel: 028 9033 3555
Fax: 028 9023 2999
Website: www.travelodge.co.uk
Rooms: 90

The Crescent Townhouse**
13 Lower Crescent, Belfast BT7 1NR
Tel: 028 9032 3349
Fax: 028 9032 0646
E-mail: info@crescenttownhouse.com
Website:www.crescenttownhouse.com

Balmoral Hotel **
Black's Road, Dunmurry
Belfast BT10 0NF
Tel: 028 9030 1234
Fax: 028 9060 1455
44 Rooms

Co Antrim

Dunadry Hotel & Country Club ****
2 Islandreagh Drive
Antrim BT41 2HA
Tel: 028 9443 4343
Fax: 028 9443 3389
Website: www.mooneyhotelgroup.com
83 Rooms

Galgorm Manor ****
136 Fenaghy Road, Cullybackey
Ballymena BT42 1EA
Tel: 028 2588 1001
Fax: 028 2588 0080
Website: www.galgorm.com
24 Rooms

Hilton Templepatrick ****
Castle Upton Estate
Templepatrick BT39 0DD
Tel: 028 9443 5500
Fax: 028 9443 5511
Website: www.templepatrick.hilton.com
130 Rooms

Adair Arms Hotel ***
Ballymoney Road
Ballymena BT43 5BF
Tel: 028 2565 3674
Fax: 028 2564 0436
Website: www.adairarms.com
44 Rooms

Ballygally Castle Hotel ***
274 Coast Road
Ballygally BT40 2QZ
Tel: 028 2858 3212
Fax: 028 2858 368
Website: www.hastingshotels.com
44 Rooms

Bushmills Inn ***
9 Dunluce Road
Bushmills BT57 8QG
Tel: 028 2073 2339
Fax: 028 2073 2048
Website: www.bushmillsinn.com
32 Rooms

Fitzwilliam International ***
Belfast International Airport
BT29 4ZY
Tel: 028 9442 2033
Fax: 028 9442 3500
108 Rooms

Glenavna House Hotel ***
588 Shore Road
Newtownabbey BT37 0SN
Tel: 028 9086 4461
Fax: 028 9086 2531
Website: www.glenavna.com
32 Rooms

Londonderry Arms Hotel ***
20 Harbour Road
Carnlough BT44 0EU
Tel: 028 2888 5255
Fax: 028 2885 5263
35 Rooms

Magherabuoy House Hotel ***
41 Magheraboy Road
Portrush BT56 8NX
Tel: 028 7082 3507
Fax: 028 7082 4687
Website: www.magherabuoy.co.uk
38 Rooms

Quality Hotel ***
75 Belfast Road
Carrickfergus BT38 8PH
Tel: 028 9336 4556
Fax: 028 9335 1620
68 Rooms

Rosspark Hotel ***
20 Doagh Road, Kells
Ballymena BT42 3LZ
Tel: 028 2589 1663
Fax: 028 2589 1477
Website: www.rosspark.com
39 Rooms

Royal Court Hotel ***
233 Ballybogey Road
Portrush BT56 8NF
Tel: 028 7082 2236
Fax: 028 7082 3176
Website: www.royalcourthotel.co.uk
18 Rooms

Templeton Hotel ***
882 Antrim Road
Templepatrick BT39 0AH
Tel: 028 9443 2984
Fax: 028 9443 3406
24 Rooms

Tullyglass Hotel ***
Galgorm Road
Ballymena BT42 1HJ
Tel: 028 2565 2639
Fax: 028 2564 6938
29 Rooms

Chimney Corner Hotel **
630 Antrim Road
Newtownabbey BT36 8RH
Tel: 028 9084 4925
Fax: 028 9084 4352
Website: chimneycorner.com
63 Rooms

Corr's Corner **
315 Ballyclare Road
Newtownabbey B36 4TQ
Tel: 028 9084 9221
Fax: 028 9083 2118
Website: corrscorner.com
30 Rooms

Co Armagh

Armagh City Hotel ****
2 Friary Road
Armagh BT60 4FR
Tel: 028 3751 8888
Fax: 028 3751 2777

Seagoe Hotel ***
22 Upper Church Lane
Portadown BT63 5JE
Tel: 028 3833 3076
Fax: 028 3835 0210
34 Rooms

Carngrove Hotel **
2 Charlestown Road
Portadown BT63 5PW
Tel: 028 3833 9222
Fax: 028 3833 2899
34 Rooms

Co Down

Slieve Donard Hotel ****
Downs Road, Newcastle BT33 0A
Tel: 028 4372 1066
Fax: 028 4372 4830
Website: www.hastingshotles.com
126 Rooms

Burrendale Hotel & Country Club ***
51 Castlewellan Road
Newcastle BT33 0JY
Tel: 028 4372 2599
Fax: 028 4372 2328
Website: www.burrendale.com
69 Rooms

Canal Court Hotel ***
Merchants Quay, Newry BT35 3HF
Tel: 028 3025 1234
Fax: 028 3025 1177
Website: www.canalcourthotel.com
51 Rooms

Clandeboye Lodge Hotel ***
10 Estate Road, Bangor BT19 1VR
Tel: 028 9185 2500
Fax: 028 9185 2772
E-mail: info@clandeboyelodge.co.uk
Website: www.clandeboyelodge.co.uk
43 Rooms

La Mon Country House Hotel ***
The Mills, 41 Gransha Road
Comber BT23 5RF
Tel: 028 9044 8631
Fax: 028 9044 8026
Website: www.lamon.co.uk
72 Rooms

Marine Court Hotel ***
The Marina, Bangor BT20 5ED
Tel: 028 9145 1100
Fax: 028 9145 1200
52 Rooms

ortaferry Hotel ***
0 The Strand
ortaferry BT22 1PE
el: 028 4272 8231
ax: 028 4272 8999
Website: www.portaferryhotel.com
4 Rooms

trangford Arms Hotel ***
2 Church Street
Newtownards BT23 4AL
el: 028 9181 4141
ax: 028 9181 1010
Website:
www.strangfordhotel.co.uk
80 Rooms

The Old Inn ***
15 Main Street
Crawfordsburn BT19 1JH
Tel: 028 9185 3255
Fax: 028 9185 2775
Website: www.theoldinn.com
32 Rooms

White Gables Hotel ***
14 Dromore Road
Hillsborough BT26 6HS
Tel: 028 9268 2755
Fax: 028 9268 9532
31 Rooms

Mourne Country Hotel **
52 Belfast Road, Newry BT34 1TR
Tel: 028 3026 7922
Fax: 028 3026 0896
43 Rooms

Co Fermanagh

Killyhevlin Hotel ****
Dublin Road, Enniskillen BT74 76RW
Tel: 028 6632 3481
Fax: 028 6632 4726
Website: www.killyhevlin.com
43 Rooms

Manor House Country Hotel ****
Killadeas, Enniskillen BT94 1NY
Tel: 028 6862 2211
Fax: 028 6862 1545
Website:
www.lakelands.net/manorhousehotel
46 Rooms

Fort Lodge Hotel **
72 Forthill Street
Enniskillen BT74 6AJ
Tel: 028 6632 3275
Fax: 028 6632 0275
36 Rooms

Lough Erne Hotel **
Main Street, Kesh BT93 1TF
Tel: 028 6863 1275
Fax: 028 6863 1921
Website: www.loughernehotel.com
16 Rooms

Mahon's Hotel **
Enniskillen Road
Irvinestown BT94 1GS
Tel: 028 6862 1656
Fax: 028 6862 8344
Website:
www.mahonshotel.co.uk
18 Rooms

Co Londonderry

Beech Hill Country House Hotel ****
32 Ardmore Road, Derry BT47 3QP
Tel: 028 7134 9279
Fax: 028 7134 5366
Website: www.beech-hill.com
27 Rooms

City Hotel ****
Queen's Quay, Derry BT48 7AS
Tel: 028 7136 5800
Fax: 028 7136 5801
Website:
www.greatsouthernhotels.com

Everglades Hotel ****
41–53 Prehen Road
Derry BT47 2NH
Tel: 028 7134 6722
Fax: 028 7134 9200
Website: www.hastingshotel.com
64 Rooms

Radisson Roe Park Hotel & Golf
Resort ****
Roe Park, Limavady BT49 9LB
Tel: 028 7772 2212
Fax: 028 7772 2313

Website: www.radissonroepark.com
64 Rooms

TOWER HOTEL DERRY

T O W E R
HOTEL - DERRY

Tower Hotel Derry ****
(4 Star RAC)

Butcher Street
Londonderry
BT48 6HL
Tel: (028) 7137 1000
Fax: (028) 7137 1234
Website: www.towerhotelgroup.com
Email: reservations@thd.ie

General Manager: Ian Hyland

This stylish new hotel is located in
the city centre. Facilities include;
90 spacious bedrooms and three
luxury suites, a Mediterranean
bistro, a chic cafe style bar, a
gymnasium and sauna.

Bohill Hotel & Country Club ***
69 Cloyfin Road
Coleraine BT52 2NY
Tel: 028 7034 4406
Fax: 028 7035 2424
37 Rooms

Broomhill Hotel ***
Limavady Road, Derry BT47 6LT
Tel: 028 7134 7995
Fax: 028 7134 9304
42 Rooms

Brown Trout Golf & Country Inn ***
209 Agivey Road
Aghadowey BT51 4AD
Tel: 028 7086 8209
Fax: 028 7086 8878
Website: www.browntroutinn.com
15 Rooms

Bushtown House Country Hotel ***
283 Drumcroone Road
Coleraine BT51 3QT
Tel: 028 7035 8367
Fax: 028 7032 0909
Website: www.bushtownhotel.com
40 Rooms

Lodge Hotel & Travel Stop ***
Lodge Road, Coleraine BT52 1NG
Tel: 028 7034 4848
Fax: 028 7035 4555
Website: www.thelodgehotel.com
56 Rooms

Quality Hotel Da Vinci's ***
15 Culmore Road, Derry BT48 8TB
Tel: 028 7127 9111
Fax: 028 7127 9222
Website: www.davincishotel.com
70 Rooms

Travel Lodge ***
22–24 Strand Road
Derry BT48 7AB
Tel: 028 7127 1271

Fax: 028 7127 1277
Website: www.thetravellodge.com
40 Rooms

Waterfoot Hotel & Country Club ***
14 Clooney Road, Derry BT47 6TB
Tel: 028 7134 5500
Fax: 028 7131 1006
48 Rooms

Edgewater Hotel **
88 Strand Road
Portstewart BT55 7LZ
Tel: 028 7083 3314
Fax: 028 7083 2224
Website: www.edgehotel.com
28 Rooms

White Horse Hotel **
68 Clooney Road, Derry BT47 3PA
Tel: 028 7186 0606
Fax: 028 7186 0371
Website: www.whitehorsehotel.biz
57 Rooms

Co Tyrone

Glenavon House Hotel ***
52 Drum Road
Cookstown BT80 8JQ
Tel: 028 8676 4949
Fax: 028 8676 4396
Website: www.glenavonhotel.co.uk
53 Rooms

Fir Trees Hotel **
Dublin Road, Strabane BT82 9EA
Tel: 028 7138 2382
Fax: 028 7138 3116
24 Rooms

Valley Hotel **
60 Main Street
Fivemiletown BT75 0PW
Tel: 028 8952 1505
Fax: 028 8952 1688
22 Rooms

Where to Eat and Drink in Northern Ireland

Northern Ireland has made great progress in recent years in terms of the overall quality and range of offerings to diners. There are an increasing number of genuinely international-class restaurants serving local and international cuisine of the highest standard. In addition many of the North's cafes and bars have upgraded their fare with many bars serving good quality local dishes at reasonable prices.

The advent of relative 'peace' in Northern Ireland has encouraged hoteliers and restaurateurs to invest in their industry and many good quality restaurants, bars and brasseries have been opened up.

The same applies to clubs and nightlife generally. The Dublin Road, Great Victoria Street stretch of South Belfast is possibly Northern Ireland's busiest district in terms of bars clubs and nightlife and is unrecognisable from the quiet area that existed 15 or 20 years ago.

Restaurants
Belfast
Aldens Restaurant
229 Upper Newtownards Road
Belfast BT4 3JH
Tel: 028 9065 0079
Fax: 028 9065 0032
A modern restaurant, Aldens has given east Belfast a taste of the gourmet experience.

ba soba Noodle Bar
38 Hill Street,
Cathedral Quarter, Belfast BT1 2LB
Tel: 028 9058 6868
ba soba is Belfast's first noodle bar modelled on noodle canteens that have been popular in Japan for centuries. Specialising in noodle dishes and curries from across South East Asia.

Beatrice Kennedy
44 University Road, Belfast BT7
Tel: 028 9020 2290
A gourmet restaurant.

Bokhara Indian Restaurant
143–149 High Street, Holywood
Tel: 028 9042 6767
Quality Indian restaurant.

Café aero Restaurant
44 Bedford Street, Belfast BT2 7FF
Tel: 028 9024 4844
Café aero Restaurant is a contemporary fine dining restaurant.

Cafe Paul Rankin
27–29 Fountain Street, Belfast
Tel: 028 9031 5090
Café Paul Rankin offers casual dining.

Cafe Milano
92–94 Lisburn Road
Belfast BT9 6AG
Tel: 028 9068 9777
A bustling new Italian restaurant.

Café Vincents
78–80 Botanic Avenue, Belfast
Tel: 028 9024 2020
Eclectic cuisine with a French influence.

Cayenne
7 Lesley House, Shaftesbury Square
Belfast BT2 7DB
Tel: 028 9033 1532
Fax: 028 9026 1575
Cayenne is the latest project from Paul and Jeanne Rankin of television's 'Gourmet Ireland'.

Christies Brasserie
7–11 Linenhall Street
Belfast BT2 8AA
Tel: 028 9031 1150
Fax: 028 9031 1151
Website: www.christies-belfaast.com
International cuisine and seafood.

Connor
11a Stranmillis Road, Belfast
Tel: 028 9066 3266
Bright, modern airy restaurant offering a wide range of dining options from coffee to evening meals.

Copperfields Bar & Restaurant
9–21 Fountain Street
Belfast BT1 5EA
Tel: 028 9024 7367
Fax: 028 9033 0436
Centrally located in the heart of Belfast, this is a traditional bar and restaurant.

Cutters Wharf
Lockview Road, Stranmillis, Belfast
Tel: 028 9066 3388
Situated on the banks of the river Lagan, what was originally an Old Boat House has now been transformed into a Californian themed restaurant.

Deanes Restaurant & Brasserie
36–40 Howard Street
Belfast BT1 6PF
Tel: 028 9056 0000
Fax: 028 9056 0001
One of Belfast's smartest eateries and home to award-winning chef Michael Deane.

East
GroundFloor,FloralBuildings
EastBridgeStreet, MarketQuarter
Belfast
Tel: 028 9024 0055
Website: www.east_online.co.uk
Trendy eaterie with Asian influences.

Giraffe
54–56 Stranmillis Road, Belfast
Tel: 028 9066 1074
Giraffe situated in the heart of the university area is a well-established eatery with a "bring your own" policy offering casual dining and an extensive menu.

Harry Ramsden's
Yorkgate Complex,
150a York Street, Belfast
Tel: 028 9074 9222
Offering world famous fish and chips in a traditional environment with a fine selection of dishes from which to choose.

Hilton Hotel
4 Lanyon Place, Belfast BT1 3LP
Tel: 028 9027 7000
Fax: 028 9027 7277
The Sonoma Restaurant offers a contemporary menu with a blend of Irish, European and Asian cuisine.

Indie
159 Stranmillis Road
Belfast BT9 5AJ
Tel: 028 9066 8100
Website: www.indiespice.com

La Salsa Mexican
23 University Road
Belfast BT7 1NA
Tel: 028 9024 4588

L'etoile
407 Ormeau Road, Belfast BT7
Tel: 028 9020 1300
French Cuisine in intimate surroundings.

Madison's
59–63 Botanic Avenue
Belfast BT7 1JL
Tel: 028 9050 9800
70 seater 'Award Winning' restaurant.

Malone House Restaurant
Barnett Demesne, Malone Road
Belfast BT9 5PB
Tel: 028 9068 1246
Fax: 028 9068 2197
Period house located in verdant surroundings in Upper Malone, offering highly regarded Irish food.

Malone Lodge Hotel

60 Eglantine Avenue
Belfast BT9 6DY
Tel: 028 9038 8000
Fax: 028 9038 8088
Located in the leafy Victorian suburbs of the University area of South Belfast.

Maloneys Restaurant

33–35 Malone Road
Belfast BT9 6RU
Tel: 028 9068 2929
Bistro-style restaurant on the busy Malone Road, offering a wide range of local and international cuisine.

McHugh's Bar & Restaurant

29–31 Queen's Square
Belfast BT1 3FG
Tel: 028 9050 9990
Famous for being the oldest building in Belfast McHugh's offers everything from Oriental cuisine, to traditional pub grub.

Merchants Brasserie

The McCausland Hotel,
34–36 Victoria Street, Belfast.
Tel: 028 9022 0200

The Morning Star

17–19 Pottinger's Entry
Belfast BT1 4DT
Tel: 028 9023 5986
Halfway down Pottinger's Entry, in the heart of Belfast, is one of the city's most historic pubs. Food is available in both the public bar and upstairs restaurant/lounge, with its discreet booths.

Nick's Warehouse

35–39 Hill Street, Belfast BT1 2LB
Tel: 028 9043 9690
Fax: 028 9023 0514
Nick's Warehouse is located in the city near to St Anne's Cathedral.

The Northern Whig

2 Bridge Street, Belfast BT1 1LU
Tel: 028 9050 9888
Formerly home to the old Northern Whig printing press, this unique building has been restored with a contemporary eastern European influence.

Olio Restaurant

17 Brunswick Street
Belfast BT2 7GE
Tel: 028 9024 0239
Fax: 028 9024 2290
Conveniently situated close to Belfast's Grand Opera House and car parks   Pasta and main course specialities blend with a selection of traditional favourites. Fresh baked fish is a speciality.

Opus One

1 University Street, Belfast BT7 1FY
Tel: 028 9059 0101
Fax: 028 9059 0606
Smart, modern restaurant in South Belfast's University quarter. Wide range of local and international dishes.

Restaurant Porcelain@ TEN sq

10 Donegall Square, Belfast
Tel: 028 9024 1001
A fusion of Japanese and European.

Ryan's Bar & Grill

116–118 Lisburn Road, Belfast
Tel: 028 9050 9851
This recently refurbished Bar and Grill offers a varied menu adding a touch of European culture with carafe's of draught wine.

The Square

89 Dublin Road, Belfast
Tel: 028 9023 9933
Always busy. Menus change regularly. Booking required.

Skye

21 Howard Street, Belfast BT1 6NE
Tel: 028 9032 3313
Fax: 028 9031 0937
Downstairs the emphasis is on bar snacks. Upstairs a full Bistro menu operates.

Suwanna Thai Restaurant

117 Great Victoria Street, Belfast
Tel: 028 9043 9007

Tedford's Restaurant

5 Donegal Quay, Belfast BT1 3EF
Tel: 028 9043 4000
Located in an historic Belfast building, formerly a ship's chandlers dating from 1851, this atmospheric restaurant overlooks the River Lagan and specialises in fish.

Ta Tu Bar & Grill

701 Lisburn Road, Belfast BT9 7GU
Tel: 028 9038 0818
Winner of the Glen Dimplex Award for Best Bar Interior in Ireland, the restaurant offers gourmet dining. Booking advisable.

The John Hewitt Bar & Restaurant

51 Donegall Street, Belfast
Tel: 028 9023 3768
The John Hewitt is very much traditional in style with the emphasis on conversation, traditional music, art displays and "craic".

The Oxford Exchange

Grill Bar Restaurant
1st Floor, St George's Market
Belfast
Tel: 028 9024 0014
Situated on the first floor of St George's Market in the developing Market Quarter of Belfast, Oxford Exchange offers quality dining in stylish surroundings.

The Red Panda Chinese Restaurant
(2 locations)
60 Great Victoria Street
Tel: 028 9080 8700
Tel: 028 9046 6644
Located opposite the Europa Hotel and recently opened in the Odyssey Pavillion, this is the largest of the Chinese restaurants in the city.

The Wok
126 Great Victoria Street, Belfast
Tel: 028 9023 3828

The Water Margin
47 High Street, Holywood
Tel: 028 9042 2333

Wine & Co.
57 High Street, Holywood
Tel: 028 9042 6083
The unique idea of Wine & Co is to choose your wine from over 400 choices downstairs and bring it upstairs to the Bistro.

Co Antrim

Bushmills Inn Hotel
25 Main Street, Bushmills BT57 8QG
Tel: 028 2073 2339
Fax: 028 2073 2048
Between the Giant's Causeway and Royal Portrush, this atmospheric restored coaching inn with its open turf fires, stripped pine and gas lights offers a selection of traditional dishes prepared from fresh local produce.

Clenaghans
48 Soldierstown Road, Aghalee
Co Antrim BT67 0ES
Tel: 028 9265 2952
Fax: 028 9265 2251
Rural hideaway (near Moira, Co Down) with bar and exclusive restaurant. Serves a range of Irish and international cuisine. Advanced booking essential.

Galgorm Manor
136 Fenaghy Road
Ballymena BT42 1EA
Tel: 028 2588 1001
Fax: 028 2588 0080
Lunch is served Mon–Sat 12.00pm–2.30pm, and in the dining room on Sunday from 12.00–2.30pm. Table d'Hote Dinner menu is served daily from 7.00–9.00pm except Sunday when service begins 6.00–8.30pm. Pub lunches are also available in 'Gillies Bar', a traditional Irish pub with open log fires

The Ginger Tree (Japanese)
29 Ballyrobert Road, Ballyclare
Tel: 028 9084 8176

Londonderry Arms Hotel
20–28 Harbour Road
Carnlough BT44 0EU
Tel: 028 2888 5255
Fax: 028 2885 5263
This family-owned hotel is a former coaching inn built by the Marchioness of Derry in 1854. The hotel is known for its fresh and simple cooking and its smoked salmon from nearby Glenarm.

Lynden Heights
97 Drumnagreagh Road
Ballygally BT40 2RP
Tel: 028 2858 3560
The Restaurant is situated on the B148 at the southern entrance to the Glens of Antrim.

Marine Hotel
1–3 North Street
Ballycastle BT54 6BN
Tel: 028 2076 2222
Fax: 028 2076 9507

Rosspark Hotel
20 Doagh Road, Kells
Ballymena BT42 3LZ
Tel: 028 2589 1663
Fax: 028 2589 1477

'Restaurant at Rosspark' offers locally caught fresh salmon and Northern Irish beef.

Templeton Hotel
882 Antrim Road
Templepatrick BT39 0AH
Tel: 028 9443 2984
Fax: 028 9443 3406

Tidy Doffer
133 Ravernet Road
Lisburn BT27 5NF
Tel: 028 9268 9188
Fax: 028 9262 8949
The Tidy Doffer is renowned as the largest thatched roof pub in Ireland. The restaurant offers a range of traditional and international dishes.

Co Armagh

De Averell House
No 3 Seven Houses
47 Upper English Street
Armagh City BT61 7LA
Tel: 028 3751 1213
Fax: 028 3751 1221
Built in the late 18th century, Basement Restaurant offers a range of menus using local and international dishes.

The Planters Tavern
4 Banbridge Road
Waringstown BT66 7QA
Tel: 028 3888 1510
Fax: 028 3888 2371
Planters Tavern is a listed 17th century coaching inn. Local beef and poultry are house specialities.

The Seagoe Hotel
22 Upper Church Lane
Portadown BT63 5JE
Tel: 028 3833 3076
Fax: 028 3835 0210
Recently refurbished Avanti Restaurant open for fine dining.

Co Down

The Brass Monkey
16 Trevor Hill, Newry BT34 1DN
Tel: 028 3026 3176
Fax: 028 3026 6013
This bar has a country farmhouse atmosphere with stone floors and a spiral staircase.

The Buck's Head
77 Main Street, Dundrum BT33 0LU
Tel: 028 4375 1868
Fax: 028 4375 1898
A country pub dating back to the 18th century which has been completely renovated, adding a conservatory and beer garden

The Burrendale Hotel and Country Club
51 Castlewellan Road
Newcastle BT33 0JY
Tel: 028 4372 2599
Fax: 028 4372 2328
The Burrendale's Vine Restaurant has an a la carte and Table d'Hote menu, a gentle ambience, fresh local food and a fine wine selection. The Cottage Kitchen Restaurant presents a Bistro Menu with an informal atmosphere.

The Cuan
The Square, Strangford BT30 7ND
Tel: 028 4488 1222
Fax: 028 4488 1770
Throughout the day there is a bar snack menu followed in the evening by Table d'Hote and a la Carte. Open 7 days a week, food served all day.

Dufferin Arms Coaching Inn
35 High Street, Killyleagh BT30 9QF
Tel: 028 4482 8229
Fax: 028 4482 8755
The Dufferin Arms Coaching Inn is renowned for its good food, music and atmosphere.

Four Trees Bar & Bistro
61–63 Main Street, Moira BT67 0LQ
Tel: 028 9261 1437
Fax: 028 9261 3939
A traditional public house with a unique stone courtyard leading to its restaurant. The public bar is quaint and charming dating back to the 19th century. The menu uses fresh local produce and incorporates modern trends.

Harry's Bar
7 Dromore Street
Banbridge BT32 4BS
Tel: 028 4066 2794
The traditional pub serves food and drink in a traditional old world atmosphere.

The Hillside
21 Main Street
Hillsborough BT26 6AE
Tel: 028 9268 2765
Fax: 028 9268 9888
The bar is housed in a 17th century building over which an antique-filled restaurant is situated. Past winner of both Egon Ronay Bar of the Year 1995 (All Ireland) and Bushmills Bar of the Year Awards.

The Lobster Pot
9–11 The Square
Strangford BT30 7ND
Tel: 028 4488 1288
Fax: 028 4488 1288
The Lobster Pot retains its old-fashioned charm with comfortable surroundings. Along with traditional Irish dished and classic European cuisine, the Lobster Pot is renowned for its seafood – especially lobster!

Normans Inn
86 Main Street, Moira BT67 0LH
Tel: 028 9261 1318
Fax: 028 9261 1318
Normans Inn is situated in the picturesque village of Moira and is a traditional bar with a bright, modern lounge. The Lounge Bistro serves food daily, Mon–Sat 12.00–8.00pm.

The Old Inn
11–15 Main Street
Crawfordsburn BT19 1JH
Tel: 028 9185 3255
Fax: 028 9185 2775
One of Ireland's oldest hostelries dating back to 1614. The highly acclaimed restaurant serving both a la carte and Table d'Hote meals is renowned for its food and extensive wine list.

The Old Schoolhouse Inn
100 Ballydrain Road
Comber BT23 6EA
Tel: 028 9754 1182
Fax: 028 9754 2583
The School House is a licensed restaurant situated in the country on the Ulster Way near Strangford Lough.

The Portaferry Hotel
10 The Strand, Portaferry BT22 1PE
Tel: 028 4272 8231
Fax: 028 4272 8999
The Portaferry Hotel makes the most of the plentiful supplies of fish and shellfish in the area. Awarded two AA Rosettes, the hotel restaurant is recommended by many international food guides.

Shanks Restaurant
The Blackwood Golf Centre
150 Crawfordsburn Road
Bangor BT19 1GB
Tel: 028 9185 3313
Fax: 028 9185 2493
Table d'Hote Lunch and Dinner menus change monthly. Shanks was awarded a Michelin star in 1996.

The Slieve Croob Inn
119 Clanvaraghan Road
Castlewellan BT31 9LA
Tel: 028 4377 1412
Fax: 028 4377 1162
Specialities include Dundrum oysters Rockerfeller and Fresh Darne of local Salmon.

Co Fermanagh

Killyhevlin Hotel
Killyhevlin, Enniskillen BT74 6RW
Tel: 028 6632 3481
Fax: 028 6632 4726

Manor House Country Hotel
Killadeas BT94 1NY
Tel: 028 6862 2200
Fax: 028 6862 1545
This elegant Victorian Manor serves up local produce.

Co Londonderry

Ardtara Country House
8 Gorteade Road, Upperlands
Maghera BT46 5SA
Tel: 028 7964 4490
Fax: 028 7964 5080
A Victorian manor, built in 1856 and set in 8.5 acres of ground. The Head Chef leads the kitchen team using fresh local produce for menus which include hand picked berries, wild boar, rabbit and salmon wrapped in Dulse (seaweed). British Airways Tourism Award Winner, 2 AA Rosettes.

Beech Hill Country House Hotel
32 Ardmore Road, Derry BT47 3QP
Tel: 028 7134 9279
Fax: 028 7134 5366
The menu is adventurous with emphasis on local produce in a classical style and attractively presented.

Bistro @ Tower Hotel Derry****
(4 Star RAC)
Butcher Street
Londonderry BT48 6HL
Tel: 028 7137 1000
Fax: 028 7137 1234
Website: www.towerhotelgroup.com
E-mail: reservations@thd.ie

Bohill Hotel & Country Club
69 Cloyfin Road, Coleraine BT52 2NY
Tel: 028 7034 4406
Fax: 028 7035 2424
The Bohill's Gourmet Restaurant – Chapter One, was built in January 1999 in the concept of a 'stand alone' restaurant for both residents and casual diners. It is distinctive in menu and ambience.

Brown Trout Golf & Country Inn
209 Agivey Road, Aghadowey (near Coleraine) BT51 4AD
Tel: 028 7086 8209
Fax: 028 7086 8878
The Inn was first licensed in the last century. The upstairs restaurant is non-smoking, but many customers eat casually around the open peat fires or out on the patio.

Decks Bar & Restaurant
1 Campsie Business Park
McLean Road, Eglinton BT47 3XX
Tel: 028 7186 0912
Fax: 028 7186 0053
Decks is essentially a Brasserie. The pine panelling in the restaurant dates back to 1902, originally in the Board Room of one of the Maiden City's oldest shirt factories.

Co Tyrone

Corick House
20 Corick Road, Clogher BT76 0BZ
Tel: 028 8554 8216
Fax: 028 8554 9531
A licensed Gourmet Restaurant offering a la Carte and Table d'Hote meals. A Grill Bar Restaurant serves Brasserie meals.

The Mellon Country Inn
134 Beltany Road, Omagh BT78 5RA
Tel: 028 8166 1224
Fax: 028 8166 2245
A recent winner of the les Routiers Silver Place Award for Best Restaurant, member of the Healthy Eating Circle and Taste of Ulster.

Viscounts Restaurant
10 Northland Row
Dungannon BT71 6AW
Tel: 028 8775 3800
Fax: 028 8775 3880
This 110 year old former church hall, has been converted into a fully licensed restaurant with a unique medieval theme.

Pubs and Clubs

Public Houses, known as 'pubs' or 'bars', are at the heart of people's social lives throughout Northern Ireland, whether as drinking places or just meeting spots. They are good places to hear live music – folk, traditional, jazz, blues and rock. Several of the pubs listed stay open until 1am.

Belfast

The Apartment
Donegall Square West, Belfast
Tel: 028 9050 9777
Fax: 028 9050 9778

Bar RED @ TENsq
10 Donegall Square, Belfast
Tel: 028 9024 1001

Benedicts of Belfast
7–21 Bradbury Place, Belfast
Tel: 028 9059 1999

The Bodega Bar
4 Callender Street, Belfast
Tel: 028 9024 3177

Culpa
1 Bankmore Square, Dublin Road
Belfast
Tel: 028 9023 3555
Mon–Thurs 9pm–1am
Fri 9pm–2am
Sat 9pm–3am
Sunday 9pm–12am

Bar 12
13 Lower Crescent, Belfast.
Tel: 028 9032 3349.
An oak panelled, imaginative Gothic style bar. Food served Monday to Saturday 12–3pm.

Bar Bacca
42 Franklin Street, Belfast
Tel: 028 9023 0200
Fax: 028 9023 0201
E-mail: info@barbacca.com
Website: www.barbacca.com
Winner of the Theme Magazine Bar and Restaurant Award for Best Bar in All Ireland in May 2002.

The Botanic Inn
23–27 Malone Road
Belfast BT9 6RU
Tel: 028 9050 9740
Popular haunt for Belfast's students and watching major sporting events.

Café Marco Polo at The McCausland Hotel
34–38 Victoria Street, Belfast
Tel: 028 9022 0200
Continental style café bar.

Chelsea Wine Bar
346 Lisburn Road, Belfast
Tel: 028 9068 7177

The Crown Liquor Saloon
46 Great Victoria Street, Belfast
Tel: 028 9027 9901
Famous traditional Irish bar opposite the Grand Opera House.

Duke of York
7–11 Commercial Court, Belfast
Tel: 028 9024 1062

The Empire
40–42 Botanic Avenue, Belfast
Tel: 028 9032 8110
Music hall and comedy club.

Irene and Nans
12 Brunswick Street, Belfast
Tel: 028 9023 9123
Fax: 028 9023 0201
E-mail: info@ireneandnans.com
Website: www.ireneandnans.com
Irene and Nans is a haven for cocktail connoisseurs and foodies with kitsch surroundings.

Kitchen Bar
16 Victoria Square, Belfast
Tel: 028 9032 4901

La Lea
43 Franklin Street, Belfast
Tel: 028 9023 0200
Fax: 0285 9023 0201
E-mail: info@lalea.com
Website:www.lalea.com

Lavery's Bar and Gin Palace
12–16 Bradbury Place, Belfast
Tel: 028 9087 1106
One of Belfast's busiest and most famous pubs with probably the widest diversity of clientele of any bar in Belfast.

McHugh's
29–31 Queen's Square, Belfast
Tel: 028 9050 9990
Fax: 028 9050 9998

Magennis's
83 May Street, Belfast
Tel: 028 9023 0295
Traditional bar close to St Georges Market and the Waterfront Hall offering live music and food.

Mezza(nine)
38–42 Great Victoria Street, Belfast
Tel: 028 9024 7447

Mercury Bar & Grill
451 Ormeau Road, Belfast
Tel: 028 9064 9017

Milk Bar-Club
10–14 Tomb Street, Belfast
Tel: 028 9027 8876
Trendy nightclub.

The Edge Bar & Restaurant
Mays Meadow, Laganbank Road
Belfast
Tel: 028 9032 2000
Waterfront facility, enjoying spectacular views from balconies.

The Empire
40–42 Botanic Avenue, Belfast
Tel: 028 9032 8110

The Morning Star
17–19 Pottinger's Entry, Belfast
Tel: 028 9032 3976

Morrisons Lounge Bars
21 Bedford Street, Belfast
Tel: 028 9032 0030

The Northern Whig
2 Bridge Street, Belfast
Tel: 028 9050 9880
Fax: 028 9050 9888

The Parlour
2–4 Elmwood Avenue, Belfast
Tel: 028 9068 6970

The Fly Bar
5–6 Lower Crescent, Belfast
Tel: 028 9050 9750
This is one of the more popular venues in Belfast, consisting of three floors, each with their very own characteristic bar.

Robinson's Bars
Great Victoria Street, Belfast
Tel: 028 9024 4774

TaTu
Lisburn Road, Belfast
Tel: 028 9038 0818
Trendy new bar and restaurant.

Pat's Bar
Prince's Dock Street, Belfast
Tel: 028 9074 4524

Rotterdam Bar
Pilot Street, off Corporation Street
Belfast BT3 5HZ
Tel: 028 9074 6021
Fax: 028 9075 3275

Derry

Castle Bar
Waterloo Street, Derry
Tel: 028 7126 3118

Clarendon Bar
46–48 Strand Road, Derry
Tel: 028 7126 3705

Cosmopolitan Bar
29 Strand Road, Derry
Tel: 028 7126 6400

Peadar O'Donnell's
Waterloo Street, Derry
Tel: 028 7137 2318

The Strand
35 Strand Road, Derry
Tel: 028 7136 6910

Grand Opera House, Belfast

Cinema, Theatre and the Arts

Cinema

After many years of decline in cinema attendances, Northern Ireland has seen a substantial increase in investment, with new multi-screen cinema complexes in many of the main population centres. Many big screen stars hail from Northern Ireland, such as Kenneth Branagh and Liam Neeson, and the region has produced award winning films and shorts.

Antrim Cineplex
1 Fountain Street
Antrim BT41 1LZ
Tel: 028 9446 1111 (info)
Tel: 028 9446 9500 (booking)

Armagh City Filmhouse
Market Street, Armagh BT61 7BU
Tel: 028 3751 1033

Bangor Multiplex
1 Valentines Road
Castle Park, Bangor BT20 4JH
Tel: 028 9146 5007

IMC Multiplex Cinema
Larne Road Link, Ballymena BT42
Tel: 028 2563 1111

Lisburn Omniplex
Lisburn Leisure Park
Governor Road, Lisburn BT28 1PR
Tel: 028 9266 3664

Movie House Cinemas Ltd
51 St Lurachs Road
Maghera BT46 5JE
Tel: 028 7964 2936

The Movie House
13 Glenwell Road
Glengormley BT36 7RF
Tel: 028 9083 3424

Movieland
Ards Shopping Centre
Blair Main Road South
Newtownards BT23 4EU
Tel: 028 9182 0000

Newry Omniplex Cinema
Quays Shopping Centre
Albert Basin, Newry
Tel: 028 3025 2233

Playhouse Cinema
Main Street, Portrush
Tel: 028 7082 3917

Queen's Film Theatre
30 University Square Mews
Belfast BT7 1JU
Tel: 028 9024 4857

Ritz Multiplex Cinemas
1–2 Burn Road
Cookstown   BT80 8DN
Tel: 028 8676 5182

Sheridan IMAX® Cinema
The Odyssey Pavilion
Queen's Quay, Belfast BT3 9QQ
Tel: 028 9046 7000
Website: www.belfastimax.com
The 380 seat Sheridan IMAX®
cinema features a host of 2D and 3D
movies.

The Strand Cinema
152–154 Holywood Road
Belfast BT4 1NY
Tel: 028 9067 3500

Strand Multiplex
Quayside Centre, Strand Road
Derry BT48
Tel: 028 7137 3900

UGC Cinemas
14 Dublin Road, Belfast BT2 7HN
Tel: 0870 155 5176

Warner Village Cinemas
Odyssey Pavilion
2 Queen's Quay, Belfast BT3 9QQ
Tel: 028 9073 9072

Theatres and Concert Halls

Northern Ireland has a relatively
small number of purpose-built
theatres and professional theatre
companies, but this should not
disguise the fact that there is great
enthusiasm for the dramatic arts
throughout the region. There is a
particularly vibrant amateur theatre
sector within Northern Ireland. The
main theatrical venues are set out
below.

Ardhowen Theatre
97 Dublin Road
Enniskillen BT74 6BR
Tel: 028 6632 3233 (Admin)
Tel: 028 6632 5440 (Box Office)
Fax: 028 6632 7012

Burnavon Arts & Cultural Centre
Burn Road, Cookstown
Tel: 028 8676 7994

Belfast Waterfront Hall
2 Lanyon Place, Belfast BT1 3WH
Tel: 028 9033 4455 (Box Office)
Tel: 028 9033 4400 (General
Enquiries)
Fax: 028 9024 9862
Website: www.waterfront.co.uk

Courtyard Theatre
Ballyearl Golf, Arts and Leisure
Centre, 585 Doagh Road
Newtownabbey BT36 5RZ
Tel: 028 9084 8287

Crescent Arts Centre
University Road, Belfast
Tel: 028 9024 2338
Converted   Victorian   school,
presenting workshops in all kinds of
dance, circus and other skills.
Occasional studio performances.

Flax International Arts Centre
Brookfield Mill, 333 Crumlin Road
Belfast BT14 7EA
Tel: 028 9035 2333

Golden Thread Theatre
333 Crumlin Road, Belfast BT14 7EA
Tel: 028 9074 5241

Grand Opera House
Great Victoria Street, Belfast
Tel: 028 9024 1919 (Box Office)
Tel: 028 9024 0411 (Admin)
Website: ww.goh.co.uk

Group Theatre
Bedford Street, Belfast BT2 7EH
Tel: 028 9032 9685

Lyric Theatre
55 Ridgeway Street, Belfast BT9 5FB

Tel: 028 9038 1081 (Box Office)
Tel: 028 9066 9660 (Admin)

Market Place
Market Street, Armagh BT61 7BX
Tel: 028 3752 1821

Old Museum Arts Centre
7 College Square North, Belfast
Tel: 028 9023 5053

Portadown Town Hall
15–17 Edward Street
Portadown BT62 3LX
Tel: 028 3833 5264

Riverside Theatre
University of Ulster
Coleraine BT52 1SA
Tel: 028 7035 1388 (Box Office)
Tel: 028 7034 4141 (Admin)
Fax: 028 7032 4924

St Columb's Theatre & Arts Centre
Orchard Street, Derry BT48 6EG
Tel: 028 7126 2880

Ulster Hall
Bedford Street, Belfast
Tel: 028 9032 3900 (admin)
Fax: 028 32 1341 (stage door)

King's Hall Exhibition & Conference
Centre
Lisburn Road, Belfast
Tel: 028 9066 5225

Ulster Orchestra
Elmwood Hall, University Road
Ticket Hotline: 028 9066 8798
The Ulster Orchestra has established
itself as one of the major symphony
orchestras in the United Kingdom.
    Much loved in Belfast and
beyond, successful tours of Europe,
Asia and America, and over 50
commercial recordings, broadcasts
for BBC television, Radio 3 and
Radio   Ulster   plus   regular
appearances at the Henry Wood
Promenade concerts, have added to
the   orchestra's   international
reputation.

Art Galleries

Ulster Museum
Botanic Gardens, Belfast
Tel: 028 9038 3000
Fax: 028 9038 3003
Irish artists include Sir John Lavery, Andrew Nicholl and William Conor.

Ormeau Baths Gallery
18a Ormeau Avenue, Belfast
Tel: 028 9032 1402
Bookshop, contemporary art.

Arches Gallery
2 Holywood Road, Belfast
Tel: 028 9045 9031
Irish artists.

Bell Gallery
13 Adelaide Park, Belfast
Tel: 028 9066 2998
Irish artistic, graphics

Elaine Somers Gallery
53a High Street, Holywood
Tel: 028 9042 3337
Contemporary Irish and International art

Nicola Russell Studio and Gallery
2–4 Church Road, Holywood
Tel: 028 9042 7133
Website: www.nicolarussell.com

Tom Caldwell Gallery
40–42 & 56 Bradbury Place, Belfast
Tel: 028 9032 3226
Living Irish artists.

Cavehill Gallery
18 Old Cavehill Road, Belfast
Tel: 028 9077 6784
Irish Artists.

Eakin Gallery
237 Lisburn Road, Belfast
Tel: 028 9066 8522
Irish Artists.

Fenderesky Gallery
2 University Road, Belfast
Tel: 028 9023 5245
Contemporary Art.

Arttank
58 Lisburn Road, Belfast BT9 6AF
Tel: 028 9023 0500
Irish and international art

McGilloway Gallery
6 Shipquay Street, Derry
Tel: 028 7136 6011
Open 10am–5.30pm Mon–Sat.
Modern Irish paintings.

Orchard Gallery
Orchard Street, Derry BT48 6EG
Tel: 028 7126 9675

Ulster Folk & Transport Museum
Tel: (028) 9042 8428
Ulster Museum
Tel: (028) 9038 3000
Ulster American Folk Park
Tel: (028) 8224 3292
Armagh County Museum
Tel: (028) 3752 3070

Events and Festivals

The Belfast Film Festival
Unit 18, North Street Arcade
Belfast BT1 1PB.
Tel: 028 9032 5913
Fax: 028 9032 5911
E-mail: info@belfastfilmfestival.org
Website: www.belfastfilmfestival.org
A week long film festival with a diverse cinematic programme of events.

Takes place annually at various venues across the city in late September/early October.

The Belfast Film Festival has seen a steady annual increase in numbers of visitors, both nationally and internationally, and has a growing prestige in the city and beyond. This coupled with the widening of the festival to include other local areas of Belfast will contribute to the establishment of the Belfast Film Festival as a significant vehicle for community, cultural and economic growth in Belfast.

The Cathedral Quarter Arts Festival
20 North Street, Belfast
Tel: 028 9023 2403
Fax: 028 9031 9884
E-mail: cqaf@hotmail.com
Website: www.cqaf.com
The Cathedral Quarter Arts Festival is a vibrant and dynamic Festival located in the historic heart of the city.

Belfast Festival at Queen's
25 College Gardens, Belfast
Tel: 028 9066 7687
Fax: 028 9066 3733
A highlight of Belfast's cultural calendar for 40 years, this is Ireland's largest arts festival.

The Festival has grown to be Ireland's largest arts festival encompassing a wide range of city venues including the Waterfront Hall, Grand Opera House, Ormeau Baths Gallery and the Lyric Theatre, as well as arts centres, community venues, pubs and hotels.

Feile an Phobail
473 Falls Road, Belfast BT12 6DD
Tel: 028 9031 3440
Fax: 028 9031 9150
Feile an Phobail West Belfast, Europe's largest community arts events. Credit card bookings for tickets available, (from UK) Telephone: 028 9028 4028 (from the Republic of Ireland) Telephone: 048 9028 4028.

Sports, Leisure and Fitness

Northern Ireland's main sports are football (soccer, Gaelic and rugby) golf, hockey and cricket. There is also a high level of interest in motorcycling and car rallying. Most other sports are to an extent minority pursuits, but Northern Ireland boasts a strong record in amateur boxing and bowls and its recently formed ice hockey team, the 'Belfast Giants', has established a regular following of 10,000 enthusiasts.

Soccer

As a small, albeit enthusiastic, footballing country Northern Ireland has limited expectations in terms of international football success, but has performed with credit in the World Cups of 1958 and 1982. Home of the legendary forward George Best, Northern Ireland has produced many top-class players (although seldom enough at one time to support a good international side). Home internationals are played at Windsor Park in Belfast, the home of Northern Ireland's biggest club, Linfield. The International team tends to be made up of professional footballers playing in the upper divisions of the English football league, although occasionally a locally based player breaks through to the International side.

At local level the 'Irish League' constitutes the main attraction. It is primarily part-time football (with a handful of full-time professionals) and comprises a number of teams from Belfast, and a team from most of Northern Ireland's largest provincial towns. The local game suffers from a number of fundamental difficulties. As a spectacle it suffers when compared with the televised glamour of the English 'premiership', and the cream of top young local players tend to leave the local game to play 'across the water'. Attendance at Irish League games are poor (except for the 'Big-Two' derby clashes between Belfast clubs Linfield and Glentoran) and crowd trouble and sectarianism on the terraces have made it very difficult for the games' promoters to push up attendances. Clubs such as Linfield, Glentoran, Crusaders and Portadown are seen as predominantly Protestant teams, while others such as Cliftonville and Newry are seen as Catholic, with little intercommunal interaction.

Like most activities in Northern Ireland soccer does not escape the impact of political divisions. A sizable minority of soccer supporters would give their first loyalty to the international team from the Irish Republic. Indeed the top team from Northern Ireland's second City 'Derry City' play in the Republic of Ireland League rather than the Irish League. This conflict of affiliation also has a negative impact on local attendances at games.

Nonetheless, despite its difficulties most of the different interests in the game have come together under the auspices of Culture Minister Michael McGimpsey to devise a strategy to improve the image and attractiveness of the game and to put Irish League football on a more sustainable financial footing. The Irish Football Association administers the game at all levels.

Gaelic Sports

There are a number of Gaelic Sports including football, hurling and camogie all administered by the Gaelic Athletic Association (GAA). Gaelic Football has now become the largest participation sport in Northern Ireland. Again Northern Ireland's political divisions are reflected in this sport which tends to be pursued

Armagh, All-Ireland Gaelic Football Champions

predominantly although not exclusively by the Catholic, Nationalist community. The GAA has only recently reversed a rule which excluded participation in Gaelic games by members of the Security Forces.

Gaelic Sport is organised on an all-island basis both at club and County level, and its highest prize is the All-Island County Championship (the 'Sam Maguire').

Northern Ireland counties have been successful in this prestigious competition in the 1990's notably Tyrone, Down, Derry and most recently Armagh. Most of the 6 counties of Northern Ireland have extensive football leagues at club level. Despite its high-level of participation and level of spectator attendances as well as TV coverage, Gaelic football remains a completely amateur sport. However pressure is building within the GAA, as it has done in recent years in athletics and rugby, to allow the top players to share in some of the commercial value created.

Hurling is played less widely than football, although areas in county Antrim and Down have a renowned passion for the sport. It is a uniquely Irish game at which the Northern counties have traditionally been weak in an all-Ireland context.

Rugby

Rugby Union has a strong following in Northern Ireland. It tends to be a predominantly, but by no means exclusively, Protestant and middle-class game. Although its organisation is all-island, the sport is based on club and provincial rather than county structures. Northern Ireland rugby is synonymous with the 'Ulster' team, which showcases Northern Ireland's best players in both the inter-provincial series against the three other Irish provinces. In recent times Ulster has also won the increasingly important European Cup, a competition featuring the best club and provincial sides from the British Isles, France and Italy. Ulster were crowned European Champions in 1999 after an exciting campaign which re-ignited wider interest in the local game.

Northern Ireland players have also contributed prominently to the Irish National Team and to the British Lions with Ballymena's Willie John McBride and North's Mike Gibson ranking among the all-time greats of the game. In more recent times players like David Humphreys, Willie Anderson and Paddy Johns have served with distinction.

Rugby Union is undergoing continuous change. Several years ago the game adopted professional status, and many top-level players departed to play outside Northern Ireland. However, with Ulster's success the best local players have largely been retained within Northern in a thoroughly professional set-up.

Cricket

As in Britain cricket is a popular summer sport in Northern Ireland although it would draw very small numbers of spectators. Much of the cricket activity outside Greater Belfast is based around village sides and villages such as Sion Mills (near Strabane) who once famously humiliated the mighty West Indies and Waringstown (near Lurgan) have become synonymous with the game.

Although a very 'British' game Cricket is organised on an all-island basis and there is a National side covering all of Ireland. This team competes with other minor cricketing countries and some of the English County sides but is not competitive at the top international level.

Hockey

Hockey (both men and ladies) is a popular sport right across Northern Ireland although more a participant than a spectator sport.

It is organised in local leagues for clubs – often closely associated with neighbouring rugby and cricket clubs although the international games are organised on an all-island basis. In the men's game Lisnagarvey (near Lisburn) have been the best team in Ireland for long stretches. In the ladies game Pegasus and Portadown have been regularly at the top.

Northern Ireland players can opt to play for Ireland or for Great Britain and many have played with distinction in major international championships including the Olympic Games.

Boxing

Although is can be seen as affirming certain stereotypical images of the 'fighting Irish' Northern Ireland has regularly produced top quality international boxers both as amateurs and professionals. There is a long history of heroic medal winning performances in Olympic and Commonwealth Championships for amateurs and for such a small place a number of local boxers have made it to World Champion in the professional ring. Names such as Barry McGuigan, Dave McAuley and Wayne McCullough have held world championship belts.

Motorsport

Northern Ireland has a large very enthusiastic following for motor sports in particular motorcycle road racing and car rallying. Although becoming increasingly expensive and specialist in nature motorsports have major spectator appeal.

A motorcycle race the North West 200 which takes place every year at Portrush is by far the largest spectator event in Northern Ireland's sporting calendar.

Golf in Northern Ireland

Northern Ireland is perfect golfing country with an abundance of fine parkland and coastal links courses exploiting the natural contours and features of the land. There are nearly a hundred 18- and 9-hole golf courses (a dozen within 5 miles of the centre of Belfast), including world-famous championship courses such as Royal Portrush and Royal County Down. Northern Ireland continues to produce world-class golfers; in recent years Ronan Rafferty, David Feherty and Darren Clarke have all reached the top international level of the game.

The following listing includes all of Northern Ireland's 18-hole golf courses, along with details of their location, best days to visit and contact information.

Belfast Area

Balmoral Golf Club
518 Lisburn Road, Belfast BT9 6GX
Tel: 028 9066 1514
Fax: 028 9066 6759
18 Holes, 6,034 yds, par 69
Parkland course, 3 miles south-west of city centre. Best days for visitors: Monday and Thursday.

Belvoir Park Golf Club
73 Church Road, Newtownbreda
Belfast BT8 7AN
Tel: 028 9049 1693
Fax: 028 9064 6113
18 Holes, 6,516 yds, par 71
Parkland course, 3 miles south of city centre. Best days for visitors: Monday, Tuesday and Thursday.

Dunmurry Golf Club
91 Dunmurry Lane, Dunmurry
Belfast BT17 9JS
Tel: 028 9061 0834
Fax: 028 9060 2540

18 Holes, 5,832 yds, par 68
Parkland course, 4 miles south-west of city centre. Best days for visitors: Tuesday and Thursday.

Fortwilliam Golf Club
Downview Avenue, Belfast BT15 4EZ
Tel: 028 9037 0770
Fax: 028 9078 1891
18 Holes, 5,973 yds, par 69
Parkland course, 3 miles north of city centre. Best days for visitors: weekday mornings.

Knock Golf Club
Summerfield
Upper Newtownards Road
Dundonald, Belfast BT16 2QX
Tel: 028 9048 3251
Fax: 028 9048 3251
18 Holes, 6,435 yds, par 71
Parkland course, 4 miles east of city centre. Best days for visitors: Monday, Wednesday and Thursday mornings; Tuesday and Friday afternoons.

Malone Golf Club
240 Upper Malone Road
Dunmurry, Belfast BT17 9LB
Tel: 028 9061 2758
Fax: 028 9043 1394
18 Holes, 6,600 yds, par 71
Parkland course, 4 miles south of city centre. Best days for visitors: any day except Tuesday and Saturday.

Mount Ober Golf & Country Club
20–24 Ballymaconaghy Road
Newtownbreda, Belfast BT8 6SB
Tel: 028 9079 5666
Fax: 028 9070 5862
18 Holes, 5,182 yds, par 68
Parkland course, 4? miles south-east of city centre. Best days for visitors: any day except Saturday.

Rockmount Golf Club
28 Drumalig Road, Carryduff
Belfast BT8 8EQ
Tel: 028 9081 2279
Fax: 028 9081 5851
18 Holes, 6,373 yds, par 72
Parkland course, 2 miles south of Carryduff. Best days for visitors: any day except Wednesday and Saturday.

Shandon Park Golf Club
73 Shandon Park, Belfast BT5 6NY
Tel: 028 9080 5030
Fax: 028 9040 2773
18 Holes, 6,282 yds, par 70
Parkland course, 4 miles east of city centre. Best days for visitors: any day except Tuesday and Saturday.

Co Antrim

Aberdelghy Golf Course
Bell's Lane, Lambeg
Lisburn BT27 4QH
Tel: 028 9266 2738
Fax: 028 9260 3432
18 Holes, 4,526 yds, par 62
Parkland course, 1? mile north of Lisburn. Best days for visitors: any day except Saturday morning.

Allen Park Golf Centre
45 Castle Road, Antrim BT41 4NA
Tel: 028 9442 9001
Fax: 028 9442 9001
18 Holes, 6,683 yds, par 72
Parkland course, 2 miles west of Antrim. Best days for visitors: any day.

Ballycastle Golf Club
Cushendall Road
Ballycastle BT54 6QP
Tel: 028 2076 2536
18 Holes, 5,940 yds, par 70
Links/Parkland course, ½ mile south-east of Ballycastle. Best days for visitors: weekdays.

Ballyclare Golf Club
25 Springvale Road
Ballyclare BT39 9JW
Tel: 028 9332 2696
Fax: 028 9332 2696
18 Holes, 5,699 yds, par 71
Parkland course, 2 miles north of town. Best days for visitors: Monday, Tuesday and Wednesday.

Ballymena Golf Club
128 Raceview Road
Ballymena BT42 4HY
Tel: 028 2586 1487
Fax: 028 2586 1487
18 Holes, 5,795 yds, par 67
Parkland course, 2 miles east of Ballymena on A42. Best days for visitors: any day except Tuesday and Saturday.

Cairndhu Golf Club
192 Coast Road, Ballygally
Larne BT40 2QG
Tel: 028 2858 3324
Fax: 028 2858 3324
18 Holes, 6,112 yds, par 69
Parkland course, 4 miles north of Larne. Best days for visitors: weekdays.

Carrickfergus Golf Club
35 North Road
Carrickfergus BT38 8LP
Tel: 028 9336 3713
Fax: 028 9336 3023
18 Holes, 5,759 yds, par 68
Parkland course, west of Carrickfergus. Best days for visitors: any day except Tuesday, Saturday and Sunday afternoon.

Galgorm Castle Golf & Country Club
Galgorm Road, Ballymena BT42 1HL
Tel: 028 2564 6161
Fax: 028 2565 1151
18 Holes, 6,736 yds, par 72
Parkland course, 1 mile south-west of Ballymena. Best days for visitors: any day.

Gracehill Golf Club
143 Ballinlea Road, Stranocum
Ballymoney BT53 8PX
Tel: 028 2075 1209
Fax: 028 2075 1074
18 Holes, 6,600 yds, par 72
Parkland course, 7 miles north-east of Ballymoney. Best days for visitors: weekdays.

Greenacres Golf Centre
153 Ballyrobert Road
Ballyclare BT39 9RT
Tel: 028 9335 4111
Fax: 028 9335 4166
18 Holes, 6,020 yds, par 71
Parkland course, 3 miles from Corr's Corner. Best days for visitors: any day except Saturday morning.

Hilton Templepatrick Golf Club
Castle Upton Estate
Templepatrick BT39 0DD
Tel: 028 9443 5542
Fax: 028 9443 5511
18 Holes, 7,100 yds, par 71
Parkland course, 5 miles from Belfast International Airport. Best days for visitors: any day.

Lisburn Golf Club
68 Eglantine Road
Lisburn BT27 5RQ
Tel: 028 9267 7216
Fax: 028 9260 3608
18 Holes, 6,672 yds, par 72
Parkland course, 2 miles south of Lisburn. Best days for visitors: weekdays.

Massereene Golf Club
51 Lough Road, Antrim BT41 4DQ
Tel: 028 9442 8096
Fax: 028 9448 7661
18 Holes, 6,375 yds, par 71
Parkland/sandy course, 1½ mile south of Antrim. Best days for visitors: any day except Friday and Saturday.

Royal Portrush Golf Club
Bushmills Road, Portrush BT56 8JQ
Tel: 028 7082 2311
Fax: 028 7082 3139
(1) 18 Holes, 6,818 yds, par 73
(2) 18 Holes, 6,273 yds, par 70
Two links courses: (1) Dunluce (2) Valley, 1 mile east or Portrush. Best days for visitors: weekdays except Wednesday and Friday afternoon (Green fees are expensive).

Whitehead Golf Club
McCrea's Brae, Whitehead BT38 9NZ
Tel: 028 9337 0820
Fax: 028 9337 0825
18 Holes, 6,050 yds, par 68
Parkland course, ½ mile north of Whitehead. Best days for visitors: any day except Saturday; members only on Sunday.

Co Armagh

Ashfield Golf Club
Freeduff, Cullyhanna
Newry BT35 0JJ
Tel: 028 3086 8180
Fax: 028 3086 8611
18 Holes, 5,645 yds, par 67
Parkland course, 4 miles north of

Crossmaglen off B30. Best days for visitors: any day.

County Armagh Golf Club
7 Newry Road, Armagh BT60 1EN
Tel: 028 3752 5861
Fax: 028 3752 5861
18 Holes, 6,212 yds, par 70
Parkland course, in palace demesne. Best days for visitors: weekdays and Sunday.

Craigavon Silverwood Golf Centre
Turmoyra Lane, Lurgan BT66 6NG
Tel: 028 3832 6606
Fax: 028 3834 7272
18 Holes, 6,188 yds, par 72
Parkland course, 2 miles north of Lurgan. Just off the M1 motorway.

Loughgall Country Park
11 Main Street, Loughgall BT61 8HZ
Tel: 028 3889 1029
Fax: 028 3889 1029
18 Holes, 5,937 yds, par 69
Parkland course, 100 yards from Loughgall village. Best days for visitors: any day.

Lurgan Golf Club
The Demesne, Lurgan BT67 9BN
Tel: 028 3832 2087
Fax: 028 3831 6166
18 Holes, 5,995 yds, par 70
Parkland course, in Lurgan. Best days for visitors: Monday, Thursday and Friday morning.

Portadown Golf Club
192 Gilford Road
Portadown BT63 5LF
Tel: 028 3835 5356
18 Holes, 6,147 yds, par 70
Parkland course, in Portadown Best days for visitors: any day except Tuesday and Saturday.

Tandragee Golf Club
Markethill Road, Tandragee
Craigavon BT62 2ER
Tel: 028 3884 1272
Fax: 028 3884 0664
18 Holes, 6,285 yds, par 70

Parkland course, ½ mile south of Tandragee. Best days for visitors: any day except Saturday and Thursday.

Co Down

Ardglass Golf Club
Castle Place, Ardglass BT30 7TP
Tel: 028 4484 1219
Fax: 028 4484 1841
18 Holes, 5,776 yds, par 68
Seaside course, in Ardglass. Best days for visitors: weekdays.

Banbridge Golf Club
116 Huntly Road
Banbridge BT32 3UR
Tel: 028 4066 2211
Fax: 028 4066 9400
18 Holes, 5,468 yds, par 67
Parkland course, 1½ miles north-west of Banbridge. Best days for visitors: any day except Tuesday and Saturday

Bangor Golf Club
Broadway, Bangor BT20 4RH
Tel: 028 9127 0922
18 Holes, 6,410 yds, par 71
Parkland course, in Bangor. Best days for visitors: Monday, Wednesday and Friday.

Blackwood Golf Centre
150 Crawfordsburn Road
Clandeboye, Bangor BT19 1GB
Tel: 028 9185 2706
Fax: 028 9185 3785
18 Holes, 6,500 yds, par 70
Parkland course, 2 miles west of Bangor. Best days for visitors: any day.

Bright Castle Golf Club
14 Coniamstown Road
Bright, Downpatrick BT30 8LU
Tel: 028 4484 1319
18 Holes, 7,143 yds, par 73
Parkland course, 4 miles south of Downpatrick.

Carnalea Golf Club
Station Road, Bangor BT19 1EZ
Tel: 028 9127 0368
Fax: 028 9127 3989
18 Holes, 5,548 yds, par 67
Seaside meadowland course, 1½ miles west of Bangor. Best days for visitors: any day except Sunday

Clandeboye Golf Club
Tower Road, Conlig
Newtownards BT23 3PN
Tel: 028 9127 1767
Fax: 028 9147 3711
(1) 18 Holes, 6,559 yds, par 71
(2) 18 Holes, 5,755 yds, par 68
Two parkland/heathland courses (1) Dufferin course (2) Ava Course. Best days for visitors: weekdays, weekend after 2.30pm.

Donaghadee Golf Club
Warren Road
Donaghadee BT21 0PQ
Tel: 028 9188 3624
Fax: 028 9188 8891
18 Holes, 6,091 yds, par 69
Seaside course, north side of Donaghadee. Best days for visitors: Monday, Wednesday and Friday.

Downpatrick Golf Club
43 Saul Road
Downpatrick BT30 6PA
Tel: 028 4461 5947
Fax: 028 4461 7502
18 Holes, 6,120 yds, par 69
Parkland course, 1 mile from Downpatrick. Best days for visitors: any day, booking is advisable.

Down Royal Park Golf Club
Dunygarton Road, Maze BT27 5RT
Tel: 028 9262 1339
Fax: 028 9262 1339
18 Holes, 6,824 yds, par 72
Heathland course, within Down Royal racecourse. Best days for visitors: any day.

Edenmore Golf Club
Edenmore House
70 Drumnabreeze Road
Magheralin, Craigavon BT67 0RH
Tel: 028 9261 1310
Fax: 028 9261 3310
18 Holes, 6,244 yds, par 71
Parkland course, 1$^1/_2$ miles southeast of Magheralin. Best days for visitors: any day except Saturday morning.

Holywood Golf Club
Nun's Walk, Demesne Road
Holywood BT18 9LE
Tel: 028 9042 3135
Fax: 028 9042 5040
18 Holes, 5,885 yds, par 67
Parkland course, 1 mile south of Holywood. Best days for visitors: any day except Thursday and Saturday

Kilkeel Golf Club
Mourne Park, Ballyardle
Newry BT34 4LB
Tel: 028 4176 5095
Fax: 028 4176 5579
18 Holes, 6,625 yds, par 72
Parkland course, 3 miles west of town. Best days for visitors: Monday, Wednesday–Friday.

Kirkistown Golf Club
142 Main Road, Cloughey
Newtownards BT22 1JA
Tel: 028 4277 1233
Fax: 028 4277 1699
18 Holes, 6,142 yds, par 70
Links course, 15 miles south-east of Newtownards – A20 and B173. Best days for visitors: any day except Saturday.

Ringdufferin Golf Course
36 Ringdufferin Road, Toye
Killyleagh BT30 9PH
Tel: 028 4482 8812
Fax: 028 4482 8812
18 Holes, 5,136 yds, par 66
Drumlin course, 2 miles north of Killyleagh. Best days for visitors: any day.

Royal Belfast Golf Club
Station Road, Craigavad
Holywood BT18 0BT
Tel: 028 9042 8165
Fax: 028 9042 1404
18 Holes, 5,961 yds, par 69
Parkland course, 7 miles north-east of Belfast. Best days for visitors: by arrangement with Club, visitors require letter of introduction (Green fees are expensive)

Royal County Down Golf Club
36 Golf Links Road
Newcastle BT33 0AN
Tel: 028 4372 3314
Fax: 028 4372 6281
(1) 18 Holes, 7,037 yds, par 74
(2) 18 Holes, 4.681 yds, par 63
Two links courses, (1) Championship (2) Annesley 30 miles south of Belfast. Best days for visitors: (1) Monday, Tuesday, Thursday and Friday (2) any day except Saturday morning

Scrabo Golf Club
233 Scrabo Road
Newtownards BT23 4SL
Tel: 028 9181 2355
Fax: 028 9182 2919
18 Holes, 6,257 yds, par 71
Undulating course, 1$^1/_2$ miles southwest of Newtownards follow Scrabo Country Park signs. Best days for visitors: Monday Tuesday and Thursday, Sunday after 11.30am.

Spa Golf Club
20 Grove Road
Ballynahinch BT24 8PN
Tel: 028 9756 2365
Fax: 028 9756 4158
18 Holes, 6,494 yds, par 72
Parkland course, 1 mile south of town. Best days for visitors: Monday–Thursday.

Warrenpoint Golf Club
Lower Dromore Road
Warrenpoint BT34 3LN
Tel: 028 4175 3695
Fax: 028 4175 2918
18 Holes, 6,200 yds, par 70
Parkland course, 1 mile west of town. Best days for visitors: Monday, Thursday and Friday.

Co Fermanagh

Castle Hume Golf Club
Castle Hume, Enniskillen BT74 6HZ
Tel: 028 6632 7077
Fax: 028 6632 7076
18 Holes, 6,900 yds, par 71
Parkland course, 3½ miles north of Enniskillen. Best days for visitors: any day.

Enniskillen Golf Club
Castle Coole, Enniskillen BT74 6HZ
18 Holes, 6,189 yds, par 69
Parkland course, in Castle Coole estate ½ mile east of town. Best days for visitors: any day

Co Derry

Castlerock Golf Club
65 Circular Road
Castlerock BT51 4TJ
Tel: 028 7084 8314
Fax: 028 7084 9440
18 Holes, 6,687 yds, par 72
Two links courses, 6 miles west of Coleraine. Best days for visitors: Monday–Thursday.

City of Derry Golf Club
49 Victoria Road, Prehen
Derry BT47 2PU
Tel: 028 7134 6369
Fax: 028 7131 0008
18 Holes, 6,487 yds, par 71
Parkland course, 2 miles south of city. Best days for visitors: weekdays until 4.30pm.

Foyle International Golf Centre

12 Alder Road, Derry BT48 8DB
Tel: 028 7135 2222
Fax: 028 7135 3967
18 Holes, 6,678 yds, par 71
Parkland course, $1^1/_2$ miles north of
Derry. Best days for visitors: any day

Moyola Park Golf Club

15 Curran Road, Shanemullagh
Castledawson BT45 8DG
Tel: 028 7946 8468
Fax: 028 7946 8626
18 Holes, 6,517 yds, par 71
Parkland course, in Castledawson.
Best days for visitors: weekdays
except Wednesday.

Portstewart Golf Club

117 Strand Road
Portstewart BT55 7PG
Tel: 028 7083 2015
Fax: 028 7083 4097
(1) 18 Holes, 6,779 yds, par 73
(2) 18 Holes, 4,730 yds, par 64
Links course, (1) Strand (2) Old – 1
mile from town centre. Best days for
visitors: (1) Monday, Tuesday,
Thursday and Friday (2) any day.

Radisson Roe Hotel & Golf Resort

Roe Park, Limavady BT49 9LB
Tel: 028 7776 0105
Fax: 028 7772 2313
18 Holes, 6,001 yds, par 70
Parkland course, 1 mile west of
Limavady. Best days for visitors: any
day.

Co Tyrone

Dungannon Golf Club

34 Springfield Lane
Dungannon BT70 1QX
Tel: 028 8772 7338
18 Holes, 5,861 yds, par 69
Parkland course, 1 mile west of
Dungannon. Best days for visitors:
Monday, Thursday and Friday
morning

Killymoon Golf Club

200 Killymoon Road
Cookstown BT80 8TW
Tel: 028 8676 3762
Fax: 028 8676 3762
18 Holes, 6,149 yds, par 69
Parkland course, south side of
Cookstown. Best days for visitors:
Monday–Wednesday and Friday,
ladies Thursday.

Newtownstewart Golf Club

38 Golf Course Road
Newtownstewart BT78 4HU
Tel: 028 8166 1466
Fax: 028 8166 2506
18 Holes, 5,341 yds, par 69
Parkland course, 2 miles south-west
of town. Best days for visitors: any
day.

Omagh Golf Club

83a Dublin Road, Omagh BT78 1HQ
Tel: 028 8224 3160
18 Holes, 5,885 yds, par 68
Parkland course, ½ mile south of
town. Best days for visitors: any day
except Tuesday and Saturday.

Strabane Golf Club

33 Ballycolman Road
Strabane BT82 9PH
Tel: 028 7138 2271
Fax: 028 7138 2007
18 Holes, 6,055 yds, par 69
Parkland course, 1 mile south of
town. Best days for visitors:
weekdays except Tuesday

Leisure Centres

Northern Ireland has a large variety
of leisure facilities for an area of its
size. The climate and landscape
facilitate outdoor pursuits such as
hiking, mountain climbing and
camping, and many of the lakes and
rivers host watersports facilities.
There are also many leisure and
activity centres, some of which are
listed below.

Andersonstown Leisure Centre

Andersonstown Road
Belfast BT11 9BY
Tel: 028 9062 5211

Antrim Forum

Lough Road, Antrim BT41 4DQ
Tel: 028 9446 4131

Ards Leisure Centre

William Street
Newtownards BT23 4EJ
Tel: 028 9181 2837
Fax: 028 9182 0807

Avoniel Leisure Centre

Avoniel Road, Belfast BT5 4SF
Tel: 028 9045 1564

Ballybeen Activity Centre

Ballybeen Square, Dundonald
Belfast BT16 2QE
Tel: 028 9048 3905

Ballyduff Community Centre

Forthill Drive, Newtownabbey
Tel: 028 9083 2516

Ballyearl Arts & Leisure Centre

585 Doagh Road
Newtownabbey BT36 5RZ
Tel: 028 9084 8287
Fax: 028 9084 4896

Ballymacarrett Recreation Centre

Connswater Street
Newtownards BT4 1SX
Tel: 028 9045 8828

Ballynahinch Community Centre
55 Windmill Street
Ballynahinch BT24 8HB
Tel: 028 9756 1950
Fax: 028 9756 5606

Ballysillan Leisure Centre
Ballysillan Road, Belfast BT14 7QQ
Tel: 028 9039 1040

Banbridge Leisure Centre
Victoria Street, Banbridge BT32 3JY
Tel: 028 4066 2799

Bangor Castle Leisure Centre
Castle Park Avenue
Bangor BT20 4BN
Tel: 028 9127 0271

Bawnacre Centre
Castle Street, Irvinestown BT94 1EE
Tel: 028 6862 1177

Beechmount Leisure Centre
Falls Road, Belfast BT12 6FD
Tel: 028 9032 8631

Belfast Indoor Tennis Arena
Ormeau Embankment
Belfast BT6 8LT
Tel: 028 9045 8024

Belvoir Activity Centre
100 Belvoir Drive, Belfast BT8 7DT
Tel: 028 9064 2174

Brandywell Sports Centre
Lone Moor Road, Derry BT48
Tel: 028 7126 3902

Brook Activity Centre
25 Summerhill Road
Twinbrook BT17 0RL
Tel: 028 9030 1848

Brooke Park Leisure Centre
Rosemount Avenue
Derry BT48 0HH
Tel: 028 7126 2637

Carrickfergus Leisure Centre
Prince William Way
Carrickfergus BT38 7HP
Tel: 028 9335 1711

Cascades Leisure Centre
51 Thomas Street
Portadown BT62 3AF
Tel: 028 3833 2802

Castlepark Recreation Centre
11 Water Road, Lisnaskea BT92 0LZ
Tel: 028 6772 1299

Comber Leisure Centre
Castle Street, Comber BT23 5DY
Tel: 028 9187 4350
Fax: 028 9187 0099

Coleraine Leisure Centre
Railway Road, Coleraine BT52 1PE
Tel: 028 7035 6432

Comber Leisure Centre
Enler Recreation Park, Castle Street
Comber BT23 5DY
Tel: 028 9187 4350

Cookstown Leisure Centre
Fountain Road, Cookstown BT80 8QF
Tel: 028 8676 3853

Craigavon Leisure Centre
Brownlow Road, Craigavon
Tel: 028 3834 1333

David Lloyd Leisure Centre
115 Old Dundonald Road
Dundonald BT16 1XT
Tel: 028 9041 3300

Derg Valley Leisure Centre
6 Strabane Road
Castlederg BT81 7HZ
Tel: 028 8167 0727

Down Leisure Centre
114 Market Street
Downpatrick BT30 6LZ
Tel: 028 4461 3426
Fax: 028 4461 6905

Dreamworld Family Entertainment Centre
Glenmachan Place, Boucher Road
Belfast BT12 6QH
Tel: 028 9020 2300

Dundonald International Ice Bowl
111 Old Dundonald Road
Dundonald, Belfast BT16 1XT
Tel: 028 9048 2611

Dungannon Leisure Centre
Circular Road, Dungannon BT71 6BH
Tel: 028 8772 0370

Dungiven Sports Pavilion
3 Chapel Road, Derry BT47 2AN
Tel: 028 7774 2074

Ecclesville Equestrian Leisure & Community Centre
11 Ecclesville Road
Fintona BT78 2EF
Tel: 028 824 0591

Falls Swim Centre
Falls Road, Belfast BT12 4PB
Tel: 028 9032 4906

Fermanagh Lakeland Forum
Broad Meadow, Shore Road
Enniskillen BT74 7EF
Tel: 028 6632 4121

Gilnahirk Golf Club
Upper Braniel Road
Belfast BT5 7TS
Tel: 028 9044 8477

Glenmore Activity Centre
43 Glenmore Park, Hilden
Lisburn, BT27 4RT
Tel: 028 9266 2830

Greenvale Leisure Centre
Greenvale Park
Magherafelt BT45 6DR
Tel: 028 7963 2796

Grove Activity Centre
15 Ballinderry Park, Knockmore
Lisburn BT28 1ST
Tel: 028 9267 1131

Grove Leisure Centre
York Road, Belfast BT15 3HF
Tel: 028 9035 1599

Kilkeel Recreation & Community Complex
Mourne Esplanade, Kilkeel BT34 4DB
Tel: 028 4176 4666

Kilmakee Activity Centre
52a Rowan Drive, Seymour Hill
Dunmurry, Belfast BT17 9QA
Tel: 028 9030 1545

The Kiltonga Leisure Centre
Belfast Road
Newtownards BT23 4TJ
Tel: 028 9181 8511
Fax: 028 9182 3400

Lagan Valley LeisurePlex
12 Lisburn Leisure Park
Governors Road, Lisburn BT28 1LP
Tel: 028 9267 2121
Fax: 028 9267 4322

Larne Leisure Centre
Tower Road, Larne BT40 1AB
Tel: 028 2826 0478

Lisnagelvin Leisure Centre
Richill Park, Waterside
Derry BT47 5QZ
Tel: 028 7134 7695

Longstone Community Association
Community Hall, Longstone Road
Annalong
Tel: 028 4376 8249

Lough Moss Centre
Hillsborough Road, Carryduff
Tel: 028 9081 4884

Loughside Leisure Centre
Shore Road, Belfast BT15 4HP
Tel: 028 9078 1524

Maghera Recreation Centre
St Lurach's Road, Maghera BT46 5JE
Tel: 028 7964 4017

Maysfield Leisure Centre
East Bridge Street
Belfast BT1 3PH
Tel: 028 9024 1633

Meadowbank Recreation Ground
Ballyronan Road, Magherafelt
Tel: 028 7963 1680

Millburn Community Centre
Linden Avenue, Coleraine BT52 2AN
Tel: 028 7034 2625

Newcastle Centre
10–14 Central Promenade
Newcastle BT33
Tel: 028 4372 5034
Fax: 028 4372 2400

Newry Sports Centre
Patrick Street, Newry BT35 8TR
Tel: 028 3026 7322

Olympia Leisure Centre
Boucher Road, Belfast BT12 6HR
Tel: 028 9023 3369

Omagh Leisure Centre
Old Mountfield Road, Omagh BT79
Tel: 028 8224 6711

Orchard Leisure Centre
37–39 Folly Lane, Armagh BT60 1AT
Tel: 028 3751 5920

The Palladium
10 Quay Street, Bangor BT20 5ED
Tel: 028 9127 0844

The Queen's Leisure Complex
Sullivan Place, Holywood BT18 9JF
Tel: 028 9042 1234

Queen's University
(Malone Sports Facilities)
Dub Lane, Belfast BT9 5NB
Tel: 028 9062 3946

Riada Centre
33 Garryduff Road
Ballymoney BT53 7DB
Tel: 028 2766 5792

Riversdale Leisure Centre
Lisnafin Park, Strabane
Tel: 028 7138 2672

The Robinson Centre
Montgomery Road
Belfast BT6 9HS
Tel: 028 9070 3948

St Columb's Park
Leisure Centre
Limavady Road, Derry BT47 6JY
Tel: 028 7134 3941

St Mary's Community Centre
Edenmore, Tempo BT92 1BN
Tel: 028 8954 1770

Seapark Sports Ground
Ballymenoch Park
Holywood BT18 0LP
Tel: 028 9042 2894

Sentry Hill Sports Complex
Old Ballymoney Road
Ballymena BT43 6NE
Tel: 028 2565 6101

Seven Towers Leisure Centre
Trostan Avenue
Ballymena BT43 7BL
Tel: 028 2564 1427

Shaftesbury Recreation Centre
Ormeau Road, Belfast
Tel: 028 9064 2801

Shankill Leisure Centre
Shankill Road, Belfast BT13 2BD
Tel: 028 9024 1434

Sheskburn Recreation Centre
7 Mary Street, Ballycastle BT54 6QH
Tel: 028 2076 3300

Sixmile Leisure Centre
Ballynure Road, Ballyclare BT39 9YU
Tel: 028 9334 1818
Fax: 028 9335 4357

Station 3000 Ltd
Mega Zone
111a Old Dundonald Road
Belfast BT16 1XT
Tel: 028 9041 0500

Station 3000 Ltd
Valley Bowling, Valley Leisure Centre
Newtownabbey
Tel: 028 9036 5642

Templemore Complex
Templemore Avenue
Belfast BT5 4FW
Tel: 028 9045 750

Templemore Sports Complex
Buncrana Road, Derry BT48 8LQ
Tel: 028 7126 5521

Trillick Enterprise Leisure Centre
Gargadis Road, Trillick BT78
Tel: 028 8956 1333

The Valley Leisure Centre
40 Church Road, Whiteabbey
Newtownabbey BT36 7LN
Tel: 028 9086 1211
Fax: 028 9085 3211

Waves Leisure Complex
22 Robert Street, Lurgan BT66 8BE
Tel: 028 3832 2906

Whiterock Leisure Centre
Whiterock Road , Belfast BT12 7RG
Tel: 028 9023 3239

Fitness Clubs

Arena Health and Fitness
Yorkgate, 100–150 York Street
Belfast BT15 1WA
Tel: 028 9074 1235
Fax: 028 9074 1239

Elysium Health and
Leisure Club
Culloden Hotel, Bangor Road, Craigavad
Tel: 028 9042 5315

Esporta
Mertoun Hall, 106 Belfast Road
Hollywood, Belfast BT18 9QY
Tel: 028 9076 5000

Fitness First
1 Circular Road
Toscana Retail Park, Bangor
Tel: 028 9147 0000

Connswater Retail Park
Connswater, Belfast
Tel: 028 9045 0505

David Lloyd Leisure
Old Dundonald Road
Belfast BT16 1DL
Tel: 028 9041 3300
Fax: 028 9041 3339

LA Fitness
Milltown Road, Shaws Bridge
Belfast BT8 7XT
Tel: 028 90 641 800
Fax: 028 90 641 611

Other Visitor Information

Currency

Northern Ireland uses the Pound Sterling, as in Great Britain. However, the main banks each issue their own banknotes, as well as the more familiar Bank of England and Bank of Scotland.   Mastercard / Access and Visa are generally accepted; Diner's Club and American Express less so.   Cheques with a bankers' card are also widely accepted.

In towns, most banks have opening hours of 9.30am – 4.30pm, sometimes closing for lunch, or closing early on Friday. A few may open on Saturday mornings, but most do not, and in smaller towns and villages the bank may not be open every day.

Cash dispensers are numerous, and accept most UK bank cards, as well as all types of credit card. Banks such as HBSC, TSB and Lloyd's do not have branches in Northern Ireland, although cash may be withdrawn via cash dispensers.

For travel to the Republic of Ireland, money must be changed into Euros, the new common currency for most of the European Union. The Euro is commonly accepted in border areas and in larger stores in Belfast and some of the bigger towns.

Shopping

Northern Ireland has most of the high street stores seen in both Great Britain and the Republic of Ireland. Shopping hours are generally 9.00am to 5.30 pm, although in smaller towns shops close for lunch and may close early (or not even open) on one day of the week. In larger towns shops are often open late on Thursday nights, and many open on Sunday from 1pm to 5pm. Some of the larger supermarkets are open 24 hours a day, except Sunday.   Most towns also have a market day once a week.

Weather

Average Annual Rainfall: 43 inches

Lost Valuables

Police Lost Property
Tel: 028 9065 0222 will put you in contact with the nearest police station.

Medical & Dental Services

Advice on medical and dental emergencies – Health Information Service. Tel: 0800 665544

Newspapers

Belfast is unusual in having three dailies, Belfast Telegraph, Irish News and Newsletter, as well as the Sunday Life. All have daily entertainment listings. The free monthly tourism newspaper "Northern Ireland Travel News", obtainable in Ports, Tourist Information Centres and travel agencies etc., has pages on current attractions and events. Monthly magazine 'InBelfast' provides a detailed 'What's On' guide to the city, and is available in newsagents and the Belfast Welcome Centre.

Belfast Telegraph

124–144 Royal Avenue
Belfast BT1 1EB
Tel: 028 9026 4000

News Letter

46–56 Boucher Crescent
Belfast BT12 6QY
Tel: 028 9068 0000

Irish News

113–117 Donegall Street
Belfast BT1 2GE

Places of Worship

Main Sunday services of major Christian denominations are advertised in the Saturday edition of the Belfast Telegraph. Places of worship for most faith communities are listed in Yellow Pages. The two cathedrals in central Belfast are St. Anne's Cathedral (Anglican/Church of Ireland) on Donegall Street and St. Peter's Cathedral (Roman Catholic) on Derby Street. Full listings of Churches are contained in Chapter 12.

Postal Services

Post Offices and red post boxes are all over the city; Main Post Office is at Castle Junction and late mailings are accepted at Tomb Street Sorting Office. Small books of UK stamps are available in most convenience stores and petrol stations.

Cars – Breakdown

Automobile Association Emergency

Tel: 0800 88 77 66

RAC

Tel: 08000 828 282

Green Flag

Tel: 0800 400 600

Ulster Automobile Club

Tel: 028 9042 6262

Average daytime/night time temperatures, °C (°F)		
	DAY	NIGHT
January/February	7 (44)	1 (34)
March/April	10 (51)	3 (38)
May/June	16 (61)	8 (46)
July/August	18 (65)	10 (51)
September/October	15 (59)	8 (46)
November/December	8 (47)	3 (37)

Travelling Distances

Road Distances from Belfast	Miles
Armagh	40
Cork	262
Dublin	103
Enniskillen	83
Larne	23
Derry	73
Newcastle	31
Newry	38
Omagh	68
Portrush	61
Rosslare	202
Shannon	211
Sligo	125

Car Parking

Multi-storey and off-street car parks have hourly tariffs dependent on location. On-street pay and display zones are clearly marked. Pay heed to restriction notices drawing attention to morning and evening rush hour clearways and bus lanes when in operation.

Disability Access

Disability Action
Tel. 028 9049 1011

Emergencies

Police, ambulance, fire service:
Dial 999

Pub Hours

Generally Mon–Sat, 11.30am–11pm, Sundays, 12.30–10pm. Many bars in Belfast have later opening hours on Thurs–Sat nights. Children are not permitted on licensed premises. No alcohol may be served to under 18s.

Smoking

No smoking applies on public transport or in most public buildings. More and more restaurants have a no-smoking policy; most have a smoke free area.

Travelling

DOE Traffic Watch

Tel: 0345 123 321

Travel Agencies

Most UK/Irish Travel Agencies and Tour Operators are represented in Belfast. Some locations may close at 1pm on Saturday.

Tipping

It is now a generally accepted practice in restaurants to leave a gratuity of 10–15 per cent for good service. Some restaurants may add on an obligatory 10 or 12.5 per cent service charge on large group bookings.

Phone Numbers

The Northern Ireland Dialling Code 028 or 28 is used as a prefix when dialling from outside the region, or when making internal calls using a mobile phone. All Belfast numbers are composed of 028 followed by 90 and six digits.

2002

	January	February	March	April	May	June
Mon	7 14 21 28	4 11 18 25	4 11 18 25	1 8 15 22 29	6 13 20 27	3 10 17 24
Tue	1 8 15 22 29	5 12 19 26	5 12 19 26	2 9 16 23 30	7 14 21 28	4 11 18 25
Wed	2 9 16 23 30	6 13 20 27	6 13 20 27	3 10 17 24	1 8 15 22 29	5 12 19 26
Thu	3 10 17 24 31	7 14 21 28	7 14 21 28	4 11 18 25	2 9 16 23 30	6 13 20 27
Fri	4 11 18 25	1 8 15 22	1 8 15 22 29	5 12 19 26	3 10 17 24 31	7 14 21 28
Sat	5 12 19 26	2 9 16 23	2 9 16 23 30	6 13 20 27	4 11 18 25	1 8 15 22 29
Sun	6 13 20 27	3 10 17 24	3 10 17 24 31	7 14 21 28	5 12 19 26	2 9 16 23 30

	July	August	September	October	November	December
Mon	1 8 15 22 29	5 12 19 26	2 9 16 23 30	7 14 21 28	4 11 18 25	2 9 16 23 30
Tue	2 9 16 23 30	6 13 20 27	3 10 17 24	1 8 15 22 29	5 12 19 26	3 10 17 24 31
Wed	3 10 17 24 31	7 14 21 28	4 11 18 25	2 9 16 23 30	6 13 20 27	4 11 18 25
Thu	4 11 18 25	1 8 15 22 29	5 12 19 26	3 10 17 24 31	7 14 21 28	5 12 19 26
Fri	5 12 19 26	2 9 16 23 30	6 13 20 27	4 11 18 25	1 8 15 22 29	6 13 20 27
Sat	6 13 20 27	3 10 17 24 31	7 14 21 28	5 12 19 26	2 9 16 23 30	7 14 21 28
Sun	7 14 21 28	4 11 18 25	1 8 15 22 29	6 13 20 27	3 10 17 24	1 8 15 22 29

2003

	January	February	March	April	May	June
Mon	6 13 20 27	3 10 17 24	3 10 17 24 31	7 14 21 28	5 12 19 26	2 9 16 23 30
Tue	7 14 21 28	4 11 18 25	4 11 18 25	1 8 15 22 29	6 13 20 27	3 10 17 24
Wed	1 8 15 22 29	5 12 19 26	5 12 19 26	2 9 16 23 30	7 14 21 28	4 11 18 25
Thu	2 9 16 23 30	6 13 20 27	6 13 20 27	3 10 17 24	1 8 15 22 29	5 12 19 26
Fri	3 10 17 24 31	7 14 21 28	7 14 21 28	4 11 18 25	2 9 16 23 30	6 13 20 27
Sat	4 11 18 25	1 8 15 22	1 8 15 22 29	5 12 19 26	3 10 17 24 31	7 14 21 28
Sun	5 12 19 26	2 9 16 23	2 9 16 23 30	6 13 20 27	4 11 18 25	1 8 15 22 29

	July	August	September	October	November	December
Mon	7 14 21 28	4 11 18 25	1 8 15 22 29	6 13 20 27	3 10 17 24	1 8 15 22 29
Tue	1 8 15 22 29	5 12 19 26	2 9 16 23 30	7 14 21 28	4 11 18 25	2 9 16 23 30
Wed	2 9 16 23 30	6 13 20 27	3 10 17 24	1 8 15 22 29	5 12 19 26	3 10 17 24 31
Thu	3 10 17 24 31	7 14 21 28	4 11 18 25	2 9 16 23 30	6 13 20 27	4 11 18 25
Fri	4 11 18 25	1 8 15 22 29	5 12 19 26	3 10 17 24 31	7 14 21 28	5 12 19 26
Sat	5 12 19 26	2 9 16 23 30	6 13 20 27	4 11 18 25	1 8 15 22 29	6 13 20 27
Sun	6 13 20 27	3 10 17 24 31	7 14 21 28	5 12 19 26	2 9 16 23 30	7 14 21 28

2004

	January	February	March	April	May	June
Mon	5 12 19 26	2 9 16 23	1 8 15 22 29	5 12 19 26	3 10 17 24 31	7 14 21 28
Tue	6 13 20 27	3 10 17 24	2 9 16 23 30	6 13 20 27	4 11 18 25	1 8 15 22 29
Wed	7 14 21 28	4 11 18 25	3 10 17 24 31	7 14 21 28	5 12 19 26	2 9 16 23 30
Thu	1 8 15 22 29	5 12 19 26	4 11 18 25	1 8 15 22 29	6 13 20 27	3 10 17 24
Fri	2 9 16 23 30	6 13 20 27	5 12 19 26	2 9 16 23 30	7 14 21 28	4 11 18 25
Sat	3 10 17 24 31	7 14 21 28	6 13 20 27	3 10 17 24	1 8 15 22 29	5 12 19 26
Sun	4 11 18 25	1 8 15 22 29	7 14 21 28	4 11 18 25	2 9 16 23 30	6 13 20 27

	July	August	September	October	November	December
Mon	5 12 19 26	2 9 16 23 30	6 13 20 27	4 11 18 25	1 8 15 22 29	6 13 20 27
Tue	6 13 20 27	3 10 17 24 31	7 14 21 28	5 12 19 26	2 9 16 23 30	7 14 21 28
Wed	7 14 21 28	4 11 18 25	1 8 15 22 29	6 13 20 27	3 10 17 24	1 8 15 22 29
Thu	1 8 15 22 29	5 12 19 26	2 9 16 23 30	7 14 21 28	4 11 18 25	2 9 16 23 30
Fri	2 9 16 23 30	6 13 20 27	3 10 17 24	1 8 15 22 29	5 12 19 26	3 10 17 24 31
Sat	3 10 17 24 31	7 14 21 28	4 11 18 25	2 9 16 23 30	6 13 20 27	4 11 18 25
Sun	4 11 18 25	1 8 15 22 29	5 12 19 26	3 10 17 24 31	7 14 21 28	5 12 19 26

Mileage Chart

Antrim
42 **Armagh**
41 84 **Ballycastle**
11 54 28 **Ballymena**
32 54 72 42 **Bangor**
19 41 58 28 14 **Belfast**
6 40 46 17 33 19 **Belfast Int Airport**
91 75 114 92 122 109 97 **Belleek**
27 70 26 16 53 39 33 108 **Carnlough**
40 61 19 28 71 58 46 95 42 **Coleraine**
28 24 57 28 60 46 33 63 45 37 **Cookstown**
25 49 63 36 5 8 26 108 44 63 53 **Craigavad**
30 73 16 19 61 48 35 110 10 35 47 49 **Cushendall**
47 68 26 35 78 65 53 92 49 7 43 71 41 **Downhill**
38 52 85 55 27 22 35 119 64 85 60 30 74 91 **Downpatrick**
45 13 67 39 56 42 42 68 55 47 11 51 58 54 53 **Dungannon**
86 50 110 82 97 84 83 25 98 91 54 101 91 88 95 43 **Enniskillen**
45 76 13 32 76 63 50 110 40 15 52 69 29 22 82 62 106 **Giant's Causeway**
22 31 59 32 24 12 19 106 49 61 45 20 53 67 18 36 82 85 **Hillsborough**
21 65 41 21 38 25 22 111 14 49 38 14 48 56 71 29 85 36 54 **Larne**
45 62 33 42 77 63 50 82 56 14 63 77 29 48 11 82 18 54 78 35 **Limavady**
84 42 125 95 96 82 82 37 111 103 59 91 114 101 93 12 118 77 104 90 63 **Lisnaskea**
55 71 51 52 87 73 61 62 68 32 48 67 81 79 63 61 47 79 76 18 73 90 **Londonderry**
26 16 66 36 37 23 23 89 52 66 30 34 55 52 22 34 70 13 46 70 13 58 81 **Lurgan**
23 40 18 40 55 41 29 79 34 21 16 47 37 28 61 27 36 44 23 45 36 24 34 48 **Maghera**
43 91 61 38 33 41 41 115 70 90 55 44 80 97 48 13 90 95 24 56 88 82 99 30 66 **Newcastle**
47 19 88 58 52 38 45 93 75 88 44 46 77 94 30 32 92 27 60 81 60 89 23 60 34 21 **Newry**
54 36 83 55 82 69 60 37 71 64 27 85 69 30 34 13 9 92 60 75 51 24 43 75 39 42 55 **Omagh**
48 60 87 57 24 29 44 128 66 87 69 43 68 13 9 99 62 103 91 24 52 102 92 38 70 21 39 88 **Portaferry**
46 67 19 34 78 64 52 102 49 6 43 68 46 89 77 99 9 77 42 48 84 54 98 13 48 9 65 55 20 **Portrush**
62 56 64 58 93 80 67 88 82 31 59 67 90 82 47 60 86 82 102 94 58 46 47 9 82 60 92 65 88 20 **Strabane**
54 25 95 65 58 45 51 100 81 94 50 52 84 101 37 39 67 99 96 34 67 88 30 66 25 7 62 46 100 81 51 **Warrenpoint**

ULSTER Business Year Planner 2003

	January	February	March	April	May	June
Tue				1		
Wed	1 New Year's Day			2		
Thu	2			3	1	
Fri	3			4	2	
Sat	4	1	1	5	3	
Sun	5	2	2	6	4	1
Mon	6	3	3	7	5 Bank Holiday	2
Tue	7	4	4	8	6	3
Wed	8	5	5	9	7	4
Thu	9	6	6	10	8	5
Fri	10	7	7	11	9	6
Sat	11	8	8	12	10	7
Sun	12	9	9	13	11	8
Mon	13	10	10	14	12	9
Tue	14	11	11	15	13	10
Wed	15	12	12	16	14	11
Thu	16	13	13	17	15	12
Fri	17	14	14	18 Good Friday	16	13
Sat	18	15	15	19	17	14
Sun	19	16	16	20	18	15
Mon	20	17	17 St. Patrick's Day	21 Easter Monday	19	16
Tue	21	18	18	22	20	17
Wed	22	19	19	23	21	18
Thu	23	20	20	24	22	19
Fri	24	21	21	25	23	20
Sat	25	22	22	26	24	21
Sun	26	23	23	27	25	22
Mon	27	24	24	28	26 Bank Holiday	23
Tue	28	25	25	29	27	24
Wed	29	26	26	30	28	25
Thu	30	27	27		29	26
Fri	31	28	28		30	27
Sat			29		31	28
Sun			30			29
Mon			31			30
Tue						
Wed						